Critical Developments and Applications of Swarm Intelligence

Yuhui Shi
Southern University of Science and Technology, China

A volume in the Advances in Computational Intelligence and Robotics (ACIR) Book Series

Published in the United States of America by
IGI Global
Engineering Science Reference (an imprint of IGI Global)
701 E. Chocolate Avenue
Hershey PA, USA 17033
Tel: 717-533-8845
Fax: 717-533-8661
E-mail: cust@igi-global.com
Web site: http://www.igi-global.com

Library of Congress Cataloging-in-Publication Data

Names: Shi, Yuhui, editor.
Title: Critical developments and applications of swarm intelligence / Yuhui Shi, editor.
Description: Hershey, PA : Engineering Science Reference, [2018] | Includes bibliographical references.
Identifiers: LCCN 2017035978| ISBN 9781522551348 (h/c) | ISBN 9781522551355 (eISBN)
Subjects: LCSH: Swarm intelligence.
Classification: LCC Q337.3 C75 2018 | DDC 006.3/824--dc23 LC record available at https://lccn.loc.gov/2017035978

This book is published in the IGI Global book series Advances in Computational Intelligence and Robotics (ACIR) (ISSN: 2327-0411; eISSN: 2327-042X)

British Cataloguing in Publication Data
A Cataloguing in Publication record for this book is available from the British Library.

For electronic access to this publication, please contact: eresources@igi-global.com.

Advances in Computational Intelligence and Robotics (ACIR) Book Series

Ivan Giannoccaro
University of Salento, Italy

ISSN:2327-0411
EISSN:2327-042X

Mission

While intelligence is traditionally a term applied to humans and human cognition, technology has progressed in such a way to allow for the development of intelligent systems able to simulate many human traits. With this new era of simulated and artificial intelligence, much research is needed in order to continue to advance the field and also to evaluate the ethical and societal concerns of the existence of artificial life and machine learning.

The **Advances in Computational Intelligence and Robotics (ACIR) Book Series** encourages scholarly discourse on all topics pertaining to evolutionary computing, artificial life, computational intelligence, machine learning, and robotics. ACIR presents the latest research being conducted on diverse topics in intelligence technologies with the goal of advancing knowledge and applications in this rapidly evolving field.

Coverage

- Intelligent control
- Natural Language Processing
- Synthetic Emotions
- Computational Intelligence
- Computational Logic
- Computer Vision
- Adaptive and Complex Systems
- Machine Learning
- Artificial life
- Brain Simulation

IGI Global is currently accepting manuscripts for publication within this series. To submit a proposal for a volume in this series, please contact our Acquisition Editors at Acquisitions@igi-global.com or visit: http://www.igi-global.com/publish/.

The Advances in Computational Intelligence and Robotics (ACIR) Book Series (ISSN 2327-0411) is published by IGI Global, 701 E. Chocolate Avenue, Hershey, PA 17033-1240, USA, www.igi-global.com. This series is composed of titles available for purchase individually; each title is edited to be contextually exclusive from any other title within the series. For pricing and ordering information please visit http://www.igi-global.com/book-series/advances-computational-intelligence-robotics/73674. Postmaster: Send all address changes to above address.

Titles in this Series

For a list of additional titles in this series, please visit: www.igi-global.com/book-series

Developments and Trends in Intelligent Technologies and Smart Systems
Vijayan Sugumaran (Oakland University, USA)
Engineering Science Reference • copyright 2018 • 351pp • H/C (ISBN: 9781522536864) • US $215.00 (our price)

Androids, Cyborgs, and Robots in Contemporary Culture and Society
Steven John Thompson (University of Maryland University College, USA)
Engineering Science Reference • copyright 2018 • 286pp • H/C (ISBN: 9781522529736) • US $205.00 (our price)

Handbook of Research on Modeling, Analysis, and Application of Nature-Inspired Metaheuristic Algorithms
Sujata Dash (North Orissa University, India) B.K. Tripathy (VIT University, India) and Atta ur Rahman (University of Dammam, Saudi Arabia)
Engineering Science Reference • copyright 2018 • 538pp • H/C (ISBN: 9781522528579) • US $265.00 (our price)

Concept Parsing Algorithms (CPA) for Textual Analysis and Discovery Emerging Research and Opportunities
Uri Shafrir (University of Toronto, Canada) and Masha Etkind (Ryerson University, Canada)
Information Science Reference • copyright 2018 • 139pp • H/C (ISBN: 9781522521761) • US $130.00 (our price)

Handbook of Research on Applied Cybernetics and Systems Science
Snehanshu Saha (PESIT South Campus, India) Abhyuday Mandal (University of Georgia, USA) Anand Narasimhamurthy (BITS Hyderabad, India) Sarasvathi V (PESIT- Bangalore South Campus, India) and Shivappa Sangam (UGC, India)
Information Science Reference • copyright 2017 • 463pp • H/C (ISBN: 9781522524984) • US $245.00 (our price)

Handbook of Research on Machine Learning Innovations and Trends
Aboul Ella Hassanien (Cairo University, Egypt) and Tarek Gaber (Suez Canal University, Egypt)
Information Science Reference • copyright 2017 • 1093pp • H/C (ISBN: 9781522522294) • US $465.00 (our price)

Handbook of Research on Soft Computing and Nature-Inspired Algorithms
Shishir K. Shandilya (Bansal Institute of Research and Technology, India) Smita Shandilya (Sagar Institute of Research Technology and Science, India) Kusum Deep (Indian Institute of Technology Roorkee, India) and Atulya K. Nagar (Liverpool Hope University, UK)
Information Science Reference • copyright 2017 • 627pp • H/C (ISBN: 9781522521280) • US $280.00 (our price)

701 East Chocolate Avenue, Hershey, PA 17033, USA
Tel: 717-533-8845 x100 • Fax: 717-533-8661
E-Mail: cust@igi-global.com • www.igi-global.com

Table of Contents

Preface xvi

Section 1
Swarm Intelligence Algorithms

Chapter 1
Unified Swarm Intelligence Algorithms 1
Yuhui Shi, Southern University of Science and Technology (SUSTech), China

Chapter 2
Local Best Particle Swarm Optimization Using Crown Jewel Defense Strategy 27
Jiarui Zhou, Harbin Institute of Technology, China
Junshan Yang, Shenzhen University, China
Ling Lin, Shenzhen University, China
Zexuan Zhu, Shenzhen University, China
Zhen Ji, Shenzhen University, China

Chapter 3
Multi-Objective Binary Fish School Search 53
Mariana Gomes da Motta Macedo, University of Pernambuco, Brazil
Carmelo J. A. Bastos-Filho, University of Pernambuco, Brazil
Susana M. Vieira, University of Lisboa, Portugal
João M. C. Sousa, University of Lisboa, Portugal

Chapter 4
City Group Optimization: An Optimizer for Continuous Problems 73
Yijun Yang, Southern University of Science and Technology, China

Chapter 5
Magnetotactic Bacteria Optimization Algorithm (MBOA) for Function Optimization: MBOA Based on Four Best-Rand Pairwise Schemes 97
Lili Liu, LiaoCheng University, China
Hongwei Mo, Harbin Engineering University, China

Chapter 6
An Analysis on Fireworks Algorithm Solving Problems With Shifts in the Decision Space and Objective Space 119
Shi Cheng, Shaanxi Normal University, China
Junfeng Chen, Hohai University, China
Quande Qin, Shenzhen University, China
Yuhui Shi, Southern University of Science and Technology, China

Section 2
Swarm Intelligence Applications

Chapter 7
Assessment of Gamma-Ray-Spectra Analysis Method Utilizing the Fireworks Algorithm for Various Error Measures 155
Miltiadis Alamaniotis, Purdue University, USA
Lefteri Tsoukalas, Purdue University, USA

Chapter 8
A Computational Comparison of Swarm Optimization Techniques for Optimal Load Shedding Under the Presence of FACTS Devices to Avoid Voltage Instability 182
G. V. Nagesh Kumar, Vignan's Institute of Information Technology (Autonomous), India
B. Venkateswara Rao, V. R. Siddhartha Engineering College (Autonomous), India
D. Deepak Chowdary, Dr. L. Bullayya College of Engineering (for Women), India
Polamraju V. S. Sobhan, Vignan's Foundation for Science, India

Chapter 9
Using Particle Swarm Optimization Algorithm as an Optimization Tool Within Developed Neural Networks 215
Goran Klepac, Raiffeisenbank Austria, Croatia

Chapter 10
Squeeze Casting Parameter Optimization Using Swarm Intelligence and Evolutionary Algorithms 245
Manjunath Patel G. C., Sahyadri College of Engineering and Management, India
Prasad Krishna, National Institute of Technology Karnataka, India
Mahesh B. Parappagoudar, Padre Conceicao College of Engineering, India
Pandu Ranga Vundavilli, Indian Institute of Technology Bhubaneswar, India
S. N. Bharath Bhushan, Sahyadri College of Engineering and Management, India

Chapter 11
Swarm-Intelligence-Based Communication Protocols for Wireless Sensor Networks 271
Lucia Keleadile Ketshabetswe, Botswana International University of Science and Technology, Botswana
Adamu Murtala Zungeru, Botswana International University of Science and Technology, Botswana
Joseph M. Chuma, Botswana International University of Science and Technology, Botswana
Mmoloki Mangwala, Botswana International University of Science and Technology, Botswana

Chapter 12
Image Reconstruction of Electrical Impedance Tomography Using Fish School Search and Differential Evolution 301
Valter Augusto de Freitas Barbosa, Universidade Federal de Pernambuco, Brazil
Wellington Pinheiro dos Santos, Universidade Federal de Pernambuco, Brazil
Ricardo Emmanuel de Souza, Universidade Federal de Pernambuco, Brazil
Reiga Ramalho Ribeiro, Universidade Federal de Pernambuco, Brazil
Allan Rivalles Souza Feitosa, Universidade Federal de Pernambuco, Brazil
Victor Luiz Bezerra Araújo da Silva, Escola Politécnica da Universidade de Pernambuco, Brazil
David Edson Ribeiro, Universidade Federal de Pernambuco, Brazil
Rafaela Covello Freitas, Escola Politécnica da Universidade de Pernambuco, Brazil
Manoela Paschoal, Universidade Federal de Pernambuco, Brazil
Natália Souza Soares, Universidade Federal de Pernambuco, Brazil
Rodrigo Beltrão Valença, Universidade Federal de Pernambuco, Brazil
Rodrigo Luiz Tomio Ogava, Universidade Federal de Pernambuco, Brazil
Ítalo José do Nascimento Silva Araújo Dias, Universidade Federal de Pernambuco, Brazil

Chapter 13
Multi-Thresholding of Histopathological Images Using Fuzzy Entropy and Parameterless Cuckoo Search 339
Krishna Gopal Gopal Dhal, Midnapore College (Autonomous), India
Mandira Sen, Tata Consultancy Services, India
Sanjoy Das, University of Kalyani, India

Chapter 14
Optimized Base Station Sleeping and Smart Grid Energy Procurement Scheme to Improve Energy Efficiency 357
Qiang Wang, Yulin Normal University, China
Hai-Lin Liu, Guangdong University of Technology, China

Detailed Table of Contents

In this chapter, the necessity of having developmental learning embedded in a swarm intelligence algorithm is confirmed by briefly considering brain evolution, brain development, brainstorming process, etc. Several swarm intelligence algorithms are looked at from a developmental learning perspective. A framework of a developmental swarm intelligence algorithm, which contains capacity developing stage and capability learning stage, is further given to help understand developmental swarm intelligence (DSI) algorithms, and to guide to design and/or implement any new developmental swarm intelligence algorithm and/or any developmental evolutionary algorithm. Following DSI, innovation is discussed and an innovation-inspired optimization (IO) algorithm is designed and developed. Finally, by combing the DSI and IO algorithm together, a unified swarm intelligence algorithm is proposed, which contains capacity developing stage and capability learning stage and with three search operators in its capability learning stage to mimic the three levels of innovations.

Particle swarm optimization (PSO) is a swarm intelligence algorithm well known for its simplicity and high efficiency on various problems. Conventional PSO suffers from premature convergence due to the rapid convergence speed and lack of population diversity. It is easy to get trapped in local optima. For this reason, improvements are made to detect stagnation during the optimization and reactivate the swarm to search towards the global optimum. This chapter imposes the reflecting bound-handling scheme and von Neumann topology on PSO to increase the population diversity. A novel crown jewel defense (CJD) strategy is introduced to restart the swarm when it is trapped in a local optimum region. The resultant algorithm named LCJDPSO-rfl is tested on a group of unimodal and multimodal benchmark functions with rotation and shifting. Experimental results suggest that the LCJDPSO-rfl outperforms state-of-the-art PSO variants on most of the functions.

Fish school search (FSS) algorithm has inspired several adaptations for multi-objective problems or binary optimization. However, there is no particular proposition to solve both problems simultaneously. The proposed multi-objective approach binary fish school search (MOBFSS) aims to solve optimization problems with two or three conflicting objective functions with binary decision input variables. MOBFSS is based on the dominance concept used in the multi-objective fish school search (MOFSS) and the threshold technique deployed in the binary fish school search (BFSS). Additionally, the authors evaluate the proposal for feature selection for classification in well-known datasets. Moreover, the authors compare the performance of the proposal with a state-of-art algorithm called BMOPSO-CDR. MOBFSS presents better results than BMOPSO-CDR, especially for datasets with higher complexity.

City group refers to a collection of cities. Through the development and growth, these cities form a chain of metropolitan areas. In a city group, cities are divided into central cities and subordinate cities. Generally, central cities have greater chances to develop. However, subordinate cities may not have great chances to develop unless they are adjacent to central cities. Thus, a city is more likely to develop well if it is near a central city. In the process, the spatial distribution of cities changes all the time. Urbanologists call the above phenomena the evolution of city groups. In this chapter, the city group optimization algorithm is presented, which is based on urbanology and mimics the evolution of city groups. The robustness and evolutionary process of the proposed city group optimization algorithm are validated by testing it on 15 benchmark functions. The comparative results show that the proposed algorithm is effective for solving complexly continuous problems due to a stronger ability to escape from local optima.

Magnetotactic bacteria is a kind of prokaryotes with the characteristics of magnetotaxis. Magnetotactic bacteria optimization algorithm (MBOA) is an optimization algorithm based on the characteristics of magnetotaxis. It mimics the development process of magnetosomes (MTSs) in magnetotactic bacteria. In this chapter, four pairwise MTSs regulation schemes based on the best individual and randomly chosen one are proposed to study which scheme is more suitable for solving optimization problems. They are tested on 14 functions and compared with many popular optimization algorithms, including PSO, DE, ABC, and their variants. Experimental results show that all the schemes of MBOA are effective for solving most of test functions but have different performance on a few test functions. The fourth MBOA scheme has superior performance to the compared methods on many test functions. In this scheme, the algorithm searches around the current best individual to enhance the convergence of MBOA and the individual can migrate to the current best individual to enhance the diversity of the MBOA.

Fireworks algorithms for solving problems with the optima shifts in decision space and/or objective space are analyzed. The standard benchmark problems have several weaknesses in the research of swarm intelligence algorithms for solving single objective problems. The optimum shift in decision space and/or objective space will increase the difficulty of problem solving. Modular arithmetic mapping is utilized in the original fireworks algorithm to handle solutions out of search range. The solutions are implicitly guided to the center of search range for problems with symmetrical search range via this strategy. The optimization performance of fireworks algorithm on shift functions may be affected by this strategy. Four kinds of mapping strategies are compared on problems with different dimensions and different optimum shift range. From experimental results, the fireworks algorithms with mapping to the boundary or mapping to limited stochastic region obtain good performance on problems with the optimum shift. This is probably because the search tendency is kept in these two strategies.

The analysis of measured data plays a significant role in enhancing nuclear nonproliferation mainly by inferring the presence of patterns associated with special nuclear materials. Among various types of measurements, gamma-ray spectra is the widest utilized type of data in nonproliferation applications. In this chapter, a method that employs the fireworks algorithm (FWA) for analyzing gamma-ray spectra aiming at detecting gamma signatures is presented. In particular, FWA is utilized to fit a set of known signatures to a measured spectrum by optimizing an objective function, where non-zero coefficients express the detected signatures. FWA is tested on a set of experimentally obtained measurements optimizing various objective functions—MSE, RMSE, Theil-2, MAE, MAPE, MAP—with results exhibiting its potential in providing highly accurate and precise signature detection. Furthermore, FWA is benchmarked against genetic algorithms and multiple linear regression, showing its superiority over those algorithms regarding precision with respect to MAE, MAPE, and MAP measures.

Voltage instability has become a serious threat to the operation of modern power systems. Load shedding is one of the effective countermeasures for avoiding instability. Improper load shedding may result in huge technical and economic losses. So, an optimal load shedding is to be carried out for supplying more demand. This chapter implements bat and firefly algorithms for solving the optimal load shedding problem to identify the optimal amount of load to be shed. This is applied for a multi-objective function which contains minimization of amount of load to be shed, active power loss minimization, and voltage profile improvement. The presence of with and without static VAR compensator (SVC), thyristor-controlled series capacitor (TCSC), and unified power flow controller (UPFC) on load shedding for IEEE 57 bus system has been presented and analyzed. The results obtained with bat and firefly algorithms were compared with genetic algorithm (GA) and also the impact of flexible AC transmission system (FACTS) devices on load shedding problem has been analyzed.

Developed neural networks as an output could have numerous potential outputs caused by numerous combinations of input values. When we are in position to find optimal combination of input values for achieving specific output value within neural network model it is not a trivial task. This request comes from profiling purposes if, for example, neural network gives information of specific profile regarding input or recommendation system realized by neural networks, etc. Utilizing evolutionary algorithms like particle swarm optimization algorithm, which will be illustrated in this chapter, can solve these problems.

This chapter is focused to locate the optimum squeeze casting conditions using evolutionary swarm intelligence and teaching learning-based algorithms. The evolutionary and swarm intelligent algorithms are used to determine the best set of process variables for the conflicting requirements in multiple objective functions. Four cases are considered with different sets of weight fractions to the objective function based on user requirements. Fitness values are determined for all different cases to evaluate the performance of evolutionary and swarm intelligent methods. Teaching learning-based optimization and multiple-objective particle swarm optimization based on crowing distance have yielded similar results.

Experiments have been conducted to test the results obtained. The performance of swarm intelligence is found to be comparable with that of evolutionary genetic algorithm in locating the optimal set of process variables. However, TLBO outperformed GA, PSO, and MOPSO-CD with regard to computation time.

Social insect communities are formed from simple, autonomous, and cooperative organisms that are interdependent for their survival. These communities are able to effectively coordinate themselves to achieve global objectives despite a lack of centralized planning, and the behaviour is referred to as swarm intelligence. This chapter presents a study of communication protocols for wireless sensor networks utilizing nature-inspired systems: social insect-based communities and natural creatures. Three types of insects are used for discussion: ants, termites, and bees. In addition, a study of the social foraging behavior of spider monkeys is presented. The performances of these swarm-intelligence-based algorithms were tested on common routing scenarios. The results were compared with other routing algorithms with varying network density and showed that swarm-intelligence-based routing techniques improved on network energy consumption with a control over best-effort service. The results were strengthened with a model of termite-hill routing algorithm for WSN.

Electrical impedance tomography (EIT) is a noninvasive imaging technique that does not use ionizing radiation with application both in environmental sciences and in health. Image reconstruction is performed by solving an inverse problem and ill-posed. Evolutionary and bioinspired computation have become a

Proposed CSA algorithm has been tested on benchmark problems addressed in the literature against other well-known algorithms. The results are presented in terms of percentage deviation (PD) of the solution from the lower bound. The results indicate that the proposed CSA algorithm is quite effective in reducing makespan because average PD is observed as 1.531, whereas the next best algorithm has result of average PD of 2.295, which is, in general, nearly 50% worse, and other algorithms start from 2.645.

This chapter introduces a model-based reinforcement learning (RL) approach for continuous state and action spaces. While most RL methods try to find closed-form policies, the approach taken here employs numerical online optimization of control action sequences following the strategy of nonlinear model predictive control. First, a general method for reformulating RL problems as optimization tasks is provided. Subsequently, particle swarm optimization (PSO) is applied to search for optimal solutions. This PSO policy (PSO-P) is effective for high dimensional state spaces and does not require a priori assumptions about adequate policy representations. Furthermore, by translating RL problems into optimization tasks, the rich collection of real-world-inspired RL benchmarks is made available for benchmarking numerical optimization techniques. The effectiveness of PSO-P is demonstrated on two standard benchmarks mountain car and cart-pole swing-up and a new industry-inspired benchmark, the so-called industrial benchmark.

Preface

Swarm intelligence originally refers to the emergent (global) collective behavior, phenomena, or intelligence of decentralized group of living/moving things through self-organization with local interactions (rules) among the group, which is credited to Gerardo Beni and Jing Wang in their paper on cellular robotic systems in1989. In 1994, Mark Millonas, from Santa Fe Institute, went further to propose five principles of swarm intelligence. The five principles are: proximity principle, which says the population of individuals in a swarm should be able to carry out simple space and time computations; quality principle, which requires that the population should be able to respond to quality factors in the environment; diverse response principle, which says that the population should not commit its activities along excessively narrow channels; stability principle, which requires that the population should not change its mode of behavior every time the environment changes; adaptability principle, which says that the population must be able to change behavior mode when it's worth the computational price. In the book "Swarm Intelligence", co-authored by James Kennedy, Russ Eberhart with Yuhui Shi, and published by Morgan Kaufmann Publisher in 2001, the authors started to call the population-based meta-heuristic optimization algorithms, which are inspired by the emergent collective behavior of the group of living/moving things, as swarm intelligence (algorithms). Consequently, swarm intelligence started to refer to a group of nature-inspired population-based meta-heuristic optimization algorithms, not the emergent collective behavior, phenomena, or intelligence of decentralized group of living/moving things at least in the community of evolutionary computation. At the beginning, a swarm intelligence algorithm generally should follow the five principles of swarm intelligence, but the requirement of which later became lessened or even be ignored eventually. In 2002, the IEEE Computational Intelligence Society established its Task Force on Swarm Intelligence with Dr. Yuhui Shi as its founding chair. In 2003, the very first conference on swarm intelligence, i.e., 2003 IEEE Symposium on Swarm Intelligence, was held in Indianapolis, Indiana, USA, April 24-26, with Dr. Yuhui Shi as its general chair. Since then, the swarm intelligence began to attract more and more researchers' attentions and involvements, and so far it has become a very popular and active research area and has grown from a non-mainstream to a mainstream population-based meta-heuristic optimization algorithm, in parallel with the four original main evolutionary computation algorithms, i.e., evolutionary programming, genetic algorithm, evolution strategy, and genetic programming. For example, according to the Google Scholar by searching "particle swarm", it comes out instantly 229,000 search results.

Swarm intelligence refers to a collection of nature-inspired population-based meta-heuristic optimization algorithms, most of which were developed in recent 20 years and more are expecting to be developed. These swarm intelligence algorithms include ant colony optimization, bacterial foraging optimization algorithm, bee colony optimization algorithm, brain storm optimization algorithm, firefly optimization algorithm, fish school search optimization algorithm, particle swarm optimization algorithm, to name just a few. These swarm intelligence algorithms were developed from different inspiration sources, and in general have different characteristics. Some are good at solving some kind of problems while bad at solving other kind of problems. As pointed out by the no free lunch theory, each has its own strength and weakness, and no single swarm intelligence algorithm can solve all kind of optimization problems. With time going on, a lot of swarm intelligence algorithms have been being developed and proposed and more are expecting to come out, therefore, novelties of these swarm intelligence algorithms are more or less different. Some show a lot of novelties, and therefore contribute a lot to the swarm intelligence community, while others may at least so far have very tiny novelty and contribute little to the community, but each should have its own uniqueness here or there. It can be expected that with the growing number (quantity) of swarm intelligence algorithms developed, quality algorithm will eventually come out of quantity of algorithms. Without accumulation of many different swarm intelligence algorithms, it is difficult, if not impossible, to come out an algorithm with much better quality, that is, one with better quality than every existing swarm intelligence algorithm. Eventually, a unified and/or standard swarm intelligence framework will be designed or developed. This unified swarm intelligence should include components similar to those components in the existing swarm intelligence algorithms, which will be utilized to take care of different scenarios of an optimization problem to be solved because of no free lunch theory. Naturally, it is one of research directions for swarm intelligence society to develop a unified or standard swarm intelligence framework so that it can take care of wider range of optimization problems under different scenarios.

Another research direction for the development of swarm intelligence can be its interpretability. Swarm intelligence algorithms have been designed for the main purpose of solving optimization problems by considering them as black-box problems, but under many situations it is necessary to know why and how a swarm intelligence algorithm solves a problem in addition to providing a good enough solution to the problem. Interpretability could be at the algorithmic level, at the calculation level, or at the solution level, respectively. Furthermore, knowledge or experience gained through applying a swarm intelligence algorithm to solve one kind of optimization problems should be utilized for solving other kind of optimization problems. Knowledge (experience) transfer will be beneficial or even critical for an algorithm to solve problem that it is difficult, if not impossible, for the algorithm to solve directly by itself.

Adaptability is another capability that every swarm intelligence algorithm should have. The adaptability can be either internal or external to the swarm intelligence algorithm. Swarm intelligence algorithms are designed for solving those optimization problems which are extremely difficult for traditional mathematical methods to solve because they are usually very complicated or complex. As a consequence, the swarm intelligence algorithm may need to have different search capability when it is within different search areas. For an algorithm to have good search capability within any search area, it should be able to adjust itself to suit for different search areas or possess different search capabilities. Common ways to achieve it are through adapting the parameters of the swarm intelligence algorithm, or even adapting the structure of the swarm intelligence algorithm, for example, the neighborhood structure in particle swarm optimization algorithms. This is the adaptability which is internal to a swarm intelligence algorithm. For applying a swarm intelligence algorithm to solve a real-world problem, the problem itself usually is not stationary, but changes with time, which can usually be represented, reflected, or revealed by a changing evaluation function, that is, the evaluation function changes over time. The changing source can be the values of evaluation function, the location of the optimal value of the evaluation function, the shape of the landscape of the evaluation function, etc. These kinds of problems with changing evaluation functions are called dynamic optimization problems which are common in real-world, for example, moving target detection. Similar to the dynamic optimization problems, there are other types of optimization problems which are challenging and difficult for swarm intelligence algorithms to solve, which include noise optimization problems and uncertain optimization problems. The swarm intelligence algorithm utilized to solve these types of optimization problem should be able to adapt to the noise environment or uncertain environment under which the swarm intelligence algorithm is run to solve the noise optimization problem or uncertain optimization problem, respectively. This is the adaptability which is external to a swarm intelligence algorithm. Adaptability of a swarm intelligence algorithm is a challenging research direction of swarm intelligence.

Most, if not all, swarm intelligence algorithms are originally designed to solve single-objective optimization problems in continuous space, in discrete space, or in binary space. The algorithms will then be modified or extended to solve constrained optimization problems, combinatorial optimization problems, and multi-objective optimization problems, but usually with not large scale. Even though these swarm intelligence algorithms can solve optimization problems with small scales satisfactorily, they will encounter problems when dealing with problems with large scale, which is usually called "curse of dimensionality". Generally speaking, an optimization problem with its dimension larger than 1000 is called a large-scale optimization problem while an optimization problem with more than 3 objectives is called many-objective optimization problems. Both the large-scale optimization problems and many-objective optimization problems are very popular and active, but very challenging research topics. Designing and/or extending swarm intelligence algorithms for large scale optimization problems and many-objective optimization problems are two hot and challenging research directions especially during the "big data" era.

Applying swarm intelligence algorithms to solve real-world problems is always the main research direction of swarm intelligence. Swarm intelligence algorithms are designed to solve problems, it is useless and meaningless to design and implement a swarm intelligence algorithm which can't be applied to solve real-world problems successfully. The design or development of a swarm intelligence algorithm is not its final goal, but its successful applications in solving real-world problems is. Since their introductions, swarm intelligence algorithms have been successfully applied to solve a lot of real-world problems, which can be formulated as a single-objective optimization problem, multi-objective optimization problem, constrained optimization problem, combinatorial optimization problem, etc., which the swarm intelligence algorithms can be designed or extended to solve. With its success in real-world applications, swarm intelligence has become more and more popular, and has been attracting more and more funding from governments and industry. For example, recently, Chinese government has announced its state strategic plan in artificial intelligence in which swarm intelligence is one of its key components. It can be expected that more and more successful applications will appear as a consequence.

WHAT IS THE BOOK ABOUT

This collection book includes selected and (more or less) enhanced papers published in the 2014, 2015, and 2016 volume years of the International Journal of Swarm Intelligence Research. Therefore, this book does not intend to fully cover all research directions on swarm intelligence but instead to provide a snapshot of current researches and developments on swarm intelligence algorithms. Hopefully, it will reflect or even reveal some research tendency on swarm intelligence. This collection book can be used as a reference book for researchers who have been conducting researches on swarm intelligence and/or evolutionary computation, and/or those who are at least interested to learn more about swarm intelligence, and/or those who have intention to conduct researches in the areas of swarm intelligence. It can also be used as a reference book for graduate students and senior undergraduate students who are interested in learning swarm intelligence.

ORGANIZATION OF THE BOOK

Swarm intelligence algorithms are basically tools to solve real-world problems which can be represented as all kinds of optimization problems. Therefore, the research on swarm intelligence should be twofold, that is, one focuses on swarm intelligence algorithms, and the other focuses on their applications to solve real-world problem. This collection book contains 16 chapters which are organized into two parts. Section 1 consists of six chapters which are about current research works on swarm intelligence algorithms. Section 2 consists of 10 chapters which are about the applications of swarm intelligence algorithms.

Section 1: Swarm Intelligence Algorithms

There exist a lot of swarm intelligence algorithms with different inspiration sources. For example, ant colony optimization algorithms are inspired by the capability of ants finding optimal paths between food sources and their nests; particle swarm optimization algorithms are inspired by the capability of flock of birds searching for foods. Most of these existing algorithms, if not all, are designed to be optimization algorithms to solve optimization problems at a single level, while in realty, a lot of learning or optimization are performed in at least two levels, that is, macro level (top level) or micro level (bottom level). The top level of learning or optimization focuses on learning the "structure" information while the bottom level of learning is where the actual learning takes place. These two levels are not stationary, but interactive and adaptive, that is, the top level will be changed according to the learning experience at the bottom level of learning, and the bottom level of learning will be adjusted according to the adapted top level of learning. As a consequence, a learning or optimization algorithm should have two levels of learning and should be developmental. In the first chapter "Unified Swarm Intelligence Algorithms", a developmental swarm intelligence (DSI) framework is first developed and illustrated by briefly looking at examples of brain evolution, brain development, learning to learn, learning to think, and brainstorming process. In the DSI framework, there are capacity developing, which corresponds to the top level of learning, and capability learning, which corresponds to the bottom level of learning. This chapter further discusses and describes the innovation process following which human being can do things differently to gain different results. Innovation could be considered at three levels, that is, at the learning level, at the emulating level, and at the exploring level. Because human being is the most intelligent animal in the world, an optimization algorithm, which mimics there level of innovations of human being, should at least intuitively be a good way to go for designing and/or implementing optimization algorithms. By considering the above, an innovation inspired optimization (IO) algorithm is also proposed in this chapter. The IO algorithm is then further combined with the framework of developmental swarm intelligence to form a unified swarm intelligence framework, which has two layers of learning as in the DSI framework, that is, the capacity developing layer which is the top level of learning, and the capability learning layer which is the bottom level of learning. But different from the DSI framework, the capability learning layer in the unified swarm intelligence framework contains three operators which corresponds to the three levels of innovations, that is, the learning level of innovation, the emulating level of innovation, and the exploring level of innovation, respectively.

There are different versions of particle swarm optimization algorithms, especially for those with different neighborhood definitions such as global version PSO, local version PSO with ring topology, local version PSO with von Neumann topology, etc. Generally speaking, global version PSO converges fast but is more like to get trapped in local optima which are often called premature convergence, while local version converges slowly but with higher possibility to find better solutions. To overcome premature convergence, in the second chapter "Local Best Particle Swarm Optimization Using Crown Jewel Defense Strategy", local version PSO with von Neumann topology is utilized together with the reflecting bound-handling scheme to increase the PSO's population diversity. Furthermore, when the PSO is trapped in a local optimum region, a novel Crown Jewel Defense strategy is introduced to restart the swarm. In this chapter, the reflecting bound-handling scheme is designed as a strategy to handle particles outside boundary, that is, a strategy to move outside boundary particles inside. The crown Jewel Defense strategy borrows an idea from business which sacrifices the most valuable assets for greater interests, that is, to give up current best for future potential much better ones. The reflecting bound-handling scheme is introduced to maintain convergence speed while the crown Jewel Defense strategy is embedded to increase population diversity and to prevent the particles from trapping into the local optimum so that for the proposed PSO to have a good balance between exploration and exploitation. Experimental results suggest that the proposed PSO algorithm outperforms state-of-the-art PSO variants on most of the tested benchmark functions with rotation and shifting.

Fish school search algorithm (FSS) has been utilized to solve multi-objective optimization problems and binary optimization problems. In the third chapter, "Multi-Objective Binary Fish School Search", the FSS has been further extended to solve multi-objective optimization problems and binary optimization problems simultaneously, that is, multi-objective binary optimization problems. The proposed algorithm utilizes both the dominance concept, which is used in multi-objective fish school search algorithms, and the threshold technique, which is used in binary fish school search algorithms. The proposed algorithm is further tested on well-known datasets for feature selection problems and compared with a state-of-art algorithm to illustrate its better performance.

A collection of cities will form a chain of metropolitan areas through their development and growth, which is called city group. The cities in a city group can be categorized as two types, that is, central cities, which have greater chances to develop, and subordinate cities, which may not have great chances to develop unless they are adjacent to central cities. Central cities or cities close to a central city are more likely to develop well, and the spatial distribution of cities therefore changes all the time which is called the evolution of city groups. Inspired by the evolution of city groups, a city group optimization algorithm is proposed in the Chapter 4, "City Group Optimization: An Optimizer for Continuous Problems". The proposed algorithm is further tested on benchmark functions to illustrate its effectiveness for solving complexly continuous problems.

In nature, there is a special kind of magnetotactic bacteria (MTB). They have different biology characteristics from chemotactic bacteria since they can orient and swim along magnetic field lines with the aid of mineral particles inside their bodies. These mineral particles with their enveloping membrane are together called magnetosomes (MTSs). Their chains are called magnetosome chains. Magnetotactic bacteria can orient themselves along geomagnetic field lines (magnetotaxis) in the earth magnetic field since they have magnetosome chains as their compass inside their bodies. Based on the interesting behavior of

MTB, Prof Hongwei Mo proposed a magnetotactic bacteria optimization algorithm (MBOA) in 2012. It mimics the development process of magnetosomes (MTSs) in magnetotactic bacteria to solve problems. In the Chapter 5, "Magnetotactic Bacteria Optimization Algorithm for Function Optimization: MBOA Based on Four Best-Rand Pairwise Schemes", based on original MBOA, four improved MBOAs are researched. Four pairwise MTSs regulation schemes based on the best individual and randomly chosen one are designed in order to study which scheme is more suitable for solving the optimization problems. In the chapter, the proposed algorithms are tested on fourteen standard function problems and compared with many popular optimization algorithms, including PSO, DE, ABC and their variants. Experimental results show that all the schemes of MBOA are effective for solving most of the benchmark functions, but have different performance on a few benchmark functions. The fourth MBOA scheme has superior performance to the compared methods on many benchmark functions. In this scheme, the algorithm searches around the current best individual to enhance the convergence of MBOA or the individual can migrate to the current best individual to enhance the diversity of the MBOA. Although the process of MBOA seems to be a little complex and has not been applied to more complex optimization problems, its realization is interesting and indeed can solve the function optimization problems. It is believable that its variants can be applied to different kinds of real-world problems at least with some modifications.

Fireworks algorithm (FWA) is a swarm intelligence optimization method that mimics the explosion process of fireworks. Fireworks algorithms for solving problems with the optima shifts in decision space and/or objective space are analyzed in Chapter 6, "An Analysis on Fireworks Algorithm Solving Problems with Shifts in the Decision Space and Objective Space". Most standard benchmark problems have several weaknesses in the original research of swarm intelligence algorithms for solving single objective problems. The optimum is in the center of search range, and is the same at each dimension of the search space. The optimum shift in decision space and/or objective space will increase the difficulty of problem solving. Modular arithmetic mapping is utilized in the original fireworks algorithm to handle solutions out of search range. The solutions are implicitly guided to the center of search range for problems with symmetrical search range via this strategy. The optimization performance of fireworks algorithm on shift functions may be affected by this strategy. Four kinds of mapping strategies, which include mapping by modular arithmetic, mapping to the boundary, mapping to stochastic region, and mapping to limited stochastic region, are compared on problems with different dimensions and different optimum shift range. From experimental results, the fireworks algorithms with mapping to the boundary, or mapping to limited stochastic region obtain good performance on problems with the optimum shift. This is probably because the search tendency is kept in these two strategies. The definitions of population diversity measurement on fireworks group and sparks group were also proposed in this chapter. From the observation on population diversity changes, the useful information of fireworks algorithm solving different kinds of problems could be obtained.

Section 2: Swarm Intelligence Applications

Gamma-ray spectra data has been used for analysis of whether there is inference of the presence of special nuclear material, which plays a significant role in enhancing nuclear nonproliferation. Gamma-ray spectra data is the most commonly used data in nuclear nonproliferation, but the gamma-ray spectrum may be masked by "background spectrum" from materials of the ambient environment, therefore, it increases the difficulty of nuclear material presence detection. In Chapter 7, "Assessment of Gamma-Ray Spectra Analysis Method Utilizing the Fireworks Algorithm for Various Error Measures", the firework algorithm is utilized for analyzing gamma-ray spectra data, which is the most commonly used data in nuclear nonproliferation, to seek for patterns of interest in order to detect gamma signature by optimizing an objective function where non-zero coefficients represent that there are gamma signatures detected.

Nowadays, voltage instability has been considered as one of the reason for the blackouts all over the world, and improper load shedding may cause voltage instability which is a serious threat to modern power systems, and which in turn may cause huge technical and economic losses, therefore, an optimal load shedding, which is to supply for more demand, has become a critical method for avoiding voltage instability. Traditionally, the optimal load shedding problem was formulated as a single objective optimization problem. In Chapter 8, "A Computational Comparison of Swarm Optimization Techniques for Optimal Load Shedding Under the Presence of FACTS Devices to Avoid Voltage Instability", the optimal load shedding problem was formulated as a multi-objective optimization problem in which the three objectives are minimization of amount of load to be shed, active power loss minimization, and voltage profile improvement. Bat and firefly algorithms were then implemented to solve the multi-objective optimization problem to identify the optimal amount of load to be shed in order to obtain an optimal load shedding. The proposed method was then tested on IEEE 57 bus system with and without Static VAR Compensator, Thyristor-controlled series capacitor and Unified Power Flow Controller on load shedding.

Customer profiling, which should consider both socio demographic characteristics and customer behavioral characteristics, is one of the most important thing in customer relationship management. Based on recognized profiles, business decisions can be made more successfully. In Chapter 9, "Using Particle Swarm Optimization Algorithm as an Optimization Tool Within Developed Neural Networks", neural networks are developed as tools for customer profiling, and particle swarm optimization algorithms are utilized for training the neural networks.

Squeeze casting process is a combination of conventional casting and forging processes, which makes squeeze casting process have many benefits over conventional casting and forging processes such as near net-shape castability, simpler tooling construction, high productivity, refined structure, improved surface finish, heat-treatability, minimum porosity and segregations, ability to cast ferrous, non-ferrous and wrought alloys. As a consequence, squeeze casting process has been commonly used in a lot of applications such as piston, cylinder, clutch housing, brake drum, engine block, connecting rod, wheels, suspension arm, hubbed flanges, barrel heads, truck hubs, etc. in automobile industry. The casting quality in squeeze casting process is mainly influenced by its process variables which are difficult and challenging to determine, especially when the number of process variables are large and the input-output relationship becomes complicated with nonlinear behaviors. Traditional optimization techniques will easily lead to local optimum solutions which can't meet user requirements. In Chapter 10, "Squeeze Casting Parameter Optimization Using Swarm Intelligence and Evolutionary Algorithms", the evolutionary and swarm intelligence algorithms, such as genetic algorithms, particle swarm optimization algorithms, and teaching learning based optimization algorithms, are used to determine the best set of process variables for the conflicting user requirements, which therefore can be represented as a multiple objective optimization problem.

Swarm intelligence refers to a collection of heuristics algorithms which are inspired by collective behaviors of social insect communities which in turn are formed by un-centralized simple, autonomous, and cooperative organisms. In Chapter 11, "Swarm-Intelligence-Based Communication Protocols for Wireless Sensor Networks", swarm intelligence algorithms inspired by ants, termites, bees, and spider monkeys are studied. The performance of these swarm intelligence algorithms are verified by testing them on common routing scenarios for wireless sensor networks. Compared with other routing algorithms with varying network density, the proposed swarm intelligence based routing techniques can have better energy consumption with a control over best-effort service.

Compared with the most commonly used medical image machines, such as Mammography, Positron Emission Tomography and X-Rays which use ionizing radiation in their process, Electrical Impedance Tomography (EIT) does not use ionizing radiation. In addition, EIT is a noninvasive imaging technique with relatively low cost and no associated risk to its use, and has therefore found a lot of applications both in environmental sciences and in health. The successful applications of EIT rely on its image reconstruction which still needs to be improved because of its low resolution and undefined borders. The EIT image reconstruction can be modeled as an inverse and ill-posed problem and new algorithms, which can create images with good resolution and has low cost, are sought for. In Chapter 12, "Image Reconstruction of Electrical Impedance Tomography Using Fish School Search and Differential Evolution", fish school search algorithm and differential evolution using Non-Blind Search are utilized for the EIT image reconstruction. Simulation results show the effectiveness of both fish school search algorithm and differential evolution for the EIT image reconstruction with large meshes and faster convergence by using Non-Blind Search.

Image thresholding, the most significant and highly complicated task in low-level image analysis, is the process of extracting the objects from its background based on threshold levels while multi-thresholding based image segmentation represents the dividing the image into different regions by selecting multiple threshold points, for which finding the threshold values is extremely time consuming. In Chapter 13, "Multi-Thresholding of Histopathological Images Using Fuzzy Entropy and Parameterless Cuckoo Search", a self-adaptive and parameter less Cuckoo Search (CS) algorithm is proposed to find the threshold values of multi-thresholding of histopathological images, in which entropy measure is to be maximized to obtain the optimal thresholds of the image and fuzzy entropy theory is utilized to consider the inexactness of the gray levels. Experimental results show that the proposed CS algorithm can lead to an accurate convergence towards the optima within less computational time, which is further compared with other meta-heuristic algorithms to illustrate its better performance. In addition, the proposed fuzzy entropy based model is compared with Shannon entropy based model both visually and statistically to establish the perceptible difference in image.

Because the carbon emission caused by the information and communication technologies accounts for more than 2% and its energy cost constitutes a significant portion of the expenditure of the operators, it is necessary and urgent to reduce the power consumption of the cellular radio networks to reduce the cost of the transmission and the pollution on the environment because of the exponential increasing of the number of the mobile terminals and traffic demands. Therefore, the energy efficacy of cellular radio networks, in which over 70%-80% power is consumed by base stations, becomes very important and an optimal base station (BS) sleeping strategy and a smart grid energy procurement Scheme are required. The BS sleeping strategy can effectively improve the energy efficiency for the wireless networks, and decrease the dependence on the traditional energy by turning off the base stations with light traffic, and the renewable energy of the distributed smart grid can decrease the carbon emission. In Chapter 14, "Optimized Base Station Sleeping and Smart Grid Energy Procurement Scheme to Improve the Energy Efficiency", a joint BS sleeping strategy, resource allocation and energy procurement scheme to maximize the profit of the network operators and to minimize the carbon emission is then proposed, which is represented as a mixed integer programming optimization problem to be solved by an optimal algorithm based on Lagrange dual domain method.

The hybrid flow shop (HFS) environment is a combination of parallel machine and flow shop environments and the corresponding HFS scheduling problems are proved to be strongly non-deterministic polynomial time-hard (NP-hard) combinatorial optimization problems, the objective of which is the minimization of makespan. In Chapter 15, "Using Cuckoo Search Algorithm for Hybrid Flow Shop Scheduling Problems Under Makespan Criterion", a cuckoo search algorithm is proposed to solve the multistage hybrid flow shop scheduling problems with parallel machines. The proposed algorithm is further tested on benchmark problems and compared with other well-known algorithms to illustrate its better performance.

Model-based reinforcement learning (RL) methods follow the strategy of nonlinear model predictive control and utilize numerical online optimization of control action sequences. In Chapter 16, "Particle Swarm Optimization for Model Predictive Control in Reinforcement Learning Environments", the model-based RL problem is first reformulated as optimization tasks which are then solved by applying a particle swarm optimization algorithm to search for optimal solutions.

Yuhui Shi
Southern University of Science and Technology, China

ACKNOWLEDGMENT

I would to thank all chapters' authors for their contributions, without whom it is impossible to have this book. I would also like to take this opportunity to thank the Ministry of Science and Technology of China for its support under the Grant No. 2017YFC0804002, the Science and Technology Innovation Committee Foundation of Shenzhen for its support under the Grant No. ZDSYS201703031748284, and the National Natural Science Foundation of China for its support under Grant Number 60975080 and 61273367. Last but not the least, I would like to thank Mariah Gilbert, Jan Travers, and Maria Rohde at the IGI Global for their supports and patience. They worked diligently with me throughout the process of editing and production. I have had a pleasure and learning experience to work with them. It is truly they that make the book a reality.

Section 1
Swarm Intelligence Algorithms

Chapter 1
Unified Swarm Intelligence Algorithms

Yuhui Shi
Southern University of Science and Technology (SUSTech), China

ABSTRACT

In this chapter, the necessity of having developmental learning embedded in a swarm intelligence algorithm is confirmed by briefly considering brain evolution, brain development, brainstorming process, etc. Several swarm intelligence algorithms are looked at from a developmental learning perspective. A framework of a developmental swarm intelligence algorithm, which contains capacity developing stage and capability learning stage, is further given to help understand developmental swarm intelligence (DSI) algorithms, and to guide to design and/or implement any new developmental swarm intelligence algorithm and/or any developmental evolutionary algorithm. Following DSI, innovation is discussed and an innovation-inspired optimization (IO) algorithm is designed and developed. Finally, by combing the DSI and IO algorithm together, a unified swarm intelligence algorithm is proposed, which contains capacity developing stage and capability learning stage and with three search operators in its capability learning stage to mimic the three levels of innovations.

INTRODUCTION

Can a swarm intelligence algorithm develop its learning capacity that can better solve an optimization problem which is unknown at the algorithm's design or implementation time? In the swarm intelligence research field, we are required to solve different types of optimization problems under different environments. For example, there are single objective optimization problems, multi-objective optimization problems, constrained optimization problems, combinatorial optimization problems, *etc*.; there are optimization problems under fixed environment, dynamically changing environment, unknown environment, *etc*. As claimed in no-free-lunch theory (Wolpert & Macready, 1997), there is no single algorithm that will work the best for all different problems. That is to say, one algorithm can be better for one kind of problems, but may be worse for other kinds of problems. It usually is not an easy, if not impossible, job to find the best algorithm for solving one kind of problems, especially when we have no prior knowledge

DOI: 10.4018/978-1-5225-5134-8.ch001

about the problem and the environment the problem is in. An ideal optimization algorithm should have the ability to change itself to have the suitable capacity to learn and solve the problem to be solved under its own environment, that is to say, it should be able to develop its own learning capacity or learning potential which has special connection with the problem and its environment, therefore, to enable the algorithm to better learn and solve the problem.

Researches on optimization algorithms have been around for many years because many real-world problems can eventually be represented or modelled as optimization problems which then require optimization algorithms to solve or to find solutions. Traditionally, hill-climbing algorithms are commonly used to solve optimization problems which usually require optimization problems to be able to be represented by mathematic functions which are further required to be continuous and differentiable. One commonly used hill-climbing algorithm is the steepest descent approach (Battiti, 1992). For an optimization problem, if it can be represented by a continuous and differentiable convex function, then the steepest descent approach can always find its global optimal solution; if the problem can't be represented by a convex function, then the steepest descent approach will find a solution which may or may not be a global optimal solution (point), and in general, it will only find a local optimal solution which may or may not be a good enough solution. What kind of local optimal solution it may find depends on the initial starting solution. Therefore, hill-climbing algorithms are usually called local search algorithms (Hoos & Stutzle, 2005). A hill-climbing algorithm has the capability to find an optimal solution, but whether it will find or not depends on its initial starting solution. To overcome this issue of failing into local optimum, some techniques have been added to modify hill-climbing algorithms to make them to have more potential to avoid local optimum and eventually find at least a good enough solution. These modified algorithms include stochastic gradient descent algorithms (Gardner, 1984), random walk algorithms (Grady, 2006), and simulated annealing algorithms (Granville *et al.*, 1994).

In order to overcome or remove the limitation that an optimization problem needs to be represented or modelled by a continuous and differentiable function and to improve its possibility of finding better solutions, population-based heuristic algorithms were proposed and studied, which can be applied to solve optimization problems which are not required to be represented by continuous and differentiable function, instead the requirement is lessened to be that any solution to the problem can be evaluated. Commonly used population-based heuristic algorithms include genetic algorithms (Holland, 1975), evolutionary programming (Fogel, 1962), genetic programming (Koza, 1992), evolution strategy (Rechenberg, 1973), and swarm intelligence algorithms (Eberhart & Shi, 2007). So far, most researches on these population-based heuristic algorithms focus on their search capability or learning capability.

To further improve performance of population-based heuristic algorithms, researches have been conducted to combine different algorithms to take advantages from each algorithm. For example, one algorithm may be good at exploration while the other may be good at exploitation (Zhu *et al.*, 2011), therefore, it is expected to have better balanced exploration and exploitation through combination. Another research trend is to adapt an algorithm's parameters to make the algorithm to dynamically fit for its search environment which usually is nonlinearly and dynamically changed (Zhan *et al.*, 2009). In general, the search process of an algorithm will be in different search "state" which requires the algorithm to be in different "potential" or to have different search capacity in addition to its learning capability. A good optimization (search) algorithm should have both learning capability and also its ability to fit into different search "state" or learning capacity (or potential). It is important for an optimization algorithm to have learning capability while it is critical for it to have learning capacity or learning potential. An optimization algorithm with both learning capability and learning capacity can be called a developmental learning algorithm, that is, an algorithm has the capability to learn while at the same time has the ability to develop its learning capacity.

There are many existing swarm intelligence algorithms, which include particle swarm optimization algorithms (Shi & Eberhart, 1998), fireworks algorithms (Tan *et al.*, 2013), firefly optimization algorithms (Yang, 2008), cultural algorithms (Reynolds, 1994), and brain storm optimization algorithms (Shi, 2011), but each has its own learning or optimization framework. So far, there is no unified swarm intelligence framework that fits well for most, if not all, swarm intelligence algorithm. In this chapter, a unified swarm intelligence framework will be developed. This chapter is organized as follows. In the Section Developmental Swarm Intelligence, the developmental learning embedded in brain evolution, brain development, cognitive process will be discussed which will form the foundation for the concept of developmental learning and developmental swarm intelligence (Shi, 2014). Furthermore, several swarm intelligence algorithms will be looked at and discussed from the developmental learning perspective, followed by an introduction of a framework for developmental swarm intelligence algorithms. In the Section Innovation Inspired Optimization Algorithm, innovation will be discussed at three levels, i.e., at the learning level, at the emulating level, and at the exploring level. Inspired by the three levels of innovations, a new population-based swarm intelligence algorithm is developed, which is called innovation inspired swarm intelligence algorithm. In the Section Unified Swarm Intelligence Algorithm, the concept of developmental swarm intelligence and innovation inspired optimization algorithm will be combined to form a unified swarm intelligence algorithm. Finally are the Section Discussions and Future Research Directions and the Section Conclusions.

DEVELOPMENTAL SWARM INTELLIGENCE

Developmental Learning

In reality, things like learning usually develop or happen in different levels. In general, there are two levels of learning that should be considered, one is at top or macro level at which "structure" or capacity of learning is formed, and the other is at the bottom or micro level at which the actual learning is conducted, therefore, the learning is developmental. Developmental learning can also be looked as hierarchical learning or two layer learning, one is learning itself (at micro level), and the other is to develop the learning capacity (at macro level). In this section, we will look at several cases with different scales.

Brain Evolution

By measuring the inside of ancient skulls, it is evident that the size of human brain has tripled across nearly seven million years and its neocortex has expanded also (Schachner, 2013). With the brain size enlarging and neocortex expanding, it is natural to think the learning capacity of the human brain has been being developed to enable human brain to have better learning capability or in better position (potentiality) to learn. On other words, brain evolution can be considered as developing brain's learning capacity while every human being is born to have the capability to learn with the learning capacity possessed by the evolved brain at that time.

Brain Development

A child is born to have almost all the neurons, but the brain itself is still under development for a while during which the nervous system will be developed (Chudler, 2012). It is natural to believe it is the developed nervous system that will determine the child's learning capacity to learn knowledge throughout his/her lifetime.If some harmful things happen, such as illness, during the time of nervous system development, which may cause the nervous system not fully developed, then the child will have developmental learning disability, that is to say, he/she is able to learn but with disability or lessened learning capacity. On other words, brain development of each child can be considered as being responsible for developing his/her learning capacity with which he/she has the learning capability to learn.

Learning to Learn

Everyone is born to be able to learn. This is the way how everyone learns the knowledge, but that is not to say, everyone will become equally knowledgeable. In reality, after many years' studies, some people become very knowledgeable and other are not. Some people are knowledgeable in some areas but not in other areas. How knowledgeable a person is and in what areas depends on his learning experience and learning attitude. If a person has the interests/attitudes to learn and he/she has followed a good learning approach and furthermore has had the luck to learn from experienced and great teachers, in general, he/she will eventually become more knowledgeable than others. Everyone is born to have the learning capability, but not everyone has followed the same learning approach, and/or has had the same learning interests, and/or has had the same luck to have the same teachers, as a consequence, everyone eventually becomes different from others. That is, everyone has the almost similar learning capability but may have different capacity. To help children and/or students to enhance its capacity to learn, schools are built, textbooks are written, teaching methods are taught to teachers to follow, and learning approaches or methodologies are introduced to students to guide them to learn. That is to say, the society is doing its best to enhance everyone's capacity to learn. Therefore, in reality, good and/or best practices are shared. As students, you should learn how to learn. But to be reality, everyone will experience different learning, therefore, it turns out everyone will be different with regards to his/her knowledge. Learning to learn will help develop a person's learning capacity so that he/she can be a better learner with his/her learning capability.

Learning to Think

It is similar when considering thinking. Any two persons may have the same knowledge about one problem, but one may be better than the other when asked to solve the problem because the two persons may look at or think the problem from different angles. A problem may be easier to be solved when being looked at from one perspective (angle). Therefore, it is important and even critical to learn the way to think. When facing a problem, if you keep on thinking the same way, you will not be able to solve the problem which you are not able to solve at the beginning. In order to solve a problem you can't solve at beginning, you should keep on thinking the problem from different perspective. The knowledge you have is your thinking capability, while the way of your thinking is your thinking capacity. You should learn both the knowledge, that is your thinking capability, and the way you think, that is your thinking capacity.

Brainstorming Process

When facing a difficult problem which one person or a small group of experts is very difficult, if not impossible, to solve, a group of persons are gathered together to brainstorm to solve (Osborn, 1963). The group of persons should include not only the experts in the areas of the problem to be solved, but also other persons with diverse background and those that know nothings about the problem to be solved. Through a brainstorming process, especially by following four rules listed in Table1 (Osborn, 1963; Smith, 2002), the problem usually will be solved with high probability. It is true that it is the experts in the brainstorming group that have the capability to finally solve the problem, but without other persons with different background in the brainstorming group, these experts will not be able to solve the problem by themselves. It is the other persons that enhance the capacity of the experts so that they have both capability and capacity to solve the problem. Otherwise, a brainstorming process is unnecessary because the experts can solve the problem themselves. In other words, the brainstorming process is utilized to increase the capacity of the person who have the capability but not the "right" capacity to solve the problem. The brainstorming process is used to develop the capacity not the capability for the experts to solve the problem.

Four Rules for Idea Generation in a Brainstorming Process

1. Suspend Judgment
2. Anything Goes
3. Cross-fertilize (Piggyback)
4. Go for Quantity

From the above discussion, it is necessary to design and/or implement swarm intelligence algorithms to have two level learnings at micro and macro level, which will then be also called developmental learning algorithms or developmental swarm intelligence algorithms when regarding swarm intelligence algorithms. Actually, a lot of existing swarm intelligence algorithms have already had developmental learning embedded in them intentionally or unintentionally, which will be looked at or discussed in the next section.

Developmental Swarm Intelligence

For a simple convex problem shown in Figure 1, the optimal solution can be found by applying the steepest gradient approach starting from an initial point x_1 according to the equation (1).

$$x_{i+1} = x_i - \delta \nabla F\left(x_i\right) \tag{1}$$

where δ is the step size and $\nabla F\left(.\right)$ is the gradient. If the step size δ in equation (1) is small enough, iterations according to equation (1) will eventually move the solution x_i approach the optimal solution as i approaches infinite. The solution finding is actually to find a mapping function $x_{i+1} = f\left(x_i\right)$ that can obtain x_{i+1} from x_i. The steepest gradient approach is one good mapping function when the optimized

Figure 1. A unimodal (convex) problem

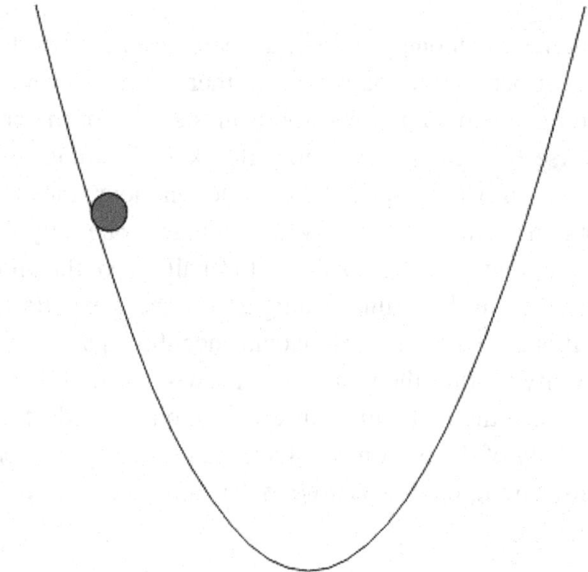

function is continuous and differentiable. Any of this kind of mapping functions represents a searching or an optimization algorithm for finding solution for an optimization problem represented by a mathematic function. The optimization algorithms such as the steepest gradient approach have the capability to find optimal or good enough solutions. Usually when designing an optimization algorithm, its search capability is considered.

For a problem shown in Figure 2, the optimization algorithms such as the steepest gradient approach may or may not find the optimal solution depending on the initial point where the algorithms starts its searching. The algorithm has the capability to search for optimal solution but may not be able to find the optimal solution. For the example shown in Figure 2, if it starts its searching from initial point b, it will find the optimal solution while if it starts from initial point a, it will not find the optimal solution,

Figure 2. A multi-modal problem

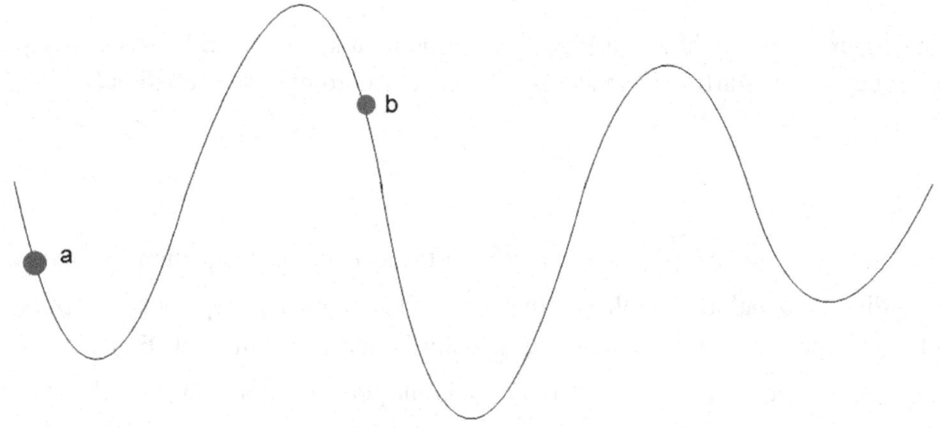

therefore, we say the algorithm has the capability to search for optimal solution from any initial point, but it has the capacity to find the optimal solution if starting from initial point b, while it does not have the capacity to find the optimal solution if starting from initial point such as a. When we design an optimization algorithm, both the search capability and search capacity need to be considered. The steepest gradient algorithm has the full capacity for the problem shown in Figure 1, but it does not always have the full capacity for the problem shown in Figure 2. How to design an optimization algorithm with both search (learning) capability and search (learning) capacity is equally important. When designing optimization algorithms for searching solutions for problems which are much complex such as those that are non-differentiable, non-continuous, and multi-modal, it is extremely important to consider both its search capability and its search capacity. For those complex problems, it is generally very difficult, if not impossible, to find optimal solution determinedly. Instead, population based approaches have been designed. By using a population of solutions, it is expected that the population of solution has more capability to cover areas where the optimal solution may lie. Therefore, it is desired to design mapping functions to generate a population of solutions from another population of solution so that eventually the population of solutions will cover the area where the optimal solution locates and/or contain the optimal solution with high probability. One of the most popular population-based optimization algorithms is swarm intelligence algorithms. Different swarm intelligence algorithm implements a different mapping function which generates a population of solutions from another population of solutions. In the designing of those swarm intelligence algorithms, researchers have paid much more attentions on algorithms' searching capability and lot of researches have been conducted on the balance between exploration (global search) and exploitation (local search). On the other hand, researchers have extensively studied population diversity and ways to improve population diversity so that to improve algorithms' search capability or search performance (Cheng *et al.*, 2011; Cheng *et al.*, 2012). These researches more and less have concerned algorithms' search capacity in addition to search capability, but not intentionally. Figure 3 shows the two major components (stages) that a developmental swarm intelligence(DSI)algorithm should contain.

Figure 3. Two major components of a developmental swarm intelligence algorithm

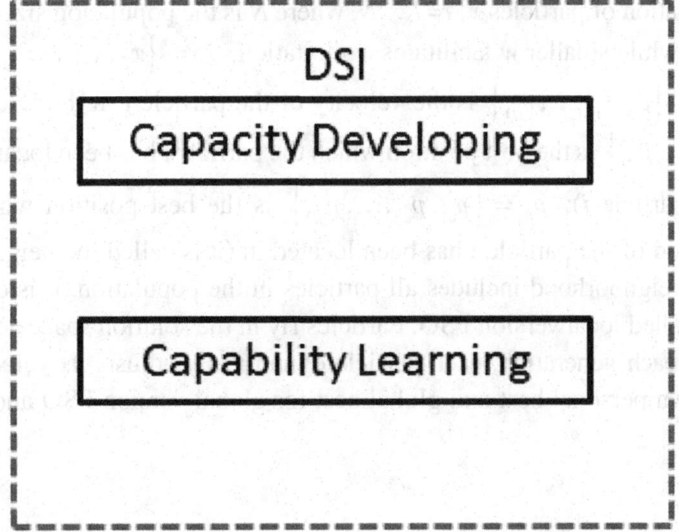

For example, the Capacity Developing shown in Figure 3 corresponds to central neuron system development while the Capability Learning in Figure 3 corresponds to the actually knowledge learning for a person throughout his/her lifetime.

By considering the case shown in Figure 2, the stage of Capacity Developing focuses on moving the algorithm's search to the area(s) around desired solutions while Capability Learning focuses on its actually searching capability from the current solution for single point based optimization algorithms and from the current population for population-based swarm intelligence algorithms.

As shown in Figure 3, a developmental swarm intelligence algorithm includes two stages of learning, that is, capacity developing and capability learning. In the remaining of this section, we are going to look at several existing swarm intelligence algorithms from developmental learning perspective, that is to look at their design or implementation in two stages with one stage focusing on algorithms' search capability and the other on algorithms' search capacity in the hope that we can come out better understanding of algorithms and eventually be able to develop algorithms with better performance by emphasizing on both search capability and search capacity.

Developmental Learning Perspective for Particle Swarm Optimization Algorithms

Particle swarm optimization (PSO) algorithm was introduced by Russell C. Eberhart and James Kennedy in 1995 (Eberhart & Kennedy, 1995). One of the most commonly used PSO algorithms can be described as (Shi & Eberhart, 1998)

$$\mathbf{v}_{ij} = w\mathbf{v}_{ij} + c_1\text{rand}()(\mathbf{p}_{ij} - \mathbf{x}_{ij}) + c_2\text{Rand}()(\mathbf{p}_{gj} - \mathbf{x}_{ij}) \tag{2a}$$

$$\mathbf{x}_{ij} = \mathbf{x}_{ij} + \mathbf{v}_{ij} \tag{2b}$$

where w is the inertia weight which is utilized to balance the exploration capability and exploitation capability of the population of particles x_i, $i=1,...N$, where N is the population size; In general, larger w facilitates exploration while smaller w facilitates exploitation. $x_i = \{x_{i1}, x_{i2}, \ldots, x_{iD}\}$ is the position of the particle i and $v_i = \{v_{i1}, v_{i2}, \ldots, v_{iD}\}$ is the velocity of the particle i in the D-dimensional solution space; $p_i = \{p_{i1}, p_{i2}, \ldots, p_{iD}\}$ is the best position which the particle i has been located in (it is called the personal best of the particle i); $p_g = \{p_{g1}, p_{g2}, \ldots, p_{gD}\}$ is the best position which all the particles within the neighborhood of the particle i has been located in (it is called the neighborhood best of the particle i). When the neighborhood includes all particles in the population, it is called global version PSO, otherwise, it is called local version PSO. Particles fly in the solution space according to the equation (2a) and (2b). In each generation, each particle dynamically adjusts its velocity according to its current velocity, its own personal best and global best for global version PSO and local best for local version PSO.

In order to improve PSO's performance, lot of researches have been conducted on dynamically changing its parameters to better reflect its current search state (Zhan *et al.*, 2009), therefore, in the hope to have better search capacity.

A PSO with fixed parameters can be considered to have fixed search capacity while a PSO with adaptive parameters can be considered to dynamically develop its search capacity. To dynamically adjust inertia weight according to dynamic searching information embedded in the search process is analogue to develop its search capacity while the actual particle updating is analogue to learn its search capability.

In PSO, there is also the concept of neighborhood. The neighborhood of the global version PSO is that each particle has all other particles as its neighbors. For local version PSO, each particle has limited number of particles as its neighbors. Depending on the definition of what particles is defined as the neighbors of each particle, there is the concept of neighborhood topology. There are many local version PSOs with different neighborhood topology, for example, there are star, ring, four clusters, and Von Neumann neighborhood topologies (Cheng *et al.*, 2011). Generally speaking, PSO with small neighborhoods might perform better on complex problems while PSO with large neighborhood would perform better for simple problems; PSO with von Neumann structured neighborhood may perform better than PSOs with other regular shaped neighborhoods including global version and local version (Kennedy & Mendes, 2002), which can be partially revealed by the population diversity over generations (Cheng *et al.*, 2011).

Lot of researchers have also been conducting researches on dynamically changing its neighborhood topology to better reflect its current search state in the hope to have better search capacity. Similarly, a PSO with fixed neighborhood topology can be considered to have fixed search capacity, while a PSO with dynamically changing neighborhood topology can be considered to dynamically develop its search capacity to better suit for its dynamically changing search environment so that the PSO achieves better performance.

A PSO algorithm can be considered to have two steps of learning as shown in Figure 4 with comparison to the two stages in a developmental swarm intelligence algorithm.

In Figure 4, a PSO with fixed parameters and/or fixed neighborhood topology can be considered to have fixed search capacity as shown in Figure 5 while a PSO with adaptive parameters and/or adaptive neighborhood topology can be considered to dynamically develop its search capacity as shown in Figure 6.

In Figure 5, the parameters and/or neighborhood topology are fixed, the PSO has fixed searching capacity while in Figure 6, the parameters and/or neighborhood topology are to be dynamically changed, the PSO is dynamically developing its search capacity, that is to say the PSO has capacity developing component implemented while the PSO implemented as shown in Figure 5 does not have capacity developing component implemented.

Figure 4. Two steps of PSO algorithm and two stages of DSI algorithm

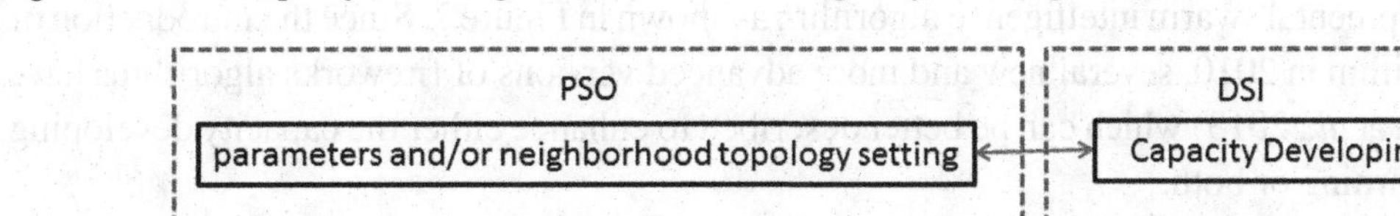

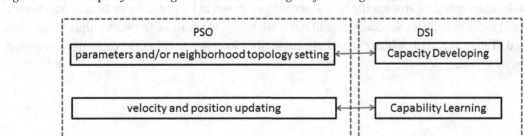

Figure 5. Two steps of PSO algorithm with fixed setting and two stages of DSI algorithm

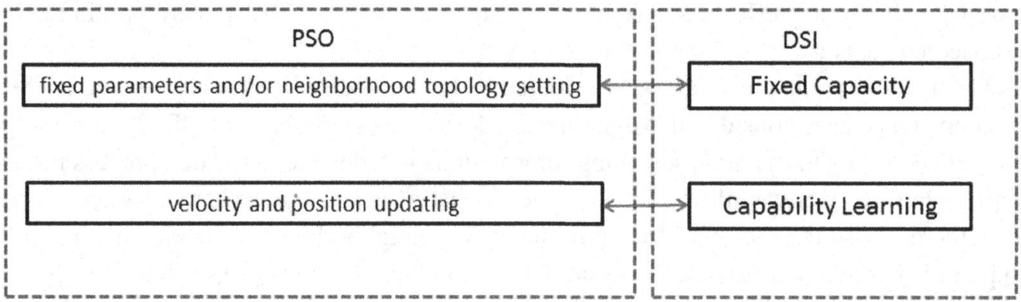

Figure 6. Two steps of PSO algorithm with adaptive setting and two stages of DSI algorithm

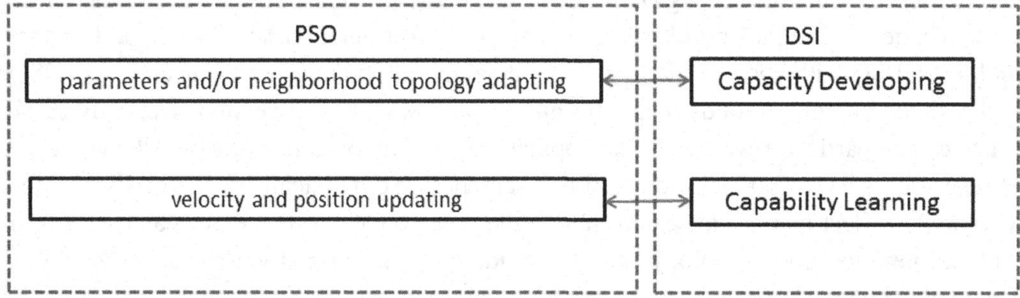

Developmental Learning Perspective for Fireworks Algorithms

Fireworks algorithm is a population-based swarm intelligence algorithm which was inspired by the firework explosion to generate sparks (Tan & Zhu, 2010). Each individual represents a location of a firework where it will explode to generate sparks which can be potential locations of fireworks for next generation. There are mainly two operations that are critical to fireworks algorithms which are explosion strategy and selection strategy. The explosion strategy determines how to explode and generate sparks while the selection strategy determines where the fireworks for the next generation will be located so that fireworks will explode at these new locations to generate sparks that become more and more closer to the location which the algorithm is searching for and which represents potential good enough solutions to the problem to be solved. The fireworks algorithm (FA) naturally matches the two stages of a developmental swarm intelligence algorithm. The selection strategy is similar to the capacity developing in a developmental swarm intelligence algorithm while the explosion strategy is similar to the capability learning in a developmental swarm intelligence algorithm as shown in Figure 7. Since the introduction of the fireworks algorithm in 2010, several new and more advanced versions of fireworks algorithms have been proposed (Tan *et al.*, 2013) which can be better described to enhance either the capacity developing or the capability learning or both.

Figure 7. A developmental learning perspective of a fireworks algorithm

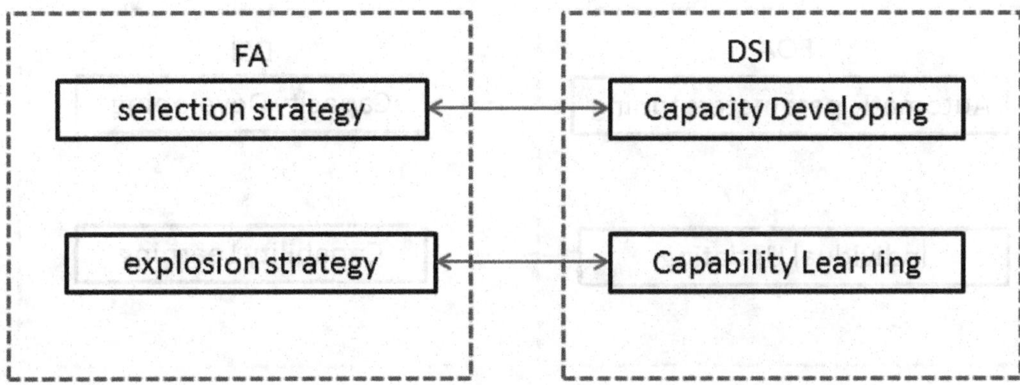

Developmental Learning Perspective for Firefly Optimization Algorithms

Firefly optimization algorithm is a population-based swarm intelligence which was inspired by PSO to simulated and/model the flashing behavior of fireflies (Yang, 2008; Yang 2010). In firefly optimization algorithm, each individual represents the location of a firefly, therefore, each individual will be updated by simulating the movement of its corresponding firefly by attracting to another firefly which is brighter. Since its introduction in 2008, more advanced version of firefly optimization algorithms have been proposed such as the chaos-enhanced firefly optimization algorithm in which movements of fireflies are controlled by automatic parameter tuning (Yang, 2011). Generally, like PSO, the original firefly optimization algorithm (FOA) mainly concerns capability learning not capacity developing or with fixed capacity as shown in Figure 8. By adding parameter controlling into a firefly optimization algorithm, it can be said that the capacity developing is therefore added into the algorithm. Here, the parameter tuning can be considered as the capacity developing stage as in a developmental swarm intelligence algorithm while the individual updating can be considered as the capability learning as in a developmental swarm intelligence algorithm as shown in Figure 9.

Figure 8. A developmental learning perspective of a FOA algorithm with fixed parameters

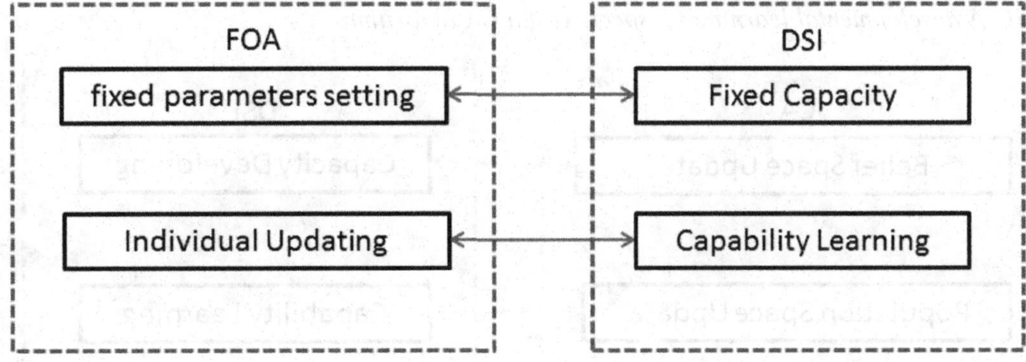

Figure 9. A developmental learning perspective of a FOA algorithm with automatic parameters tuning

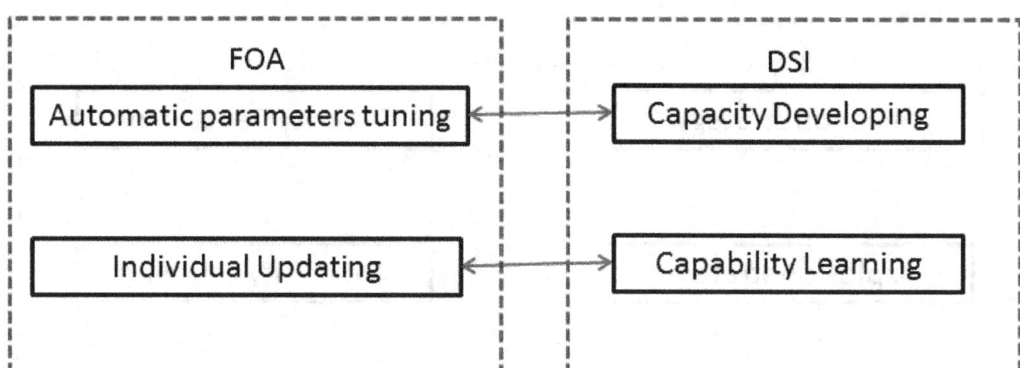

Developmental Learning Perspective for Cultural Algorithms

Cultural Algorithm (CA) was originally developed by Reynolds in 1994 (Reynolds, 1994). CA consists of two major components, *i.e.*, a belief space and a population space, and a protocol that exchanges knowledge between the two spaces. Any population-based learning algorithm could be used in the population space to evolve or learn knowledge at micro-level. The potential good knowledge learnt in the population space will be passed to belief space to update its knowledge structure. In the other hand, the knowledge stored in the belief space will be utilized to help knowledge learning in the population space. Therefore, from the developmental learning perspective, the belief space is more like to be responsible for capacity developing in the Cultural Algorithm while the population space is responsible for knowledge learning, i.e. capability learning as shown in Figure 10.

Developmental Learning Perspective for Brain Storm Optimization Algorithms

Brain storm optimization (BSO) algorithm is a new population-based swarm intelligence algorithm, which was inspired by one of human creative problem solving skills, *i.e.*, brainstorming process (Shi, 2011a; Shi, 2011b). Since its introduction in 2011, several modified versions of BSOs have been pro-

Figure 10. A developmental learning perspective of a CA algorithm

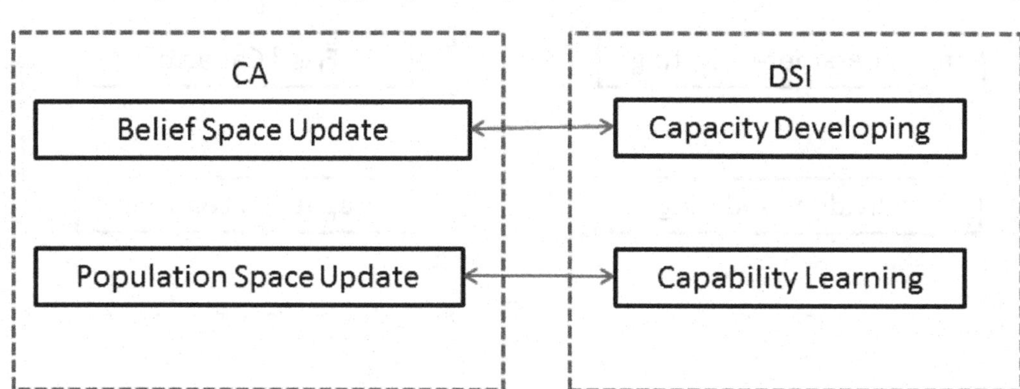

posed (Yang *et al.*, 2013; Zhan *et al.*, 2012; Zhou *et al.*, 2012;) and two versions of multi-objective brain storm optimization algorithms have also been proposed to solve multi-objective optimization problems (Shi *et al.*, 2013; Xue *et al.*, 2012). Furthermore, BSO has been applied to solve real-world applications (Duan *et al.*, 2013; Jadhav *et al.*, 2012; Krishnanand *et al.*, 2013; Radakrishnan, 2013; Ramanand *et al.*, 2012; Sun *et al.*, 2013).

BSO consists of two major operations (or components), that is, convergent operation and divergent operation. With the convergent operation, a population of individuals, say 100 individuals, is operated to generate a small number of clue individuals, say 5 clue individuals which represent good and diversely distributed individuals inside the population. With divergent operation, a new population of individuals is generated mainly based on the clue individuals. Originally, *k*-means clustering algorithm was proposed to be the convergent operation which generates a small number of clue individuals from a population of individuals, but other clustering algorithm can also be utilized to generate clue individuals. Furthermore, any other algorithm or operation could be used to generate clue individuals from a population of individuals because clustering is not purpose but a means to map from a population of individuals to a small number of clue individuals. Originally, Gaussian distribution noise is used in divergent operation which adds noise to clue individuals to generate a new population of individuals, but other distribution noises, such as Cauchy distribution noise, Levy flight, can also be used to generate new individuals. Initially, noise is added to either one individual or two individuals to generate new individuals, but it also can be added to more than two individuals, say three individuals as was done in differential evolution, to generate new individuals (Sun *et al.*, 2013; Zhan *et al.*, 2012). Comparing these two operations in a BSO algorithm with the two stages in a developmental swarm intelligence algorithm, it can be easily seen, the convergent operation in a BSO algorithm is similar to the capacity developing stage in a developmental swarm intelligence algorithm while the divergent operation in a BSO algorithm is similar to the capability learning in a developmental swarm intelligence algorithm as shown in Figure 11. Therefore, it can be easily seen that a BSO algorithm naturally matches the two stages of a developmental swarm intelligence algorithm.

Figure 11. A developmental learning perspective of a BSO algorithm

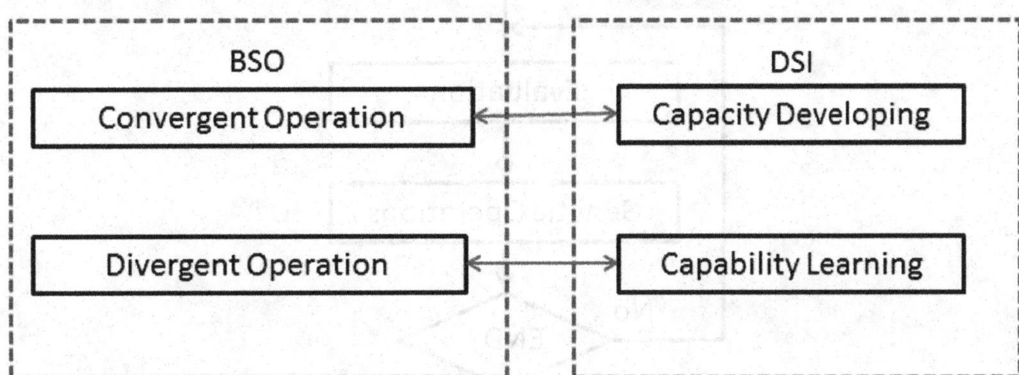

Developmental Learning Perspective for Evolutionary Algorithms

There are many other swarm intelligence algorithms reported in the literature, we are not going to go through all of them, instead, we took the above discussed algorithms as examples to demonstrate how to look at swarm intelligence algorithms from the developmental learning perspective. In addition to the swarm intelligence algorithms, evolutionary algorithms can also be looked from the developmental learning perspective. For example, for a genetic algorithm (Holland, 1975), it usually consists of five major components and follow the procedure as shown in Figure 12 below in which genetic operations include selection, mutation, and crossover operations.

For each original evolutionary algorithm (EA) including GA shown in Figure 12, the parameters are fixed, therefore, it can be considered to have fixed learning capacity. In the literature, there are lot of researches on dynamic parameter adapting to improve its performance for which the parameter adapting can be considered as capacity developing as in a developmental swarm intelligence algorithm and the individual updating can be considered as capability learning as in a developmental swarm intelligence algorithm which is shown in Figure 13. Furthermore, there are a lot of researches on hybrid algorithms (HA), especially those hybrid algorithms such as memetic algorithms (Moscato & Cotta, 2002) in which one algorithm is more responsible for finding starting points or parameters for the second algorithm. In this case, the first algorithm can be considered to be responsible for capacity developing while the second algorithm can be considered to be responsible for capability learning as shown in Figure 14.

Figure 12. A general procedure of genetic algorithm

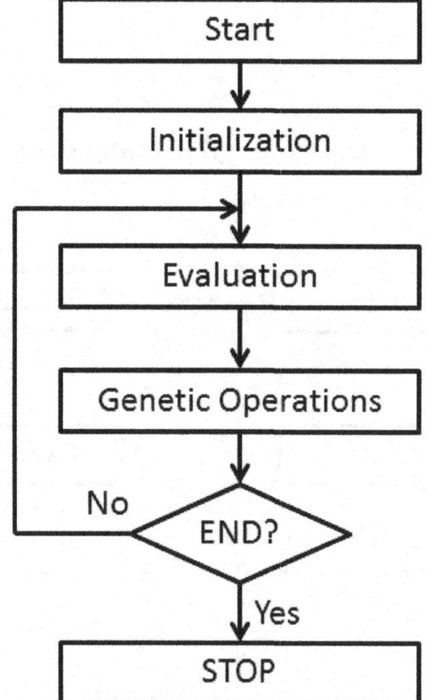

Figure 13. A developmental learning perspective of an EA algorithm with parameter adapting

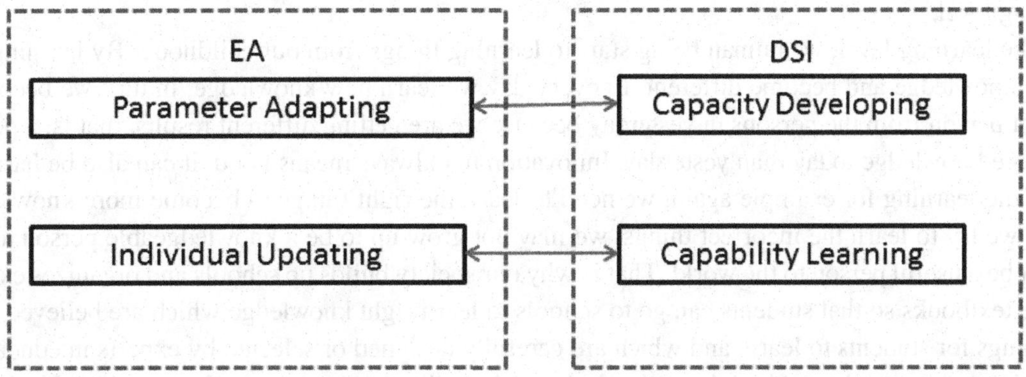

Figure 14. A developmental learning perspective of a hybrid algorithm

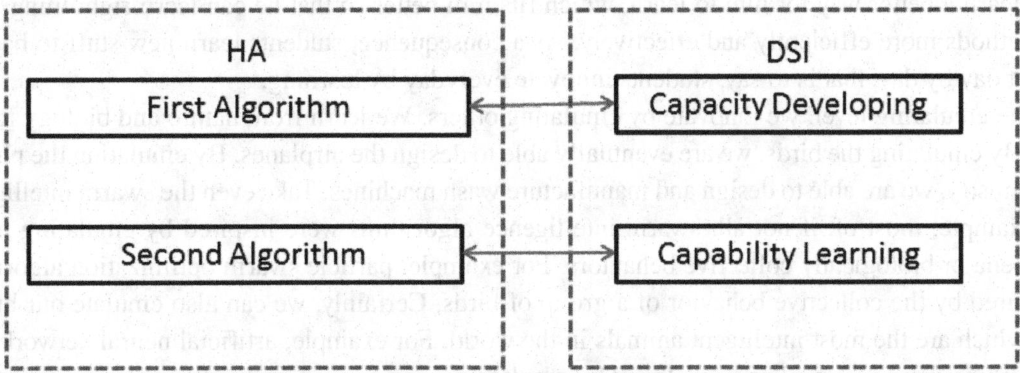

INNOVATION-INSPIRED OPTIMIZATION ALGORITHM

Innovation

The world has been changing quickly especially for the recently one hundred years. It is the innovation that is behind the changes. Generally speaking, innovation is about changes. In another word, change means to have different results, which in turn requires you to do things differently. If doing the same thing in the same way, you will get the same results. In order to get different results, you need to do differently. To do differently, you need to think differently. If you think the same thing in the same way, you will do the thing in the same way. There are different levels of innovations, and there are innovations in different scales. With regards to innovations in different scales, innovation can be international, which is unique to the whole world, for example, international patents; innovation can be national, which is unique to the whole country, for example, national patents; innovation can be local, which is unique to those with local culture; innovation can also be individual, which is unique to every individual person.

We, human being, are making innovations everywhere and all the time either intentionally or unintentionally. For example, children go to schools to learn things to become different so they innovate by learning to make them different day by day. Taking individual person for example, in general innovation can be at three different levels, which are at the learning level, at the emulating level, and at the exploring level.

At the learning level, we human being start to learning things from our childhood. By learning, we acquire knowledge and become different. In every day we learn new knowledge, in turn we become a different person from the persons in yesterday because we are getting different results, that is, a person with more knowledge today than yesterday. Innovation not always means good, it can also be harmful. Taking the learning for example again, we need to learn the right things to become more knowledgeable. If we try to learn the incorrect things, we may not grow up to be a knowledgeable person and in turn not be a useful person to the world. That is why our society builds up schools and organizes experts to write textbooks so that students can go to schools to learn right knowledge which are believed to be right things for students to learn, and which are carefully designed or selected by experts in education. In addition to learn right stuff, students should learn the right stuff by using a right method. If a bad or wrong method is used, students may not be able to learn useful knowledge at least in an efficient and effective way. That is why students are told to use the right method to study or learn. Finally, a student should learn a better way for him to learn, which fits him better so that he can learn right things with right methods more efficiently and effectively. As a consequence, students learn new stuff to become different day by day, that is to say, students innovate everyday by learning.

At the emulating level, we innovate by emulating others. We learn from nature and biology for example. By emulating the birds, we are eventually able to design the airplanes. By emulating the physics and chemistry, we are able to design and manufacture wash machines. Take even the swarm intelligence as an example, most of, if not all, swarm intelligence algorithms were inspired by emulating nature phenomena or biologically collective behaviors. For example, particle swarm optimization algorithms are inspired by the collective behavior of a group of birds. Certainly, we can also emulate our human being, which are the most intelligent animals in the world. For example, artificial neural networks and deep learning were designed and developed by emulating our human neural systems; brain storm optimization algorithms were designed and developed by emulating the brainstorming process, which our human being uses to solve difficult problems which can't be solved by a single expert. We should learn to emulate or copy stuff from somewhere which is not what we are familiar with. A method used in other areas, which the researchers there take it for granted, may easily solve the problem which researchers in this area can't solve for long time.

At the exploring level, to innovate, you should do what other people have not done or you should do things quite differently from what you have been doing all the time, which in turn requires you to think in a way in which you have not thought. To have a break-through thought, you need to pay attention to the differences not the similarities. Novelty is what we should focus on to have innovation at the exploring level. As Albert Einstein said a great thought begins by seeing something differently, with a shift of the mind's eye.

Innovation-Inspired Optimization Algorithm

As mentioned in the last section, we, human being, have been making the world better and better by doing innovations. There are in general three levels of innovations. Without innovation, the world will never change. With innovations, we have been making the world different, if not better and better. Innovation is similar to the learning capability in the developmental swarm intelligence algorithms. You have to make things different to be able to make them better, which is similar to that new solutions have to generated in order to find better solution in a swarm intelligence algorithm. Swarm intelligence should have learning capabilities, i.e. innovations, to have better optimization capability or search capability. Therefore, analogous to the innovation, to make an optimization algorithm to have better performance, it should also have three levels of innovations or learning capabilities, that is, learning capabilities at the learning level, at the emulating level, and at the exploring level, respectively, which will be discussed in this section.

Innovation-Inspired Optimization Algorithm

By taking the three levels of innovations into consideration, a new population-based swarm intelligence algorithm can be designed and developed by implementing the capability learning in a developmental swarm intelligence algorithm with the three levels of learning capabilities. Figure 15 shows the framework of the new population-based swarm intelligence algorithm in which three levels of innovations are

Figure 15. Framework of Innovation-Inspired Optimization Algorithm

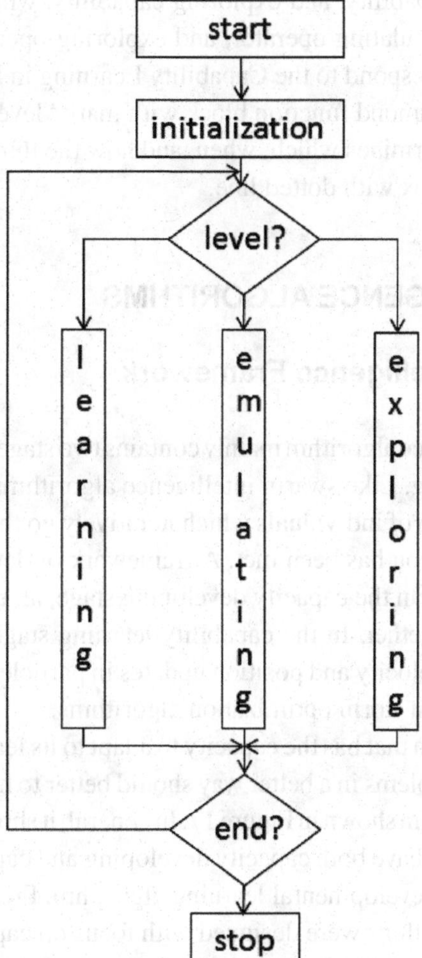

utilized as three optimization/search operators, therefore this algorithm is called an innovation-inspired optimization (IO) algorithm with three operators, i.e. learning, emulating, and exploring (LEE) operators.

As shown in Figure 15, the major difference between the IO algorithm and other swarm intelligence is its mapping function which involves learning operator, emulating operator, and exploring operator in parallel. In each iteration, which operators are to be executed and how are they executed depend on the diamond function block with mark "level?", which determines how to execute these three operators by considering current situation. It is more or less like a decision maker. With different considerations, different decision makers could be designed. A simple one can be to run these three operators probabilistically. For example, each operator will be selected to run with a probability, i.e., only one operator will be selected to run during any iteration. Another simple scenario can be that in each iteration, all three operators will be run, but with different probabilities. In summary, the IO algorithm possess the three search capabilities, that is, learning capability, emulating capability, and exploring capability.

Developmental Learning Perspective for Innovation-Inspired Optimization Algorithm

As discussed in the previous section, there are three search capabilities in an IO algorithm. They are learning capability, emulating capability, and exploring capability, which come out from the LEE operators, i.e., learning operator, emulating operator, and exploring operator, respectively. As shown in Figure 16, the LEE operators correspond to the Capability Learning in DSI, which is marked in a green box with dotted line, while the diamond function block with mark "level?" corresponds to the Capacity Developing in DSI because it determines which, when, and how the three operators are to be run, which is also marked in another green box with dotted line.

UNIFIED SWARM INTELLIGENCE ALGORITHMS

Developmental Swarm Intelligence Framework

A developmental swarm intelligence algorithm mainly contains two stages of learning, that is, the capacity developing and capability learning. Like swarm intelligence algorithms, a developmental swarm intelligence algorithm has a population of individuals which iteratively go through the two stages of learning until at least a termination condition has been met. A framework of developmental swarm intelligence algorithms is shown in Figure 17. In the capacity developing stage, all the individuals in the population develop the learning capacity together. In the capability learning stage, the population of individuals learns to solve problem, such as velocity and position updates in particle swarm optimization algorithms and individual updates in the brain storm optimization algorithms.

A swarm intelligence algorithm that has the capacity to adapt to its learning environment so that it can learn to solve large amount of problems in a better way should better to have a framework of the developmental swarm intelligence algorithm shown in Figure 17. In general, it should have developmental learning embedded, that is to say, it should have both capacity developing and capability learning embedded in it, or in other words, it should be a developmental learning algorithm. From author's understanding, most existing swarm intelligence algorithms were designed with focus on capability learning not on capacity developing. For example, as discussed in the previous section, particle swarm optimization algorithms

Figure 16. A developmental learning perspective of innovation-inspired optimization algorithm

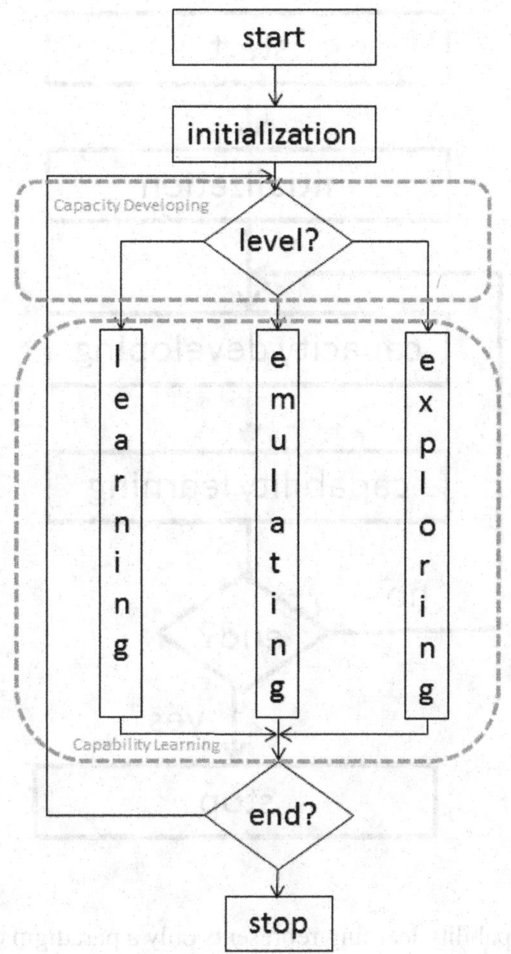

were originally designed to have learning capability, but by considering adapting its parameter and/or neighborhood topology, it turns the algorithm to be able to adapt to its learning environment, therefore, to develop its learning capacity in addition to learning capability. This is true for other swarm intelligence algorithms, such as a firefly optimization algorithm. In general, a developmental swarm intelligence algorithm has both capacity developing and capability learning, and it usually is implemented in two separate layers, that is, it usually has the hierarchal learning structure. One layer focuses on capacity developing while the other layer focuses on capability learning. Or in other words, capacity developing is a top-level learning or macro-level learning, and capability learning is a bottom-level learning or a micro-level learning. A few swarm intelligence algorithms were designed with consideration of both capacity developing and capacity learning either intentionally or unintentionally, which include the brain storm optimization algorithms, the cultural algorithms, and the fireworks algorithms as discussed in the previous section. For example, in a brain storm optimization algorithm, two layers of learning are implemented in each generation. The converging operation corresponds to capacity developing while the diverging operation corresponds to capability learning. As a consequence, any developmental swarm intelligence algorithm should have the framework shown in Figure 17. A different implementation for

Figure 17. A framework of a developmental swarm intelligence algorithm

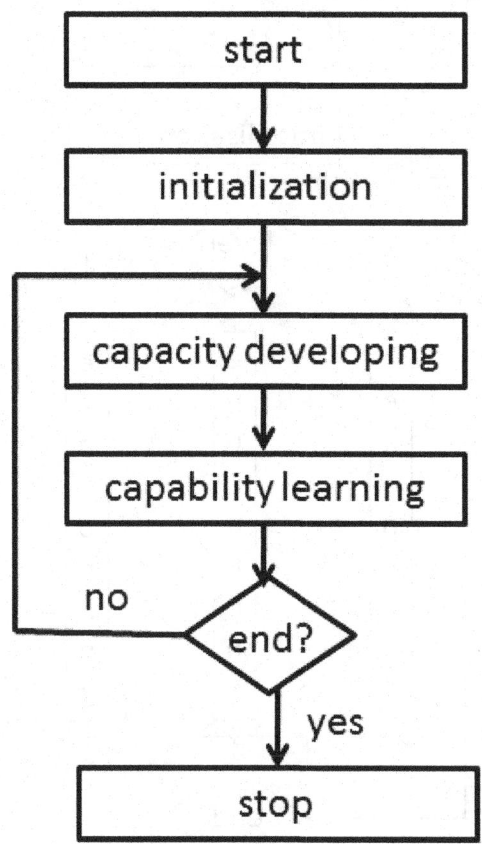

capacity developing and/or capability learning represents only a paradigm of the developmental swarm intelligence. Therefore, the Figure 17 can be considered as a standard developmental swarm intelligence algorithm framework under which different paradigms could be designed and/or implemented to fit for different kind of problems.

Unified Swarm Intelligence Framework

The developmental swarm intelligence framework specifies that a good optimization algorithm should have two layers of learning, which are capacity developing and capability learning, while the framework of innovation-inspired optimization algorithms specifies that a good optimization algorithm should have three types of search operators in its capability learning, which are learning operator, emulating operator, and exploring operator. It will be natural to believe that an even better swarm intelligence framework should be one that combines the developmental swarm intelligence framework and the framework of the innovation-inspired optimization algorithm. Figure 18 shows one that combines both, which can be called as a unified swarm intelligence framework. A swarm intelligence algorithm should be designed to follow the unified swarm intelligence framework shown in Figure 18 to have good or better performance.

Figure 18. Unified swarm intelligence framework

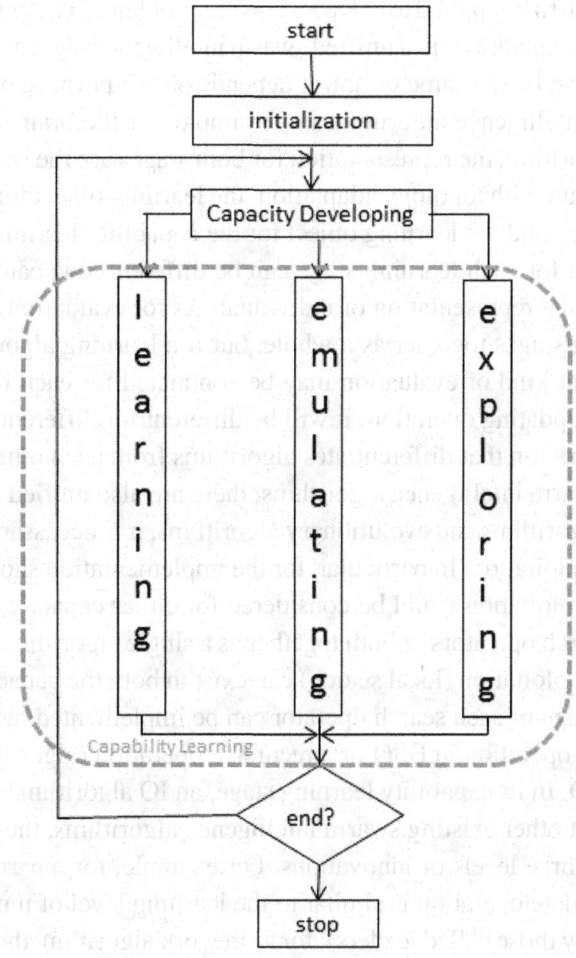

DISCUSSIONS AND FUTURE RESEARCH DIRECTIONS

The unified swarm intelligence framework shown in Figure 18 contains both capacity developing stage and capability learning stage, therefore the unified swarm intelligence framework is also a developmental swarm intelligence framework, but with LEE operators in its capability learning stage, which are learning operator, emulating operator, and exploring operator. By considering these three operators in the capability learning stage together, a unified swarm intelligence framework is the same as a developmental swarm intelligence framework. With three operators in its capability learning stage in a unified swarm intelligence framework, a unified swarm intelligence algorithm should possess much more abundant searching capabilities.

Capacity developing stage and three search operators in the capability learning stage usually are implemented as one operation each, but it is possible that each can be implemented by a learning algorithm which can be any kind of learning algorithms including population-based swarm intelligence algorithms. In this way, there are iterations inside each algorithm.

Like in any swarm intelligence algorithm, there are three factors that need to be considered for a unified swarm intelligence algorithm to be applied to solve real-world problems. They are representation, evaluation, and individual updating operation. In a unified swarm intelligence algorithm, the representation for the two stages of learning can be the same or not. It depends on the purpose or object of each learning stage for a unified swarm intelligence algorithm. For example, for the brain storm optimization algorithm and the fireworks algorithm, the representation for both stages are the same, while for the particle swarm optimization algorithm with topology adaptation, the learning object for the capacity developing is the neighborhood topology and the learning object for the capability learning is the individual itself, therefore, the representation for each learning stage can be different, one can be the representation of topology while the other is the representation of individual. As for evaluation, in general, evaluation is conducted for both learning stages together as a whole, but if a learning algorithm is utilized for each learning stage, then different kind of evaluation may be conducted for each learning stage separately. With regards to individual updating operation, it will be different for different algorithms. It is usually the individual updating operation that differentiates algorithms from each other.

In addition to unified swarm intelligence algorithms, there are also unified evolutionary algorithms. As in swarm intelligence algorithms and evolutionary algorithms, it is necessary to consider the balance between exploration and exploitation. In particular, for the implementation shown in Figure 18, balance between exploration and exploitation could be considered for either capacity developing or capability learning including three search operators or both together as a single algorithm. That is to say that exploration (global search) and exploitation (local search) can exist in both the capacity developing stage and capability learning. Each stage or each search operator can be implemented by a feed-forward mapping operation such as divergent operation in BSO or a recursive operation (algorithm) such as the *k*-means clustering algorithm in BSO. In its capability learning stage, an IO algorithm has three search operators included, but so far for most other existing swarm intelligence algorithms, they do not contain all three search operators to mimic three levels of innovations. For example, for a particle swarm optimization algorithm, its individual update operation is similar to the learning level of innovation, i.e., individuals learning from others (usually those called leaders); for a firework algorithm, there are mainly two operations that are critical to fireworks algorithms which are explosion strategy and selection strategy. The explosion strategy is similar to the emulating level of innovation, i.e., individuals emulating the explosion of fireworks, while the selection strategy is similar to the learning level, i.e., individual selecting (learning) better positions to explode; With three search operators in its capability learning stage, a unified swarm intelligence algorithm intuitively should have better balance between exploration and exploitation by considering the three search operators being inspired by three levels of innovations, i.e., learning level, emulating level, and exploring level, therefore a unified swarm intelligence algorithm should have better search capability, especially when solving complicated and complex optimization problems.

Furthermore, it will be helpful and useful but also very challenging to design a unified capacity developing operation (or algorithm) and capability learning operation (or algorithm) that work the best for at least most of problems because of its capacity developing component. Certainly, the starting point is to come out more and different capacity developing and capability learning operations before considering designing unified operations.

CONCLUSION

In this chapter, swarm intelligence algorithms were looked at from the developmental learning perspective. A framework of developmental swarm intelligence algorithms was provided so that it helps understand a developmental swarm intelligence algorithm and guide to design or to implement any new paradigm of developmental swarm intelligence algorithms. By briefly looking at brain evolution, brain development, brainstorming process, *etc*., it is natural to think that a swarm intelligence algorithm should include both capacity developing and capability learning stage to have better performance. It is the capacity developing stage that put the algorithm at the right position to learn knowledge or solve problem while it is the capability learning stage that actually learns knowledge or solves problems. For existing swarm intelligence algorithms, some of them have fixed capacity in their original versions, but they will have so-called capacity developing stage when their parameters are dynamically adjusted. Some examples discussed in this chapter are particle swarm optimization algorithms and firefly optimization algorithms. Some of existing algorithms were designed or implemented with consideration of capacity developing either intentionally or unintentionally. Examples discussed in this chapter are brain storm optimization algorithms, cultural algorithms, and fireworks algorithms. Following the developmental swarm intelligence algorithms, a new population-based swarm intelligence algorithm, called innovation-inspired optimization algorithm, was further designed and developed, which is inspired by the three levels of innovations, that is, the learning level of innovation, the emulating level of innovation, and the exploring level of innovations. By combining the innovation-inspired optimization algorithm and the developmental swarm intelligence framework together, a unified swarm intelligence framework was proposed which, like the developmental swarm intelligence, has capacity developing stage and capability learning stage but with three search operators in its capability learning stage to mimicking three levels of innovations, therefore, an algorithm designed under the unified swarm intelligence framework should have better balance between exploration and exploitation and could fit well for solving wider range of optimization problems.

ACKNOWLEDGMENT

This work is partially supported by the Ministry of Science and Technology (MOST) of China under the Grant No. 2017YFC0804002, Science and Technology Innovation Committee Foundation of Shenzhen under the Grant No. ZDSYS201703031748284

REFERENCES

Battiti, R. (1992). First-and second-order methods for learning: Between steepest descent and Newton's method. *Neural Computation*, *4*(2), 141–166. doi:10.1162/neco.1992.4.2.141

Cheng, S., Shi, Y., & Qin, Q. (2011). Experimental study on boundary constraints handling in particle swarm optimization: From population diversity perspective. *International Journal of Swarm Intelligence Research*, *2*(3), 43–69. doi:10.4018/jsir.2011070104

Cheng, S., Shi, Y., & Qin, Q. (2012). Population diversity of particle swarm optimizer solving single and multi-objective problems. *International Journal of Swarm Intelligence Research, 3*(4), 23–60. doi:10.4018/jsir.2012100102

Chudler, E. H. (2012). Brain development. *Neuroscience For Kids*. Retrieved from http://faculty.washington.edu/chudler/dev.html

Duan, H., Li, S., & Shi, Y. (2013). Predator-Prey Based Brain Storm Optimization for DC Brushless Motor. *IEEE Transactions on Magnetics, 49*(3), 5336–5240. doi:10.1109/TMAG.2013.2262296

Eberhart, R., & Kennedy, J. (1995). A new optimizer using particle swarm theory. *Proceedings of the Sixth International Symposium on Micro Machine and Human Science*, 39--43. doi:10.1109/MHS.1995.494215

Eberhart, R., & Shi, Y. (2007). *Computational Intelligence, Concepts to Implementation* (1st ed.). Morgan Kaufmann Publishers.

Fogel, L. J. (1962). Autonomous automata. *Industrial Research, 4*, 14–19.

Gardner, W. A. (1984). Learning characteristics of stochastic-gradient-descent algorithms: A general study, analysis, and critique. *Signal Processing, 6*(2), 113–133. doi:10.1016/0165-1684(84)90013-6

Grady, L. (2006). Random walks for image segmentation. *IEEE Transactions on Pattern Analysis and Machine Intelligence, 28*(11), 1768–1783. doi:10.1109/TPAMI.2006.233 PMID:17063682

Holland, J. H. (1975). *Adaptation in natural and artificial systems*. Ann Arbor, MI: Univ. of Michigan Press.

Hoos, H. H., & Stutzle, T. (2005). *Stochastic Local Search: Foundations and Applications*. Morgan Kaufmann.

Jadhav, H. T., Sharma, U., Patel, J., & Roy, R. (2012). Brain storm optimization algorithm based economic dispatch considering wind power. *2012 IEEE International Conference on Power and Energy (PECon)*, 588-593. doi:10.1109/PECon.2012.6450282

Kennedy, J., & Mendes, R. (2002). Population structure and particle swarm performance. *Proceedings of The Fourth Congress on Evolutionary Computation (CEC 2002)*, 1671-1676.

Koza, J. R. (1992). *Genetic Programming: On the Programming of Computers by Means of Natural Selection*. MIT Press.

Krishnanand, K. R., Hasani, S. M. F., Panigrahi, B. K., & Panda, S. K. (2013). Optimal Power Flow Solution Using Self–Evolving Brain–Storming Inclusive Teaching–Learning–Based Algorithm. In *Advances in Swarm Intelligence* (pp. 338–345). Springer Berlin Heidelberg. doi:10.1007/978-3-642-38703-6_40

Moscato, P., & Cotta, C. (2002). Memetic algorithms. Handbook of Applied Optimization, 157-167.

Osborn, A. F. (1963). *Applied imagination: Principles and procedures of creative problem solving* (3rd ed.). New York, NY: Charles Scribner's Son.

Radakrishnan, K. K. (2013). Optimal Power Flow Solution Using Self-Evolving Brain-Storming Inclusive Teaching-Learning-Based Algorithm. *4th International Conference on Swarm Intelligence*.

Ramanand, K. R., Krishnanand, K. R., Panigrahi, B. K., & Mallick, M. K. (2012). Brain Storming Incorporated Teaching–Learning–Based Algorithm with Application to Electric Power Dispatch. In Swarm, Evolutionary, and Memetic Computing, (pp. 476-483). Springer Berlin Heidelberg. doi:10.1007/978-3-642-35380-2_56

Rechenberg, I. (1973). *Evolutionsstrategie: Optimierung technischer Systeme nach Prinzipien der biologischen Evolution*. Stuttgart, Germany: Frommann-Holzboog.

Reynolds, R. G. (1994). An introduction to cultural algorithms. *Proceedings of the Third Annual Conference on Evolutionary Programming*, 131-139.

Schachner, E. (2013). How Has the Human Brain Evolved? *Scientific American Mind*, *24*(3). Retrieved from http://www.scientificamerican.com/article/how-has-human-brain-evolved/

Shi, Y. (2014). Developmental Swarm Intelligence: Developmental Learning Perspective of Swarm Intelligence Algorithms. *International Journal of Swarm Intelligence Research*, *5*(1), 36–54. doi:10.4018/ijsir.2014010102

Shi, Y., & Eberhart, R. (1998). A modified particle swarm optimizer. *Proceedings of the 1998 Congress on Evolutionary Computation (CEC1998)*, 69-73. doi:10.1109/ICEC.1998.699146

Shi, Y., Xue, J., & Wu, Y. (2013). Multi-Objective Optimization Based on Brain Storm Optimization Algorithm. *International Journal of Swarm Intelligence Research*, *4*(3), 1–21. doi:10.4018/ijsir.2013070101

Smith, R. (2002). *The 7 Levels of Change* (2nd ed.). Tapeslry Press.

Sun, C., Duan, H., & Shi, Y. (2013). Optimal Satellite Formation Reconfiguration Based on Closed-Loop Brain Storm Optimization. *Computational Intelligence Magazine, IEEE*, *8*(4), 39–51. doi:10.1109/MCI.2013.2279560

Tan, Y., Yu, C., Zheng, S., & Ding, K. (2013). Introduction to fireworks algorithm. *International Journal of Swarm Intelligence Research*, *4*(4), 39–70. doi:10.4018/ijsir.2013100103

Tan, Y., & Zhu, Y. (2010). Fireworks algorithm for optimization. In *Advances in Swarm Intelligence* (Vol. 6145, pp. 355–364). Springer Berlin Heidelberg. doi:10.1007/978-3-642-13495-1_44

Wolpert, D. H., & Macready, W. G. (1997). No free lunch theorems for optimization. *IEEE Transactions on Evolutionary Computation*, *1*(1), 67–82. doi:10.1109/4235.585893

Xue, J., Wu, Y., Shi, Y., & Cheng, S. (2012). Brain storm optimization algorithm for multi-objective optimization problems. In *Advances in Swarm Intelligence* (pp. 513–519). Springer Berlin Heidelberg. doi:10.1007/978-3-642-30976-2_62

Yang, X. S. (2008). *Nature-Inspired Metaheuristic Algorithms*. Luniver Press.

Yang, X. S. (2010). Firefly algorithm, stochastic test functions and design optimisation. *International Journal of Bio-inspired Computation*, *2*(2), 78–84. doi:10.1504/IJBIC.2010.032124

Yang, X. S. (2011). Chaos-Enhanced Firefly Algorithm with Automatic Parameter Tuning. *International Journal of Swarm Intelligence Research*, *2*(4), 1–11. doi:10.4018/jsir.2011100101

Yang, Y., Shi, Y., & Xia, S. (2013). Discussion mechanism based brain storm optimization algorithm. *Journal of Zhejiang University (Engineering Science)*, *47*(10), 1705–1711. doi:10.3785/j.issn.1008-973X.2013.10.002

Zhan, Z., Zhang, J., Li, Y., & Chung, H. S. (2009). Adaptive particle swarm optimization. *IEEE Trans. Syst., Man, Cybern. Part-B. Appl. Rev.*, *39*(6), 1362–1381.

Zhan, Z., Zhang, J., Shi, Y., & Liu, H. (2012). A modified brain storm optimization. *Evolutionary Computation (CEC), 2012 IEEE Congress on,* 1-8. doi:10.1109/CEC.2012.6256594

Zhou, D., Shi, Y., & Cheng, S. (2012). Brain storm optimization algorithm with modified step-size and individual generation. In *Advances in Swarm Intelligence* (pp. 243–252). Springer Berlin Heidelberg. doi:10.1007/978-3-642-30976-2_29

Zhu, Z., Zhou, J., Ji, Z., & Shi, Y. (2011). DNA Sequence Compression Using Adaptive Particle Swarm Optimization Based Memetic Algorithm. *IEEE Transactions on Evolutionary Computation*, *15*(5), 643–658. doi:10.1109/TEVC.2011.2160399

Chapter 2
Local Best Particle Swarm Optimization Using Crown Jewel Defense Strategy

Jiarui Zhou
Harbin Institute of Technology, China

Junshan Yang
Shenzhen University, China

Ling Lin
Shenzhen University, China

Zexuan Zhu
Shenzhen University, China

Zhen Ji
Shenzhen University, China

ABSTRACT

Particle swarm optimization (PSO) is a swarm intelligence algorithm well known for its simplicity and high efficiency on various problems. Conventional PSO suffers from premature convergence due to the rapid convergence speed and lack of population diversity. It is easy to get trapped in local optima. For this reason, improvements are made to detect stagnation during the optimization and reactivate the swarm to search towards the global optimum. This chapter imposes the reflecting bound-handling scheme and von Neumann topology on PSO to increase the population diversity. A novel crown jewel defense (CJD) strategy is introduced to restart the swarm when it is trapped in a local optimum region. The resultant algorithm named LCJDPSO-rfl is tested on a group of unimodal and multimodal benchmark functions with rotation and shifting. Experimental results suggest that the LCJDPSO-rfl outperforms state-of-the-art PSO variants on most of the functions.

DOI: 10.4018/978-1-5225-5134-8.ch002

INTRODUCTION

Particle swarm optimization (PSO) was first introduced by Kennedy and Eberhart (Eberhart & Kennedy, 1995) based on a social-psychological model of social influence and learning. Like most swarm intelligence algorithms, PSO is a population-based stochastic search technique. Each member of the PSO swarm, called a particle, represents a candidate solution in the search space. During the optimization, each particle iteratively adjusts its position and flying direction according to the velocity, which is dependent on the best experiences of the swarm and the particle itself. A fitness value is used to estimate the quality of the particle's position. The subsequent flying direction is determined accordingly.

PSO is easy to implement while highly effective in searching the solution space. It has been successfully applied to various optimization problems such as spam detection (Tan, 2010), breast cancer diagnosis (Sheikhpour, Sarram, & Sheikhpour, 2016), building energy performance simulation (Delgarm, Sajadi, Kowsary, & Delgarm, 2016), log-periodic antenna design (Zaharis et al., 2017), and radiotherapy planning (Modiri, Gu, Hagan, & Sawant, 2017). However, the conventional PSO commonly gets trapped in local optima when solving complex multimodal problems. It converges quickly in that information transmits throughout the swarm rapidly, while the search scope is also shrinking fast, which usually leads to the lack of population diversity and premature convergence. If the particles are initialized in proper areas, PSO can quickly reach a superior solution. However, in more common cases it is likely to converge to an inferior solution and result in mediocre performance.

Many PSO improvements have been proposed to address this problem by increasing the population diversity. For instance, Qin *et al.* improved PSO with an inter-swarm interactive learning strategy (Qin, Cheng, Zhang, Li, & Shi, 2016); Wang *et al.* introduced the idea of hybrid Krill herd and quantum-behaved in PSO to increase the local search ability and individual diversity (Wang, Gandomi, Alavi, & Deb, 2016); Dong *et al.* used supervised learning and control method to optimize the parameters and to maintain diversity for PSO (Dong & Zhou, 2017); Du *et al.* proposed a novel heterogeneous strategy PSO, which enhances the converging speed while prevents premature convergence (Du, Ying, Yan, Zhu, & Cao, 2017).

In this paper, we impose the reflecting bound-handling scheme and von Neumann topological neighborhood on a local best PSO (LPSO), which helps to achieve a better balance between diversity and convergence speed. Moreover, a novel Crown Jewel Defense (CJD) strategy is proposed to direct the algorithm toward a better solution when the particles are trapped in a local optimum region. We evaluate the performance of the proposed algorithm, namely LCJDPSO-rfl, through a series of experiments on both unimodal and multimodal benchmark functions. The experimental results demonstrate the stability and efficiency of LCJDPSO-rfl on most of the functions.

BACKGROUND

Global Optimization

Global optimization is the process for seeking variables that minimize or maximize the result of the target function. It's an important research area in the field of artificial intelligence and machine learning. Conventional deterministic optimization methods, e.g., Quasi-Newton methods and gradient descent achieve promising performance on unimodal and low dimensional problems. However, these "greedy" algorithms depend on the assumptions of the shape of the solution space. Their performance is sensitive to the selection of the searching starting point and decreases dramatically on high dimensional multimodal problems. The conventional methods are easily getting trapped in local optima. Improvement algorithms try to utilize stochastic searching strategies. Prominent methods include the Davies, Swann, and Campey with Gram-Schmidt orthogonalization (Swann, 1964), Davidon, Fletcher and Powell strategy (Powell, 1964), Solis and Wets algorithm (Solis & Wets, 1981), and Random walks in a Dirichlet environment (Enriquez & Sabot, 2006).

Nowadays the global optimization problems have formed a major category in the real-world applications. Their solution spaces are usually multimodal and sometimes contain discontinuous regions. The dimensions can be hundreds or even thousands. In many cases, the target function does not have an explicit mathematical definition. For this reason, the heuristic algorithms are proposed to search the optimal solution effectively and efficiently, while relaxing the assumptions of the problems' determinism and observability (Russell & Norvig, 2002). These algorithms normally involve a population to represent the candidate solutions, and use competitive selection, recombination, mutation or other stochastic operators to improve the overall search result (Nguyen, Ong, & Lim, 2009). Representative methods include genetic algorithm (Spears, De Jong, Bäck, Fogel, & De Garis), particle swarm optimization, differential evolution (Storn & Price, 1997), and brain storm optimization (Shi, 2011). These algorithms have achieved great success in the recent years.

According to the No Free Lunch Theorem (Wolpert & Macready, 1997), any two optimization algorithms are equivalent when their performance is averaged across all possible functions. One optimizer can outperform another only when it is more specialized to the target problem (Ho & Pepyne, 2002). Therefore, more sophisticated search strategies are adopted by the heuristic algorithms. This sometimes makes the optimization oversensitive to the parameter settings, and lead to unexpected performance decrease when the environmental conditions are slightly changed, which is common in real world applications. An alternative is to combine different optimization methods in the so-called memetic algorithm framework (Neri & Cotta, 2012). Some of the algorithms have reported promising results on a wide range of global optimization problems.

Particle Swarm Optimization

Inspired by the swarm behavior of birds flocking, Kennedy and Eberhart first proposed PSO as a population-based heuristic algorithm to handle complex optimization problems. PSO is invented to exploit the simulation of social interaction instead of the purely individual cognition. In a conventional PSO, a swarm of particles is defined to represent candidate solutions to the optimization problem to be solved. The swarm is first initialized randomly. Then each particle is moved iteratively in the direction adjusted by its own personal best position and the global best position of the swarm. In this way, the particles discover optimal regions of the solution space through learning from the historical information of themselves and the other particles. The moving direction, known as velocity, and the position of each particle are defined as vectors $\boldsymbol{v}_i$ and $\boldsymbol{x}_i$, respectively. In each iteration of PSO, each dimension of $\boldsymbol{v}_i$ and $\boldsymbol{x}_i$, denoted as v_i^d and x_i^d, are updated according to the following formulas:

$$v_i^d = v_i^d + c_1 \times r1_i^d \times \left(pbest_i^d - x_i^d\right) + c_2 \times r2_i^d \times \left(nbest - x_i^d\right)$$

$$x_i^d = x_i^d + v_i^d$$

where c_1 and c_2 are the acceleration parameters, $r1_i^d$ and $r2_i^d$ are two uniformly distributed random numbers in range [0, 1], $pbest_i^d$ is the best position yielding the best fitness value in the historical search of the *i*th particle, and *nbest* is the best position found by the particles in the neighborhood of the *i*th particle so far. The neighborhood of one particle is defined by a topology structure. Based on the size of the neighborhood, PSO algorithms can be categorized as global best PSOs and local best PSOs. In the global best PSO, the neighborhood includes the whole swarm, where *nbest* is also called *gbest*. In the local best PSO, *nbest* is the best *pbest* of the particles in a predefined neighborhood topology. The performance of PSO varies with different topological structures. The topological structure of the neighborhood can be configured statically or changed dynamically (Kennedy & Mendes, 2002).

In each generation of the iteration, after a particle has updated its flying direction and position, a comparison is conducted between the particle's current fitness value and its personal best fitness value, and the better one will be taken as the new personal best. The algorithm repeats this procedure until the stopping criteria are reached. Procedure of the conventional PSO is summarized in Algorithm 1.

The model of PSO is simple. It requires only few parameters. The PSO is flexible to be integrated with other optimization techniques. Accordingly, PSO has attracted increasing interest, and has been successfully used to solve a wide range of real-world problems. However, the researchers are still facing some major issues. One of them is that PSO usually suffers from premature convergence when applied to the complex multimodal optimization problems.

The PSO Improvements

A large number of PSO variants have been proposed to solve the issues and improve the performance. For instance, to control the balance between exploration and exploitation in PSO, the inertia weight ω was introduced to conventional PSO by Shi and Eberhart (Shi & Eberhart, 1998) to form the PSO*w*. With the inertia weight, the velocity update equation is changed to:

$$v_i^d = \omega \times v_i^d + c_1 \times r1_i^d \times \left(pbest_i^d - x_i^d\right) + c_2 \times r2_i^d \times \left(nbest - x_i^d\right)$$

Algorithm 1. The Procedure of PSO

```
1. Initialize the position and velocity of each particle in PSO swarm;
2. Update pbest and nbest;
3. While stopping criteria not satisfied do
4.     Calculate the velocity and position of each particle according to the
update formulas;
5.     Evaluate the fitness of each particle;
6.     Update pbest and nbest if necessary;
7. End while
```

where a larger ω emphasizes exploration and a smaller ω emphasizes exploitation. However, the explicit line between exploration and exploitation is hard to draw. Therefore, the inertia weight usually changes adaptively during the search. A widely used linear changing of ω is proceeded with the following equation:

$$\omega = \omega_{max} - \frac{\left(\omega_{max} - \omega_{min}\right) \times g}{G}$$

where ω_{max} and ω_{min} denote the predefined maximum and minimum vales of ω respectively. Variable g is the current generation number, and G is the predefined maximum number of generations. Based on this equation, PSO*w* starts with more exploration and gradually turns to favor exploitation as the g increases. Several adaptive methods are proposed afterwards.

The restart mechanism is another major research topic in PSO. For instance, Lovbjerg *et al.* (Lovbjerg & Krink, 2002) proposed a random relocation scheme to increase population diversity. García-Nieto *et al.* (García-Nieto & Alba, 2011) proposed RPSOvm by introducing the velocity modulation and restarting mechanisms to PSO to enhance its scalability on high-dimensional problems. Particularly, the velocity modulation mechanism is used to guide the particle movements towards the region of interests, and the restarting mechanism is imposed to avoid the early convergence and redirect the particles to promising areas in the search space. It is reported to preserve population diversity and obtain superior solutions.

A representative PSO improvement is the comprehensive learning PSO (CLPSO), which was proposed by Liang *et al.* (Liang, Qin, Suganthan, & Baskar, 2006). It utilizes a comprehensive learning strategy to address the issue of premature convergence. Unlike conventional PSOs that updates all dimensions of a particle only according to its own *pbest*, CLPSO allows each dimension to learn from different particles' *pbest*. This strategy successfully balances the search speed and the swarm's diversity. CLPSO has been demonstrated to perform excellently on complex multimodal optimization problems (Liang, Suganthan, & Deb, 2005). It is one of the most widely used PSO variants. Zhan *et al.* (Zhan, Zhang, Li, & Shi, 2011) proposed a novel orthogonal learning PSO (OLPSO). It employs orthogonal experimental design to discover useful information that lies in the above of a particle's historical best experience and its neighborhoods' best experiences. This strategy can guide the particles to fly in better directions by constructing a much promising and efficient exemplar. The OLPSO obtains high-quality solutions with strong robustness on different types of benchmark functions. More comprehensive review on PSO improvements can be found in (Bonyadi & Michalewicz, 2017; Zhang, Wang, & Ji, 2015). In this study, we combine the reflecting bound-handling scheme, the von Neumann topological neighborhood, and a newly defined Crown Jewel Defense (CJD) strategy to form a new LCJDPSO-rfl algorithm.

LOCAL BEST PSO USING CROWN JEWEL DEFENCE STRATEGY

The flowchart of the proposed CJDPSO-rfl is shown in Figure 1. It combines local best PSO with the reflecting bound-handling scheme to maintain the convergence speed. A CJD strategy is introduced to enhance the swarm's diversity and prevent the particles from trapping into the local optimum.

Figure 1. The flowchart of CJDPSO-rfl

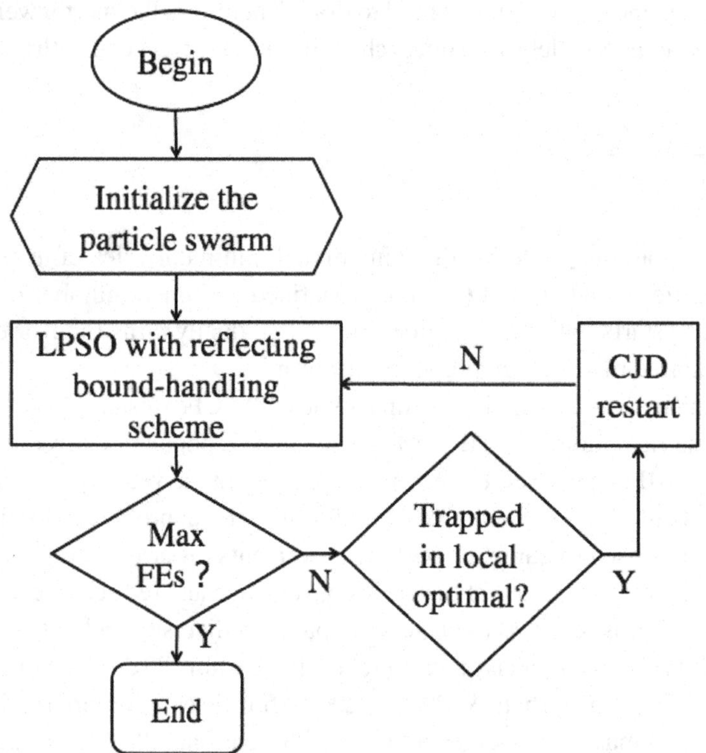

The von Neumann Topology

The von Neumann topology is chosen as the neighborhood structure for CJDPSO-rfl. As shown in Figure 2, the von Neumann topology is a closed surface where the neighbors above, below, and on a two-dimensional lattice of the updating particle were connected. The particle velocity is updated according to the *nbest*, i.e., the best particle position in the von Neumann topology neighborhood. It has been shown in several studies to outperform other social structures on various problems (Kennedy & Mendes, 2002; Peer, van den Bergh, & Engelbrecht, 2003).

The Reflecting Bound-Handling Scheme

During the optimization, the swarm in PSO can only search a limited range of the solution space on each dimension. A particle will be relocated within the boundary if it flies out of the range. In the reflecting bound-handling scheme, the boundary is like a mirror to reflect the projection of the out-of-bound particles. As shown in Figure 3, on a dimension a particle originally located in position x_{i-1} is supposed to move to $\tilde{x}_i$ on its next move, which is beyond the boundary by a distance L1. This particle will be rebounded to x_i instead. The reflecting scheme has been compared to other bound-handling schemes (Chu, Gao, & Sorooshian, 2011) and proved to be more effective in high-dimensional problems.

Figure 2. The von Neumann topology

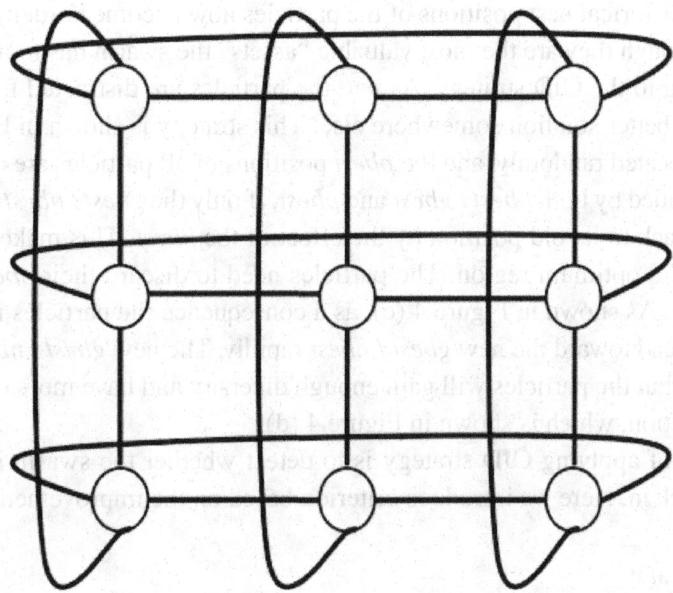

Figure 3. The reflecting bound-handling scheme

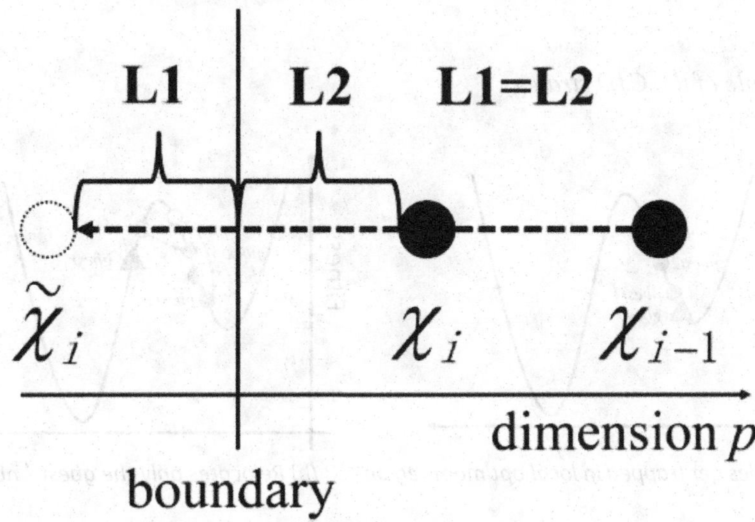

The Crown Jewel Defense Strategy

The idea of CJD restart mechanism is derived from the Crown Jewel Defense strategy in business (Berkovitch & Khanna, 1990). According to this strategy, to protect from the takeover, a company sells off its most valuable assets to a third party to become a less attractive acquisition target. That is, the sacrifice of the most valuable assets is made for greater interest. In this paper, we borrow the idea in PSO to restart the particle swarm when it is trapped in a local optimum.

As shown in Figure 4 (a), the swarm oscillates around a local optimum region and wastes computational resources. The historical best positions of the particles now become burdens that confine them in this inferior area. Although they are the most valuable "assets" the swarm has found so far, they should be discarded according to the CJD strategy. As par, the particles are distracted from the local optimal and forced to search a better solution somewhere else. This strategy is shown in Figure 4 (b), in which the *gbest* / *nbest* is relocated randomly, and the *pbest* positions of all particles are reinitialized. The particle's movement is guided by both *nbest* / *gbest* and *pbest*. If only the *gbest* / *nbest* is changed, a particle will still be dragged back to its old position by the effect of the *pbest*. This makes the swarm difficult to escape from the local optimum region. The particles need to discard their *pbest* to follow the new relocated *nbest* / *gbest*. As shown in Figure 4 (c), as a consequence the particles move out of the local optimum region and head toward the new *gbest* / *nbest* rapidly. The new *gbest* / *nbest* position could be either better or worse, but the particles will gain enough diversity and have more opportunities to reach a more promising solution, which is shown in Figure 4 (d).

An essential issue of applying CJD strategy is to detect whether the swarm is trapped, i.e., when the strategy should kick in. Here we introduce criterion based on the improvement of the *pbest*. Given:

$$I_g^i = \frac{pbestV_{g-1}^i - pbestV_g^i}{pbestV_{g-1}^i}$$

Figure 4. An example of the CJD strategy

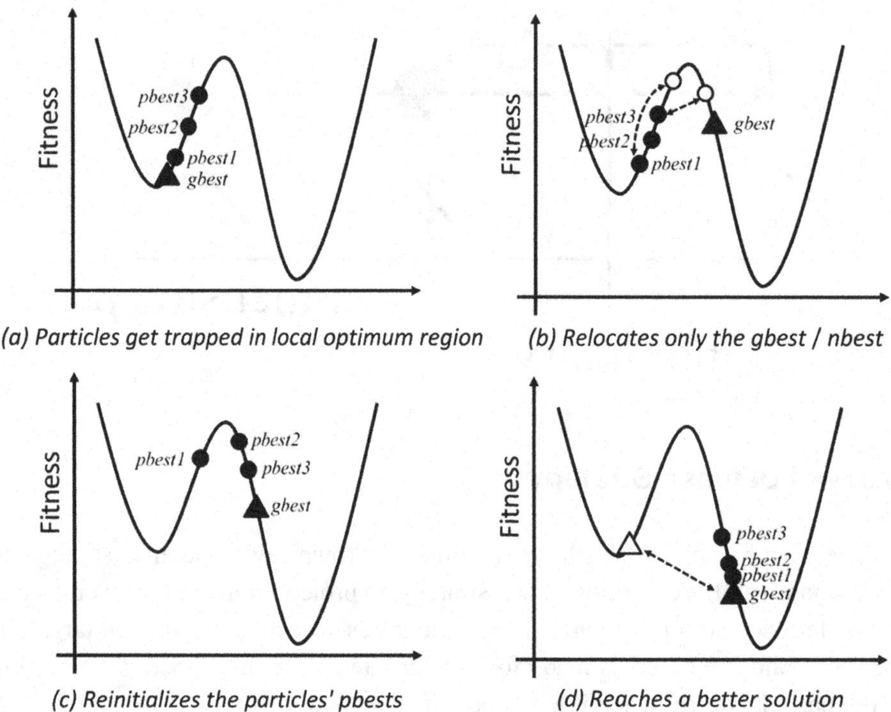

Algorithm 2. The Procedure of LCJDPSO-rfl

```
Initialize the position and velocity of each particle in PSO swarm ps;
Update pbest and nbest;
g = 0, k = 0;
While g < G do
    g = g + 1, k = k + 1;
    For i = 1 to |ps| do
        Update the velocity of particle i with the nbest in the von Neumann topology neighborhood;
        Update the position of particle i with the reflecting bound-handling scheme;
        Calculate the fitness value of particle i;
        If personal best pbest_i is improved then
            Update pbest_i;
            Calculate the improvement I_g^i;
            If I_g^i > δ then k = 0;
        End if
        Update nbest_i if necessary;
    End for
    Store the ever found global best solution;
    If k >= K then
        Apply CJD strategy;
        For i = 1 to |ps| do
            Reinitialize pbest_i and nbest_i;
        End for
        k = 0;
    End if
End while
```

where I_g^i is the improvement achieved by the *i*th particle in the *g*th iteration, and $pbestV_{g-1}^i$ and $pbestV_g^i$ denote the corresponding personal best fitness value before and after the update, respectively. If I_g^i is larger than a predefined threshold δ, the *pbest* improvement is considered as valid, i.e., the particle is reaching a better solution. In contrary, if I_g^i is smaller than δ, the improvement is negligible due to the oscillation. After a continuous *K* iterations, if no valid improvement can be detected in any particle, the CJD strategy is activated and the *pbest* of all particles are replaced with randomly generated positions. Note that the ever-found global best solution is stored separately before the CJD restart takes into effect so that it won't be lost.

Unlike conventional random restart methods, where the search process simply reruns from scratch, the CJD strategy only reinitializes the particles' *pbest* and *gbest* / *nbest*, meanwhile their current positions remain unchanged. These positions are obtained in previous evolution iterations. They contain useful information about the solution space. By retaining the current positions, the particle swarm can still learn from its historical experiences and avoid from where it has fallen.

By combining the von Neumann topology neighborhood, the reflecting bound-handling scheme, and the Crown Jewel Defense restart mechanism, we propose the LCJDPSO-rfl as given in Algorithm 2, in which *nbest* is the *pbest* of the best particle in the von Neumann topology.

EXPERIMENTAL STUDY

Benchmark Functions

A group of 26 benchmark functions from (Liang et al., 2005; Suganthan et al., 2005; Zhan et al., 2011) are used in the experiments to evaluate the performance of LCJDPSO-rfl. The benchmark functions are summarized in Table 1.

Table 1. The benchmark functions

	Function	Dimension	Search Range	Reference
f_1	Sphere	30	[-100, 100]	(Yao, Liu, & Lin, 1999)
f_2	Schwefel's Problem 2.22	30	[-10, 10]	(Yao et al., 1999)
f_3	Rosenbrock	30	[-10, 10]	(Yao et al., 1999)
f_4	Noise	30	[-1.28, 1.28]	(Yao et al., 1999)
f_5	Schwefel	30	[-500, 500]	(Yao et al., 1999)
f_6	Rastrigin	30	[-5.12, 5.12]	(Yao et al., 1999)
f_7	Ackley	30	[-32, 32]	(Yao et al., 1999)
f_8	Griewank	30	[-600, 600]	(Yao et al., 1999)
f_9	Generalized Penalized 1	30	[-50, 50]	(Yao et al., 1999)
f_{10}	Generalized Penalized 2	30	[-50, 50]	(Yao et al., 1999)
f_{11}	Rotated Schwefel	30	[-500, 500]	(J. J. Liang et al., 2006)
f_{12}	Rotated Rastrigin	30	[-5.12, 5.12]	(J. J. Liang et al., 2006)
f_{13}	Rotated Ackley	30	[-32, 32]	(J. J. Liang et al., 2006)
f_{14}	Rotated Griewank	30	[-600, 600]	(J. J. Liang et al., 2006)
f_{15}	Shifted Rosenbrock	30	[-100, 100]	(Suganthan et al., 2005)
f_{16}	Shifted Rastrigin	30	[-5, 5]	(Suganthan et al., 2005)
f_{17}	CF1	30	[-5, 5]	(J. Liang et al., 2005)
f_{18}	CF2	30	[-5, 5]	(J. Liang et al., 2005)
f_{19}	CF3	30	[-5, 5]	(J. Liang et al., 2005)
f_{20}	CF4	30	[-5, 5]	(J. Liang et al., 2005)
f_{21}	CF5	30	[-5, 5]	(J. Liang et al., 2005)
f_{22}	CF6	30	[-5, 5]	(J. Liang et al., 2005)
f_{23}	F15	30	[-5, 5]	(Suganthan et al., 2005)
f_{24}	F18	30	[-5, 5]	(Suganthan et al., 2005)
f_{25}	F21	30	[-5, 5]	(Suganthan et al., 2005)
f_{26}	F24	30	[-5, 5]	(Suganthan et al., 2005)

The benchmark functions consist of four groups: unimodal functions f_1 - f_4, primary multimodal functions f_5 - f_{10}, rotated and shifted functions f_{11} - f_{16}, and complex hybrid functions f_{17} - f_{26}. The complexity of solving these functions increases from group 1 to group 4. For all 26 functions, the dimension of solution space is set to $D = 30$. The representative PSO improvements, the proposed LCJDPSO-rfl, and their variants are compared. Each algorithm is conducted independently for 30 runs on each benchmark function, and the average result is reported. All the algorithms are terminated when the maximum number of function evaluations (FEs) is reached. For f_1 - f_{16} the maximum FEs is set to 2E+5, and for f_{17} - f_{26} it is 5E+4.

Four experiments are carried out to evaluate the performance of LCJDPSO-rfl. Experiment 1 compares PSO algorithms with and without the reflecting bound-handling scheme, the von Neumann topology, and the CJD strategy. Experiment 2 investigates the settings of the crucial parameters ω and K for LCJDPSO-rfl. In Experiment 3, the effects of different restarting strategies are studied. Finally, Experiment 4 compares the performance of LCJDPSO-rfl with other representative PSO algorithms.

Parameter Settings

The population sizes of LCJDPSO-rfl and its variants are set to $|ps| = 30$. Improvement threshold is δ = 1E-6, inertia weight is $\omega = 0.4$, and the maximum generation to activate CJD reinitialization is $K = 6$. The settings of ω and K are further studied in Experiment 2. Acceleration parameters are set to $c_1 = 1$ and $c_2 = 2$, respectively. Larger c_2 allows the particles fly toward their *nbest* more quickly and accelerate the convergence speed. Their optimal value settings are determined according to the empirical studies.

Experiment 1: Effects of the Reflecting Bound-Handling Scheme, the Von Neumann Topology, and the CJD Strategy

To study the effects of the reflecting bound-handling scheme, the von Neumann topology neighborhood, and the CJD strategy, six variant algorithms with different combinations of these strategies are compared:

- **PSO:** Conventional global best PSO;
- **PSO-rfl:** Global best PSO with reflecting bound-handling scheme;
- **CJDPSO-rfl:** Global best PSO with reflecting bound-handling scheme and CJD strategy;
- **LPSO-rfl:** Local best PSO with von Neumann topology neighborhood and reflecting bound-handling scheme;
- **LCJDPSO:** Local best PSO with von Neumann topology neighborhood and CJD strategy;
- **LCJDPSO-rfl:** Local best PSO with von Neumann topology neighborhood, reflecting bound-handling scheme, and CJD strategy.

The mean fitness values of all the algorithms over 30 runs are listed in Table 2.

The comparisons between PSO, PSO-rfl, LCJDPSO, and LCJDPSO-rfl show that the algorithms with reflecting bound-handling scheme obtain better results than the counterparts. Results in CJDPSO-rfl and LCJDPSO-rfl indicate that the von Neumann topology neighborhood can improve the optimization performance in PSO. The superiority of utilizing CJD strategy is demonstrated in the comparison between LPSO-rfl and LCJDPSO-rfl. Experimental results show that the LCJDPSO-rfl, taking the advantages of all three strategies, outperforms all other variants on most of the benchmark functions.

Table 2. Experimental results of different combinations of the strategies

		PSO	PSO-rfl	CJDPSO-rfl	LPSO-rfl	LCJDPSO	LCJDPSO-rfl
f_1	Mean	1.20E+03	2.22E-163	7.77E-125	1.48E-167	2.29E-170	**2.73E-172**
	Var.	1.06E+07	0.00E+00	1.40E-247	0.00E+00	0.00E+00	**0.00E+00**
f_2	Mean	3.48E+01	1.46E-90	7.55E-73	7.88E-92	7.52E-70	**3.47E-94**
	Var.	4.17E+02	3.17E-179	1.37E-143	1.07E-184	1.36E-137	**2.45E-186**
f_3	Mean	4.10E+04	1.10E+00	3.68E+01	2.84E+00	3.35E+00	**1.96E+00**
	Var.	3.46E+10	2.59E+02	1.07E+03	4.04E+00	1.52E+01	**1.01E+01**
f_4	Mean	3.28E-01	1.39E-02	1.13E+00	3.32E-02	6.06E-04	**1.74E-04**
	Var.	5.31E-01	2.41E-03	2.57E+00	1.01E-05	9.56E-07	**4.57E-08**
f_5	Mean	3.73E+03	2.56E+03	**2.18E+03**	3.77E+03	3.39E+03	2.51E+03
	Var.	2.31E+05	4.88E+05	**3.77E+05**	1.15E+05	1.45E+05	9.25E+04
f_6	Mean	1.43E+02	9.10E+01	7.62E+01	9.47E+01	5.81E+01	**5.42E+01**
	Var.	2.09E+03	5.58E+02	4.06E+02	8.93E+01	1.74E+02	**4.08E+01**
f_7	Mean	9.48E+00	1.92E+00	4.83E-01	1.98E+00	3.73E-02	**4.74E-11**
	Var.	6.02E+01	9.38E-01	5.22E-01	5.83E-12	3.33E-02	**5.38E-20**
f_8	Mean	2.17E+01	3.70E-02	4.71E-02	1.45E-02	3.11E-17	**1.78E-17**
	Var.	1.49E+03	6.14E-03	2.57E-02	1.30E-33	5.44E-33	**2.64E-33**
f_9	Mean	3.04E-01	4.92E-01	7.98E+01	1.33E+00	**2.12E-33**	5.84E-33
	Var.	2.43E-01	6.59E-01	6.52E+04	4.13E-04	**1.24E-65**	8.55E-65
f_{10}	Mean	1.64E+07	1.01E-02	1.31E+00	1.66E-01	5.71E-32	**1.81E-32**
	Var.	6.46E+15	2.21E-04	4.05E+01	2.81E-63	3.40E-62	**1.56E-63**
f_{11}	Mean	8.58E+03	8.28E+03	9.21E+03	8.52E+03	**7.60E+03**	7.62E+03
	Var.	3.13E+05	4.54E+05	1.67E+05	2.18E+05	**9.09E+04**	1.23E+05
f_{12}	Mean	2.59E+02	1.63E+02	2.46E+02	1.32E+02	8.89E+01	**8.77E+01**
	Var.	5.78E+03	1.27E+03	6.21E+03	2.35E+02	2.02E+02	**2.29E+02**
f_{13}	Mean	2.03E+01	1.81E+01	1.83E+01	8.27E+00	4.76E+00	**3.80E+00**
	Var.	9.12E+00	2.74E+01	2.86E+01	3.47E-01	1.29E+00	**6.09E-01**
f_{14}	Mean	2.33E+02	1.92E-02	6.63E-02	1.05E-02	**8.85E-04**	2.85E-03
	Var.	5.27E+04	3.80E-04	2.36E-02	1.01E-05	**1.88E-05**	8.53E-05
f_{15}	Mean	4.25E+09	1.97E+01	8.21E+02	1.99E+01	1.47E+06	**1.92E+01**
	Var.	2.44E+19	1.56E+03	4.42E+06	4.42E+02	1.60E+13	**1.09E+03**
f_{16}	Mean	1.44E+02	6.50E+01	6.21E+01	1.01E+02	6.88E+01	**4.41E+01**
	Var.	1.04E+03	4.00E+02	1.58E+03	4.99E+01	1.35E+02	**4.21E+01**
f_{17}	Mean	2.09E+02	9.60E+01	8.21E+01	4.40E+01	3.52E+00	**0.00E+00**
	Var.	1.24E+04	1.32E+04	6.60E+03	0.00E+00	2.98E+02	**0.00E+00**
f_{18}	Mean	3.13E+02	2.12E+02	8.78E+01	8.53E+01	2.12E+01	**2.23E+00**
	Var.	1.89E+04	1.51E+04	7.50E+03	6.08E+00	1.52E+02	**2.18E+00**

continued on following page

Table 2. Continued

		PSO	PSO-rfl	CJDPSO-rfl	LPSO-rfl	LCJDPSO	LCJDPSO-rfl
f_{19}	Mean	3.36E+02	2.22E+02	2.87E+02	2.04E+02	1.39E+02	**1.19E+02**
	Var.	2.22E+04	7.68E+03	1.60E+04	2.08E+02	4.72E+02	**2.85E+02**
f_{20}	Mean	4.89E+02	4.59E+02	4.31E+02	3.74E+02	3.01E+02	**2.91E+02**
	Var.	2.70E+04	2.61E+04	1.29E+04	1.41E+02	1.35E+02	**1.40E+02**
f_{21}	Mean	2.98E+02	1.19E+02	7.27E+01	3.68E+01	2.04E+01	**2.84E+00**
	Var.	4.57E+04	2.00E+04	4.59E+03	2.03E+00	3.96E+02	**2.53E+00**
f_{22}	Mean	8.46E+02	8.36E+02	5.06E+02	7.27E+02	5.36E+02	**5.13E+02**
	Var.	1.64E+04	2.08E+04	3.79E+01	2.08E+04	9.43E+03	**3.50E+03**
f_{23}	Mean	5.40E+02	3.52E+02	3.01E+02	3.25E+02	1.88E+02	**1.65E+02**
	Var.	2.72E+04	5.48E+04	2.43E+04	1.31E+03	6.47E+03	**4.21E+03**
f_{24}	Mean	9.62E+02	8.29E+02	9.26E+02	7.94E+02	6.68E+02	**5.52E+02**
	Var.	8.47E+03	2.84E+04	6.49E+03	1.51E+04	7.26E+03	**2.30E+04**
f_{25}	Mean	1.19E+03	9.38E+02	7.95E+02	8.55E+02	6.31E+02	**5.14E+02**
	Var.	1.41E+04	8.94E+04	1.12E+05	6.40E+03	4.08E+04	**2.18E+04**
f_{26}	Mean	1.10E+03	4.33E+02	3.75E+02	2.68E+02	8.57E+02	**2.00E+02**
	Var.	1.97E+04	1.19E+05	8.02E+04	1.16E-12	6.14E+04	**1.09E-12**

Experiment 2: Effects of Parameters K and ω

The parameter K is introduced in LCJDPSO-rfl to specify the maximum number of stagnant iterations the swarm could endure before the CJD strategy is applied. It plays a major role in controlling the intensity of exploitation. A small K results in quick turn to exploration by relocating the *pbest* positions, while large K allows the swarm to exploit more in the local region. Nevertheless, K should not be set too small, say, less than six generations so that the swarm can search the current area thoroughly and avoid falsely detect the stagnant. We study the effect of K by setting it to 6, 12, and 30 respectively. The average results of LCJDPSO-rfl using different Ks are reported in Table 3. It is shown that LCJDPSO obtains best performance with $K = 6$ especially on complex hybrid functions f_{17} - f_{26}, suggesting that *pbest* should be relocated as soon as the stagnant is confirmed. Whereas, in f_1 - f_{16}, the performance of using $K = 6$ is competitive with that of $K = 12$. Overall, $K = 6$ is the best choice for all functions.

The second parameter we study is the inertia weight ω. It has been shown that PSOs with dynamic ω tend to outperform the counterparts with constant ω. However, this is not the case in LCJDPSO-rfl. We compare the performance of LCJDPSO-rfl using linear changing ω and constant $\omega = 0.1, 0.4, 0.9$. The results are reported in Table 4. It is shown that LCJDPSO-rfl with a constant $\omega = 0.4$ obtains the best results. The reason may rely on the usage of the CJD strategy. When CJD is activated, i.e., the personal best positions are relocated, large ω is preferred to drag the particles out of the local optimum area. In a linear changing ω, its value reduces as the iteration number increases. Therefore, the impact of CJD strategy is suppressed at the late stage of the search. The constant $\omega = 0.4$ happens to obtain the best balance between exploitation and exploration. It maximizes the positive impact of CJD to LCJDPSO-rfl.

Table 3. Experimental results of different K setting

	$K = 6$	$K = 12$	$K = 30$		$K = 6$	$K = 12$	$K = 30$
f_1	**2.73E-172**	4.80E-171	3.93E-168	f_{14}	2.85E-03	**1.47E-03**	3.64E-03
	± 0.00E+00	± 0.00E+00	± 0.00E+00		± 8.53E-05	**± 1.50E-05**	± 9.27E-05
f_2	3.47E-94	**7.39E-95**	1.17E-92	f_{15}	1.92E+01	**7.43E+00**	3.11E+01
	± 2.45E-186	**± 2.03E-188**	± 3.23E-183		± 1.09E+03	**± 3.55E+02**	± 3.06E+03
f_3	1.96E+00	**1.54E+00**	2.67E+00	f_{16}	**4.41E+01**	4.66E+01	4.57E+01
	± 1.01E+01	**± 3.14E+00**	± 6.30E+00		**± 4.21E+01**	± 5.76E+01	± 8.30E+01
f_4	**1.74E-04**	4.36E-04	7.55E-04	f_{17}	**0.00E+00**	**0.00E+00**	**0.00E+00**
	± 4.57E-08	± 4.11E-07	± 2.00E-06		**± 0.00E+00**	**± 0.00E+00**	**± 0.00E+00**
f_5	2.51E+03	**2.39E+03**	2.59E+03	f_{18}	**2.23E+00**	2.62E+00	3.14E+00
	± 9.25E+04	**± 1.80E+05**	± 1.11E+05		**± 2.18E+00**	± 4.04E+00	± 9.79E+00
f_6	5.42E+01	5.29E+01	**5.18E+01**	f_{19}	**1.19E+02**	1.23E+02	1.36E+02
	± 4.08E+01	± 6.09E+01	**± 9.33E+01**		**± 2.85E+02**	± 2.61E+02	± 6.41E+02
f_7	**4.74E-11**	5.36E-02	2.13E-01	f_{20}	**2.89E+02**	2.93E+02	2.97E+02
	± 5.38E-20	± 6.90E-02	± 1.84E-01		**± 1.40E+02**	± 2.98E+02	± 2.16E+02
f_8	**1.78E-17**	3.11E-17	3.11E-17	f_{21}	**2.43E+00**	3.20E+00	3.60E+00
	± 2.64E-33	± 1.14E-32	± 6.43E-33		**± 2.53E+00**	± 2.69E+00	± 1.33E+00
f_9	5.84E-33	**2.17E-33**	4.15E-03	f_{22}	**5.13E+02**	**5.13E+02**	5.18E+02
	± 8.55E-65	**± 1.89E-65**	± 4.13E-04		**± 3.50E+03**	**± 6.67E+03**	± 6.18E+03
f_{10}	**1.81E-32**	5.18E-32	1.89E-32	f_{23}	**1.65E+02**	1.76E+02	1.73E+02
	± 1.56E-63	± 1.95E-62	± 1.92E-63		**± 4.21E+03**	± 6.56E+03	± 5.90E+03
f_{11}	7.62E+03	**7.59E+03**	**7.59E+03**	f_{24}	**5.52E+02**	6.07E+02	5.87E+02
	± 1.23E+05	**± 1.75E+05**	**± 1.14E+05**		**± 2.30E+04**	± 2.84E+04	± 2.60E+04
f_{12}	8.77E+01	**8.30E+01**	8.65E+01	f_{25}	5.14E+02	**4.99E+02**	5.63E+02
	± 2.29E+02	**± 2.21E+02**	± 3.83E+02		± 2.18E+04	**± 8.49E+03**	± 3.19E+04
f_{13}	**3.80E+00**	4.06E+00	4.07E+00	f_{26}	**2.00E+02**	**2.00E+02**	**2.00E+02**
	± 6.09E-01	± 4.51E-01	± 6.50E-01		**± 1.09E-12**	**± 1.90E-14**	**± 3.80E-18**

Experiment 3: Comparison of the Different Restarting Strategies

In this experiment, we investigate the effects of the CJD strategy and other restart methods. Following algorithms with different strategies are compared:

- **LSPSO-rfl:** The LPSO-rfl algorithm with whole swarm restarting, which reinitializes the current and *pbest* positions of all particles;
- **LPPSO-rfl:** The LPSO-rfl algorithm with a strategy that only the current positions of the particles are reinitialized;
- **LPPSO-1/D-rfl:** The LPSO-rfl algorithm with a strategy that each dimension of the particle position is reinitialized randomly with probability 1/D;

Table 4. Experimental results of different ω setting

	Linear ω	$\omega = 0.1$	$\omega = 0.4$	$\omega = 0.9$		Linear ω	$\omega = 0.1$	$\omega = 0.4$	$\omega = 0.9$
f_1	**1.2E-184**	8.1E-178	2.7E-172	1.8E+04	f_{14}	3.5E-03	**2.6E-03**	2.9E-03	6.1E+02
	± 0.0E+00	± 0.0E+00	± 0.0E+00	± 5.3E+06		± 4.1E-05	**± 3.2E-05**	± 8.5E-05	± 2.9E+03
f_2	2.8E-58	1.6E-45	**3.5E-94**	6.3E+01	f_{15}	**1.4E+01**	7.3E+01	1.9E+01	9.3E+09
	± 1.9E-114	± 5.9E-89	**±2.5E-186**	± 4.0E+01		**± 9.6E+02**	± 8.8E+03	± 1.1E+03	± 9.8E+18
f_3	5.2E+00	6.2E+00	**2.0E+00**	3.2E+05	f_{16}	5.2E+01	5.9E+01	**4.4E+01**	3.1E+02
	± 1.7E+02	± 1.7E+02	**± 1.0E+01**	± 2.5E+09		± 8.1E+01	± 7.5E+01	**± 4.2E+01**	± 1.6E+02
f_4	1.4E-03	3.1E-03	**1.7E-04**	4.0E+00	f_{17}	**0.0E+00**	**0.0E+00**	**0.0E+00**	1.6E+02
	± 1.7E-06	± 6.8E-06	**± 4.6E-08**	± 6.7E-01		**± 0.0E+00**	**± 0.0E+00**	**± 0.0E+00**	± 2.4E+02
f_5	2.9E+03	3.1E+03	**2.5E+03**	7.3E+03	f_{18}	3.0E+00	4.3E+00	**2.2E+00**	1.4E+02
	± 1.8E+05	± 1.1E+05	**± 9.3E+04**	± 1.2E+05		± 6.4E+00	± 1.2E+01	**± 2.2E+00**	± 4.2E+02
f_6	5.4E+01	5.5E+01	**5.4E+01**	2.6E+02	f_{19}	1.3E+02	1.3E+02	**1.2E+02**	4.4E+02
	± 6.8E+01	± 3.9E+01	**± 4.1E+01**	± 2.4E+02		± 3.8E+02	± 5.6E+02	**± 2.9E+02**	± 2.8E+03
f_7	5.7E-01	1.3E+00	**4.7E-11**	1.8E+01	f_{20}	2.9E+02	2.9E+02	**2.9E+02**	5.2E+02
	± 4.6E-01	± 5.3E-01	**± 5.4E-20**	± 1.4E-01		± 2.9E+02	± 3.7E+02	**± 1.4E+02**	± 9.5E+02
f_8	8.0E-17	2.4E-16	**1.8E-17**	1.6E+02	f_{21}	4.2E+00	6.1E+00	**2.4E+00**	1.3E+02
	± 1.3E-32	± 8.6E-32	**± 2.6E-33**	± 8.3E+02		± 1.5E+00	± 7.7E+00	**± 2.5E+00**	± 3.0E+02
f_9	6.2E-32	2.6E-31	**5.8E-33**	2.2E+07	f_{22}	5.2E+02	5.6E+02	**5.1E+02**	5.6E+02
	± 3.0E-62	± 1.0E-60	**± 8.6E-65**	± 4.9E+13		± 6.2E+03	± 1.7E+04	**± 3.5E+03**	± 2.7E+02
f_{10}	8.8E-04	2.3E-03	**1.8E-32**	8.4E+07	f_{23}	1.6E+02	**1.5E+02**	1.7E+02	5.1E+02
	± 8.9E-06	± 1.9E-05	**± 1.6E-63**	± 2.3E+14		± 1.9E+03	**± 1.5E+03**	± 4.2E+03	± 4.5E+03
f_{11}	**7.6E+03**	7.6E+03	7.6E+03	9.4E+03	f_{24}	6.1E+02	6.5E+02	**5.5E+02**	9.7E+02
	± 1.8E+05	± 9.1E+04	± 1.2E+05	± 2.2E+04		± 1.5E+04	± 1.0E+04	**± 2.3E+04**	± 4.8E+03
f_{12}	**8.6E+01**	8.7E+01	8.8E+01	4.4E+02	f_{25}	5.2E+02	**4.9E+02**	5.1E+02	1.2E+03
	± 3.4E+02	± 2.5E+02	± 2.3E+02	± 4.8E+02		± 1.6E+04	**± 1.0E+04**	± 2.2E+04	± 9.6E+03
f_{13}	5.1E+00	6.1E+00	**3.8E+00**	2.1E+01	f_{26}	**2.0E+02**	**2.0E+02**	**2.0E+02**	9.4E+02
	± 1.2E+00	± 9.6E-01	**± 6.1E-01**	± 5.3E-03		**± 2.4E-13**	**± 5.5E-13**	**± 1.1E-12**	± 7.9E+03

- **LCJDPSO-rfl:** The proposed algorithm.

The average best fitness values of these algorithms over 30 independent runs are reported in Table 5. All four algorithms use the same von Neumann topology neighborhood and reflecting bound-handling scheme. Their parameter settings are the same. The results show that LCJDPSO-rfl outperforms other counterpart algorithms particularly on the complex hybrid functions.

The experimental results show that different restart strategies affect the performance differently. The whole swarm reinitialization works well on some functions. However, it is generally inefficient due to the discarding of all previous experiences. The LPPSO-rfl and LPPSO-1/D-rfl obtain promising results on several unimodal and multimodal functions. Retaining the old *pbest* positions, particles are easily trapped in local optimum regions particularly on complex benchmark functions. In general, the CJD strategy is superior to the counterpart methods.

Table 5. Experimental results of different restart strategies

		LSPSO-rfl	LPPSO-rfl	LPPSO-1/D-rfl	LCJDPSO-rfl
f_1	Mean	1.26E-167	4.65E-171	1.11E-171	**2.73E-172**
	Var.	0.00E+00	0.00E+00	0.00E+00	**0.00E+00**
f_2	Mean	5.51E-93	3.47E-93	2.27E-93	**3.47E-94**
	Var.	3.97E-184	2.28E-184	6.95E-185	**2.45E-186**
f_3	Mean	2.18E+00	2.41E+00	2.22E+00	**1.96E+00**
	Var.	4.30E+00	3.23E+00	5.70E+00	**1.01E+01**
f_4	Mean	3.25E-04	8.74E-03	**1.83E-05**	1.74E-04
	Var.	2.09E-07	1.28E-04	**6.64E-09**	4.57E-08
f_5	Mean	2.58E+03	3.84E+03	**3.32E+01**	2.51E+03
	Var.	1.24E+05	4.78E+05	**5.07E+03**	9.25E+04
f_6	Mean	5.58E+01	1.07E+02	**4.12E-15**	5.42E+01
	Var.	1.10E+02	6.57E+02	**5.82E-29**	4.08E+01
f_7	Mean	3.73E-02	2.59E+00	**2.63E-14**	4.74E-11
	Var.	3.33E-02	3.37E+00	**1.53E-28**	5.38E-20
f_8	Mean	**1.33E-17**	1.81E-02	1.74E-02	1.78E-17
	Var.	**2.29E-33**	4.74E-04	3.05E-04	2.64E-33
f_9	Mean	1.66E-02	5.73E-01	3.76E-31	**5.84E-33**
	Var.	4.02E-03	4.41E-01	3.18E-60	**8.55E-65**
f_{10}	Mean	**1.62E-32**	2.03E-01	9.62E-31	1.81E-32
	Var.	**1.26E-63**	2.91E-01	1.65E-59	1.56E-63
f_{11}	Mean	**7.55E+03**	8.40E+03	8.58E+03	7.62E+03
	Var.	**7.11E+04**	4.85E+05	1.41E+05	1.23E+05
f_{12}	Mean	8.94E+01	1.30E+02	1.23E+02	**8.77E+01**
	Var.	2.87E+02	1.06E+03	1.10E+03	**2.29E+02**
f_{13}	Mean	4.10E+00	7.33E+00	7.45E+00	**3.80E+00**
	Var.	6.42E-01	8.72E+00	6.82E+00	**6.09E-01**
f_{14}	Mean	**1.24E-03**	1.91E-02	1.41E-02	2.85E-03
	Var.	**1.02E-05**	5.06E-04	3.61E-04	8.53E-05
f_{15}	Mean	1.23E+01	**8.96E+00**	1.36E+01	1.92E+01
	Var.	9.60E+02	**5.89E+02**	7.15E+02	1.09E+03
f_{16}	Mean	4.50E+01	9.01E+01	**1.41E-13**	4.41E+01
	Var.	4.44E+01	5.80E+02	**4.68E-27**	4.21E+01
f_{17}	Mean	**0.00E+00**	6.00E+01	5.20E+01	**0.00E+00**
	Var.	**0.00E+00**	5.60E+03	4.90E+03	**0.00E+00**
f_{18}	Mean	3.14E+00	1.09E+02	1.01E+02	**2.23E+00**
	Var.	5.20E+00	6.72E+03	8.59E+03	**2.18E+00**
f_{19}	Mean	1.21E+02	2.02E+02	1.68E+02	**1.19E+02**
	Var.	2.58E+02	4.03E+03	2.23E+03	**2.85E+02**

continued on following page

Table 5. Continued

		LSPSO-rfl	LPPSO-rfl	LPPSO-1/D-rfl	LCJDPSO-rfl
f_{20}	Mean	2.95E+02	3.49E+02	4.45E+02	**2.91E+02**
	Var.	8.83E+01	9.34E+03	2.95E+04	**1.40E+02**
f_{21}	Mean	3.05E+00	3.66E+01	6.07E+01	**2.84E+00**
	Var.	1.90E+00	1.95E+03	1.02E+04	**2.53E+00**
f_{22}	Mean	5.41E+02	4.90E+02	8.39E+02	**5.13E+02**
	Var.	1.21E+04	9.42E+02	2.15E+04	**3.50E+03**
f_{23}	Mean	1.71E+02	3.48E+02	3.36E+02	**1.65E+02**
	Var.	2.89E+03	1.33E+04	2.47E+04	**4.21E+03**
f_{24}	Mean	5.59E+02	8.03E+02	8.19E+02	**5.52E+02**
	Var.	2.18E+04	1.80E+04	2.24E+04	**2.30E+04**
f_{25}	Mean	**4.84E+02**	8.65E+02	8.48E+02	5.14E+02
	Var.	**2.94E+03**	8.50E+04	8.05E+04	2.18E+04
f_{26}	Mean	**2.00E+02**	2.48E+02	2.48E+02	**2.00E+02**
	Var.	**9.76E-13**	1.21E+04	1.21E+04	**1.09E-12**

Table 6. Parameter settings for the counterpart algorithms

Algorithm	Parameters
PSO*w*	$\|ps\| = 20$, $c_1 = c_2 = 2$, $\omega = 0.4$
RPSOvm	$\|ps\| = 10$, $c_1 = c_2 = 1.5$, $\omega_0 = 0.1$, $\omega_1 = 0.0$
CLPSO	$\|ps\| = 20$, $c = 1.49445$, $\omega_0 = 0.9$, $\omega_1 = 0.7$, $m = 8$
OLPSOG	$\|ps\| = 40$, $c = 2$, $\omega = 0.9$, $G = 5$
OLPSOL	$\|ps\| = 40$, $c = 2$, $\omega = 0.9$, $G = 5$

Experiment 4: Comparison With State-of-the-Art PSO Variants

In this experiment, performance of LCJDPSO-rfl is compared to the representative PSO variants including PSO*w*, RPSOvm, CLPSO and OLPSO (both global version OLPSOG and local version OLPSOL). Particularly, RPSOvm is selected because it outperforms other state-of-the-art PSO improvements that contain restart mechanism. The parameter settings of counterpart algorithms are summarized in Table 6, which have been adjusted to obtain best performance on the benchmark functions. The average best fitness values and the variances of all algorithms over 30 runs are reported in Table 7, where the "†" indicates that the differences of the mean values are statistical significant in a Wilcoxon rank-sum test with level $\alpha = 0.05$.

Experimental results show that the LCJDPSO-rfl significantly outperforms other algorithms. It searches different types of benchmark functions effectively and efficiently. PSO*w* obtains promising results on the unimodal functions. However, the high variances indicate that the algorithm performance is not stable. The RPSOvm is comparable to LCJDPSO-rfl on simple multimodal functions f_5 - f_{10}. Yet it is no match to LCJDPSO-rfl on other functions.

Table 7. Experimental results of LCJDPSO-rfl and counterpart PSO variants

		PSOw	RPSOvm	CLPSO	OLPSOL	OLPSOG	LCJDPSO-rfl
f_1	Mean	1.20E+03	9.20E-40	1.25E-15	4.82E+00	2.92E-09	**2.73E-172†**
	Var.	1.06E+07	2.27E-78	1.52E-30	2.19E+01	7.29E-18	**0.00E+00**
f_2	Mean	3.48E+01	9.25E-24	1.27E-10	2.65E+00	4.32E-07	**3.47E-94†**
	Var.	4.17E+02	1.29E-46	6.29E-21	9.08E+00	5.52E-14	**2.45E-186**
f_3	Mean	4.10E+04	1.30E+01	2.93E+01	2.63E+02	4.48E+01	**1.96E+00**
	Var.	3.46E+10	6.35E+02	5.72E+02	1.06E+04	9.02E+02	**1.01E+01**
f_4	Mean	3.28E-01	**9.61E-24†**	3.93E-02	3.33E-01	6.55E-07	1.74E-04
	Var.	5.31E-01	**5.85E-46**	3.59E-02	6.23E-02	4.26E-12	4.57E-08
f_5	Mean	3.73E+03	6.48E+02	**3.04E+02†**	3.04E+03	4.74E+02	2.51E+03
	Var.	2.31E+05	1.24E+05	**8.47E+04**	1.67E+05	9.10E+04	9.25E+04
f_6	Mean	1.43E+02	**0.00E+00†**	9.95E-01	6.64E+01	5.13E+00	5.42E+01
	Var.	2.09E+03	**0.00E+00**	2.38E+01	1.27E+02	5.68E+00	4.08E+01
f_7	Mean	9.48E+00	**5.84E-15†**	3.39E-08	2.15E+00	3.80E-06	4.74E-11
	Var.	6.02E+01	**3.15E-30**	5.04E-16	3.58E-01	2.25E-12	5.38E-20
f_8	Mean	2.17E+01	1.02E-02	2.02E-11	9.78E-01	9.55E-03	**1.78E-17†**
	Var.	1.49E+03	7.07E-04	1.08E-21	1.67E-02	1.54E-04	**2.64E-33**
f_9	Mean	3.04E-01	7.22E-16	9.65E-17	4.20E+00	1.28E-11	**5.84E-33†**
	Var.	2.43E-01	1.44E-31	2.38E-32	1.73E+01	3.58E-22	**8.55E-65**
f_{10}	Mean	1.64E+07	3.19E-15	2.61E-15	1.57E+01	4.39E-04	**1.81E-32†**
	Var.	6.46E+15	9.45E-31	1.13E-29	5.83E+01	4.64E-06	**1.56E-63**
f_{11}	Mean	8.58E+03	8.98E+03	8.40E+03	8.52E+03	8.26E+03	**7.62E+03†**
	Var.	3.13E+05	2.83E+05	1.89E+05	6.28E+04	4.73E+05	**1.23E+05**
f_{12}	Mean	2.59E+02	2.24E+02	1.91E+02	2.30E+02	1.41E+02	**8.77E+01†**
	Var.	5.78E+03	3.35E+03	1.24E+03	1.26E+03	3.00E+03	**2.29E+02**
f_{13}	Mean	2.03E+01	9.39E+00	2.00E+01	2.03E+01	1.87E+01	**3.80E+00†**
	Var.	9.12E+00	7.50E+00	1.32E-03	1.18E+00	2.82E+01	**6.09E-01**
f_{14}	Mean	2.33E+02	1.67E-02	1.11E+00	1.94E+01	3.44E-01	**2.85E-03†**
	Var.	5.27E+04	9.25E-04	5.27E-02	1.13E+02	2.79E-02	**8.53E-05**
f_{15}	Mean	4.25E+09	3.74E+02	4.69E+01	4.51E+06	1.01E+02	**1.92E+01†**
	Var.	2.44E+19	5.75E+05	2.05E+03	2.94E+13	2.57E+03	**1.09E+03**
f_{16}	Mean	1.44E+02	**2.39E-01†**	1.32E+00	8.90E+01	5.52E+00	4.41E+01
	Var.	1.04E+03	**1.81E-01**	2.41E+00	2.76E+02	6.31E+00	4.21E+01
f_{17}	Mean	2.09E+02	1.24E+02	1.09E+02	1.21E+02	8.41E+01	**0.00E+00†**
	Var.	1.24E+04	1.70E+04	9.53E+03	1.92E+03	8.53E+03	**0.00E+00**
f_{18}	Mean	3.13E+02	2.48E+02	1.41E+02	1.59E+02	9.04E+01	**2.23E+00†**
	Var.	1.89E+04	3.24E+04	1.10E+04	6.12E+03	8.90E+03	**2.18E+00**
f_{19}	Mean	3.36E+02	3.85E+02	2.59E+02	3.31E+02	2.00E+02	**1.19E+02†**
	Var.	2.22E+04	5.45E+04	1.59E+04	3.43E+03	9.47E+03	**2.85E+02**
f_{20}	Mean	4.89E+02	6.52E+02	4.29E+02	4.87E+02	3.61E+02	**2.91E+02†**
	Var.	2.70E+04	9.84E+03	8.52E+03	3.51E+03	5.42E+03	**1.40E+02**
f_{21}	Mean	2.98E+02	1.99E+02	9.44E+01	1.22E+02	7.36E+01	**2.84E+00†**
	Var.	4.57E+04	3.18E+04	4.64E+03	1.31E+03	5.67E+03	**2.53E+00**

continued on following page

Table 7. Continued

		PSOw	RPSOvm	CLPSO	OLPSOL	OLPSOG	LCJDPSO-rfl
f_{22}	Mean	8.46E+02	8.51E+02	7.24E+02	6.42E+02	7.42E+02	**5.13E+02†**
	Var.	1.64E+04	1.91E+04	2.63E+04	1.72E+04	3.26E+04	**3.50E+03**
f_{23}	Mean	5.40E+02	2.76E+02	**1.54E+02**	2.88E+02	1.88E+02	1.65E+02
	Var.	2.72E+04	6.23E+04	**2.53E+04**	1.17E+04	3.39E+04	4.21E+03
f_{24}	Mean	9.62E+02	1.17E+03	9.20E+02	9.39E+02	8.16E+02	**5.52E+02†**
	Var.	8.47E+03	7.65E+03	1.35E+04	1.74E+04	1.87E+04	**2.30E+04**
f_{25}	Mean	1.19E+03	1.26E+03	8.54E+02	1.09E+03	8.91E+02	**5.14E+02†**
	Var.	1.41E+04	2.73E+04	1.00E+05	2.61E+04	6.83E+04	**2.18E+04**
f_{26}	Mean	1.10E+03	1.15E+03	3.09E+02	8.41E+02	3.54E+02	**2.00E+02†**
	Var.	1.97E+04	1.23E+05	5.40E+04	7.29E+04	6.96E+04	**1.09E-12**

Figure 5. Convergence traces on unimodal functions (Group 1)

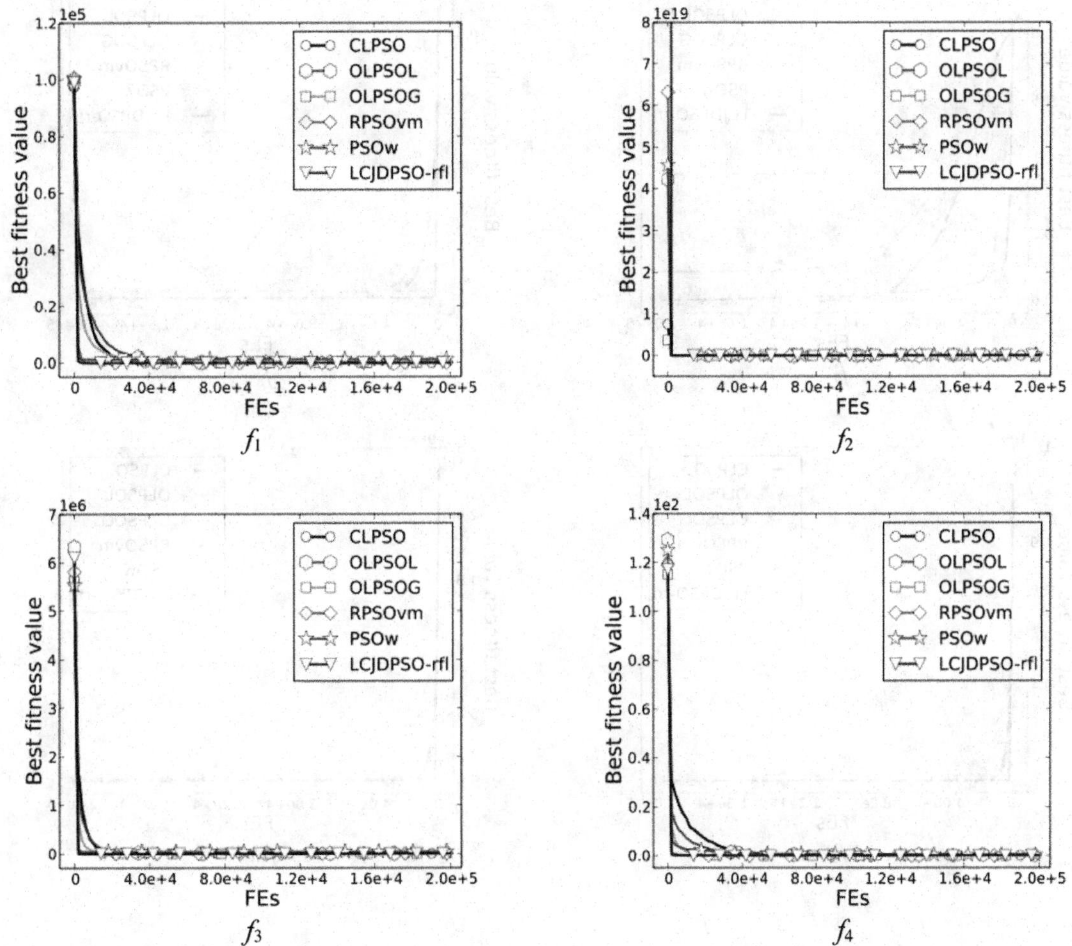

Figure 6. Convergence traces on primary multimodal functions (Group 2)

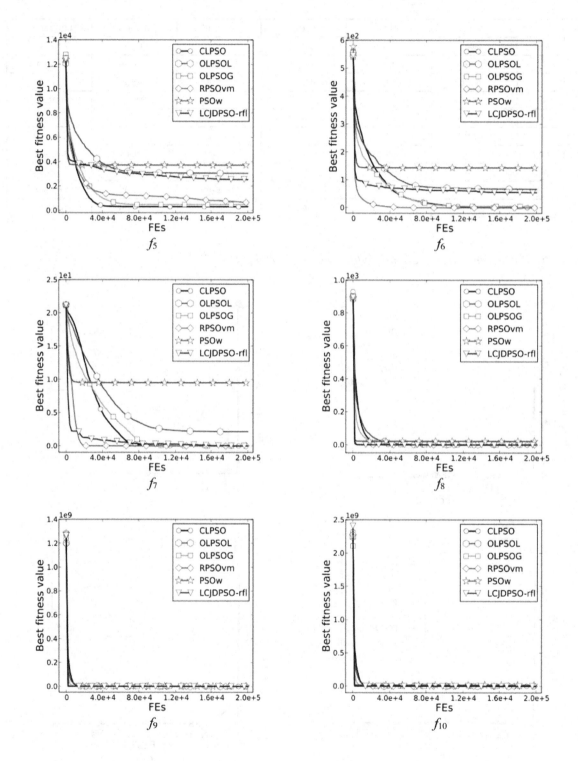

f_5 f_6

f_7 f_8

f_9 f_{10}

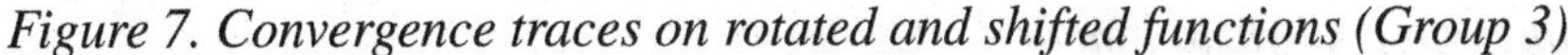

Figure 7. Convergence traces on rotated and shifted functions (Group 3)

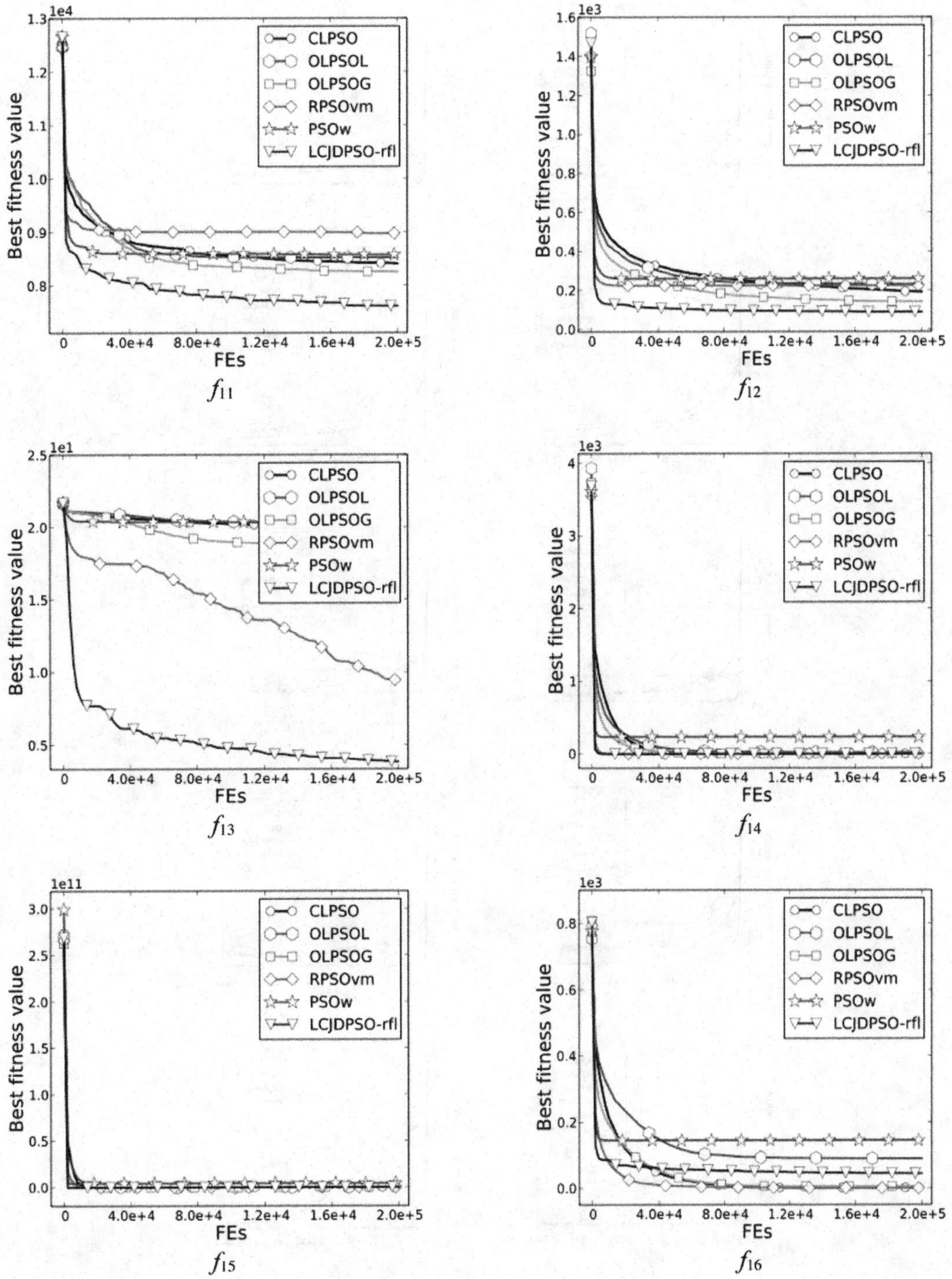

f_{11} f_{12}

f_{13} f_{14}

f_{15} f_{16}

Figure 8. Convergence traces on complex hybrid functions (Group 4)

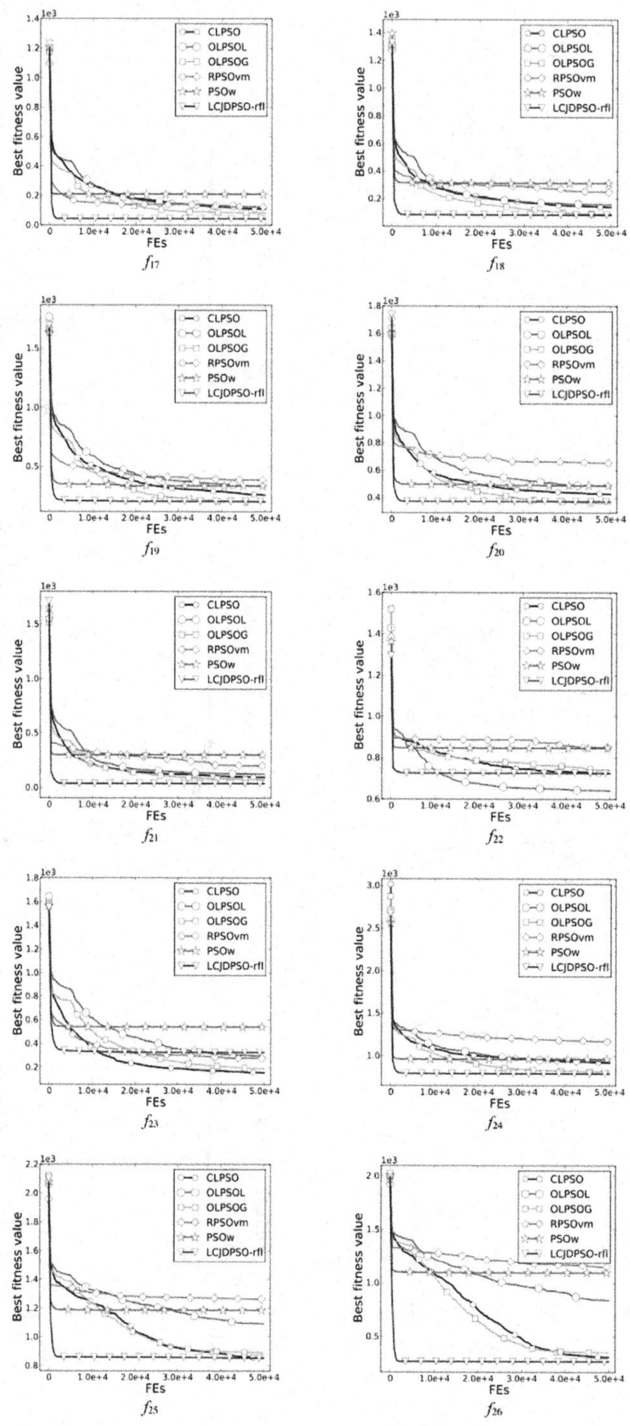

Average convergence traces of all algorithms on the four groups of benchmark functions are illustrated in Figures. 5 - 8. In Figure 5 all algorithms are managed to solve the simple unimodal functions efficiently. In Figure 6 the LCJDPSO-rfl is observed to converge much faster than other algorithms on most of the functions. Figure 7 and 8 show that LCJDPSO-rfl obtains better results than counterparts while maintaining the higher convergence speed.

CONCLUSION

In this paper, we combine the reflecting bound-handling scheme, the von Neumann topology neighborhood, and the CJD restart strategy in a local best PSO to form the LCJDPSO-rfl algorithm. This algorithm is easy to implement as it requires no complex operators. A group of 26 benchmark functions including the unimodal, primary multimodal, rotated and shifted, and hybrid global optimization problems are utilized to evaluate the performance of the proposed algorithm. Experimental results demonstrate that the LCJDPSO-rfl outperforms other representative PSO variants on most of the functions. It can obtain promising results with less computational time and meanwhile effectively prevent premature convergence.

ACKNOWLEDGMENT

This work was supported in part by the National Natural Science Foundation of China (61471246 and 61501138), in part by China Postdoctoral Science Foundation (2015M580265), in part by Guangdong Foundation of Outstanding Young Teachers in Higher Education Institutions (Yq2013141), in part by Guangdong Special Support Program of Topnotch Young Professionals (2014TQ01X273), in part by Shenzhen Scientific Research and Development Funding Program (KQC201108300045A, ZYC201105170243A, JCYJ20170302154328155, and JCYJ20150403161923539), in part by Nanshan Innovation Institution Construction Program (KC2014ZDZJ0026A), and in part by Nanshan Innovation Research and Develop Project (KC2014JSQN0008A).

REFERENCES

Berkovitch, E., & Khanna, N. (1990). How target shareholders benefit from value-reducing defensive strategies in takeovers. *The Journal of Finance*, *45*(1), 137–156. doi:10.1111/j.1540-6261.1990.tb05084.x

Bonyadi, M. R., & Michalewicz, Z. (2017). Particle Swarm Optimization for Single Objective Continuous Space Problems: A Review. *Evolutionary Computation*, *25*(1), 1–54. doi:10.1162/EVCO_r_00180 PMID:26953883

Chu, W., Gao, X., & Sorooshian, S. (2011). Handling boundary constraints for particle swarm optimization in high-dimensional search space. *Information Sciences*, *181*(20), 4569–4581. doi:10.1016/j.ins.2010.11.030

Delgarm, N., Sajadi, B., Kowsary, F., & Delgarm, S. (2016). Multi-objective optimization of the building energy performance: A simulation-based approach by means of particle swarm optimization (PSO). *Applied Energy*, *170*, 293–303. doi:10.1016/j.apenergy.2016.02.141

Dong, W., & Zhou, M. (2017). A Supervised Learning and Control Method to Improve Particle Swarm Optimization Algorithms. *IEEE Transactions on Systems, Man, and Cybernetics. Systems*, *47*(7), 1135–1148. doi:10.1109/TSMC.2016.2560128

Du, W. B., Ying, W., Yan, G., Zhu, Y. B., & Cao, X. B. (2017). Heterogeneous Strategy Particle Swarm Optimization. *IEEE Transactions on Circuits and Wystems. II, Express Briefs*, *64*(4), 467–471. doi:10.1109/TCSII.2016.2595597

Eberhart, R., & Kennedy, J. (1995). *A new optimizer using particle swarm theory*. Paper presented at the International Symposium on Micro Machine and Human Science. doi:10.1109/MHS.1995.494215

Enriquez, N., & Sabot, C. (2006). Random walks in a Dirichlet environment. *Electronic Journal of Probability*, *11*(31), 802–817.

García-Nieto, J., & Alba, E. (2011). Restart particle swarm optimization with velocity modulation: A scalability test. *Soft Computing*, *15*(11), 2221–2232. doi:10.1007/s00500-010-0648-1

Ho, Y.-C., & Pepyne, D. L. (2002). Simple explanation of the no-free-lunch theorem and its implications. *Journal of Optimization Theory and Applications*, *115*(3), 549–570. doi:10.1023/A:1021251113462

Kennedy, J., & Mendes, R. (2002). *Population structure and particle swarm performance*. Paper presented at the IEEE Congress on Evolutionary Computation.

Liang, J., Qin, A. K., Suganthan, P. N., & Baskar, S. (2006). Comprehensive learning particle swarm optimizer for global optimization of multimodal functions. *IEEE Transactions on Evolutionary Computation*, *10*(3), 281–295. doi:10.1109/TEVC.2005.857610

Liang, J., Suganthan, P., & Deb, K. (2005). *Novel composition test functions for numerical global optimization*. Paper presented at the IEEE Swarm Intelligence Symposium. doi:10.1109/SIS.2005.1501604

Lovbjerg, M., & Krink, T. (2002). *Extending particle swarm optimisers with self-organized criticality*. Paper presented at the IEEE World on Congress on Computational Intelligence. doi:10.1109/CEC.2002.1004479

Modiri, A., Gu, X., Hagan, A. M., & Sawant, A. (2017). Radiotherapy Planning Using an Improved Search Strategy in Particle Swarm Optimization. *IEEE Transactions on Biomedical Engineering*, *64*(5), 980–989. doi:10.1109/TBME.2016.2585114 PMID:27362755

Neri, F., & Cotta, C. (2012). Memetic algorithms and memetic computing optimization: A literature review. *Swarm and Evolutionary Computation*, *2*, 1–14. doi:10.1016/j.swevo.2011.11.003

Nguyen, Q. H., Ong, Y.-S., & Lim, M. H. (2009). A probabilistic memetic framework. *IEEE Transactions on Evolutionary Computation*, *13*(3), 604–623. doi:10.1109/TEVC.2008.2009460

Peer, E. S., van den Bergh, F., & Engelbrecht, A. P. (2003). *Using neighborhoods with the guaranteed convergence PSO*. Paper presented at the IEEE Swarm Intelligence Symposium.

Powell, M. J. D. (1964). An efficient method for finding the minimum of a function of several variables without calculating derivatives. *The Computer Journal*, *7*(2), 155–162. doi:10.1093/comjnl/7.2.155

Qin, Q., Cheng, S., Zhang, Q., Li, L., & Shi, Y. (2016). Particle Swarm Optimization With Interswarm Interactive Learning Strategy. *IEEE Transactions on Cybernetics*, *46*(10), 2238–2251. doi:10.1109/TCYB.2015.2474153 PMID:26357418

Russell, S. J., & Norvig, P. (2002). Artificial intelligence: a modern approach (International Edition). Academic Press.

Sheikhpour, R., Sarram, M. A., & Sheikhpour, R. (2016). Particle swarm optimization for bandwidth determination and feature selection of kernel density estimation based classifiers in diagnosis of breast cancer. *Applied Soft Computing*, *40*, 113–131. doi:10.1016/j.asoc.2015.10.005

Shi, Y. (2011). *Brain storm optimization algorithm*. Academic Press.

Shi, Y., & Eberhart, R. (1998). *A modified particle swarm optimizer*. Paper presented at the IEEE International Congress on Evolutionary Computation.

Solis, F. J., & Wets, R. J. B. (1981). Minimization by random search techniques. *Mathematics of Operations Research*, *6*(1), 19–30. doi:10.1287/moor.6.1.19

Spears, W. M., De Jong, K. A., Bäck, T., Fogel, D. B., & De Garis, H. (1993). *An overview of evolutionary computation*. Academic Press.

Storn, R., & Price, K. (1997). Differential evolution-a simple and efficient heuristic for global optimization over continuous spaces. *Journal of Global Optimization*, *11*(4), 341–359. doi:10.1023/A:1008202821328

Suganthan, P. N., Hansen, N., Liang, J. J., Deb, K., Chen, Y., Auger, A., & Tiwari, S. (2005). *Problem definitions and evaluation criteria for the CEC 2005 special session on real-parameter optimization*. KanGAL Report, 2005005.

Swann, W. H. (1964). *Report on the development of a new direct search method of optimization*. Research Note (64).

Tan, Y. (2010). Particle Swarm Optimization Algorithms Inspired by Immunity-Clonal Mechanism and Their Applications to Spam Detection. *International Journal of Swarm Intelligence Research*, *1*(1), 64–86. doi:10.4018/jsir.2010010104

Wang, G.-G., Gandomi, A. H., Alavi, A. H., & Deb, S. (2016). A hybrid method based on krill herd and quantum-behaved particle swarm optimization. *Neural Computing & Applications*, *27*(4), 989–1006. doi:10.1007/s00521-015-1914-z

Wolpert, D. H., & Macready, W. G. (1997). No free lunch theorems for optimization. *IEEE Transactions on Evolutionary Computation, 1*(1), 67–82. doi:10.1109/4235.585893

Zaharis, Z. D., Gravas, I. P., Yioultsis, T. V., Lazaridis, P. I., Glover, I. A., Skeberis, C., & Xenos, T. D. (2017). Exponential Log-Periodic Antenna Design Using Improved Particle Swarm Optimization With Velocity Mutation. *IEEE Transactions on Magnetics, 53*(6), 1–4. doi:10.1109/TMAG.2017.2660061

Zhan, Z., Zhang, J., Li, Y., & Shi, Y. (2011). Orthogonal learning particle swarm optimization. *IEEE Transactions on Evolutionary Computation, 15*(6), 832–847. doi:10.1109/TEVC.2010.2052054

Zhang, Y., Wang, S., & Ji, G. (2015). A comprehensive survey on particle swarm optimization algorithm and its applications. *Mathematical Problems in Engineering*.

Chapter 3
Multi-Objective Binary Fish School Search

Mariana Gomes da Motta Macedo
University of Pernambuco, Brazil

Carmelo J. A. Bastos-Filho
University of Pernambuco, Brazil

Susana M. Vieira
University of Lisboa, Portugal

João M. C. Sousa
University of Lisboa, Portugal

ABSTRACT

Fish school search (FSS) algorithm has inspired several adaptations for multi-objective problems or binary optimization. However, there is no particular proposition to solve both problems simultaneously. The proposed multi-objective approach binary fish school search (MOBFSS) aims to solve optimization problems with two or three conflicting objective functions with binary decision input variables. MOBFSS is based on the dominance concept used in the multi-objective fish school search (MOFSS) and the threshold technique deployed in the binary fish school search (BFSS). Additionally, the authors evaluate the proposal for feature selection for classification in well-known datasets. Moreover, the authors compare the performance of the proposal with a state-of-art algorithm called BMOPSO-CDR. MOBFSS presents better results than BMOPSO-CDR, especially for datasets with higher complexity.

INTRODUCTION

Binary optimization is a class of problems in which the input variables to be determined are binary, which means that the variables just can assume two states. This type of approach is applied to feature selection problems. In the feature selection problem, one has to define which features must be chosen for a particular task. Feature selection can be used to identify which features are relevant for a specific task, such as for classification, regression or forecasting.

DOI: 10.4018/978-1-5225-5134-8.ch003

Consider a classification problem as an example. In general, one has several possible features as inputs to find the best class of each instance, and it is useful for all types of knowledge, such as medical diagnosis (Shenfield & Rostami, 2015), text classification (Forman, 2003) and fingerprint segmentation (Sankaran et al., 2017). One important aspect of the classification task is the amount of deployed features to guarantee an accurate result, which for real problems can be high. As a consequence of using many input features, the classifier may need a high processing time. Another issue is that a large number of features can obscure important relationships between instances because of the irrelevant or redundant features. Thus, feature selection is a relevant problem for an efficient classification procedure (Guyon & Elisseeff, 2003). Many approaches for feature selection using swarm-based approaches and evolutionary computation have been proposed recently (Xue, 2013a) (Xue, 2013b) (Xue, 2014)(Xue, 2015)(Xue, 2016). In the literature, one can find many classification methods. Support Vector Machine (SVM) (Hearst et al., 1998) is a widely used and well-known technique for classification tasks. Although SVM is not the fastest one, it is considered robust. Since the goal of the chapter is not to propose a classification method, but it is to introduce a technique for feature selection, the authors use SVM in all the experiments for the validation of our proposal.

On the other hand, from the optimization perspective, the authors highlight that most of the real-world engineering problems present more than one optimization targets. This last affirmative means that one may need to optimize simultaneous fitness functions that are conflicting among them. As an example, suppose that one must design a classifier that uses a low number of features and presents a small error in the classification process. One can observe that if the authors diminish the number of required features below an unknown threshold, the accuracy of the classifier can be worsened. This kind of conflict constitutes a typical multi-objective optimization problem. In this chapter, the authors use this optimization problem for validating our proposal and for the sake of comparison with other state-of-the-art algorithms.

Several propositions of feature selection can be found in the literature (Peng et al., 2005)(Tasca et al., 2017). However, there are not too many approaches for multi-objective binary optimization (Argyris, 2011)(de Souza, 2014)(Collette, 2013)(de Souza, 2014), especially when one considers swarm intelligence based methods. Four versions can be highlighted in the literature as binary multi-objective methods: CMDPSO and NSPSO proposed by Xue et al. (2013a), and BMOPSO and BMOPSO-CDR introduced by Souza et al. (2011). Those versions were designed inspired on Particle Swarm Optimization (PSO) (Clerc, 2010). PSO proposed by Kennedy and Ebehart (1995) simulates the movement of a flock. This movement uses a topology of communication to share information between the birds, and they change position influenced by neighbors and its inertia. Between those versions, the authors chose to perform a comparison of the proposal with BMOPSO-CDR algorithm because of its performance, and it is the best proposition on the literature that directly addresses a binary multi-objective problem using swarm intelligence technique.

The proposal of this chapter is an algorithm to solve binary problems, which presents conflicting objectives to resolve, using the movements of fish proposed by Fish School Search (FSS) (Bastos-Filho et al., 2008; 2009). The authors introduce Multi-Objective Binary Fish School Search (MOBFSS) combining adaptations of the Binary Fish School Search and the Multi-Objective Fish School Search (MOFSS) (Bastos-Filho & Guimarães, 2015). Along the chapter, the authors describe all the operators and its usefulness. Moreover, the authors encourage the deployment of MOBFSS for feature selection by presenting the results for three UCI datasets (UCI, 2017) composed of different number of attributes.

The remainder of the chapter is divided as follows. The first section is about the background which presents a brief review concerning the approaches based on Fish School Search and its characteristics.

The second section explains the proposed Multi-Objective Binary Fish School Search algorithm and its operators. Subsequently, the next section provides the simulation setup. The fourth section presents the results and its analysis. The following section exposes the author's proposition for possible future works. Finally, in the last section, the authors summarize the main achievements.

BACKGROUND

The encoding of problems and the operators of the Fish School Search algorithm inspired several approaches. This section aims to present some of the previous works and the central concepts, which inspired the MOBFSS. First, the subsection about Fish School Search Algorithm shows the key features of it and its process. Secondly, the subsection named Binary Fish School Search reveals the adaptations realized on FSS regarding its transformation. Finally, the last subsection explains the multi-objective version of Fish School Search, which alters all the operators to optimize two or three conflict objectives.

Fish School Search Algorithm

The Fish School Search algorithm (FSS) was proposed by Bastos Filho et al. (2008; 2009). The movement of fish and their feeding processes inspired FSS. The main idea of FSS is to move to feed, and the movement is divided into three types: individual, collective instinctive and collective volitive. The individual movement gives the possibility to go to new positions that other fishes would not go. The collective instinctive movement attracts the fish to the best region found by the school. Finally, the collective volitive movement provides the capacity of expanding or contracting the school, which gives a way to get out of bad regions or refines the search in promising ones. Another important aspect of FSS is the weight of the fish. It represents the accumulated success of the fish along the iterations. Thus, the feeding operator updates this parameter. The feeding represents the proportion of the fish success in the weight of each fish through the iterations.

In Algorithm 1, the pseudocode simplifies all the process developed by FSS. Each fish is a simple reactive agent, which is represented by a position within the allowed search space and its weight is limited to a maximum value. Before starting the process, it is necessary to initialize the school randomly inside the search space and to update the fitness of each position. Next, a loop is going to be processed while the stop criterion is not satisfied.

The first step of the loop is to apply the individual movement and feeding for each fish. The individual movement, represented by Equation (1) and the temporary position ($\vec{n}_i(t)$. $\vec{n}_i(t)$ is the addition of the fish's current position ($\vec{x}_i(t)$. $\vec{x}_i(t)$ and a random value between -1 and 1 ($\vec{r}[-1,1]$) multiplied by the step individual ($S_{ind}(t)$) that constrains the length of the movement.

$$\vec{n}_i(t) = \vec{x}_i(t) + \vec{r}[-1,1] \cdot S_{ind}(t). \quad (1)$$

The step individual is initialized at the beginning of the algorithm, and the suggested starting value by Bastos-Filho and Nascimento (2013) is in the range [0.10,0.001] when 10.000 iterations are used. Subsequent, the feeding is updated as shown in Equation (2). The new weight ($w_i(t+1)$) adds the

Algorithm 1. FSS Pseudocode

```
Initialize the position, the weight and the fitness of the school;
While stop criterion is not met do
    For each fish do
        Execute individual movement;
        Execute feeding;
    End For
    Calculate drift;
    For each fish do
        Execute collective instinctive movement;
     End For
     Calculate barycenter;
     For each fish do
         Execute collective volitive movement;
     End For
 End While
 Export the best fish found;


 Update step
 end while
```

variation of fitness of the fish ($\Delta f_i(t)$) normalized by the best current fish, which improved more in the current iteration ($\max\left[\Delta f(t)\right]$). Moreover, the variation of the fitness ($\Delta f_i(t)$) is the fitness of the new position ($f\left[\vec{n}_i(t)\right]$) subtracts to the old position ($\left[\Delta f(t)\right]$), as shown in Equation (3). It is important to highlight that only the fishes, which improved the fitness, actually move.

$$w_i(t+1) = w_i(t) + \frac{\Delta f_i(t)}{\max\left[\Delta f(t)\right]}, \tag{2}$$

$$\Delta f_i(t) = f\left[\vec{n}_i(t)\right] - f\left[\vec{x}_i(t)\right]. \tag{3}$$

Secondly, the collective instinctive movement has to be applied, and the drift is calculated as presented in Equation (4). This drift uses only the fish that improved its fitness within the current iteration to calculate it. The variation of the position ($\Delta\vec{x}_i(t)$) multiplies the variation of the fitness ($\Delta f_i(t)$), and this sum for all the school, divided by the sum of all the variation of their fitness. The variation of position is shown in Equation (5), which is calculated as the distance between the new position and the old position. After the calculation of the drift, the fish are going to move in the direction of the drift ($\vec{I}(t)$) as described in Equation (6).

$$\vec{I}(t) = \frac{\sum_{i=1}^{N} \Delta\vec{x}_i(t)\Delta f_i(t)}{\sum_{i=1}^{N} \Delta f_i(t)}, \tag{4}$$

$$\Delta\vec{x}_i(t) = \vec{n}_i(t) - \vec{x}_i(t), \tag{5}$$

$$\vec{x}_i(t+1) = \vec{x}_i(t) + \vec{I}(t). \tag{6}$$

The third step is to execute the collective volitive movement after calculates the evaluation of the barycenter as shown in Equation (7). The barycenter ($\vec{B}(t)$) divides the sum of the current position and the weight of each fish to the sum of all weights. After that, Equation (8) can be applied to contract or expand the school. This equation subtracts when the weight of the school increases, and it sums when the opposite happens. The new movement is in the direction of the barycenter, but it is constrained by the step volitive (S_{vol}) and a random value between 0 and 1. The volitive step can be initialized as the double of the current step individual. When the stop criterion finally is achieved inside the loop, it exports the best fish found by the FSS.

$$\vec{B}(t) = \frac{\sum_{i=1}^{N} \vec{x}_i(t) w_i(t)}{\sum_{i=1}^{N} w_i(t)}, \tag{7}$$

$$\vec{x}_i(t+1) = \vec{x}_i(t) + S_{vol} \cdot rand[0,1] \frac{\vec{x}_i(t) - \vec{B}(t)}{\sqrt{\left[\vec{x}_i(t) - \vec{B}(t)\right]^2}}. \tag{8}$$

Binary Fish School Search Algorithm

The Binary version of the Fish School Search (BFSS) was proposed by Sargo et al. (2013;2014). Carneiro and Bastos-Filho added some improvements to BFSS (Carneiro & Bastos-Filho, 2016). Therefore, the binary version uses the same inspiration of the FSS movements, but it differs from the original once a binary decision vector is used as the input. Because of this, it is necessary to adapt the movements. The BFSS can be represented by the same pseudocode of FSS, described in Algorithm 1.

BFSS initializes all the dimensions of the fish using a threshold as follow: if a random number uniformly generated is greater than 0.5, the value is 1, and if this is not true, the value is 0, as the initialization of positions in line 1 of Algorithm 1. Next, the individual movement, as line 4 of Algorithm 1, is based on flipping some dimensions of the position. The control is done by the step individual $(S_{ind}(t))$ that if the value is less than $(S_{ind}(t))$, the dimension is going to flip (0 to 1, or 1 to 0). The individual step decreases along the iterations. Thus, the movement (flip) is executed only if the new position is better than the old one.

The feeding is performed in the same way of FSS, as line 5 of Algorithm 1. Next, the drift of the collective instinctive movement uses the new position instead of the variation of positions, as line 7 of Algorithm 1. The new vector calculated by the drift is going to be constructed by binary numbers depending on the threshold that is equal to the multiplication of threshold *(thres_c)* with the maximum value of the drift vector. Each number greater than this multiplication will be 1, and the others will be 0. All the different dimensions compared to the drift vector can be randomly selected to flip.

Finally, before the collective volitive movement, the barycenter is calculated in the same way of FSS as line 11 of Algorithm 1, but the vector will be transformed into a binary format. The same way of the drift will be performed on the barycenter vector. The threshold is the multiplication of *(thres_v)* with the maximum value of the barycenter vector to be used in the collective volitive movement as line 13 of Algorithm 1. If the overall weight of the school is greater than before, the flip is in one of the dimensions that are different from the barycenter. In contrast, if the overall weight of the school is less than before, the anti-barycenter vector replaces the barycenter, which all the dimensions flipped to be compared to the fish.

Carneiro and Bastos-Filho proposed the Improved Binary Fish School Search (IBFSS) (Carneiro & Bastos-Filho, 2016) that is an extension of BFSS. The differences of them are: (i) the threshold used in the initialization is 0.75; (ii) The step individual $(S_{ind}(t))$ is the number of dimensions that may flip (it can not achieve 0 because it will not change any dimension), and it can be initialized as a percentage of the search space; (iii) The flip of dimensions in the collective instinctive movement is more than 1, and the drift is based on the variation of positions; (iv) The step volitive (S_{vol}) can be set as the double of the individual step, and it is utilized as the number of dimensions that should be flipped.

Multi-Objective Fish School Search Algorithm

The Multi-objective Fish School Search (MOFSS), which was proposed by Bastos-Filho and Guimarães (2015), is based on the original FSS algorithm, and the operators were adapted for multi-objective problems. An important addition was the External Archive (EA) that stores the best non-dominated solutions (Deb et al., 2002; Nebro et al., 2009), and it can be important to guide the school and to maintain good solutions. EA should be limited in size to maintain the computational cost under control. This restriction is controlled by the Crowding Distance method, which is deployed in other relevant algorithms Non-dominated Sorting Genetic Algorithm II (NSGA-II) (Deb et al., 2002) and Strength Pareto Evolutionary Algorithm 2 (SPEA2) (Zitzler et al., 2001). Another operator added to MOFSS is the turbulence operator to improve the fine-tuning abilities within the EA. In Algorithm 2, the pseudocode of the MOFSS is detailed like the original chapter of Bastos-Filho and Guimarães (2015).

Before the loop of MOFSS, the initialization of all the parameters, fish and external archive is executed. Next, the loop runs all the movements and operators while the stop criterion is not achieved. Firstly, it updates both steps, individual and volitive. Secondly, the individual movement always permits fish to explore new positions. The individual movement is applied as Equation (9) and (10). The leader ($\vec{x}_g(t)$) is chosen from the External Archive and guides the movement.

$$\vec{n}_i(t) = \vec{x}_i(t) + \Delta\vec{x}_i(t), \tag{9}$$

$$\Delta\vec{x}_i(t) = S_{ind}(t) \cdot U[0,1] \frac{\vec{x}_g(t) - \vec{x}_i(t)}{\sqrt{\left[\vec{x}_g(t) - \vec{x}_i(t)\right]^2}}. \tag{10}$$

Next, the feeding operator updates the weight of the school using Equation (11). The multi-objective approaches use the dominance concept to assess the solutions, which defines that one solution only dominates another if it is better that the other solutions in all the objectives. If one solution is better than the other in one objective, but it is worse in another objective, the solutions are considered as not comparable. Moreover, the solutions that are worse than the others in all objective functions are called dominated solutions. One can use this criterion to differentiate solutions. $\Delta w_i(t)$ is then determined by using the dominance concept using the following rules: (i) is equal to *a*, if the solution is non-dominated; (ii) is equal to –*a*, if the solution is dominated; (iii) is equal to *b*, if the new position is not comparable but presents a higher value calculating the Crowding Distance of new position and old position; (iv) is equal to –*b*, otherwise. The parameters *a* and *b* are initialized by the user, and it weights the feed-

Algorithm 2. MOFSS Pseudocode

```
Initialize parameters;
Initialize randomly all fish;
Initialize external archive AE;
While stop criterion is not meet do
      Update step_ind and step_vol;
      Execute individual movement;
      Update AE;
      Execute feeding;
      Execute collective instictive movement;
      Execute collective volitive movement;
      Update AE;
      Execute turbulence AE;
      Update AE;
End while
Return AE
```

ing process. The authors mention that this allowed the spread of non-dominated solutions inside the EA. The dominance degree factor $D_i(t)$ is inspired on SPEA2 (Zitzler et al., 2001 and De et al., 2001), so it is calculated by the sum of the number of fish that a fish i dominates normalized by the maximum value found considering all the other fish, as shown in Equation (12).

$$w_i(t+1) = w_i(t) + \Delta w_i(t) D_i(t), \tag{11}$$

$$D_i(t) = 1 - \frac{\sum_{j \in N, j \prec i} s_j(t)}{Max[\sum_{j \in N, j \prec i} s_j(t)]}, \forall i. \tag{12}$$

The collective instinctive movement operator aims to attract the fish to better regions if the search is improving. In Equation (13), the drift is calculated differently from the FSS algorithm. Instead of using the variation of fitness, as the weight is the sum of improvements of iterations, the authors use the variation of the weight. Next, the collective instinctive movement can update the new position using Equation (14).

$$\vec{I}(t) = \sum_{i=1}^{N} \frac{\Delta w_i(t) \Delta \vec{x}_i(t)}{MAX[1, \Delta w]}, \tag{13}$$

$$\vec{x}_i(t+1) = \vec{x}_i(t) + \vec{I}_i(t). \tag{14}$$

The collective volitive movement, depicted in Equation (15), should impose to the swarm a contraction or expansion, so that the school may perform exploitation or exploration, respectively. In MOFSS, a leader of the External Archive is randomly chosen to attract or push away the fish with the strength of the maximum step (S_{vol}). Moreover, Equation (16) calculates the intensity and direction of the displacement weighted by (S_{vol}), the direction is defined by the result of the function *sign*(.) that returns the signal of its parameter.

$$\vec{x}_i(t+1) = \vec{x}_i(t) + V_i(t) \frac{\vec{x}_i(t) - \vec{x}_g(t)}{\sqrt{\vec{x}_i(t)^2 - \vec{x}_g(t)^2}}, \tag{15}$$

$$V_i(t) = S_{vol}(t)\, sign(\Delta w)\, U[0,1]. \tag{16}$$

Finally, the turbulence operator is applied to the external archive solutions to avoid stagnation, but this is only applied as a greedy operator, i.e. the movement just occurs if the new position is better than the current one. This turbulence is the same deployed in the Multiple Objective Particle Swarm Optimization (MOPSO) algorithm (Coello et al., 2004).

MULTI-OBJECTIVE BINARY FISH SCHOOL SEARCH ALGORITHM

This section aims to present our proposal and detail all the operators and techniques utilized in the Multi-Objective Binary Fish School Search (MOBFSS) algorithm. MOBFSS is inspired by: (i) the movements utilized in Fish School Search (FSS) (Bastos Filho et al., 2008; 2009); (ii) the multi-objective approach used in Multi-Objective Fish School Search (MOFSS) (Bastos-Filho & Guimarães, 2015); (iii) the binary strategy employed in Binary Fish School Search (BFSS) (Sargo, 2013;2014), and its extension Improved Binary Fish School Search (IBFSS) (Carneiro & Bastos-Filho, 2016).

In MOBFSS, each fish is represented by its position (a binary vector), fitness and weight. The algorithm aims to solve two or three conflicting objectives. Therefore, the essential idea of MOBFSS is the movement of a school using individual and collective information. The operators are based on the flip of a binary dimension (change zero to one or the opposite) defined as movements. The calculation of feeding depends on the dominance concept (Bastos-Filho & Guimarães, 2015). Moreover, the use of external archive is to maintain good solutions found during the search process so far, and the application of a truncation method named Crowding Distance limits the size of the external archive (Deb et al., 2002) (Zitzler et al., 2001) (Bastos-Filho & Guimarães, 2015) (Santana & Bastos-Filho, 2009).

In summary, the pseudocode of the proposal can be seen in Algorithm 3. The first step of the algorithm is the initialization: the size of the school, the maximum number of iterations, the size of the external archive, the initial weight of each fish, the initial and final values for the individual and volitive step and the instinctive step. The second step is to execute the individual movement as a greedy operator. The third step is to calculate the dominance of each fish to feed the school. The fourth step is to execute the collective instinctive movement towards a convergence of good regions. The fifth step is the execution of the collective volitive movement to provide exploitation in a good region or to expand the school to find other regions. The external archive should be updated after the feeding and after the collective volitive movement operator. At last, the operator of turbulence tries to diversify the external archive to avoid fishes stuck in local minima. Moreover, the external archive is updated using the Crowding Distance. This method adds the external archive with the current school, and the solutions are sorted according to the dominance criterion and crowding distance to maintain the best solutions.

Individual Movement Operator

The individual movement operator is performed to generate diversity in the school. Its motivation is to provide freedom to each fish to find new areas and to avoid minimum local points. The pseudocode of the individual movement operator is shown in Algorithm 4. The diversity is controlled by the parameter individual flip ($Flip_{ind,}$), which quantifies the maximum number of dimensions that might be flipped in each fish. The movement is only applied to the fish that move to better positions. Moreover, a random number decides if each one of the dimensions is flipped or not. If the random number is greater than the individual step ($S_{ind}(t)$), and the maximum number of dimensions flipped are less than $Flip_{ind}$, the

Algorithm 3. MOBFSS Pseudocode

```
Initialize parameters, school and external archive
While stop criterion is not met do
     For each fish do
          Execute individual movement
     End For
     For each fish do
          Calculate dominance
     End For
     Feed the school
     Update external archive
     Calculate drift
     For each fish do
          Execute collective instinctive movement
     End For
     Calculate barycenter
     For each fish do
          Execute collective volitive movement
     End For
     Update external archive
     Execute turbulence operator at External Archive
End While
```

dimension is flipped, as shown in line 1, 2 and 3 of Algorithm 4. The algorithm should calculate which fish improved the fitness after the individual movement, so a true or false parameter can be added to the fish's object related to the improvement, and it can be updated while the individual operator is applied.

In this mechanism, the goal is to provide diversity and to avoid stagnation in a local minimum. The authors analyzed this operator by debugging the code, and the authors could perceive that the goals were achieved. Moreover, it is important to highlight the importance of the initialization of the parameters, specially $S_{ind}(t)$ *and* $Flip_{ind}$. They are fundamental to prevent the swarm to move only to certain regions.

Feeding Operator

The feeding operator uses the same methodology of MOFSS. The weight of each fish is updated by the addition of the multiplication of the variation of weight and the dominance of the fish as Equation (11). The variation of the weight is calculated by parameters given by the user (a, b). If the new position dominates the old one, the variation of the weight is a. If the old position dominates the new one, the variation of the weight is $-a$. If they are indifferent to each other, the Crowding Distance is applied to analyze the fish comparing the new position and the old position. If the new position presents a higher value of Crowding Distance than the old position, the variation of the weight is b, and if this does not happen, the variation of the weight is $-b$. The dominance of the fish is calculated depending on the proportion of how many fish are dominated by each fish and the maximum number of dominated fish as presented in Equation (12).

Algorithm 4. Individual movement operator pseudocode

```
For each dimension do
    If  random value > S_ind(t) and number dimensions flipped < Flip_ind :
        Flip(fish[dimension])
    End If
End For
Evaluate the fish by the new position
If the fitness improved by individual movement:
    Fish moves
Else:
    Fish does not move
```

Collective Instinctive Movement Operator

The collective instinctive movement operator considers only the fish that had successfully moved during the individual operator within the current iteration. For each dimension, the authors apply the difference between the value in this dimension in the current position and compare it to the value in the old position. If the sum of all dimensions exceeds a percentage of the school's size positively or negatively, these dimensions are flipped to the direction of the function sign, and the number of dimensions that can be flipped is constrained by the step instinctive $S_{inst}(t)$. Moreover, the threshold instinctive flip ($flip_{inst}$) is used for defining if the dimension can be flipped or not. Thus, this operator aims to attract fish to better regions, and the step instinctive and threshold are important in the definition of how fast the school is allowed to converge.

Take a fish with an old position equal to {0,1,1,0,1} and a new position equal to {1,1,1,0,0}. The difference of both vectors is equal to {1,0,0,0, -1}. The instinctive vector is going to similarly calculate for all the fish that improved their fitness. The sum, for example, is equal to {7, -2, 4, 2, -5}, and the number of fish that improved in this iteration is equal to 8. Consequently, only the dimensions, which are greater than 4 ($flip_{inst}$) or less than -4 ($flip_{inst}$), can flip the same index of dimension on the fish in the respective direction to 1 or 0. As the example, the position {1,1,1,0,0} does not have any dimension to flip because the only possibilities are the first index to 1 and the last index to 0. However, a fish with a position equal to {0,0,1,0,1} can change to {1,0,1,0,1} or {1,0,1,0,0} or {0,0,1,0,1}.

In this operator, the main intention is to help the swarm to converge for promising regions, which means helping the swarm to explore better regions. Therefore, this operator intensifies the exploration of the algorithm, and the absence of this operator impacts in the convergence.

Collective Volitive Movement Operator

The collective volitive movement operator randomly chooses a leader of External Archive to compare to each fish of the school. If the leader has a better weight than the fish, different dimensions between them are flipped. If the opposite happens, the similar dimensions should be flipped instead. The step volitive $S_{vol}(t)$ is the parameter that constrains the maximum number of dimensions that can be flipped.

The most important operator of MOBFSS is the collective volitive movement. The lack of this operator does not provide sufficient exploration and exploitation. The authors performed a preliminary assessment of this operator, and it impacts considerably in the convergence of the algorithm. Thus, the exploration and exploitation of this operator seem to be the key point to reach good results in multi-objective problems.

Turbulence Operator

The turbulence operator deployed in this chapter is the same used in the MOFSS (Bastos-Filho and Guimarães, 2015). The goal is to avoid getting stuck in local minima. In this operator, a new position is created by a randomly flip. If the flip causes a better non-dominated solution, the leader assumes the new solution. Moreover, this operator impacts on the stagnation of the swarm. This operator helps the swarm to continue looking for good solutions, and it is controlled by the parameter turbulence *(turb),* which restricts the number of dimensions that can be flipped.

EXPERIMENTS

The algorithms were programmed in Java language using the Jmetal library (Durillo, 2010; 2011). Moreover, the authors used the WEKA implementation of SVM because it is robust (Hall et al., 2009). Those libraries provide several techniques and metrics well established by the scientific community. In addition, the computer that performed the experiments was a MacBook Pro composed of 3 GHz Intel Core i7 and 16 GB 1600 MHz DDR3, and the operating system macOS Sierra version 10.12.6.

The number of features is what determined the selection of datasets used for testing the algorithms. The authors selected three different datasets, which are the UCI datasets. They are Wine, Ionosphere, and Sonar (UCI, 2017) and present 13, 34 and 60 features, respectively. The authors would like to emphasize that the complexity increases when the numbers of features are higher. The goal is to analyze three different scenarios that reveal various complexities.

The authors performed a parametrical analysis for each one of the three datasets. The choice of values was decided by the general best solution, which means that for each dataset is possible to find a better combination of parameters. The authors aimed to set parameters that might bring several good solutions for any dataset. In summary, the authors used the valued for the parameters determined in preliminary experiments depicted in Table 1.

The authors executed 30 trials for each experiment in each dataset. The authors used the same stop criterion adopted in Souza et al. (2011), which determined the maximum of the number of evaluations of the fitness function equal to 200,000 and the maximum number of iterations without improvement equal to 100. Moreover, the results of MOBFSS are compared with the BMOPSO-CDR results, in which the authors adopted the same values of Souza et al. (2011).

The metrics used for comparison of algorithms are Hypervolume (HVR), Spacing (SP) and Maximum-Spread (MS) (Zitzler & Thiele, 1999) (Zitzler et al., 2000). Hypervolume calculates the area between the Pareto Front and a reference point (datum point). HVR measures the union of the areas formed by the solutions within the Pareto Front and the Datum point. Thus, a larger area means a better solution. On the other hand, SP measures the diversity of solutions within the Pareto Front, so a small value of SP means better diversity for a solution. Finally, MS calculates the Euclidean distance between the

Table 1. MOBFSS Parameters

Description	Parameter	Value
Number of dimensions (for each fish)	n_{dim}	Dependent on dataset
Number of fishes in the internal population	N	$5 * n_{dim}$
Size of the External Archive	AE_{size}	n_{dim}
Maximum number of evaluation	e_{max}	200,000
Number of trials per scenario	s_{max}	30
Number of iterations without improvements to stop the optimization	t_{imp}	100
Initial weight of each fish	W_i	0.5
Weight limits for each fish	W_{i_min}, W_{i_max}	[0.1; 1]
Fish feeding (dominance criterion)	a	0.3
Fish feeding (indifference criterion)	b	0.1
Maximum number of flipped dimensions in the individual movement	S_{ind}	$0.3 * n_{dim}$
Comparison to random value on individual movement	$flip_{ind}$	[0.25,0.75]
Maximum number of flipped dimensions in the instinctive movement	S_{inst}	[0.30, 0.50] ($*n_{dim}$)
Threshold used for defining if a flip can be performed in the instinctive movement	$flip_{inst}$	N / 4
Maximum number of flipped dimensions in the volitive movement	S_{vol} (t)	[0.15, 0.30] ($*n_{dim}$)
Turbulence threshold	turb	$0.3 * n_{dim}$

solutions that are more distant. As a consequence, MS considers the extension of the Pareto Front, and higher values are considered as better solutions.

RESULTS

Figure 1, 2 and 3 depicts the evolution of the average value for the HVR metrics for the three deployed datasets, and its respectively standard deviation. One can observe that the HVR for MOBFSS converges faster and usually presents higher or at least similar values to the ones presented by the BMOPSO-CDR. The HVR of the MOPFSS is better after the convergence for the most complex datasets, *i.e.*, Sonar and Ionosphere. In Figure 4 and 5, the authors present the obtained Pareto Fronts for the Sonar and Ionosphere datasets, respectively. The best Pareto Front found by the Sonar dataset is the one obtained by the MOBFSS approach. The same occurs for the Ionosphere dataset. The authors do not show the Pareto Front for the Wine dataset because it is an elementary problem and both algorithms found the same Pareto Front with only two solutions.

In Table 2, the authors present the results of the metrics for the Sonar and Ionosphere datasets. The results for the Sonar show the highest difference between BMOPSO-CDR and MOBFSS, which means that for more complex problems (higher number of features) the MOBFSS far outperforms the BMOPSO-CDR approach. The authors calculated the p-value for the signal-ranked Wilcoxon Statistical Test (using 95% of confidence) for each dataset. The results for the Sonar and Ionosphere datasets presented statistical significance showing that the MOBFSS approach outperformed BMOPSO-CDR.

Figure 1. Hypervolume metric evolution for the best solution on the sonar dataset

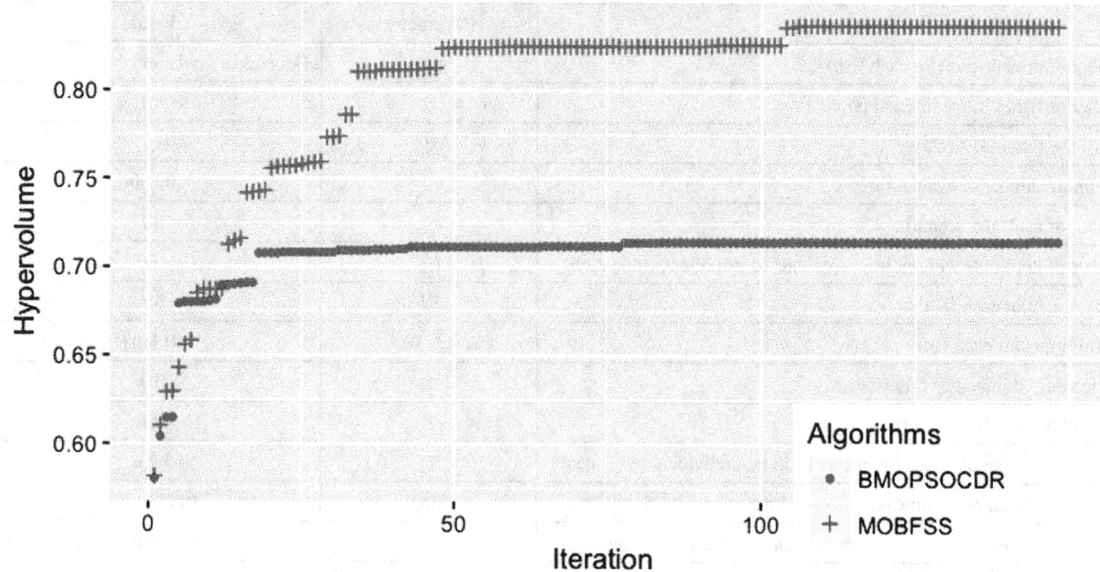

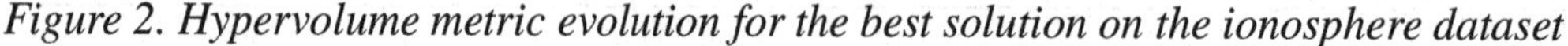

Figure 2. Hypervolume metric evolution for the best solution on the ionosphere dataset

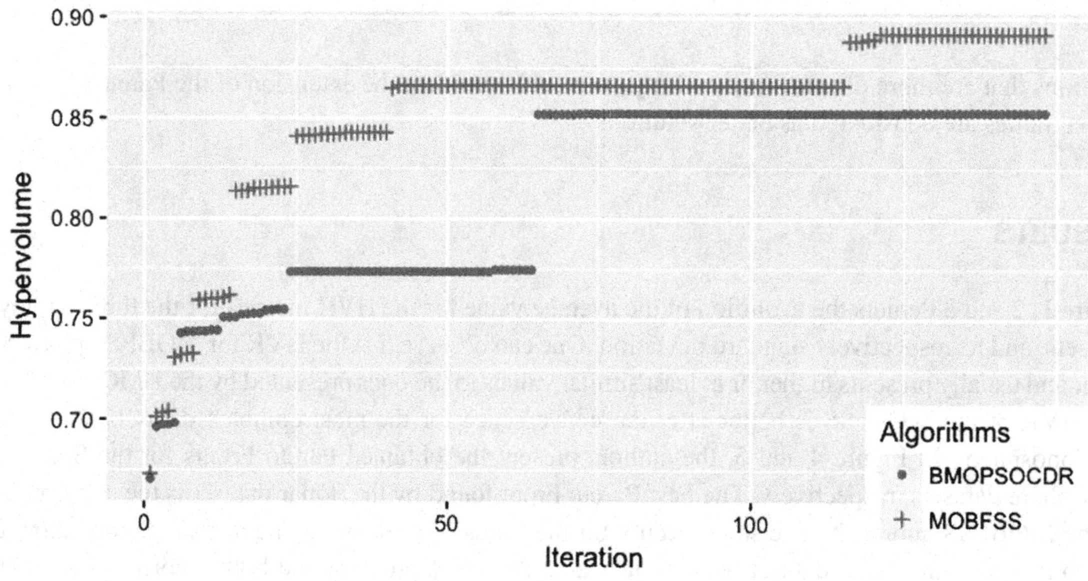

Specifically, about MOBFSS, the authors performed some preliminary results to show that the removal of any one of the operators reduces the performance and/or impacts in the convergence process. However, the withdrawal of the collective volitive movement diminishes approximately 0.05-0.15 in the value of the HVR metrics, which means that it is the most important operator of the algorithm. Without the collective volitive movement, the swarm does not have the capability of exploration and exploitation.

Figure 3. Hypervolume metric evolution for the best solution on the wine dataset

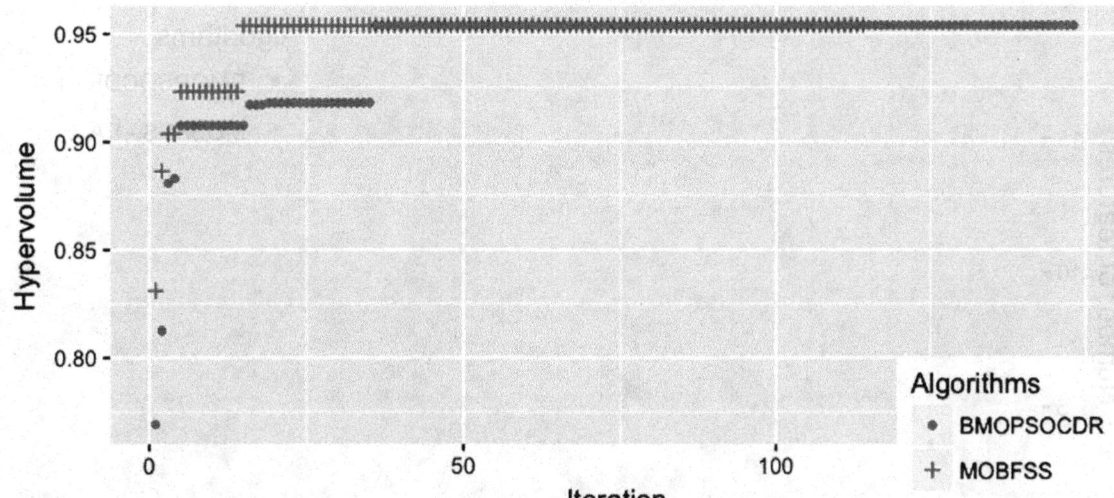

Figure 4. Pareto front for the best external archive on the sonar dataset

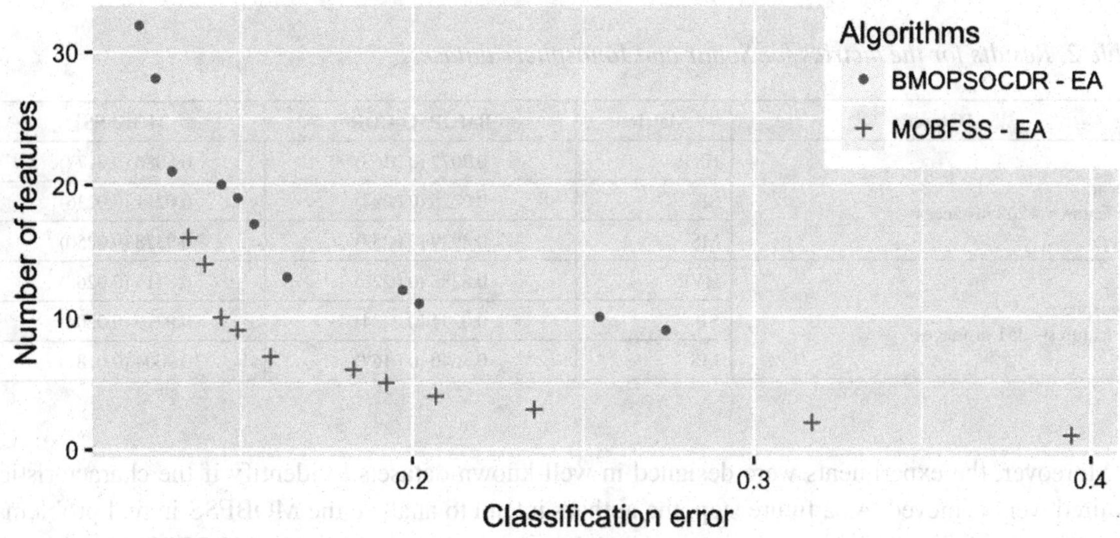

FUTURE RESEARCH DIRECTIONS

The authors aimed to introduce the first version of a Multi-Objective Binary algorithm. The MOBFSS merges operators and strategies that could intensify the diversity and convergence without concerning about complexity. The next goal is to minimize the complexity and the number of parameters, which control the operators. Additionally, the MOBFSS requires two evaluations per fish in each iteration, but BMOPSO-CDR only evaluates once per fish by iteration. Thus, a future possibility is to reduce the number of evaluations so that several adaptations may be necessary to this particular modification, but it will impact positively in the complexity.

Figure 5. Pareto front for the best external archive on the ionosphere dataset

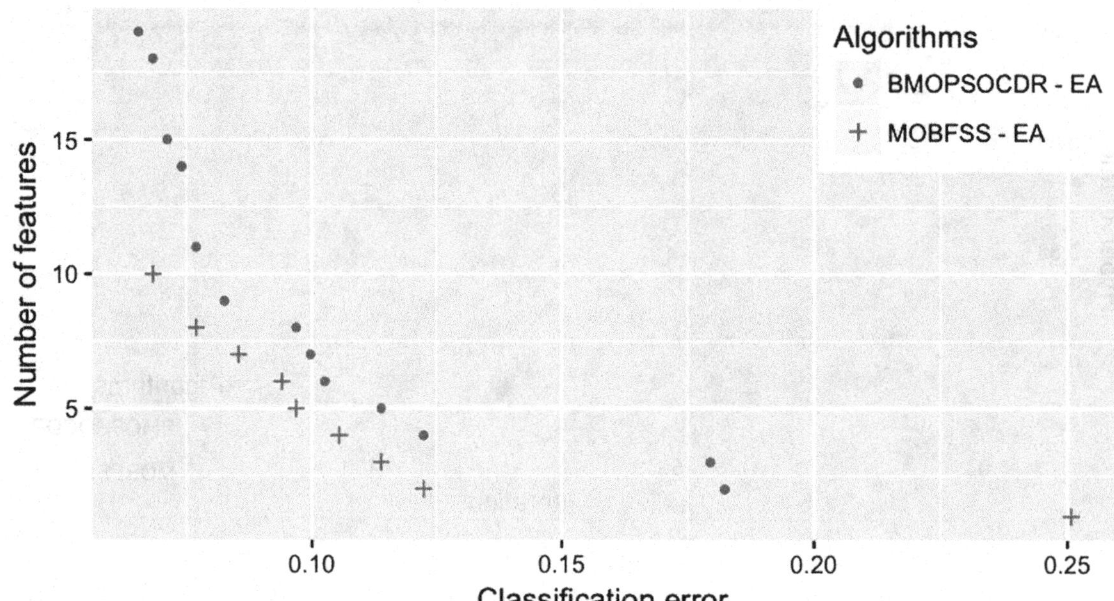

Table 2. Results for the metrics for Sonar and Ionosphere datasets

Dataset	Metrics	BMOPSO-CDR	MOBFSS
Sonar 60 features – 208 instances	HVR	0.7072 (0.0163)	0.8086 (0.0177)
	SP	0.0226 (0.0094)	0.0211 (0.0236)
	MS	0.8939 (0.0253)	0.9328 (0.0250)
Ionosphere 34 features – 351 instances	HVR	0.8286 (0.0226)	0.8418 (0.0268)
	SP	0.0291 (0.0134)	0.0279 (0.0204)
	MS	0.8640 (0.0167)	0.9004 (0.0181)

Moreover, the experiments were designed in well-known datasets to identify if the characteristics required were achieved. As a future step, the authors intend to analyze the MOBFSS in real problems. Consequently, this analysis may bring several insights about new extensions for MOBFSS that will optimize the metrics results, and it simultaneously decreases its complexity and required a priori information.

CONCLUSION

The main proposal of this chapter is to present a new algorithm, MOBFSS, which can directly address the optimization of conflicting objectives using binary decision variables. MOBFSS focus on maintaining the inspirations of the operators in FSS. BFSS and MOFSS were used to motivate the adaptations made in MOBFSS.

Each operator in MOBFSS has a specific goal. Firstly, the individual movement proposed by us diversifies the current population. Secondly, the feeding operator updates the weight of the fish, which represents the accumulation of discoveries. Thirdly, the collective instinctive movement attracts the swarm to better regions. Next, the collective volitive movement acts as a refiner of good areas or a mechanism to expand the swarm aiming to find other regions. Finally, the turbulence operator causes little changes in the External Archive with the aid to avoid early stagnation.

Therefore, the adaptations indicate that the goals established by us were accomplished. The exam of the operators and the results reveal the potential usefulness of MOBFSS. The feature selection problem is relevant, and the authors contribute, in this chapter, with a good proposition for this issue.

Moreover, the convergence of MOBFSS points out to be a state-of-art swarm-based technique for binary optimization in multi-objective problems. As for disadvantages, MOBFSS evaluates the swarm after the individual and collective volitive movement, and the number of parameters is higher than for the BMOPSO-CDR. However, the authors, in the future, intend to solve these points and also expect to assess the proposal in real-world problems.

ACKNOWLEDGMENT

Mariana Macedo thanks the Academic Strengthening Program of the University of Pernambuco (PFA - UPE) and Coordination for the Improvement of Higher-Education Personnel (CAPES), Brazil, for the partial financial support for this chapter.

REFERENCES

Argyris, N., Figueira, J. R., & Morton, A. (2011). Identifying preferred solutions to Multi-Objective Binary Optimisation problems, with an application to the Multi-Objective Knapsack Problem. *Journal of Global Optimization*, *49*(2), 213–235. doi:10.1007/s10898-010-9541-9

Bastos-Filho, C. J., & Guimarães, A. C. (2015). Multi-objective fish school search. *International Journal of Swarm Intelligence Research*, *6*(1), 23–40. doi:10.4018/ijsir.2015010102

Bastos-Filho, C. J. A., Lima-Neto, F. B., Lins Sousa, M. F. C., Pontes, M. R., & Madeiro, S. S. (2009). On the influence of the swimming operators in the fish school search algorithm. *2009 IEEE International Conference on Systems, Man and Cybernetics*, 5012–5017. doi:10.1109/ICSMC.2009.5346377

Bastos-Filho, C. J. A., Lima-Neto, F. B., Lins, A. J. C. C., Nascimento, A. I. S., & Lima, M. P. (2008). A novel search algorithm based on fish school behavior. *IEEE International Conference on Systems, Man and Cybernetics*, 2646–2651. doi:10.1109/ICSMC.2008.4811695

Bastos-Filho, C. J. A., & Nascimento, D. O. (2013, September). An enhanced fish school search algorithm. In *Computational Intelligence and 11th Brazilian Congress on Computational Intelligence (BRICS-CCI & CBIC), 2013 BRICS Congress on* (pp. 152-157). IEEE. doi:10.1109/BRICS-CCI-CBIC.2013.34

Carneiro, R. F., & Bastos-Filho, C. J. (2016, November). Improving the Binary Fish School Search Algorithm for feature selection. In *Computational Intelligence (LA-CCI), 2016 IEEE Latin American Conference on* (pp. 1-6). IEEE. doi:10.1109/LA-CCI.2016.7885708

Clerc, M. (2010). *Particle swarm optimization*. John Wiley & Sons.

Coello Coello, C. A., Lamont, G. B., & Veldhuizen, D. A. V. (2007). *Evolutionary Algorithms for Solving Multi-Objectives Problems*. Springer.

Coello Coello, C. A., Pulido, G., & Lechuga, M. S. (2004). Handling multiple objectives with particles swarm optimization. *IEEE Transactions on Evolutionary Computation*, *8*(3), 256–279. doi:10.1109/TEVC.2004.826067

Collette, Y., & Siarry, P. (2003). *Multiobjective Optimization - Principles and Case Studies*. Springer.

de Souza, L. S., de Miranda, P. B., Prudencio, R. B., & Barros, F. D. A. (2011, November). A multi-objective particle swarm optimization for test case selection based on functional requirements coverage and execution effort. In *Tools with Artificial Intelligence (ICTAI), 2011 23rd IEEE International Conference on* (pp. 245-252). IEEE. doi:10.1109/ICTAI.2011.45

de Souza, L. S., Prudêncio, R. B., & Barros, F. D. A. (2014, October). A hybrid binary multi-objective particle swarm optimization with local search for test case selection. In *Intelligent Systems (BRACIS), 2014 Brazilian Conference on* (pp. 414-419). IEEE.

Deb, K., Pratap, A., Agarwal, S., & Meyarivan, T. (2002). A fast and elitist multiobjective genetic algorithm: NSGA-II. *IEEE Transactions on Evolutionary Computation*, *6*(2), 182–197. doi:10.1109/4235.996017

Deb, K., Thiele, L., Laumanns, M., & Zitzler, E. (2001). *Scalable Test Problems for Evolutionary Multi-Objective Optimization. TIK Report 112, Computer Engineering and Networks Laboratory (TIK)*. ETH Zurich.

Deb, K., Thiele, L., Laumanns, M., & Zitzler, E. (2002). Scalable Multi-Objective Optimization Test Problems. *IEEE Congress on Evolutionary Computation*, 825–830.

Deb, K., Thiele, L., Laumanns, M., & Zitzler, E. (2005). Scalable Test Problems for Evolutionary Multi-Objective Optimization. In A. Abraham, R. Jain, & R. Goldberg (Eds.), *Evolutionary Multiobjective Optimization: Theoretical Advances and Applications* (pp. 105–145). Springer. doi:10.1007/1-84628-137-7_6

Durillo, J., Nebro, A., & Alba, E. (2010). The jmetal framework for multi-objective optimization: Design and architecture. *IEEE Congress on Evolutionary Computation*, 4138–4325. doi:10.1109/CEC.2010.5586354

Durillo, J. J., & Nebro, A. J. (2011). jmetal: A java framework for multi-objective optimization. *Advances in Engineering Software*, *42*(10), 760–771. doi:10.1016/j.advengsoft.2011.05.014

Eberhart, R., & Kennedy, J. (1995, October). A new optimizer using particle swarm theory. In *Micro Machine and Human Science, 1995. MHS'95., Proceedings of the Sixth International Symposium on* (pp. 39-43). IEEE. doi:10.1109/MHS.1995.494215

Engelbrecht, A. P. (2007). *Computational Intelligence: An Introduction*. John Wiley and Sons. doi:10.1002/9780470512517

Forman, G. (2003). An extensive empirical study of feature selection metrics for text classification. *Journal of Machine Learning Research*, *3*(Mar), 1289–1305.

Guyon, I., & Elisseeff, A. (2003). An introduction to variable and feature selection. *Journal of Machine Learning Research*, *3*(Mar), 1157–1182.

Hall, M., Frank, E., Holmes, G., Pfahringer, B., Reutemann, P., & Witten, I. H. (2009). The WEKA data mining software: An update. *SIGKDD Explorations*, *11*(1), 10–18. doi:10.1145/1656274.1656278

Hearst, M. A., Dumais, S. T., Osuna, E., Platt, J., & Scholkopf, B. (1998). Support vector machines. *IEEE Intelligent Systems & their Applications*, *13*(4), 18–28. doi:10.1109/5254.708428

Kennedy, J., & Eberhart, R. C. (2001). *Swarm Intelligence*. Morgan Kaufmann Publishers.

Nebro, A. J., Durillo, J. J., Garça-Nieto, J., Coello Coello, C. A., Luna, F., & Alba, E. (2009). SMPSO: A new PSO-based metaheuristic for multi-objective optimization. *IEEE Symposium on Computational Intelligence in Multicriteria Decision-Making*, 66–73. doi:10.1109/MCDM.2009.4938830

Peng, H., Long, F., & Ding, C. (2005). Feature selection based on mutual information criteria of max-dependency, max-relevance, and min-redundancy. *IEEE Transactions on Pattern Analysis and Machine Intelligence*, *27*(8), 1226–1238. doi:10.1109/TPAMI.2005.159 PMID:16119262

Sankaran, A., Jain, A., Vashisth, T., Vatsa, M., & Singh, R. (2017). Adaptive latent fingerprint segmentation using feature selection and random decision forest classification. *Information Fusion*, *34*, 1–15. doi:10.1016/j.inffus.2016.05.002

Santana, R. A., Pontes, M. R., & Bastos-Filho, C. J. A. (2009). A multiple objective particle swarm optimization approach using crowding distance and roulette wheel. *Ninth International Conference on Intelligent Systems Design and Applications*, 237–242. doi:10.1109/ISDA.2009.73

Sargo, J. A., Vieira, S. M., Sousa, J. M., & Bastos Filho, C. J. (2014, July). Binary Fish School Search applied to feature selection: Application to ICU readmissions. In *Fuzzy Systems (FUZZ-IEEE), 2014 IEEE International Conference on* (pp. 1366-1373). IEEE.

Sargo, J. A. G. (2013). *Binary Fish School Search applied to Feature Selection*. Academic Press.

Shenfield, A., & Rostami, S. (2015, August). A multi objective approach to evolving artificial neural networks for coronary heart disease classification. In *Computational Intelligence in Bioinformatics and Computational Biology (CIBCB), 2015 IEEE Conference on* (pp. 1-8). IEEE. doi:10.1109/CIBCB.2015.7300294

Souza, L. S., de Miranda, P. B., Prudencio, R. B., & Barros, F. D. A. (2011, November). A multi-objective particle swarm optimization for test case selection based on functional requirements coverage and execution effort. In *Tools with UCI Machine Learning Repository: Data Sets*. Retrieved 21 June 2017, from https://archive.ics.uci.edu/ml/datasets.html

Tasca, M., Plastino, A., Ribeiro, C., & Zadrozny, B. (2017). A Fast and Effective Strategy for Feature Selection in High-dimensional Datasets. *Journal of Information and Data Management*, *7*(2), 155.

Xue, B., Cervante, L., Shang, L., Browne, W. N., & Zhang, M. (2014). Binary PSO and rough set theory for feature selection: A multi-objective filter based approach. *International Journal of Computational Intelligence and Applications*, *13*(2). doi:10.1142/S1469026814500096

Xue, B., Zhang, M., & Browne, W. N. (2013a). Particle swarm optimization for feature selection in classification: A multi-objective approach. *IEEE Transactions on Cybernetics, 43*(6), 1656-1671. doi:10.1109/TSMCB.2012.2227469

Xue, B., Zhang, M., & Browne, W. N. (2013b). Particle swarm optimization for feature selection in classification: A multi-objective approach. *IEEE Transactions on Cybernetics*, *43*(6), 1656–1671. doi:10.1109/TSMCB.2012.2227469 PMID:24273143

Xue, B., Zhang, M., & Browne, W. N. (2015). A comprehensive comparison on evolutionary feature selection approaches to classification. *International Journal of Computational Intelligence and Applications*, *14*(2). doi:10.1142/S146902681550008X

Xue, B., Zhang, M., Browne, W. N., & Yao, X. (2016). A survey on evolutionary computation approaches to feature selection. *IEEE Transactions on Evolutionary Computation*, *20*(4), 606–626. doi:10.1109/TEVC.2015.2504420

Zitzler, E., Deb, K., & Thiele, L. (2000). Comparison of multiobjective evolutionary algorithms: Empirical results. *Evolutionary Computation*, *8*(2), 173–195. doi:10.1162/106365600568202 PMID:10843520

Zitzler, E., Laumanns, M., & Thiele, L. (2001). *SPEA2: Improving the strength Pareto evolutionary algorithm for multiobjective optimization*. Evolutionary Methods for Design Optimization and Control with Applications to Industrial Problems.

Zitzler, E., & Thiele, L. (1999). Multiobjective evolutionary algorithms: A comparative case study and the strength pareto approach. *IEEE Transactions on Evolutionary Computation*, *3*(4), 257–271. doi:10.1109/4235.797969

KEY TERMS AND DEFINITIONS

Dominance: In a multi-objective problem, a solution dominates another solution if it outperforms in all the objectives.

External Archive: A space to store non-dominated solutions.

Feature Selection Problem: A problem that should be solved by finding the best minimal number of features to optimize task.

Fish: The abstraction of solution for the fish school search algorithm.

Fitness Function: A function in which qualify a solution.

Indifference: In a multi-objective problem, a solution is indifferent to another solution if none of them dominates.

Pareto Front: A subset of the set which is composed of all the solutions of a multi-objective problem.

Weight: An abstract term which accumulates the efficiency of a fish.

Chapter 4
City Group Optimization: An Optimizer for Continuous Problems

Yijun Yang
Southern University of Science and Technology, China

ABSTRACT

City group refers to a collection of cities. Through the development and growth, these cities form a chain of metropolitan areas. In a city group, cities are divided into central cities and subordinate cities. Generally, central cities have greater chances to develop. However, subordinate cities may not have great chances to develop unless they are adjacent to central cities. Thus, a city is more likely to develop well if it is near a central city. In the process, the spatial distribution of cities changes all the time. Urbanologists call the above phenomena the evolution of city groups. In this chapter, the city group optimization algorithm is presented, which is based on urbanology and mimics the evolution of city groups. The robustness and evolutionary process of the proposed city group optimization algorithm are validated by testing it on 15 benchmark functions. The comparative results show that the proposed algorithm is effective for solving complexly continuous problems due to a stronger ability to escape from local optima.

1. INTRODUCTION

City group, the sub-discipline of urbanology, first, is found by the twentieth century urbanologist, i.e., Ebenezer (Ebenezer, 2010). Until 1915, Patrick wrote a book "Cities in Evolution" and first presented "city-region" (Patrick, 1968). The "city-region" is defined as "conurbation" by Patrick, a chain of inter-linked urban districts or metropolitan areas. In 1957, Gottmann used "megalopolis" to describe a chain of metropolitan areas along the northeastern seaboard of U.S. According to the research of urbanologists, they discovered that different terms are used to denote the concept of metropolitan areas. Thus, to avoid confusion, we use a constant term "city group" to express the same concept in this chapter. By now, many scholars have researched abundant information about city groups (Peter, & Kathy, 2006). During twenty-first century, a quick population growth leads to the expansion of cities. City groups have drawn more people's attention, especially in China (Yao, et al., 2006). With the fast development of China, many city groups, such as the Pearl River Delta, Beijing-Tianjin-Hebei Region and Central

DOI: 10.4018/978-1-5225-5134-8.ch004

Plains Urban Agglomeration, have already deeply influenced the public life. City groups have become common phenomena. However, we investigate the Engineering Index (EI) and Science Citation Index Expanded (SCIE), and discover that no one tries to utilize advantages of city groups to solve optimization problems. Therefore, this chapter is written to study advantages of city groups, and these may contribute to design new metaheuristics.

The development of city group is an evolutionary process. The process can be classified into the following two stages. In the first stage, cities cluster together in a group. A city with more residents is deemed to have a higher population size index (***PSI***). A city has prosperous economies, excellent geographic positions and convenient transportations, naturally, its ***PSI*** is high. A city group contains central cities and subordinate cities. It is obvious that ***PSI***s of central cities are higher than subordinate cities. Usually, subordinate cities that are nearer central cities are easier to improve their ***PSI***s. Hence, the central cities are magnetic for subordinate cities. In this case, subordinate cities will be gathered around central cities as shown in Figure 1(a). In the second stage, cities are diffused in a limit area. Suppose subordinate cities have higher ***PSI***s than central cities over time, and then the subordinate cities will displace former central cities. So the center of city group will change from the previous position to another position. New central cities will be surrounded by subordinate cities, thus the cities are diffused as shown in Figure 1(b). Due to the unceasing clustering and diffusion, a city group maintains the internal balance and development (Gregory, 2002).

In the last decade, more and more metaheuristics are presented and developed to balance the population diversity and convergence speed. For metaheuristics, fine population diversity is beneficial to escape from local optima, and a fast convergence speed contributes the improvement of efficiency in solving problems. Genetic algorithm (GA) adopts evolutionary operators. Because of a series of genetic transformations, selection, mutation and crossover, GA preserves population diversity. But GA lacks effective mechanisms to accelerate convergence. Particle swarm optimization (PSO) adopts kinetic particle swarms to find the best solutions. Swarms follow leaders, and search the solution space of a problem. Due to the directivity of particles, PSO exhibits a fast convergence speed. But on multimodal problems, the leader located at a local optimum may lead to the premature convergence of swarms. In order to solve this problem, many

Figure 1. (a) Clustering (b) Diffusion

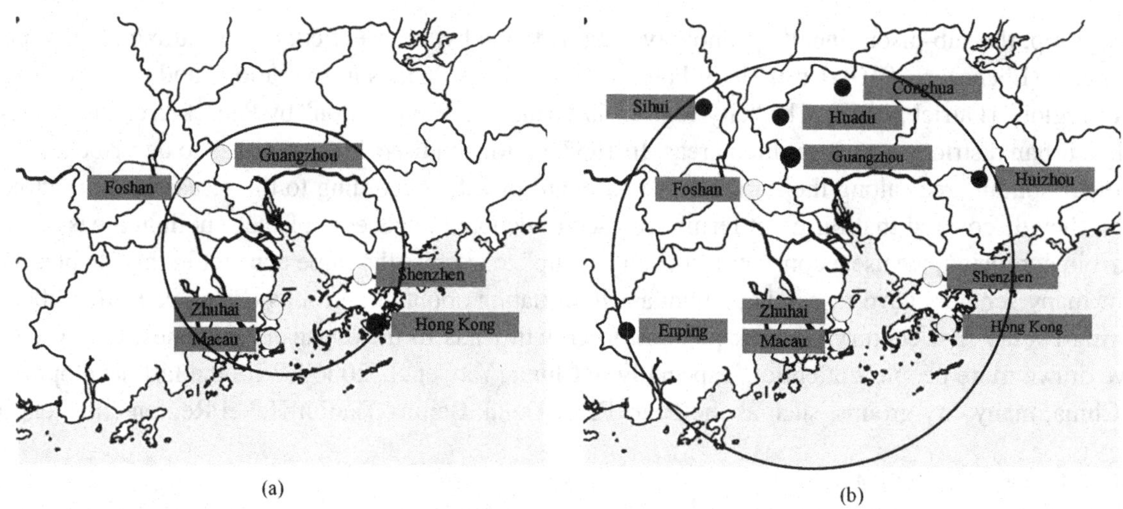

researchers have proposed varied strategies to modify PSO. Nevertheless, these versions of PSO lead complicated algorithmic structures, and some even lose the fast-converging characteristic. Artificial bee colony (ABC) is inspired by smart search behaviors of bee colony, and it is a burgeoning metaheuristic. The algorithm emphasizes the cooperation of honey bee colony. Each honey bee has chances to explore the whole search space. Therefore, ABC has a strong ability to maintain population diversity. However, due to the lack of directivity, the convergence speed of ABC is low. From the above discussions, ensuring diversity and convergence speed are concurrently excellent; it is still a tough problem.

From the above phenomena, we conclude that the evolution of city group is a process of distributing cities, and it is similar to searching the best solution of a problem. We build an artificial city group in the search space of a certain problem, and then let the artificial city group imitates the evolution of real city group. Each artificial city represents a potential solution, and the quality of solution reflects the value of ***PSI***. Furthermore, the city with the highest ***PSI*** magnetizes the whole city group just like what the leader does in PSO. Thus, the excellent convergence of PSO is retained. Owing to the second stage of the evolution of city group, diffusion just like the mutation and crossover in GA, the diversity is also maintained. In the artificial city group, cities continually cluster and diffuse so as to jump out of local optima. Therefore, the metaheuristic inspired by the evolution of city group should be superior for complex optimization problems. We call this new metaheuristic as city group optimization (CGO). As such, the merit of CGO is to balance the diversity and convergence speed without complicated algorithmic structures.

We organize the remainder of this chapter as follows: Section II briefly describes some basic concepts of existing metaheuristics, and introduces the evolution of real city group. Section III discusses the basic framework of CGO. The evolutionary process of CGO is investigated in Section IV. Section V expounds experimental settings, and provides experimental results by comparing CGO with several metaheuristics. Section VI and VII give some discussions and conclusions for further work.

2. BACKGROUND

2.1. Swarm Intelligence

With the increase of complex problems optimizing, many practical optimization design problems have been raised, which give rise to the boom of swarm intelligence algorithms. Many algorithms such as ant colony optimization (ACO), PSO, ABC, differential evolution (DE) (Storn, & Price, 1995), harmony search algorithm (Duan, & Li, 2014), pigeon-inspired optimization (Duan, & Qiao, 2014), chemical reaction optimization (Lam, & Li, 2010), biogeography-based optimization (Simon, 2008) and brain storm optimization (Shi, 2011) have been presented and developed. At the very beginning, two major methods were developed for different kinds of problems: ACO and PSO.

ACO utilizes artificial ants to find a shortest path from their nests to destinations. In ACO, paths between nests and destinations represent potential solutions to optimization problems. Pheromone, a kind of volatile chemical, stimulates neurons of ants. An ant deposits a certain amount of pheromone along the path, while it finds a satisfactory destination. The amount of pheromone is related to the quality of resources, and influences the path selection of other ants. A better path appeals to ants, and then more ants deposit more pheromone. By the mechanism of positive feedback, ACO leads ant colonies to discover the shortest path (Dorigo, et al., 1996). This metaheuristic has been successfully applied to solving the traveling salesman problem (Dorigo, & Gambardella, 1997). Kennedy and Eberhart studied the swarm phenomenon in nature, and presented a PSO algorithm (Kennedy, & Eberhart, 1995; Eberhart, & Kennedy, 1995). PSO uses particle swarm to mimic a flock of birds or a school of fishes. In PSO, each individual is treated as a no-volume particle in the D-dimensional space, and each particle represents a potential solution to a certain problem. The particle swarm is roughly led by their own best position and the best position of entire swarm (Clerc, & Kennedy, 2002). In swarm intelligence, scholars cost a large amount of time to learn from bees (Parpinelli, & Lopes, 2011). In order to mimic intelligent behaviors of bees, Karaboga and Basturk presented the ABC algorithm (Karaboga, & Basturk, 2007). In ABC, the bees are sorted by their tasks (searchers, explorers and scouts). The first two kinds of bees gather honey according to the quality of resources. High-quality resources are worthy of being exploited. Oppositely, the scouts randomly fly in the search space, and the movement is similar to random walk. Scouts help a bee colony to find out better resources. If a new resource has more honey than the former one, more bees will exploit the new resource and give up the previous one (Karaboga, & Basturk, 2008). The above three swarm intelligence algorithms have been applied to solving a vast range of problems (Duan, et al, 2013; Duan, et al., 2008; Zhang, et al., 2008).

Because researchers have investigated many group behaviors in nature (fire fly, fruit fly, wolves, et al.), and model those, so swarm intelligence algorithms are rapidly developing. One of the reasons why researchers model those behaviors is that animals or insects live together can increase the possibility of successful foraging and reduce the energy cost. Researchers studied many social behaviors in animals or insects so as to facilitate analysis of social behaviors. They have come up with two models: information sharing (IS) model (Clark, & Mangel, 1984) and producer-scrounger (PS) model (Barnard, & Sibly, 1981). In the IS model, individuals share information with others, and the cooperation of population is very important. In the PS model, individuals are classified into leaders and followers, and the leaders can guide the followers to find better resources. S. He *et al* (He, et al., 2009) presented group search optimizer based on these models.

As mentioned above, researchers have analyzed a large amount of natural phenomena to design algorithms (PSO, ABC, ACO, etc.). There are some biological examples: foraging, division of labor, corpse clustering, larval sorting, nest building and cooperative transport, etc. These examples have been modelled in detail, and have a common characteristic: they need to consume a certain amount of resources and time to attain optimizing conditions. But sometimes these examples may not get desirable results due to the existence of unpredictability. In our view, when some natural phenomena are compared with human beings, they are not indeed intelligent. We cannot blindly imitate nature. Human beings develop all the time by natural selection. From theories of Darwin, human beings have evolved to the most intelligent species on the Earth. Human society is also the most complex and intelligent. In human society, the population migration, the evolution of city group, the evolution of society, the wealth accumulation and seeking optimized solutions (brainstorm process) are all valuable phenomena. The phenomena are related to human beings, and humans may be more acquainted with them. On the condition that researchers study these uniquely social phenomena, they will discover something beneficial to design new swarm intelligence algorithms. Shi first presented a BSO algorithm based on the human brainstorm process (Shi, 2011), and the algorithm is an outstanding example of learning experience from the human activities. In conclusion, appropriate human activities should inspire more swarm intelligence algorithms. Through abundant research, no-one methods can perform well for all optimizing problems. Hence, more effective methods should be proposed to adapt to different problems, e.g., (Wolpert, & Macready, 1997).

2.2. City Group

In this section, three phenomena about the evolution of city group are introduced in brief. It needs to be stressed: authors are not fully professional researchers into urbanology, so just introduce some phenomena related to designing the CGO algorithm.

2.2.1. Phenomenon 1

Transportation is very necessary for cities. In a city group, laborers build many roads to connect cities in order to transport goods and travel to places. A number of roads make up a road network. Every city make itself a node of the network. The city with the most roads is a transportation hub (***TH***), and the road with the most volume of traffic is a trunk road (***TR***). The phenomenon can be described by using mathematical models. According to the research of urbanologists, the basically topological structures that a road network contains are given in Figure 2. Urbanologists have compared these structures on the stability and space utilization. For stability, when researchers delete one line, structure (a) and structure (c) still keep the balance of road networks. However, structure (b) and structure (d) are both out of contact with a city. Therefore, the balance of networks is broken. It is undoubted that structure (a) and structure (c) have a stronger ability to resist interference. For space utilization, clearly, the area of structure (c) is smaller than structure (a) when they are the same at the number of cities. Analytical results indicate "Figure 2(c)" is the best structure for road networks. The structure is crucial for designing the CGO algorithm in Section III.

2.2.2. Phenomenon 2

A real example is provided to elucidate the clustering and diffusion in a city group. The Pearl River Delta, where there were only several small fishing villages in the past China, and we call it as an underdeveloped place. However, nowadays the place possesses the most prosperous economy in China, which is contributed by Hong Kong. Gradually, more and more cities arise around Hong Kong. This is a clustering phenomenon (see Figure 1(a)). With the development of subordinate cities, cities become bigger in size, they will expand towards far places in order to improve ***PSI***s. It is clear that the ***PSI*** of Guangzhou exceeds Hong Kong (see Figure 3). The data in Figure 3 are provided by National Bureau of Statistics of the People's Republic of China. Guangzhou becomes the central city of the city group. Hence, the center of the city group changes from one position to another position. The new central city magnetizes more subordinate cities, so the city group becomes bigger in size (see Figure 1(b)). This is

Figure 2. The structures of road networks

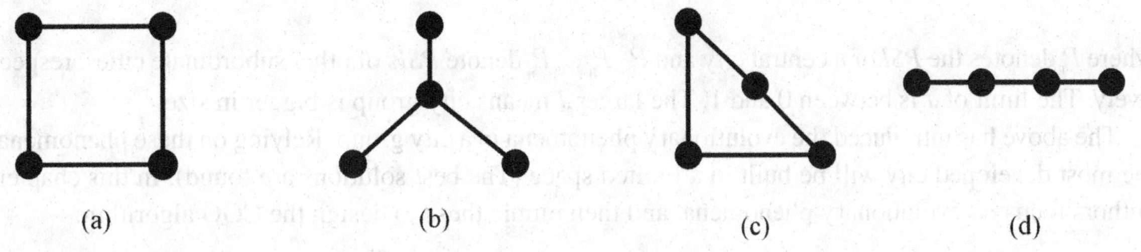

Figure 3. PSIs of Guangzhou and Hong Kong (1960-2010)

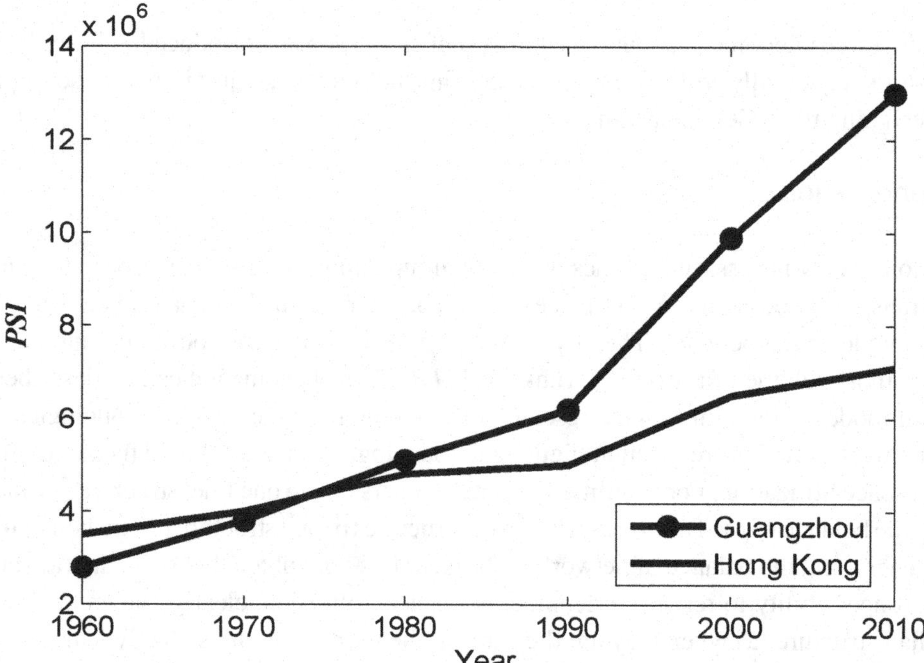

a diffusion phenomenon. Subordinate cities have certain probability to transform into central cities due to the clustering and diffusion. On the one hand, a developed city is attractive for subordinate cities, and more cities will cluster around the central city. On the other hand, central cities are likely to be replaced by subordinate cities, and then the size of city group will change.

2.2.3. Phenomenon 3

The size is an important index for evaluating the development of a city group. Usually, a diminutive city group contains fewer cities, i.e., a central city and several subordinate cities. By comparing these subordinate cities, you will find plenty of similar places. Thus, we can see that the diversity is low. In contrast, a large city group contains more varied cities. Therefore, the diversity is high. Urbanologists have proposed a mathematical equation to evaluate the size of a city group. The equation is given as follows:

$$J = \frac{P_1}{P_1 + P_2 + \ldots + P_n}$$

where P_1 denotes the *PSI* of a central city and $P_2, P_3 \ldots P_n$ denote *PSIs* of other subordinate cities, respectively. The limit of J is between 0 and 1. The larger J means city group is bigger in size.

The above has introduced the evolutionary phenomena in a city group. Relying on these phenomena, the most developed city will be built in a limited space (The best solutions are found). In this chapter, authors focus on evolutionary phenomena, and then mimic these to design the CGO algorithm.

3. CITY GROUP OPTIMIZATION ALGORITHM

In this section, the total components of CGO algorithm are introduced, i.e., the road network, the positions update rules, the evaluation of the size of a city group, the *TH* (transportation hub) updating. Then we give the procedure of CGO. Finally, the search process of CGO is analyzed in brief.

CGO uses positions of cities in a search space to denote potential solutions to a continuous problem. In CGO, cities are represented by $X\,(X_1, X_2, X_3 \ldots X_i)$.

3.1. Road Network

According to the *Phenomenon 1*, a road network is necessary for a city group. Hence, CGO uses the steps devised to generate a fictitious network in a search space. Firstly, cities are classified into a central city and subordinate cities, and the initial position of a TH is generated randomly within a D-dimensional search space. Secondly, a central city and a TH form a TR (trunk road). Thirdly, all subordinate cities and a TR form a fictitious road network. Finally, subordinate cities search the solution space among the road network. The above steps involved can be achieved as follows: $\boldsymbol{TR} = P \times (X_{best} - G^t)$

$$X_{ic}^t = X_i^t + rand \times (\boldsymbol{TR} - (X_i^t - G^t))$$

where X_{best} (central city) denotes the historically best position of an entire city group, and X_i represents the one city of subordinate cities. G denotes a TH. The rand is a random number, ranging from 0 and 1. The range of P, a random number, is from -1 to 1. X_i, X_{ic}, G and X_{best} are vectors whose dimension is same as the dimension of optimization problems. In the Eq. (2), a TR is generated by X_{best} and G. In the Eq. (3), a TR and subordinate cities make up a road network, and the subordinate cities search the solution space among the road network.

3.2. Positions Update Rules

For problems of minimization, we assume the *F*(*X*) represents the function value of *X*. In CGO algorithm, a smaller *F*(*X*) denotes that the *PSI* of a city is higher. Positions of cities are evaluated and updated as follows:

$$\begin{cases} X_i^{t+1} = X_{ic}^t & F(X_{ic}^t) < F(X_i^t) \\ X_i^{t+1} = X_i^t & F(X_{ic}^t) \geq F(X_i^t) \end{cases}$$

The Eq. (4) judges which is better between X_{ic} and X_i. A better solution is saved. After positions of all cities are evaluated according to Eq. (4), finding the city with the highest *PSI* among all cities, also defining it as X_{best}. Positions update rules get a better solution or ensure that the known X_{best} is not replaced (greedy selection strategy). Of course, the Eq. (4) is adopted to update positions of cities in order to obtain a simple algorithmic structure. Other updating rules can also be adopted, i.e., roulette wheel selection, tournament selection strategy, etc. These new rules may bring a better diversity.

3.3. Evaluating the Size of City Group

For complex optimization problems, a low diversity leads to the premature convergence in search processes. So as to prevent this case, a city group must be adaptively adjusted based on the diversity. According to *Phenomenon 3*, the size of a city group reflects the diversity. Thus the Eq. (5) evaluates the size of city group to facilitate an advantageous adjustment.

$$\boldsymbol{R} = \frac{1}{2} \times \frac{\sum_{i=1}^{n} D(X_i, X_{best})}{n}$$

where $\boldsymbol{R}$ denotes the size of a city group, $D\,(X_i, X_{best})$ denotes the distance between X_i and X_{best}, n is the number of cities. In the evolutionary process, Eq. (5) can objectively reflect the size of a city group. Here, the distance can use different strategies, for example, Euclidean distance, Chebyshev distance or Cityblock distance, etc. For simplifying algorithmic principle, the Euclidean distance is appropriate to complete the Eq. (5).

3.4. *TH* Updating

Subordinate cities search around *TR* in order to improve their *PSI*s, and *TR* is formed by *TH* and X_{best}. Thus, the position of *TH* is adjacent to global optima, and then subordinate cities have a greater probability to seek out better solutions. So the position of *TH* is an integral part of the CGO algorithm. In order to update the *TH*, CGO utilizes the equations devised as follows:

$$Sm = D \times \beta$$

$$Gc = X_{best}^{m} + \boldsymbol{R} \times \alpha \times a$$

$$\begin{cases} G^{t+1} = Gc & F(Gc) < F(G^t) \\ G^{t+1} = G^t & F(Gc) \geq F(G^t) \end{cases}$$

where α is a random number among the search scope (for example, the random $\alpha \in [-100,100]$), $\boldsymbol{R}$ denotes the size of a city group, a is an random number from "-1" to "1", m represents the mth dimension of $X_{best} = (x_1, x_2, x_3, \ldots, x_D)$, *Sm* represents the number of inner iterations (the role of *Sm* is explained in Figure 4), D equals the dimension of optimization problems, and β is a predefined number. So *Sm* can be adjusted for different problems. In order to make the above description clearer, reader can find *Sm* and Eq. 7-8 in Figure 4.

3.5. Procedure of CGO

The pseudocode of CGO algorithm is provided in Figure 4, and the flowchart involved is illustrated in Figure 5.

Figure 4. Pseudocode of the CGO

```
procedure CGO
    initialize city group: random X_i; TH: random G; Sm;
    find out the best position among all cities: X_best;
    for Nc = 1 to Nc_max
        for i = 1 to n
            Eq. (2); Eq. (3); Eq. (4);
        end for
        find out the best position among all cities: X_best;
        evaluating the size of city group;
        for p = 1 to Sm
            Eq. (7); Eq. (8);
        end for
    end for
    best solution=X_best
end procedure
```

3.6. Search Process of CGO

In this section, the search process of a city group is illuminated in Figure 6 and Figure 7.

As shown in Figure 6, A is X_{best}, the line AB and line AC represent two ***TR***s, and then G denotes a ***TH***. According to the Eq. (2), a ***TH*** and a central city form a ***TR***. There are different ***TH***s as shown in Figure 6 (G^1 or G^2). Theoretically, if G is adjacent to global optima; subordinate cities are easier to find out better solutions. For the point of view of mathematics, actually, the change of G is equivalent to Cartesian coordinate transformation. The line AB represents a ***TR***, and then a subordinate city (point E) searches the solution space. The temporary position of the subordinate city is random inside triangle ABE. In the next iteration, the location of the ***TH*** is updated. The new ***TH*** is G^2. Another subordinate city (point D) searches a new solution space (triangle ACD). Furthermore, G^2 is closer to X_{best} (point A), and then the subordinate city (point D) has a narrower search scope. In contrast, the point E has a larger search scope. Thus, the diversity of a city group will increase. In conclusion, a long ***TR*** contributes to diversity improvement, and a short ***TR*** contributes to convergence speed improvement.

We have discussed how the length of a *TR* affects the diversity and convergence speed of CGO algorithm. Next, we expound how to adjust the length of a *TR*. As shown in Figure 7, the point A represents a global optimum, and surrounding points denote cities. The point B represents a local optimum; the point C denotes X_{best}, and around point C, these points are potential positions of a *TH*. Assuming the city group clusters around a global optimum (see Figure 7(a)), and R is small according to the Eq. (5). So the central city will select a closer position to build a *TH* (see Figure 7(c)), and the length of *TR* is short. Hence, the city group will cluster to increase the convergence speed. Suppose a city group clusters around a local optimum (see Figure 7(b)), but some cities are still scattered. Thus, R is large according to the Eq. (5). The central city will select a more far position to build a *TH* (see Figure 7(d)), and the length of *TR* is long. Then city group will diffuse to increase the diversity until these cities seek out a great enough

Figure 5. Flowchart of the CGO

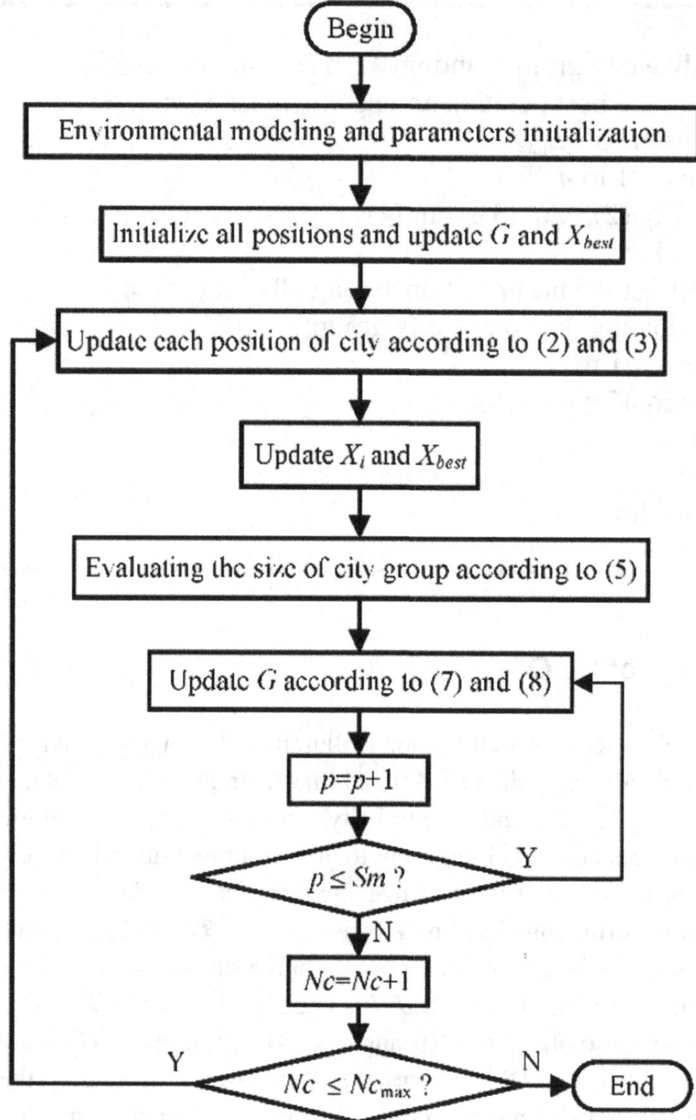

position to build a central city. Overall, a city group is adaptively adjusted according to the diversity. This is the reason why CGO should have an outstanding performance for complexly continuous problems.

4. EVOLUTION OF ARTIFICIAL CITY GROUP

In this section, the evolution of artificial city group in complex function spaces is detailedly shown by a series of experiments. Here, we propose two questions: 1) how does CGO evolve on complex function spaces, and 2) what's the best combination of parameters to solve problems.

Figure 6. An example of length of TR. $AG^1=BG^1$; $AG^2=CG^2$

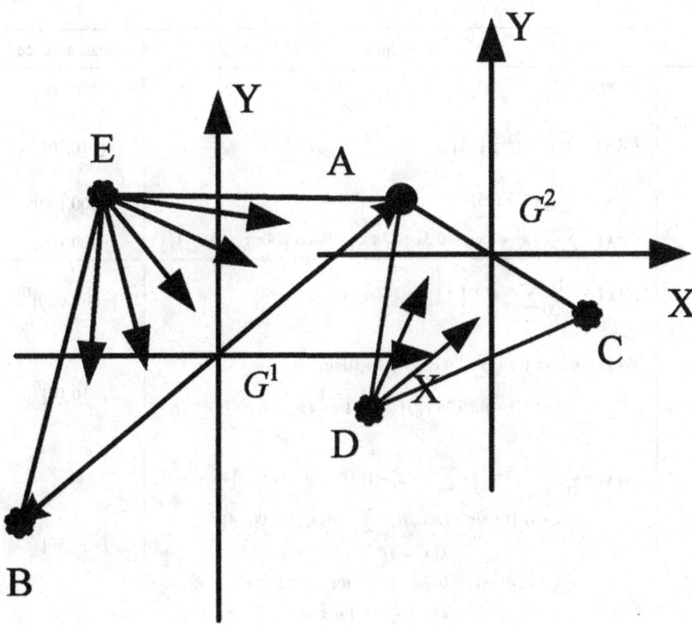

Figure 7. An example of adjusting the length of TR

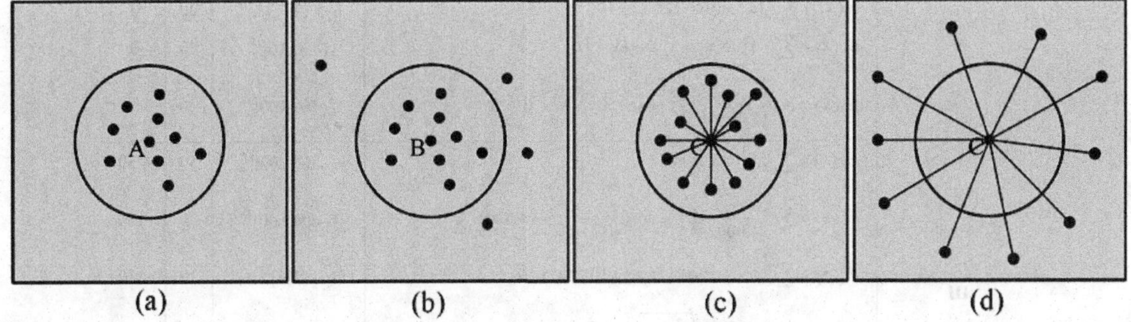

4.1. Analysis of Evolutionary Process

To analyze the evolutionary process of CGO, two kinds of functions are used. These functions are shown in Table 1 as F_4 (unimodal function) and F_9 (multimodal function), respectively. To make this presentation clearer, we set search space to be $[-100,100]^D$, and $D = 20$. Experimental results involved are provided in Figure 8, and these results are all based on a typical run. Hence, the experiment can represent the most cases. Figure 8, (a) and (b) give convergence curves of CGO; (c) shows the unstable size of a city group (the $\boldsymbol{R}$ value). From the preceding discussion, on F_4, because a city group needs the slightest effort to find out better and better solutions, the central city is more attractive to subordinate cities. More subordinate cities are built around the central city, and thus the size of city group is convergent. According to the Eq. (5), $\boldsymbol{R}$ should rapidly decrease to accelerate convergence. On the contrary, for F_9, the central city may be

Table 1. Benchmark Functions List

Group	Function	Search Space	D	$F_{\min}$
I	$F_1(\boldsymbol{x})=\sum_{i=1}^{D}x_i^2$	$[-100,100]^D$	20	0
	$F_2(\boldsymbol{x})=\sum_{i=1}^{D}\lvert x_i\rvert+\prod_{i=1}^{D}\lvert x_i\rvert$	$[-10,10]^D$	20	0
	$F_3(\boldsymbol{x})=\sum_{i=1}^{D}(x_i+0.5)^2$	$[-100,100]^D$	20	0
	$F_4(\boldsymbol{x})=\sum_{i=1}^{D-1}[x_i^2+2x_{i+1}^2-0.3\cos(3\pi x_i)-0.4\cos(4\pi x_{i+1})+0.7]$	$[-100,100]^D$	20	0
II	$F_5(\boldsymbol{x})=\frac{1}{4000}\sum_{i=1}^{D}x_i^2-\prod_{i=1}^{D}\cos(\frac{x_i}{\sqrt{i}})+1$	$[-600,600]^D$	20	0
	$F_6(\boldsymbol{x})=\sin^2(\pi y_1)+\sum_{i=1}^{D-1}(y_i-1)^2[1+10\sin^2(y_{i+1})]+(y_D-1)^2[1+\sin^2(2\pi y_D)]$, $y_i=1+\frac{1}{4}(x_i+1)$	$[-10,10]^D$	20	0
	$F_7(\boldsymbol{x})=\frac{1}{10}\{\sin^2(3\pi x_1)+\sum_{i=1}^{D-1}(x_i-1)^2[1+\sin^2(3\pi x_{i+1})]+(x_D-1)^2[1+\sin^2(2\pi x_D)]\}+\sum_{i=1}^{D}u(x_i,5,100,4)$ $u(x_i,a,k,m)=\begin{cases}k(x_i-a)^m & \text{for } x_i>a\\ 0 & \text{for } -a\le x_i\le a\\ k(-x_i-a)^m & \text{for } x_i<-a\end{cases}$	$[-50,50]^D$	20	0
	$F_8(\boldsymbol{x})=\frac{\pi}{D}\{10\sin^2(\pi y_1)+\sum_{i=1}^{D-1}(y_i-1)^2[1+10\sin^2(\pi y_{i+1})]+(y_D-1)^2\}+\sum_{i=1}^{D}u(x_i,10,100,4)$, $y_i=1+\frac{1}{4}(x_i+1)$	$[-50,50]^D$	20	0
	$F_9(\boldsymbol{x})=\sum_{i=1}^{D}[x_i^2-10\cos(2\pi x_i)+10]$	$[-5.12,5.12]^D$	20	0
	$F_{10}(\boldsymbol{x})=\sum_{i=1}^{D-1}[100(x_{i+1}-x_i^2)^2+(x_i-1)^2]$	$[-30,30]^D$	20	0
	$F_{11}(\boldsymbol{x})=\{(D-1)\sum_{i=1}^{D-1}[\sqrt{y_i}+\sin(50y_i^{0.2})\sqrt{y_i}]\}^{-2}$, $y_i=\sqrt{x_i^2+x_{i+1}^2}$	$[-100,100]^D$	20	0
III	$F_{12}(\boldsymbol{x})=\sum_{i=1}^{D}z_i^2, \boldsymbol{z}=\boldsymbol{x}-\boldsymbol{o}$	$[-100,100]^D$	50	-450
	$F_{13}(\boldsymbol{x})=\sum_{i=1}^{D}\frac{z_i^2}{4000}-\prod_{i=1}^{D}\cos(\frac{z_i}{\sqrt{i}})+1, \boldsymbol{z}=(\boldsymbol{x}-\boldsymbol{o})\times\boldsymbol{M}$	$[-600,600]^D$	50	-180
	$F_{14}(\boldsymbol{x})=\sum_{i=1}^{D}(z_i^2-10\cos(2\pi z_i)+10), \boldsymbol{z}=\boldsymbol{x}-\boldsymbol{o}$	$[-5,5]^D$	10	-330
	$F(x,y)=0.5+\frac{(\sin^2(\sqrt{x^2+y^2})-0.5)}{(1+0.001(x^2+y^2))^2}$ $F_{15}(\boldsymbol{x})=F(z_1,z_2)+F(z_2,z_3)+...+F(z_{D-1},z_D)+F(z_D,z_1)$ $\boldsymbol{z}=(\boldsymbol{x}-\boldsymbol{o})\times\boldsymbol{M}$	$[-100,100]^D$	10	-300

built in a local optimum. The attraction of central city is low, and thus subordinate cities are scattered. Therefore, $\boldsymbol{R}$ should be large. According to the Eq. (7), the central city will select a far position to build a ***TH***. Every city will has a bigger search scope. Hence, CGO can preserve the diversity of city group to jump out of local optima and seek out better solutions.

From the experimental results, it is certified that the above analysis about the search process of CGO. On the unimodal function F_4, CGO is easier to find a better solution. The central city has a stronger ability to attract other cities. In Figure 8(c), the F_4 line quickly declines. That represents that the size of city group rapidly decreases. Hence, CGO have a rapid convergence speed. On the contrary, the F_9

Figure 8. Search process of CGO on unimodal and multimodal functions. (a) F_4 (b) F_9 (c) the R value

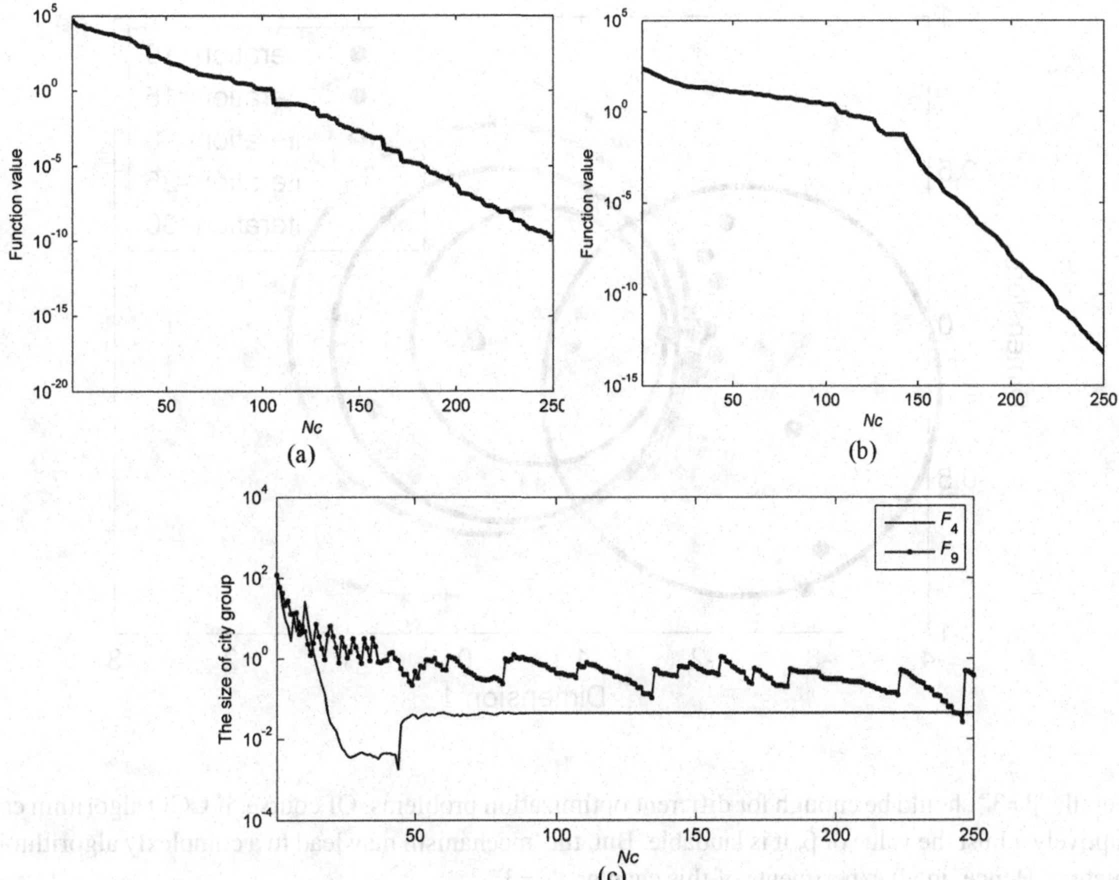

line is wobbly. That denotes that the spatial distribution of cities is not stable. To make this presentation more visual, the varied size is investigated using a multimodal function (F_9, and $D = 2$). The results are illustrated in Figure 9. Each circle represents a size of city group, respectively. It is clear that the size of city group decreases firstly, and then increases. Accordingly, the diversity does not decrease with iteration numbers increasing. In this sense, CGO preserves the diversity. It is worth stressing that CGO still maintains a fast convergence speed in multimodal function F_9 (see Figure 8(b)).

4.2. Analysis of Parameters Setting

In Section III, we proposed that *Sm* can be adjusted for different problems. For a determinate problem, its dimension is constant. Hence, we just need to set β to adapt different problems. Here we use a unimodal function and a multimodal function that are given in Table 1 as *F3* and *F7* to study how β is the best set. In Figure 10, we plot different convergence curves according to different β (β = {1, 2, 3, 4, 5}). From results, a large β should contribute to fast convergence speed and high accuracy. However, overlarge β is not efficient. According to Figure 4, it can be seen that an overlarge β leads to excessive iteration numbers and produces prodigious computational burden. That means the run efficiency of CGO is unsatisfactory.

Figure 9. Search process of CGO on a multimodal function

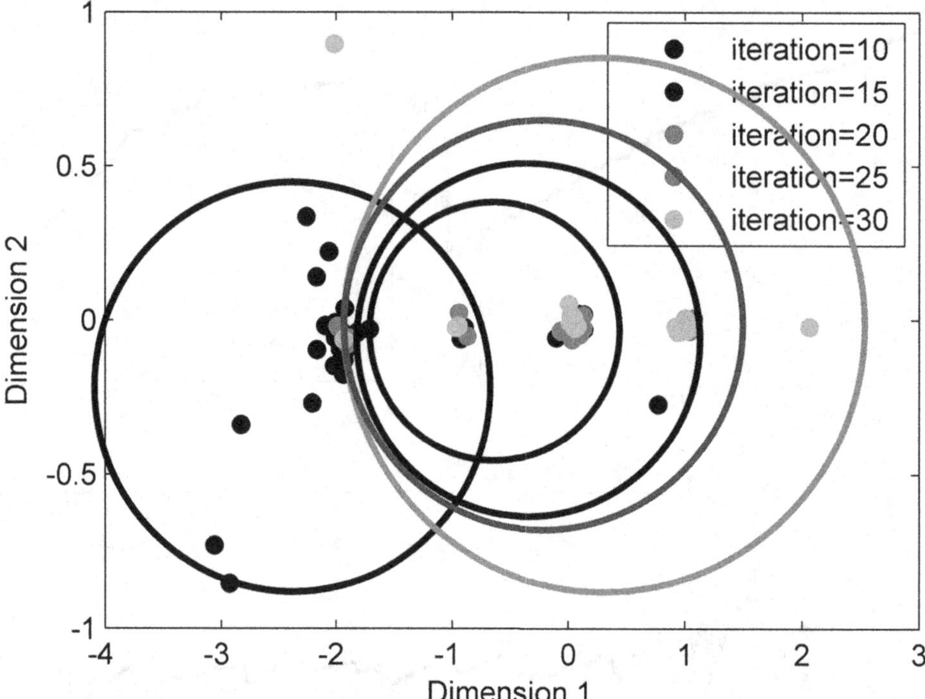

Overall, "β=3" should be enough for different optimization problems. Of course, if CGO algorithm can adaptively adjust the value of β, it is laudable. But, this mechanism may lead to a complexly algorithmic structure. Hence, in all experiments of this chapter, "β=3".

5. EXPERIMENTAL RESULTS

5.1. Benchmark and Experimental Settings

In order to evaluate the performance of CGO, 15 benchmark functions are used in experiments. Readers can obtain these functions from (Yao, et al., 1999; Suganthan, et al., 2005).

All algorithms are implemented using MATLAB 8.0 under Microsoft Windows 8 operating system. All experiments are implemented on a computer with a CPU 2.60GHz and a 4.0 GB RAM. In order to evaluate the performance of CGO, we have compared it with other metaheuristics including PSO, ABC, GA, BSO and BSO-II, and then we obtain part source codes from Internet (Karaboga, 2014). As we know, the traditional version of PSO algorithm has some undesirable properties. The original algorithm has been altered in ways that eliminate problems and improve abilities of particle swarm to find optima of problems (Chen, et al., 2013). But the traditional PSO is still the most widely applied to optimization problems due to its simple framework, so we use the traditional PSO. ABC is a new metaheuristic, and

Figure 10. Performance of CGO under different β values. (a) and (c) F_3. (b) and (d) F_7

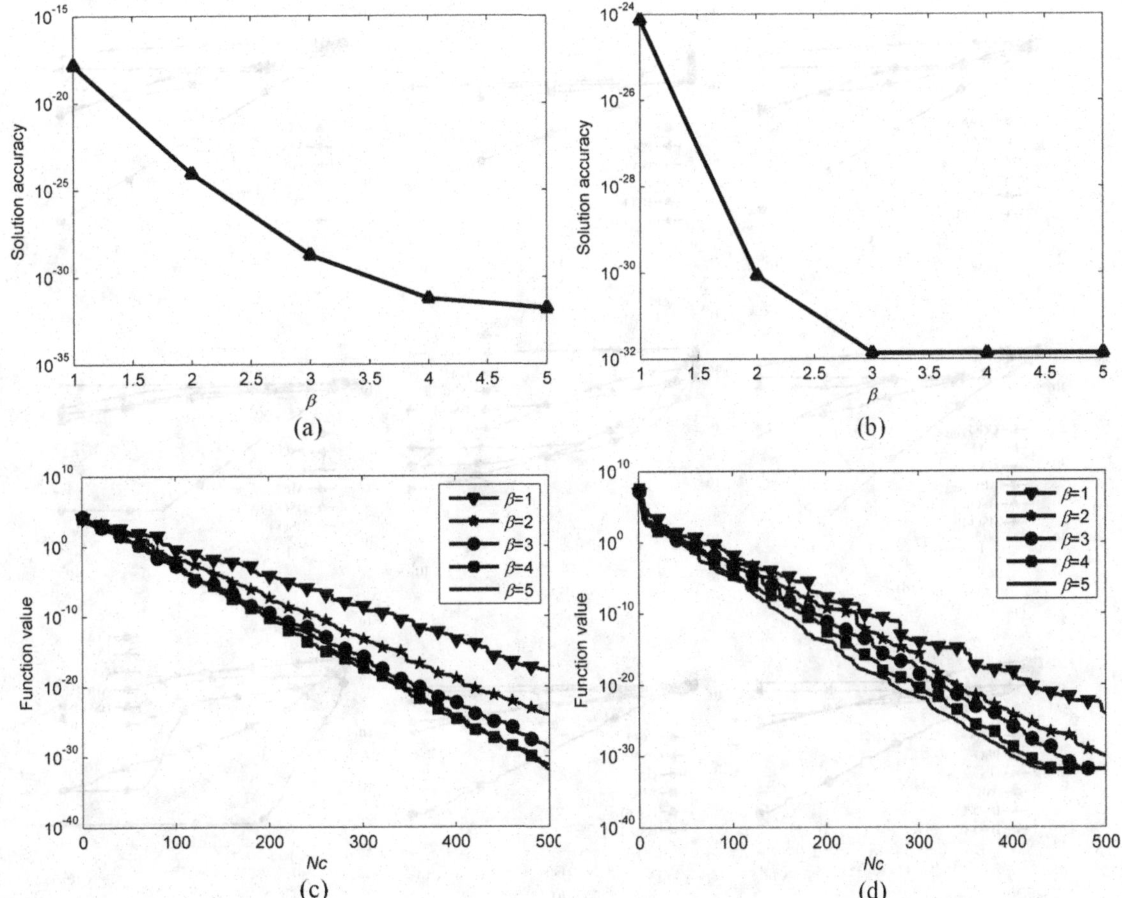

has advantages over PSO in some conditions. The population size of bees is 30, and other parameters are set as the same as the original source files. For PSO, the population is 30, acceleration factors, namely, c_1 and c_2 equal 2.0 and the decaying inertia weight w_{max}=0.9 and w_{min}=0.4. For CGO, the number of cities is 30 and $\beta = 3$. GA's population equals to 30, and other parameters are set as appropriately as possible. The parameters of BSO are set according to the Shi's paper (Shi, 2011).

In each run, a maximum number of function evaluations is set to be 50000. Each function is repeatedly evaluated for 20 times. The Mean, Best, Worst and Standard Deviation are recorded in Table 2, 3 and 4. Standard deviation can show the stability of algorithms. Generally, a smaller standard deviation is better. In practical engineering, users usually have less experience about the characters of optimization algorithms. In this case, users may not continually change the inner parameters (including population, weight factors, and limiting factors, etc.) of algorithms. They always care if an algorithm can get satisfactory solutions with less evaluation numbers. Hence, we use the same evaluations number to compare different algorithms. For studying the convergent performance of optimization algorithms, we collect data to plot convergence curves. Each algorithm runs 20 times, and we calculate average function values.

Figure 11. Convergence graphs on benchmark functions

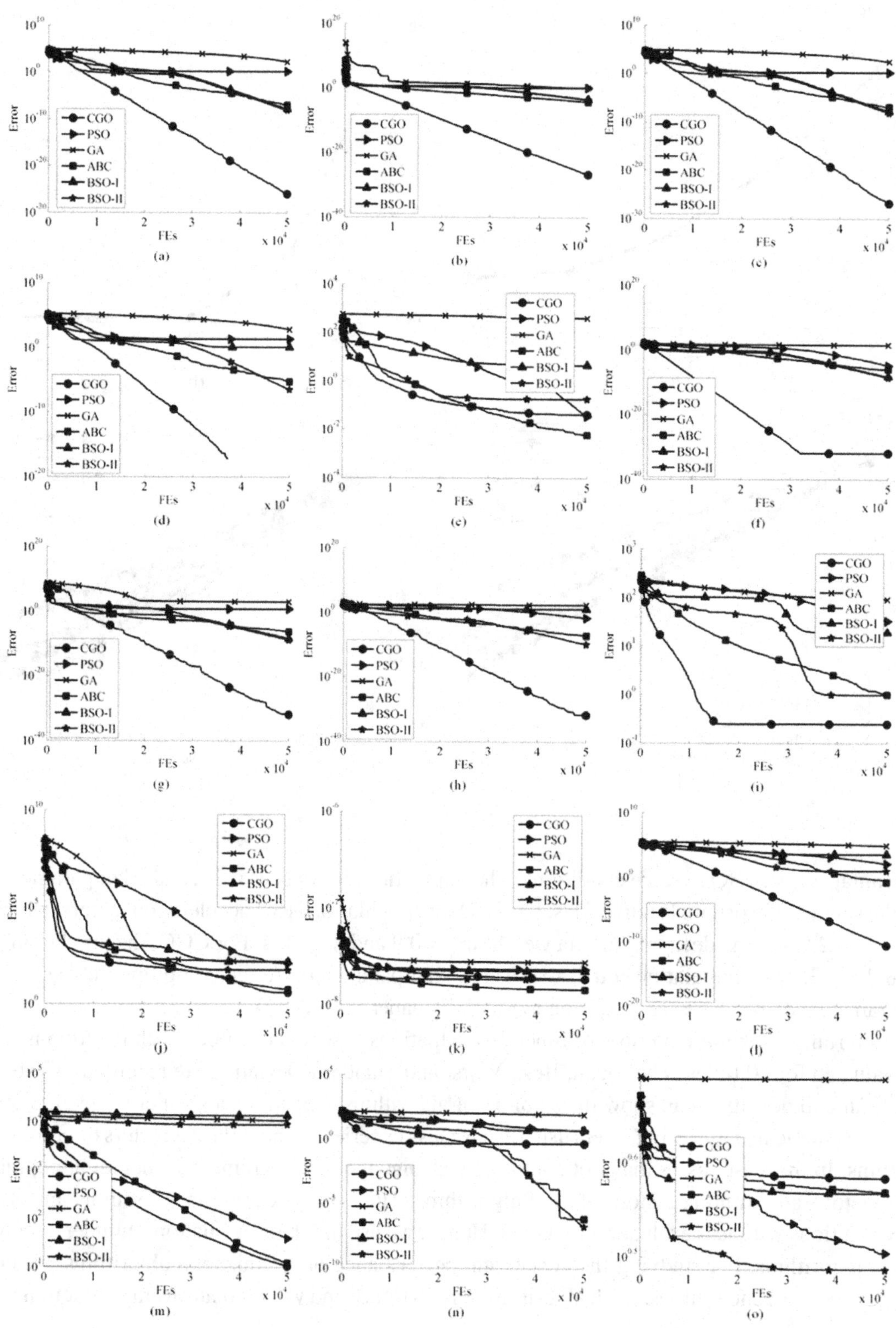

Table 2. Results on Unimodal Functions

Test Function		CGO	PSO	GA	ABC	BSO-I	BSO-II
F_1	Best	8.78E-30	1.32E-04	0.2233	5.32E-09	1.35E-08	6.59E-09
	Mean	**3.79E-27**	0.0021	230.7859	7.06E-08	1.67E-08	8.50E-09
	Worst	3.06E-26	0.0113	1.54E+03	2.22E-07	2.12E-08	9.96E-09
	Std. Dev	**9.28E-27**	0.0026	394.3919	5.68E-08	3.57E-09	1.37E-09
F_2	Best	5.64E-29	6.91E-04	1.3065	2.75E-05	3.54E-04	2.40E-04
	Mean	**2.18E-27**	0.0025	1.5868	6.58E-05	3.86E-04	2.98E-04
	Worst	9.81E-27	0.007	1.7947	1.54E-04	4.30E-04	3.36E-04
	Std. Dev	**2.80E-27**	0.0018	0.144	3.46E-05	2.92E-05	3.55E-05
F_3	Best	8.84E-31	9.16E-05	0.1464	1.25E-10	1.09E-08	6.74E-09
	Mean	**1.99E-27**	8.80E-04	0.1849	9.42E-10	1.60E-08	8.25E-09
	Worst	1.51E-26	0.0026	0.2194	3.71E-09	2.32E-08	9.20E-09
	Std. Dev	**3.71E-27**	8.02E-04	0.0197	1.07E-09	4.77E-09	9.33E-10
F_4	Best	0	0.0112	8.5479	1.79E-07	7.38E-07	3.12E-07
	Mean	**0**	0.7611	1.57E+03	7.73E-06	1.32E+00	3.52E-07
	Worst	0	3.6704	1.07E+04	5.83E-05	2.98E+00	4.26E-07
	Std. Dev	**0**	1.0875	2.81E+03	1.61E-05	1.08E+00	4.69E-08

5.2. Comparative Results

1. **Results on Unimodal Functions:** On unimodal functions (F_1-F_4), algorithms are not trapped into local optima, so global optimum is not hidden. In Table 2, the Best and the Mean worked out by different algorithms after 50000 evaluation numbers are reported. It can be seen that the proposed CGO shows higher accuracy. According to Section IV, the size of city group rapidly decreases on unimodal functions. Thus, subordinate cities are easy to locate better positions. It is no accident that the solution accuracy is high. To test the convergence speed, convergence curves of different algorithms are reported in Figure 11 (a-d). It can be indicated that CGO performs the most rapid convergence speed on F_1-F_4.
2. **Results on Multimodal Functions:** On multimodal functions (F_5-F_{11}), the global optimum is more difficult to be found. Thus, we compare the accuracy, speed and reliability of different algorithms. On multimodal functions, the solution accuracy and reliability are given in Table 3. According to the results of tests in Table 3, the Mean shows the solution accuracy of different algorithms. It can be seen that CGO performs the best on four of seven multimodal functions, and ABC performs the best on three of seven multi modal functions. Thus, the results demonstrate that CGO shows high solution accuracy. In Table 3, the Standard Deviation and Mean indicate the reliability on multimodal functions, and smaller Standard Deviation and Mean represent better reliability. As is given in Table 3, CGO still has the best performance due to the ability to escape from local optima.

Table 3. Results on Multimodal Functions

Test Function		CGO	PSO	GA	ABC	BSO-I	BSO-II
F_5	Best	7.33E-14	0.0041	301.5632	1.18E-06	0.0416	0.0246
	Mean	0.0355	0.0651	387.0306	**0.0077**	4.5973	0.1806
	Worst	0.1425	0.4139	501.8206	0.0243	12.3171	0.3185
	Std. Dev	0.0341	0.0942	59.9751	**0.0095**	5.0863	0.1188
F_6	Best	1.50E-32	3.95E-07	0.0806	3.98E-08	5.66E-09	3.28E-09
	Mean	**1.50E-32**	1.78E-05	40.4229	1.78E-06	8.18E-09	4.10E-09
	Worst	1.50E-32	1.04E-04	118.4602	9.62E-06	1.02E-08	4.84E-09
	Std. Dev	**5.62E-48**	3.05E-05	38.6262	2.52E-06	1.79E-09	6.01E-10
F_7	Best	1.35E-32	1.41E-04	227.8385	5.52E-09	2.42E-09	1.14E-09
	Mean	**3.01E-32**	0.0054	1.09E+03	2.59E-07	3.79E-09	1.58E-09
	Worst	2.23E-31	0.0289	3.97E+03	1.32E-06	4.76E-09	1.85E-09
	Std. Dev	**5.09E-32**	0.0078	1.01E+03	3.61E-07	8.94E-10	2.72E-10
F_8	Best	2.36E-32	1.58E-06	103.4073	6.78E-10	4.011	1.08E-10
	Mean	**7.19E-32**	0.0413	332.5715	2.50E-08	13.6443	1.62E-10
	Worst	9.83E-31	0.3356	675.7509	1.43E-07	26.5373	2.37E-10
	Std. Dev	**2.14E-31**	0.1026	180.3684	4.09E-08	9.4145	4.82E-11
F_9	Best	0	14.7113	63.5641	5.69E-05	11.9395	1.30E-06
	Mean	**0.199**	28.7152	90.3256	1.0652	19.3022	0.995
	Worst	0.995	43.8434	117.9911	2.9862	27.8588	2.9849
	Std. Dev	**0.4083**	7.9982	14.2358	1.0317	6.4327	1.4071
F_{10}	Best	0.0067	9.7219	32.7096	0.3818	17.2545	13.8402
	Mean	18.7429	99.8561	36.8469	**5.7804**	51.1012	19.2931
	Worst	130.1956	476.2107	43.47	18.0468	118.0149	75.8479
	Std. Dev	31.0238	132.852	**2.9201**	4.2861	38.1059	15.6605
F_{11}	Best	1.57E-08	1.91E-08	2.25E-08	1.42E-08	2.01E-08	1.67E-08
	Mean	1.87E-08	2.08E-08	2.78E-08	**1.43E-08**	2.25E-08	1.85E-08
	Worst	2.11E-08	2.44E-08	3.93E-08	1.48E-08	2.92E-08	2.09E-08
	Std. Dev	1.38E-09	1.37E-09	4.55E-09	**1.43E-10**	2.15E-09	1.10E-09

In addition, the convergence speed of different algorithms is reported in Figure 11. Although CGO preserves diversity, CGO still keeps a fast convergence speed. In Figure 11 (e-k), CGO has the fastest convergence speed on five of seven functions, especially on F_6 to F_9. The result demonstrates that CGO skillfully balances diversity and convergence speed.

3. **Results on Shifted and Rotated Functions:** To test the performance of CGO, we also use shifted and rotated (SR) functions. Here F_{12} is a unimodal function, and F_{13}-F_{15} are multimodal functions. By shifting and rotating, search spaces of these functions become more complex. Hence, the global search ability of algorithms is thoroughly verified. Comparative results are given in the Table 4,

Table 4. Results on Shifted and Rotated Functions

Test Function		CGO	PSO	GA	ABC	BSO-I	BSO-II
F_{12}	Best	-450	-390.4338	5.43E+04	-449.9909	834.2457	-450
	Mean	**-450**	-328.2076	9.00E+04	-449.7334	3.50E+03	-440.0194
	Worst	-450	-197.3574	1.58E+05	-449.3376	6.39E+03	-350.1945
	Std. Dev	**2.68E-12**	54.7099	2.68E+04	0.2186	1.56E+03	31.5613
F_{13}	Best	-174.7617	-162.9958	7.11E+03	-174.9604	1.26E+04	7.95E+03
	Mean	-168.3667	-147.0208	1.05E+04	**-169.0398**	1.34E+04	8.64E+03
	Worst	-161.3267	-125.3653	1.52E+04	-152.5403	1.38E+04	9.34E+03
	Std. Dev	**3.2817**	10.6679	2.29E+03	6.3135	332.9248	464.1593
F_{14}	Best	-330	-328.9791	-271.679	-330	-327.0151	-330
	Mean	-329.7513	-326.2908	-245.7827	**-330**	-324.9257	**-330**
	Worst	-329.005	-323.0353	-197.4891	-330	-320.0504	-330
	Std. Dev	0.442	1.5184	18.7057	1.01E-05	2.4574	**3.95E-08**
F_{15}	Best	-296.8394	-297.6256	-295.4245	-296.6569	-296.6831	-297.7171
	Mean	-296.0435	-296.6913	-295.1293	-296.3638	-296.3014	**-296.9338**
	Worst	-295.4939	-295.9799	-295.0051	-295.9802	-295.9021	-296.3171
	Std. Dev	0.3907	0.363	**0.1471**	0.1684	0.3092	0.3763

and convergence curves are given in Figure 11 (l-o). If the optimum of a benchmark function is represented by *optimum*, and an algorithm finds the best function value is *best*. So the *error* = *best-optimum*. According to experimental results, CGO shows faster convergence speed, higher solution accuracy and better reliability on F_{12} and F_{13}.

6. DISCUSSION

Swarm intelligence algorithm (SIA) is similar in structure that includes mutation strategies and selection operators. Generally, different algorithms are distinguished by mutation strategies. CGO is part of SIA, so it also has an analogical structure. From the mutation strategy of CGO, this algorithm is related to DE and BSO. In order to highlight the characteristic of CGO, we compare it with the above two algorithms.

1. **Comparison With DE:** In CGO, the mutation strategy includes Eq. (2), (3) and (7). Eq. (2) and (3) are similar to the differential operator of DE as shown in Figure 12. Hence, CGO adopts a differential operator in mutation strategy. However, the operator with a guide point (point *G*) can expand the search scope of swarm (see Figure 6). By updating the guide point (*G*), CGO is more likely to escape from local solutions.
2. **Comparison With BSO:** CGO mimics the clustering and diffusion of real city groups, and then this mechanism is also used in BSO. For BSO, different solutions are clustered by the K-means algorithm, and then BSO utilizes a local search method to optimize solutions in different categories. By the linear combination of different categories of solutions, BSO is likely to jump out of local

Table 5. Comparison with Different Algorithms on 15 Benchmark Functions

Test Function		CGO	PSO	GA	ABC	BSO-I	BSO-II
F_1	Mean	1	5	6	4	3	2
	Std. Dev	1	5	6	4	3	2
F_2	Mean	1	5	6	2	4	3
	Std. Dev	1	5	6	3	2	4
F_3	Mean	1	4	5	2	4	3
	Std. Dev	1	5	6	3	4	2
F_4	Mean	1	4	6	3	5	2
	Std. Dev	1	5	6	3	4	2
F_5	Mean	2	3	6	1	5	4
	Std. Dev	2	3	6	1	5	4
F_6	Mean	1	5	6	4	3	2
	Std. Dev	1	5	6	4	3	2
F_7	Mean	1	5	6	4	3	2
	Std. Dev	1	5	6	4	3	2
F_8	Mean	1	4	6	3	5	2
	Std. Dev	1	4	6	3	5	2
F_9	Mean	1	5	6	3	4	2
	Std. Dev	1	5	6	2	4	3
F_{10}	Mean	2	6	4	1	5	3
	Std. Dev	4	6	1	2	5	3
F_{11}	Mean	3	4	6	1	5	2
	Std. Dev	4	3	6	1	5	2
F_{12}	Mean	1	4	6	2	5	3
	Std. Dev	1	4	6	2	5	3
F_{13}	Mean	2	3	5	1	6	4
	Std. Dev	1	3	6	2	4	5
F_{14}	Mean	3	4	6	1	5	1
	Std. Dev	3	4	6	2	5	1
F_{15}	Mean	5	2	6	3	4	1
	Std. Dev	6	4	1	2	3	5
Average rank		1.83	4.3	5.53	2.43	4.2	2.6
Overall rank		**1**	**5**	**6**	**2**	**4**	**3**

Figure 12. The operators of CGO and DE

	Operators
CGO	$X_{new} = X_i + rand \times (P \times (X_{best} - G) - (X_i - G)).$
DE	$X_{new} = X_{best} + F \times (X_{r1} - X_{r2}),$ $X_{new} = X_i + F \times (X_{best} - X_i) + F \times (X_{r1} - X_{r2}),$ $X_{new} = X_{best} + F \times (X_{r1} - X_{r2}) + F \times (X_{r3} - X_{r4}),$ $X_{new} = X_{r1} + F \times (X_{r2} - X_{r3}) + F \times (X_{r4} - X_{r5}).$

optima. CGO adopts a differential operator with guide point to implement the clustering of solutions, concurrently, implement a local search. By evolving guide point, solutions can be diffused. From the above discussion, CGO utilizes a more compact structure to improve the implementation efficiency.

7. CONCLUSION

A new optimization algorithm called CGO has been presented. The CGO is characterized by mimicking the evolution of city group. In a statistical way, experimental results show that the proposed CGO algorithm can outperform several well-known metaheuristics on 15 standard benchmark functions. CGO seems to be effective for solving continuous problems. Furthermore, for complex functions, CGO commendably balances the diversity and convergence speed, and avoids premature or slow convergence.

In real world, some city groups are multicentric. In future research, it would be necessary to study if a multicentric city group model can be adopted in CGO. In this chapter, it has been verified that a unicentric city group model is effective for continuous problems. Intuitively, multicentric city group should have a stronger ability to escape from local optima. This model should be helpful to increase the diversity of solutions. On the other hand, it would be significant to test if a multicentric and multigroup model can be applied to niching techniques (Qu, et al., 2013).

PSO, ABC, GA and DE have solved many engineered problems. PSO and ABC have successfully solved different problems (Kennedy, & Eberhart, 1997; Karaboga, & Gorkemli, 2011). And DE and GA also have many applications (Zhang, et al., 2010). Last but not least, it would be interesting to identify practical applications which can be addressed using CGO effectively and efficiently.

ACKNOWLEDGMENT

This work was partially supported by Aeronautical Foundation of China under grant #2015ZA51013

REFERENCES

Barnard, C., & Sibly, R. (1981). Producers and scroungers: A general model and its application to captive flocks of house sparrows. *Animal Behaviour*, *29*(2), 543–550. doi:10.1016/S0003-3472(81)80117-0

Chen, W. N., Zhang, J., Lin, Y., Chen, N., Zhan, Z. H., Chung, H. S. H., & Shi, Y. H. et al. (2013). Particle swarm optimization with an aging leader and challengers. *IEEE Transactions on Evolutionary Computation*, *17*(2), 241–258. doi:10.1109/TEVC.2011.2173577

Clark, C. W., & Mangel, M. (1984). Foraging and flocking strategies: Information in an uncertain environment. *American Naturalist*, *123*(5), 626–641. doi:10.1086/284228

Clerc, M., & Kennedy, J. (2002). The particle swarm-explosion, stability, and convergence in a multidimensional complex space. *IEEE Transactions on Evolutionary Computation*, *6*(1), 58–73. doi:10.1109/4235.985692

Dorigo, M., & Gambardella, L. M. (1997). Ant colony system: A cooperative learning approach to the traveling salesman problem. *IEEE Transactions on Evolutionary Computation*, *1*(1), 53–66. doi:10.1109/4235.585892

Dorigo, M., Maniezzo, V., & Colorni, A. (1996). Ant system: Optimization by a colony of cooperating agents. *IEEE Transactions on Systems, Man, and Cybernetics. Part B, Cybernetics*, *26*(1), 29–41. doi:10.1109/3477.484436 PMID:18263004

Duan, H. B., & Li, J. N. (2014). Gaussian harmony search algorithm: A novel method for loney's solenoid problem. *IEEE Transactions on Magnetics*, *50*(3), 83–87. doi:10.1109/TMAG.2013.2284764

Duan, H. B., Luo, Q. N., Ma, G. J., & Shi, Y. H. (2013). Hybrid particle swarm optimization and genetic algorithm for multi-UAVs formation reconfiguration. *IEEE Computational Intelligence Magazine*, *8*(3), 16–27. doi:10.1109/MCI.2013.2264577

Duan, H. B., & Qiao, P. X. (2014). Pigeon-inspired optimization: A new swarm intelligence optimizer for air robot path planning. *International Journal of Intelligent Computing and Cybernetics.*, *7*(1), 24–37. doi:10.1108/IJICC-02-2014-0005

Duan, H. B., Yu., Y. X., & Zhou, R. (2008). UCAV path planning based on ant colony optimization and satisficing decision algorithm. In *Proceedings of IEEE Congress on Evolutionary Computation*. (pp. 957–962). IEEE. doi:10.1109/CEC.2008.4630912

Ebenezer, H. (2010). *Garden Cities of Tomorrow*. Nabu Press.

Eberhart, R. C., & Kennedy, J. (1995). A new optimizer using particle swarm theory. In *Proceedings of the 1995 6th International Symposium on Micro Machine and Human Science*. (pp. 39–43). Academic Press. doi:10.1109/MHS.1995.494215

Gregory, S. (2002). *Urban Sprawl: Causes, Consequences and Policy Responses*. Washington, DC: The Urban Institute Press.

He, S., Wu, Q. H., & Saunders, J. R. (2009). Group search optimizer: An optimization algorithm inspired by animal searching behavior. *IEEE Transactions on Evolutionary Computation, 13*(5), 973–990. doi:10.1109/TEVC.2009.2011992

Karaboga, D. (n.d.). *Artificial bee colony homepage*. Available: http://mf.erciyes.edu.tr/abc/

Karaboga, D., & Basturk, B. (2007). A powerful and efficient algorithm for numerical function optimization: Artificial bee colony. *Journal of Global Optimization, 39*(3), 459–471. doi:10.1007/s10898-007-9149-x

Karaboga, D., & Basturk, B. (2008). On the performance of artificial bee colony algorithm. *Applied Soft Computing, 8*(1), 687–697. doi:10.1016/j.asoc.2007.05.007

Karaboga, D., & Gorkemli, B. (2011). A combinatorial artificial bee colony algorithm for traveling salesman problem. In *Proceedings of International Symposium on INnovations in Intelligent SysTems and Applications*. (pp. 50–53). Academic Press. doi:10.1109/INISTA.2011.5946125

Kennedy, J., & Eberhart, R. C. (1995). Particle swarm optimization. In *Proceedings of the 1995 IEEE International Conference on Neural Networks. Part 1 (of 6)*. (pp. 1942–1948). IEEE.

Kennedy, J., & Eberhart, R. C. (1997). A discrete binary version of the particle swarm algorithm. In *Proceedings of the IEEE International Conference on Systems, Man and Cybernetics* (pp. 4104–4108). IEEE. doi:10.1109/ICSMC.1997.637339

Lam, A. Y. S., & Li, V. O. K. (2010). Chemical-reaction-inspired metaheuristic for optimization. *IEEE Transactions on Evolutionary Computation, 14*(3), 381–399. doi:10.1109/TEVC.2009.2033580

Parpinelli, R. S., & Lopes, H. S. (2011). New inspirations in swarm intelligence: A survey. *International Journal of Bio-inspired Computation, 3*(1), 1–16. doi:10.1504/IJBIC.2011.038700

Patrick, G. (1968). *Cities in Evolution*. New York: Harper & Row.

Peter, H., & Kathy, P. (2006). *The Polycentric Metropolis: Learning from Mega-city Regions in Europe*. London: Earthscan Press.

Qu, B. Y., Suganthan, P. N., & Das, S. (2013). A distance-based locally informed particle swarm model for multimodal optimization. *IEEE Transactions on Evolutionary Computation, 17*(3), 387–402. doi:10.1109/TEVC.2012.2203138

Shi, Y. H. (2011). Brain storm optimization algorithm. In Y. Tan, Y. Shi, Y. Chai, & G. Wang (Eds.), *Proceedings of the Second International Conference On Advances in Swarm Intelligence, Chongqing, China* (LNCS 6728, pp. 303-309). Springer. doi:10.1007/978-3-642-21515-5_36

Shi, Y. H. (2011). An optimization algorithm based on brainstorming process. *International Journal of Swarm Intelligence Research, 2*(4), 35–62. doi:10.4018/IJSIR.2011100103

Simon, D. (2008). Biogeography-based optimization. *IEEE Transactions on Evolutionary Computation, 12*(6), 702–713. doi:10.1109/TEVC.2008.919004

Storn, R., & Price, K. (1995). Differential evolution: A simple and efficient heuristic for global optimization over continuous spaces. *Journal of Global Optimization*, *11*(4), 341–359. doi:10.1023/A:1008202821328

Suganthan, P.N., Hansen, N., Liang, J.J., Deb, K., Chen, Y.-P., Auger, A., & Tiwari, S. (2005). *Problem definitions and evolution criteria for the CEC 2005 special session on real-parameter optimization.* Nanyang Technol. Univ., Singapore, Tech. Rep. and KanGAL Rep. 2005005.

Wolpert, D. H., & Macready, W. G. (1997). No free lunch theorems for optimization. *IEEE Transactions on Evolutionary Computation*, *1*(1), 67–82. doi:10.1109/4235.585893

Yao, S. M., Chen, Z. G., & Zhu, Y. M. (2006). *The Urban Agglomerations of China*. Hefei, China: Univ. Science and Technology of China Press.

Yao, X., Liu, Y., & Lin, G. M. (1999). Evolutionary programming made faster. *IEEE Transactions on Evolutionary Computation*, *3*(2), 82–102. doi:10.1109/4235.771163

Zhang, X. Y., Duan, H. B., & Jin, J. Q. (2008). DEACO: hybrid ant colony optimization with differential evolution. In *Proceedings of IEEE Congress on Evolutionary Computation*. (pp. 921–927). IEEE.

Zhang, X. Y., Duan, H. B., & Yu, Y. X. (2010). Receding horizon control for Multi-UAVs close formation control based on differential evolution. *Science China. Information Sciences*, *53*(2), 223–235. doi:10.1007/s11432-010-0036-6

Chapter 5
Magnetotactic Bacteria Optimization Algorithm (MBOA) for Function Optimization:
MBOA Based on Four Best-Rand Pairwise Schemes

Lili Liu
LiaoCheng University, China

Hongwei Mo
Harbin Engineering University, China

ABSTRACT

Magnetotactic bacteria is a kind of prokaryotes with the characteristics of magnetotaxis. Magnetotactic bacteria optimization algorithm (MBOA) is an optimization algorithm based on the characteristics of magnetotaxis. It mimics the development process of magnetosomes (MTSs) in magnetotactic bacteria. In this chapter, four pairwise MTSs regulation schemes based on the best individual and randomly chosen one are proposed to study which scheme is more suitable for solving optimization problems. They are tested on 14 functions and compared with many popular optimization algorithms, including PSO, DE, ABC, and their variants. Experimental results show that all the schemes of MBOA are effective for solving most of test functions but have different performance on a few test functions. The fourth MBOA scheme has superior performance to the compared methods on many test functions. In this scheme, the algorithm searches around the current best individual to enhance the convergence of MBOA and the individual can migrate to the current best individual to enhance the diversity of the MBOA.

DOI: 10.4018/978-1-5225-5134-8.ch005

INTRODUCTION

Bio-inspired computing (BIC) has been extensively studied for solving the optimization problems. It is a field that develops new computational tools based on or inspired by biology mechanisms for problem solving (De Castro, L.N, 2006). It is one of the important branches of natural computing. As we know, the biology and many kinds of life systems have been the greatest inspiration sources for a long time in many different fields. In the field of computational intelligence, Evolutionary Computing (Back, T., 1996) is the first group of bio-inspired computing methods which were inspired by evolutionary biology in 1960s.

In the past two decadess, many BIC algorithms were developed including Ant Colony Optimization (ACO) (Dorigo, M., Manianiezzo, V., & Colorni, A., 1996) and Particle Swarm Optimization (PSO) (Kennedy, J., & Eberhart, R.,1995), which are known as Swarm Intelligence (SI) (Bonabeau, E., Dorigo, M., & Theraulaz, G., 2000) based on the behaviors of ant colony and bird flocks, respectively. Some other developed SI techniques include Artificial Bee Colony. (ABC) (Karaboga, D., & Akay, B., 2009), Biogeography-Based Optimization Algorithm (BBO) (Simon, D., 2008), etc. All of them are also known as population based optimization algorithms. Besides animals on earth can inspire people to design new problems solving methods, researchers have proposed Bacterial Foraging Optimization Algorithm (BFOA) (Müeller, S., Marchetto, J., Airaghi, S., & Koumoutsakos, P., 2002), which was inspired by chemotactic phenomena of bacteria. In recent years, many new optimization algorithms inspired by nature were proposed, such as Invasive Weed Optimization Algorithm (IWOA) (Mehrabian, A. R. & Lucas, C., 2006), Monkey Search (MS) (Mucherino, A. & Seref, O. 2007), Artificial Glowworm Swarm Optimization(AGSO) (Krishnanand, K. N. & Ghose, D., 2009), Firefly Algorithm (FA)(Yin, Tan.,2015), Brain storm optimization algorithm(Shi, Y. H., 2011), Chemical-Reaction Optimization(Lam, A.Y.S. & Li, V.O.K, 2010). Most of them were inspired by biology and few of them were inspired by physical and chemical phonmenon.

In nature, there is a special kind of magnetotactic bacteria (MTB) (Faivre, D., & Schuler, D., 2008). They have different biology characteristics from chemotactic bacteria since they can orient and swim along magnetic field lines with the aid of mineral particles inside their bodies. These mineral particles with their enveloping membrane are together called magnetosomes (MTSs). Their chains are called magnetosome chains. Magnetotactic bacteria can orient themselves along geomagnetic field lines (magnetotaxis) in the earth magnetic field (Mitchell J.G., & Kogure K., 2006) since they have magnetosome chains as their compass inside their bodies.

Based on the biology principle of MTB, Mo proposed an original magnetotactic bacteria optimization algorithm (Mo H.W., 2012, Mo H.W., & Xu L.F., 2013). The ability of solving problems of the original MBOA depends on the replacement operation that some worse solutions are replaced by some randomly solutions. The moment mechanism in the original MBOA doesn't work well, but the original MBOA shows the potential ability of solving optimization problems and has very fast convergence speed.

For the MTB, each cell carries a remanent magnetic moment, the direction of which is determined by the orientation of the magnetosome-chain axis and its magnetic polarity (Michael W, Leida G.A, & Alfonso F.D, et al., 2007). If each cell is to align its magnetosome chain parallel to the other ones, with the same polarity, each cell would yield the most efficient swimming way for living. This behavior is thought to increase the efficiency with which such bacteria find their optimal oxygen concentrations at sediment water interfaces or in water columns (Duin-Borkowski R, McCartney M. R., & Frankel R. B. et al., 1998). This specific behavior is the inspiration source of the MBOA. For the MBOA, we consider the state that each cell is to align its magnetosome chain parallel to the other ones, with the same polarity, each cell would yield the most efficient swimming way for living as finding the optimal solution. The interaction energy between different chains in different cells makes MTB strive for better living.

In recent years, some improved MBOAs had been proposed. In the moments of the best individual-based magnetotactic bacteria optimization algorithm (BIMBOA), the problem solutions are generated by moment mechanisms based on interaction energy among solutions (Mo, H.W., Liu, L.L., Xu, L.F. & Zhao, Y.Y.,2014). In the magnetotactic bacteria optimization algorithm based on best-rand scheme (MBOA-BR) it regulates the moments based on the information exchange between best individual's moments and some randomly one (Mo, H.W. and Geng, M.J. (2014)). In the magnetotactic bacteria optimization algorithm based on best-target (MBOA-BT) some cells receive MTS information from the interaction between the local best one and the target one to balance the local search and global search (Mo, H.W. & Liu, L.L.,2014). In the power spectrum-based magnetotactic bacteria algorithm (PSMBA), it is based on the models of power spectra of the magnetic field noise produced by Brownian rotation of nonmotile bacteria in zero magnetic field (Mo, H.W., Liu, L.L. & Geng, M.J.,2014). In the magnetotactic bacteria moment migration algorithm (MBMMA), the moments of relative good solutions can migrate each other to enhance the diversity of the MBMMA. Magnetotactic Bacteria Optimization Algorithm with the Best Individual-guided Differential Interaction Energy (MBOA-BIDE) (Mo H.W., Liu L.L.,& Zhao J., 2015), Magnetotactic Bacteria Moment Migration Algorithm (MBMMA) (Mo H.W., Liu L.L.,& Zhao J., 2017), have been proposed to modify the performance of MBOA. In MBOA-BIDE, The way to calculate the interaction energy adopted the linear combination of the distance between the optimal individual and the target individual and the distances between the optimal individual and the random individual. It can overcome the shortcomings of complicated interaction energy calculation of the original MBOA. In the Magnetotactic Bacteria Moment Migration Algorithm (MBMMA), the moments of relative good solutions can migrate each other to enhance the diversity of the MBMMA.

In this paper, the original MBOA is further improved based on four different schemes. The main idea is to regulate the moments of MTSs based on the combination of the best cell and some other randomly chosen one. All of the improved algorithms work mainly according to three steps: MTSs generation, MTSs regulation, and MTSs replacement. Four schemes are realized at the step of MTSs regulation.

The remainder of this paper is organized as follows: Section MBOA BASED ON FOUR BEST-RAND PAIRWISE SCHEMES describes the basic biology concepts related to MTB and the model of MBOA. In Section Simulation Results, experiments on fourteen standard functions' optimization and analysis are provided and results are summarized. In Section Future, the future of the MBOA is considered. Finally is the Section CONCLUSIONS.

MBOA BASED ON FOUR BEST-RAND PAIRWISE SCHEMES

Hypothesis of Interaction Energy of Magnetosome Chains

The simplest hypothesis for magnetotaxis is the passive orientation of a swimming bacterium along its magnetic field lines by the torque exerted by the field on its magnetic moment. Considering a chain of magnetosomes as a cylinder of infinite length in a magnetic field B, its energy Em of the bacterial moment can be estimated as follows (Frankel R. B., 1984).

$$E_m = -M \cdot B = -MB\cos\theta \tag{1}$$

where θ is the angle between M and B. M is the total magnetic moments of a magnetosome.

According to (Philipse A.P., & Maas D., 2002), the interaction energy between two dipoles from different magnetosome chains is:

$$E_{n,m} = \left(\frac{D}{1+nD+mD}\right)^3 \tag{2}$$

where $n, m = 0, 1, 2, \ldots$ are the number of magnetosomes of two cells, D is the distance between neighbor centers in a chain.

Suppose the interaction energy between two cells in a MTB is as follows:

$$\frac{1}{2}(E_n + E_m) = E_{n,m} \tag{3}$$

where E_n, E_m are the energy of two cells, respectively. If two cells have the same number of magnetosomes, that is, $n = m$, and $E_n = E_m$, then $E_{n,m} = E_n = E_m$.

Procedures of MBOA

Before describing the MBOA, some basic metaphor concepts are given as follows. A population is a magnetotactic bacterium with multi-cells. A cell is a candidate solution, that is, a vector. The attributes of a solution vector are considered as magnetosomes. The values of attributes of a solution vector are considered as the moments of a cell. The interaction between two cells is represented by the differential vector between them. In the following, we describe the main procedures of MBOA.

Initialization of the Population

The initial population is filled with *N* number of randomly generated n-dimensional real-valued vectors (i.e., cells of a MTB). Let $X_i = (x_{i,1}, x_{i,2}, \ldots, x_{i,n})$ represents the ith cell (for generation index *t*=0) initialized randomly. Then each cell is generated as follows:

$$x_{i,j} = x_{\min,j} + rand(0,1) \times (x_{\max,j} - x_{\min,j}) \tag{4}$$

where *i* =1, 2,..., *N*, *j* =1, 2,..., *n*. $x_{\max,j}$ and $x_{\min,j}$ are upper and lower bounds for the dimension *j*, respectively. *rand*(0,1) is a random number between 0 and 1.

Interaction Distance

Interaction distance is used to calculate the interaction energy for generating the magnetosomes of cells. The distance D_i of two cells X_i and X_r calculated as follows:

$$D_i = X_i - X_r \tag{5}$$

where X_r is a randomly chosen cell, where i and r is mutually different integer indices from{1, 2,…,N}, and r is randomly chosen one. Thus, we can get a $N \times n$ distance matrix $D = [D_1, D_2, ..., D_N]'$. In order to improve the diversity and expand the search space of the MBOA, D is a randomly chosen distance matrix and D_i is not unique.

MTSs Generation

Based on the distances among cells, the interaction energy e_i between two cells based on (2) is defined as

$$e_{i,j}(t) = \left(\frac{d_{i,j}(t)}{1 + c_1 \times norm(D_i) + c_2 \times d_{p,q}(t)} \right)^3 \tag{6}$$

where t is the generation index, c_1 and c_2 are constants. D_i is calculated according to the equation (5). D_i stands for the Euclidean distance between two cells, X_i, X_r. $d_{p,q}$ is randomly selected from D_p. $norm(D_i)$ is the Euclidean length of vector D_i. p and r are mutually different and randomly chosen integer indices from {1, 2, ..., N}. $q \in \{1, 2, ..., n\}$ stands for one randomly chosen integer. n is the number of dimensions of a cell.

After obtaining interaction energy, for simplifying calculation, ignore where θ is the angle between M and B and direction in (1), the moments $M_i = (m_{i1}, m_{i2}, ..., m_{in})$ are generated as follows:

$$M_i(t) = \frac{E_i(t)}{B} \tag{7}$$

where B is a constant named magnetic field strength.

Then the total moments of a cell is regulated as follows:

$$x_{i,j}(t) = x_{i,j}(t) + m_{r,q}(t) \times rand \tag{8}$$

where $m_{r,q}$ is randomly chosen from M_i. $rand$ is a random number in interval (0,1).

MTSs Regulation Based on Best-Rand Scheme

After moments generation, evaluating the population according to cells' fitness, then the moments regulation is realized as follows: setting a magnetic fieldstrength probability mp.

If rand > mp, the moments in the cell migrate as follows:

$$X_i(t+1) = X_{best}(t) + (X_{best}(t) - X_i(t)) \times rand \tag{9}$$

Otherwise,

$$X_i(t+1) = X_i(t) + (X_{best}(t) - X_r(t)) \times rand \tag{10}$$

or

$$X_i(t+1) = X_r(t) + (X_{best}(t) - X_i(t)) \times rand \tag{11}$$

or

$$X_i(t+1) = X_r(t) + (X_{best}(t) - X_r(t)) \times rand \tag{12}$$

or

$$X_i(t+1) = X_i(t) + (X_{best}(t) - X_i(t)) \times rand \tag{13}$$

where *rand* is a random number in interval (0,1). r is randomly chosen from $\{1, 2 \ldots, N\}$.

In this step, four pairwise schemes (9) and (10), (9) and(11), (9) and(12), (9) and (13) are designed in order to study which scheme is suitable for solving optimization problems. All the schemes are based on the best cell's moments to regulate the moments of the cells in next generation. Based on (8), it will generate some cells close to the best one, thus it has an enhanced local search ability. Based on (10), (11), (12), or (13), some randomly chosen cell which may be far from the best cell will approximate to the best one. Thus, it may enhance the ability of global search. This step can be described as a MBOA/best-rand scheme. Based on this step, some cells in the population will have chance to be regulated based on the moments of the best cell.

MTSs Replacement

After the moments regulation, evaluating the population according to cells' fitness, then some cells with worse moments are replaced by the following way:

$$X_i(t+1) = m_{r,q}(t) \times ((rand(1,n) - 1) \times rand(1,n)) \tag{14}$$

where $m_{i,q}$ is randomly chosen from M_i. r is randomly chosen from $\{1, 2 \ldots, N\}$. $q \in \{1, 2 \ldots, n\}$ stands for one randomly chosen integer. $rand(1.n)$ is a random vector with n dimensions.

At last, evaluating the population according to cells' fitness after replacement.

Generally, a pseudo code of MBOA with variants is as follows:

```
Step 1: Define the simple bounds, determination of algorithm parameters.
Step 2: Initialization: Randomly create the initial population in the search
space based on (4).
Step 3: while stopping criteria is not met for i=1:N Calculate interaction
distance according to (5)
  end for
  for i=1:N
      for j=1:n
      Calculate interaction energy according to (6)
      end for
      Obtain moments according to (7)
      for j=1:n
      MTSs generation according to (8)
      end for
  end for
  Evaluate the population according to fitness
      for i=1:N
          if rand > mp
          MTSs regulation according to (9)
          else
          MTSs regulation according to (10) or (11) or (12) or (13)
          end if
          end for
  Evaluate the population according to fitness
      for i=N/5:N
      MTSs replacement to (14)
      end for
      Memorize the best solution achieved so far
Step 4: End while
```

In the algorithm, one fifth of MTSs with relative worse moments will be replaced.

SIMULATION RESULTS

To test the performance of the proposed four schemes of the MBOA, the effectiveness of MBOA variants are demonstrated by comparing the performance of MBOA variants with the state-of-the-art evolutionary algorithms on 14 benchmark functions collected from (Gao W.F., & Liu S.Y., 2011). These benchmark functions are widely used in evaluating global numerical optimization algorithms. In this section, the benchmark functions are presented firstly. Secondly, the parameter settings of MBOA variants and the algorithms chosen for comparison are presented. Finally, the simulation results obtained from different experimental studies are analyzed and discussed.

Benchmark Functions and Experiments Settings

A short description of 14 benchmark functions is shown in Tables 1. These functions can be classified into two groups. $f_1 - f_6$ are unimodal; f_7 is a noisy quartic function. The minimum of them is 0. The unimodal functions here are used to test whether MBOA variants can still maintain the fast-converging feature. The next seven functions $f_8 - f_{14}$ are multimodal functions and the number of local minima increases exponentially with the problem dimension. These functions can be used to test the global search ability of an algorithm in avoiding premature convergence.

To validate the effectiveness of the proposed algorithms, we compare MBOA variants with the standard GA (Holland, J. H., 1975), standard DE (Vesterstroem, J., & Thomsen, R., 2004), HPSO-TVAC (Ratnaweera, A., Halgamuge, S., & Watson, H., 2004), CLPSO (Liang J.J., Qin A.K., Suganthan P.N., & Baskar S., 2006), APSO (Zhan Z.H., Zhang, J., Li, Y., & Chung S. H., 2009), CABC (Alatas, B., 2010), GABC (Zhu G.P, & Kwong S., 2010) and RABC (Kang F., Li J. J., & Ma Z.Y., 2011). For a fair comparison, the same initial random population is used to evaluate different algorithms. The population size of GA and DE is 50. For DE, the other parameter values are chosen as in (Vesterstroem, J., & Thomsen, R., 2004). For GA, single point crossover operation with the rate of 0.8 is employed. Mutation rate in our experiments is 0.01. Additionally, we follow the parameter settings in the original paper of HPSO-TVAC (Ratnaweera, A., Halgamuge, S., & Watson, H., 2004), CLPSO (Liang J.J, Qin A.K, Suganthan P.N, & Baskar S., 2006), APSO(Zhan Z.H., Zhang, J., Li, Y., Chung S. H., 2009), CABC (Alatas, B., 2010), GABC (Zhu G.P, & Kwong S., 2010) and RABC (Kang F., Li J. J., & Ma Z.Y., 2011). In the MBOA variants, the parameters to be set includ the magnetic field strength B, c_1, c_2, and magnetic field strength probability mp. The parameter settings are discussed in the following section.

Parameter Settings of MBOA

In order to apply MBOA algorithm to a problem, its adjustable parameters have to be tuned. The effects of the parameters (c_1, c_2, mp and B) will be analyzed in detail. Five test functions which are chosen from those given in Table 1 were used as objective functions in order to show the effects of the parameters (including c_1, c_2, mp and B). For each function, 30 trials were performed for each method. The number of particles is set 50 and the maximum number of FEs is set 200000 for test problems. There are no other stopping criteria and all the experiments are run for 200000 FES.

Table 1. Benchmark functions used in experiments.

Function	Range	D	Formulation
f_1: Sphere	[-100, 100]	30	$f(x)=\sum_{i=1}^{n} x_i^2$
f_2: Schwefel2.22	[-10, 10]	30	$f(x)=\sum_{i=1}^{n}\lvert x_i\rvert+\prod_{i=1}^{n}\lvert x_i\rvert$
f_3: Schwefel1.2	[-100, 100]	30	$f(x)=\sum_{i=1}^{n}(\sum_{j=1}^{i} x_j)^2$
f_4: Zakharov	[-5, 10]	30	$f(x)=\sum_{i=1}^{n} x_i^2+(\sum_{i=1}^{n} 0.5ix_i)^2+(\sum_{i=1}^{n} 0.5ix_i)^4$
f_5: Step	[-100, 100]	30	$f(x)=\sum_{i=1}^{n}(\lfloor x_i+0.5\rfloor)^2$
f_6: Schwefel2.21	[-100, 100]	30	$f(x)=\max\{\lvert x_i\rvert, 1\le i\le n\}$
f_7: Noisy Quartic	[-1.28, 1.28]	30	$f(x)=\sum_{i=1}^{n} ix_i^4+random[0,1)$
f_8: Rosenbrock	[-30, 30]	30	$f(x)=\sum_{i=1}^{n-1}[100(x_{i+1}-x_i^2)^2+(x_i-1)^2]$
f_9: Schwefel	[-500, 500]	30	$f(x)=\sum_{i=1}^{n} -x_i\sin(\sqrt{\lvert x_i\rvert})$
f_{10}: Rastrigin	[-5.12, 5,12]	30	$f(x)=\sum_{i=1}^{n}[x_i^2-10\cos(2\pi x_i)+10$
f_{11} :Griewank	[-600, 600]	30	$f(x)=\frac{1}{4000}\sum_{i=1}^{n} x_i^2-\prod_{i=1}^{n}\cos\left(\frac{x_i}{\sqrt{i}}\right)+1$
f_{12}: Ackley	[-32, 32]	30	$f(x)=-20\exp\left(-0.2\sqrt{\frac{1}{n}\sum_{i=1}^{n} x_i^2}\right)-\exp\left(\frac{1}{n}\sum_{i=1}^{n}\cos(2\pi x_i)\right)+20+e$
f_{13}: Penalty1	[-50, 50]	30	$f(x)=\frac{\pi}{n}\left\{10\sin^2(\pi y_1)+\sum_{i=1}^{n-1}(y_i-1)^2\left[1+10\sin^2(\pi y_{i+1})\right]+(y_n-1)\right\}+\sum_{i=1}^{n} u(x_i,10,100,4)$ $y_i=1+\frac{1}{4}(x_i+1)$
f_{14}: Penalty2	[-50, 50]	30	$f(x)=0.1\left\{\sin^2(\pi x_1)+\sum_{i=1}^{n-1}(x_i-1)^2\left[1+\sin^2(3\pi x_{i+1})\right]+(x_n-1)^2\left[1+\sin^2(2\pi x_n)\right]\right\}$ $+\sum_{i=1}^{n} u(x_i,5,100,4)$

Table 2 presents the results of MBOA under different c_1 (c_1=10, 20, 30, 40, 50). In Table 3, MBOA with different c_1 values are ranked based on their mean performances. They are ranked according to their performances using a standard competition ranking scheme. In competition ranking, algorithms receive the same rank if their performances are same. The next performing algorithm is assigned a rank with a gap (gap is determined based on the number of equally performing algorithms). Table 3 provides the ranks of the different c_1 and the average rank for all the functions based on mean performances. Based on the average ranking, the order of performance obtained is c_1 =10, 20, 30, 40 followed by c_1 =50.

From Tables 2, we can see that MBOA under c_1=10, c_1=30 and c_1= 40 show worse performance on function f_{14}. And MBOA under c_1=20 gives better performance compared with MBOA under c_1=50.

Figure 1 presents the histograms that indicate the number of times each c_1 have achieved the ranks in the range of 1 to 5. It can be seen that c_1=20 achieves the top rank as compared to the other different c_1 values.

Table 4 presents the results of MBOA under different c_2(0.001~0.009) for test functions. As seen from Tables 4, it is clear that MBOA under c_2=0.003, c_2=0.006 and c_2=0.009 show worse performance on function f_{14}. And MBOA under c_2=0.002 gives better performance compared with MBOA under c_2=0.001, c_2=0.004, c_2=0.005, c_2=0.007 and c_2=0.008.

Table 5 presents the results of MBOA under different *mp(0.1~0.9)* for test functions. From Tables 5, we can see that MBOA under *mp*=0.2, 0.3 and 0.7 show worse performance on function f_{14}. And MBOA under *mp*=0.5 gives better performance.

Table 2. The results for the test functions of MBOA under different c_1 values (c_2=0.005, mp=0.5 and B=3)

Fun	c_1=10	c_1=20	c_1= 30	c_1= 40	c_1=50
f_7:Noisy Quartic	**8.8833e-06**	1.5174e-05	1.3849e-05	1.6079e-05	1.5814e-05
f_8: Rosenbrock	25.8083	25.3302	25.3876	**24.6095**	25.9463
f_9: Schwefel	**-12226.3056**	-12105.2245	-12180.3250	-12138.6513	-11965.2836
f_{13}: Penalty1	5.7988e-11	6.5032e-12	4.3998e-12 4.39982867371919e-12	**3.9821e-12**	4.4016e-12
f_{14}: Penalty2	0.0989	**1.2034e-09**	0.0993	0.0993	6.0368e-05

Table 3. Rank table for the mean values

Fun	c_1=10	c_1=20	c_1= 30	c_1= 40	c_1=50
f_7:Noisy Quartic	**1**	**3**	**2**	**5**	**4**
f_8: Rosenbrock	**4**	**2**	**3**	**1**	**5**
f_9: Schwefel	**1**	**4**	**2**	**3**	**5**
f_{13}: Penalty1	**5**	**4**	**2**	**1**	**3**
f_{14}: Penalty2	**3**	**1**	**5**	**4**	**2**
Avg.rank	2.8	2.8	2.8	2.8	**3.8**

Figure 1. Histogram of individual mean ranks

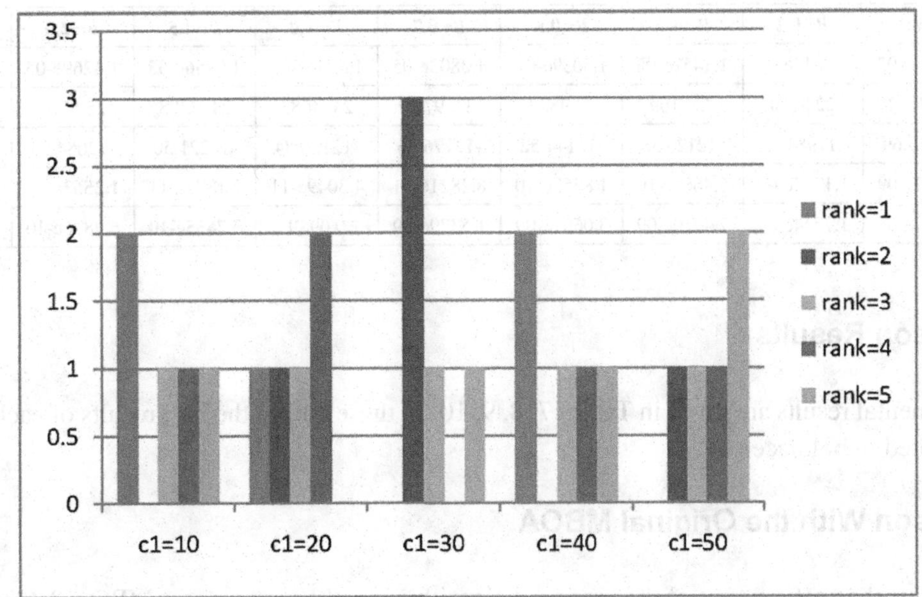

Table 4. The results for the test functions of MBOA under different c_2 values (c_1=20, mp=0.5 and B=3)

Fun	c_2=0.001	c_2=0.002	c_2=0.003	c_2=0.004	c_2=0.005	c_2=0.006	c_2=0.007	c_2=0.008	c_2=0.009
f_7:	2.2701e-05	1.2914e-05	1.1250e-05	1.9003e-05	2.1910e-05	1.4114e-05	1.8885e-05	1.8991e-05	1.7756e-05
f_8	26.2252	25.5120	25.8110	**24.9490**	25. 4178	26.3875	26. 0288	25.3971	25. 9295
f_9	-12202.00	-12221.83	-12126.56	-12186.82	-12276.69	-12093.73	**-12253.16**	-12015.64	-12224.30
f_{13}	7.5146e-12	7.3667e-12	7.9935e-12	7.3363e-12	7.0337e-12	1.7642e-10	7.9280e-12	7.3285e-12	**6.9246e-12**
f_{14}	7.8988e-09	**5.0283e-10**	0.0989	3.6625e-04	3.0104e-07	0.0997	1.6459e-08	7.8781e-10	0.0132

Table 5. The results for the test functions of MBOA under different mp values (c_1=20, c_2=0.002, and B=3)

Fun	mp=0.1	mp=0.2	mp=0. 3	mp=0.4	mp=0.5	mp=0.6	mp=0. 7	mp=0.8	mp=0. 9
f_7:	1.4840e-05	1.7403e-05	1.5374e-05	1.8154e-05	1.4617e-05	1.4058e-05	1.2062e-05	1.5654e-05	**1.1111e-05**
f_8	26. 5976	26.3719	25.8329	25.8490	**25. 4328**	25. 7334	26. 2443	26.9164	27. 7434
f_9	-11389.78	-11956.65	-11793.07	-11971.49	-12050.63	-12306.82	-12115.53	**-12363.09**	-12359.07
f_{13}	1.1823e-09	5.7445e-12	**4.6424e-12**	5.9673e-12	7.2274e-12	8.3232e-12	1.4074e-11	2.3434e-11	7.3392e-12
f_{14}	1.4125e-09	**0.0993**	0.0989	**9.5565e-10**	1.3374e-09	3.6625e-04	0.1979	8.1072e-04	9.2557e-06

Table 6 presents the results of MBOA under different *B* (0.1~3.0) for test functions. From Tables 6, we can see that MBOA under *B*=1.5 gives best performance compared with MBOA under some different parameter settings.

So Parameter sets (c_1=20, c_2=0.002, *mp*=0.5 and *B*=1.5) of MBOA are best selected for the 5 tested functions in this paper.

Table 6. The results for the test functions of MBOA under different B values (c_1=20, c_2=0.002, and mp=0.5)

Fun	*B*=0.1	*B*=0.2	*B*=0. 3	*B*=0.5	*B*=0.7	*B*=1,0	*B*=1.5	*B*=2.0	*B*=3.0
f_7:	1.5623e-05	1.7514e-05	1.1452e-05	1.5039e-05	1.3803e-05	1.4736e-05	**1.0166e-05**	1.4269e-05	1.1008e-05
f_8	23. 7372	**22.8716**	23.8109	23.9803	23. 9757	24. 4683	24. 8208	25.5500	25. 6568
f_9	-12039.69	-11984.19	-12126.38	-12144.52	**-12276.76**	-12126.84	-12221.50	-12084.93	-12097.30
f_{13}	4.3882e-09	1.1734e-09	5.4660e-10	1.8258e-10	8.2821e-11	4.3049e-11	2.1872e-11	**1.2563e-12**	6.3314e-12
f_{14}	6.4039e-08	1.7744e-08	7.4920e-09	3.0601e-09	1.5379e-09	0.0989	**3.7855e-10**	6.9876e-10	0.2971

Comparison Results

The experimental results are given in Tables 7, 8, 9, 10. In these tables, the best results of each function are highlighted in boldface.

Comparison With the Original MBOA

In order to test the performance of the proposed algorithm, firstly, we compare MBOA-1 (pairwise (9) and (10)), MBOA-2 pairwise (9) and (11)), MBOA-3 (pairwise (9) and (12)), MBOA-4 (pairwise (9) and (13)) with the original MBOA to demonstrate the effectiveness of the MBOA variants. The experimental results in terms of statistical parameters (mean and standard deviations) yielded by MBOA variants and the original MBOA after 2×10^5 FEs are tabulated in Table 7. In order to make a fair comparison, the population size is uniformly set to 50 in all algorithms. To reduce statistical errors, each test is repeated 30 times independently.

As can be seen from Table 7, it is clear that MBOA-1, MBOA-2, MBOA-3 and MBOA-4 perform much better than the original MBOA on test functions except function f_7. And MBOA-4 shows the best performance on most of the test functions among the four MBOA schemes. The four MBOA schemes improve the quality of optimum solution of test functions as compared to the original MBOA.

The results are shown in Table 8 in terms of the mean, standard deviation (st.d), mid, best, and worst of the solutions obtained in the 30 independent runs by each algorithm.

As is given in Table 8, we can see that MBOA variants outperform GA and DE on most of the test functions. For solving the unimodal problems, the MBOA-4 offers the best performance on all the test functions. In particular, MBOA variants offer the highest accuracy on functions f_1 to f_7. And for functions f_2 and f_5, both MBOA variants and GA can obtain the optimal solutions. For multimodel and high-dimensional function f_8, although the results of MBOA variants are a little far from the global optimums, the MBOA variants perform better than GA and have worse performance compared with DE. The MBOA variants and GA can also find the optimal solutions on the complex multimodal functions f_{10} and f_{12}. The MBOA variants have better performance than GA and DE on function f_{11}. For functions f_9 and f_{13}, MBOA variants perform better than DE but have worse performance when compared with GA. Among MBOA-1, MBOA-2, MBOA-3 and MBOA-4, MBOA-4 shows the best performance for all the test functions.

In Figure 2, the convergence of GA, DE and MBOA-1, MBOA-2, MBOA-3, MBOA-4 on some benchmark examples are shown for 1000 generations.

Table 7. The results for the test functions of original MBOA and the four schemes of MBOA

Fun	Original MBOA	MBOA-1	MBOA-2	MBOA-3	MBOA-4
$f_{1:}$ Sphere	4.1187e-12 (5.8137e-13)	**0(0)**	**0(0)**	**0(0)**	**0(0)**
$f_{2:}$ Schwefel 222	7.8687e-05 (4.7642e-06)	**0(0)**	**0(0)**	**0(0)**	**0(0)**
$f_{3:}$ Schwefel 12	5.4672e-10 (7.5964e-11)	**0(0)**	**0(0)**	**0(0)**	**0(0)**
$f_{4:}$ Zakharov	6.5792e-10 (1.5148e-10)	**0(0)**	**0(0)**	**0(0)**	**0(0)**
$f_{5:}$ Step	**0(0)**	**0(0)**	**0(0)**	**0(0)**	**0(0)**
$f_{6:}$ Schwefel2.21	7.9478e-07 (5.6896e-08)	**0(0)**	**0(0)**	**0(0)**	**0(0)**
$f_{7:}$ Noisy Quartic	1.2355e-05 (1.2594e-05)	2.6615e-05 (2.4255e-05)	2.4378e-05 (2.0330e-05)	1.5036e-05 (1.8283e-05)	**1.1956e-05 (1.1163e-05)**
$f_{8:}$ Rosenbrock	29.0000 (2.9841e-06)	28.4605 (0.6956)	28.2280 (0.9348)	28.7793 (0.3952)	**25.4865 (2.2272)**
$f_{9:}$ Schwefel	-2384.9947 (516.3535)	-12343.9637 (241.7416)	-12324.9340 (436.3097)	**-12404.1490 (211.1639)**	-12192.4781 (497.2549)
$f_{10:}$ Rastrigin	2.9460e-07 (3.9366e-08)	**0(0)**	**0(0)**	**0(0)**	**0(0)**
$f_{11:}$ Griewank	4.4261e-15 (6.9409e-16)	**0(0)**	**0(0)**	**0(0)**	**0(0)**
$f_{12:}$ Ackley	4.5078e-06 (3.4832e-07)	**-8.8816e-16(0)**	**-8.8816e-16(0)**	**-8.8816e-16(0)**	**-8.8816e-16(0)**
$f_{13:}$ Penalty1	1.6631 (2.3597e-05)	0.0010 (4.1619e-04)	9.5015e-04 (3.3930e-04)	1.6331e-04 (6.0487e-05)	**1.9889e-11 (7.4963e-12)**
$f_{14:}$ Penalty1	3.0000 (2.5556e-07)	0.0295 (0.0157)	0.0988 (0.3509)	1.0932 (1.3576)	**3.7719e-10 (2.3743e-10)**

From Figure2, it can be seen that all of the MBOA variants have faster convergence speed than those of GA and DE except f_9. The results show that all the schemes can solve the benchmark problems with high efficiency.

Comparison With HPSO-TVAC, CLPSO and APSO

In Table 9, we compare MBOA-4 with HPSO-TVAC, CLPSO and APSO on 11 benchmark functions described in (Ratnaweera, A., Halgamuge, S., & Watson, H., 2004), all the algorithms use the same number of 2.0×10^5 FEs for each test function. The results of HPSO-TVAC, CLPSO and APSO are adopted from (Gao W. F., & Liu S. Y., 2011) directly.

As can be seen from Table 9, MBOA-4 greatly outperforms HPSO-TVAC, CLPSO and APSO with better mean and standard deviation except on functions f_8, f_9 and f_{13}. And for function f_5, all the methods can obtain the optimal solutions.

Table 8. Performance comparisons of MBOA variants, GA and DE

Func.		GA	DE	MBOA-1	MBOA-2	MBOA-3	MBOA-4
f_1	Mean	7.0759e-05	5.2647e-48	**0**	**0**	**0**	**0**
	St.d	2.6597e-04	8.8136e-48	**0**	**0**	**0**	**0**
	Mid	0	2.2481e-48	**0**	**0**	**0**	**0**
	best	0	1.2781e-49	**0**	**0**	**0**	**0**
	worst	0.0012	4.0574e-47	**0**	**0**	**0**	**0**
f_2	Mean	**0**	4.6407e-25	**0**	**0**	**0**	**0**
	St.d	**0**	6.2699e-25	**0**	**0**	**0**	**0**
	Mid	**0**	2.5100e-25	**0**	**0**	**0**	**0**
	best	**0**	1.67901e-26	**0**	**0**	**0**	**0**
	worst	**0**	3.1359e-24	**0**	**0**	**0**	**0**
f_3	Mean	4.9326e+03	1.4882e-05	**0**	**0**	**0**	**0**
	St.d	2.0358e+03	2.3849e-05	**0**	**0**	**0**	**0**
	Mid	5.0155e+03	3.3783e-06	**0**	**0**	**0**	**0**
	best	1.9515e+03	1.0107e-07	**0**	**0**	**0**	**0**
	worst	1.0925e+04	8.6312e-05	**0**	**0**	**0**	**0**
f_4	Mean	5.2554	7.3646e-08	**0**	**0**	**0**	**0**
	St.d	2.6819	1.4330e-07	**0**	**0**	**0**	**0**
	Mid	4.6712	2.7059e-08	**0**	**0**	**0**	**0**
	best	0.5279	1.9935e-09	**0**	**0**	**0**	**0**
	worst	13.8492	7.1667e-07	**0**	**0**	**0**	**0**
f_5	Mean	**0**	0.0333	**0**	**0**	**0**	**0**
	St.d	**0**	0.1826	**0**	**0**	**0**	**0**
	Mid	**0**	0	**0**	**0**	**0**	**0**
	best	**0**	0	**0**	**0**	**0**	**0**
	worst	**0**	1	**0**	**0**	**0**	**0**
f_6	Mean	8.6009	9.4631	**0**	**0**	**0**	**0**
	St.d	2.4472	4.2385	**0**	**0**	**0**	**0**
	Mid	8	8.3893	**0**	**0**	**0**	**0**
	best	4	3.2321	**0**	**0**	**0**	**0**
	worst	14	18.0622	**0**	**0**	**0**	**0**
f_7	Mean	0.2112	5.4e-03	2.6270e-05	1.2778e-05	1.8272e-05	**7.5250e-06**
	St.d	0.1758	1.7e-03	2.5862e-05	2.0055e-05	1.9057e-05	**6.8837e-06**
	Mid	0.1773	5.1e-03	1.4693e-05	6.1626e-06	1.3098e-05	**5.1280e-06**
	best	0.0362	2.7567e-03	1.4977e-06	2.3272e-07	7.3925e-08	**2.8292e-08**
	worst	0.6914	0.0106	8.7097e-05	6.8721e-05	6.0779e-05	**2.9347e-05**

continued on following page

Table 8. Continued

Func.		GA	DE	MBOA-1	MBOA-2	MBOA-3	MBOA-4
f_8	Mean	102.8566	**19.6130**	28.5880	28.8087	28.3769	25.0222
	St.d	52.2624	15.1547	0.6034	0.0673	1.1934	**2.5887**
	Mid	95.6286	**18.6721**	28.7823	28.8119	28.9398	24.4530
	best	13.4641	**0.0048**	26.8860	28.70143	26.0968	21.8180
	worst	230.9496	73.1609	28.8620	28.9267	28.9868	**28.7978**
f_9	Mean	**-12569.4827**	-10305.0957	-12323.230	-12387.910	-12517.3355	-12411.5675
	St.d	**0.0032**	511.3140	272.8015	199.6219	90.5377	507.6040
	Mid	**-12569.4833**	-10355.1119	-12440.6982	-12479.15494	-12563.200	-12569.486
	best	**-12569.4839**	-11380.5521	-12557.352	-12564.096	-12569.162	-12569.486
	worst	**-12569.4655**	-9233.3923	-11686.1994	-12046.453	-12276.827	-10437.597
f_{10}	Meann	**0**	33.2069	**0**	**0**	**0**	**0**
	St.d	**0**	33.0204	**0**	**0**	**0**	**0**
	Mid	**0**	19.2384	**0**	**0**	**0**	**0**
	best	**0**	8.9678	**0**	**0**	**0**	**0**
	worst	**0**	161.0427	**0**	**0**	**0**	**0**
f_{11}	Mean	0.0031	1.2271	**0**	**0**	**0**	**0**
	St.d	0.0035	2.7257	**0**	**0**	**0**	**0**
	Mid	0.0011	1.5878e-04	**0**	**0**	**0**	**0**
	best	0.0014	7.8211e-10	**0**	**0**	**0**	**0**
	worst	0.0043	6.1031	**0**	**0**	**0**	**0**
f_{12}	Mean	**-8.8818e-16**	5.3883e-15	**-8.8818e-16**	**-8.8818e-16**	**-8.8818e-16**	**-8.8818e-16**
	St.d	**0**	1.5283e-15	**0**	**0**	**0**	**0**
	Mid	**-8.8818e-16**	6.2172e-15	**-8.8818e-16**	**-8.8818e-16**	**-8.8818e-16**	**-8.8818e-16**
	best	**-8.8818e-16**	2.6645e-15	**-8.8818e-16**	**-8.8818e-16**	**-8.8818e-16**	**-8.8818e-16**
	worst	**-8.8818e-16**	6.2172e-15	**-8.8818e-16**	**-8.8818e-16**	**-8.8818e-16**	**-8.8818e-16**
f_{13}	Mean	**1.5705e-32**	0.0138	7.8691e-04	8.4821e-04	1.3648e-04	1.1621e-11
	St.d	**5.5674e-48**	0.0757	2.5924e-04	2.5129e-04	5.0231e-05	3.5566e-12
	Mid	**1.5705e-32**	**1.5705e-32**	7.1711e-04	8.9617e-04	1.2899e-04	1.2899e-04
	best	**1.5705e-32**	**1.5705e-32**	3.8578e-04	4.4120e-04	5.5310e-05	4.9444e-12
	worst	**1.5705e-32**	0.4147	0.0014	0.0012	2.9970e-04	1.9143e-11
f_{14}	Mean	**1.3498e-32**	3.6625e-04	0.2284	0.1699	1.2369	1.7835e-10
	St.d	**5.5674e-48**	0.0020	0.7342	0.5528	1.3150	3.9507e-11
	Mid	**1.3498e-32**	**1.3498e-32**	0.0232	0.0217	0.8473	1.8451e-10
	best	**1.3498e-32**	**1.3498e-32**	0.0049	0.0087	0.0016	9.3698e-11
	worst	**1.3498e-32**	0.0110	2.9706	2.2414	2.9937	2.4334e-10

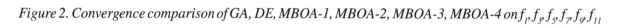

Figure 2. Convergence comparison of GA, DE, MBOA-1, MBOA-2, MBOA-3, MBOA-4 on $f_1, f_3, f_5, f_7, f_9, f_{11}$

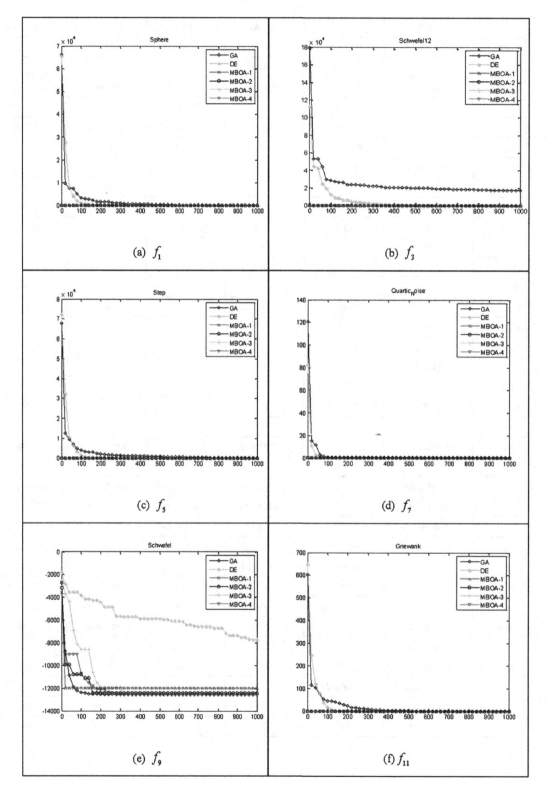

(a) f_1

(b) f_3

(c) f_5

(d) f_7

(e) f_9

(f) f_{11}

Table 9. Performance comparisons of HPSO-TVAC, CLPSO APSO and MBOA-4

Fun		HPSO-TVAC	CLPSO	APSO	MBOA-4
f_1 : Sphere	Mean	3.38e-41	1.89e-19	1.45e-150	**0**
	St.d	8.50e-41	1.49e-19	5.73e-150	**0**
f_2 : Schwefel2.22	Mean	6.9e–23	1.01e–13	5.15e–84	**0**
	St.d	6.89e–23	6.51e–14	1.44e–83	**0**
f_3 : Schwefel1.2	Mean	2.89e–07	395	1.0e–10	**0**
	St.d	2.97e–07	142	2.13e–10	**0**
f_5 : Step	Mean	0	0	0	0
	St.d	0	0	0	0
f_7 :Noisy Quartic	Mean	5.54e–02	3.92e–03	4.66e–03	**1.5785e-05**
	St.d	2.08e–02	1.14e–03	1.7e–03	**1.2477e-05**
f_8 : Rosenbrock	Mean	1.3e+01	11	**2.84**	28.0048
	St.d	1.65e+01	1.45e+01	**3.27**	1.4389
f_9 : Schwefel	Mean	−10869.57	−12557.7	**−12569.5**	-12330.74
	St.d	289	36.2	**5.22e–11**	487.6509
f_{10} : Rastrigin	Mean	2.39	2.57e–11	5.8e–15	**0**
	St.d	3.71	6.64e–11	1.01e–14	**0**
f_{11} : Griewank	Mean	**1.07e–02**	6.45e–13	1.67e–02	**0**
	St.d	**1.14e–02**	2.07e–12	2.41e–02	**0**
f_{12} : Ackley	Mean	2.06e–10	2.01e–12	1.11e–14	**-8.8818e-16**
	St.d	9.45e–10	9.22e–13	3.55e–15	**0**
f_{13} : Penalty1	Mean	7.07e–30	1.59e–21	**3.76e–31**	1.9075e-11
	St.d	4.05e–30	1.93e–21	**1.2e–30**	1.0470e-11

Comparison With CABC, GABC and RABC

At last, MBOA-4 is compared with CABC, GABC and RABC. The parameter configurations for these ABC variants are identical to that used in (Alatas, B., 2010). The results are given in Table 10 in terms of the mean and standard deviation of the solutions obtained in the 50 independent runs by each algorithm.

The results show that MBOA-4 performs much better than these ABC variants on 8 test functions and worse than these ABC variants on 4 test functions. And MBOA-4 and these ABCs show the same performance on function f_5. Therefore, it can be concluded that MBOA-4 is more efficient than these ABCs on unimodal problems. For multimodal problems, it is clear that MBOA-4 is consistently superior to these ABC variants on functions f_{10}, f_{11} and f_{12}.

In total, as seen from the results, MBOA variants achieve better performance than compared methods in terms accuracy of global optima for unimodal as well as multimodal functions (f_{10}, f_{11} and f_{12}).

Table 10. Performance comparisons of MBOA-4, CABC, GABC and RABC.

Fun	FEs		CABC	GABC	RABC	MBOA-4
f_1 : Sphere	1.5×10^5	Mean	2.3e–40	3.6e–63	9.1e–61	**0**
		St.d	1.7e–40	5.7e–63	2.1e–60	**0**
f_2 : Schwefel2.22	2.0×10^5	Mean	3.5e–30	4.8e–45	3.2e–74	**0**
		St.d	4.8e–30	1.4e–45	2.0e–73	**0**
f_3 : Schwefel1.2	5.0×10^5	Mean	8.4e+02	4.3e+02	2.9e–24	**0**
		St.d	9.1e+02	8.0e+02	1.5e–23	**0**
f_5 : Step	1.0×10^5	Mean	**0**	**0**	**0**	**0**
		St.d	**0**	**0**	**0**	**0**
f_6 : Schwefel2.21	5.0×10^5	Mean	6.1e–03	3.6e–06	2.8e–02	**0**
		St.d	5.7e–03	7.6e–07	1.7e–02	**0**
f_7 : Noisy Quartic	3.0×10^5	Mean	3.8e–02	1.1e–02	3.6e–02	**7.5106e-06**
		St.d	5.2e–01	5.3e–02	6.8e–03	**7.9287e-06**
f_8 : Rosenbrock	2.0×10^6	Mean	2.1e–02	6.7e–03	**6.4e–23**	27.7699
		St.d	3.5e–02	8.6e–02	**3.8e–22**	1.5948
f_9 : Schwefel	5.0×10^4	Mean	5.3e+02	9.7e+01	**9.2e–02**	118.2298
		St.d	4.8e+02	9.2e+01	**1.5e–02**	406.9618
f_{10} : Rastrigin	5.0×10^4	Mean	1.3e–00	1.5e–10	2.3e–02	**0**
		St.d	2.7e–00	2.7e–10	5.1e–01	**0**
f_{11} : Griewank	5.0×10^4	Mean	1.2e–04	6.0e–13	8.7e–08	**0**
		St.d	4.6e–04	7.7e–13	2.1e–08	**0**
f_{12} : Ackley	5.0×10^4	Mean	1.0e–05	1.8e–09	9.6e–07	**-8.8818e-016**
		St.d	2.4e–06	7.7e–10	8.3e–07	**0**
f_{13} : Penalty1	5.0×10^4	Mean	4.2e–11	**8.5e–20**	5.4e–16	1.9075e-11
		St.d	5.3e–11	**4.1e–20**	2.8e–16	1.0470e-11
f_{14} : Penalty2	5.0×10^4	Mean	7.4e–09	**5.3e–18**	1.5e–12	3.6656e-04
		St.d	8.1e–09	**4.8e–18**	2.7e–12	0.0020

FUTURE RESEARCH DIRECTIONS

In this paper, the MBOA is mainly improved in the respect of diversity of solutions. By desiging different types of MTSs regulation schemes, the MBOA show different performance on the functions optimziation. But as we can see that the MBOA is different from the other kinds of optimization algorithms in that it consists of three parts: MTSs generation,MTSs regulation and MTSs replacement. While in the part of MTSs generation, we design an function named interaction energy. It is mainly used to generate the first generation candidate solutions based on initialization. It should play important role in the algorithm when it is used to solve different kinds of problems. So in the future, we have two directions to research the MBOA. One hand, we will pay attention to how to design different types of energy functions in order to study its influences on the performance of the algorithms. On the other hand, it will be analyzed in theory and will be further modified to improve their performance for solving the problems including constrained optimization, multi-objective optimization, and some real engineering problems. It would also be used to solve the problems of machine learning. And, for different kinds of problems, we will design more types of MTSs diversity and different energy functions. We will try to find a right scheme for the algorithm that adapts to different solutions spaces both in theory and in practice.

CONCLUSION

MBOA is a new optimization algorithm insipired by the behavior of magnetotactic bacteria in nature. It mainly focuse on mimicing the moments interaction with the magnetic field of the earth. The original MBOA has similar disadvantages as some other optimziation algorithms, such as GAs, that is, it is easy to stay at local miminal values. In order to improve its performance to solve more practice problems, in this paper, an improved magnetotactic bacteria optimization algorithm with four variants is improved, which are based on the interaction between the best cell's moments and some randomly chosen cell. All the variants with different schemes use the best individual's moments to balance the ability of exploration and exploitation. The MBOA variants are compared with many state-of-the-art methods including standard GA, standard DE, HPSO-TVAC, CLPSO, APSO, CABC, and GABC. The comparison results showed that the MBOA-4 has superior performance on many benchmark functions. All the variants have faster convergence speed than GA and DE.

ACKNOWLEDGMENT

This research was supported by the National Natural Science Foundation of China [grant numbers No.61075113]

REFERENCES

Alatas, B. (2010). Chaotic bee colony algorithms for global numerical optimization. *Expert Systems with Applications*, *37*(8), 5682–5687. doi:10.1016/j.eswa.2010.02.042

Back, T. (1996). *Evolutionary Algorithms in Theory and Practice*. Oxford, UK: Oxford Univ. Press.

Bonabeau, E., Dorigo, M., & Theraulaz, G. (2000). Inspiration for optimization from social insect behavior. *Nature*, *406*(6791), 39–42. doi:10.1038/35017500 PMID:10894532

De Castro, L. N. (2006). *Fundamentals of Natural Computing*. Champman & Hall/CRC.

Dorigo, M., Manianiezzo, V., & Colorni, A. (1996). The ant system: Optimization by a colony of cooperating agents. *IEEE Transactions on Systems, Man, and Cybernetics. Part B, Cybernetics*, *26*(1), 29–41. doi:10.1109/3477.484436 PMID:18263004

Duin-Borkowski, R., McCartney, M. R., & Frankel, R. B. (1998). Magnetic Microstructure of magnetotactic bacteria by electron holography. *Science*, *282*(5395), 1868–1870. doi:10.1126/science.282.5395.1868 PMID:9836632

Faivre, D., & Schuler, D. (2008). Magnetotactic bacteria and magnetosomes. *Chemical Reviews*, *108*(11), 4875–4898. doi:10.1021/cr078258w PMID:18855486

Frankel, R. B. (1984). Magnetic guidance of organisms. Ann. Reo. *Biophys. Bioeng.*, *13*(1), 85–10. doi:10.1146/annurev.bb.13.060184.000505 PMID:6378076

Gao, W. F., & Liu, S. Y. (2011). Improved artificial bee colony algorithm for global optimization. *Information Processing Letters*, *111*(17), 871–882. doi:10.1016/j.ipl.2011.06.002

Holland, J. H. (1975). *Adaptation in Natural and Artificial Systems*. University of Michigan Press.

Kang, F., Li, J. J., & Ma, Z. Y. (2011). Rosenbrock artificial bee colony algorithm for accurate global optimization of numerical functions. *Inform. Sci.*, *12*(16), 3508–3531. doi:10.1016/j.ins.2011.04.024

Karaboga, D., & Akay, B. (2009). A comparative study of Artificial Bee Colony algorithm. *Applied Mathematics and Computation*, *214*(1), 108–132. doi:10.1016/j.amc.2009.03.090

Kennedy, J., & Eberhart, R. (1995). Particle swarm optimization. *IEEE International Conference on Neural Networks*, 1942-1948.

Krishnanand, K. N., & Ghose, D. (2009). Glowworm swarm optimization for simultaneous capture of multiple local optima of multimodal functions. *Swarm Intelligence*, *3*(2), 87–124. doi:10.1007/s11721-008-0021-5

Lam, A. Y. S., & Li, V. O. K. (2010). Chemical reaction inspired metaheuristic for optimization. *IEEE Transactions on Evolutionary Computation*, *14*(3), 381–400. doi:10.1109/TEVC.2009.2033580

Liang, J. J., Qin, A. K., Suganthan, P. N., & Baskar, S. (2006). Comprehensive learning particle swarm optimizer for global optimization of multimodal functions. *IEEE Transactions on Evolutionary Computation*, *10*(3), 281–295. doi:10.1109/TEVC.2005.857610

Mehrabian, A. R., & Lucas, C. (2006). A novel numerical optimization algorithm inspired from weed colonization. *Ecological Informatics*, *1*(4), 355–366. doi:10.1016/j.ecoinf.2006.07.003

Michael, W., Leida, G. A., & Alfonso, F. D. (2007). Barros magnetic optimization in a multicellular magnetotactic organism. *Biophysical Journal*, *92*(2), 661–670. doi:10.1529/biophysj.106.093823 PMID:17071652

Mitchell, J. G., & Kogure, K. (2006). Bacterial motility: Links to the environment and a driving force for microbial physics. *FEMS Microbiology Ecology*, *55*(1), 3–16. doi:10.1111/j.1574-6941.2005.00003.x PMID:16420610

Mo, H. W. (2012). Research on magnetotactic bacteria optimization algorithm. *The Fifth International Conference on Advanced Computational Intelligence*, 423-428.

Mo, H. W., & Geng, M. J. (2014). Magnetotactic bacteria optimization algorithm based on best-rand scheme. The 6th Naturei and Biologically Inspired Computing, 59-64.

Mo, H. W., & Liu, L. L. (2014). Magnetotactic bacteria optimization algorithm based on best-target scheme. *International Conference on Nature Computing and Fuzzy Knowledge*, 103-114. doi:10.1109/ICNC.2014.6975877

Mo, H. W., Liu, L. L., & Geng, M. J. (2014). A new magnetotactic bacteria optimization algorithm based on moment migration. *International Conference on Swarm Intelligence*, 103-114. doi:10.1007/978-3-319-11857-4_12

Mo, H. W., Liu, L. L., & Xu, L. F. (2014). A power spectrum optimization algorithm inspired by magnetotactic bacteria. *Neural Computing & Applications*, *25*(7), 1823–1844. doi:10.1007/s00521-014-1672-3

Mo, H. W., Liu, L. L., Xu, L. F., & Zhao, Y. Y. (2014). Research on magnetotactic bacteria optimization-algorithm based on the best individual. *The Sixth International Conference on Bio-inspired Computing*, 318-322.

Mo, H. W., Liu, L. L., & Zhao, J. (2015). Performance research on Magnetotactic Bacteria Optimization Algorithm with the Best Individual-guided Differential Interaction Energy. *Journal of Computer and Communications.*, *03*(05), 127–136. doi:10.4236/jcc.2015.35016

Mo, H. W., Liu, L. L., & Zhao, J. (2017). A new magnetotactic bacteria optimization algorithm based on moment migration. *IEEE/ACM Transactions on Computational Biology and Bioinformatics*, *14*(1), 15–26. doi:10.1109/TCBB.2015.2453949 PMID:28182541

Mo, H. W., & Xu, L. F. (2013). Magnetotactic bacteria optimization algorithm for multimodal optimization. *Swarm Intelligence (SIS), IEEE Symposium on,* 240-247.

Mucherino, A. & Seref, O. (2007). Monkey search: A novel metaheuristic search for global optimization. *Proceedings of Data Mining, Systems Analysis and Optimization in Biomedicine,* 162-173.

Müeller, S., Marchetto, J., Airaghi, S., & Koumoutsakos, P. (2002). Optimization based on bacterial chemotaxis. *IEEE Transactions on Evolutionary Computation*, *6*(1), 16–29. doi:10.1109/4235.985689

Philipse, A. P., & Maas, D. (2002). Magnetic colloids from magnetotactic bacteria: Chain formation and colloidal stability. *Langmuir*, *18*(25), 9977–9984. doi:10.1021/la0205811

Ratnaweera, A., Halgamuge, S., & Watson, H. (2004). Self-organizing hierarchical particle swarm optimizer with time-varying acceleration coefficients. *IEEE Transactions on Evolutionary Computation*, *8*(3), 240–255. doi:10.1109/TEVC.2004.826071

Shi, Y. H. (2011). Brain storm optimization algorithm. Advances in Swarm Intelligence in Lecture Notes in Computer Science, 728, 303-309.

Simon, D. (2008). Biogeography-based optimization. *IEEE Transactions on Evolutionary Computation*, *12*(6), 702–713. doi:10.1109/TEVC.2008.919004

Vesterstroem, J., & Thomsen, R. (2004). A comparative study of differential evolution, particle swarmoptimization, and evolutionary algorithms on numerical benchmark problems. *Proc. IEEE Congr. Evolutionary Computation,* 1980–1987.

Yin, T. (2015). *Firefly Algorithm*. Science Publisher.

Zhan, Z. H., Zhang, J., Li, Y., & Chung, S. H. (2009). Adaptive particle swarm optimization. *IEEE Transactions on Systems, Man, and Cybernetics. Part B, Cybernetics*, *39*(6), 1362–1381. doi:10.1109/TSMCB.2009.2015956 PMID:19362911

Zhu, G. P., & Kwong, S. (2010). Gbest-guided artificial bee colony algorithm for numerical function optimization. *Applied Mathematics and Computation*, *217*(7), 3166–3173. doi:10.1016/j.amc.2010.08.049

Chapter 6
An Analysis on Fireworks Algorithm Solving Problems With Shifts in the Decision Space and Objective Space

Shi Cheng
Shaanxi Normal University, China

Junfeng Chen
Hohai University, China

Quande Qin
Shenzhen University, China

Yuhui Shi
Southern University of Science and Technology, China

ABSTRACT

Fireworks algorithms for solving problems with the optima shifts in decision space and/or objective space are analyzed. The standard benchmark problems have several weaknesses in the research of swarm intelligence algorithms for solving single objective problems. The optimum shift in decision space and/or objective space will increase the difficulty of problem solving. Modular arithmetic mapping is utilized in the original fireworks algorithm to handle solutions out of search range. The solutions are implicitly guided to the center of search range for problems with symmetrical search range via this strategy. The optimization performance of fireworks algorithm on shift functions may be affected by this strategy. Four kinds of mapping strategies are compared on problems with different dimensions and different optimum shift range. From experimental results, the fireworks algorithms with mapping to the boundary or mapping to limited stochastic region obtain good performance on problems with the optimum shift. This is probably because the search tendency is kept in these two strategies.

DOI: 10.4018/978-1-5225-5134-8.ch006

1. INTRODUCTION

An optimization problem in $\mathcal{R}^n$, or simply an optimization problem, is a mapping $f : \mathcal{R}^n \rightarrow \mathcal{R}^k$, where $\mathcal{R}^n$ is termed as decision space (Adra, Dodd, & Griffin, *et al*., 2009) (or parameter space (Jin & Sendhoff, 2009), problem space), and $\mathcal{R}^k$ is termed as objective space (Sundaram, 1996). Swarm intelligence is based on a population of individuals (Kennedy, Eberhart, & Shi, 2001). In swarm intelligence, an algorithm maintains and successively improves a collection of potential solutions until some stopping condition is met. The solutions are initialized randomly in the search space. The search information is propagated through the interaction among solutions. With solutions' converging and/or diverging behaviors, solutions are guided toward the better and better areas.

In swarm intelligence algorithms, there is a population of solutions which exist at the same time. The premature convergence may happen due to solutions getting clustered together too fast. The population diversity is a measure of exploration and exploitation status. Based on the population diversity changing measurement, the state of exploration and exploitation can be obtained. The population diversity definition is the first step to give an accurate observation of the search state. Many studies of population diversity in evolutionary computation algorithms and swarm intelligence have been developed (Burke, Gustafson, & Kendall, 2002; Cheng, & Shi, 2011; Cheng, Shi, & Qin, 2011; Cheng, 2013; Cheng, Shi, & Qin, 2013; Mauldin, 1984; Shi, & Eberhart, 2008; Shi, & Eberhart, 2009).

The concept of developmental swarm intelligence algorithms was proposed in Shi (2014). The developmental swarm intelligence algorithm should have two kinds of ability: capability learning and capacity developing. The Capacity Developing focuses on moving the algorithm's search to the area(s) where higher searching potential may be possessed, while the capability learning focuses on its actual searching from the current solution for single point based optimization algorithms and from the current population for population-based swarm intelligence algorithms.

The capacity developing is a top-level learning or macro-level learning. The capacity developing could be the learning ability of an algorithm to adaptively change its parameters, structures, and/or its learning potential according to the search states on the problem to be solved. In other words, the capacity developing is the search strength possessed by an algorithm. The capability learning is a bottom-level learning or micro-level learning. The capability learning is the ability for an algorithm to find better solution(s) from current solution(s) with the learning capacity it is possessing (Shi, 2014).

The Fireworks algorithm (FWA) (Tan, & Zhu, 2010; Tan, Yu, & Zheng, *et al*., 2013) and brain storm optimization (BSO) (Cheng, Shi, & Qin, *et al*., 2014; Shi, 2011a; Shi, 2011b; Cheng, Qin, & Chen, *et al*., 2016;) algorithm are two good examples of developmental swarm intelligence (DSI) algorithms. The "good enough" optimum could be obtained through solutions' diverging and converging in the search space. In FWA algorithm, mimicking the fireworks exploration, the new solutions are generated by the exploration of existed solutions. While in BSO algorithm, the solutions are clustered into several categories, and new solutions are generated by the mutation of clusters or existed solutions. The capacity developing, i.e., the adaptation in search, is another common feature in these two algorithms.

Swarm intelligence is based on a population of individuals. In swarm intelligence, an algorithm maintains and successively improves a collection of potential solutions until some stopping condition is met. The solutions are initialized randomly in the search space, and are guided toward the better and better areas through the interaction among solutions. Mathematically, the updating process of population of individuals over iterations can be viewed as a mapping process from one population of individuals to another population of individuals from one iteration to the next iteration, which can be represented as $P_{t+1} = f(P_t)$, where P_t is the population of individuals at the iteration t, $f()$ is the mapping function.

As a general principle, the expected fitness of a solution returned should be improved as the search method is given more computational resources in time and/or space. More desirable, in any single run, the quality of the solution returned by the method should be improved monotonically - that is, the quality of the solution at time $t+1$ should be no worse than the quality at time t, i.e., $fitness(t+1) \leq fitness(t)$ for minimum problems (Cheng, Shi, & Qin, *et al.*, 2013; Ficici, 2005).

The capacity developing ability of FWA means that FWA could dynamically change its search ability on different problems. This ability is shown on the parameters adaptation in new solution generation. In fireworks algorithm, the parameters to control the number and range of new solutions are adaptively determined by the fitness of fireworks. The capability learning ability of FWA means that the obtained solutions are getting better and better iteratively.

In this chapter, the fireworks algorithms for solving problems with the optima shifts in the decision space and/or objective space are analyzed. This chapter is organized as follows: Section 2 reviews the basic fireworks algorithm. Section 3 introduces and analyzes four kinds of mapping strategies. Section 4 defines two kinds of population diversities in fireworks and sparks, respectively. Experiments are conducted in Section 5 followed by the discussion on the firework diversity and spark diversity changing curves in Section 6. Finally, Section 7 concludes with some remarks and future research directions.

2. FIREWORKS ALGORITHM

Fireworks algorithm (FWA) is a swarm intelligence optimization method that mimics the explosion process of fireworks (Tan, & Zhu, 2010; Tan, Yu, & Zheng, *et al.*, 2013; Tan, 2015; Zheng, Janecek, & Tan, 2013). The basic framework of fireworks algorithm is given in Figure 1 (Tan, 2015). The procedure of fireworks algorithm is given in Algorithm 1. There are four operators/strategies in FWA, which are explosion operator, mutation operator, mapping strategy, and selection strategy, respectively.

Algorithm 1. The Procedure of Fireworks Algorithm

```
1.  Initialize n locations;
2.  While have not found "good enough" solution or not reached the pre-deter-
mined maximum number of iterations do
3.      Set off fireworks at n locations;
4.      Generate sparks through explosion operator;
5.      Generate sparks through mutation operator;
6.      Obtain the locations of sparks;
7.      Map the locations into feasible search space;
8.      Evaluate the quality of the locations;
9.      Select n locations as new fireworks;
```

Figure 1. The framework of fireworks algorithm

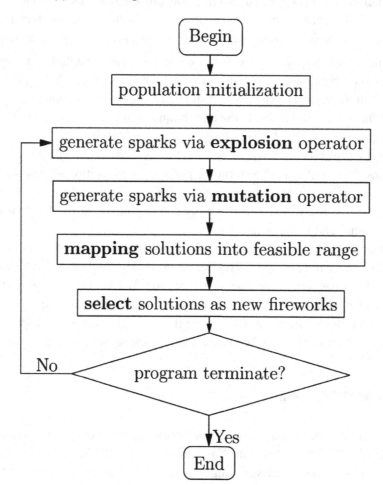

2.1 Explosion Operator

In explosion operator, the number of sparks and amplitude of explosion are calculated for each firework.

2.1.1 Number of Sparks

Based on the concept that more sparks should be generated from a firework with good fitness value, the number of sparks generated by firework i is defined as follows:

$$s_i = m \times \frac{y_{\max} - f(\mathbf{x}_i) + \varepsilon}{\sum_{i=1}^{n} (y_{\max} - f(\mathbf{x}_i)) + \varepsilon} \tag{1}$$

where m is a parameter that controlling the total number of sparks generated by the n fireworks, $y_{\max}$ is the maximum (worst for minimum problem) fitness value among the n fireworks, $y_{\max} = \max(f(\mathbf{x}_i))$, $i = 1,2,\ldots,n$, and ε, which is a tiny constant number, is utilized to avoid zero-division-error.

To keep the population diversity of fireworks, sparks should be generated from all fireworks. To avoid that many sparks are generated from one firework, the greatest lower bound $a{\cdot}m$ and the least upper bound $b{\cdot}m$ are set to sparks number s_i (Tan, & Zhu, 2010; Tan, 2015):

$$\hat{s}_i = \begin{cases} \text{round}(a \cdot m) & \text{if } s_i < a \cdot m \\ \text{round}(b \cdot m) & \text{if } s_i > b \cdot m \\ \text{round}(s_i) & \text{otherwise.} \end{cases} \tag{2}$$

where a and b are constant parameters, and $a < b < 1$.

2.1.2 Amplitude of Explosion

For a firework with good fitness value, the sparks are generated close to the firework. This could enhance the exploitation ability of the algorithm. While for a firework with a bad fitness value, the sparks are generated far from the firework. This is aimed to enhance the exploration ability of algorithm.

$$A_i = \hat{A} \times \frac{f(\mathbf{x}_i) - y_{\min} + \varepsilon}{\sum_{i=1}^{n}(f(\mathbf{x}_i) - y_{\min}) + \varepsilon} \tag{3}$$

where $\hat{A}$ is the maximum explosion amplitude, and $y_{\min}$ is the minimum (best for minimum problem) fitness value among the n fireworks, $y_{\min} = \min(f(\mathbf{x}_i))$, $i = 1,2,\ldots,n$.

2.2 Mutation Operator

The Gaussian mutation is utilized to generate new sparks from a firework. For a firework i, randomly select z dimensions,

$$x_i^k = x_i^k \times \mathcal{N}(1,1), \forall k \in z \tag{4}$$

The Gaussian operator could help solutions "jumping out" of the local optima.

2.3 Mapping Strategy

In the explosion operator and mutation operator, a new solution may be generated out of search space. Then the mapping strategy is utilized to set the solution into the feasible search range. The mapping by modular arithmetic is used in the original fireworks algorithm (Tan, & Zhu, 2010). The mapping equation is shown in equation (5).

$$x_i^k = x^k_{\min} + | x_i^k | \text{mod}(x^k_{\max} - x^k_{\min}) \quad (5)$$

The solution could be reset to the feasible search range via this strategy.

2.4 Selection Strategy

At the beginning of each explosion generation, n locations are selected for the fireworks explosion. The current best location $\mathbf{x}^*$, corresponding to the objective value $f(\mathbf{x}^*)$ that is best among current locations, is always kept for the next explosion generation. The other $n-1$ locations are selected based on the distance among a solution and other solutions. The distance between a solution $\mathbf{x}_i$ and other solutions is defined in Eq. (6):

$$R(\mathbf{x}_i) = \sum_{j \in K} d(x_x, x_j) = \sum_{j \in K} \left\| x_x, x_j \right\| \quad (6)$$

The selection probability of a location x_i is defined as follows:

$$p(x_i) = \frac{R(x_i)}{\sum_{j \in K} R(x_j)} \quad (7)$$

3. MAPPING STRATEGIES IN FIREWORKS ALGORITHM

3.1 Mapping by Modular Arithmetic

The mapping by modular arithmetic is used in the original fireworks algorithm (Tan, & Zhu, 2010). The solution could be reset to the feasible search range via this strategy. However, in most cases, the distance between a solution, which exceeds the feasible search space, and the search boundary is very close. In other words, the value of $| x_i^k - x^k_{\max} |$ for x_i^k is larger than $x^k_{\max}$, or $| x^k_{\min} - x_i^k |$ for x_i^k is smaller than $x^k_{\min}$, is very tiny when solution x_i^k exceeds the feasible search space.

Moreover, for most optimization problems, the search space is symmetrical, i.e., $-x^k_{\min} = x^k_{\max}$, and the center of search range is 0. We define that $x^k_{\max} = -x^k_{\min} = x^k_{\text{half}}$, and the distance between solution and boundary is Δx_i^k, $0 < \Delta x_i^k < x_{half}^k$. Then we have solution $x_{i,up}^k = x_{max}^k + \Delta x_i^k = x_{half}^k + \Delta x_i^k$ for $x_{i,up}^k$ exceeding the upper bound x_{max}^k, and solution $x_{i,low}^k = x_{min}^k - \Delta x_i^k = -x_{half}^k - \Delta x_i^k$ for $x_{i,low}^k$ exceeding the lower bound x_{min}^k. For the first case, $x_{i,up}^k = x_{half}^k + \Delta x_i^k$, then

$$x_{i,up}^k = x_{min}^k + | x_i^k | \mod (x_{max}^k - x_{min}^k)$$

$$= -x_{half}^k + | x_{half}^k + \Delta x_i^k | \mod 2x_{half}^k$$

$$= -x_{half}^k + x_{half}^k + \Delta x_i^k$$

$$= \Delta x_i^k$$

For the second case, $x_{i,low}^k = -x_{half}^k - \Delta x_i^k$, then

$$x_{i,low}^k = x_{min}^k + | x_i^k | \mod (x_{max}^k - x_{min}^k)$$

$$= -x_{half}^k + | -x_{half}^k - \Delta x_i^k | \mod 2x_{half}^k$$

$$= -x_{half}^k + x_{half}^k + \Delta x_i^k$$

$$= \Delta x_i^k$$

From the analysis, mapping by modular arithmetic strategy always set the solution to a position value Δx_i^k when the distance Δx_i^k is less than half of the search range x_{half}^k. The closer to 0 the Δx_i^k is, the closer the solution will be reset to the center of the search range.

For problem with symmetrical search space, $| x_i^k |$ is less than $x_{max}^k - x_{min}^k$ when $\Delta x_i^k < x_{half}^k$. The result of $| x_i^k | \mod (x_{max}^k - x_{min}^k)$ is $| x_i^k |$. This conclusion is not accurate for problems with asymmetrical search space. The value of $| x_i^k |$ may be larger than $x_{max}^k - x_{min}^k$ even $\Delta x_i^k < x_{half}^k$. The result of $| x_i^k | \mod (x_{max}^k - x_{min}^k)$ is affected by the initialized value of x_{max}^k or x_{min}^k.

The problems with asymmetrical search space are rare in the standard benchmark functions; and it can be shifted to problems with symmetrical search space by adding or subtracting a certain value. For the problems with asymmetrical search space, it is difficult to analyze the result of mapping by modular arithmetic strategy. The sign of x_{max}^k, and x_{min}^k, and the relation between x_{max}^k, x_{min}^k and x_{half}^k should be considered in the investigation. For example, the $\Delta x_i^k = 2$, in the following three scenarios:

1. for $x_{max}^k = 40$, $x_{min}^k = 0$,

$x_i^k = 0 + |-2| \mod (40 - 0) = 2$

The new solution x_i^k is close to the lower bound x_{min}^k.

2. for $x_{max}^k = 30$, $x_{min}^k = -10$,

$x_i^k = -10 + |-12| \mod (30 - (-10)) = 2$

The new solution x_i^k is in the lower range of search space.

3. for $x_{max}^k = 120$, $x_{min}^k = 80$,

$x_i^k = 80 + |78| \mod (120 - 80) = 118$

The new solution x_i^k is in the upper range of search space, and it is close to the upper bound x_{max}^k.

To overwhelm the implicit guiding to the center of the search space, random mapping in the whole search range is proposed to replace mapping by modular arithmetic strategy in Zheng, Janecek, & Tan (2013). The equation of random mapping in the whole search range is given in equation (8)

$$x_i^k = x_{min}^k + r_1 \times (x_{max}^k - x_{min}^k) \tag{8}$$

where r_1 is an uniformly distributed random numbers in the range $[0,1)$. This strategy could avoid implicit guiding to the center; however, the search tendency is also abandoned.

3.2 Mapping to the Boundary

The conventional boundary handling methods try to keep the solutions inside the feasible search space S. Search information is obtained only when solutions stay in the search space. If a solution exceeds the boundary limit in one dimension at one iteration, that search information will be abandoned. Instead, a new solution will replace the previous solution in that dimension. The classic strategy is to set the solution at boundary when it exceeds the boundary (Zhang, Xie, & Bi, 2004). The equation of this strategy is as follows:

$$x_i^k = \begin{cases} x_{min}^k & x_i^k < x_{min}^k \\ x_{max}^k & x_i^k > x_{max}^k \\ x_i^k & \text{otherwise.} \end{cases} \tag{9}$$

This strategy resets solutions in a particular point—the boundary, which constrains solutions to stay in the search space limited by boundary.

3.3 Mapping to Stochastic Region

The stochastic strategy can also be used to reset the solutions into feasible range when solutions exceed the search boundary (Cheng, 2013; Cheng, Shi, & Qin, 2011; Eberhart, & Shi, 2007). The equation is shown in equation (10),

$$x_i^k = \begin{cases} x_{\min}^k + r_1 \times \frac{1}{2}(x_{\max}^k - x_{\min}^k) & x_i^k < x_{\min}^k \\ x_{\max}^k - r_2 \times \frac{1}{2}(x_{\max}^k - x_{\min}^k) & x_i^k > x_{\max}^k \\ x_i^k & \text{otherwise.} \end{cases} \tag{10}$$

where r_1 and r_2 are two uniformly distributed random numbers in the range $[0,1)$. The $\frac{1}{2}(x_{\max}^k - x_{\min}^k) = x_{\text{half}}^k$ is half of the search range on dimension k. By this strategy, solutions will be reset within the half search space when solutions exceed the boundary limit. This will increases the algorithm's exploration, that is, solutions have higher possibilities to explore new search areas. However, it decreases the algorithm's ability of exploitation at the same time.

3.4 Mapping to Limited Stochastic Region

A solution exceeding the boundary may mean that the global or local optimum may be close to the boundary region. An algorithm should spend more iterations in this region. With the consideration of keeping the ability of exploitation, the resetting scope should be taken into account. The equation of resetting solution into a special area is as follows:

$$x_i^k = \begin{cases} x_{\min}^k + r_1 \times c \times \frac{1}{2}(x_{\max}^k - x_{\min}^k) & x_i^k < x_{\min}^k \\ x_{\max}^k - r_2 \times c \times \frac{1}{2}(x_{\max}^k - x_{\min}^k) & x_i^k > x_{\max}^k \\ x_i^k & \text{otherwise.} \end{cases} \tag{11}$$

where c is a parameter to control the resetting scope. When $c = 1$, this strategy is the same as the equations (10), that is, solutions are reset within a half space. On the contrary, when $c = 0$, this strategy is the same as the equation (9), i.e., it is the same as the classic strategy. The closer to 0 the c is, the more particles have a high possibility to be reset close to the boundary.

4. POPULATION DIVERSITY

In a fireworks optimization algorithm, the population diversity should be measured on the two groups of individuals at the same time. The first group is the population of fireworks, which contains n individuals. The second group is the population of sparks, which contains m individuals.

4.1 Population Diversity in Fireworks

The fireworks are the "seeds" of new solutions. Population diversity in fireworks, or firework diversity, is a measurement of fireworks' distribution. The definition of the firework diversity, which is dimension-wise and based on the L_1 norm, is given below.

$$\overline{x}^k = \frac{1}{n}\sum_{i=1}^{n} x_i^k$$

$$\text{div}^k = \frac{1}{n}\sum_{i=1}^{n} |x_i^k - \overline{x}^k|$$

$$\text{div}_f = \sum_{k=1}^{D} w^k \text{Div}^k$$

where $\overline{x}^k$ represents the pivot of fireworks in dimension k, and Div^k measures firework diversity for dimension k. Then we define $\overline{\mathbf{x}} = [\overline{x}^1, \ldots, \overline{x}^k, \ldots, \overline{x}^D]$, $\overline{\mathbf{x}}$ represents the mean of current fireworks on each dimension, and $\mathbf{div} = [\text{div}^1, \ldots, \text{div}^k, \ldots, \text{div}^D]$, which measures firework diversity for each dimension. w^k is a weight for dimension k. div_f measures the whole firework group's population diversity.

4.2 Population Diversity in Sparks

The sparks are generated via the operations on the fireworks. The distribution of sparks shows the algorithm's exploration or exploitation ability. The definition of the spark diversity is as follows:

$$\overline{x}^k = \frac{1}{m}\sum_{i=1}^{m} x_i^k$$

$$\text{div}^k = \frac{1}{m}\sum_{i=1}^{m} |x_i^k - \overline{x}^k|$$

$$\mathrm{div}_s = \sum_{k=1}^{D} w^k \mathrm{Div}^k$$

where $\overline{x}^k$ represents the pivot of sparks in dimension k, and div^k measures spark diversity for dimension k. Then we define $\overline{\mathbf{x}} = [\overline{x}^1,\ldots,\overline{x}^k,\ldots,\overline{x}^D]$, $\overline{\mathbf{x}}$ represents the mean of current sparks on each dimension, and $\mathbf{div} = [\mathrm{div}^1,\ldots,\mathrm{div}^k,\ldots,\mathrm{div}^D]$, which measures spark diversity for each dimension. div_s measures the whole spark group's population diversity.

Without loss of generality, every dimension is considered equally. Setting all weights $w^k = \frac{1}{D}$, then the dimension-wise population diversity in fireworks and sparks can be rewritten as:

$$\mathrm{div} = \sum_{k=1}^{D} \frac{1}{D} \mathrm{div}^k = \frac{1}{D} \sum_{k=1}^{D} \mathrm{div}^k$$

5. EXPERIMENTAL STUDY

5.1 Benchmark Functions

The experiments have been conducted to test the fireworks algorithm with different mapping strategies on the benchmark functions listed in Table 1. Considering the generality, twelve standard benchmark functions are selected, which include six unimodal functions and six multimodal functions (Liang, Qin, & Suganthan, *et al.*, 2006; Yao, Liu, & Lin, 1999). All functions are run 50 times to ensure a reasonable statistical result. There are 5000 iterations for 100 dimensional problems, and 20000 iterations for 200 in every run. For problems with the shifted search space, randomly shifting of the location of optimum is utilized in each dimension for every run.

In all experiments, the parameters of fireworks algorithm are set as follows: $n = 5$, $m = 50$, $a = 0.04$, $b = 0.8$, $\hat{A} = 40$, and $\hat{m} = 5$ (Tan, & Zhu, 2010).

5.2 Experimental Results on 100 Dimensional Problems

Several performance measurements are utilized in the experiments below. The best, median, worst, and mean fitness values are attained after a fixed number of iterations. Standard deviation values of the best fitness values are also utilized, which gives the solution's distribution. These values give a measurement of goodness of the algorithm.

Table 1. The benchmark functions used in experimental study, where D is the dimension of each problem, $\mathbf{z} = (\mathbf{x} - \mathbf{o})$, $\mathbf{x} = [x_1, x_2, ..., x_D]$, o_i is an randomly generated number in problem's search space S and it is different in each dimension, global optimum $\mathbf{x}^* = \mathbf{o}$, $f_{\min}$ is the minimum value of the function, and $S \subseteq \mathcal{R}^D$.

Name	Function	S	$f_{\min}$
Parabolic	$f_0(\mathbf{x}) = \sum_{i=1}^{D} z_i^2 + \text{bias}_0$	$[-100, 100]^D$	-450.0
Schwefel's P2.22	$f_1(\mathbf{x}) = \sum_{i=1}^{D} \lvert z_i \rvert + \prod_{i=1}^{D} \lvert z_i \rvert + \text{bias}_1$	$[-10, 10]^D$	-330.0
Schwefel's P1.2	$f_2(\mathbf{x}) = \sum_{i=1}^{D} (\sum_{k=1}^{i} z_k)^2 + \text{bias}_2$	$[-100, 100]^D$	450.0
Step	$f_3(\mathbf{x}) = \sum_{i=1}^{D} (\lfloor z_i + 0.5 \rfloor)^2 + \text{bias}_3$	$[-100, 100]^D$	330.0
Quartic Noise	$f_4(\mathbf{x}) = \sum_{i=1}^{D} i z_i^4 + \text{random}[0, 1) + \text{bias}_4$	$[-1.28, 1.28]^D$	-450.0
Zakharov	$f_5(\mathbf{x}) = \sum_{i=1}^{D} x_i^2 + \left(\sum_{i=1}^{D} 0.5 i x_i \right)^2 + \left(\sum_{i=1}^{D} 0.5 i x_i \right)^4 + \text{bias}_5$	$[-100, 100]^D$	120.0
Rosenbrock	$f_6(\mathbf{x}) = \sum_{i=1}^{D-1} [100(z_{i+1} - z_i^2)^2 + (z_i - 1)^2] + \text{bias}_6$	$[-10, 10]^D$	180.0
Rastrigin	$f_7(\mathbf{x}) = \sum_{i=1}^{D} [z_i^2 - 10\cos(2\pi z_i) + 10] + \text{bias}_7$	$[-5.12, 5.12]^D$	-330.0
Noncontinuous Rastrigin	$f_8(\mathbf{x}) = \sum_{i=1}^{D} [y_i^2 - 10\cos(2\pi y_i) + 10] + \text{bias}_8$ $y_i = \begin{cases} z_i & \lvert z_i \rvert < \frac{1}{2} \\ \frac{\text{round}(2z_i)}{2} & \lvert z_i \rvert \geq \frac{1}{2} \end{cases}$	$[-5.12, 5.12]^D$	450.0

continued on following page

Table 1. Continued

Name	Function	S	f_{min}
Ackley	$f_9(\mathbf{x}) = -20\exp\left(-0.2\sqrt{\frac{1}{D}\sum_{i=1}^{D} z_i^2}\right) - \exp\left(\frac{1}{D}\sum_{i=1}^{D}\cos(2\pi z_i)\right) + 20 + e + \text{bias}_9$	$[-32, 32]^D$	180.0
Griewank	$f_{10}(\mathbf{x}) = \frac{1}{4000}\sum_{i=1}^{D} z_i^2 - \prod_{i=1}^{D}\cos(\frac{z_i}{\sqrt{i}}) + 1 + \text{bias}_{10}$	$[-600, 600]^D$	120.0
Generalized Penalized	$f_{11}(\mathbf{x}) = \frac{\pi}{D}\{10\sin^2(\pi y_1) + \sum_{i=1}^{D-1}(y_i - 1)^2 \times [1 + 10\sin^2(\pi y_{i+1})] + (y_D - 1)^2\} + \sum_{i=1}^{D} u(z_i, 10, 100, 4) + \text{bias}_{11}$ $y_i = 1 + \frac{1}{4}(z_i + 1)$ $u(z_i, a, k, m) = \begin{cases} k(z_i - a)^m & z_i > a, \\ 0 & -a < z_i < a \\ k(-z_i - a)^m & z_i < -a \end{cases}$	$[-50, 50]^D$	330.0

5.2.1 Optima Shifted in Objective Space

In this experimental test, the fitness values of all functions are shifted, *i.e.*, the optima are shifted in the objective space. Except Rosenbrock f_6 which has the optimum 1 in each dimension, all optima for other optimized problems are zero, and in the center of each dimension. Tables II give results of fireworks algorithm with variants of mapping strategies on problems with 100 dimensions. Almost for all functions, exclude Zakharov f_5 and Rosenbrock f_6, a solution close to the global optima could be found. This indicates the good global search ability of FWA algorithm on unshifted problems or problems only shifted in objective space.

The function value of the best solution found by an algorithm in a run is denoted by $f(\mathbf{x}_{\text{best}})$. The error of this run is denoted as $error = f(\mathbf{x}_{\text{best}}) - f(\mathbf{x}^*)$. Figure 2 shows the mean error convergence curves of fireworks algorithm with variants of mapping strategies on problems with 100 dimensions. In the Figure 2, the optimal solutions of all problems are not shifted in the decision space, *i.e.*, the optimal solutions are in the original position.

Table 2. Results of fireworks algorithm solving unimodal and multimodal benchmark functions with 100 dimensions. All algorithms are run for 50 times, where "best", "median", "worst", and "mean" indicate the best, median, worst, and mean of the best fitness values for all runs, respectively.

Func.	f_{min}	Strategy	Best	Median	Worst	Mean	Std. Dev.
f_0	-450.0	module	-449.3444	-448.9598	-448.0658	-448.9147	0.277065
		boundary	-449.3933	-448.8824	-448.1283	-448.8809	0.269637
		half	**-449.4268**	-449.0027	-448.3215	**-448.9606**	0.222348
		limit	-449.3760	-448.9099	-448.1133	-448.8917	0.240857
f_1	-330.0	module	**-328.4559**	-324.0381	-322.4086	**-324.2528**	1.248930
		boundary	-326.6667	-324.1527	-320.7364	-324.2165	1.120473
		half	-326.8668	-324.2639	-321.2152	-324.2125	1.125782
		limit	-326.2929	-323.6833	-321.2341	-323.7082	1.081387
f_2	450.0	module	466.7780	546.6010	714.5826	**552.9967**	64.1812
		boundary	463.4458	575.6690	794.2512	578.5310	76.4414
		half	460.5627	538.5312	745.8827	555.7664	70.3049
		limit	**456.9129**	547.6564	874.6852	563.8786	82.8116
f_3	330.0	module	**330**	336	345	335.96	4.35871
		boundary	**330**	335	347	334.6	3.74699
		half	**330**	336	349	335.72	4.29902
		limit	**330**	334	343	**334.38**	3.34598
f_4	-450.0	module	-449.2060	-448.2023	-445.1228	-447.7778	0.982955
		boundary	**-449.9999**	-449.9049	-449.5053	**-449.8794**	0.106480
		half	-449.5537	-449.07995	-448.5039	-449.0770	0.203279
		limit	-449.9862	-449.8835	-449.7018	-449.8774	0.065388
f_5	120.0	module	154.4391	810.4756	2991.5770	951.9720	628.2422
		boundary	**148.8349**	790.9108	4181.2270	1018.600	719.174
		half	190.5590	756.5600	2577.424	**908.3718**	577.2972
		limit	162.5348	679.6599	4990.6583	945.4303	815.660
f_6	180.0	module	295.9601	323.2955	342.7281	323.6606	9.85196
		boundary	305.3805	325.0340	362.4316	325.9969	10.7647
		half	**203.5266**	322.2850	346.0957	318.8226	19.6244
		limit	243.9741	320.6150	348.5671	**318.8161**	15.2322
f_7	-330.0	module	-329.3937	-313.2504	-279.8374	**-311.3391**	12.6960
		boundary	-329.3313	-305.3798	-279.3557	-305.8558	12.8952
		half	-327.1825	-309.3691	-281.2410	-307.2591	12.8290
		limit	**-329.8486**	-312.1943	-279.7763	-310.4771	11.5374
f_8	450.0	module	456.4441	479.1351	511.2062	480.6478	12.7667
		boundary	**451.4516**	476.0076	500.5704	**475.8197**	13.2851
		half	457.5641	475.5994	514.1108	477.5237	12.2246
		limit	454.4522	478.2005	506.8727	478.0259	11.8877

continued on following page

Table 2. Continued

Func.	f_{min}	*Strategy*	*Best*	*Median*	*Worst*	*Mean*	*Std. Dev.*
f_9	180.0	module	180.3149	180.9512	182.1143	180.9825	0.398409
		boundary	180.3529	180.9668	182.0348	181.0494	0.437793
		half	180.2285	181.1495	182.3711	181.1747	0.531463
		limit	**180.0838**	180.9081	181.9618	**180.9706**	0.410570
f_{10}	120.0	module	120.0206	120.0358	120.1574	120.0411	0.022477
		boundary	120.0129	120.0374	120.0664	**120.0365**	0.013280
		half	120.0105	120.0356	120.1430	120.0372	0.019784
		limit	**120.0038**	120.0345	120.0955	120.0367	0.016191
f_{11}	330.0	module	330.0000	330.0000	330.0000	330.0000	2.784E-08
		boundary	330.0000	330.0000	330.0000	330.0000	5.460E-08
		half	330.0000	330.0000	330.0000	330.0000	4.942E-08
		limit	330.0000	330.0000	330.0000	330.0000	5.511E-08

5.2.2 Optima Shifted in Whole Decision Space

For each problem, both the optimal solution in decision space and fitness value in the objective space are shifted in this experimental test. All the optimal solutions are shifted at a random position in each dimension. The shifted range for new optimal solution is the whole decision space, *i.e.*, the new optimal solution $x_i^\star$ is a random value in the range $[x_i^{\text{lower}}, x_i^{\text{upper}}]$. The x_i^{lower} and x_i^{upper} are the lower and upper search bound for optimized problem at the ith dimension, respectively. Tables 3 give results of fireworks algorithm with variants of mapping strategies on problems with 100 dimensions. The optimal results found on problems with shift in decision space are significantly worse than the problems with original solutions. This indicates that the shift in decision space could affect the algorithm's search performance.

Figure 3 shows the convergence curves of fireworks algorithm with variants of mapping strategies on problems with 100 dimensions. In the Figure 3, the optimal solutions of all problems are shifted to random positions of the whole decision space.

5.2.3 Optima Shifted in Half Decision Space

To test the impact of different shifted ranges, the optimal solutions are shifted in the half search range. All the optimal solutions are shifted at a random position in each dimension. The shifted range for new optimal solution is the half decision space, *i.e.*, the new optimal solution $x_i^\star$ is a random value in the range $[x_i^{\text{lower}} + x_i^{\text{quarter}}, x_i^{\text{upper}} - x_i^{\text{quarter}}]$. The x_i^{lower} and x_i^{upper} are the lower and upper search bound for optimized problem at the ith dimension, respectively. The x_i^{quarter} is a quarter of search range in the i th dimension.

In this experiments, the optimal solutions are shifted away the original positions, but the shift range for each dimension is only half of search dimension. Tables 4 give results of fireworks algorithm with

Figure 2. The average performance of the fireworks algorithm solving unimodal and multimodal problems. The optima of each problem are only shifted in objective space; and the dimension of each problem is 100.

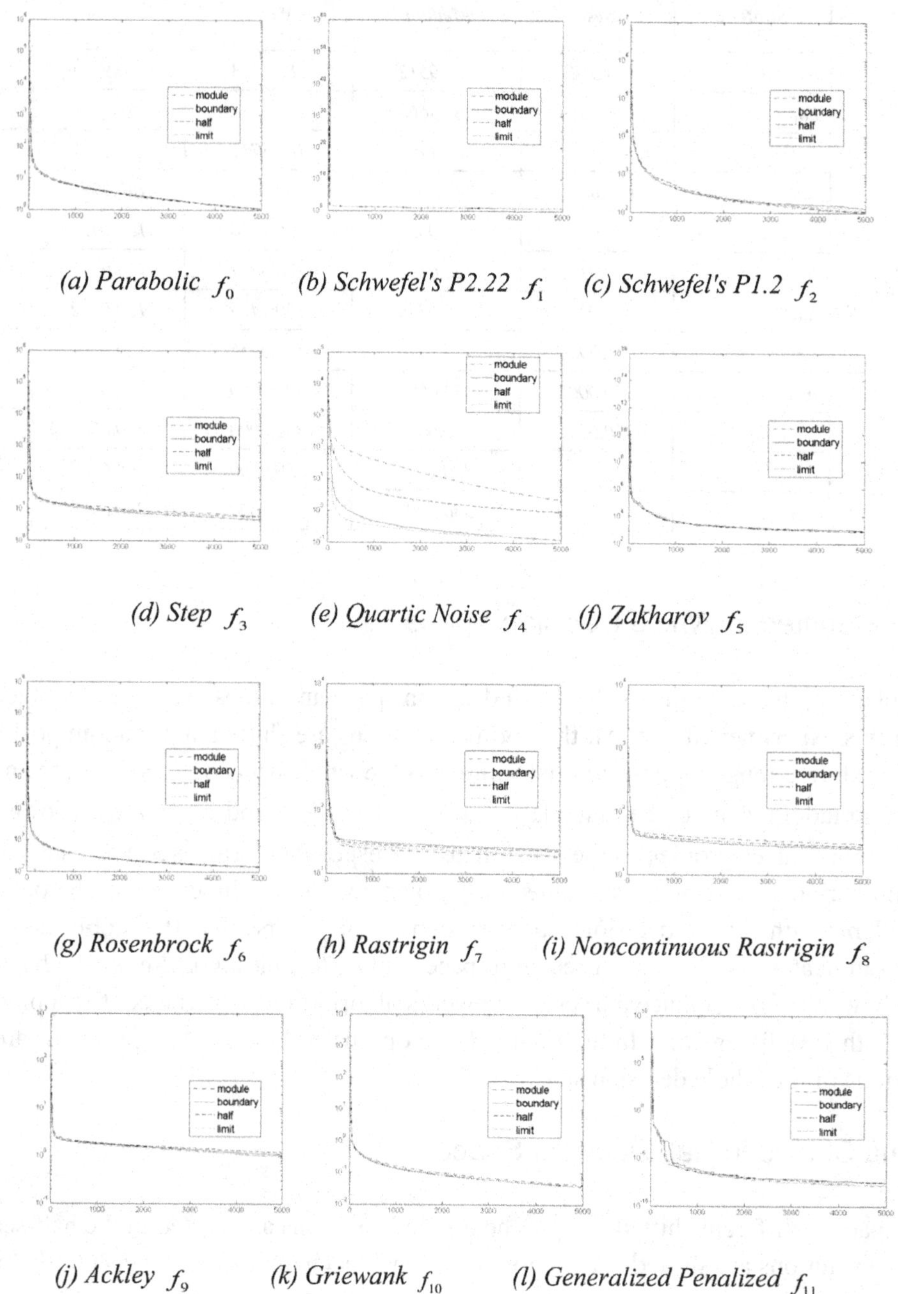

(a) Parabolic f_0 (b) Schwefel's P2.22 f_1 (c) Schwefel's P1.2 f_2

(d) Step f_3 (e) Quartic Noise f_4 (f) Zakharov f_5

(g) Rosenbrock f_6 (h) Rastrigin f_7 (i) Noncontinuous Rastrigin f_8

(j) Ackley f_9 (k) Griewank f_{10} (l) Generalized Penalized f_{11}

Table 3. Results of fireworks algorithm solving unimodal and multimodal benchmark functions with 100 dimensions. All algorithms are run for 50 times, where "best", "median", "worst", and "mean" indicate the best, median, worst, and mean of the best fitness values for all runs, respectively.

Func.	f_{min}	Strategy	Best	Median	Worst	Mean	Std. Dev.
f_0	-450.0	*module*	123.38703	443.5230	1024.782	471.1070	207.9864
		boundary	**-446.2835**	279.5694	645.2740	257.7740	195.3318
		half	15.00762	325.4885	740.7109	328.8860	154.7432
		limit	-27.8817	247.1299	626.7375	**238.2201**	157.8467
f_1	-330.0	*module*	-297.4991	-279.6044	-239.9893	-278.3370	12.97823
		boundary	**-328.0924**	-310.2071	-284.0640	**-309.9837**	9.525181
		half	-313.2956	-307.4991	-295.1823	-307.0945	3.801982
		limit	-319.1543	-309.5740	-281.7188	-307.7595	7.662498
f_2	450.0	*module*	190329.82	231705.97	310290.72	235824.79	26547.04
		boundary	**167252.70**	228470.79	290612.78	228660.62	27511.23
		half	178236.02	221880.83	275190.32	**223549.86**	22957.08
		limit	167518.92	227517.45	272639.00	227843.97	24968.41
f_3	330.0	*module*	1186	1717	2286	1714.72	286.861
		boundary	849	1118	1887	1141.56	211.747
		half	895	1467	3066	1508.5	347.288
		limit	**806**	1091	1509	**1108.88**	157.111
f_4	-450.0	*module*	-132.4733	-41.7221	516.0298	-21.7028	95.46532
		boundary	**-176.7556**	-170.7187	-162.4072	**-170.3907**	3.404519
		half	-143.7480	-110.7060	3.395777	-106.3327	25.8994
		limit	-170.9285	-150.3782	-112.2938	-150.4278	10.6696
f_5	120.0	*module*	**233004.90**	281065.51	303928.92	278050.29	13639.96
		boundary	236792.74	278681.803	307744.19	278568.44	12960.83
		half	243372.02	280375.01	306615.69	278327.38	12064.30
		limit	234127.21	281461.05	304418.64	**277011.29**	14991.12
f_6	180.0	*module*	4944.945	6932.558	14801.02	7923.657	2561.422
		boundary	**1877.569**	3057.027	7633.572	**3433.112**	1279.323
		half	3172.771	5496.0507	13117.97	6138.764	2313.946
		limit	2605.176	3963.499	7196.590	4036.601	1124.613
f_7	-330.0	*module*	-178.2166	-125.5192	-68.2343	-121.5790	24.4702
		boundary	-175.1720	-129.2962	-95.6616	-131.1400	19.2129
		half	-184.2904	-126.8511	-71.6192	-129.8883	23.9738
		limit	**-187.1445**	-132.5406	-82.3374	**-133.4027**	20.7342
f_8	450.0	*module*	595.4057	643.4495	702.5768	642.4688	20.6502
		boundary	601.8870	636.1157	699.7248	633.6486	20.2862
		half	590.4379	634.3766	694.2829	633.9112	24.9922
		limit	**567.0588**	622.7443	710.5508	**627.0450**	30.0756

continued on following page

Table 3. Continued

Func.	f_{min}	Strategy	Best	Median	Worst	Mean	Std. Dev.
f_9	180.0	*module*	*186.2686*	*187.7935*	*190.8406*	*187.9336*	*0.943194*
		boundary	*185.0179*	*185.8210*	*186.9406*	***185.8798***	*0.444148*
		half	*185.7822*	*187.1204*	*188.7718*	*187.1224*	*0.712018*
		limit	***184.8649***	*185.9802*	*187.4313*	*186.0757*	*0.522148*
f_{10}	120.0	*module*	*126.8078*	*130.9325*	*137.7229*	*131.6190*	*2.623525*
		boundary	***124.4869***	*126.9145*	*132.5153*	*127.1530*	*1.688852*
		half	*125.6894*	*130.0155*	*134.8119*	*129.9716*	*2.033134*
		limit	*124.5314*	*127.0915*	*131.5167*	***127.0913***	*1.574195*
f_{11}	330.0	*module*	*338.2957*	*344.8616*	*384.4356*	*346.0932*	*6.868677*
		boundary	*335.6560*	*339.3348*	*349.1999*	*339.3016*	*2.212450*
		half	*337.1561*	*341.4568*	*348.4833*	*341.4121*	*2.710028*
		limit	***334.8988***	*338.4259*	*344.13725*	***338.4819***	*2.049914*

variants of mapping strategies on problems with 100 dimensions. The optimal results found on problems with shift in small range are better than the problems with a large shifted range. This indicates that the shifted range in decision space could also affect the algorithm's search performance. In general, the larger the shifted range is in the decision space, the harder the optimized problem is.

Figure 4 shows the convergence curves of fireworks algorithm with variants of mapping strategies on problems with 100 dimensions. In the Figure 4, the optimal solutions of all problems are shifted to random positions, which is in a half search range of each dimension.

5.3 Experimental Results on 200 Dimensional Problems

5.3.1 Optima Shifted in Objective Space

The dimension of each problem is increased to 200 in this experiment. The best fitness value of each problem is shifted in the objective space. Tables 5 give results of fireworks algorithm with variants of mapping strategies on problems with 200 dimensions. Similar to the results on the problems with 100 dimensions, almost for all functions, exclude Zakharov f_5 and Rosenbrock f_6, a solution close to the global optima could be found.

Figure 5 shows the convergence curves of fireworks algorithm with variants of mapping strategies on problems with 200 dimensions. In the Figure 5, the optimal solutions of all problems are not shifted in the decision space.

Figure 3. The average performance of the fireworks algorithm solving unimodal and multimodal problems. The optima of each problem are shifted in both decision and objective space; and the dimension of each problem is 100.

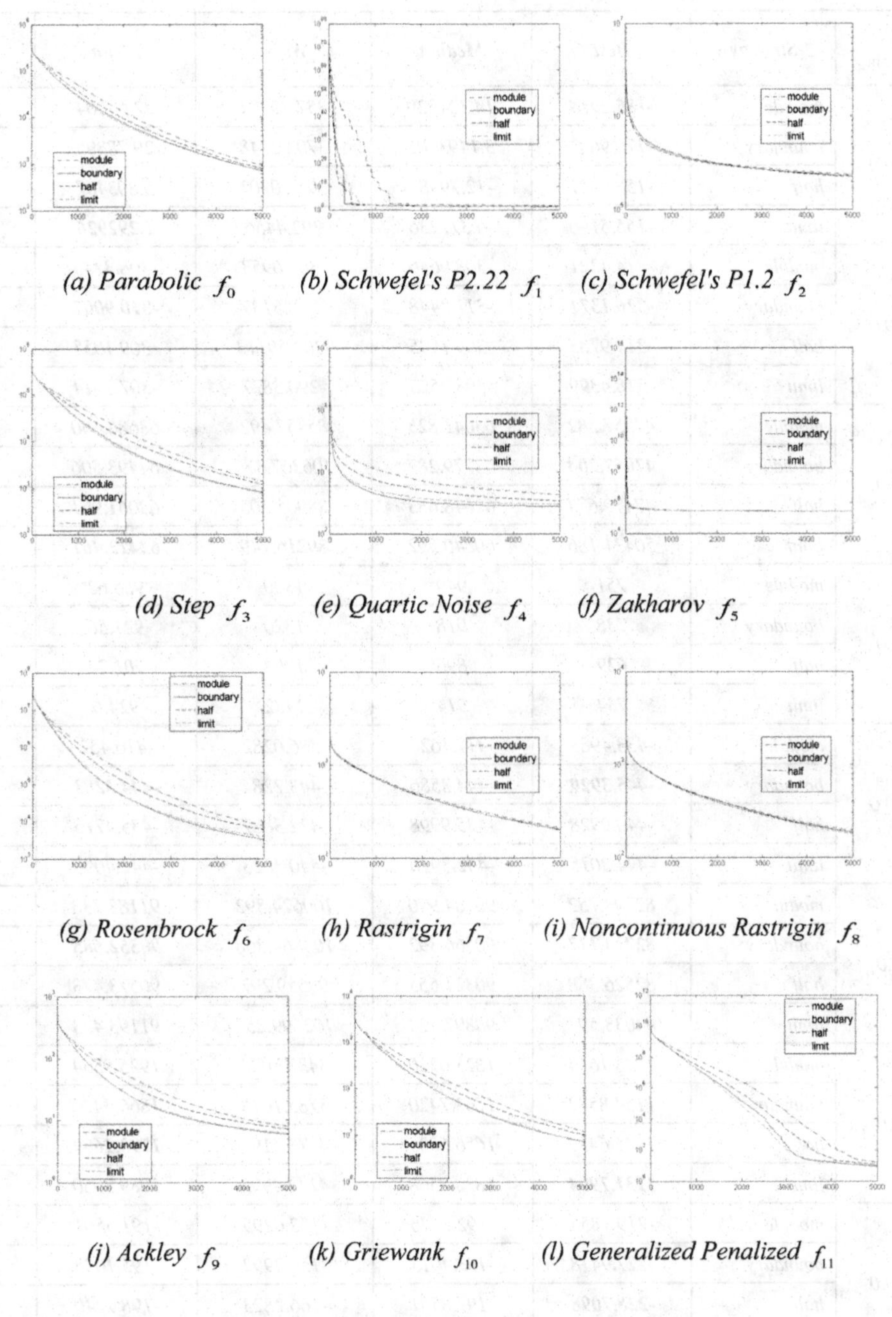

(a) Parabolic f_0 *(b) Schwefel's P2.22* f_1 *(c) Schwefel's P1.2* f_2

(d) Step f_3 *(e) Quartic Noise* f_4 *(f) Zakharov* f_5

(g) Rosenbrock f_6 *(h) Rastrigin* f_7 *(i) Noncontinuous Rastrigin* f_8

(j) Ackley f_9 *(k) Griewank* f_{10} *(l) Generalized Penalized* f_{11}

Table 4. Results of fireworks algorithm solving unimodal and multimodal benchmark functions with 100 dimensions. All algorithms are run for 50 times, where "best", "median", "worst", and "mean" indicate the best, median, worst, and mean of the best fitness values for all runs, respectively.

Func.	f_{min}	Strategy	Best	Median	Worst	Mean	Std. Dev.
f_0	-450.0	module	**-185.2914**	14.124529	357.49391	22.65004	112.39337
		boundary	-170.9602	3.1493202	370.92748	29.78895	120.7512
		half	-158.6821	-12.79981	397.20201	6.803467	106.20981
		limit	-155.5196	-6.377236	292.4456	**1.292926**	103.8833
f_1	-330.0	module	-314.4221	-308.9646	-301.6953	-308.3745	2.783527
		boundary	**-326.1371**	-311.2448	-298.5137	**-310.9007**	5.826472
		half	-314.9783	-309.1535	-302.59113	-309.1055	3.336730
		limit	-318.4399	-308.2525	-290.3827	-307.7114	5.4887411
f_2	450.0	module	47557.582	63642.825	85357.492	63686.660	8761.1986
		boundary	**47057.204**	63779.287	106367.379	64493.506	10147.306
		half	47479.674	62648.683	88905.105	63061.961	8241.791
		limit	50431.186	60840.592	89216.749	**62422.461**	8719.6751
f_3	330.0	module	751	949	1300	965.62	139.2567
		boundary	738	918	1320	921.56	109.4660
		half	**629**	896	1293	**901.24**	117.3573
		limit	734	914	1132	924.6	100.3035
f_4	-450.0	module	-433.4983	-417.1620	-386.0282	-416.452	11.51628
		boundary	**-445.3929**	-444.3586	-443.2284	**-444.3283**	0.537208
		half	-440.9928	-435.9998	-422.3887	-435.4715	3.449639
		limit	-444.3015	-442.3910	-440.3623	-442.4090	0.758719
f_5	120.0	module	82793.752	90584.970	100624.392	91183.738	4211.676
		boundary	**82713.117**	90566.392	103864.368	**90552.685**	4347.262
		half	82826.388	90321.555	99659.297	90573.473	3713.694
		limit	84033.593	90897.924	102699.253	91193.423	4259.793
f_6	180.0	module	1248.1614	1823.0720	3437.7023	1925.9554	527.1532
		boundary	1154.8582	1762.7420	3785.1613	1866.3426	558.5631
		half	1141.6439	1656.6525	4073.5192	**1793.1689**	540.0707
		limit	**1131.7994**	1830.8568	4144.4995	1989.3950	639.3603
f_7	-330.0	module	-219.1855	-192.3446	-152.0295	-191.5501	15.12473
		boundary	-227.9418	-193.4013	-156.2992	-195.1035	14.73017
		half	**-228.7098**	-197.8581	-166.2823	-198.7240	13.74228
		limit	-223.1445	-192.7464	-146.8072	-191.8345	14.74619
f_8	450.0	module	542.0665	564.9106	598.6952	**567.1226**	13.16895
		boundary	**542.0561**	573.9182	606.0742	574.0390	15.47853
		half	542.3951	568.8122	603.5879	568.1229	12.79338
		limit	544.1801	570.7855	604.5505	572.7924	16.63077

continued on following page

Table 4. Continued

Func.	f_{min}	Strategy	Best	Median	Worst	Mean	Std. Dev.
f_9	180.0	module	184.5027	185.2573	186.7207	**185.3615**	0.521935
		boundary	184.7380	185.4617	186.6033	185.5006	0.460228
		half	184.7292	185.4794	186.64792	185.4792	0.398503
		limit	**184.4612**	185.3615	186.5080	185.4033	0.435109
f_{10}	120.0	module	123.4223	125.0873	127.7308	125.2388	1.160101
		boundary	123.6241	124.8859	128.4585	**124.9565**	0.932499
		half	123.7914	124.8900	126.5411	124.9768	0.670491
		limit	**123.2259**	125.0623	127.1870	125.1186	0.739124
f_{11}	330.0	module	334.3172	337.1139	341.8405	337.2946	1.544227
		boundary	**334.2016**	336.9861	343.3512	337.2948	1.616435
		half	334.2971	337.1736	341.5528	337.1456	1.557392
		limit	335.2080	337.07096	342.2122	**337.1267**	1.314208

5.3.2 Optima Shifted in Decision Space

The optimal solutions in the decision space are shifted to random positions and the best fitness values are also shifted in the objective space. The shifted range in the decision space is the whole dimension. Tables 6 give results of fireworks algorithm with variants of mapping strategies on problems with 200 dimensions. All optimized results are significantly affected by the shift in the decision space. Even the function evaluation times are doubled in this experiment, the results obtained on the problems with 200 dimensions are worse than the problems with 100 dimensions under the same optimal solutions shift conditions.

Figure 6 shows the convergence curves of fireworks algorithm with variants of mapping strategies on problems with 200 dimensions. In the Figure 6, the optimal solutions of all problems are shifted to random positions of the whole decision space.

5.4 Experimental Results Discussion

From the experimental results on the problems with different dimensions, the problems with different shifted space (objective space and/or decision space), and the problem with different shifted search range (the whole dimension or the half dimension), several conclusions could be made as follows:

- The optima shift in objective space has tiny or no effect on the difficulty of the optimization problem. The fireworks algorithms could find the equivalent solutions on problems with or without optima shift in the objective space.
- The optimization problems are getting harder when the optima are shifted in the decision space, i.e., the optima are more difficult to obtain when the optima are different in each dimension and/or not located in the center of search space.

Figure 4. The average performance of the fireworks algorithm solving unimodal and multimodal problems. The optima of each problem are shifted in both decision and objective space; and the dimension of each problem is 100.

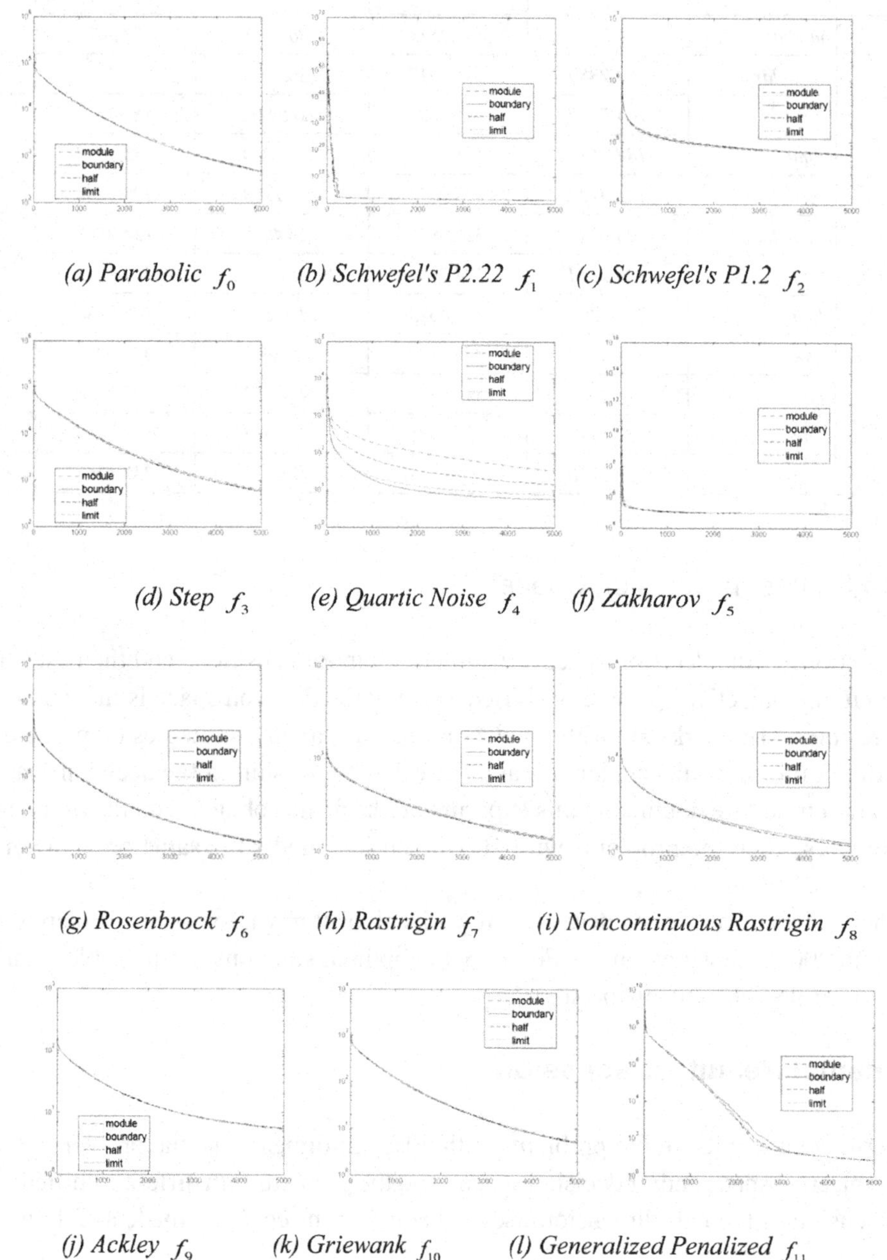

(a) Parabolic f_0 *(b) Schwefel's P2.22* f_1 *(c) Schwefel's P1.2* f_2

(d) Step f_3 *(e) Quartic Noise* f_4 *(f) Zakharov* f_5

(g) Rosenbrock f_6 *(h) Rastrigin* f_7 *(i) Noncontinuous Rastrigin* f_8

(j) Ackley f_9 *(k) Griewank* f_{10} *(l) Generalized Penalized* f_{11}

Table 5. Results of fireworks algorithm solving unimodal and multimodal benchmark functions with 200 dimensions. All algorithms are run for 50 times, where "best", "median", "worst", and "mean" indicate the best, median, worst, and mean of the best fitness values for all runs, respectively.

Func.	f_{min}	Strategy	Best	Median	Worst	Mean	Std. Dev.
f_0	-450.0	module	**-449.2836**	-447.9331	-447.2188	-447.9011	0.351210
		boundary	-448.5346	-448.0384	-447.0821	**-447.9858**	0.306007
		half	-448.7739	-447.9997	-447.1211	-447.9708	0.295745
		limit	-449.0540	-447.8710	-447.3707	-447.9279	0.331783
f_1	-330.0	module	**-327.3319**	-317.4173	-312.2510	-317.3661	2.563841
		boundary	-323.1203	-317.9470	-311.9309	**-318.1197**	2.165784
		half	-325.3018	-317.6230	-310.5166	-317.9416	2.884145
		limit	-321.8501	-317.1449	-311.0070	-317.2362	1.922750
f_2	450.0	module	**496.5504**	729.0643	1369.7020	**766.9991**	176.0479
		boundary	557.2692	796.3215	1311.5603	835.1774	176.7223
		half	518.0539	793.2134	2028.4127	842.6432	248.2963
		limit	531.0513	835.5607	1609.3941	843.3504	191.1417
f_3	330.0	module	**330**	338	354	339.88	7.146019
		boundary	**330**	338	366	340.94	8.331650
		half	**330**	338	359	**339.36**	7.024983
		limit	**330**	338	357	339.6	6.702238
f_4	-450.0	module	-447.4834	-442.8298	-370.4542	-437.4525	13.96694
		boundary	-449.9728	-449.5250	-448.4757	-449.4665	0.360087
		half	-448.4886	-447.5657	-446.2801	-447.5325	0.492155
		limit	**-449.9761**	-449.7147	-449.1239	**-449.6729**	0.180545
f_5	120.0	module	525.5551	2708.646	6734.9040	2722.429	1474.514
		boundary	338.8051	3055.294	14271.281	3566.716	2933.513
		half	**171.0216**	2378.5118	8330.3818	**2696.532**	1838.365
		limit	285.0780	2554.061	17667.789	3332.777	3026.411
f_6	180.0	module	436.1458	467.1124	493.9468	466.4139	15.05203
		boundary	433.7179	467.3060	501.9691	**465.5784**	14.18886
		half	**424.7823**	467.2277	495.5025	467.7276	13.68348
		limit	438.4786	469.0342	501.8399	469.0162	13.59741
f_7	-330.0	module	-326.8973	-289.4301	-222.7455	-283.8403	26.5466
		boundary	-328.1163	-288.2729	-206.3530	**-287.4119**	28.7910
		half	**-328.4341**	-289.5011	-203.8046	-287.0577	27.1837
		limit	-326.9404	-283.1533	-236.4542	-285.4177	24.7744
f_8	450.0	module	462.7835	504.1687	558.7536	505.8180	23.4710
		boundary	460.6350	501.0622	565.1147	501.9267	26.0457
		half	**460.2330**	495.4389	549.2493	**496.4361**	21.9924
		limit	462.9024	497.0098	557.4533	501.3018	25.0063

continued on following page

Table 5. Continued

Func.	f_{min}	Strategy	Best	Median	Worst	Mean	Std. Dev.
f_9	180.0	module	180.5112	181.0231	181.8271	181.0744	0.376529
		boundary	**180.3096**	180.9057	182.0348	181.0780	0.449329
		half	180.4998	180.9239	182.4185	181.0551	0.438899
		limit	180.4222	180.9975	181.5995	**180.9861**	0.337914
f_{10}	120.0	module	**120.0139**	120.0424	120.0638	120.0427	0.010187
		boundary	120.0155	120.0412	120.0665	120.0401	0.010327
		half	120.0152	120.0398	120.0607	**120.0400**	0.010177
		limit	120.0177	120.0419	120.0653	120.0413	0.010468
f_{11}	330.0	module	330	330.0000	330.0000	330.0000	2.757E-09
		boundary	330	330.0000	330.0000	330.0000	1.386E-09
		half	330	330.0000	330.0000	330.0000	2.938E-09
		limit	330	330.0000	330.0000	330.0000	1.615E-09

- The difficulty of shifted optimization problems are affected by the dimension of problems. The difficulty is significantly increased when the number of problems' dimensionality is increased. The performance of the algorithm on optima shift problems is getting worse when number of dimensions increases. For optima shifted problems with double number of dimensions (from 100 dimensions to 200 dimension), even doubled the number of iterations, the performance is not linearly improved.
- The difficulty of optimization problems is affected by the shift range in decision space. The problems are getting harder when the optima are shifted in large space. It is more difficult to obtain optima when the optima are shifted far away to the center of search space.

6. POPULATION DIVERSITY DISCUSSION

The population diversities measurements on the fireworks group and sparks group are given in Figures 7, 8, 9, and 10. The Figure 7 and Figure 8 are curves of population diversities changing for FWA solving unimodal problem f_2, while the Figure 9 and Figure 10 are curves of population diversities changing for FWA solving multimodal problem f_6. For problems f_2 and f_6, the firework diversity and spark diversity are vibrated during whole search process, and the firework diversity vibrated in a large range than the spark diversity. In all figures, there is no significant difference among FWA algorithms with different mapping strategies.

The population diversities are vibrated in the different search ranges. The range of firework diversity may be related to the setting of ε value. The range of spark diversity may be related to the step size of new solution generation.

Figure 5. The average performance of the fireworks algorithm solving unimodal and multimodal problems. The optima of each problem are only shifted in objective space; and the dimension of each problem is 200.

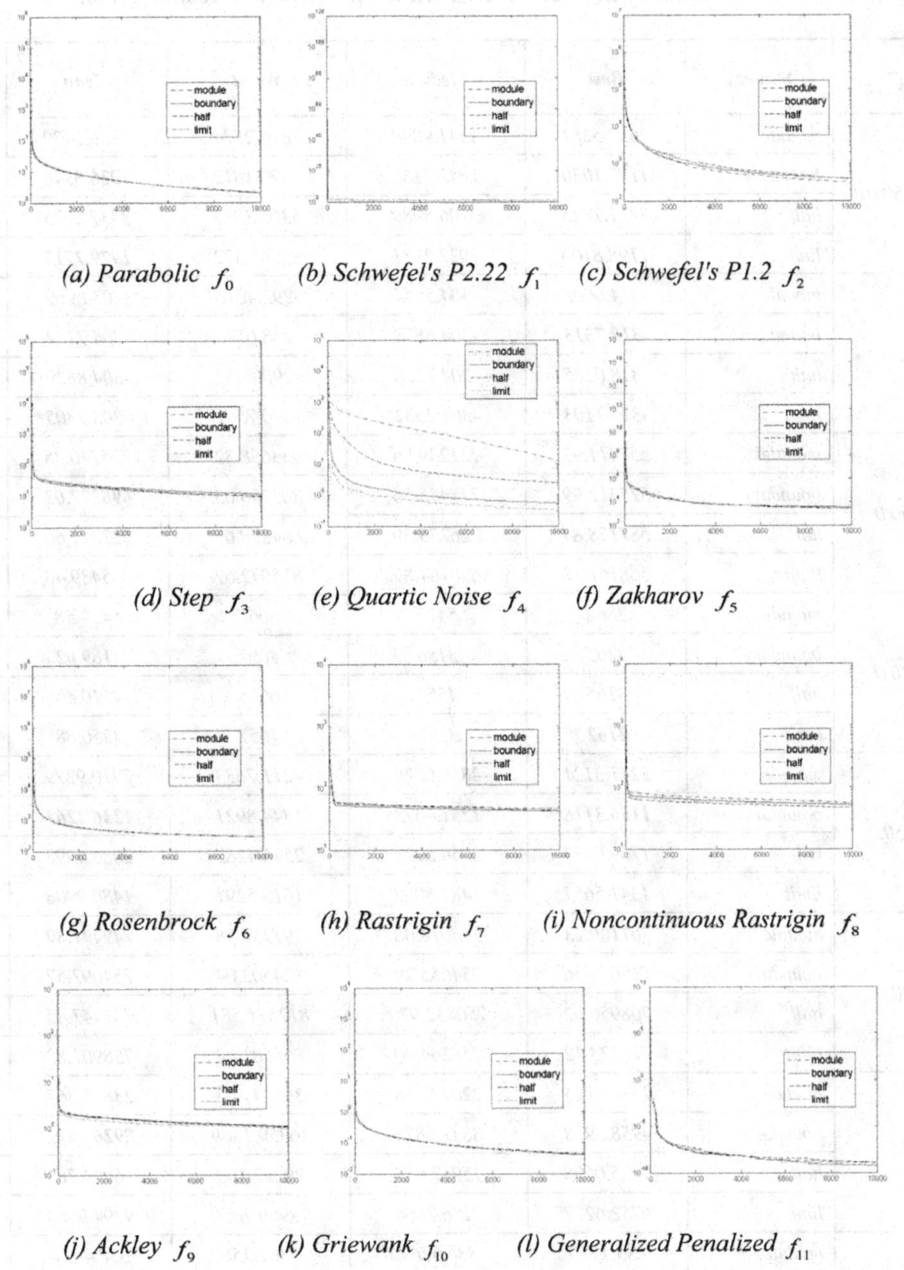

(a) Parabolic f_0 *(b) Schwefel's P2.22* f_1 *(c) Schwefel's P1.2* f_2

(d) Step f_3 *(e) Quartic Noise* f_4 *(f) Zakharov* f_5

(g) Rosenbrock f_6 *(h) Rastrigin* f_7 *(i) Noncontinuous Rastrigin* f_8

(j) Ackley f_9 *(k) Griewank* f_{10} *(l) Generalized Penalized* f_{11}

Table 6. Results of fireworks algorithm solving unimodal and multimodal benchmark functions with 200 dimensions. All algorithms are run for 50 times, where "best", "median", "worst", and "mean" indicate the best, median, worst, and mean of the best fitness values for all runs, respectively.

Func.	f_{min}	Strategy	Best	Median	Worst	Mean	Std. Dev.
f_0	-450.0	module	2633.5281	4541.9890	7896.2774	4736.1439	1068.09
		boundary	**1177.1030**	1842.7156	3370.1812	1926.8348	412.118
		half	2411.7845	3206.3989	5305.3913	3337.2975	653.833
		limit	1198.8100	1927.2931	3376.7372	**1979.7717**	441.416
f_1	-330.0	module	-314.6008	-304.5344	-292.4016	-303.8969	4.87418
		boundary	**-318.7313**	-304.6878	-288.6522	-304.7134	4.89172
		half	-318.0285	-304.7728	-290.8962	**-304.8829**	5.19988
		limit	-315.1103	-304.2532	-290.7561	-303.7305	4.68894
f_2	450.0	module	557411.97	721239.96	953638.32	725740.38	68419.2
		boundary	**525312.99**	714435.56	803750.03	**696277.02**	58846.4
		half	587178.84	726235.39	864398.05	722311.60	61986.5
		limit	568161.72	696164.80	855042.67	705439.46	63807.4
f_3	330.0	module	3868	5473	8067	5429.58	1027.13
		boundary	2205	3186	4097	**3189.02**	376.496
		half	3165	4552	6975	4510.46	782.330
		limit	**2162**	3293	4657	3250.88	416.908
f_4	-450.0	module	2241.3121	2839.0026	4211.7633	2910.9279	435.221
		boundary	**1156.3118**	1231.4673	1344.8921	**1236.2261**	35.7139
		half	1769.0354	2056.5928	2516.4782	2086.4998	89.8391
		limit	1341.5657	1481.8088	1615.5291	1480.9908	70.2946
f_5	120.0	module	**707100.23**	748014.08	797751.58	**749491.89**	19327.1
		boundary	717639.56	754655.29	824502.04	754097.57	22249.4
		half	708950.02	750832.970	812571.581	751447.45	8664.82
		limit	719123.12	758264.90	805581.84	758901.82	19770.6
f_6	180.0	module	15345.225	22013.788	39844.803	23815.367	6221.89
		boundary	**4958.8938**	8831.6828	16359.1349	**8926.5821**	1923.07
		half	9335.0608	15917.656	29292.100	16094.783	4194.44
		limit	6752.6277	9136.7606	13969.7060	9394.9959	1657.57
f_7	-330.0	module	233.7510	336.5764	436.6258	338.4481	50.2967
		boundary	176.9333	270.6839	378.2411	**274.6178**	49.7996
		half	205.1035	313.4778	424.9427	309.3778	55.1056
		limit	**153.9582**	298.8610	408.2567	292.5787	46.6232
f_8	450.0	module	953.2389	1062.5557	1193.8228	1070.1834	58.7348
		boundary	**896.6237**	1048.3495	1215.6763	**1051.9569**	57.2677
		half	955.6467	1050.5059	1170.9600	1055.7335	56.9554
		limit	939.6675	1071.7209	1213.1681	1060.4554	60.8931

continued on following page

Table 6. Continued

Func.	f_{min}	*Strategy*	*Best*	*Median*	*Worst*	*Mean*	*Std. Dev.*
f_9	180.0	module	189.3461	191.0274	193.5268	191.04263	0.97840
		boundary	**186.3560**	187.5791	188.8159	**187.6379**	0.54196
		half	187.7469	189.4291	190.8975	189.3868	0.69846
		limit	186.3658	187.76619	189.1711	187.7668	0.58992
f_{10}	120.0	module	164.0023	184.5372	212.4104	187.6732	11.8809
		boundary	136.4422	141.0826	149.9158	141.4925	3.10751
		half	147.7439	160.3801	180.6264	161.4745	7.38680
		limit	**136.3016**	142.3075	158.0976	142.4169	3.91170
f_{11}	330.0	module	369.0072	1310.812	26983.41	2975.131	4716.50
		boundary	**342.5246**	351.9261	366.2908	352.2404	5.25540
		half	351.9593	376.7778	1273.1508	440.3222	181.216
		limit	344.2784	351.0091	367.6420	**351.6486**	4.58822

7. CONCLUSION

The fireworks algorithms for solving problems with the optima shift in the decision space and/or objective space were analyzed in this chapter. The benchmark problems have several weaknesses in the original research of swarm intelligence algorithms for solving single objective problems. The optimum is in the center of search range, and is the same at each dimension of the search space. The optimum shift in decision space and/or objective space could increase the difficulty of problem solving.

The solutions are implicitly guided to the center of the search range for problems with symmetrical search range via mapping by modular arithmetic strategy. The optimization performance of fireworks algorithm on the shift functions may be affected by this strategy. Four kinds of mapping strategies, which include mapping by modular arithmetic, mapping to the boundary, mapping to stochastic region, and mapping to limited stochastic region, were compared on problems with different dimensions and different optimum shift range. From the experimental results, the fireworks algorithms with mapping to the boundary, or mapping to limited stochastic region had good performance on problems with the optimum shift. This is probably because the search tendency is kept in these two strategies.

The definitions of population diversities measurement were also proposed in this chapter, from observation on population diversity changes, the useful information of fireworks algorithm solving different kinds of problems could be obtained.

Figure 6. The average performance of the fireworks algorithm solving unimodal and multimodal problems. The optima of each problem are shifted in both decision and objective space; and the dimension of each problem is 200.

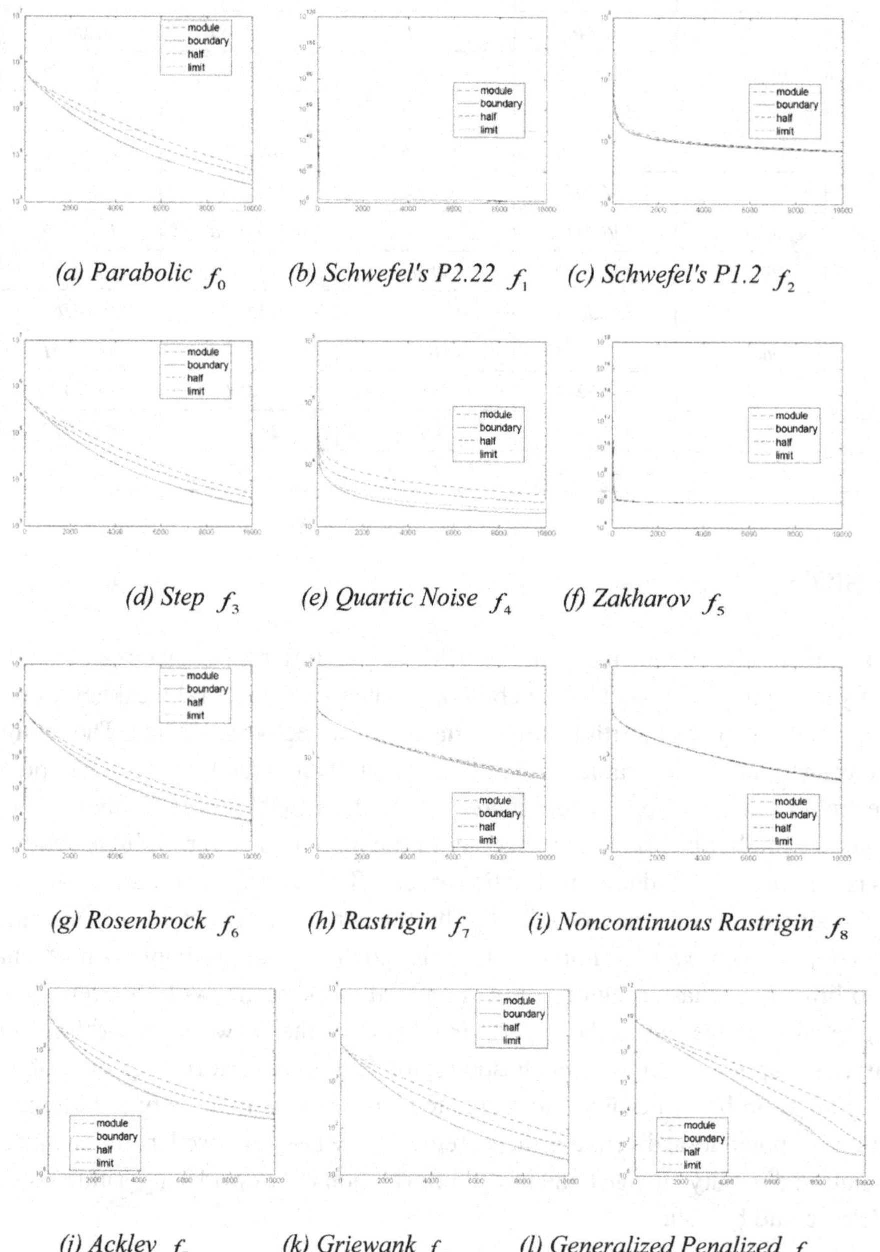

(a) Parabolic f_0 *(b) Schwefel's P2.22* f_1 *(c) Schwefel's P1.2* f_2

(d) Step f_3 *(e) Quartic Noise* f_4 *(f) Zakharov* f_5

(g) Rosenbrock f_6 *(h) Rastrigin* f_7 *(i) Noncontinuous Rastrigin* f_8

(j) Ackley f_9 *(k) Griewank* f_{10} *(l) Generalized Penalized* f_{11}

Figure 7. The population diversities of the fireworks algorithm solving shifted unimodal problem f_2. The fitness value of the problem is only shifted in objective space; and the dimension of the problem is 200.

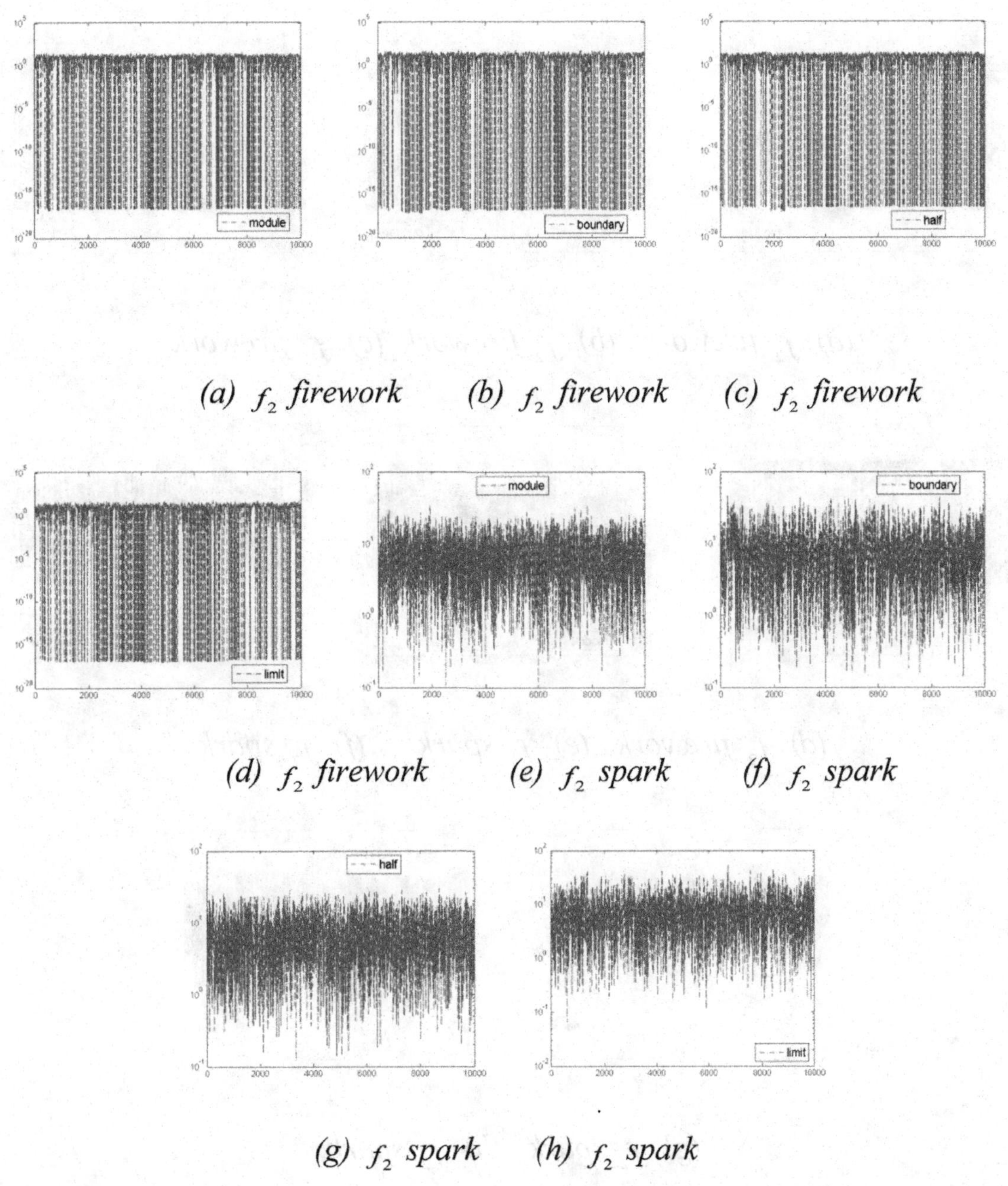

(a) f_2 *firework* *(b)* f_2 *firework* *(c)* f_2 *firework*

(d) f_2 *firework* *(e)* f_2 *spark* *(f)* f_2 *spark*

(g) f_2 *spark* *(h)* f_2 *spark*

Figure 8. The population diversities of the fireworks algorithm solving shifted unimodal problem f_2. The optima of the problem are shifted in both decision and objective space; and the dimension of the problem is 200.

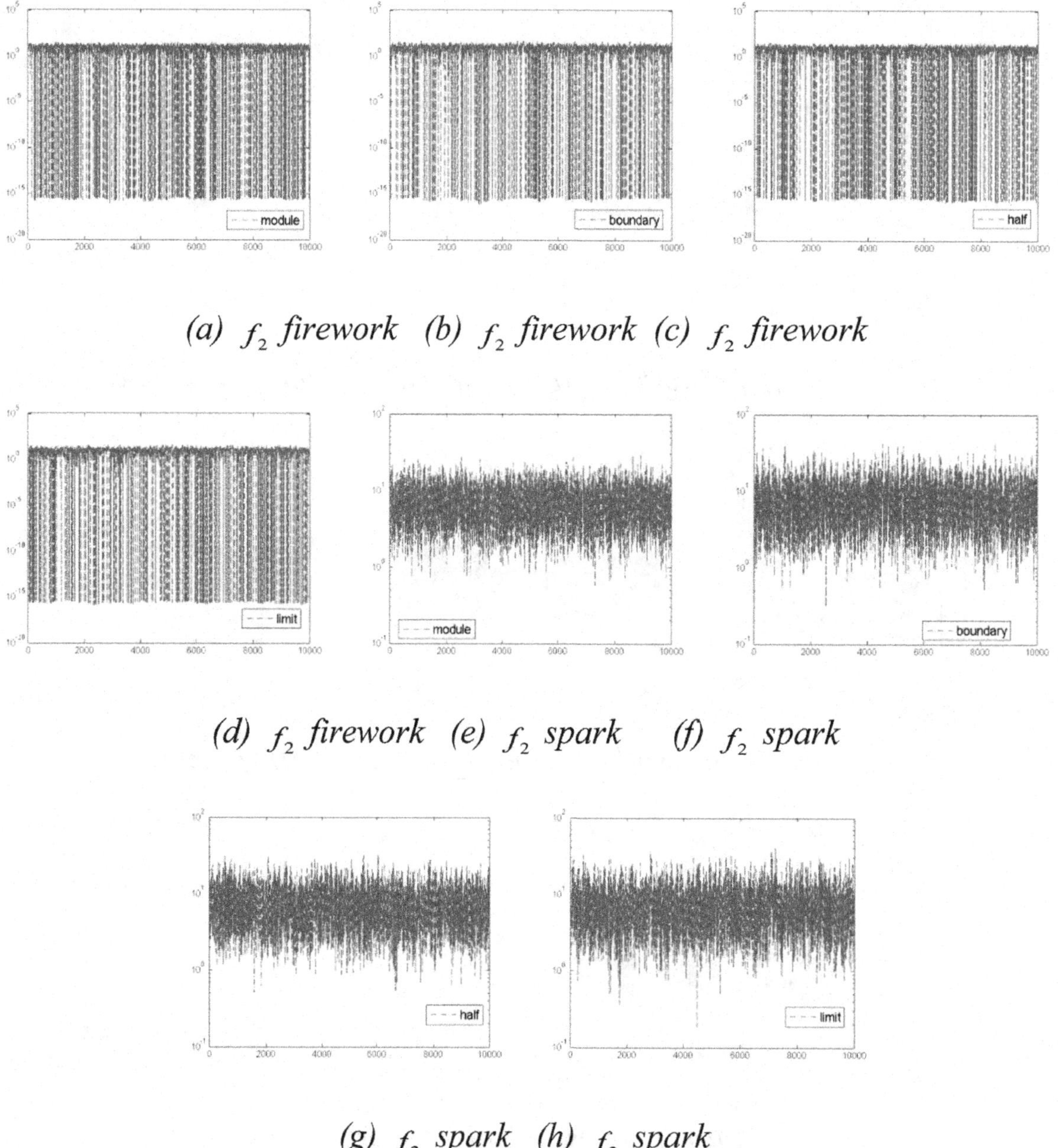

(a) f_2 firework (b) f_2 firework (c) f_2 firework

(d) f_2 firework (e) f_2 spark (f) f_2 spark

(g) f_2 spark (h) f_2 spark

Figure 9. The population diversities of the fireworks algorithm solving shifted multimodal problem f_6. The fitness value of the problem is only shifted in objective space; and the dimension of the problem is 200.

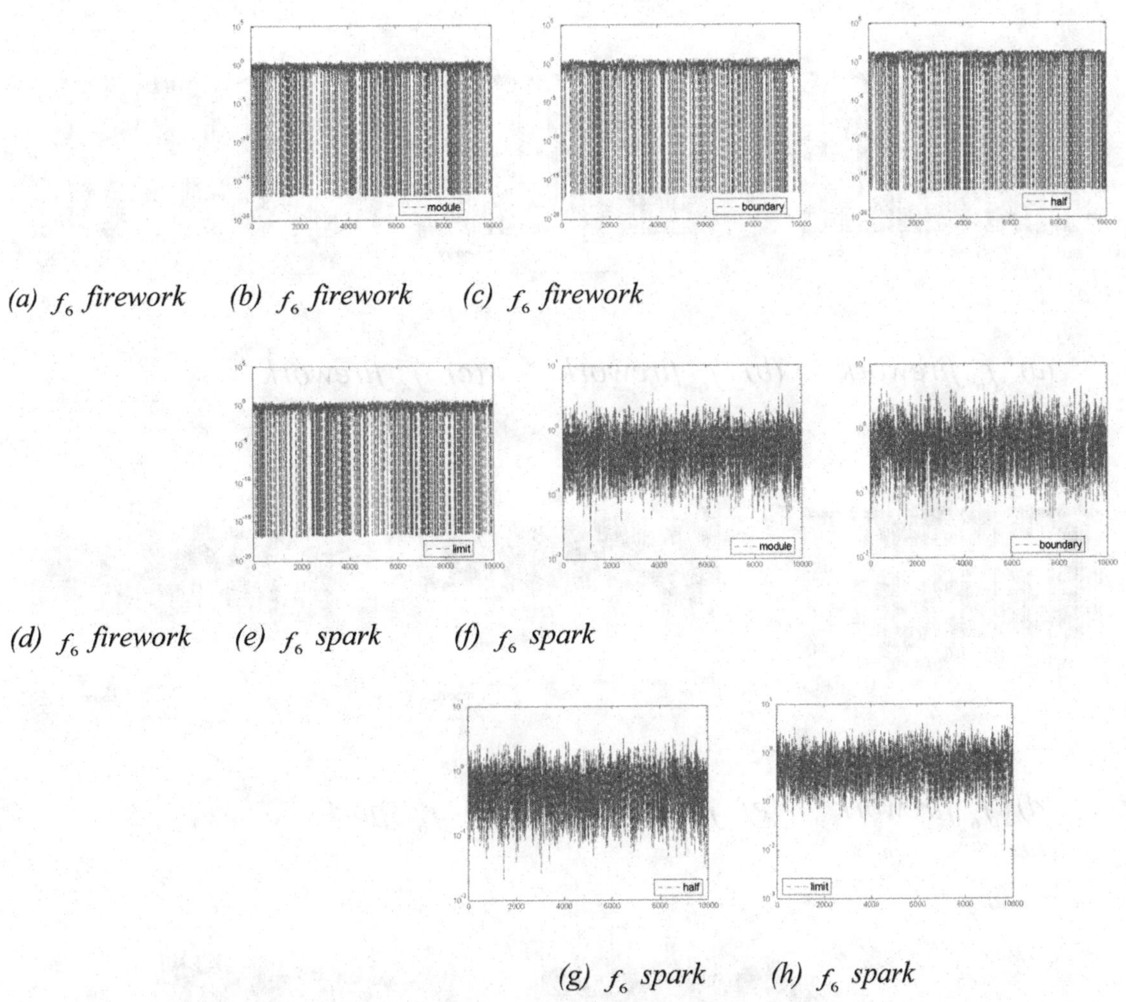

(a) f_6 firework *(b) f_6 firework* *(c) f_6 firework*

(d) f_6 firework *(e) f_6 spark* *(f) f_6 spark*

(g) f_6 spark *(h) f_6 spark*

In this chapter, population diversities were monitored on FWA for solving single-objective problems. Multi-objective problems have different goals of the optimization, it does not find one single solution, but many. The concept of convergence has different meanings between single and multiple objective problems (Jin & Sendhoff, 2009). Population diversity is also important when applying FWA to solve multi-objective problems (Adra, & Fleming, 2011; Cheng, Shi, & Qin, 2012). Defining population diversity for a multi-objective fireworks algorithms and monitoring its change during the search process is our future research work.

Figure 10. The population diversities of the fireworks algorithm solving shifted multimodal problem f_6. The optima of the problem are shifted in both decision and objective space; and the dimension of the problem is 200.

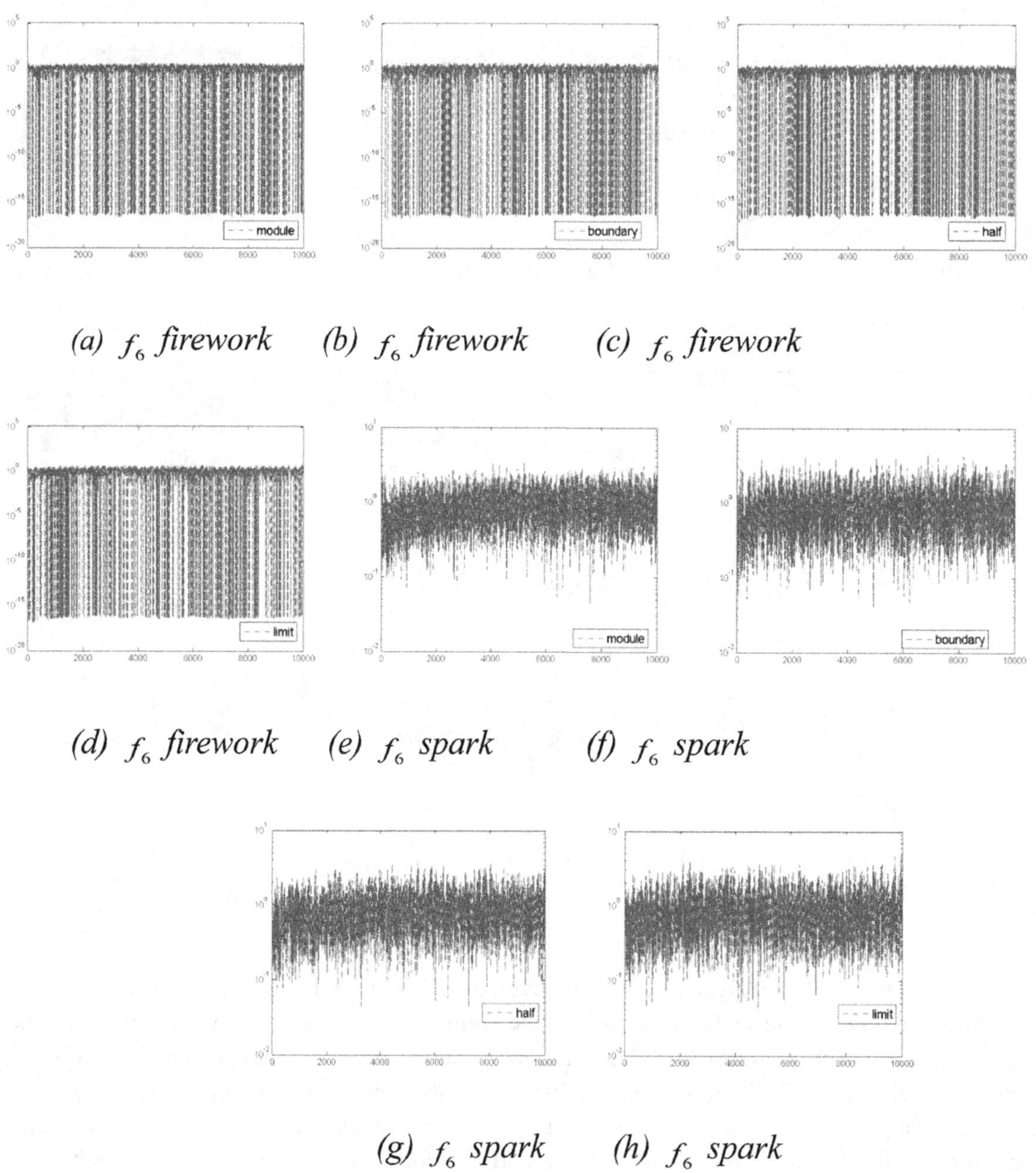

(a) f_6 firework *(b) f_6 firework* *(c) f_6 firework*

(d) f_6 firework *(e) f_6 spark* *(f) f_6 spark*

(g) f_6 spark *(h) f_6 spark*

ACKNOWLEDGMENT

This work is partially supported by the National Natural Science Foundation of China under Grant Number 61403121, 71402103, and 61273367, the Fundamental Research Funds for the Central Universities under Grant GK201703062 and 2015B20214, the sponsorship of Jiangsu Overseas Research & Training Program for University Prominent Young & Middle-aged Teachers and Presidents, China.

REFERENCES

Adra, S. F., Dodd, T. J., Griffin, I. A., & Fleming, P. J. (2009). Convergence acceleration operator for multiobjective optimization. *IEEE Transactions on Evolutionary Computation*, *12*(4), 825–847. doi:10.1109/TEVC.2008.2011743

Adra, S. F., & Fleming, P. J. (2011). Diversity management in evolutionary many-objective optimization. *IEEE Transactions on Evolutionary Computation*, *15*(2), 183–195. doi:10.1109/TEVC.2010.2058117

Burke, E. K., Gustafson, S., & Kendall, G. (2002). A survey and analysis of diversity measures in genetic programming. In *Proceedings of the Genetic and Evolutionary Computation Conference (GECCO 2002)*. San Francisco, CA: Morgan Kaufmann Publishers Inc. (pp. 716-723).

Cheng, S. (2013). *Population diversity in particle swarm optimization: Definition, observation, control, and application* (Ph.D. dissertation). Department of Electrical Engineering and Electronics, University of Liverpool.

Cheng, S., Qin, Q., Chen, J., & Shi, Y. (2016). Brain storm optimization algorithm: A review. *Artificial Intelligence Review*, *46*(4), 445–458. doi:10.1007/s10462-016-9471-0

Cheng, S., & Shi, Y. (2011). Diversity control in particle swarm optimization. In *Proceedings of 2011 IEEE Symposium on Swarm Intelligence (SIS 2011)* (pp. 110-118). IEEE.

Cheng, S., Shi, Y., & Qin, Q. (2011). Experimental study on boundary constraints handling in particle swarm optimization: From population diversity perspective. *International Journal of Swarm Intelligence Research*, *2*(3), 43–69. doi:10.4018/jsir.2011070104

Cheng, S., Shi, Y., & Qin, Q. (2012). Population diversity of particle swarm optimizer solving single and multi-objective problems *International Journal of Swarm Intelligence Research*, *3*(4), 23–60. doi:10.4018/jsir.2012100102

Cheng, S., Shi, Y., & Qin, Q. (2013). A study of normalized population diversity in particle swarm optimization. *International Journal of Swarm Intelligence Research*, *4*(1), 1–34. doi:10.4018/jsir.2013010101

Cheng, S., Shi, Y., Qin, Q., & Gao, S. (2013). Solution clustering analysis in brain storm optimization algorithm. In *Proceedings of The 2013 IEEE Symposium on Swarm Intelligence, (SIS 2013)*. Singapore: IEEE. doi:10.1109/SIS.2013.6615167

Cheng, S., Shi, Y., Qin, Q., Zhang, Q., & Bai, R. (2014). Population diversity maintenance in brain storm optimization algorithm. *Journal of Artificial Intelligence and Soft Computing Research*, *4*(2), 83–97. doi:10.1515/jaiscr-2015-0001

Eberhart, R., & Shi, Y. (2007). *Computational Intelligence: Concepts to Implementations*. Morgan Kaufmann Publisher. doi:10.1016/B978-155860759-0/50002-0

Ficici, S. G. (2005). Monotonic solution concepts in coevolution. In *Genetic and Evolutionary Computation Conference (GECCO 2005)*, (pp. 499-506). Academic Press.

Jin, Y., & Sendhoff, B. (2009). A systems approach to evolutionary multiobjective structural optimization and beyond. *IEEE Computational Intelligence Magazine*, *4*(3), 62–76. doi:10.1109/MCI.2009.933094

Kennedy, J., Eberhart, R., & Shi, Y. (2001). Swarm Intelligence. Morgan Kaufmann Publisher.

Liang, J. J., Qin, A. K., Suganthan, P. N., & Baskar, S. (2006). Comprehensive learning particle swarm optimizer for global optimization of multimodal functions. *IEEE Transactions on Evolutionary Computation*, *10*(3), 281–295. doi:10.1109/TEVC.2005.857610

Mauldin, M. L. (1984). Maintaining diversity in genetic search. In *Proceedings of the National Conference on Artificial Intelligence (AAAI 1984).* (pp. 247-250). Academic Press.

Shi, Y. (2011a). Brain storm optimization algorithm. In Advances in Swarm Intelligence. Springer Berlin/Heidelberg. doi:10.1007/978-3-642-21515-5_36

Shi, Y. (2011b). An optimization algorithm based on brainstorming process. *International Journal of Swarm Intelligence Research*, *2*(4), 35–62. doi:10.4018/IJSIR.2011100103

Shi, Y. (2014). Developmental swarm intelligence: Developmental learning perspective of swarm intelligence algorithms. *International Journal of Swarm Intelligence Research*, *5*(1), 36–54. doi:10.4018/ijsir.2014010102

Shi, Y., & Eberhart, R. (2008). Population diversity of particle swarms. In *Proceedings of the 2008 Congress on Evolutionary Computation (CEC 2008)* (pp. 1063-1067). Academic Press. doi:10.1109/CEC.2008.4630928

Shi, Y., & Eberhart, R. (2009). Monitoring of particle swarm optimization. *Frontiers of Computer Science*, *3*(1), 31–37. doi:10.1007/s11704-009-0008-4

Sundaram, R. K. (1996). *A First Course in Optimization Theory*. Cambridge University Press. doi:10.1017/CBO9780511804526

Tan, Y. (2015). *Fireworks Algorithm: A Novel Swarm Intelligence Optimization Method*. Springer. doi:10.1007/978-3-662-46353-6

Tan, Y., Yu, C., Zheng, S., & Ding, K. (2013). Introduction to fireworks algorithm. *International Journal of Swarm Intelligence Research*, *4*(4), 39–70. doi:10.4018/ijsir.2013100103

Tan, Y., & Zhu, Y. (2010). Fireworks algorithm for optimization. In Advances in Swarm Intelligence. Springer Berlin Heidelberg. doi:10.1007/978-3-642-13495-1_44

Yao, X., Liu, Y., & Lin, G. (1999). Evolutionary programming made faster. *IEEE Transactions on Evolutionary Computation*, *3*(2), 82–102. doi:10.1109/4235.771163

Zhang, W., Xie, X.-F., & Bi, D.-C. (2004). Handling boundary constraints for numerical optimization by particle swarm flying in periodic search space. In *Proceedings of the 2004 Congress on Evolutionary Computation*, (pp. 2307-2311). Academic Press. doi:10.1109/CEC.2004.1331185

Zheng, S., Janecek, A., & Tan, Y. (2013). Enhanced fireworks algorithm. In *Proceedings of 2013 IEEE Congress on Evolutionary Computation, (CEC 2013)*. Cancun, Mexico: IEEE. doi:10.1109/CEC.2013.6557813

Section 2
Swarm Intelligence Applications

Chapter 7
Assessment of Gamma-Ray-Spectra Analysis Method Utilizing the Fireworks Algorithm for Various Error Measures

Miltiadis Alamaniotis
Purdue University, USA

Lefteri Tsoukalas
Purdue University, USA

ABSTRACT

The analysis of measured data plays a significant role in enhancing nuclear nonproliferation mainly by inferring the presence of patterns associated with special nuclear materials. Among various types of measurements, gamma-ray spectra is the widest utilized type of data in nonproliferation applications. In this chapter, a method that employs the fireworks algorithm (FWA) for analyzing gamma-ray spectra aiming at detecting gamma signatures is presented. In particular, FWA is utilized to fit a set of known signatures to a measured spectrum by optimizing an objective function, where non-zero coefficients express the detected signatures. FWA is tested on a set of experimentally obtained measurements optimizing various objective functions—MSE, RMSE, Theil-2, MAE, MAPE, MAP—with results exhibiting its potential in providing highly accurate and precise signature detection. Furthermore, FWA is benchmarked against genetic algorithms and multiple linear regression, showing its superiority over those algorithms regarding precision with respect to MAE, MAPE, and MAP measures.

DOI: 10.4018/978-1-5225-5134-8.ch007

INTRODUCTION

Globalization, and the viability of the interstate system upon which it rests, crucially depend on international security that includes nuclear security, safeguards and nonproliferation. This is more true today than any other time since 1648 when the Treaty of Westphalia gave birth to the modern notion of interstate system (Mock, 2011). Besides the apocalyptic specter of nuclear war, failure to check nuclear proliferation may lead to chaotic instabilities and a global system in rapid and irreversible decline, especially in view of the devastating effects of nuclear and radiological weaponry on urban communities (Alamaniotis et al., 2013). Lack of effective nuclear security may very well unleash forces of disintegration and decay in the modern global system. Thus, nonproliferation treaty enforcement is of paramount importance (Bunn, 2003).

Nonproliferation is an area within the field of nuclear security that highly relies on interdisciplinary knowledge culminating in precise analysis of measurements in order to detect and identify the use, storage and transport of special nuclear materials (SNM) (Runkle et al., 2010). To that end, data and information analysis aiming at detecting and identifying patterns of interest is one of the cornerstones in nuclear nonproliferation (Alamaniotis et al., 2015). Data collection refers to the process of collecting information, content and contributions from various radiological and non-radiological sources. However, the most common (i.e., widest used) type of data in nonproliferation is the gamma spectroscopic measurements. Analysis of gamma spectroscopic measurements is performed with specialized algorithms that seek for patterns of interest in the obtained measurements (Burr & Hamada, 2009). Gamma-ray measurements are obtained in the form of energy spectra, where a single spectrum is the aggregation of contributions coming from various sources. It should be noted, that a gamma-ray spectrum also contains contribution from materials of the ambient environment; this contribution is known as "background spectrum" (Alamaniotis et al., 2013a). Therefore, the variety of contributions increase the complexity of the gamma-ray spectrum, and as a result, low contributed sources may be masked by high contributed ones.

Analysis of gamma-ray spectra aims at identifying the constituents of a measured spectrum. On one hand, several analysis algorithms seek to extract features that may be utilized for identification of the spectrum constituents. On the other hand, a high number of algorithms focus on utilizing the whole spectral curve instead of extracting features. Following the latter approach, a common strategy in gamma-ray spectrum analysis is the fitting of the measured spectrum with a set of predetermined spectra, which are obtained either through measurements or simulations (Tsoulfanidis & Landsberger, 2013).

In this chapter, the focal point is the analysis of gamma-ray spectra into their constituents by adopting a fitting process. The fitting process is conducted by formulating an optimization problem whose solution is sought by the Fireworks Algorithm (Tan & Zhu, 2010). It should be noted that spectrum fitting denotes the minimization of the distance between the linear combination of available signature patterns and the measured signal (Hogan et al., 1970). The goal of fitting is to analyze the measurement into those constituents whose synthesis best matches the initial measurement. Notably, in nonproliferation applications there is no prior information about the contents of the spectrum. In other words, the measured spectrum is considered as totally "unknown". The degree of fitting (i.e., distance) is expressed quantitively as the value of a measure (i.e., error) function between the linear combination and the measured signal (Tsoulfanidis & Landsberger, 2013). The signatures with statistically significant non-zero coefficients are indicated as the final list of constituents in the measured spectrum.

The roadmap of this chapter is as follows: i) a literature review on FWA applications, as well as on gamma-ray analysis algorithms is given, ii) the FWA framework is described, iii) the intelligent analysis method is presented, iv) results for various objective functions are provided and discussed, and finally v) chapter conclusions are highlighted.

LITERATURE REVIEW

Fireworks Algorithm Applications

The explosion of fireworks and the dispersion of sparks that follows them, inspired researchers at Peking University in China (Tan & Zhu, 2010) to come up with a new stochastic optimization algorithm called the fireworks algorithm. Since then, FWA has gained popularity and found application in various areas, while still being applied to new problems, where optimal solutions are required.

In particular, the FWA has been successfully applied to a disperse set of problems up to this point. FWA has been used in nonnegative matrix factorization (Janecek, & Tan, 2011), spam detection introduced by (He et al, 2013), power loss minimization of power systems presented in (Imran, & Kowsalya, 2014), recognition tasks (Zheng, & Tan, 2013 March), power distribution networks (Imran, Kowsalya, & Kothari, 2014), 0/1 Knapsack problem solving (Jiaqin, 2011), digital filter design introduced in (Gao & Diao, 2011), variable-rate fertilization in oil crop production (Zheng, Song, & Chen, 2013), and non-linear equations and systems solving (Zhen-xin, 2013),

Another significant application of FWA incurs in the forecasting of icing thickness on power lines as presented in (Ma & Ni, 2016). In addition, Bacanin & Tuba (2015) presented the use of FWA in portfolio optimization under various constraints, while Tuba et al. (2015a) introduced FWA in image processing. Moreover, FWA was applied to optimization of RFID network planning (Tuba et al., 2015b), and to web information retrieval in (Bouarara et al., 2015). A method for scheduling of multi-satellite control resources is presented in (Liu et al., 2015 May), and a novel method for preserving privacy in big data environments in (Rahmani et al., 2015). Further, a novel approach for thermal unit commitment that utilizes FWA proved to be of high efficiency as discussed in (Panwar et al., 2015), while high efficiency was also exhibited by applying FWA in Abstract Ultrasonic Machining process (Goswami & Chakraborty, 2015a).

The parameter evaluation of support vector machines is also a problem in which FWA found application with high accurate results (Tuba et al., 2016 June). Additionally, maximizing power harnessing from solar PV by use of FWA is presented and tested in (Sangeetha et al., 2016). Other engineering problems in which FWA contributed includes wireless sensor networks localization (Arsic et al., 2016), resource allocation in smart grids (Reddy et al., 2016), optimizing economic emission in power microgrids (Sarfi et al., 2016), gamma-ray spectrum fitting (Alamaniotis, Choi & Tsoukalas, 2015), optimization of laser machining processes (Goswami & Chakraborty, 2015b), and selective elimination in PWM inverters (Rajaram et al., 2014). Additionally, a discrete FWA was applied to detecting communities in social networks as presented in (Gouendouz et al., 2017), and to predicting of De Novo Motif in (Lihu & Holban, 2015).

Overall, it is clear that FWA has been already successfully applied to a high variety of various problems, and it is expected that its use will further proliferate to various problems in diverse domains. Therefore, it is safe to assume that FWA is a highly promising optimization algorithm, that gains popularity in research community.

Gamma-Ray Analysis Algorithms

The analysis algorithms of gamma ray spectra are mainly classified into two categories: i) peak based algorithms where the algorithms utilize spectral peaks and their features to identify the constituents of a spectrum, and ii) fitting algorithms in which the algorithm utilizes the full spectrum, by adopting known nuclide signatures to fit a measurement.

The most widely used method for gamma-ray spectrum analysis is the multiple linear regression fitting introduced in (Hogan et al., 1970). A more advanced linear fitting using Pareto optimality and evolutionary computing is presented in (Alamaniotis et al., 2013b). Furthermore, spectrum fitting using Levenberg-Marquardt optimization is discussed in (Fatah & Ahmed 2011) and in (Mattingly & Mitchell, 2010). Fuzzy logic has been proposed in several studies such as in (Alamaniotis et al., 2011), (Murray et al., 2000) and (Alamaniotis et al., 2013). Genetic algorithms have been also used in optimal gamma-ray analysis as described in (Carlevaro et al., 2008) and (Garcia-Talavera & Ulicny, 2003). Additionally, genetic algorithms are applied to seeking an optimal combination of signatures synergistically with other intelligent tools such as fuzzy logic (Alamaniotis & Jevremovic, 2015), while hybrid fuzzy-wavelets methods have been proposed in (Alamaniotis & Tsoukalas, 2016 November) and (Alamaniotis et al., 2010). Gamma-ray analysis with B-spline functions is presented in (Zhu et al., 2009), while a hybrid evolutionary-fuzzy in (Huang et al. 2011). Other analysis methods adopted the use of Bayesian Statistics as described in (Stinnett & Sullivan, 2013) and (Sullivan & Stinnett, 2015), likelihood ratios (Forsberg et al., November 2009), Local-Global graphs (Bourbakis et al., 2008; Pantelopoulos et al., 2009), and neural networks (Yoshida et al., 2003; Kamuda et al., 2017; Kangas et al., 2008). In addition, a synthetically enhanced detector resolution algorithm has been proposed in (Sjoden et al., 2009; Sjoden et al., 2012), while standalone wavelet processing for gamma ray spectra has been discussed in (Sullivan et al., 2006).

Overall, algorithms are imposed to several difficulties in effectively analyzing complex measured spectra into their constituents. Those difficulties come mainly from i) random background contribution, ii) random spectral fluctuation, iii) nonlinear detector characteristics, and iv) electronic noise (Tsoulfanidis & Landsberger, 2013). In addition, highly complex spectra, which contain the aggregated contributions of a high number of sources - with some of them having very small contribution - are difficult to be accurately analyzed.

FIREWORKS ALGORITHM

Swarm Intelligence (SI), is that area of artificial intelligence, that includes tools whose development was inspired by the behavioral patterns observed in swarm systems (Alamaniotis et al., November 2012) found in natural environment. SI is applied to complex optimization problems, where conventional optimization algorithms either fail or are computationally expensive (Engelbrecht, 2007). FWA is identified as an SI optimization algorithm that has been developed at Peking University in China (Tan & Zhu, 2010) and mimics the firework explosion in the sky.

The key idea is that by mimicking the firework explosion and the subsequent spark dispersion, a search strategy for an optimal solution in the parameter space is "invented". Solution search takes place in the vicinity of locations in which the fireworks are set off. In practice, the search is conducted by the sparks that are generated in the proximity of the set off locations (Tan & Zhu, 2010). Spark locations stand for potential solutions to the optimization problem at hand, and are evaluated according to an analytical function, which evaluates the solution quality, i.e., how "optimal" the current solution is. FWA is iterated continuously until an optimal solution is located; each algorithmic iteration is simply called with the biological term "generation" (Tan & Zhu, 2010). The FWA block diagram is depicted in Figure 1 (Tan & Zhu, 2010), where the execution order of algorithmic steps is provided. For details on FWA and its individual steps, the interested reader is referenced to check (Tan & Zhu, 2010) and (Tan et al, 2013).

In the beginning, the parameter *N*, which expresses the population of fireworks used in the current problem, is evaluated. Every single firework is analytically expressed as a *D*-dimensional vector, i.e., a firework is a vector of length *D*, where *D* coincides with the dimension of the problem solution space. At each FWA generation, a new population of solutions is generated, with the population of sparks remaining equal to *N*. In the following step, a set of *N* locations from all over the search space is chosen, and a single firework is placed at each location.

Every firework is set off at its current location, and subsequently generates a number of sparks that get dispersed around the firework location; appearance of sparks designates the disappearance of the firework. Hence, the generated sparks are located around the initial firework set off point. The population of sparks generated by each firework is given by:

$$S_i = S_o \frac{Y_{max} - f(x_i) + \varepsilon}{\sum_{i=1}^{N} \left(Y_{max} - f(x_i)\right) + \varepsilon} \quad (1)$$

where $f(x_i)$ is the fitness value of the firework x_i, S_i stands for the number of sparks generated by the firework *i*, Y_{max} is the worst fitness value in the current generation, S_o is a predefined constant, and ε is a small value that ensures that denominator does not drop to zero. To prevent the non- desirable overwhelming effects of the explosion, S_i is bound as follows:

$$S_i = \left\{ round(a \cdot m) \right\} \quad if\ S_i < a \cdot m$$

Figure 1. Block diagram of the fireworks algorithm used for optimization (Tan & Zhu, 2010)

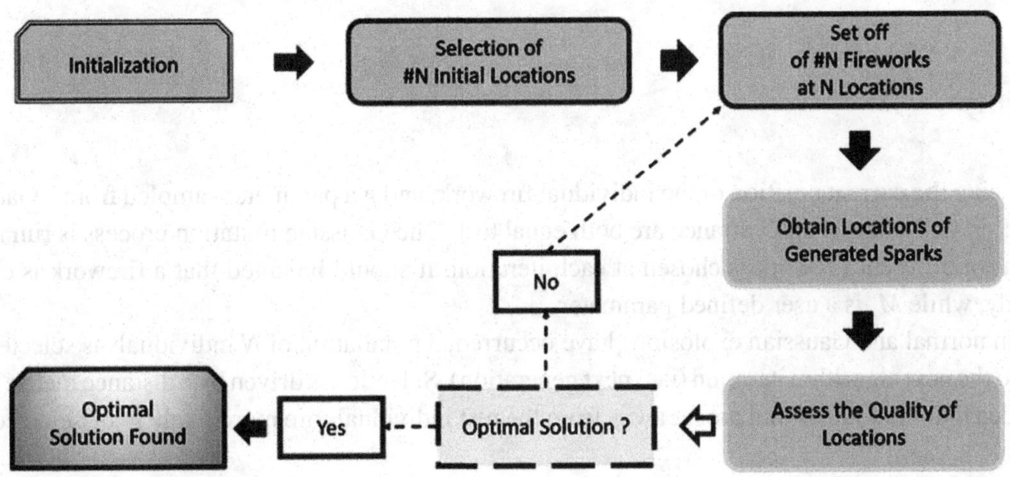

$$S_i = \left\{ round\left(b \cdot m\right) \right\} \quad if\, S_i > b \cdot m \tag{2}$$

$$S_i = \left\{ round\left(S_i\right) \right\} \quad otherwise$$

with α and b being constants that satisfy $\alpha < b < 1$. Furthermore, the area of spark dispersion in the initial location is defined by the parameter named as "amplitude of explosion". The amplitude is evaluated by:

$$A_i = A_o \frac{Y_{min} - f\left(x_i\right) + \varepsilon}{\sum_{i=1}^{N} \left(Y_{min} - f\left(x_i\right)\right) + \varepsilon} \tag{3}$$

where A_i is the explosion amplitude of the firework i, A_o is a constant, and Y_{min} is the best fitness value of the current generation. In the extreme case where an individual firework is close to the boundary of the feasible solutions space, it is likely that some of the dispersed sparks may result outside of the feasible space. This is something undesirable, and thus, a mapping strategy is required to secure feasibility of all located solutions. To compensate for this extreme case, the sparks that lie outside the feasible space are mapped back to the feasible space by utilizing the following formula:

$$x_i = x_{min} + \left|x_i\right| \% (x_{max} - x_{min}) \tag{4}$$

where x_i is the location of a spark outside of the feasible space, x_{min} and x_{max} are the respective minimum and maximum boundaries of allowable spark positions, and % is the modular operation. To ensure diversity of the spark population, and therefore attain a good search strategy, another type of sparks are also generated right after the occurrence of a firework explosion. The generated sparks are obtained by a Gaussian mutation process that is analytically expressed by:

$$x_k = x_k \cdot \mathrm{g} \tag{5}$$

$$\mathrm{g} = N(1,1) \tag{6}$$

with x_k being the current position of the individual firework, and g a parameter sampled from a Gaussian distribution whose mean and variance are both equal to 1. The Gaussian mutation process is run for M_g iterations; a different firework is chosen at each iteration. It should be noted that a firework is chosen arbitrarily, while M_g is a user defined parameter.

When normal and Gaussian explosions have occurred, a population of N individuals is selected and passed to the next algorithm iteration (i.e., next generation). Selection is driven by a distance metric based on the idea that individuals that are far away from the rest individuals are more likely to be selected than individuals that are close to other individuals. Euclidean distance (Lu et al, 2002) is used as the distance metric formula that is given below:

$$d(x_i, x_j) = \left\| x_i - x_j \right\| \tag{7}$$

where $d(x_i,x_j)$ denotes the distance between the locations x_i and x_j. In general, any valid distance measure may be used in (7), for example, Euclidean, Mahalanobis, and Manhattan distance. Generally speaking distance between a location x_i and the rest locations is expressed as:

$$R(x_i) = \sum_{j \in K} d\left(x_i, x_j\right),\ i \neq j \tag{8}$$

with K denoting the locations of all fireworks and the respective sparks. Hence, inclusion of an individual in the next generation is based on a probability value computed by a roulette wheel method:

$$p(x_i) = \frac{R\left(x_i\right)}{\sum_{j \in K} R\left(x_i, x_j\right)}. \tag{9}$$

The roulette wheel method shown in Eq. (9) provides the (N-1) individuals of the next generation, while the last, i.e., N^{th} individual, is identified as the best individual of the current generation. The aforementioned selection is iterated with a new set of N fireworks in each FWA generation.

Notably, since its inception, several modifications of the main FWA have been proposed. The proposals include: the enhanced fireworks algorithm proposed by Zheng, Janecek and Tan (2013), the adaptive fireworks algorithm (Tan, 2015a), the cooperative FWA (Tan, 2015b), the introduction of transfer functions in FWA by Liu at al. (2013), and the study of fitting methods of FWA by Pei et al., (2012). Further work proposed improvements based on mutation (Yu, Li, & Tan, 2014 October), integration with dynamic search (Tan, 2015c), adaptive amplitude methods (Li, Zheng, & Tan, 2014 July), the use of new Gaussian explosion selections (Zhang, Zhang, & Zheng, 2014), differential evolution operators (Zheng et al, 2015), and dynamic control (Janecek, & Tan, 2011 July). Recently, a new improved FWA was proposed by introducing a novel guiding spark as described in (Li, Zheng & Tan, 2017).

Overall, there is still active research in improving FWA as well as establishing a solid mathematical foundation of it.

INTELLIGENT IDENTIFICATION METHODOLOGY

The proposed methodology aims at analyzing a measured spectrum into its constituents by utilizing a set of pre-defined signature spectra (i.e., nuclide templates). The methodology adopts a linear combination of the preselected template spectra (Garcia-Talavera, & Ulicny, 2003) to fit the measured spectrum. In particular, the linear combination is comprised of a set of coefficients whose population is equal to the

Figure 2. Block diagram of the FWA based gamma-ray spectrum analysis methodology

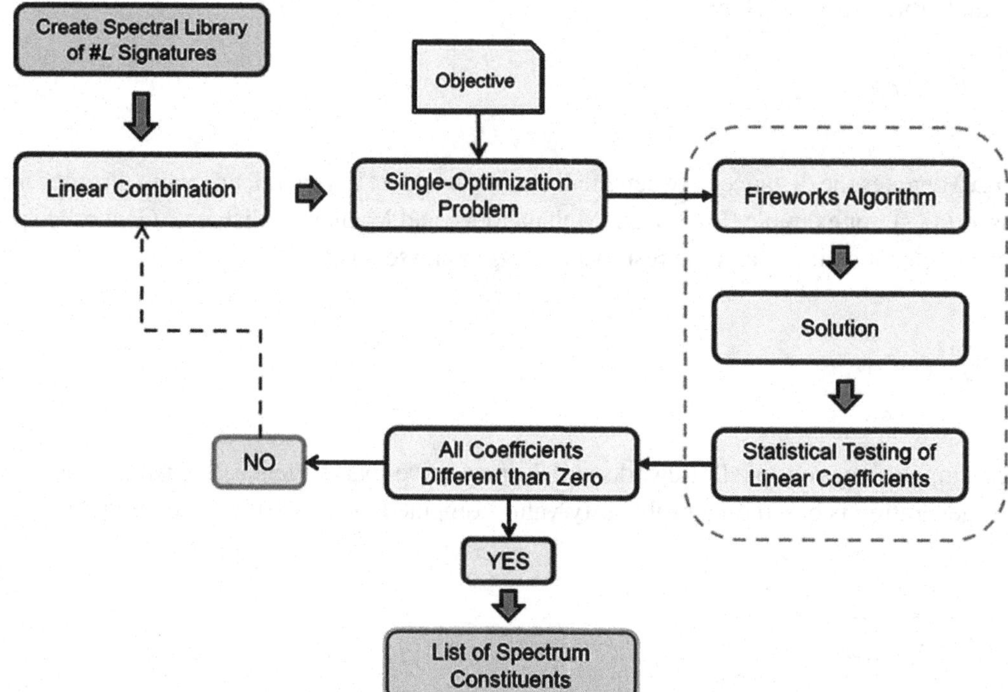

number of templates employed for spectrum fitting. Quantitatively, the linear coefficients express the *nuclide fractional abundance* in the measured spectrum, and are evaluated as the solution to a well-defined optimization problem. To that end, an objective function is needed that quantifies the degree of similarity between the linear estimated spectrum and the measured one; error functions are utilized as objective functions of the optimization problem.

The block diagram of the proposed gamma-ray analysis methodology is presented in Figure 2. It is comprised of several steps whose details are given below:

1. Populate a template library with #L nuclide signature templates (T_l).
2. Determine a linear combination of templates:

$$F = \alpha_1 T_1 + \alpha_2 T_2 + \ldots + \alpha_L T_L \tag{10}$$

3. Employ a metric function as an objective function:

$$Obj = f(M, F) \tag{11}$$

where M is the measured and F is the linearly estimated spectrum.

4. Formulate the optimization problem:

$$\underset{\alpha_i}{\text{minimize}}\{Obj\} \quad \text{w.r.t. } 1 \geq \alpha_j \geq 0 \tag{12}$$

5. Use FWA to locate an optimal solution of the optimization problem.
6. Statistically test the computed coefficients whether they are significantly different than zero: A *t*-statistical test is adopted as given below:

$$H_0 : \alpha_i = 0 \quad H_a : \alpha_i > 0 \tag{13}$$

and the *t-statistic* is obtained by:

$$t = \frac{\hat{a}_i - a_i}{se} \tag{14}$$

with $\hat{a}_i$ being the coefficient value estimated by FWA, α_i is the value according to H_0, and *se* is the standard error. Given that α_i =0, then Eq. (14) gets the form:

$$t = \frac{\hat{a}_i}{se}. \tag{15}$$

The standard error of a linear coefficient is taken as:

$$se\{\alpha_i\} = \sqrt{\frac{\sum_{c=1}^{C}\left(M_c - \hat{M}_c\right)^2}{(\mathrm{C}-L)\sum_{c=1}^{C}\left(T_{i_c} - \bar{T}_{i_c}\right)^2}} \tag{16}$$

where C is the number of spectrum bins, L is the number of available templates, M is the measured spectrum, and T_i are the respective template for isotope i.

7. In case one or more coefficient is found to be zero, then go back to step 2 and perform a new fitting excluding the zero coefficient templates.
8. If no coefficient is found to be significantly equal to zero then terminate the fitting process. Templates associated with non-zero coefficients are identified as the spectrum constituents.

It should be noted that the FWA consists of the "heart" of the gamma ray analysis algorithm. The overall performance of the analysis algorithm is strongly correlated to FWA performance with respect to accuracy and execution time.

Error Metrics

In the current work, a group of six error measures is employed with the intention to evaluate the fitting accuracy. It should be noted that each error function will be used as the objective function of the single objective optimization problem. Assuming that M_t is the measured value and F_t the fitted value for energy bin *t*, then the formulas of the six error measures are given by:

1. Mean Square Error (MSE)

$$MSE = \frac{1}{T}\sum_{t=1}^{T}(M_t - F_t)^2 \tag{17}$$

2. Root Mean Square Error (RMSE)

$$RMSE = \sqrt{MSE} \tag{18}$$

3. Theil-2 Coefficient (Theil-2)

$$Theil = \frac{\sqrt{\sum_{t=1}^{T}(M_t - F_t)^2}}{\sqrt{\sum_{t=1}^{T}(M_t)^2}\sqrt{\sum_{t=1}^{T}(F_t)^2}} \tag{19}$$

4. Maximum Absolute Percentage Error (MAP)

$$MAP = \max_{t=1,\ldots,T}\left(100 \times \left|\frac{M_t - F_t}{M_t}\right|\right) \tag{20}$$

5. Mean Absolute Error (MAE)

$$MAE = \frac{1}{N}\sum_{t=1}^{N}\left|R_t - P_t\right| \tag{21}$$

6. Mean Absolute Percentage Error (MAPE)

$$MAPE = \frac{100}{N}\sum_{t=1}^{N}\left|\frac{R_t - P_t}{R_t}\right| \tag{22}$$

where T represents the total number of energy bins in the gamma-ray spectrum.

ASSESSMENT OF IDENTIFICATION RESULTS

Introduction

In this section, the FWA analysis methodology is applied on a set of gamma-ray spectra obtained with a low-resolution handheld *2x2*" NaI detector (Tsoulfanidis & Landsberger, 2013). The spectra have been experimentally measured in the laboratory environment, and consist of 1024 energy bins (i.e., analytically the spectra are expressed as histograms of 1024 bins) spanning the energy range [0 3.2] MeV. The analysis methodology is assessed by computing the accuracy and precision ratios that express the number of signatures (a) correctly identified, (b) missed, and (c) incorrectly detected. For convenience, the formulas of accuracy and precision are given below:

$$Accuracy = \frac{\#\, correct\, detections}{\#\, correct\, detections + \#\, missed\, detections} 100\% \tag{23}$$

$$Precision = \frac{\#\, correct\, detections}{\#\, correct\, detections + \#\, false\, detections} 100\%\,. \tag{24}$$

Analysis results obtained with FWA are compared to those taken with i) a genetic algorithm and ii) multiple linear regression (MLR) (Burr & Hamada, 2009). It should be noted that the genetic algorithm optimizes the same objective functions as FWA, while MLR does use the least squares fitting (Mitchell et al., 1989). With regard to gamma-ray signatures list, we adopt a set of six nuclide signatures that have been simulated using the GADRAS platform which has been developed by Sandia National Laboratory (Mattingly & Mitchell, 2010). In particular the following signatures are adopted in the current work: ^{235}U (Uranium), ^{239}Pu (Plutonium), ^{137}Cs (Cesium), ^{241}Am (Americium), ^{192}Ir (Iridium) and ^{60}Co (Cobalt). It should be noted that a basis assumption in our work is that there is a prior variable selection mechanism that has selected among the 700 nuclides only the above 6 for our scenarios; in the ideal case, our approach should have used to fit all the 700 nuclides, which is currently computationally infeasible. With respect to FWA optimization, the population of fireworks is set equal to 8, while the GA has a population of 30 individuals and mutation probability equal to 0.01 (Tsoukalas & Uhrig, 1997).

In the next two subsections, a step-by-step demonstration case is given, and further results on a set of experimentally obtained spectra are given and discussed. Initial results of the presented FWA gamma-ray analysis algorithms were also presented in (Alamaniotis, Choi & Tsoukalas, 2015).

Demonstration Case Using the MSE Measure

In this section, the FWA analysis methodology is applied to analysis of a single gamma-ray spectrum, which is depicted in Figure 3. The spectrum contains only one signature that is the Cobalt signature. In this case, we assume that background spectrum is not available; therefore, we try to fit the nuclides signatures in the presence of background contribution.

Initially, the MSE measure is selected and the optimization problem is formed as given below:

$$\underset{\alpha_i}{\text{minimize}}\{\frac{1}{1024}\sum_{t=1}^{1024}(M_t - F_t)^2\}$$
$$\text{w.r.t. } 1 \geq \alpha_j \geq 0 \;\; j=1,\ldots,6 \tag{25}$$

where the problem is optimized using the FWA. The obtained coefficients α_1, α_2, α_3, α_4, α_5, α_6 for Am, Co, Cs, Ir, Pu, U are given below:

- **Americium:** $\alpha_1 = 0.02584$
- **Cobalt:** $\alpha_2 = 0.89422$
- **Cesium:** $\alpha_3 = 0.03150$
- **Iridium:** $\alpha_4 = 0.00043$
- **Plutonium:** $\alpha_5 = 0.06141$
- **Uranium:** $\alpha_6 = 0.08705$.

A t-test is conducted to check whether those coefficients are significantly different than zero. The results of the significance test provide that:

α_1 equals to Zero (Americium is not detected)

Figure 3. Measured gamma-ray spectrum of the demonstration scenario

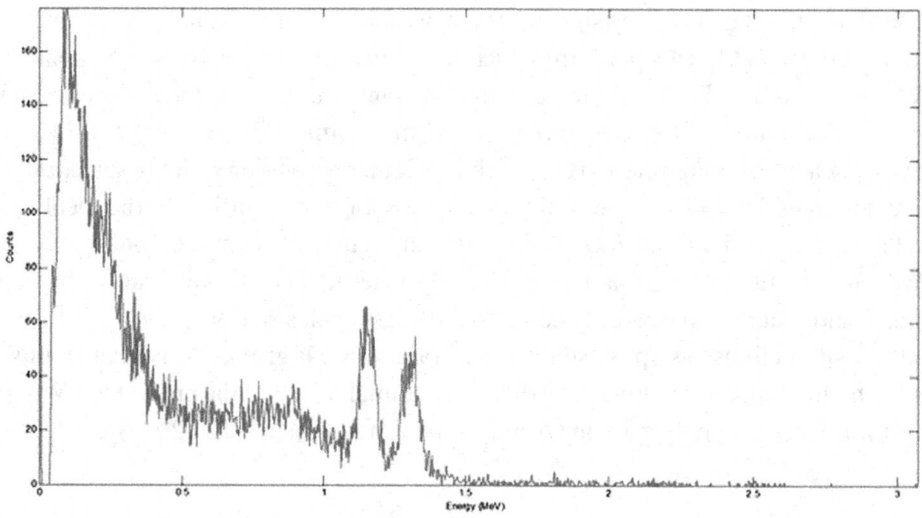

α_4 equals to Zero (Iridium is not detected).

Next, the optimal process is iterated with the rest four signatures. The new FWA iteration provides:

- **Cobalt:** $\alpha_2 = 0.0354$
- **Cesium:** $\alpha_3 = 0.0478$
- **Plutonium:** $\alpha_5 = 0.8502$
- **Uranium:** $\alpha_6 = 0.0500$

while the t-test designates that:

α_3 equal to Zero (Cesium is not detected)
α_6 equal to Zero (Uranium is not detected).

The third iteration includes only two nuclides, i.e., Co and Pu. Application of FWA provides the following results:

$\alpha_2 = 0.75541$
$\alpha_5 = 0.76277$

where both are found to be non-zero. Therefore, the analysis ends with the final list of detected signatures to contain Cobalt and Plutonium. The entropy obtained at each iteration by FWA is given in Figure 4.

Overall, the FWA analysis designates as final result that the spectrum is consisted of Cobalt and Pu, a result that is interpreted as 1 correct detection and 1 false detection. In terms of accuracy and precision ratios we get: Accuracy = 100% and Precision = 50%.

Analysis of the spectrum of Figure 3, adopting the same objective function, i.e., MSE, with a genetic algorithm fitting identifies Am, Co, Pu, Ir, and U. Therefore, we get Accuracy=100%, and Precision=20%. In addition, the MLR analysis identifies Co, Cs, Ir, Pu, and U, thus, giving Accuracy=100% and Precision=20%.

The above demonstration case intends to exhibit the steps of the FWA based analysis methodology. In this section, we used only one objective function, namely MSE. In the next section results will be obtained for all six aforementioned measures.

Results on Various Error Measures

In this section, the FWA based analysis methodology is applied on a set of experimentally obtained spectra. It this section, we assume that background measurements are available and hence, we are able to subtract the background from the measurement. The test spectra are depicted in Figures 5 and 6. It should be noted that the gamma-ray spectra are obtained with various acquisition times in order to obtain various signal-to-noise ratios. Table 1 presents the statistics of the measured spectra. We observe in Figures 5 and 6 that we have employed a set of eight spectra, with each spectrum exhibiting strong fluctuation. It is this fluctuation that imposes difficulties to spectrum analysis methods, and drives analysis algorithms to false alarms.

Figure 4. FWA entropy curves for each iteration

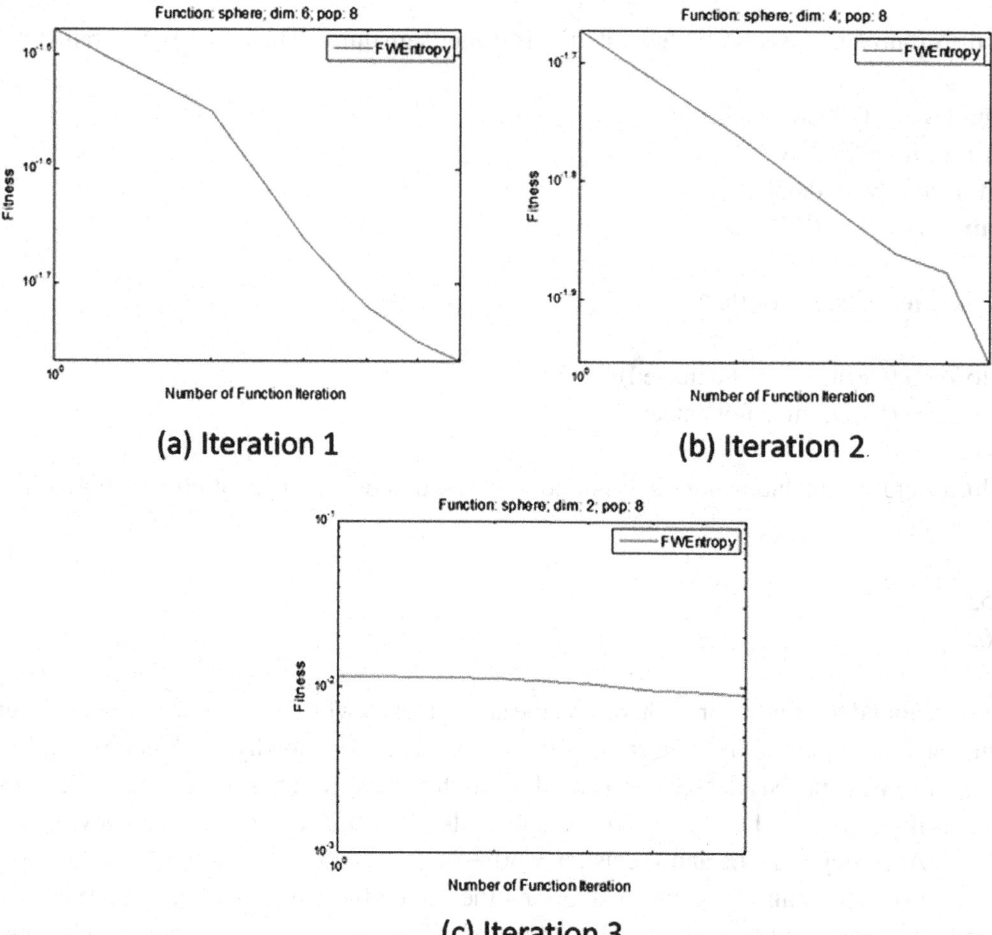

Initially, we perform analysis of the eight test spectra by adopting the MSE measure. The results of this analysis are given for FWA and GA in Table 2. In addition, results taken with the MLR are also presented in the same Table. MLR results will be given in all respective tables in the remainder of this chapter, though they will be the exactly the same, because no objective function is adopted by MLR. The analysis results with respect to accuracy and precision ratios are given in Figure 7, where the average values for the analysis of the 8 scenarios are provided. It is worth mentioning that results taken with RMSE coincide with those of MSE; this is expected given that RMSE is the square root of MSE.

In Figure 7, we observe that all three methods had similar (also high) performance. However, the GA analysis approach was slightly better than the rest in terms of precision, while it had provided the same accuracy as MLR. With regard to accuracy, FWA with MSE provided the lowest accuracy and second highest precision among the three tested methods. Same behavior was also observed for RMSE measure.

In the next step, we test the analysis approaches by using the Theil-2 measure. Analysis results are provided in Table 3, while the average accuracy and precision ratios in Figure 8. We observe that all three methods provide high accuracy with MLR having the highest one, i.e., 100%. The FWA method

Figure 5. Measured gamma-ray spectra labeled 1-4

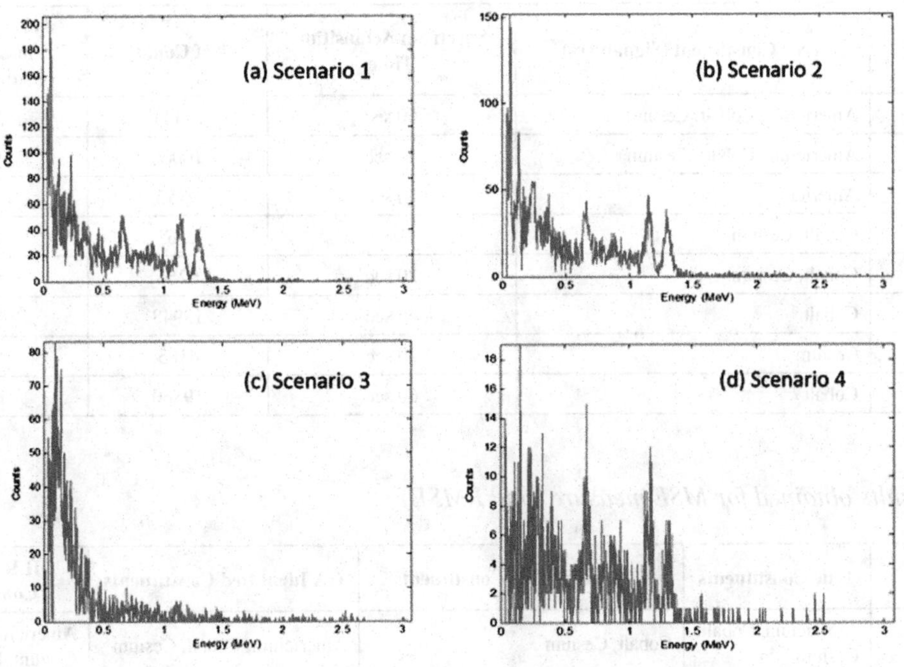

Figure 6. Measured gamma-ray spectra labeled 5-8

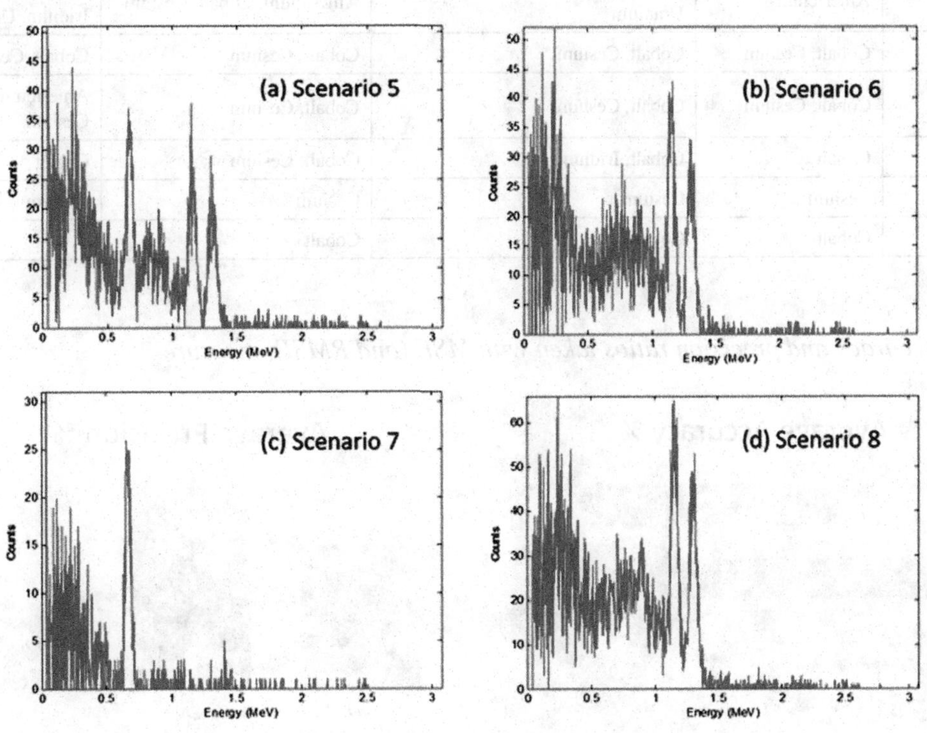

Table 1. Description of tested scenarios depicted in Figures 5 and 6

Scenario #	True Constituent (Signatures)	Spectrum Acquisition Time	# of Counts	# of Counts after background subtraction
Scenario 1	Americium, Cobalt, Cesium	60 sec	22111	13064
Scenario 2	Americium, Cobalt, Cesium	40 sec	16006	9922
Scenario 3	Americium	40 sec	9952	4013
Scenario 4	Cobalt, Cesium	5 sec	2363	1623
Scenario 5	Cobalt, Cesium	20 sec	9256	6332
Scenario 6	Cobalt	40 sec	12948	6921
Scenario 7	Cesium	20 sec	4185	1455
Scenario 8	Cobalt	60 sec	19860	10806

Table 2. Results obtained for MSE measure (and RMSE)

Scenario #	True Constituents	FWA Identified Constituents	GA Identified Constituents	MLR Identified Constituents
Scenario 1	Americium, Cobalt, Cesium	Cobalt, Cesium	Americium, Cobalt, Cesium	Americium, Cobalt, Cesium, Plutonium
Scenario 2	Americium, Cobalt, Cesium	Americium, Cobalt, Cesium	Americium, Cobalt, Cesium	Americium, Cobalt, Cesium
Scenario 3	Americium	Americium, Cesium, Iridium, Uranium	Americium, Cobalt, Cesium	Americium, Cesium, Iridium, Uranium
Scenario 4	Cobalt, Cesium	Cobalt, Cesium	Cobalt, Cesium	Cobalt, Cesium
Scenario 5	Cobalt, Cesium	Cobalt, Cesium	Cobalt, Cesium	Americium, Cobalt, Cesium
Scenario 6	Cobalt	Cobalt, Iridium	Cobalt, Cesium	Cobalt
Scenario 7	Cesium	Cesium	Cesium	Cesium
Scenario 8	Cobalt	Cobalt	Cobalt	Cobalt

Figure 7. Accuracy and precision ratios taken with MSE (and RMSE) measure

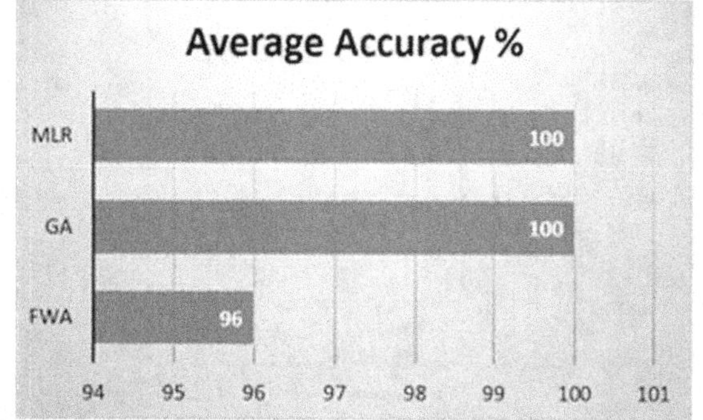

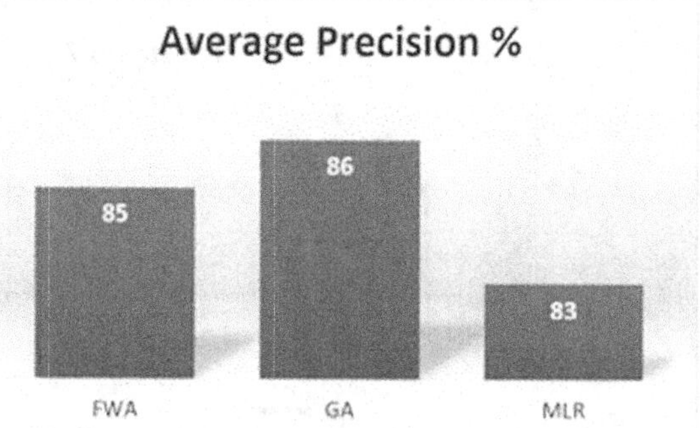

provides 96% accuracy but at the same time provides the highest precision ratio for Theil-2 measure that is equal to 87%. Both GA and MLR provide precision above 80%, but still lower than that of FWA.

Going further, the methods are assessed on using the MAE measure. Similar to previous measures, analysis results are presented in Table 4, while the accuracy and precision ratios are given in Figure 9. In this case, we observe that FWA provides the highest precision, i.e., 94%, and the second highest accuracy, which may be also characterized as very high (96%). In the current case, MLR is proven to be the most accurate algorithm, but at the same time is the least precise. GA analysis gives the lowest accuracy and the second highest precision, which is equal to 88%.

Next, we adopt the MAPE measure as the objective function of the analysis methods. Analysis results obtained for MAPE are presented in Table 5, while the average accuracy and precision are depicted in Figure 10. With respect to MAPE, we observe that MLR and GA provide the highest possible accuracy; FWA has an accuracy of 96%, which is high but still behind the other two methods. However, FWA outperforms both MLR and GA in terms of precision; it provides the highest precision ratio, which is equal to 90%.

The last tested measure is the MAP measure. Results obtained with that measure are given in Table 6, while accuracy and precision ratios are depicted in Figure 11. Both methods exhibit the same behavior likewise in MAPE measure. In particular, GA and MLR outperform FWA with respect to accuracy - they provide a perfect accuracy of 100%, while FWA gives 96%. However, we may safely state that FWA provides high accuracy and its difference with the rest is not very significance. Further, observation of the precision ratio exhibits that FWA is more precise than both GA and MLR. It should be noted, that the difference between GA and FWA may not seem to be high, but has a magnitude of 5%.

Overall, we have tested the FWA gamma ray analysis method with a variety of six measures, and assess its performance based on signature detection accuracy and precision. One of the main conclusions made is that FWA seems to provide high accuracy in gamma spectrum analysis. In all tested cases, FWA provided a 96% average accuracy. On one hand, this value may be characterized as satisfactory. On the other hand, FWA accuracy was less than MLR and GA in the majority of the cases, though their differences were not high. However, the FWA provided higher precision for most of the tested measures.

Table 3. Results obtained for Theil-2 measure

Scenario #	True Constituents	FWA Identified Constituents	GA Identified Constituents	MLR Identified Constituents
Scenario 1	Americium, Cobalt, Cesium	Cobalt, Cesium	Americium, Cobalt	Americium, Cobalt, Cesium, Plutonium
Scenario 2	Americium, Cobalt, Cesium	Americium, Cobalt, Cesium	Americium, Cobalt, Cesium	Americium, Cobalt, Cesium
Scenario 3	Americium	Americium, Iridium, Plutonium, Uranium	Americium, Cesium, Iridium, Uranium	Americium, Cesium, Iridium, Uranium
Scenario 4	Cobalt, Cesium	Cobalt, Cesium	Cobalt, Cesium	Cobalt, Cesium
Scenario 5	Cobalt, Cesium	Americium, Cobalt, Cesium	Americium, Cobalt, Cesium	Americium, Cobalt, Cesium
Scenario 6	Cobalt	Cobalt	Cobalt	Cobalt
Scenario 7	Cesium	Cesium	Cesium, Uranium	Cesium
Scenario 8	Cobalt	Cobalt	Cobalt	Cobalt

Figure 8. Accuracy and precision ratios taken with Theil-2 measure

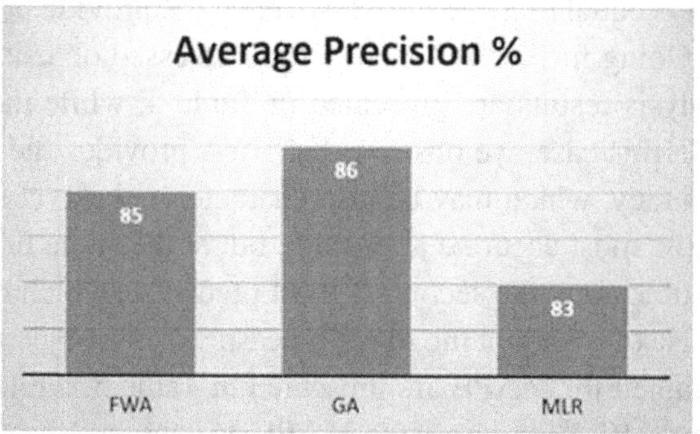

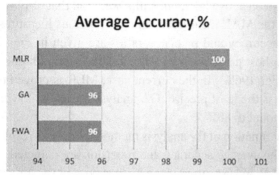

Table 4. Results obtained for MAE measure

Scenario #	True Constituents	FWA Identified Constituents	GA Identified Constituents	MLR Identified Constituents
Scenario 1	Americium, Cobalt, Cesium	Americium, Cobalt, Cesium	Americium, Cobalt, Cesium	Americium, Cobalt, Cesium, Plutonium
Scenario 2	Americium, Cobalt, Cesium	Cobalt, Cesium	Americium, Cobalt, Cesium	Americium, Cobalt, Cesium
Scenario 3	Americium	Americium, Iridium	Cesium, Iridium	Americium, Cesium, Iridium, Uranium
Scenario 4	Cobalt, Cesium	Cobalt, Cesium	Cobalt, Cesium	Cobalt, Cesium
Scenario 5	Cobalt, Cesium	Cobalt, Cesium	Cobalt, Cesium	Americium, Cobalt, Cesium
Scenario 6	Cobalt	Cobalt	Cobalt	Cobalt
Scenario 7	Cesium	Cesium	Cesium	Cesium
Scenario 8	Cobalt	Cobalt	Cobalt	Cobalt

Figure 9. Accuracy and precision ratios taken with MAE measure

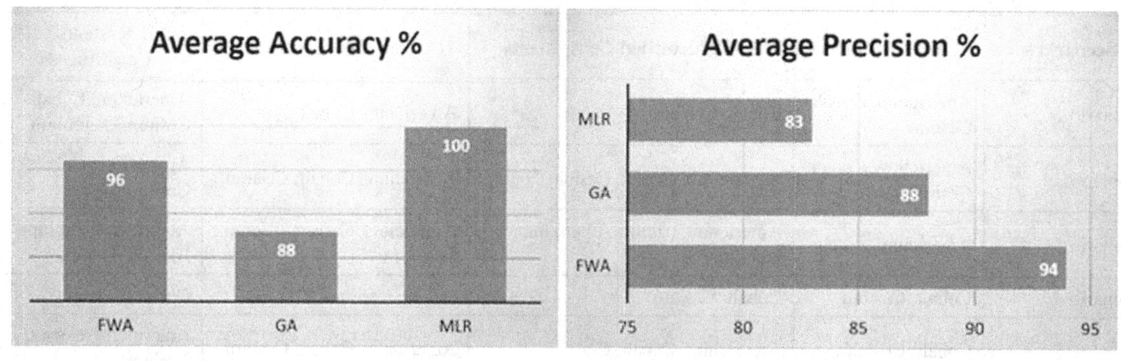

Table 5. Results obtained for MAPE measure

Scenario #	True Constituents	FWA Identified Constituents	GA Identified Constituents	MLR Identified Constituents
Scenario 1	Americium, Cobalt, Cesium	Americium, Cobalt, Cesium	Americium, Cobalt, Cesium	Americium, Cobalt, Cesium, Plutonium
Scenario 2	Americium, Cobalt, Cesium	Cobalt, Cesium	Americium, Cobalt, Cesium	Americium, Cobalt, Cesium
Scenario 3	Americium	Americium, Iridium	Americium, Cesium	Americium, Cesium, Iridium, Uranium
Scenario 4	Cobalt, Cesium	Americium, Cobalt, Cesium	Cobalt, Cesium	Cobalt, Cesium
Scenario 5	Cobalt, Cesium	Cobalt, Cesium	Cobalt, Cesium	Americium, Cobalt, Cesium
Scenario 6	Cobalt	Cobalt	Cobalt	Cobalt
Scenario 7	Cesium	Cesium	Cesium	Cesium
Scenario 8	Cobalt	Cobalt	Cobalt	Cobalt

Figure 10. Accuracy and precision ratios taken with MAPE measure

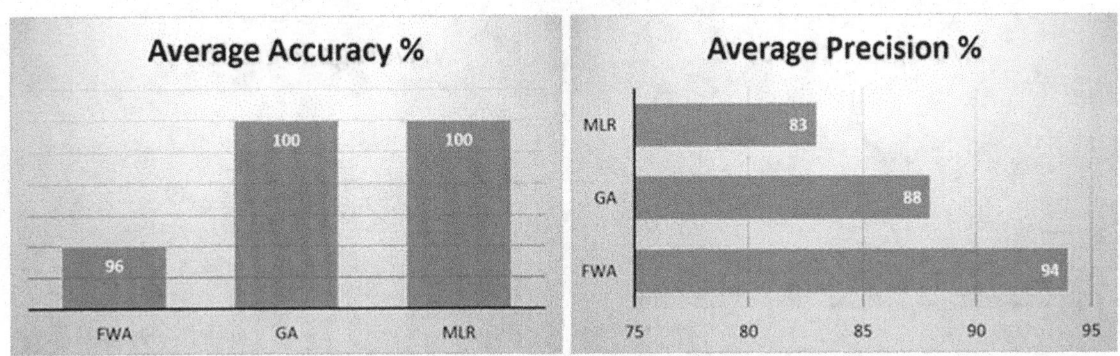

It should be noted that FWA provided the highest precision for the MAP measure, which was equal to 95.5%. It should be also marked that the FWA combined with MAE, MAPE and MAP provided very high precision ratio (>90%). Furthermore, the best dual performance, i.e., the dual of joint values for accuracy-precision, was taken when FWA adopted the MAP as its objective function, with MAPE and MAE being very close as well.

Therefore, we conclude that the simple FWA combined with MAP, MAPE and MAE may provide robust gamma-ray analysis, especially in the case in which precision is of interest. It is expected that the use of improved versions of FWA, like the proposed Enhanced FWA, will further boost the performance of the main FWA based gamma-ray analysis method.

Table 6. Results obtained for MAP measure

Scenario #	True Constituents	FWA Identified Constituents	GA Identified Constituents	MLR Identified Constituents
Scenario 1	Americium, Cobalt, Cesium	Americium, Cobalt, Cesium	Americium, Cobalt, Cesium	Americium, Cobalt, Cesium, Plutonium
Scenario 2	Americium, Cobalt, Cesium	Cobalt, Cesium	Americium, Cobalt, Cesium	Americium, Cobalt, Cesium
Scenario 3	Americium	Americium, Iridium	Americium, Uranium	Americium, Cesium, Iridium, Uranium
Scenario 4	Cobalt, Cesium	Cobalt, Cesium	Cobalt, Cesium	Cobalt, Cesium
Scenario 5	Cobalt, Cesium	Cobalt, Cesium	Americium, Cobalt, Cesium	Americium, Cobalt, Cesium
Scenario 6	Cobalt	Cobalt	Cobalt	Cobalt
Scenario 7	Cesium	Cesium	Cesium	Cesium
Scenario 8	Cobalt	Cobalt	Cobalt	Cobalt

Figure 11. Accuracy and precision ratios taken with MAPE measure

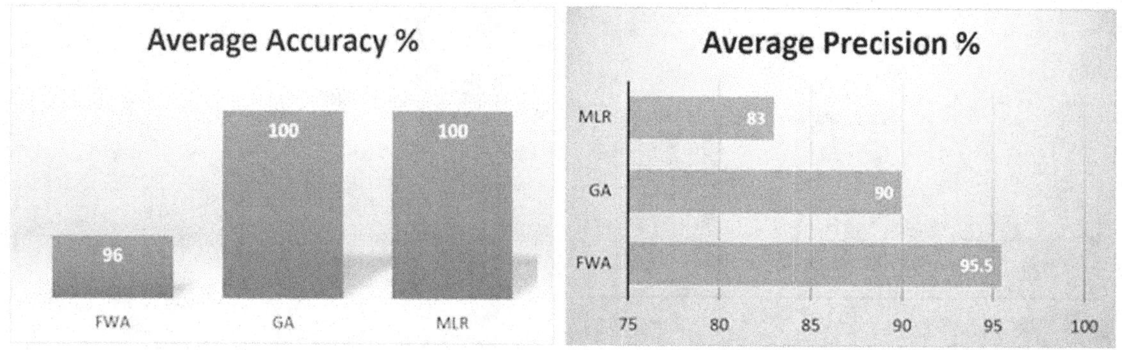

CONCLUSION

FWA is an algorithm that belongs to the field of swarm intelligence, and mimics the explosion and dispersion of fireworks in the sky. Despite its "short lifetime", it has been applied to various problems where optimization is required. This chapter aspired in enlisting the majority of applications in which FWA has been applied up to the current time, in addition to the various FWA improvements that have been proposed so far.

Moreover, the main goal of the chapter is to introduce and assess an intelligent gamma-ray spectrum analysis method whose cornerstone is the use of FWA and that had been previously introduced by Alamaniotis, Choi & Tsoukalas (2015). In particular, FWA is adopted to seek a solution to an optimization problem that models the fitting of predetermined gamma-ray signatures to a measured spectrum. The goal of the optimization problem is to find the combination of signatures that coincides with the actual constituents of the measured spectrum. The difficulty in spectrum analysis stems from the spectrum fluctuation as well as from various dynamic parameters such as the background spectrum.

In this chapter, we assessed the performance of FWA with respect to a set of various error measures and more specifically, MSE, RMSE, Theil-2, MAE, MAPE and MAP. We found that the combination of FWA with MAP provided the best joint performance with respect to accuracy and precision. However, MAE and MAPE provided also high performance and not very far from that of MAP. In addition, the presented method was benchmarked against optimization with GA and MLR fitting method on a set of experimentally obtained gamma-ray spectra. On one hand, GA and MLR slightly outperformed FWA with respect to accuracy, but on the other hand gave worse precision ratios in the majority of the cases. Therefore, a FWA-MAP (or MAE, or MAPE) will be preferable if precision is important compared to GA and MLR.

It should be noted, that only the basic FWA was employed in the current work, hence, growing the belief that the improved versions of FWA, (like EFWA) will likely provide higher performance in terms of accuracy as well. Therefore, future work will be directed to i) testing improved versions of FWA, and ii) extensive apply FWA in more complex gamma-ray spectra.

ACKNOWLEDGMENT

This material is based upon work supported by the Department of Energy National Nuclear Security Administration under Award Number(s) DE-NA0002576.

NOTE

REFERENCES

Alamaniotis, M., Choi, C. K., & Tsoukalas, L. H. (2015). Application of fireworks algorithm in gamma-ray spectrum fitting for radioisotope identification. *International Journal of Swarm Intelligence Research*, *6*(2), 102–125. doi:10.4018/IJSIR.2015040105

Alamaniotis, M., Gao, R., Tsoukalas, L. H., & Jevremovic, T. (2009). Intelligent Order-based Method for Synthesis of NRF Spectra and Detection of Hazardous Materials. In *21st IEEE International Conference on Tools with Artificial Intelligence*, (pp. 658-665). Newark, NJ: IEEE. doi:10.1109/ICTAI.2009.96

Alamaniotis, M., Heifetz, A., Raptis, A. C., & Tsoukalas, L. H. (2013). Fuzzy-logic radioisotope identifier for gamma spectroscopy in source search. *IEEE Transactions on Nuclear Science*, *60*(4), 3014–3024. doi:10.1109/TNS.2013.2265307

Alamaniotis, M., Ikonomopoulos, A., Jevremovic, T., & Tsoukalas, L. H. (2011). Intelligent recognition of signature patterns in NRF spectra. *Nuclear Technology*, *175*(2), 480–497. doi:10.13182/NT11-A12319

Alamaniotis, M., Ikonomopoulos, A., & Tsoukalas, L. H. (2012). *Swarm Intelligence Optimization: Applications of Particle Swarms in Industrial Engineering and Nuclear Power Plants.* In C. Kahraman (Ed.), *Computational Intelligence Systems in Industrial Engineering* (pp. 181–202). Springer & Atlantis Press.

Alamaniotis, M., & Jevremovic, T. (2015). Hybrid fuzzy-genetic approach integrating peak identification and spectrum fitting for complex gamma-ray spectra analysis. *IEEE Transactions on Nuclear Science*, *62*(3), 1262–1277. doi:10.1109/TNS.2015.2432098

Alamaniotis, M., Mattingly, J., & Tsoukalas, L. H. (2013a). Kernel-Based Machine Learning for Background Estimation of NaI Low-Count Gamma-Ray Spectra. *IEEE Transactions on Nuclear Science*, *60*(3), 2209–2221. doi:10.1109/TNS.2013.2260868

Alamaniotis, M., Mattingly, J., & Tsoukalas, L. H. (2013b). Pareto-Optimal gamma spectroscopic radionuclide identification using evolutionary computing. *IEEE Transactions on Nuclear Science*, *60*(3), 2222–2231. doi:10.1109/TNS.2013.2260869

Alamaniotis, M., & Tsoukalas, L. H. (2015, November). Developing Intelligent Radiation Analysis Systems: A Hybrid Wave-Fuzzy Methodology for Analysis of Radiation Spectra. In *Tools with Artificial Intelligence (ICTAI), 2015 IEEE 27th International Conference on* (pp. 1114-1121). IEEE. doi:10.1109/ICTAI.2015.158

Alamaniotis, M., Young, J., & Tsoukalas, L. H. (2010). An insight in wavelet denoising of nuclear resonance fluorescence spectra for identification of hazardous materials. *1st National Conference on Advanced Tools and Solutions for Nuclear Material Detection*, (pp. 1-6), Salt Lake City, UT: Academic Press.

Alamaniotis, M., Young, J., & Tsoukalas, L. H. (2015). Assessment of fuzzy logic radioisotopic pattern identifier on gamma-ray signals with application to security. In Research Methods: Concepts, Methodologies, Tools, and Applications (pp. 1052-1071). IGI Global. doi:10.4018/978-1-4666-7456-1.ch046

Arsic, A., Tuba, M., & Jordanski, M. (2016). Fireworks algorithm applied to wireless sensor networks localization problem. In *Evolutionary Computation (CEC), 2016 IEEE Congress on* (pp. 4038-4044). IEEE. doi:10.1109/CEC.2016.7744302

Bacanin, N., & Tuba, M. (2015, May). Fireworks algorithm applied to constrained portfolio optimization problem. In *Evolutionary Computation (CEC), 2015 IEEE Congress on* (pp. 1242-1249). IEEE. doi:10.1109/CEC.2015.7257031

Bouarara, H. A., Hamou, R. M., Amine, A., & Rahmani, A. (2015). A fireworks algorithm for modern web information retrieval with visual results mining. *International Journal of Swarm Intelligence Research*, *6*(3), 1–23. doi:10.4018/IJSIR.2015070101

Bourbakis, N., Pantelopoulos, A., & Kannavara, R. (2008). A NRF Spectra Signature Detection Model using loca- global graphs. In *20st International Conference on Tools with Artificial Intelligence*, (pp. 547-550), Dayton, OH: Academic Press. doi:10.1109/ICTAI.2008.125

Bunn, G. (2003). The Nuclear Nonproliferation Treaty: History and Current Problems. *Arms Control Today*, *33*(10), 4.

Burr, T., & Hamada, M. (2009). Radio-isotope identification algorithms for NaI γ spectra. *Algorithms*, *2*(1), 339–360. doi:10.3390/a2010339

Carlevaro, C. M., Wilkinson, M.V., & Barrios, L.A. (2008). A genetic algorithm approach to routine gamma spectra analysis. *Journal of Instrumentation, 3*.

Engelbrecht, A. P. (2007). *Computational intelligence: An introduction*. John Wiley & Sons. doi:10.1002/9780470512517

Fatah, A. H., & Ahmed, A. H. (2011). Analysis of gamma-ray spectra using Levenberg-Marquardt method. *Engineering Technologies*, *73*, 269–274.

Forsberg, P., Agarwal, V., Gao, R., Tsoukalas, L. H., & Jevremovic, T. (November 2009). Peakseek: A statistical processing algorithm for radiation spectrum peak identification. In *21th IEEE International Conference on Tools with Artificial Intelligence*, (pp. 674-678). Newark, NJ: IEEE. doi:10.1109/ICTAI.2009.97

Gao, H., & Diao, M. (2011). Cultural firework algorithm and its application for digital filters design. *International Journal of Modelling. Identification and Control*, *14*(4), 324–331. doi:10.1504/IJMIC.2011.043157

Garcia-Talavera, M., & Ulicny, B. (2003). A genetic algorithm approach for multiplet deconvolution in γ-ray spectra. *Nuclear Instruments & Methods in Physics Research. Section A, Accelerators, Spectrometers, Detectors and Associated Equipment*, *512*(3), 585–594. doi:10.1016/S0168-9002(03)02052-7

Goswami, D., & Chakraborty, S. (2015a). Parametric optimization of ultrasonic machining process using gravitational search and fireworks algorithms. *Ain Shams Engineering Journal*, *6*(1), 315–331. doi:10.1016/j.asej.2014.10.009

Goswami, D., & Chakraborty, S. (2015b). A study on the optimization performance of fireworks and cuckoo search algorithms in laser machining processes. *Journal of The Institution of Engineers (India): Series C, 96*(3), 215-229.

Guendouz, M., Amine, A., & Hamou, R. M. (2017). A discrete modified fireworks algorithm for community detection in complex networks. *Applied Intelligence*, *46*(2), 373–385. doi:10.1007/s10489-016-0840-9

He, W., Mi, G., & Tan, Y. (2013). Parameter optimization of local-concentration model for spam detection by using fireworks algorithm. In *Advances in swarm intelligence* (pp. 439–450). Springer Berlin Heidelberg. doi:10.1007/978-3-642-38703-6_52

Hogan, M. A., Yamamoto, S., Covell, D. F., & Brown, M. (1970). Multiple linear regression analysis of scintillation gamma-ray spectra: Automatic candidate selection. *Nuclear Instruments and Methods*, *80*(1), 61–68. doi:10.1016/0029-554X(70)90298-3

Huang, H., Pasquier, M., & Quek, C. (2011). Decision Support System based on hierarchical co-evolutionary fuzzy approach: A case study in detecting gamma ray signals. *Expert Systems with Applications*, *38*(9), 10719–10729. doi:10.1016/j.eswa.2010.10.011

Imran, A. M., & Kowsalya, M. (2014). A new power system reconfiguration scheme for power loss minimization and voltage profile enhancement using Fireworks Algorithm. *International Journal of Electrical Power & Energy Systems*, *62*, 312–322. doi:10.1016/j.ijepes.2014.04.034

Imran, A. M., Kowsalya, M., & Kothari, D. P. (2014). A novel integration technique for optimal network reconfiguration and distributed generation placement in power distribution networks. *International Journal of Electrical Power & Energy Systems*, *63*, 461–472. doi:10.1016/j.ijepes.2014.06.011

Janecek, A., & Tan, Y. (2011). Using population based algorithms for initializing nonnegative matrix factorization. In *Advances in swarm intelligence* (pp. 307–316). Springer Berlin Heidelberg. doi:10.1007/978-3-642-21524-7_37

Janecek, A., & Tan, Y. (2011, July). Iterative improvement of the multiplicative update nmf algorithm using nature-inspired optimization. In *Natural Computation (ICNC), 2011 Seventh International Conference on* (Vol. 3, pp. 1668-1672). IEEE. doi:10.1109/ICNC.2011.6022356

Jiaqin, Z. (2011). Fireworks Algorithm for Solving 0/1 Knapsack Problem. *Journal of Wuhan Engineering Institute, 3*, 21.

Kamuda, M., Stinnett, J., & Sullivan, C. (2017). Automated Isotope Identification Algorithm Using Artificial Neural Networks. *IEEE Transactions on Nuclear Science*, *64*(7), 1858–1864. doi:10.1109/TNS.2017.2693152

Kangas, L. J., Keller, P. E., Siciliano, E. R., Kouzes, R. T., & Ely, J. H. (2008). The use of artificial neural networks in PVT-based radiation portal monitors. *Nuclear Instruments & Methods in Physics Research. Section A, Accelerators, Spectrometers, Detectors and Associated Equipment*, *587*(2), 398–412. doi:10.1016/j.nima.2008.01.065

Li, J., Zheng, S., & Tan, Y. (2014, July). Adaptive Fireworks Algorithm. In *Evolutionary Computation (CEC), 2014 IEEE Congress on* (pp. 3214-3221). IEEE. doi:10.1109/CEC.2014.6900418

Li, J., Zheng, S., & Tan, Y. (2017). The effect of information utilization: Introducing a novel guiding spark in the fireworks algorithm. *IEEE Transactions on Evolutionary Computation*, *21*(1), 153–166. doi:10.1109/TEVC.2016.2589821

Lihu, A., & Holban, Ș. (2015). De novo motif prediction using the fireworks algorithm. *International Journal of Swarm Intelligence Research*, *6*(3), 24–40. doi:10.4018/IJSIR.2015070102

Liu, J., Zheng, S., & Tan, Y. (2013). The improvement on controlling exploration and exploitation of firework algorithm. In *Advances in Swarm Intelligence* (Vol. 7923, pp. 11–23). Springer Berlin Heidelberg. doi:10.1007/978-3-642-38703-6_2

Liu, Z., Feng, Z., & Ke, L. (2015, May). Fireworks algorithm for the multi-satellite control resource scheduling problem. In *Evolutionary Computation (CEC), 2015 IEEE Congress on* (pp. 1280-1286). IEEE. doi:10.1109/CEC.2015.7257036

Lu, G., Tan, D., & Zhao, H. (November 2002). Improvement on regulating definition of antibody density of immune algorithm. In *Neural Information Processing 2002. ICONIP'02. Proceedings of the 9th International Conference on* (*vol. 5*, pp. 2669-2672). IEEE.

Ma, T., & Niu, D. (2016). Icing forecasting of high voltage transmission line using weighted least square support vector machine with fireworks algorithm for feature selection. *Applied Sciences*, *6*(12), 438. doi:10.3390/app6120438

Mattingly, J., & Mitchell, D. J. (2010). A framework for the solution of inverse radiation transport problems. *IEEE Transactions on Nuclear Science*, *57*(6), 3734–3743.

Mitchell, D. J., Sanger, H. M., & Marlow, K. W. (1989). Gamma-ray response functions for scintillation and semiconductor detectors. *Nuclear Instruments & Methods in Physics Research. Section A, Accelerators, Spectrometers, Detectors and Associated Equipment*, *276*(3), 547–556. doi:10.1016/0168-9002(89)90582-2

Mock, W. B. (2011). Treaty of Westphalia. In *Encyclopedia of Global Justice* (pp. 1095–1096). Springer Netherlands. doi:10.1007/978-1-4020-9160-5_660

Murray, W. S., Butterfield, K. B., & Baird, W. (2000). Automated radioisotope identification using fuzzy logic and portable CZT detectors. In *Nuclear Science Symposium Conference Record*, 2000 *IEEE* (*Vol. 2*, pp. 9-129). IEEE. doi:10.1109/NSSMIC.2000.949884

Pantelopoulos, A., Alamaniotis, M., Jevremovic, T., Park, S. M., Chung, S. M., & Bourbakis, N. (2009, November). LG-graph based detection of NRF spectrum signatures: Initial results and comparison. In *Tools with Artificial Intelligence, 2009. ICTAI'09. 21st International Conference on* (pp. 683-686). IEEE.

Panwar, L. K., Reddy, S., & Kumar, R. (2015). Binary fireworks algorithm based thermal unit commitment. *International Journal of Swarm Intelligence Research*, *6*(2), 87–101. doi:10.4018/IJSIR.2015040104

Pei, Y., Zheng, S., Tan, Y., & Takagi, H. (2012). An empirical study on influence of approximation approaches on enhancing fireworks algorithm. In *Systems, Man, and Cybernetics (SMC), 2012 Conference on*, (pp.1322-1327). IEEE.

Rahmani, A., Amine, A., Hamou, R. M., Rahmani, M. E., & Bouarara, H. A. (2015). Privacy preserving through fireworks algorithm based model for image perturbation in big data. *International Journal of Swarm Intelligence Research*, *6*(3), 41–58. doi:10.4018/IJSIR.2015070103

Rajaram, R., Palanisamy, K., Ramasamy, S., & Ramanathan, P. (2014). Selective harmonic elimination in PWM inverter using fire fly and fire works algorithm. *International Journal of Innovative Research in Advanced Engineering*, *1*, 55–62.

Reddy, K. S., Panwar, L. K., Kumar, R., & Panigrahi, B. K. (2016). Distributed resource scheduling in smart grid with electric vehicle deployment using fireworks algorithm. *Journal of Modern Power Systems and Clean Energy*, *4*(2), 188–199. doi:10.1007/s40565-016-0195-6

Runkle, R. C., Bernstein, A., & Vanier, P. E. (2010). Securing special nuclear material: Recent advances in neutron detection and their role in nonproliferation. *Journal of Applied Physics*, *108*(11), 13. doi:10.1063/1.3503495

Sangeetha, K., Babu, T. S., & Rajasekar, N. (2016). Fireworks algorithm-based maximum power point tracking for uniform irradiation as well as under partial shading condition. In *Artificial Intelligence and Evolutionary Computations in Engineering Systems* (pp. 79–88). New Delhi: Springer. doi:10.1007/978-81-322-2656-7_8

Sarfi, V., Niazazari, I., & Livani, H. (2016, September). Multiobjective fireworks optimization framework for economic emission dispatch in microgrids. In *North American Power Symposium (NAPS)*, 2016 (pp. 1-6). IEEE. doi:10.1109/NAPS.2016.7747896

Sjoden, G. E., Detwiler, R., LaVigne, E., & Baciak, J. E. Jr. (2009). Positive SNM gamma detection achieved through synthetic enhancement of sodium iodide detector spectra. *IEEE Transactions on Nuclear Science*, *56*(3), 1329–1339. doi:10.1109/TNS.2009.2014757

Sjoden, G. E., Maniscalco, J., & Chapman, M. (2012). Recent advances in the use of ASEDRA in post processing scintillator spectra for resolution enhancement. *Journal of Radioanalytical and Nuclear Chemistry*, *291*(2), 365–371. doi:10.1007/s10967-011-1335-0

Stinnett, J., & Sullivan, C. J. (2013). An automated isotope identification algorithm using Bayesian statistics. *IEEE Nuclear Science Symposium Conference Record.*

Sullivan, C. J., Martinez, M. E., & Garner, S. E. (2006). Wavelet analysis of sodium iodide spectra. *IEEE Transactions on Nuclear Science*, *53*(5), 2916–2922. doi:10.1109/TNS.2006.881909

Sullivan, C. J., & Stinnett, J. (2015). Validation of a Bayesian-based isotope identification algorithm. *Nuclear Instruments & Methods in Physics Research. Section A, Accelerators, Spectrometers, Detectors and Associated Equipment*, *784*, 298–305. doi:10.1016/j.nima.2014.11.113

Tan, Y. (2015). Fireworks Algorithm with Dynamic Search. In *Fireworks Algorithm* (pp. 103–117). Springer Berlin Heidelberg. doi:10.1007/978-3-662-46353-6_7

Tan, Y. (2015a). Adaptive Fireworks Algorithm. In *Fireworks Algorithm* (pp. 119–131). Springer Berlin Heidelberg. doi:10.1007/978-3-662-46353-6_8

Tan, Y. (2015b). Cooperative Fireworks Algorithm. In *Fireworks Algorithm* (pp. 133–149). Springer Berlin Heidelberg. doi:10.1007/978-3-662-46353-6_9

Tan, Y., Yu, C., Zheng, S., & Ding, K. (2013). Introduction to fireworks algorithm. *International Journal of Swarm Intelligence Research*, *4*(4), 39–70. doi:10.4018/ijsir.2013100103

Tan, Y., & Zhu, Y. (2010). Fireworks algorithm for optimization. In *Advances in Swarm Intelligence* (pp. 355–364). Springer Berlin Heidelberg. doi:10.1007/978-3-642-13495-1_44

Tsoukalas, L. H., & Uhring, R. E. (1997). *Fuzzy and Neural Approaches in Engineering*. John Wiley and Sons.

Tsoulfanidis, N., & Landsberger, S. (2013). *Measurement and detection of radiation*. CRC press.

Tuba, E., Tuba, M., & Beko, M. (2016, June). Support vector machine parameters optimization by enhanced fireworks algorithm. In *International Conference in Swarm Intelligence* (pp. 526-534). Springer International Publishing. doi:10.1007/978-3-319-41000-5_52

Tuba, M., Bacanin, N., & Alihodzic, A. (2015a, April). Multilevel image thresholding by fireworks algorithm. In *Radioelektronika (RADIOELEKTRONIKA), 2015 25th international conference* (pp. 326-330). IEEE. doi:10.1109/RADIOELEK.2015.7129057

Tuba, M., Bacanin, N., & Beko, M. (2015b, April). Fireworks algorithm for RFID network planning problem. In *Radioelektronika (RADIOELEKTRONIKA), 2015 25th International Conference* (pp. 440-444). IEEE. doi:10.1109/RADIOELEK.2015.7129049

Yoshida, E., Shizuma, K., Endo, S., & Oka, T. (2003). Application of neural networks for the analysis of gamma-ray spectra measured with a Ge spectrometer. *Nuclear Instruments & Methods in Physics Research. Section A, Accelerators, Spectrometers, Detectors and Associated Equipment*, *484*(1-3), 557–563. doi:10.1016/S0168-9002(01)01962-3

Yu, C., Li, J., & Tan, Y. (2014, October). Improve enhanced fireworks algorithm with differential mutation. In *Systems, Man and Cybernetics (SMC), 2014 IEEE International Conference on* (pp. 264-269). IEEE. doi:10.1109/SMC.2014.6973918

Zhang, B., Zhang, M., & Zheng, Y. J. (2014). Improving Enhanced Fireworks Algorithm with New Gaussian Explosion and Population Selection Strategies. In *Advances in Swarm Intelligence* (pp. 53–63). Springer International Publishing. doi:10.1007/978-3-319-11857-4_7

Zhen-xin, D. U. (2013). Fireworks Algorithm for Solving Nonlinear Equation and System. *Modern Computer, 4*, 6.

Zheng, S., & Tan, Y. (2013, March). A unified distance measure scheme for orientation coding in identification. In *Information Science and Technology (ICIST), 2013 International Conference on* (pp. 979-985). IEEE. doi:10.1109/ICIST.2013.6747701

Zheng, Y., Janecek, A., & Tan, Y. (2013). Enhanced fireworks algorithm. In *IEEE Congress on Evolutionary Computation* (pp. 2069-2077). IEEE.

Zheng, Y. J., Song, Q., & Chen, S. Y. (2013). Multiobjective fireworks optimization for variable-rate fertilization in oil crop production. *Applied Soft Computing*, *13*(11), 4253–4263. doi:10.1016/j.asoc.2013.07.004

Zheng, Y. J., Xu, X. L., Ling, H. F., & Chen, S. Y. (2015). A hybrid fireworks optimization method with differential evolution operators. *Neurocomputing*, *148*, 75–82. doi:10.1016/j.neucom.2012.08.075

Zhu, M. H., Liu, L. G., Qi, D. X., You, Z., & Xu, A. A. (2009). Least square fitting of low resolution gamma ray spectra with cubic B-spline basis functions. *Chinese Phys. C.*, *33*(1), 24–29. doi:10.1088/1674-1137/33/1/006

Chapter 8
A Computational Comparison of Swarm Optimization Techniques for Optimal Load Shedding Under the Presence of FACTS Devices to Avoid Voltage Instability

G. V. Nagesh Kumar
Vignan's Institute of Information Technology (Autonomous), India

B. Venkateswara Rao
V. R. Siddhartha Engineering College (Autonomous), India

D. Deepak Chowdary
Dr. L. Bullayya College of Engineering (for Women), India

Polamraju V. S. Sobhan
Vignan's Foundation for Science, India

ABSTRACT

Voltage instability has become a serious threat to the operation of modern power systems. Load shedding is one of the effective countermeasures for avoiding instability. Improper load shedding may result in huge technical and economic losses. So, an optimal load shedding is to be carried out for supplying more demand. This chapter implements bat and firefly algorithms for solving the optimal load shedding problem to identify the optimal amount of load to be shed. This is applied for a multi-objective function which contains minimization of amount of load to be shed, active power loss minimization, and voltage profile improvement. The presence of with and without static VAR compensator (SVC), thyristor-controlled series capacitor (TCSC), and unified power flow controller (UPFC) on load shedding for IEEE 57 bus system has been presented and analyzed. The results obtained with bat and firefly algorithms were compared with genetic algorithm (GA) and also the impact of flexible AC transmission system (FACTS) devices on load shedding problem has been analyzed.

DOI: 10.4018/978-1-5225-5134-8.ch008

INTRODUCTION

Nowadays, voltage instability has been considered as one of the reason for the blackouts all over the world. Blackouts occurs due to contingency, such as the outage of an important transmission line or the outage of a major generator, or insufficient reactive power support at important buses due to a high loading condition or a combination of both the aspects. The requirement for improved efficiency at the same time as maintaining system stability necessitates the development of improved system analysis approaches and the improvement of advanced technologies. The Load shedding is a type of emergency control that is designed to ensure system stability by curtailing system load to match generation. It is an effective corrective control action in which a part of the system loads are disconnected according to certain priority in order to protect the power system. Load shedding is considered as the last resort tool for use in that extreme situation and usually the less preferred action to be adopted, but in this kind of problem it is vital to prevent the system from collapsing (Kundur, 1993). Load shedding schemes are mainly classified into two types those are under frequency load shedding scheme and under voltage load shedding scheme. Under frequency load shedding scheme has been used, to protect the power system stability from major disturbances. However, the analysis of recent blackouts suggests that voltage collapse and voltage-related problems are also important concerns in maintaining system stability. For this reason, voltage also needs to be taken into account in load shedding schemes. This type of scheme is called under voltage load shedding scheme. The load shedding problem is formulated using optimization methods. These methods are used to find the amount of load to be shed based on Optimal Power Flow frame work. The purpose of an Optimal Power Flow (OPF) function is to schedule the power system control parameters which optimize a certain objective function while satisfying its equality and inequality constraints, power flow equations, system security and equivalent operating limits. The equality constraints are the nodal power balance equations, while the inequality constraints are the limits of all control or state variables. OPF has been widely used for both the operation and planning of a power system. Introduced by Tinney (1967) and discussed by Carpentier (1979), the control variables include generator active powers, generator bus voltages, transformer tap ratios and the reactive power generation of shunt compensators.

A wide variety of classical optimization techniques have been applied in solving the OPF problems considering a single objective function, such as nonlinear programming, quadratic programming, linear programming, Newton-based techniques sequential unconstrained minimization technique, interior point methods and the parametric method but unfortunately these methods are infeasible in practical systems because of non-linear characteristics like valve point effects. Hence, it becomes essential to develop optimization techniques which are capable of overcoming these drawbacks and handling such difficulties. Optimization problems have been solved by many population-based optimization techniques in the recent past. These techniques have been successfully applied to non-convex, non-smooth and non-differentiable optimization problems. Some of the population-based optimization methods are genetic algorithm, Cuckoo Search Algorithm (Dung A. Le &Dieu N. Vo, 2016), bat Search Algorithm (Rao & Kumar, 2015), Quasi-Oppositional Biogeography-Based Optimization, Hybridization of Biogeography Based Optimization (HBBO) (Prabhneetkaur and Taranjotkaur, 2014), Anticipatory Multi objective Cuckoo Search (AMOCS) algorithm (SamikshaGoel, Arpita Sharma and V. K. Panchal, 2014),Teaching Learning Based Optimization (Aparajita Mukherjee, Sourav Paul & Provas Kumar Roy, 2015)artificial bee colony optimization (Rahul Khandelwal, J. Senthilnath, S. N. Omkar and Narendra Shivanath, 2016).

Flexible AC Transmission System (FACTS) controllers could be a suitable alternative to provide reactive power support at the load centers locally and hence keep the voltages within their safe operating limits to minimize the load shedding (Hingorani & Gyugyi, 2000). The FACTS devices use reliable high-speed thyristor based controllable elements such as SVC, TCSC, and UPFC etc. are designed based on state of the art developments in power semiconductor devices. J. G. Singh et al. suggested a new sensitivity based approach to locate Thyristor Controlled Series Compensator (TCSC) and Unified Power Flow Controller (UPFC) to enhance power system loadability. The new sensitivity factors may be effectively used for placement of TCSC and UPFC for increasing the system's loadability. Voltage stability analysis of large power systems using the modal analysis technique has further been proposed by B Gao et al. Modal analysis through bus, branch and generation participation factors provide useful information, which can then be utilized for placement of FACTS devices. Bus participation factors have been taken into consideration for determining the most suitable sites by Y.Mansour et al. Various optimization techniques have also been used for determining suitable locations for FACTS device to improve voltage profile and damping of the system.

A. Ramasamy et al brought into view the correlation between FVSI index and UVLS scheme. Under Voltage Load Shedding (UVLS) is one of the various methods used to sustain voltage stability. Alternatively, Fast Voltage Stability Index (FVSI) index has proven to be a good indicator for voltage stability in a system. From the simulation, results clearly indicate that FVSI index can be used to identify location to be load shed and thus reduce probability of Voltage Instability.

In (H. Am briz-Perez, E.Acha, C.R. Fuerte-Esquivel & A.De la Torre, 1998), has been showed the issue of UPFC modeling within the context of OPF solutions. The nonlinear optimization problem is solved by newton's method leading to highly robust iterative solutions even for cases of large scale power networks, where hundreds of variables are to be optimized is presented in literature. (RR Aparna, 2016), explains the use of swarm intelligence techniques for different applications. In 2016 (Dung A. Le & Dieu N. Vo, 2016), uses a cuckoo search algorithm (CSA) to solve the optimal reactive power dispatch (ORPD) problem in power system operation considering the power loss and voltage deviation. The advantages of the CSA method are few control parameters and high optimal solution quality. The objective of the ORPD problem is to minimize real power losses or bus voltage deviation satisfying equality and inequality constraints of real and reactive power balance. In this the authors use the single objective function for solving ORPD problem. Static synchronous series compensator (SSSC) is one of the most effective flexible AC transmission systems (FACTS) devices used for enhancing power system security. Optimal location and sizing of SSSC are investigated for solving the optimal reactive power dispatch (ORPD) problem in order to minimize the active power loss in the transmission networks. Optimal reactive power dispatch (ORPD), a sub problem of OPF, has significant influence on the economic and secure operation of power systems. (SusantaDutta, Provas Kumar Roy & Debashis Nandi, 2016) use chemical reaction optimization (CRO) to solve the above problem with minimization of single objective function. Out of the several FACTS devices UPFC is one of the most important shunt-series connected FACTS devices to improve voltage stability and minimize the amount of load to be shed (Padiyar & Uma Rao, 1999; Lashkar Ara & Kazemi, 2012).

In this chapter, FACTS devices like SVC, TCSC and UPFC are considered to minimize the load curtailment. An optimal power flow problem is formulated with the objective to minimize the amount of load to be shed, the total real power losses and voltage deviation subjected to constraints along with FACTS devices limits. To deal with the above problem new metaheuristic optimization techniques called bat and firefly algorithms have been proposed. In this chapter the impact of SVC, TCSC and UPFC on minimization of load shedding problem has been examined with bat and firefly algorithms. The effectiveness of the proposed algorithms has been tested on IEEE 57-bus system without and with SVC, TCSC and UPFC. The obtained results are compared with Genetic algorithm. To show the effectiveness of the algorithms, their population size and parameters are also varied. In this chapter voltage stability has been analyzed using line based voltage stability index called 'Fast Voltage Stability Index' (FVSI).

The remaining organization of the chapter is as follows. Section 2 presents the various FACTS devices like SVC, TCSC and UPFC; Section 3 presents multi objective OPF problem formulation. The implementation of Meta heuristic optimization algorithms to the problem is given in Section 4. Numerical results and discussion are followed in Section 5. Section 6 presents' future research directions finally, the conclusion is given in section 7.

FACTS DEVICES

Static VAR Compensator (SVC)

Static VAR Compensator is the simple and popular shunt connected FACTS device. The SVC is modeled as a variable susceptance device. The SVC device can either inject reactive power (capacitive) or absorb it (inductive) as per system requirements. The sizing of the SVC located at a bus is done until the voltage at the bus is 1.0 p.u. The variable susceptance model is shown in Figure 1.

Current drawn by the SVC is

$$I_{svc} = jB_{svc}V_k \tag{1}$$

SVC absorbed or injected reactive power at bus k is

$$Q_{svc} = -V_k^2 B_{SVC} \tag{2}$$

Figure 1. Variable Shunt Susceptance

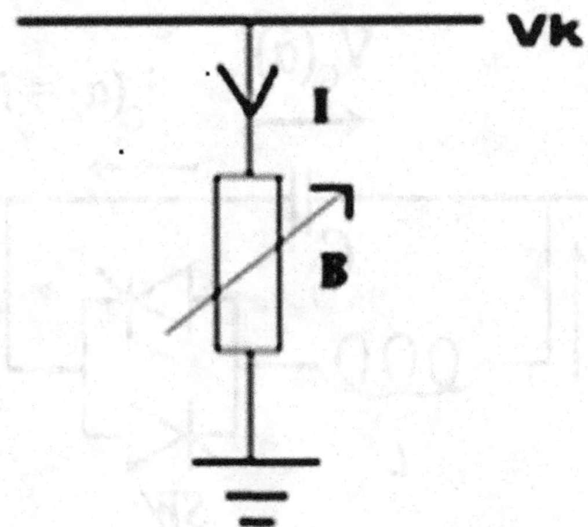

The real and reactive power variations at k[th] bus related to the susceptance of the SVC are given in equation 3. The total susceptance B_{svc} is taken as the state variable.

$$\begin{bmatrix} \Delta P_k \\ \Delta Q_k \end{bmatrix}^i = \begin{bmatrix} 0 & 0 \\ 0 & Q_k \end{bmatrix}^i \begin{bmatrix} \Delta \theta_k \\ \Delta B_{svc} / B_{svc} \end{bmatrix}^i \tag{3}$$

After completion of iteration, susceptance value of the SVC is updated as per the optimization rules. Initial values of the SVC susceptance is consider to be B=0.02p.u, B_{min}= -1.0p.u, B_{max}=1.0p.u

Thyristor-Controlled Series Capacitor (TCSC)

Thyristor-controlled series capacitor scheme is developed by Vithaythil and others. TCSC also enhances a system's stability. The basic module of the TCSC is represented in Figure 2. It consists of a series compensating capacitor shunted by thyristor controlled reactor. Thyristor inclusion in the TCSC module enables it to have a smoother control of reactance against system parameter variations. This is modeled as a controllable reactance, is inserted in series with the transmission line to adjust the line impedance and thereby controls power flow.

In this study, reactance of the transmission line is adjusted by using TCSC directly. The TCSC is modeled as variable impedance and its rating depends on the reactance of the transmission line where the TCSC is located. The impedance equations are written as in equations 4 and 5.

$$Z_{line} = R_{line} + X_{line} \tag{4}$$

$$X_{ij} = X_{line} + X_{TCSC} \tag{5}$$

Figure 2. Basic TCSC model

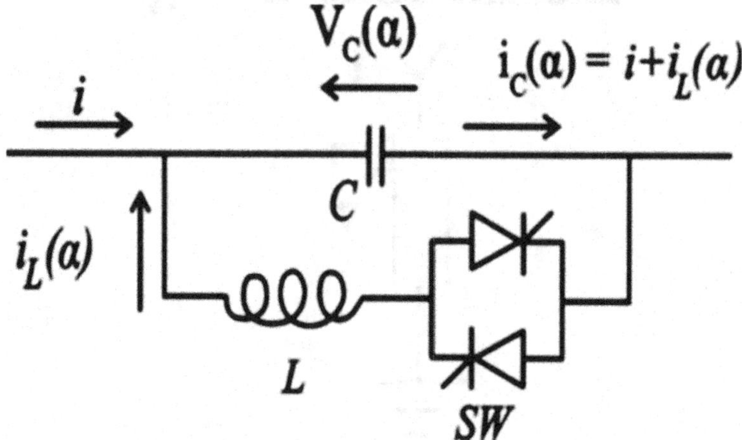

where XTCSC is reactance of TCSC, in order to avoid over compensation, the working range of the TCSC is selected between -0.8Xline and 0.6Xline.

The transfer admittance matrix of the TCSC is given by

$$\begin{bmatrix} I_i \\ I_j \end{bmatrix} = \begin{bmatrix} jB_{ii} & jB_{ij} \\ jB_{ji} & jB_{jj} \end{bmatrix} \begin{bmatrix} Vi \\ V_j \end{bmatrix} \tag{6}$$

For capacitive operation, equations are given in 7 and 8

$$B_{ii} = B_{jj} = \frac{1}{X_{TCSC}} \tag{7}$$

$$B_{ij} = B_{ji} = -\frac{1}{X_{TCSC}} \tag{8}$$

For inductive operation the signs are reversed

The active and reactive power equations at bus k are:

$$P_i = V_i V_j B_{ij} \sin(\theta_i - \theta_j) \tag{9}$$

$$Q_i = -V_i^2 B_{ii} - V_i V_j B_{ij} \cos(\theta_i - \theta_j) \tag{10}$$

When the series reactance regulates the amount of active power flowing from bus i to bus j the change in reactance of TCSC is

$$\Delta X_{TCSC} = X^{i}_{TCSC} - X^{(i-1)}_{TCSC} \tag{11}$$

Based on optimization rules, the state variable XTCSC of the series controller is updated.

Unified Power Flow Controller

Gyugyi proposed the UPFC concept is used for real time control and dynamic compensation of the ac transmission system (Tiwari & Sood, 2012; Ghahremani & Kamwa, 2013). UPFC provides multi-functional flexibility required to solve many of the problems in the power system. The UPFC is able to control simultaneously or selectively all the parameters affecting power flow in the transmission line (i.e. voltage magnitude, line impedance and phase angle). This capability signifies the term ‘unified’ in the UPFC (Radu, 2006; Padiyar & Kulakarni, 1998).

The UPFC consists of two voltage-source converters, one connected in shunt and one connected in a series. The series converter of the UPFC injects an AC voltage with the controllable magnitude and phase angle in a series with the transmission line via a series connected coupling transformer. The basic function of shunt converter is to supply or absorb the real power demanded by the series converter at the common DC link. It can also generate or absorb controllable reactive power and provide independent shunt reactive compensation for the line which is shown in Figure 3. Thereby, the UPFC can fulfil the functions of reactive shunt compensation, series compensation and phase shifting (Mihalie, Zunko & Povh, 1994). The device is an amalgamation of a shunt connected Static Synchronous Compensator (STATCOM) and a series connected Static Synchronous Series Compensator (SSSC). The combination of above two devices is UPFC. In UPFC exchange of real and reactive has been obtained through shared DC linkage. It is also capable of generation or absorption of controlled reactive power, thus providing autonomous shunt reactive compensation. The UPFC not only performs the functions of STATCOM, SSSC, and the phase angle regulator but also provides additional flexibility by combining some of the functions of these controllers (Tiwari, 2012; Gyugyi, 1995).

UPFC voltage sources are written in equations 12 and 13,

$$V_{vR}(\cos\delta_{vR} + j\sin\delta_{vR}) \tag{12}$$

$$V_{cR}(\cos\delta_{cR} + j\sin\delta_{cR}) \tag{13}$$

where V_{vR} and δ_{vR} are the controllable voltage magnitude and phase angle of the voltage source representing the shunt converter. Similarly, V_{cR} and δ_{cR} are the controllable voltage magnitude and phase angle of the voltage source representing the series converter. The source impedance is considered to be resistance less. (i.eR_{vR}=0, R_{cR}=0)

Figure 3. Schematic arrangement of the Unified Power Flow Controller

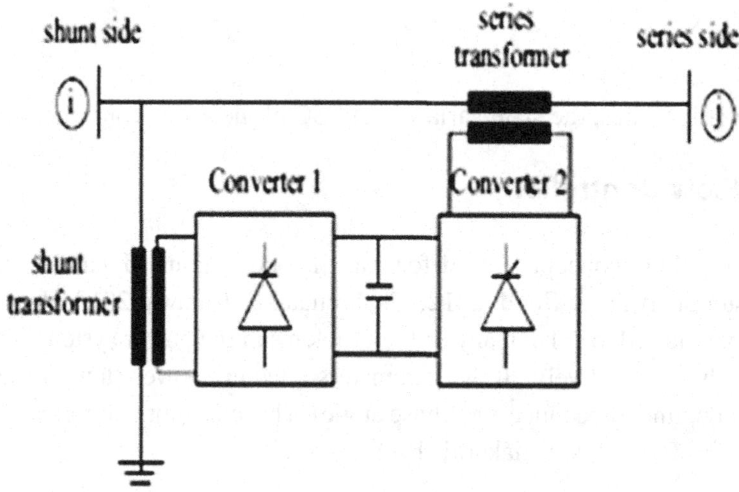

The UPFC using solid state controllers provides functional flexibility to handle practically all the power flow control and transmission line compensation problems which are generally not obtained by variable impedance type thyristor-controlled controllers. Installing UPFC in the system improves the voltage profile that will reduce the amount of load to be shed. The starting values of the UPFC voltage sources are taken to be V_{cr} =0.04 p.u, δ_{cr}=87.13^0, V_{vr} =1 p.u. and δ_{vr} = 0^0. The source reactances are taken as X_{cr}=X_{vr} = 0.1 p.u.

PROBLEM FORMULATION

In this chapter, the optimal amount of load to be shed is identified by new optimisation techniques namely bat and firefly algorithms to avoid voltage instability. Impact of SVC, TCSC and UPFC on load shedding problem has been analysed with optimization techniques. In this chapter multi objective function is formulated to improve the stability of the system which consists of three parameters. These three components are active power loss minimisation, minimization of voltage deviation and minimization of amount of load to be shed.

Objective Function

In multi objective optimization problem, each objective would be considered for the optimal solution. The multi objective index for the performance calculation of amount of load to be shed is considered along with the active power loss and voltage deviation is given in equation 14.

$$\text{Min F} = \text{Min}\left(W_1 {}^*F_{Ploss} + W_2 {}^*F_{VD} + W_3 {}^*F_{LS}\right) \tag{14}$$

where W_1+W_2+W_3 =1 and

$W_1 = 0.3$, $W_2 = 0.3$, $W_3 = 0.4$

Select these values based on trial and error method.

- **Active Power Loss:** This objective consists of minimizing the active power losses in the transmission lines. It can be expressed as in equation 15,

$$F_{PLoss} = \min\left(P_{Loss}\right) = \min\left(\sum_{k=1}^{ntl} \text{real}(S_{ij}^k + S_{ji}^k)\right) \tag{15}$$

where ntl=no. of transmission lines

S_{ij} is the total complex power flow of line i – j

- **Voltage Deviation:** To have a good voltage performance, the voltage deviation at each bus must be made as small as possible. The Voltage Deviation (VD) can be expressed in equation 16,

$$F_{VD} = \min\left(VD\right) = \min\left(\sum_{k=1}^{Nbus} \left|V_k - V_k^{ref}\right|^2\right) \tag{16}$$

V_k is the voltage magnitude at bus k

V_k^{ref} is the reference voltage magnitude at bus k

- **Amount of Load to be Shed:** This objective function is interruption load minimisation. Load interruption can be defined as the total load to be shed in order to maintain the voltage at appropriate level (Arief, 2010; Yasin, 2013; Cheraghi Valujerdi, 2012; Fernandes, 2008).

$$F_{LS} = \min\left(\text{Amount of Load to be shed}\right) = \min\left(\Delta S_{shed\ i}\right) \tag{17}$$

where $\Delta S_{shed\ i}$ is the total amount of load to be shed at bus i.

Equality constraints:

$$\sum_{i=1}^{N} P_{Gi} = \sum_{i=1}^{N} P_{Di} + P_L \tag{18}$$

$$\sum_{i=1}^{N} Q_{Gi} = \sum_{i=1}^{N} Q_{Di} + Q_L \tag{19}$$

where i=1,2,3,.......,N and N = no. of. Buses

P_L is total active power losses; Q_L is total reactive power losses

Inequality constraints:

$$V_{Gi}^{\min} \leq V_{Gi} \leq V_{Gi}^{\max} \tag{20}$$

$$P_{Gi}^{\min} \leq P_{Gi} \leq P_{Gi}^{\max} \tag{21}$$

$$Q_{Gi}^{\min} \leq Q_{Gi} \leq Q_{Gi}^{\max} \quad (22)$$

SVC Limits

$$B_{svc}^{\min} \leq B_{svc} \leq B_{svc}^{\max} \quad (23)$$

TCSC Limits

$$X_{tcsc}^{\min} \leq X_{tcsc} \leq X_{tcsc}^{\max} \quad (24)$$

UPFC device limits:

$$V_{vr}^{\min} \leq V_{vr} \leq V_{vr}^{\max} \quad (25)$$

Vvr is the shunt converter voltage magnitude (p.u)

$$V_{cr}^{\min} \leq V_{cr} \leq V_{cr}^{\max} \quad (26)$$

Vcr is the series converter voltage magnitude (p.u)where P_L is the active power loss in the system, P_{Gi} is the active power generation at bus i, P_{Di} is the real power demand at bus i, Q_{Gi} is the reactive power generation at bus i. Q_{Di} is the reactive power demand at bus i, N and ng are the number of buses and no of generators in the system respectively.

Load curtailment limits:

$$0 \leq P_{shed\,i} \leq P_{Di}$$

$$0 \leq Q_{shed\,i} \leq Q_{Di}$$

where $P_{shed,i}$ is the amount of load to be shed at bus i in MW

$Q_{shed,i}$ is the amount of load to be shed at bus i in MVAR

Fast Voltage Stability Index (FVSI)

The voltage stability indices referred to indicate the voltage collapse. In this chapter, line-based voltage stability index is implemented to evaluate the voltage stability analysis in a power system. This index is called as Fast Voltage Stability Index (FVSI). It is given in equation 27. The system becomes unstable if FVSI is equal to or greater than unity.

$$FVSI_{ij} = \frac{4\ Z^2 Q_j}{V_i^2\ X} \tag{27}$$

where

Z = Impedance of the line
X = Reactance of the line
Q_j = reactive power at bus j
(receiving end bus)
V_i = voltage magnitude at bus i
(sending end bus)
$FVSI_{ij}$ = FVSI for line connected between bus i and bus j.

Any line in the system that exhibits FVSI close to unity indicate that the line is may lead to system violation. So FVSI has to be maintained less than unity in order to maintain a stability of the system (Ratniyomcha & Kulworawa-nichpong, 2009).

OPTIMIZATION METHODS FOR OPTIMAL LOADSHEDDING

Overview of the Optimization techniques

Modern engineers are facing with problems like system design, construction and maintenance. In all these problems, the main goal is to obtain a better solution with less effort. The effort required for the desired output is usually formulated as a function with considered limitations. Optimization is also defined as the technique employed to get the maximum or minimum value of a function. It has been used widely in several technical fields. Some of these are design of aircraft and aerospace structures for minimum weight, calculating optimal trajectories of space vehicles, designing civil engineering structures like frames, foundations, towers, chimneys, bridges, and dams for minimum cost, designing water resource systems for maximum benefit, Optimal plastic design of structures, developing material handling equipment such as conveyors, trucks, and cranes at minimal costs, designing maximum efficiency pumps, turbines, and heat transfer equipment, Optimum electrical machinery design for motors, generators, and transformers, Optimum design of electrical networks, power systems, Optimal production planning, controlling, and scheduling, Selecting site for an industry, Planning of maintenance and replacement of equipment to reduce operating costs, Devising best strategies to obtain maximum profit in the presence of competition and Optimum design of control systems.

A multi-objective optimization problem is an optimization problem that involves multiple objective functions. In mathematical terms, a multi-objective optimization problem can be formulated as

$$\text{Min } f\left(X\right) = \min(f_1\left(x\right), f_2\left(x\right), f_3\left(x\right), \ldots. f_k\left(x\right) \tag{28}$$

S.t $x \in X$

Subjected to the constraints

$$g_i\left(X\right) \leq 0, \quad i = 1,2,3,\ldots,p$$

$$h_i\left(X\right) = 0, \quad i = 1,2,3,\ldots,q$$

where X is an m-dimensional vector called the design vector, f(X) is termed the objective function, and g_i (X) and h_i (X) are known as inequality and equality constraints, respectively. The number of variables m and the number of inequality constraints p and the number of equality constraints q. The problem stated in Eq. (28) is called a constrained multi objective optimization problem.

Genetic Algorithm

Genetic Algorithms (GAs) are one of various techniques amongst the Evolutionary Algorithms, which search for solutions to optimization problems through "evolving" better solutions. Genetic Algorithms have found application in science, engineering, business and social sciences. GAs has been developed by John Holland, his colleagues and students at the University of Michigan during the early 1970's. Also, they have gained popularity over the recent years in fields of science and engineering. GAs have been successfully applied to optimization problems like wire routing, scheduling, adaptive control, game playing, cognitive modelling, transportation issues, traveling salesman problems, optimal control problems, etc. GAs are general-purpose search techniques based on principles inspired from the genetic and evolution mechanisms observed in natural systems and populations of living beings.

In lieu to Optimal Power Flow, the major steps of the GA as applied can be summarized as under:

1. "Creation of an initial population through the random generation of a set of feasible solutions (chromosomes).
2. Evaluation of each chromosome by solving the objective function.
3. Determining fitness function for each chromosome in the population.
4. Application of GA operators to generate new populations.
5. Copying the optimal solution from the current into the new population.
6. Generating new members (typically 1-10% of the population size), as neighbors to solutions in the current population, and adding them to the new population.
7. Applying crossover operators to complete members of the new population.
8. Applying mutation operator to the new population".

Bat Algorithm

Bat algorithm (BA) is a metaheuristic method which uses population of points to search for a global minimum of a function over continuous search space. This bat algorithm is developed using the concept of echolocation behaviour of micro bats with varying pulse rates of emission and loudness. This method is based upon the certain approximations that all bats use echolocation to sense distance, and distinguish between food and background barriers in some magical way. To search for prey, Bats usually fly haphazardly with velocity v at position x with a fixed frequency f_{min}, varying wavelength and loudness (Yang, 2008; Yang, X. S 2011). Depending on the proximity of their target, they can automatically adjust the frequency of their emitted pulses and adjust the rate of pulse emission assuming that the loudness varies from a large value A_0 to a minimum constant value A_{min}. It is even assumed that frequency ranges from 0 to f_{max} because higher frequencies have short wavelengths and travel shorter distances, so that the rate of pulse can be 0 or 1, where 0 means no pulses and 1 means maximum rate of pulse emission. Search for prey is intensified by a local random walk and selection of the best continues until certain stop criteria are met. This essentially uses a frequency-tuning technique to control the dynamic behaviour of a swarm of bats, and the balance between exploration and exploitation can be controlled by tuning algorithm-dependent parameters in bat algorithm (Yang, X. S, 2010). The basic steps of the bat algorithm are summarized and are given bellow in the pseudo code.

"Objective function f(x), $x = (x_1, x_2, ..., x_d)^T$
Initialize the bat population x_{ii} $(ii = 1, 2, ..., n)$ *and* v_{ii}
Define pulse frequency f_{ii} *at* x_{ii}
Initialize pulse rates r_{ii} *and the loudness* A_{ii}
while(t <Max number of iterations)
Generate a new solution by changing frequency,
And modifying velocities and solutions [equations (2) to (4)]
if(rand $>r_{ii}$*)*
Select a best solution in the available solutions
Create a local solution around the selected best solution
end if
Create a new solution by flying randomly
if(rand $<A_{ii}$ *&* $f(x_{ii}) < f(x_o)$*)*
Accept the new solutions
Increase r_{ii} *and reduce* A_{ii}
end if
Rank the bats and find the current best x_o
End while
Post process results and visualization"

The step by step implementation of bat algorithm can be described as follows:

Step 1: *Initialize the load flow data, and bat parameters such as the size of population (N), the maximum number of generations (N_gen), Loudness (L), Pulse rate (PR) and the number of variables to be optimized (D).*

Step 2: *Generate the initial population of N individuals randomly in the feasible area. Consider the optimized variables. Therefore, all the solutions are practicable solutions and the object is to find the best possible one.*

Step 3: *Evaluate the fitness for each individual in the population according to the objective function.*

Step 4: *Generate a new resident.*
Step 5: *Stop the process and print the best individual if the stopping criterion is satisfied, else go back to step 4.*

Firefly Algorithm

Firefly algorithm (FA) is a kind of stochastic search techniques based on the mechanism of natural behavior of fireflies. The firefly algorithm is a metaheuristic algorithm, enthused by the sporadic behavior of fireflies. The primary objective for a firefly's flash is to act as a signal system to entice other fireflies (X.S. Yang, 2009; Yang 2010). This algorithm is based upon the following assumptions those are all fireflies are unisexual, so that one firefly will be a focus for all other fireflies. Charismatic is proportional to their vividness, and for any two fireflies, the less bright one will catch the fancy of the brighter one. However, the vividness can decrease as their distance increases. If there are no fireflies dazzling than a given firefly, it will move haphazardly and the vividness should be associated with the objective function. Vividness is proportional to value of search-space function in case of maximization problem.

There are two important disputes in firefly algorithm, first is light intensity variation and other is vividness variation. It is assumed that vividness of firefly is ascertained by its vividness which in turn associated with search-space function. The vividness of the firefly is calculated objective value F(x) at a particular location x. Vividness is relative and it varies with distance between two fireflies. Light is also absorbed by the air and it also gets decreased with increasing distance so vividness is allowed to show a discrepancy with degree of absorption. The firefly algorithm function can be described as: initially consider an objective function F(x). Generate an initial population of n fireflies X_i, i=1, 2, 3…n. Calculate Light intensity at X_i which is determined by F (X). Delineate the light absorption coefficient. Now compare the light intensities of fireflies and move the firefly which is having lesser light intensity towards the brighter one. Then vary the vividness with distance. Now echelon the fireflies and discover the best solution. It may create as gbest. In optimization problem where number of fireflies are greater than number of local optima, the initial locations of the n fireflies should be distributed relatively uniformly throughout the entire search space. During the execution, the fireflies converge into all of these local optima, the global optima is determined. Firefly algorithm will approach the global optima when n tends to infinite and number of iterations is greater than 1 but in reality it has abrupt convergence. The basic steps of the Firefly algorithm can be summarized in the pseudo code given below (Lukasik & Zak, 2009).

***x*), *x* =** *(x1,…,xd)T*
Generate initial population of fireflies $\mathbf{x}_{ii}$*(i=1, 2…, n)*
Light intensity I_{ii} *at* x_{ii} *is determined by* $f(\mathbf{x}_{ii})$
Define light absorption coefficient γ
while*(t <MaxGeneration)*
for*ii = 1: n all n fireflies*
for*jj = 1: ii all n fireflies*
if*(I_{jj}> I_{ii}), More firefly ii towards jj in d-dimension;* ***end if***
Attractiveness varies with distance r
Evaluate new solutions and modify the light intensity
***end for** jj*

***end for** ii*
Rank all the fireflies and find the current best firefly
end while
Post process results and visualization

The bat and firefly algorithms are implemented to find the optimal amount of load to be shed by considering without and with SVC, TCSC and UPFC. In this study, the real and reactive loads at buses, real power generation and voltages of the generator buses are considered as variables to optimize the multi objective function. For the considered IEEE-57 bus system, the Genetic algorithm, bat algorithm and firefly algorithm are applied. The simulation is carried out with an initial population having 20 individuals with a maximum generation number equal to 50.

RESULTS AND DISCUSSION

Load shedding is one of the effective solutions for avoiding instability. However, optimal load shedding needs to be carried out to meet more demand. This chapter implements the bat and firefly algorithms for solving the optimal load shedding problem. The objective function consists of minimizing the amount of load to be shed, active power loss minimization and voltage profile improvement. The load shedding problem is analyzed for the IEEE 57 bus system. Further, the effect of FACTS devices like SVC, TCSC and UPFC on load shedding problem is examined. IEEE 57 bus system is considered for case study. In this system, bus 1 is considered as slack bus and 2, 3, 6, 8, 9 & 12 are considered as generator buses. All other buses are considered as load buses. All these buses are interconnected by 80 transmission lines. Multi objective optimization for optimal load shedding is simulated using GA, BA & FA and results have been presented and analyzed. Table 1 and Table 2 represent the input parameters of the bat and firefly algorithms respectively. Table 3 represents the generator characteristics of IEEE 57 bus system.

Optimal Load Shedding With SVC Device Using Bat And Firefly Techniques

SVC is placed at bus number 31 because it is lowest voltage bus. Table 4 and Table 5 showcase the voltage profiles without and with the placement of SVC at 31-bus in IEEE57 bus system using bat algorithm and firefly algorithm respectively. There is an observable change in the voltage profile of the system with the installation of SVC. The firefly algorithm is established to be a better technique than bat algorithm in improving the voltage profile.

Table 1. Input parameters of bat algorithm

S.No	Parameters	Quantity
1	Population size	20
2	Number of generations	50
3	Loudness	0.5
4	Pulse rate	0.5

Table 2. Input parameters of Firefly Algorithm

S.No	Parameters	Quantity
1	Number of fireflies	20
2	Max Generation	50
3	Alpha	0.5
4	Beta	0.5
5	Gama	1

Table 3. Generator Characteristics of IEEE 57 Bus System

Generator Bus no	a ($/MW²/hr)	b ($/MW/hr)	c ($/hr)	P_G^{min} (MW)	P_G^{max} (MW)
1	0.0775	20	0	0	575
2	0.01	40	0	0	100
3	0.25	20	0	0	140
6	0.1	40	0	0	100
8	0.02222	20	0	0	550
9	0.01	40	0	0	200
12	0.32258	20	0	0	410

Table 4. Voltage Profiles Comparison before and after installing SVC in optimal load shedding using bat algorithm

	Load Shedding Without SVC		Load Shedding With SVC	
Bus No	Voltage (p.u)	Phase Angle	Voltage (p.u)	Phase Angle
1	1.04	0	1.04	0
2	1.0357	1.1509	1.01	1.3632
3	1.0183	1.5235	1	-0.8131
4	1.0066	0.888	0.9954	-1.5834
5	0.9986	0.682	0.9949	-2.0035
6	1	1.0228	1	-1.7632
7	0.9863	0.137	0.9917	-0.8225
8	1.005	1.7483	1.005	2.0214
9	1	0.9849	1	0.4627
10	0.987	-2.2244	0.9986	-2.376
11	0.9804	-0.9579	0.9943	-1.6717
12	1.015	-1.7333	1.015	-1.6877
13	0.9808	-1.687	1.0005	-2.4608
14	0.956	-2.5766	0.9933	-3.6137
15	1.0122	-0.3215	1.0177	-1.3241
16	1.0153	-2.5607	1.0187	-1.7305
17	1.0204	-2.1404	1.0204	-2.1235

continued on following page

Table 4. Continued

	Load Shedding Without SVC		Load Shedding With SVC	
Bus No	**Voltage (p.u)**	**Phase Angle**	**Voltage (p.u)**	**Phase Angle**
18	0.9686	-3.8159	0.9708	-6.0589
19	0.9117	-5.1436	0.9598	-7.9972
20	0.9094	-5.1921	0.9661	-8.4447
21	0.9009	-5.133	0.9882	-7.6203
22	0.9081	-5.0077	0.9929	-7.6212
23	0.9069	-5.0834	0.9898	-7.6393
24	0.9038	-5.3594	0.9536	-7.1524
25	0.9012	-12.3353	0.906	-12.5987
26	0.9069	-4.9091	0.952	-6.8645
27	0.9208	-3.7698	0.961	-5.0101
28	0.9471	-2.8134	0.9712	-3.802
29	0.9679	-2.1723	0.9818	-2.9656
30	0.9077	-13.2257	0.9478	-13.3322
31	**0.9043**	**-14.4136**	**1**	**-14.3372**
32	0.9097	-13.3153	0.9490	-13.6936
33	0.9069	-13.3758	0.9250	-13.7383
34	0.9197	-6.8281	0.9457	-8.7034
35	0.9289	-6.5386	0.9543	-8.4939
36	0.9408	-6.2075	0.9651	-8.2502
37	0.9487	-5.9002	0.9737	-8.0997
38	0.9698	-4.8285	0.9937	-7.5878
39	0.9481	-5.9684	0.9719	-8.106
40	0.9411	-6.3062	0.9635	-8.2415
41	0.9334	-6.0772	0.9744	-6.5012
42	0.9022	-7.5211	0.938	-8.37
43	0.9658	-2.4314	0.9871	-3.0908
44	0.9687	-4.4081	1.0032	-6.5556
45	0.9715	-2.7193	1.0213	-3.6266
46	0.9291	-4.251	0.9957	-5.1542
47	0.906	-5.3731	0.9902	-6.6341
48	0.9898	-5.1941	0.9929	-6.8905
49	0.9094	-5.3855	0.9901	-6.2493
50	0.9113	-5.5914	0.9717	-6.0461
51	0.9724	-3.8773	0.9945	-3.8155
52	0.9286	-3.0633	0.9399	-3.7593
53	0.9142	-3.3455	0.9241	-3.9934
54	0.9464	-2.1355	0.9521	-2.6997
55	0.9879	-0.596	0.9896	-1.0857
56	0.9037	-7.817	0.9326	-9.2341
57	0.9083	-8.4341	0.9272	-10.1059

Table 5. Voltage Profile Comparison before and after installing SVC in optimal load shedding using Firefly algorithm

	Load Shedding Without SVC		Load Shedding With SVC	
Bus No	**Voltage (p.u)**	**Phase Angle**	**Voltage (p.u)**	**Phase Angle**
1	1.04	0	1.04	0
2	1.0332	0.4692	1.01	0.2648
3	1.0126	-0.2266	1	-0.69
4	1.0027	-0.9924	0.9953	-1.3541
5	0.9973	-1.429	0.9949	-1.5885
6	1	-1.1993	1	-1.2585
7	0.9859	-1.0545	0.9922	-1.5323
8	1.005	1.2752	1.005	0.4903
9	0.9974	-0.4728	1	-0.9862
10	0.9859	-3.0882	0.9986	-3.1467
11	0.9786	-2.0752	0.9946	-2.6423
12	1.015	-2.1506	1.015	-2.0134
13	0.9795	-2.5101	1.0006	-3.0423
14	0.9547	-3.4093	0.9934	-4.1786
15	1.0104	-1.0342	1.0177	-1.4167
16	1.018	-2.2126	1.0198	-1.6988
17	1.0224	-1.8422	1.0246	-1.2846
18	0.9644	-5.644	0.971	-5.8956
19	0.9096	-6.6723	0.959	-8.0714
20	0.9086	-6.5097	0.9648	-8.6694
21	0.9088	-6.1049	0.9884	-8.0484
22	0.9065	-5.9188	0.993	-8.0869
23	0.9053	-6.0011	0.9899	-8.11
24	0.9124	-6.3838	0.9539	-7.7125
25	0.9001	-13.3715	0.9062	-13.1505
26	0.9178	-5.9451	0.9525	-7.4361
27	0.92	-4.9103	0.9616	-5.6786
28	0.9465	-3.9893	0.9719	-4.507
29	0.9673	-3.3697	0.9835	-3.6934
30	0.9076	-14.2577	0.9498	-13.8799
31	**0.9005**	**-15.4298**	**1**	**-14.8749**
32	0.9019	-14.293	0.9498	-14.2165
33	0.9051	-14.3538	0.9280	-14.2612
34	0.9178	-7.75	0.9455	-9.2171
35	0.927	-7.4568	0.9541	-9.0062
36	0.9389	-7.1225	0.9649	-8.7615

continued on following page

Table 5. Continued

	Load Shedding Without SVC		Load Shedding With SVC	
Bus No	**Voltage (p.u)**	**Phase Angle**	**Voltage (p.u)**	**Phase Angle**
37	0.9469	-6.8088	0.9735	-8.6024
38	0.9282	-5.7116	0.9674	-8.0531
39	0.9462	-6.8804	0.9717	-8.6147
40	0.9392	-7.2266	0.9632	-8.7625
41	0.9315	-7.1683	0.9744	-7.3676
42	0.9059	-8.5905	0.9384	-9.173
43	0.964	-3.5421	0.9873	-4.0334
44	0.9971	-5.2513	1.0033	-6.9393
45	0.97	-3.484	1.0218	-3.8415
46	0.9277	-5.1011	0.9956	-5.6937
47	0.9469	-6.2396	0.9901	-7.1472
48	0.9883	-6.0651	0.9929	-7.3928
49	0.908	-6.2498	0.99	-6.7949
50	0.9101	-6.459	0.9716	-6.6641
51	0.9713	-4.7449	0.9943	-4.5569
52	0.9274	-4.323	0.9403	-4.6469
53	0.9128	-4.6399	0.9244	-4.9709
54	0.9443	-3.5044	0.952	-3.8905
55	0.9853	-2.0285	0.989	-2.4661
56	0.9211	-8.8577	0.9335	-9.9703
57	0.9068	-9.4549	0.9282	-10.794

The maximum and minimum limits of bus voltage magnitude are considered as 1. 1p.u and 0.9p.u, respectively while B_{SVC} limits range from -1 to 1 p.u. The MATLAB program is simulated for optimal load shedding problem using Genetic, bat and firefly algorithms for both the cases i.e without SVC and with SVC. Results of the various parameters in the considered objective function are presented in Table 6.

The system load curtailment in the absence of SVC, with bat algorithm is 137.9777 MW, while it is reduced to 135.5223 MW with the Firefly algorithm. On placement of SVC, the load to be tripped is reduced measurably. The load to be shed is found to be the least with Firefly algorithm.

Fast Voltage Stability Index is employed in determining the stability of the system. The influence of load shedding on stability index along with the SVC is analysed. The results are presented in Table 7 for both bat and firefly algorithms. A remarkable change is observed in the FVSI values with the incorporation of SVC, which is further improved with Firefly algorithm. The results are plotted in Figure 4 and Figure 5.

The computational capabilities of the two techniques are analysed. Figure 6 and Figure 7 indicates the convergence of the objective function using bat and firefly algorithm without SVC. These figures show that the Firefly algorithm gives a better value as compared to the bat algorithm, but the bat algorithm takes lesser number of generations to get the final steady value. The same thing holds well without SVC also, and this can be seen from the Figure 8 and Figure 9.

Table 6. Objective function parameters without and with SVC using bat and firefly Algorithm in Load Shedding problem

	Without SVC	With SVC	Without SVC	With SVC	Without SVC	With SVC
	GA-OPF		BA-OPF		FA-OPF	
Real Power Losses (MW)	17.4023	14.5279	16.7969	14.0070	16.4094	11.6515
Voltage Deviation in all Buses (p.u)	5.1236	2.5682	4.9117	2.2587	4.9726	2.1763
Amount of Load Shed (MW)	138.638	125.342	137.977	123.921	135.522	121.653
Objective Function	3423.65	1867.25	3333.64	1806.64	3273.59	1776.45
FVSI value for all lines (p.u)	6.6794	4.1027	6.5773	3.9025	6.5396	3.7716
Size of SVC (p.u)	---	0.2135	---	0.2121	-----	0.1958

Table 7. Comparison of Maximum FVSI value using bat and firefly algorithms

Algorithm	Power System Status	Maximum FVSI value in single line
GA	Without SVC	0.2896
	With SVC	0.1904
BA	Without SVC	0.2863
	With SVC	0.1891
FA	Without SVC	0.2847
	With SVC	0.1883

Figure 4. Comparison of FVSI with and without SVC using bat Algorithm

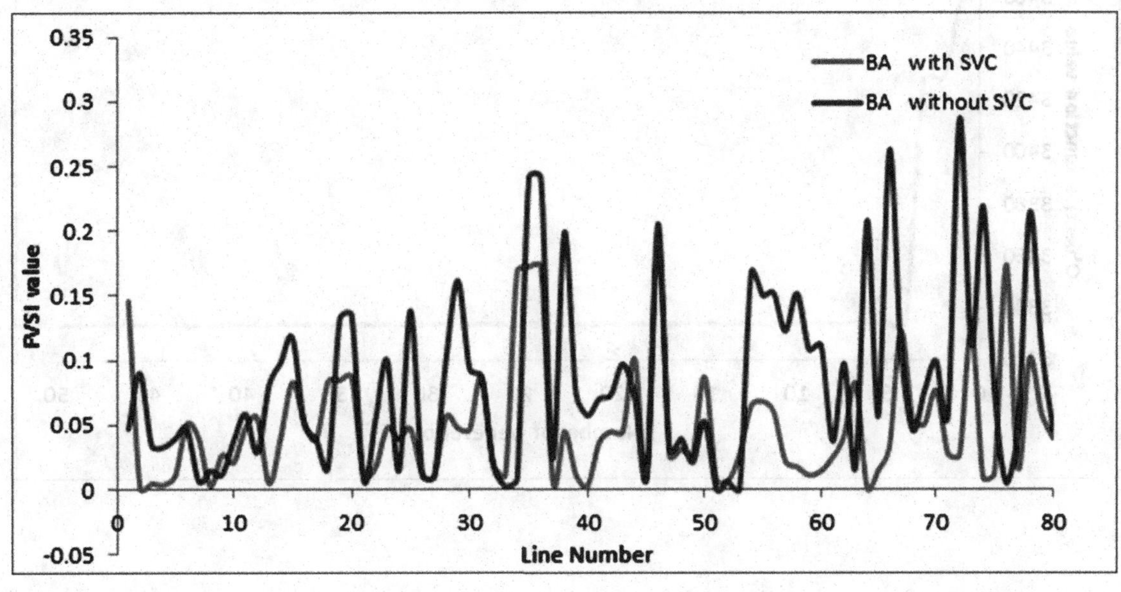

Figure 5. Comparison of FVSI with and without SVC using Firefly Algorithm

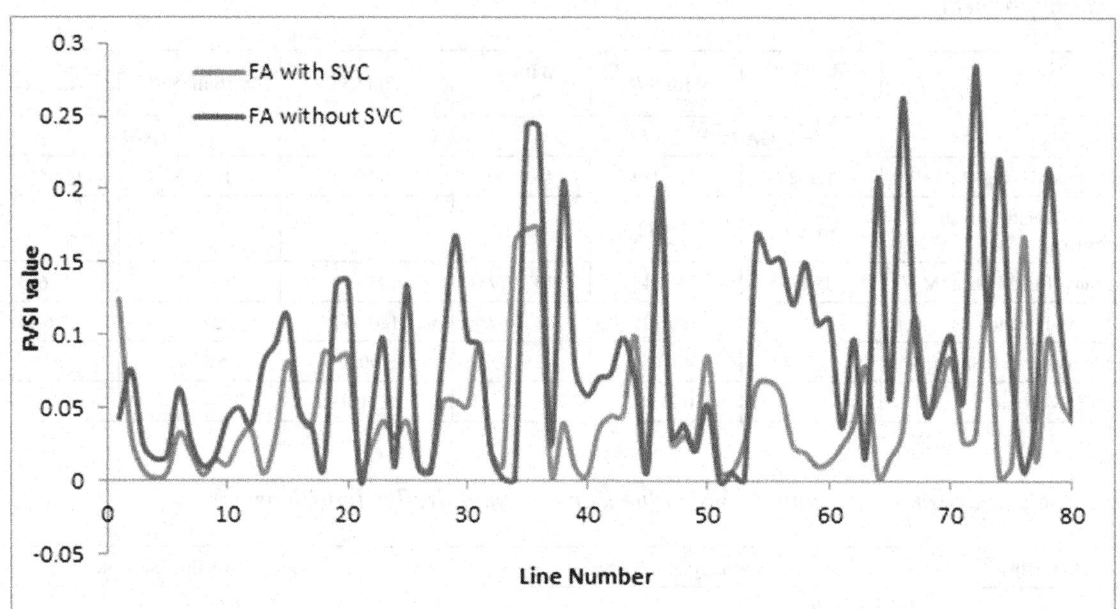

Figure 6. Convergence of the objective function using BA without SVC

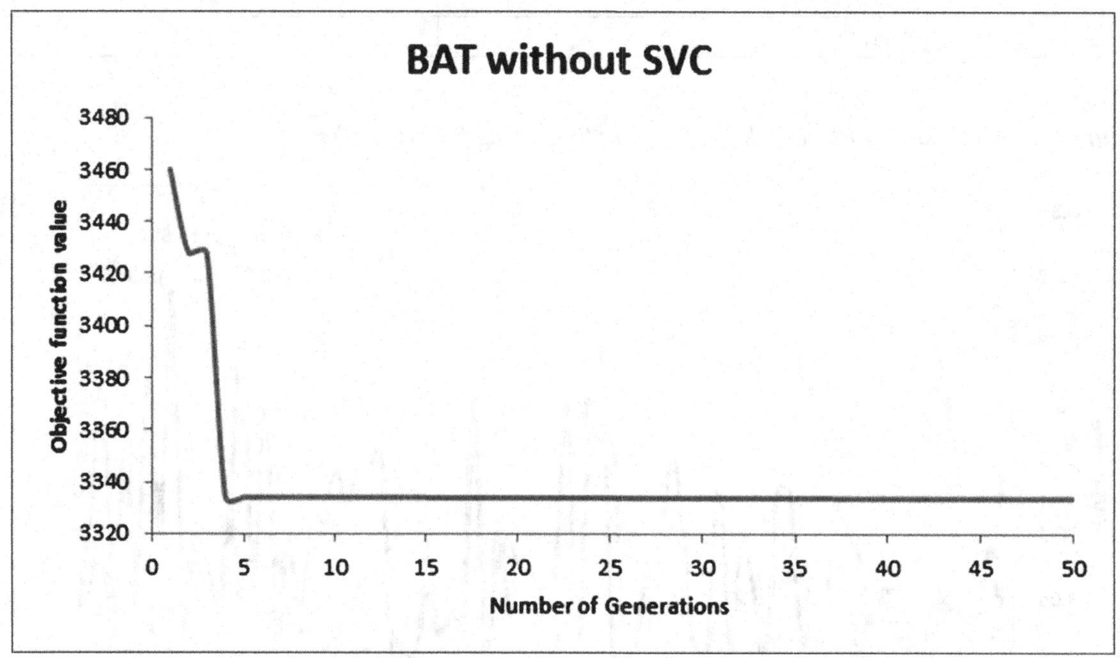

Figure 7. Convergence of the objective function using FA without SVC

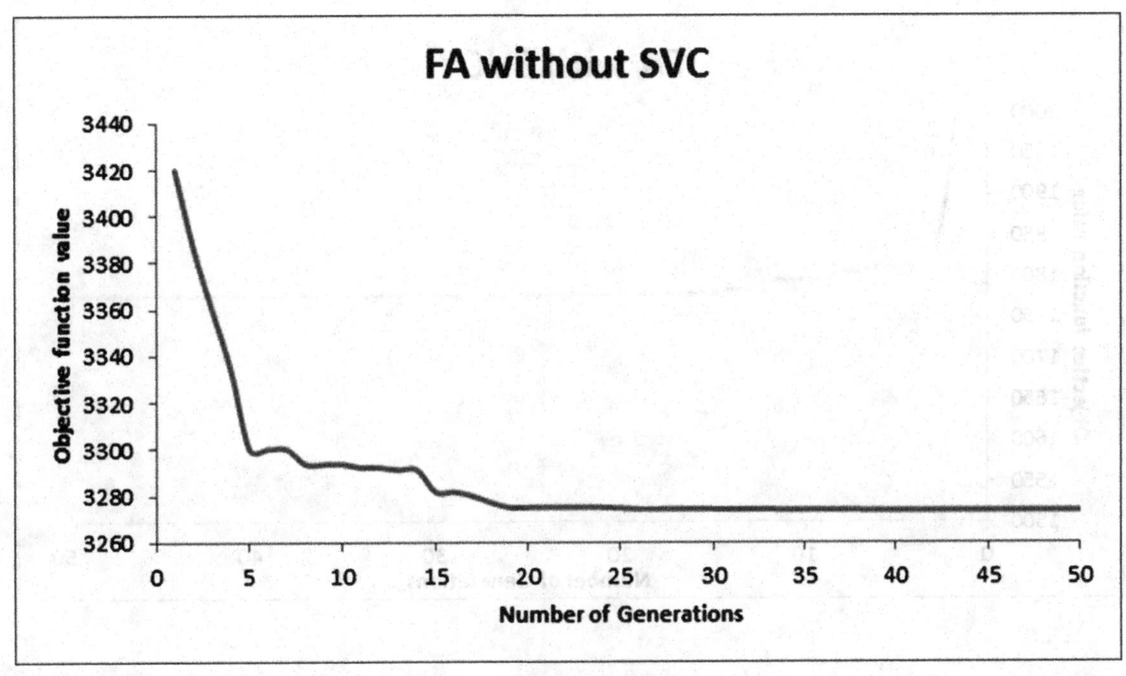

Figure 8. Convergence of the objective function using BA with SVC

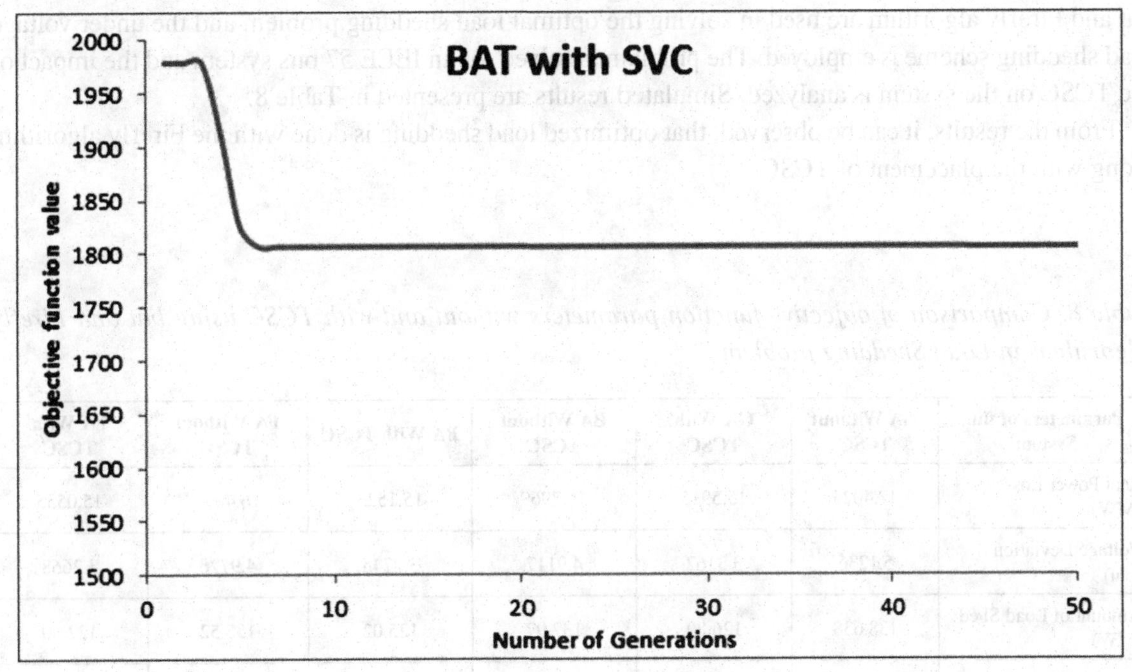

Figure 9. Convergence of the objective function using FA with SVC

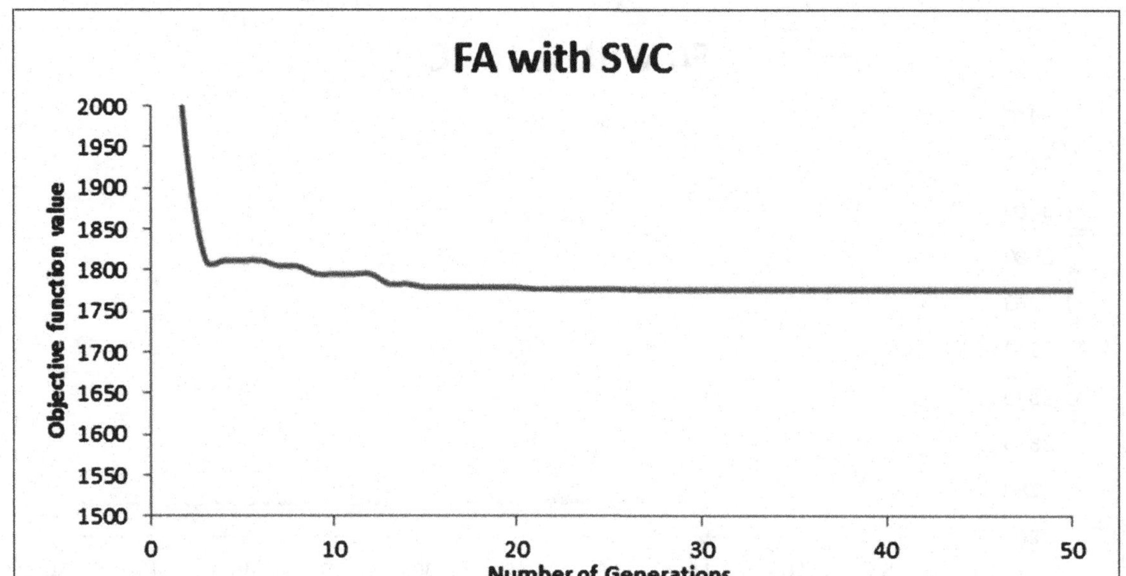

Optimal Load Shedding With TCSC Device Using Bat and Firefly Techniques

The optimal load shedding problem is analyzed with the placement of series FACTS controller TCSC. bat and Firefly algorithm are used in solving the optimal load shedding problem and the under voltage load shedding scheme is employed. The problem is solved for an IEEE 57 bus system and the impact of the TCSC on the system is analyzed. Simulated results are presented in Table 8.

From the results, it can be observed, that optimized load shedding is done with the Firefly algorithm along with the placement of TCSC.

Table 8. Comparison of objective function parameters without and with TCSC using bat and Firefly Algorithms in Load Shedding problem

Parameters of the System	GA Without TCSC	GA With TCSC	BA Without TCSC	BA With TCSC	FA Without TCSC	FA With TCSC
Real Power Losses (MW)	17.4023	15.5915	16.7969	15.1523	16.4094	15.0535
Voltage Deviation (p.u)	5.1236	3.3162	4.9117	3.2745	4.9726	3.2668
Amount of Load Shed (MW)	138.638	126.89	137.97	125.02	135.52	122.00
Objective Function	3423.65	1915.34	3333.64	1895.15	3273.59	1795.05
FVSI for all lines (p.u)	6.6794	4.6841	6.5773	4.3363	6.5396	4.3084
Reactance of TCSC (p.u)	---	0.23	-----	0.2	------	0.18

Optimal Load Shedding With UPFC Device Using Bat and Firefly Techniques

UPFC is a combination of shunt and series controllers and the load shedding problem is analyzed with a UPFC device. Power system problems can be effectively solved by using metaheuristic optimization methods because of their execution flexibility and controlling ability. With the same objective of minimizing the amount of load to be shed, analysis is carried out incorporating the UPFC device and optimal load shedding is done by two different Metaheuristic optimization techniques, bat and Firefly algorithm and it is compared with Genetic algorithm. On simulating the MATLAB program results are obtained for IEEE 57 bus system and are presented in Table 9. From this it is observed that the amount of load to be shed is 118.6538 MW in firefly algorithm incorporating with UPFC which is less as compared to bat and genetic algorithms.

Overall results obtained with the placement of SVC, TCSC and UPFC for optimal load shedding are presented in Table 10. The series cum shunt controller UPFC had a better edge over the other FACTS devices. Optimal load shedding through Firefly algorithm technique excelled over the bat algorithm.

Table 11 indicates the FVSI values. From this it is observed that by incorporating the UPFC in Firefly algorithm maximum FVSI value is 0.2045p.u obtained for line no 46 and without UPFC maximum

Table 9. Objective function parameters without and with UPFC using bat and firefly algorithms in Load Shedding problem

	GA-OPF		BA-OPF		FA-OPF	
	Before Installing UPFC	**Before Installing UPFC**	**Before Installing UPFC**	**After Installing UPFC**	**Before Installing UPFC**	**After Installing UPFC**
Real Power Losses (MW)	17.4023	13.9468	16.7969	12.8415	16.409	11.565
Voltage Deviation (p.u)	5.1236	2.1845	4.9117	1.9311	4.9726	1.9071
Amount of Load Shed (MW)	138.638	122.829	137.9777	120.9992	135.52	118.65
Objective Function	3423.65	1752.94	3333.64	1716.62	3273.59	1647.93
FVSI for all lines (p.u)	6.6794	4.0926	6.5773	3.8392	6.5396	3.6410

Table 10. Comparison of amount of load to shed with different FACTS controllers using bat and firefly algorithms

	BA-OPF			FA-OPF		
	Size of SVC 0.2121p.u	**Size of TCSC 0.2p.u**	**Size of UPFC Vcr =0.1205, Vvr = 1.1393**	**Size of SVC 0.1958p.u**	**Size of TCSC 0.18p.u**	**Size of UPFC Vcr =0.1131, Vvr =1.1392**
Amount of Load Shed (MW)	123.921	125.02	120.999	121.653	122.008	118.653

Table 11. Comparison of Maximum FVSI value using bat and firefly algorithms

	Power System Status	Minimum Bus Voltage (p.u) and Bus No	Maximum FVSI Value and Line Connected Between Bus No (Sending End – Receiving End)
GA	Without UPFC	0.8892 (31)	0.2896 (line no 72) (44-45)
	With UPFC	1 (31)	0.2125 (line no 46) (34-32)
BA	Without UPFC	0.9043 (31)	0.2863 (line no 72) (44-45)
	With UPFC	1 (31)	0.2091 (line no 46) (34-32)
FA	Without UPFC	0.9050 (31)	0.2847 (line no 72) (44-45)
	With UPFC	1 (31)	0.2045 (line no 46) (34-32)

FVSI value is 0.2847p.u obtained for line no 72. So by incorporating the UPFC, FVSI values are reduced which indicates the improvement of the voltage stability.

Figure 10 and Figure 11 indicates the convergence of the objective function using bat and firefly algorithm with UPFC, these figures shows that Firefly algorithmgives best value compared to bat algorithm but bat algorithms takes less number of generations to get the final steady value. Same thing is holds good for the convergence of the objective function using bat and firefly algorithms without UPFC, it can be observed from the Figure 12 and Figure 13, Figure 14 represents the Fast Voltage Stability Index for lines with and without UPFC using bat Algorithm. Figure 15 represents the Fast Voltage Stability Index for lines with and without UPFC using Firefly Algorithm. From these figures it has been observed that by incorporating the UPFC in the system FVSI values at lines are reduced which are near to the zero, indicates that voltage stability has been improved.

Figure 10. Convergence of the objective function using BA with UPFC

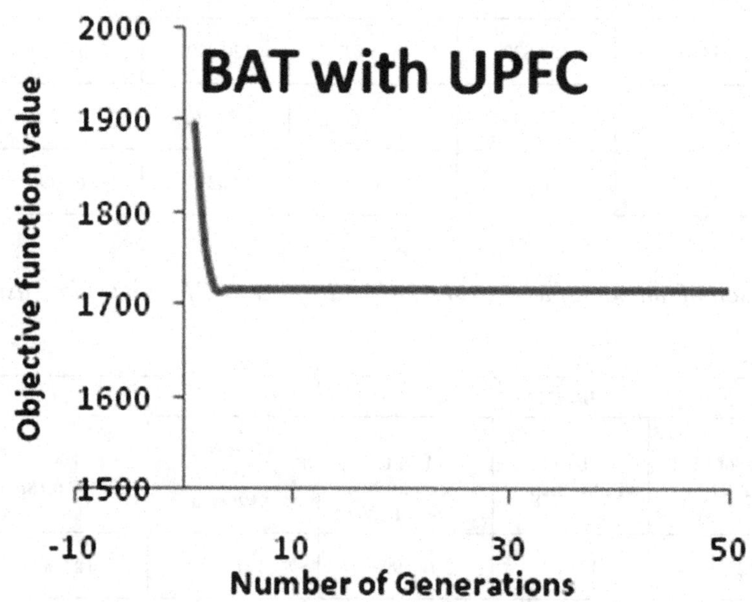

Figure 11. Convergence of the objective function using FA with UPFC

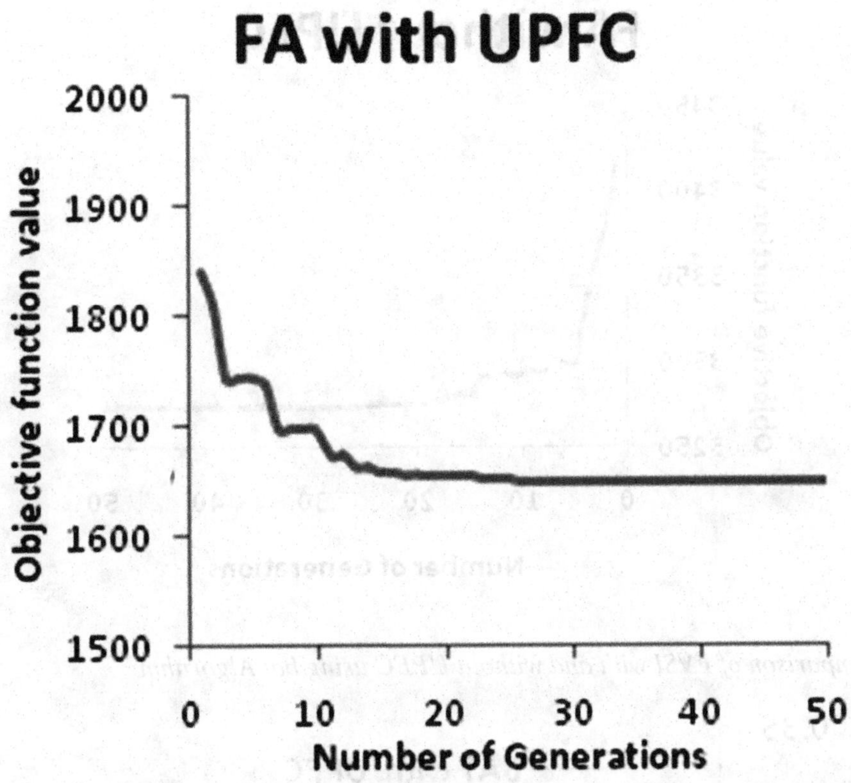

Figure 12. Convergence of the objective function using BA without UPFC

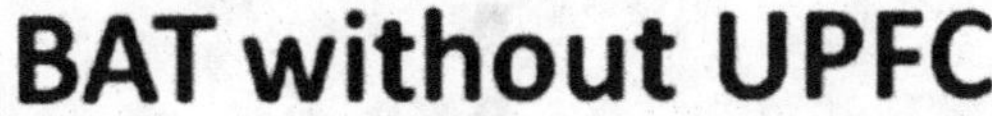

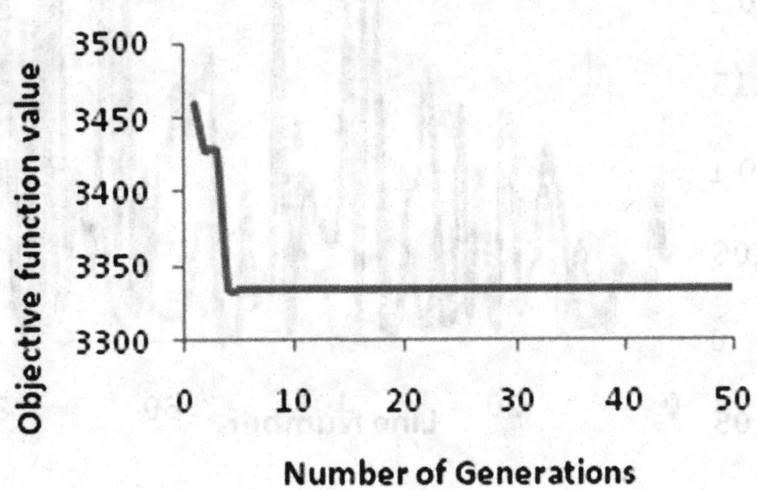

Figure 13. Convergence of the objective function using FA without UPFC

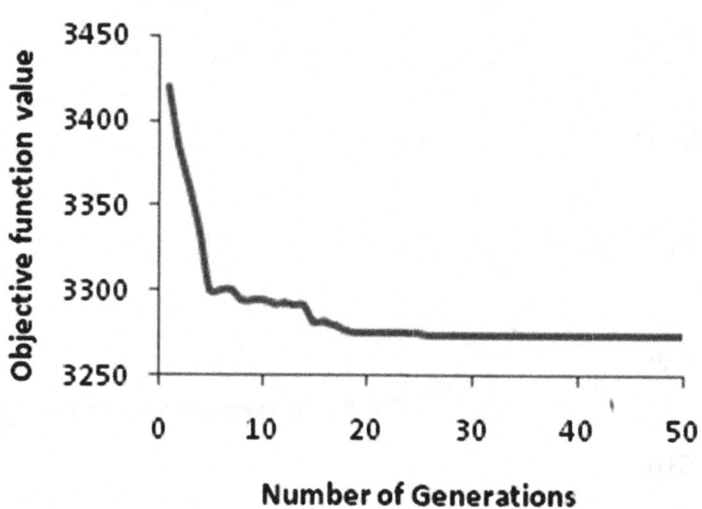

Figure 14. Comparison of FVSI with and without UPFC using bat Algorithm

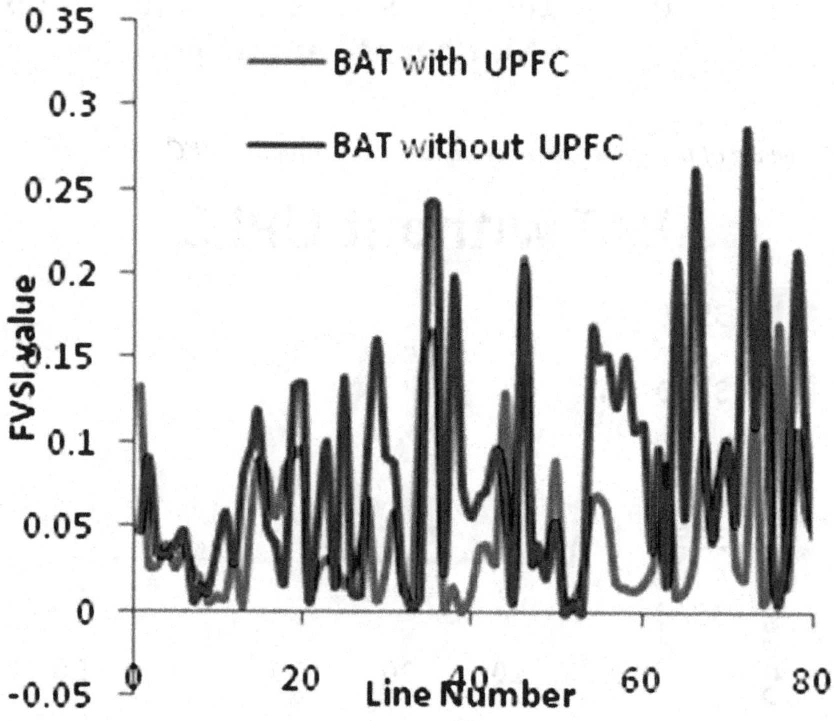

Figure 15. Comparison of FVSI with and without UPFC using Firefly Algorithm

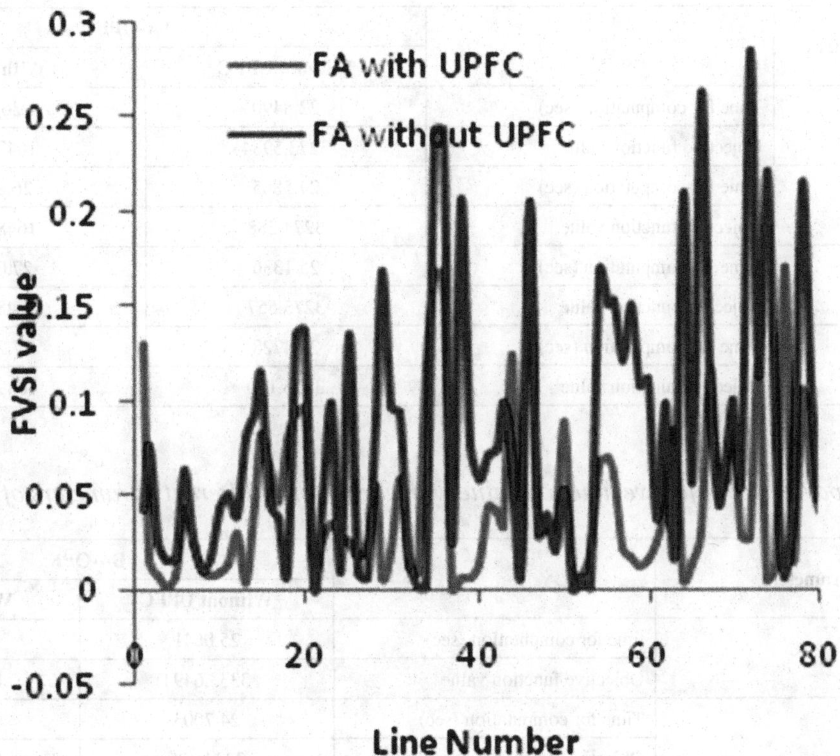

Table 12 and Table 13 indicate the objective function value and time for computation with variation of parameters of Firefly and bat algorithms. From these it has been observed that by taking loudness and pulse rate as 0.5 in bat algorithm gives better results similarly in firefly algorithm α=β=0.5,γ==1 gives better results. Table 14 represents the objective function value, time for computation for different population size using bat and firefly algorithms. From this it is observed that by increasing the population size objective function value improved but time for computation increases so the population size 20 is the best value from the view point of objective function value and time of computation.

FUTURE RESEARCH DIRECTIONS

A combination of these optimization techniques as hybrid optimization techniques can be implemented for future work to get better results. In this chapter power system performance has been enhanced by using single FACTS device that is SVC, TCSC and UPFC individually only it can be implemented with multi type FACTS devices for future work and to achieve better performance. Here optimization planning is done for static environment. For future work this can be a challenging topic for planning for dynamic environment.

Table 12. Comparison of objective function value with variation of different parameters of Firefly algorithm

Firefly Parameters		FA-OPF	
		Without UPFC	With UPFC
α=β=0.5,γ=1	Time for computation (sec)	22.8490	26.859
	Objective function value	3273.5984	1647.9307
α=β=0.4,γ=1	Time for computation (sec)	24.5865	26.22001
	Objective function value	3274.288	1648.2474
α=β=0.3,γ=1	Time for computation (sec)	25.1336	27.03758
	Objective function value	3275.557	1648.9013
α=β=0.2,γ=1	Time for computation (sec)	24.4728	27.20770
	Objective function value	3276.150	1649.4731

Table 13. Comparison of objective function value with variation of different parameters of bat algorithm

Bat Parameters		BA-OPF	
		Without UPFC	With UPFC
Loudness=0.5 Pulse rate=0.5	time for computation (sec)	25.0641	29.59813
	Objective function value	3333.6494	1716.6244
Loudness=0.4 Pulse rate=0.4	Time for computation (sec)	24.7003	31.98822
	Objective function value	3334.405	1716.9387
Loudness=0.3 Pulse rate=0.3	Time for computation (sec)	25.3972	32.36781
	Objective function value	3334.9504	1717.6386
Loudness=0.2 Pulse rate=0.2	Time for computation (sec)	26.0541	34.37184
	Objective function value	3335.123	1718.0408

Table 14. Comparison of objective function value with different population sizes

*P- Size		FA-OPF		BA-OPF	
		Without UPFC	With UPFC	Without UPFC	With UPFC
10	Time for computation (sec)	12.649134	17.362509	13.220731	16.159404
	Objective function value	3275.3937	1649.2125	3334.9235	1717.0186
20	Time for computation (sec)	22.84907	26.32859	25.06411	29.59813
	Objective function value	3273.5984	1647.9307	3333.6494	1716.6244
30	Time for computation (sec)	38.542848	44.499639	40.897537	50.007029
	Objective function value	3273.5691	1647.2289	3333.1784	1715.8954
40	Time for computation (sec)	48.982572	54.908505	49.594485	71.198184
	Objective function value	3273.3010	1647.2073	3332.7003	1715.6118

*P-Size = Population size

CONCLUSION

This chapter presents bat and firefly algorithms for optimal load shedding problem to avoid voltage instability. The bat and Firefly algorithms were applied to solve the optimization problem formulated in the optimal power flow framework with the consideration of various network constraints. It is shown from the simulation results that the methods can effectively improve voltage stability of the power system. The Firefly algorithm processes at a fast speed compared to bat and genetic algorithms. Statistical studies based on multiple independent runs also reveal that Firefly algorithm is a quite robust tool compared to bat and genetic algorithms because of its ability to generate nearly identical results. The load-shedding system has undoubtedly benefited in terms of avoiding voltage instability and minimizing real power losses. This chapter also presents the impact of FACTS controllers like SVC, TCSC and UPFC on load shedding problem. Stability analysis is carried out by computing Fast Voltage Stability Index. The result shows that incorporating the FACTS devices like SVC, TCSC and UPFC in the IEEE 57 bus system reduces the real power loss, improves the voltage profile and enhances the system stability. However, optimal load shedding is attained with Firefly algorithm. Device-wise UPFC showed a better result than SVC and TCSC. Utilizing the FACTS controllers in load shedding problem improved the voltage stability.

REFERENCES

Am briz-Perez, Acha, Fuerte-Esquivel, & De la Torre. (1998). Incorporation of a UPFC model in an Optimal Power Flow Using Newton's method. *IEE Proceedings. Generation, Transmission and Distribution, 145*(3).

Aparna, R. R. (2016). Swarm Intelligence for Automatic Video Image Contrast Adjustment. *International Journal of Rough Sets and Data Analysis, 3*(3), 21–37. doi:10.4018/IJRSDA.2016070102

Ara, Kazemi, & NabaviNiaki. (2012). Multi objective Optimal Location of FACTS Shunt-Series Controllers for Power System Operation Planning. *IEEE Transactions on Power Delivery, 27*(2), 481-490.

Carpentier. (1979). Optimal Power Flows. *Electrical Power and Energy Systems, 1*, 959-972.

Dutta, S., Roy, P. K., & Nandi, D. (2016). Optimal Allocation of Static Synchronous Series Compensator Controllers using Chemical Reaction Optimization for Reactive Power Dispatch. *International Journal of Energy Optimization and Engineering, 5*(3), 43–62. doi:10.4018/IJEOE.2016070103

Gao, Morison, & Kundur. (1992). Voltage Stability Evaluation using Modal Analysis. *IEEE Transactions on Power Systems, 7*(4), 1529–1542.

Ghahremani, E., & Kamwa, I. (2013, May). Optimal Placement of Multiple-Type FACTS Devices to Maximize Power System Loadability Using a Generic Graphical User Interface. *IEEE Transactions on Power Systems, 28*(2), 764–778. doi:10.1109/TPWRS.2012.2210253

Goel, S., Sharma, A., & Panchal, V. K. (2014). Multiobjective Cuckoo Search for Anticipating the Enemy's Movements in the Battleground. *International Journal of Applied Metaheuristic Computing*, *5*(4), 26–46. doi:10.4018/ijamc.2014100102

Gyugyi, Schauder, Williams, Rictman, Torgerson, & Edris. (1995). The Unified Power Flow Controller; A New Approach to Power Transmission Control. *IEEE Trans on Power Delivery, 10*(2), 1085-1097.

Hingorani, N. G., & Gyugyi, L. (2000). *Understanding FACTS: Concepts and Technology of Flexible AC Transmission System*. IEEE Press.

Kundur, P. (1993). *Power System Stability and Control*. New York: McGraw-Hill, Inc.

Le, D. A., & Vo, D. N. (2016). Cuckoo Search Algorithm for Minimization of Power Loss and Voltage Deviation. *International Journal of Energy Optimization and Engineering*, *5*(1), 23–34. doi:10.4018/IJEOE.2016010102

Mansour, Xu, Alvarado, & Chhewangrinzin. (1994). SVC placement using Critical Modes of voltage stability. *IEEE Transactions on Power Systems*, *9*(2), 757–763.

Mihalie, Zunko, & Povh. (1994). Improvement of Transient using Unified Power Flow Controller. *IEEE Trans*.

Mukherjee, A., Paul, S., & Roy, P. K. (2015). Transient Stability Constrained Optimal Power Flow Using Teaching Learning Based Optimization. *International Journal of Energy Optimization and Engineering*, *4*(1), 18–35. doi:10.4018/ijeoe.2015010102

Padiyar, K. R., & Kulakarni, A. M. (1998). Control design and simulation of unified power flow controller. *IEEE Transactions on Power Delivery*, *13*(4), 1348–1354. doi:10.1109/61.714507

Padiyar, K.R., & Uma Rao, K. (1999). Modeling and Control of Unified Power Flow Controller For Transient Stability. *Electrical Power and Energy Systems, 21*.

Prabhneetkaur & Taranjotkaur. (2014). A Comparative Study of Various Metaheuristic Algorithms. *International Journal of Computer Science and Information Technologies*, *5*(5), 6701–6704.

Rahul Khandelwal, J. (2016). A Novel Multiobjective Optimization for Cement Stabilized Soft Soil based on Artificial Bee Colony. *International Journal of Applied Metaheuristic Computing*, *7*(4), 1–17. doi:10.4018/IJAMC.2016100101

Ramasamy, V. & ZainalAbidin. (2009). A study on FVSI index as an indicator for under voltage load shedding (UVLS). *Proceedings of ICEE 2009 3rd International Conference on Energy and Environment*, 84-88. doi:10.1109/POWERI.2006.1632526

Ratniyomcha, T., & Kulworawanichpong, T. (2009). Evaluation of voltage stability indices by using Monte Carlo simulation. *Proceedings of the 4th IASME / WSEAS International Conference on Energy & Environment (EE'09)*, 297-302.

Singh, J. G., Singh, S. N., & Srivastava, S. C. (2006). Placement of FACTS controllers for enhancing power system loadability. In *Power India Conference*. IEEE.

Tinney, W. F., & Hart, C. E. (1967, November). Power Flow- Solution by Newton's Method. *IEEE Transactions*, *86*, 1449.

Tiwari, P. K., & Sood, Y. R. (2012). Efficient and optimal approach for location and parameter setting of multiple unified power flow controllers for a deregulated power sector. *IET Generation, Transmission & Distribution*, *6*(10), 958–967. doi:10.1049/iet-gtd.2011.0722

VenkateswaraRao, B., & Nagesh Kumar, G. V. (2014). Optimal Location of Thyristor Controlled Series Capacitor for reduction of Transmission Line losses using bat Search Algorithm. *WSEAS Transactions on Power Systems, 9*, 459-470.

Yang, X. S. (2008). *Nature-Inspired Metaheuristic Algorithms*. Luniver Press.

Yang, X.-S. (2009). Firefly algorithms for multimodal optimization. *Stochastic Algorithms: Foundation and Applications SAGA*, *5792*, 169–178. doi:10.1007/978-3-642-04944-6_14

Yang, X. S. (2010). A New Metaheuristic bat Inspired Algorithm. Nature Inspired Cooperative Strategies for Optimization (NISCO 2010), Studies in Computational Intelligence. Springer. doi:10.1007/978-3-642-12538-6_6

Yang, X. S. (2010). *Firefly algorithm, Levy flights and global optimization. In Research and Development in Intelligent Systems XXVI* (pp. 209–218). London, UK: Springer. doi:10.1007/978-1-84882-983-1_15

Yang, X. S. (2011). Bat Algorithm for Multi objective Optimization. *International Journal of Bio-inspired Computation*, *3*(5), 267–274. doi:10.1504/IJBIC.2011.042259

KEY TERMS AND DEFINITIONS

Bat Algorithm: Bat algorithm was developed by X. S. Yang in 2010 and works based on echo location behavior of micro bats.

FA: Firefly algorithm was developed by X. S. Yang in 2008 and works based on flashing behavior of fire fly.

FACTS: Alternating current transmission systems incorporating power electronic-based and other static controllers to enhance controllability and increase power transfer capability.

FACTS Devices or FACTS Controllers: A power electronic-based system and other static equipment that provide control of one or more AC transmission system parameters.

Optimization: It is the action of making the best or most effective use of a situation or resource.

SVC: Static VAR compensator is the most popular shunt connected FACTS controller. The SVC is modeled as a variable susceptance device and its value is tuned in order to achieve a specified voltage magnitude that meets the constraints. The SVC device can either inject reactive power (capacitive) or absorb it (inductive) as per system requirements.

TCSC: The basic Thyristor-controlled series capacitor is a method of "rapid adjustment of network impedance". Apart from controlling line power transfer capability, TCSC also enhances a system's stability. It consists of a series compensating capacitor shunted by thyristor controlled reactor. Thyristor inclusion in the TCSC module enables it to have a smoother control of reactance against system parameter variations.

UPFC: A combination of static synchronous compensator (STATCOM) and a static series compensator (SSSC) which are coupled via a common dc link, to allow bidirectional flow of real power between the series output terminals of the SSSC and the shunt output terminals of the STATCOM, and are controlled to provide concurrent real and reactive series line compensation without an external electric energy source.

Chapter 9
Using Particle Swarm Optimization Algorithm as an Optimization Tool Within Developed Neural Networks

Goran Klepac
Raiffeisenbank Austria, Croatia

ABSTRACT

Developed neural networks as an output could have numerous potential outputs caused by numerous combinations of input values. When we are in position to find optimal combination of input values for achieving specific output value within neural network model it is not a trivial task. This request comes from profiling purposes if, for example, neural network gives information of specific profile regarding input or recommendation system realized by neural networks, etc. Utilizing evolutionary algorithms like particle swarm optimization algorithm, which will be illustrated in this chapter, can solve these problems.

INTRODUCTION

Neural networks are not self-explainable regarding to their nature, and it is challenging to find out right methodology, which will find logical and explainable connections between inputs and outputs. These connections and their explanation are not linear and it cannot be observed in that way, but finding typical (optimal) mixture of input values in a neural network for achieving desired output is a great movement. Usage of neural networks for constructing predictive models is a demanding process. It demands precise and objective determination of sample construction, target variable construction, attribute relevance analysis, model testing and many other activities, which will guarantee that developed model is robust, stable, reliable and predictive.

DOI: 10.4018/978-1-5225-5134-8.ch009

If we are talking about predictive models with binominal output and predictive models based on logistic regression, neural networks or similar techniques, than determination of initial states of variable values for achieving specific output are relatively simple. It can be a manual process, but achievable from perspective of human effort.

Reason why someone would like to find out which values of input variables will cause best fit for specific output is that we would like to find out typical case, or profile. That means if we would like to find out typical profile of churner based on developed binominal predictive model we should find combination of input values which will result with maximum output value in zone of wanted output.

Things became more complicated when we have multinomial output from predictive models.

Main advantage of binominal output usage is ability to understand relations between target variable and potential predictors and business logic check.

From technical point of view, data mining techniques like neural networks, and logistic regression by the nature of their algorithms, prefer to operate with values between 0 and 1. Dummy variables could be interpreted as membership declaration with 0 and 1values. If some value belongs into specific class represented as dummy variable, it is true and dummy variable has value "1" otherwise "0".

Robust and stable predictive models have few attributes incorporated into model. It could be 6-10 of most predictive attributes. As it is evident initial data sample could contain more than hundreds of potential predictors. Some of them are original variables from databases as socio demographic values assigned to each customer, and other has behavioural characteristics defined by experts and extracted from existing transactional data.

Attribute relevance analyse has two important functions:

- Recognition of most important variables which has greatest impact on target variable
- Understanding relations and logic between most important predictor and target variable, and understanding relations and logic between most important predictors from target variable perspective

Contrary to assurance that powerful hardware and sophisticated software can substitute need for attribute relevance analysis, attribute relevance analysis is important part of each kind of analysis which operates with target variable. Recognition of most important variables which has greatest impact on target variable reduces redundancy and uncertainty at model development process stage. It provides robustness of the model and model reliability. Attribute relevance analyi beside importance measuring, evaluates attribute characteristics. Attribute characteristics evaluation includes measuring attribute values impact on target variables. It helps on understanding relations and logic between most important predictor and target variable, and understanding relations and logic between most important predictors from target variable perspective. After attribute relevance analysis stage, analyst has initial picture about churner profile and behaviour. This stage often opens many additional questions related to revealed relations and sometimes induces construction of new behavioural (derived) variables, which also should pass attribute relevance analysis process.

From perspective of predictive modelling there are two basic data sample types for predictive churn model development:

- Data sample with binomial target variable
- Data sample with multinomial target variable

Data sample with multinomial target variable contains target variable with more than two finite states.

Biggest challenge is to find out combination of input values which will result with maximum output value in zone of wanted output in situation when we have multinomial output (multinomial target variable) from predictive models and predictive models based on structures like neural networks.

Reason for that is in their complexity based on links between chance nodes. It means that predictive models based on Bayesian networks demands different approach in situation when we would like to use it for finding of optimal combination of input values which will produce desired output.

In those cases it is almost impossible to find out optimal combination of variable values for achieving desired output. For that purpose appropriate approach can be usage of evolutionary computing for finding optimal values of input variables with respect of desired output and interaction within Bayesian network.

Evolutionary algorithms like particle swarm optimization algorithm will not always propose best solution, but solution which is plausible and acceptable.

Other problem is related to fact that evidence means certain event, which implies potential usage of binary states as outputs from chance nodes within Bayesian network. It leads us to on binary PSO usage and adoption, except in situation when we do not have intention to set all chance nodes as a certain events. It depends on potential solution, but for sure it demands additional research and conclusions for finding optimal approach for usage neural networks with PSO algorithm for finding optimal solution.

As an illustration the proposed methodology will be applied as a tool for profiling on developed neural network. Model, which regarding input variables as predictors evaluate shopping preferences, will be used for finding optimal values of predictor for buying specific product.

Most important feature of presented methodology is the ability to recognize important areas and customer characteristics where changes became significant in comparison with previous period. Particle swarm optimization algorithm as a profiling tool usage, in combination with predictive models, has additional advantage. This could be the base for strategic business decisions, regarding observed market trends.

Predictive models complexity rise with number of input variables, as well as number of states in output variable. Greater impact on complexity has increasing number of states in output variable.

In other words, it is a great challenge to recognize typical profile of customer which prefers buying, or usage product of service e.g. "A" in situation where we use predictive models which has function to predict probability of buying, or usage for n product where n >2.

Complexity from other side rises with higher number of predictors, because they cause numerous potential combinations regarding state from output variable.

Main advantage of the proposed solution is the automatic determination of profiles in situation, where we have combinatory explosion caused by numerous nodes and their states within neural network model.

Variables which are part of predictive models should contain strong business logic approved and checked with people from business practice. Approved and checked business logic assures also trust into developed model, because a business user also on quantitative models looks as on black boxes, especially when it is complex. Understanding inputs and logic of those inputs, which is in line with their perception of their problem area, could result on better cooperation and better results in decision making. Particle swarm optimization algorithm operates on trusted variables for seeking additional information on profiles.

Profiling could be wrongly identified as segmentation modeling. Those two types of models have common points but it is a different type of models. Profiling models gives holistic picture of typical churner/buyer/ users as member of some population or as a member of the segment recognized thought segmentation process. Profiling models does not lay on social demographic data only; they also could be constructed by using behavioral and temporal characteristics. Profiling models could provide differentiation between profiles within segments. It could be trigger for decision about churn mitigation policy, or further analysis processes. Profiling analysis could include variety of data mining techniques.

Integral part of the chapter is a case study in domain of insurance.

The case study will present the usage of the particle swarm optimization algorithm as a tool for finding profiles based on previously developed neural network. As explained in introduction, particle swarm optimization algorithm will be used as a tool which should find optimal values of input variables (within developed predictive models) as referent values for maximization of probability value of some risky event. It means that particle swarm optimization algorithm will be used as a tool which should find optimal values of input variables within developed predictive models as referent values for maximization value of probability that customer will select/ buy some product or service. Using given results, insurance company can make profiles of the riskiest insurance users, even in the situation affected by combinatory explosion, caused by numerous nodes and their states within neural network model. the proposed methodology is applicable not only on neural networks, it can be applied on each complex predictive model. Additional advantage of the proposed solution is that it is not focused only on previously determined aim variable.

Such methodology is fruitful ground for profile transition evaluation and monitoring. In case of temporal component introduction within model, it is possible to monitoring profile changes with respect of selected target variable. It means that profile transition in case of complex analytical environment can be analyzed and compared, which is valuable piece of information for business decision purposes.

BACKGROUND

Profiling is always hot topic when we are talking about customer relationship management. Knowing right customer profile is key for successful marketing strategy.

Predictive modeling is often use as a tool for profiling.

There are numerous case studies dedicated to predictive modeling in business, and usage of data mining techniques for building predictive models for purposes like churn detection, next best offer, fraud detection (Larose, 2005; Klepac, 2010; Klepac, 2014, Klepac, 2015).

In case of predictive modeling, particle swarm optimization (PSO) algorithm is mostly used as an algorithm for learning optimization in neural networks (Clerck, 2013; Kurbatsky, 2014, Russel, 2001).

Particle swarm optimization algorithm are used in many areas, mostly for solving problems in domain of optimization (Adhikari, 2013 ;Anagnostopoulos, 2012; Babahajyani 2014 ; El-Shorbagy, 2013).

In literature particle swarm optimization algorithm is not recognized as a methodology that can directly contribute on customer profiling. Mostly it is used as a tool for neural networks optimization which could be used as a tool for profiling or for clustering purposes (Devi, 2014; Konstantinos, 2010; Xing, 2014).

Particle swarm optimization algorithm has great potential for solving problems which are not only primary focused on optimization (Singh, 2010; Tosun, 2014; Yosuf, 2010).

Problems in domain of business could be used by adoption and inventive usage of PSO algorithm (Olson, 2011; Rajesh 2013; Xing, 2014a).

Besides optimization for neural networks in domain of business, PSO are also used as learning optimization tool in domain of engineering, environmental science, social science (Clerk, 2013; Olson, 2011, Russel, 2001).

Neural networks and particle swarm optimization algorithm could be also used in area of time series forecasting (Adhikari, 2013). This approach is the same as in the situation where particle swarm optimization algorithm has been used as a tool for learning optimization for neural networks on non temporal data. Main differences are related to nature of temporal data and their characteristics which demands different approach in building predictive models by using neural networks.

Different types of neural network algorithms (Alexander, 1995) demands different approaches in usage of soft computing techniques (Devi, 2014) along with neural networks. It means that e.g. in the situation where particle swarm optimization algorithm has been used as a tool for learning optimization for neural network, regarding fact do we try to optimize learning for error back propagation model or for self organizing maps it demands different approaches in particle swarm optimization algorithm usage.

Evolutionary algorithms, as well as particle swarm optimization algorithm could be applied on various business areas (Arora, 2013; Nguyen, 2010; Taleizadeh, 2013).

One of the application area could be customer relationship management systems.

Usage of data mining techniques in customer relationship management systems, are mostly concentrated on finding typical profile of churner, buyer or subscriber (Giudici, 2003; Giudici, 2009). Neural networks play significant role in predictive modeling as well as for profiling. Taking in consider anatomy of neural networks, and final output after modeling with neural network it is obvious that profiling in case of multinomial output from the model is not an easy task (Larose, 2005).

Profiling could be interpreted as diversification task. In case when predictive model exists, it could be used as a base for diversification. Particle swarm optimization algorithm has potential for diversification tasks (Cheng, 2013 ; Kress, 2010; Konstantinos, 2010). This idea leads us to ideas presented in this chapter, where particle swarm optimization algorithm became tool for diversification (profiling) based on predictive model constructed by neural network usage.

Evolutionary approach, which is one of the particle swarm optimization algorithm characteristics, gives opportunity for finding optimal solution regarding aimed profiles. This approach saves time and human work on *manual* profiling, and speed up profiling process.

From the other side, it could give a perspective on changes in customer profile characteristic through time, in case when it is appropriate used as a part of more complex system for profile analysis.

Customer relationship management paradigm demands fast information about customers. It includes information about changes in buying preferences, which implies changes in customer profiles. In situation when company operates with numerous items, or group of items, it is unrealistic to make customer profiling without some sophisticated tool like it will be presented in this chapter.

Presented methodology gives opportunity to companies for faster reaction, and faster revelation in customer profile changes. Customer profile changes imply market changes and have an influence on changes in market strategies. Most important feature of presented methodology is the ability to recognize important areas and customer characteristics where changes became significant in comparison with previous period. Particle swarm optimization algorithm as a profiling tool usage, in combination with predictive models has additional advantage. Each predictive model calibration, which should be done periodically, could potentially have an influence on customer profiles. Profiles after predictive model calibration could be extracted by particle swarm optimization algorithm usage. This could be the base for strategic business decisions, regarding observed market trends.

In presented solution PSO algorithm has more active role in customer profiling, based on developed predictive model.

IMPORTANCE OF CUSTOMER PROFILING

Customer Profiling Purpose

Customer profiling is one of the most important thing in customer relationship management. Campaign planning, new product development, cross selling activities, up selling activities and other activities in relation with customer portfolio management are closely related with customer profiles.

It is unrealistic to expect that whole customer portfolio has the same profile characteristics. Profile characteristics vary by product usage, product group usage and regarding time component, because, as time goes by, the same customer group can change their attitudes and preferences. Profile monitoring and customer profile recognition is a key factor of successful customer relationship management.

For companies which have low number of products and services in selling assortments, customer profiling is an easier task in comparison to companies with high number of products and services in selling assortments. Even in situation where a company has narrow set of product and services in selling assortments, profiling is a non trivial task. Profiling is not (should not be) concentrated on socio demographic characteristics only. Profiling should take also in consideration customer behavioral characteristics. Customer behavioral characteristics are not obvious and recognizable as socio demographic variables. Even socio demographic characteristics could be represented with set of standard variables like age, gender, region etc., and if company wants to base profiles on these variables (which is not recommended) profiling is not a trivial task. It should be done by taking in consideration of aim variable which represents usage of some product or group of products. Taking in consideration of customer behavioral characteristic as a part of profiling makes profiling more complicated. First problem in situation when companies decide to include behavioral characteristics as profiling elements is relevant behavioral characteristics recognition, significant for profiling. Behavioral characteristics are more powerful determinants for profiling than socio demographic characteristics. Problem with them is in fact that it is not easy to recognize key behavioral characteristics which will show typical customer profile.

Extracting Behavioral Characteristic for Profiling

For behavioral characteristic recognition useful auxiliary tool is hypothesis consideration. Hypothesis deliberation leads us to understanding, and discovering causalities of some observed problems. We recommend that analytical process should not be only pure pattern extraction from disposable data sources. It should be supervised and supported by business experts, which can express their opinions about causalities, which can be proved or disproved on analytical way.

In that case, some incorrect consumption, which has an influence on business decisions by decision makers, could be challenged and rejected.

It is possible to skip this stage, but it is recommended, because on that way a company has opportunity for better understanding causalities of observed problem.

For example, if a company as aim has up selling, it could be solved by making predictive models which also contains patterns / profiles of buyers of targeted products. After this stage experts also can generate hypothesis based on revealed patterns, about causalities as well as in first phase, before making predictive models.

While using hypotheses, common question is which hypothesis is true or most probable. Analyst will choose most probable answer using intuition and then will look for hypothesis confirmation using available data. By using hypotheses, analyst must be aware of wider perspective, avoiding to be focused only on one hypothesis and always looking for approval and alternatives.

This approach gives opportunity to experts to express their expert knowledge about key profiling factors. Most important thing is, if we are observing this methodology through prism of predictive model development and attribute relevance analysis, that each hypothesis generated by expert will be approved or rejected on analytical way.

Attribute relevance analysis is a key process in model development. It assures right variable selection and avoids model building with irrelevant attributes, which can cause with unpredictable outputs. Beside mentioned function, attribute relevance analysis has important role in understanding of key factors in relation with customer relationship management. It does not mean that this stage in modeling will provide all the answers important for customer understanding, but it for sure raises right questions and opens horizons in customer understanding for specific portfolio.

Sometimes important relation and patterns could be found in attribute relevance analysis stage. Often customer needs are not so obvious, but combination of several reveled relations could be good direction for getting idea where is the root of the problem. Developed predictive model could have high predictive power, but it does not mean that company fully understands reasons why some product is more popular for one customer segment, and other customer segment does not like it. Unfortunately, further investigation about these trends often stops, after predictive model has been done, and it is a mistake, because company in that case only has probability calculator for buying some product without deeper understanding what is actually going on. By using predictive models as probability calculator it is possible to recognize who will buy some product, but without deeper understanding of causes it is impossible to make good strategy for further selling activities. That is the reason why predictive model development should not be only aim of customer relationship modeling projects.

Extracted relations and knowledge about influences on some event, like willingness for buying some product or service became powerful tool for strategic business planning in marketing. It can be used for making effective commercials which targeted customer's specific motivators and fits with behavioral characteristics recognized through attribute relevance analysis.

Business Decisions Based on Recognized Profiles

Customer willingness for buying some product or service can vary through time. Reason for that can be in seasonal factors, or in attitude changes which can be caused by customer lifetime cycle. Predictive models in process of calibration can recognize those relations, but it is most important that business side is aware of those facts, and to use it for strategic business planning. Example for that could be situation with buyers with small kids. In certain period of time they could be oriented on buying items for small children. After some time, they change their habits, because the same children have different needs regarding needed items, and companies should recognize this shift.

Additional problem is that all buyers do not have children at the same age, and they changes preferences and needs in different period of time. From this point it is possible that this coherent segment after specific point starts to divide on sub segments with different needs which can be visible from profile characteristics.

A predictive model which calculates probability of buying for many products, are too complex as a tool for profiling, because there is too many combinatory states for precise profiling. Hypothetically, it could be used for this purpose, but it is not convenient for practical business purposes.

For successful periodic profiling based on complex predictive model automatic procedure should be used. There is no prescribed methodology or method for that purpose. This chapter will represent a novel methodology which includes existence of developed predictive model. Predictive model could be based on different data mining models like neural networks (which will be represented in this chapter), Bayesian network, logistic regression, linear regression, decision trees etc.

Analyst knows basic relations based on attribute relevance analysis, but regarding combinatory explosion caused with variety of outputs in output variable, it is very hard, or almost impossible to make precise profiling in that conditions.

Solution is to use evolutionary approach, in our case particle swarm optimization algorithm to make profiling. That approach gives us opportunity for automatic profile detection. It could speed up profiling process and also gives an opportunity for profile comparison. It also could be use as a part of a tool for monitoring profile changes.

Segment migration could be recognized trough profile migration, and that could be signal for changes in company policy regarding company strategy. Presented methodology could be also used as a part of early warning system

Early warning systems, for example can be much more effective based on presented methodology if it uses presented methodology as a part of it.

That approach can result with extended framework for early warning system, which can be extended regarding specifics of some company and business area. Changes in profiles which prepare to buy some product or group of products for sure belongs in early warning system area.

PARTICLE SWARM OPTIMISATION ALGORITHM AND PROFILING FROM PREDICTIVE MODELS

Relation Between Predictive Modeling and Profiling

Final result of predictive modeling should not be predictive model as only aim of that process. Predictive modeling should be also concentrated on understanding reasons and causes of events, which is object of predictive modeling. In case of predictive modeling for recommendation systems, next best offer, buying preferences it is important to understand profiles and characteristics, which has highest odds for selection of specific items. In general, a predictive model contains determined number of variables, and profiles are determined with their values. It means that referent profile, in light of predictive model is determined with final number of variables, which contains specific values, or scales within variables.

Understanding of those relations and values, leads us in deeper understanding of client preferences, which could be base for further hypothesis generation concentrated on deeper understanding and further analytics of customer behavior and preferences.

Predictive model development at final stage provides tool for probability calculation, but development phase should reveal main characteristic of portfolio structure, basic information about important variables that has greatest influence on customer decisions.

Data cleaning, data preprocessing, factor analysis, attribute relevance analysis, makes significant contribution to this aim.

Predictive model complexity increases with number of input variables, as well as number of states in output variable. Greater impact on complexity has increasing number of states in output variable.

In other words, it is great challenge to recognize typical profile of customer which prefers buying, or usage product of service *e.g.*"A" in situation where we use predictive model which has function to predict probability of buying, for n product (where n >2).

Complexity from other side rises with higher number of predictors, because they cause numerous potential combinations regarding state from output variable.

During developing phase in case of models with output variables with two possible states, it is easier to determine profiles for two different states. First reason lays in fact that measures for attribute relevance analysis like Information Value and Weight of evidence gives clear picture of zones, which has higher impact on observed binary states.

When number of states in output variable from predictive model is greater than two, complexity rises, and in stage of model development common task for understanding profiles is recognition of attributes which has greatest impact on aim variables with multiple states.

It could be on help for general picture about impact on preferences, but it is not sufficient for typical profile recognition for specific product or service. Often in that case, users try to find out manually typical profile, by varying values of predictors for each state in output variable within model.

It is time consuming and imprecise process, and in case of numerous states in output variable few of the output states are usually covered on this way.

Profiling is important, because it introduces new dimension in predictive modeling, which is on help for decision support process. Knowing typical user profiles for certain product or service means adequate marketing strategy for those product or services. It leads us to the fact that based on that knowledge company could design campaigns for existing and future customers.

Finding right customer characteristics leads us to recognition of motivators and reasons for buying some specific product or service.

From the other hand, market is dynamic environment, and as predictive models should be calibrated, typical profiles for products and services should be calibrated as well in line with model calibration.

It is nontrivial task, taking in consider all difficulties connected with profiling from predictive models in situation especially where number of states in output variable from predictive model is greater than two.

Attribute Relevance Analysis and Profiling

Robust and stable predictive models have few attributes incorporated into model. It could be 6-12 of most predictive attributes.

Initial data sample could contain more than hundreds of potential predictors. Some of them could be socio demographic values assigned to each customer, and other has behavioral characteristics defined by experts and extracted from existing transactional data as derived variables.

Attribute relevance analysis has two important functions:

- Recognition of most important variables which has greatest impact on target variable.
- Understanding relations and logic between most important predictor and target variable, and understanding relations and logic between most important predictors from target variable perspective.

Both functions are in line with customer profile recognition, especially in situation when we are developing predictive model for probability calculation product or services buying.

Attribute relevance analysis besides importance measuring, evaluates attribute characteristics. Attribute characteristics evaluation includes measuring attribute values impact on target variables. It helps on understanding relations and logic between most important predictor and target variable, and understanding relations and logic between most important predictors from target variable perspective.

After attribute relevance analysis stage, analyst has initial picture about profiles, which includes behavioral characteristics as well.

From perspective of predictive modeling there are two basic types of predictive models important from profiling point:

- Predictive models with binomial target variable.
- Predictive models with multinomial target variable.

In case of predictive models with binomial target variable common approach for attribute relevance analysis is usage of Weight of Evidence and Information Value calculation by using following formulas:

$$WoE = \ln\left(\frac{\mathrm{Dnb}}{\mathrm{Db}}\right)$$

$$\mathrm{IV} = \sum_{i=1}^{n}\left(\mathrm{Dnb}_{\mathrm{i}} - \mathrm{Db}_{\mathrm{i}}\right) * \ \ln\left(\frac{\mathrm{Dnb}_{\mathrm{i}}}{\mathrm{Db}_{\mathrm{i}}}\right)$$

Weight of evidence is calculated as a natural logarithm of ratio between distributions of e.g. non-buyers (D_{nb}) and e.g. buyers (D_b) in distribution spans. Information value is calculated as sum of differences between distribution of non-buyers and buyers in distribution spans and product of corresponding weight of evidence.

Advantage in this situation is clear diversification regarding two output states, presented through Weight of Evidence measure, as it is shown in Figure 1.

Let assume, that graph on Figure 1 represents Weight of evidence measure result for variable *District.* All customers, which lives in districts with positive Weight of evidence value, prefer to buy product (aim variable is constructed as buying product X = Yes or buying product X = No).

All customers which lives in districts with negative Weight of evidence value, do not buy product X. After attribute relevance analysis and recognition of most predictive variables, analyst has relatively clear picture about customers, which prefer to by product X.

It is still manual work, but it is not impossible to recognize typical profile "buyer of product X" by maximizing probability for buying product "X" through predictive model. Attribute relevance analysis done by Weight of evidence gives pretty good starting point for doing this.

In situation with multinomial target variable it is much more complicated and almost impossible even manually to make typical profiles like: "buyer of product A", "buyer of product B", ... "buyer of product N".

In case of predictive models with multinomial target variable common approach for attribute relevance analysis is usage of e.g. information gain calculation.

Information gain can be calculated by following formula (Han, 2006):

Figure 1. Illustration Weight of evidence result

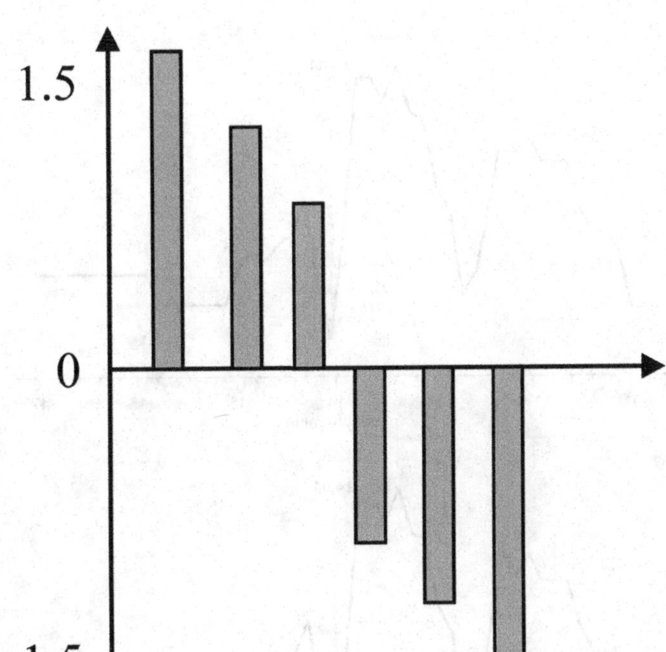

$$Info(D) = -\sum_{i=1}^{n} p_i \log_2(p_i)$$

where p_i is probability that an arbitrary tuple in D belongs to class C_i (Han, 2006). This measure is recommended for usage in situation where output variable has more than two states for prediction. There are many measures which can be used for this purpose. *Info gain* is presented as one possible solution for attribute relevance analysis in situation when we are operating with more than two states in output variable.

Figure 2 shows hypothetic example of information gain calculation for three classes.

As it is visible from Figure 2, we do not have clear cuts in impact zones, it is overlapped. It complicates profiling and it is hard, or even impossible to make profiling like in is presented in situation with binary output.

As it is also visible from the Figure 2, different output classes for the same predictor, in the same zones could have significant influences for several output classes. Also, those zones (bins) could be different for different output classes, with different info gain values through observed zones.

Information gain is valuable measure for attribute relevance analysis and for finding appropriate predictors, which will be base for predictive model.

In both situation aim is to maximize probability for buying specific product, in case when we try to recognize typical profile. Manually it is relatively easy task in situation with binary output from predictive model.

In situation when predictive model has more than two output states and 6-12 predictors, efficient profiling became hard task.

Figure 2. Illustration of info gain calculation

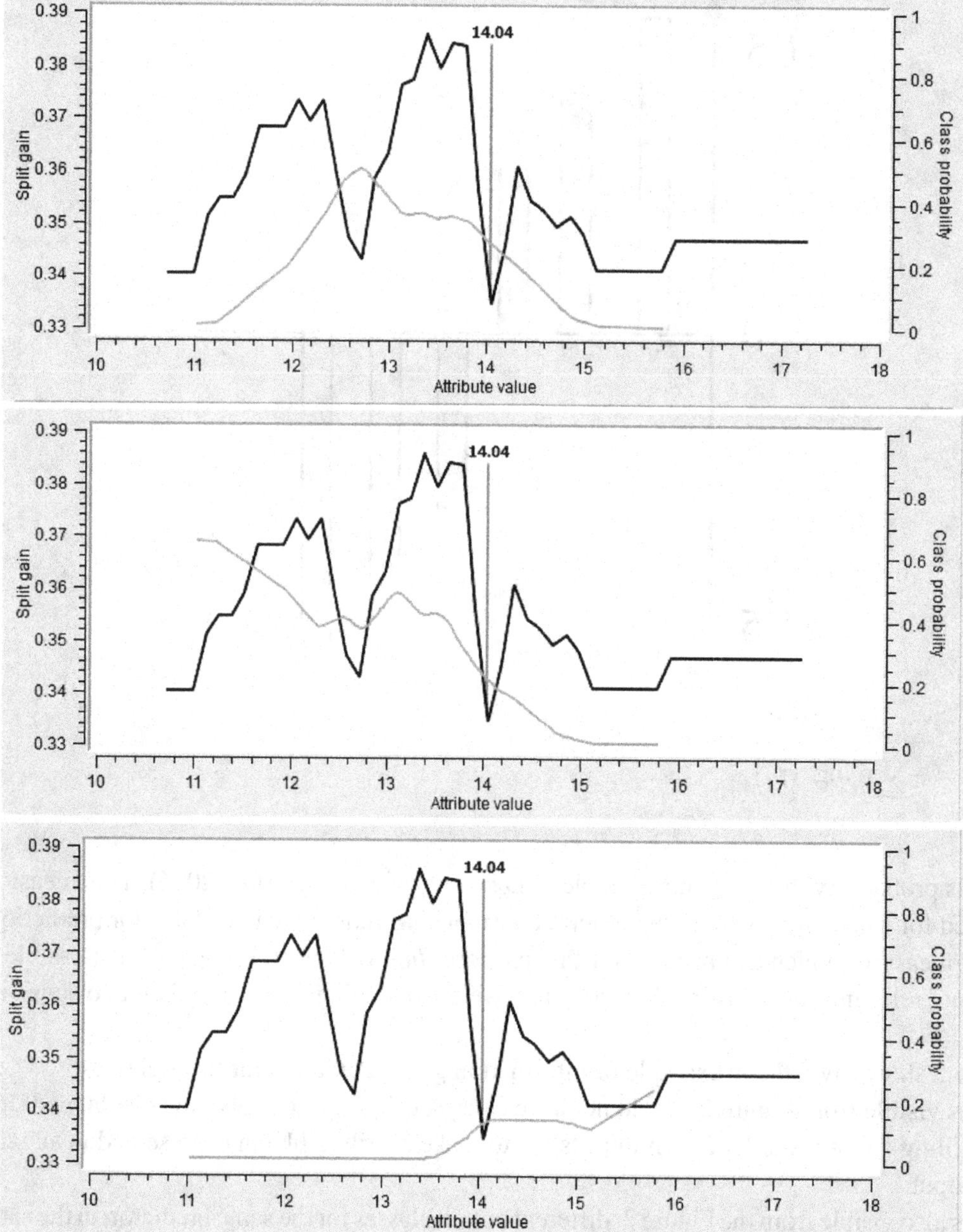

Let assume that we have business problem where company developed predictive model with more than two output states. Output states represent probability for buying specific product or service. Predictive model contains ten variables as predictors. Taking in consider fact that predictive model contains in output variable several states, and taking in consider expected situation like it is visible from Figure 2, overlapping for different predictors for different output states is expected.

This situation is main reason beside many output states in aim variable, for difficulties in profiling based on predictive models.

This is the main reason of difficulties for finding clear cut in predictors regarding profiling, and for finding clear distinction between profiles which are related to specific value of output state.

Using Particle Swarm Optimization Algorithm as Automatic Profiling Tool From Predictive Models

Profiling by using particle swarm optimization algorithm could be done for each predictive model based on different methods (neural networks, support vector machines, Bayesian networks). As an illustration we will present situation when predictive model is based on error back propagation neural network model.

Important step after attribute relevance analysis and before modeling is continuous variables normalization. For each input variable, normalization is crucial factor.

Normalization is important step in modeling. Normalization transforms each predictor values on same scale. Scale can vary, but it is common procedure for using scale between zero and one.

Normalization has function for giving opportunity to all predictors to contribute to model predictive power. Without normalization there are few potential problems which we can expect regarding different scale of predictors.

First problem is connected with higher influence of variables which contains bigger numbers. It is especially visible in situation where we are using values without normalization for k- means clustering purposes. Let suppose that variables, which we are taking in consideration for k-mean clustering are: gender, age, yearly income, number of buying in shop …

Regarding nature of k-mean clustering and nature of distance functions, variables with higher scale (values) will have strongest influence on final output. At the end, in some extreme situation it can result with output where k-mean clustering results are based on one variable, by neglecting other variables.

In mentioned situation where we operate with variables: gender, age, yearly income, number of buying in shop, it is easy to assume that yearly income could became more influencing variable. As a result clustering without normalization would be based on this variable, with weak, or almost no influence of other variables. To avoiding this situation, normalization as a step is very important.

Presented arguments are in high correlation with models like k-means clustering, but it also has significant influence on other models like neural networks.

That leads us to the second problem, which is in line with nature of models like neural networks, or logistic regression. Expected outputs from those models are between zero and one. Neural networks, regarding their anatomy and construction operates (prefer to operate) with input values between zero and one. Regarding that facts, preferred normalization should be done in way that all input variables are in range from zero to one.

Analyst should make additional analysis regarding missing values within predictors, how to declare it, does it have some special meaning, and should it be part of the model. For example, if we have missing values in customer phone number value; it can be interpreted on different ways, depending on problem for which we are developing predictive model.

Let suppose that company has 60% of missing values in variable phone number. If it is data sample which contains customers which bought some product, and after e-mail campaign for some additional product, they left phone number for contact because, they want to buy additional product. Empty field means that customer is not interested for buying additional product.

Different situation could be if 60% of missing values in variable phone number represents data sample of loan users. Paying debt preferences could be in correlation with willingness to provide phone number to bank. Data preparation before normalization process depends on data interpretation, and it is in service for achieving as much as possible better predictive power of the model.

Suppose that continuous variable has a minimum value min (y) and a maximum value max(y), than formula for min max transformation is:

$$y_i' = \frac{y_i - \min(y)}{\max(y) - \min(y)} *(\max(y') - \min(y')) + \min(y')$$

where Y_i' is the transformed value of continuous variable Y for case i. In case of normalization for modeling with error back propagation neural network and sigmoid function as activation function usage, recommendation is that normalization should be done with min(y') = 0 and max(y') =1.

After neural network training on empirical data (development sample), neural network calculates probability of buying specific j-th product or service. P_j represents probability that customer with characteristic from Y_1' ..Y_n' will buy j-th product or service, where *j*>0.

Figure 3 shows neural network model for calculation probability of buying j-th product for customers with characteristic from Y_1' .. Y_n'.

Output Z_k are linear combinationbs of input variables Y'_I weighted by W_{ik} expressed by formula:

Figure 3. Neural network model for calculation probability of buying j-th product

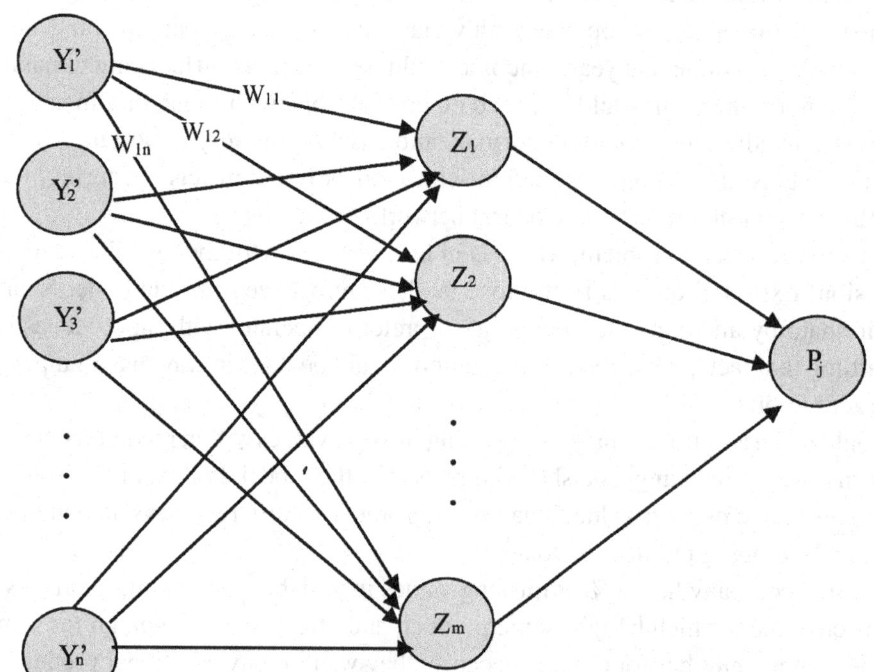

$$Z_{k=}\sum_{i=1}^{n} Y_i' w_{ik}$$

Output from neuron Z_k are calculated by using sigmoid function:

$$Output\left(Z_k\right) = \frac{1}{1+e^{-Z_k}}$$

Error back propagation model has main two stages in model training. First stage is concentrated on output calculation regarding empirical input. Second stage is concentrated on error calculation between empirical result and calculated result as well as error back propagation and correction to each existing neuron.

Process stops when termination criteria has meet, it can be satisfactory value of overall error, or number of defined epochs.

For discovering client profile which has highest preference of buying j-th product, it is necessary to find such combination of Y_1' to Y_n' values which gives maximum value of P_j.

Maximum value of P_j for j-th product, in model should not always be 1.

Manual approach which includes *trial and error* approach could easily be interpreted as manual evolutional process, similar to algorithms based on evolutional principles. This process is time consuming, too costly, imprecise and with uncertain outcome.

In situation when we have numerous products which is included in model (huge number of *j*) it is almost impossible to finish this task manually with satisfactory results.

From the other hand, taking in consider all problems regarding overlapping values from information gain calculation with respect to aim variable, it is nontrivial task, and for solution we propose usage of particle swarm optimization algorithm.

Usage of particle swarm optimization algorithm in combination with neural networks is not new idea.

Main difference in common usage of particle swarm optimization algorithm in combination with neural networks and proposed usage in fact that particle swarm optimization algorithm are mostly used as a tool for learning optimization in neural network.

Proposed approach use trained neural network in combination with particle swarm optimization algorithm for finding optimal customer profile, which are inclined for buying specific product or service.

This approach results in improvement of fast profiling in situation when we would like to determine profiles from complex predictive models with many predictors and many outputs from the aim variable. This leads to the fact that same methodology could be used periodically for monitoring changes in customer profiles. From perspective of decision support system it is valuable information.

Particle swarm optimization for this purpose could be used as:

$$v=v_c+c_1r_1(pbest\text{-}\ Y_i') + c_2r_2(gbest\text{-}\ Y_i')$$

$$Y_i'= Y_i'+v$$

where Y_i' is i-th particle in swarm. It is input value from neural network initially generated randomly or by random selection from empirical data. We generate swarm of size N randomly using uniform distribution. Values of particle are in range (0,1), which represents normalized value into neural network.

gbest is best solution of swarm

pbest is best solution for particular particle

c_1,c_2 is acceleration factors range (0,4)

r_1,r_2 is random value range (0,1), factor which stops quick converging

v is velocity

v_c is current velocity

Number of particles is determined with number of input variables into the predictive model.

Basic algorithm for each j-th product where criteria is maximization of P_j using predictive model (neural network in presented case) using Y_1' to Y_n' as particles and swarm of size N is:

1. *For each j-th product*
2. *Initialize swarm of size N and randomly assign initial values of particles from Y1' to Yn' in range (0,1)*
3. *Evaluate fitness (for each particle)*
4. *Calculate pbest, gbest and v*
5. *Calculate new position for each particle*
6. *Go to 3 until reaching stopping criteria (stopping criteria could be convergence, predefined number of iteration or decreasing fitness trend)*

As a final result after stopping condition is satisfied, profiles (values of Y_1' to Y_n') should be appointed for each product (*j-th* product).

Values of Y_1' to Y_n' for *j-th* product shows typical customer profile which prefer to chose *j-th* product with maximized P_j value which represents probability for buying *j-th* product or service.

Particle swarm optimization algorithm, presented on that way became powerful tool for automatic profile detection based on created predictive model. Evolutionary approach, integrated within particle swarm optimization algorithm speed up process of finding profiles which best fits to specific state into output variable.

This approach gives opportunity to companies for making periodic, frequent profiling in service of profile monitoring and strategic marketing planning.

These methodologies are convenient for early detection for changes in market trends. That could be the base for new product development, or base for cross selling, and up selling activities.

Other advantage of proposed methodology could be in recognition of dominant behavioral characteristics. If some behavioral characteristic for buying some specific product or many of them became dominant in comparison with previous period, and if their influence rise, it means that it should be seriously observed as significant factor in further selling activities.

Let suppose that using shopping coupons which buyers can take from specific magazine, is in great correlation with increasing number of buying some specific product. If previously, that characteristic was not so evident, or significant, that can lead us to few hypotheses (conclusions).

One of than can be that this magazine within its content motivate readers for buying those product, directly or indirectly.

Another one can be that readers are targeted market for that product and that they prefer to by that product.

Company can generate many hypotheses, and it can be triggers and motivators for additional ideas for selling strategies. Each hypothesis should be tested, and after hypothesis confirmation, marketing department can make strategy for further selling activities which should result with higher income for the company.

As it is visible from presented example, automatic profiling beside automatic profile detection purpose has additional service. It is base for generating hypothesis which should serve as milestones for better strategic planning, as well as an early warning market signals strongly related to specific product, or group of product which company sells.

It is obvious, that presented methodology, has multipurpose usability for strategic marketing planning.

Beside recognized profiles using PSO algorithm, in situation when output variable has many states, interesting information could be found, about similarity between generated profiles based on input values for each correspondent output value, which represents willingness for buying specific product or service.

It could be extracted by using Euclidian distances by formula:

$$D(o,i) = \sqrt{\left(Y'_{o,1} - Y'_{i,1}\right)^2 + \left(Y'_{o,2} - Y'_{i,2}\right)^2 + \ldots + \left(Y'_{o,n} - Y'_{i,n}\right)^2}$$

where:

D(o,i) is distance between observed profile and tested profile (observed profile ($Y'_{o,n}$) is profile for which we would like to find most similar one, and tested profiles ($Y'_{i,n}$) are remain profiles) .

$Y'_{o,n}$ are input values from observed profile calculated with PSO algorithm, for which we are searching nearest profile in list of candidates for comparison, determined with PSO algorithm.

$Y'_{i,n}$ are input values from predictive models calculated with PSO algorithm which makes list of candidates for comparison as nearest profile, calculated with PSO algorithm.

This information about similarity could be used for cross selling purposes in situation where significant similarity between two profiles which represents willingness for buying specific product or service exists. It implies that two similar characteristic profiles has propensity for buying two or more different products or services.

Proposed methodology could be base for new clustering approach. These clustering methods are concentrated on similarity of product or service usage/buying.

Such recognized patterns can discover interesting relationships between customers segments. Company can discover that for example, buyers of product “A” are similar to buyers of product “B” and “C”. Difference can be e.g. in minor behavior characteristic like part of the day preferred for buying activities.

This detail can be used for planning marketing activities, or for generating hypothesis which can be usable for testing. Confirmed hypothesis, company can use for further marketing activities.

Additional advantage of calculating distances is periodical observing changes in distances which can show changes in characteristics between recognized segments. This approach can be usable for trend monitoring, as well as a part of the early warning system.

Distances can be calculated partially, in way that algorithm takes in account only socio demographics data, or behavioral data only. Also, analyst can take in account only targeted set of variables, for which exist special reason for observing, with neglecting other variables.

During the time, distance between two or more segments can remain the same, or distance can be higher or lower. If it remains the same, it means that there are no changes between segment characteristics.

If distance became greater, it implies that segments regarding their characteristic became more different, and it is possible that in the future it loose most of their mutual characteristics.

If calculated distance during period of time became lower, it implies that segments regarding their characteristic became more similar, and it is possible that in the future it has more and more mutual characteristics.

It is the opportunity for the company for potential cross selling, if we are talking about different type of products.

Strategy, regarding distance calculation can be focusing on characteristics which are main factors for segments discrimination. This approach gives an opportunity for monitoring unstable characteristics and their trends.

From the other hand, stable characteristics which are mainly mutual characteristics for several segments, should also be monitored. Reason for that is an early recognition factor which shows early trend of changes in some group characteristic.

It could not be determined in advance, which approach should be used in general. It depends on company position on the market, number of recognized segments, number of predictors which consists predictive models, and other factors.

As it is recommended that profiling process should be automated, distance calculation based on proposed methodology should also be automated. Automatic solution should be in line with previously recognized business needs. It includes decisions about variables which will be in focus for distance calculations. It also includes observation and recognition of stable and unstable characteristics within profiles, as well as analytical output design.

Preliminary Results Based on Empirical Data

Described methodology has been applied on empirical data of one Croatian retailer. In his assortment he has more than 10 000 products which he sales through shopping malls.

It is unrealistic and inconvenient to make predictive model for each product.

Strategy was to make predictive models on product group level. Products groups have been made on products, which were recognized as strategic products for this company.

Fourteen groups of product were created.

Criteria for recognition buyer X as a buyer of product in product group was buying product/products in product group in at least 80% cases when he or she visited mall in last year. If buyer satisfied this condition, his/hers profile characteristics has been assigned for buying defined group of products.

It was possible to assign same profile characteristics to different group of products. It was base for predictive mode learning sample construction.

Based on that, learning sample has been divided on development sample and test sample on 80:20 ratio. Neural network model has been developed, and it was base for applying particle swarm optimization algorithm.

Developed model of neural network had 12 input variables, and that determine number of particles in individual case.

Initial swarm was constructed with 7 members, for each of fourteen groups.

Stopping criteria for PSO algorithm was achieving fitness of any particle within swarm greater or equal than 0.82 (on scale from 0..1 which represents probability for buying observed product), or keeping similar (5% changes) or repeating fitness (recognized repeating patterns similar to e.g.: 0.5, 0.6,0.5, 0.6, 0.5) on swarm in last 200 epoch with fitness within swarm less than 0.80.

In case of meeting criteria where any particle within swarm are greater or equal than 0.80, algorithm has remembered values and tries to achieve better results until convergence.

Final profiling results by using PSO algorithm are shown in Table 1.

Success rate for profiling was 71.42% (10 successfully recognized profiles of 14). From Table 1 it is evident that successfully recognized profiles have lower number of epochs. One of the reasons was that successfully recognized profiles met stopping criteria earlier. In case of unsuccessful profiling number of epoch are longer. Reason for that is observing 200 epochs in which fitness changes are within 5% or recognition of repeating patterns above fitness value of 0.82.

Table 1. Profiling result

Group number	Best fitness (0..1)	Number of epochs in PSO	Successful profiling
1.	0.21	1431	No
2.	0.73	1527	No
3.	0.84	893	Yes
4.	0.91	784	Yes
5.	0.92	754	Yes
6.	0.88	801	Yes
7.	0.85	384	Yes
8.	0.54	1566	No
9.	0.33	1721	No
10.	0.87	932	Yes
11.	0.86	1016	Yes
12.	0.89	1155	Yes
13.	0.92	711	Yes
14.	0.87	802	Yes

It is interesting that significant numbers of recognized profiles was in strong correlation with eating habits. Vegetarians, customers who prefer mostly to buy dairy products and customers which mostly buys meet were recognized by particle swarm optimization algorithm in low number of epochs.

It leads us to conclusion that they have distinctive profiles. Detailed analysis on profile characteristics confirms that conclusion.

Other profiles were not so distinctive and were recognized by particle swarm optimization algorithm in higher number of epochs.

For several type of products swarm optimization algorithm was unable to find appropriate solution.

Recognized profiles give a good hint about typical profile of buyer vegetarian product, or typical buyer of dairy products, as well as for customers which mostly buys meet.

There were some behavioral patterns, as well as socio demographics characteristics which shows great discriminative power regarding eating habits.

Other recognized profiles were not so distinctive, because they have more similar mutual characteristics and it became evident after detailed analysis on profile characteristics for those segments.

With successfully recognized profiles similarity has been calculated. Similarity definition was that two profiles are similar if they have differences less than 15%. Reason for that was avoiding situation where two profiles are declared as similar because other are much more different from observed one and difference between them are e.g. 60%. From business perspective it is not similar profiles from perspective of decision-making.

Result of similarity calculation is shown in Table 2.

Further analysis shows that similar profiles are different in average with 2-3 variables of 12. Variables *age* and *number of buying in last 3 months* as predictors in predictive model mostly caused differences. From business perspective it implies profile characteristics which are creditable for profile differentiation which makes differentiation for buying two different product /group of products.

Similarity was mostly case in situation where profiles were not so distinctive and were recognized by particle swarm optimization algorithm in higher number of epochs.

Similarity was mostly the case in situation with profiles which buys similar products like specific kind of tools (construction tools, gardening tools, house maintenance tools …) .

For example, main difference between construction tools, gardening tools, house maintenance tools buyers were in preferred period where buyers buys tools.

Buyers mostly buy house maintenance tools during weekend in the morning. Buyers mostly buy gardening tools in the second part of the week, and construction tools buyers mostly buy during whole week, but not during the weekend.

This variable can give us a hint about customers' behavior characteristics regarding buying habits.

Hypothesis is that house maintenance tool buyers use those tools during weekends for making small works on houses.

Table 2. Similar profiles

Profile based on group number	Similar to profile based on group number
2	10
4	13
7	12

Hypothesis is that gardening tools buyers, plan to spend weekend on garden, and they are buying gardening tools the second part of the week as a preparation for those activities.

Hypothesis is that construction tools buyers buys those tools for business purposes, and that is the reason why they buy it during whole week, but not during the weekend.

From reveled result, it is visible power of presented methodology, which first recognize profiles from predictive models, and in the next step it opens many optional ways for making deeper analysis and for applying additional methods, like distance functions in service of deeper understanding of client portfolio.

It leads us to possibility for creating queries, based on recognized profiles like:*"Find all profiles similar to profile A, and which is not similar to profile B"* or: *"Find all profiles similar to profile A or C, and which has more than two factors similar with profile B".*

Same methodology could be useful also for detecting trend changes in profiling, like it was situation with observed case study.

After initial analyze, same analyze has been done several times each quarter in one year.

It shows that some dominant buyer characteristics have been changed.

Few profile variables (buyer characteristics for specific product) changed expected value through time, as well as variables itself.

It was base for changing tactical plans regarding future campaigns.

FUTURE RESEARCH DIRECTIONS

Presented methodology is based on using neural network model with PSO algorithm for profiling. As it was stipulated, same methodology could be applied on any type of trained predictive model. Most similar situation regarding model type if we are talking about neural networks are predictive models based on other type of neural networks not only error back propagation model like Hopfield model, or radial basis function. Similar situation regarding methodology as well could be with support vector machines, multinomial regression, and decision trees.

Subject of future research could be aimed on usage of presented methodology with predictive models based on Bayesian networks. Reason for that is in their complexity based on links between chance nodes. It means that predictive models based on Bayesian networks demands different approach in situation when we would like to use it in combination with PSO algorithm for profiling.

Other problem is related to fact that evidence means certain event, which implies potential usage of binary states as outputs from chance nodes within Bayesian network. It leads us to on binary PSO usage and adoption, except in situation when we do not have intention to set all chance nodes as a certain events. It depend on potential solution, but for sure it demands additional research and conclusions for finding optimal approach for usage Bayesian networks with PSO algorithm for customer profiling purposes.

Other interesting topic is clustering and usage of e.g. *K-means clustering* on profiles recognized by PSO algorithm usage based on predictive model.

Clustering could recognize similar profiles and consolidate similar profiles together. At the end it could imply revelation that customers which buys product groups *A,B,C,D* are similar to customers which buys product groups *E,F,G,H.*

Additionally, decision trees could be used for finding common denominator within clusters, as well as common differences between clusters. All those information are valuable from perspective of business decision-making.

DISCUSSION

Predictive model developing should not be only aim in cases when company develops predictive models for churn detection, best next offer, up sell, cross sell and similar models. Developing process should be way for understanding relations, and key driven factors for appearance which we are modeling. It is much easier to achieve in situation where we have binary output in aim variable, and it became complicated in situations with models which have more than two states in aim variable.

Predictive models should not be only used as a probabilistic calculator, because in that case business background remains unknown and unhidden. Understanding of business background is crucial factor for strategic management. Knowledge about typical users of some specific product is base for strategic business activities. If for example, typical buyer of black beer with specific flavor, meets matching criteria of age between 20-30 years, lives in specific regions, shows increasing trend for buying those product from June till October, visits stores in average once a week, drives mostly red cars, it is significant information for making business strategy regarding marketing activities.

Typical buyer of black beer with specific flavor could change its habits or characteristics during period of time. It could be changed in way that typical buyer of black beer with specific flavor, meets matching criteria of age between 30-35 years, lives in specific regions, shows increasing trend for buying those product from May till August, visits stores in average once a month.

Changing in characteristics could be caused by time component because same buyers became older, and we have loyal buyers because they did not give up to by same product. Changing in habits connected with increasing buying trends from May till August instead June till October could imply changing in factors like preferred period of holidays.

Profile changes demands changes in marketing strategies and marketing planning.

Significant profile transformation demands greater changes in marketing strategies.

This hypothetic example illustrates strong connection between analytics and strategic business thinking.

Portfolio management demands continuous portfolio monitoring, and in situation where company operates with numerous products on market, which are covered with some predictive models which calculates probability for buying, or next best offer, it is impossible to operate or monitoring portfolio without systematic approach.

Presented model is appropriate solution in this case, and it can be used as well as element for more complex systems. Particle swarm optimization algorithm in combination with built predictive model (based on e.g. neural network) is a solid base for automation of profiling processes.

Periodical processing on available data with particle swarm optimization algorithm in combination with built predictive model should result with derived typical profiles, and what is more important with migration trends (differences) of some characteristic within profiles.

Those results observed during period of time could give pretty clear picture about changes in customers/buyers profiles, and could be trigger for further market activities, as well as generator of new ideas for product development.

As it was seen from presented empirical results, there is no guarantee that proposed model will be successful for generating typical profiles for all the products covered with predictive model. However, empirical results show that it is efficient for most of the modalities of output variable. It implies that proposed methodology could be efficient for intended purpose.

Additional advantage which proposed model offers is ability to calculate similarity between profiles. It is useful functionality in situation where companies try to find "profile clusters". Profile clustering is useful in situation where company try to optimize market activities and to save costs regarding marketing budget. On the other side, it could be generator for new ideas for new product development.

For example, if a buyer of black beer with specific flavor has similar profile like chips buyers, and garden equipment buyers, it could be good starting point for cross selling activities, or good starting point for new product development.

Generic profile calculation has additional advantage in combination with functions for distance calculation. In combination, that methodology could give an answer on questions, which is the main similarity between garden equipment buyer and buyers which prefer to buy construction material.

Also, same methodology can give the answers on questions like, which is the main differences between buyer of black beer with specific flavor, and buyer of beer without flavors.

Regarding nature of market, which can change their characteristics during period of time, same methodology can provide information about profile migration, which could be presented with profile migration maps for specific products or group of products. Also, it can give an answer does profiles for several targeted products became more diversified or became more similar during period of time.

That information is valuable source for portfolio management, as well as for market trends recognition.

It is important to have in mind, that a good predictive model mostly contains behavioral variables which holds the model, and has great influence on predictive power. That fact, leads us to conclusion that proposed methodology could be good tool for recognition and differentiation based on behavioral characteristics. Behavioral characteristics, like for example, buying habits, preferred buying time, buying frequency, store visiting, could be valuable source for good profiling. Changes in those characteristics could imply different buying patterns or preferences. Taking in account all factors which makes differentiation between typical consumers of specific products, supported with presented methodology based on particle swarm optimization algorithm, in combination with built predictive model, outputs can provide valuable information for understanding customer behavior.

It is not hard to assume benefits of applying additional data mining methods like Self Organizing Maps and decision trees. In case where we have generated profiles based on particle swarm optimization algorithm, in combination with built predictive model, Self Organizing Maps could be used for customer profile clustering. Clustered profiles, which contain behavioral characteristics processed with decision trees, could give insight about key driven factors about main differences in recognized buyer's segments.

Generally speaking, it leads us to conclusion that company instead of single profile monitoring, could also monitor profile groups. Also, same as for single profiles, periodical processing on profile group level during period of time could give pretty clear picture about changes in customers/buyers profiles on recognized group level, and could be trigger for further market activities, as well as generator of new ideas for product development and cross selling.

CONCLUSION

Particle swarm optimization algorithm is mostly used as a learning optimization tool for neural networks. It implies changing on weights for achieving optimal fitness.

Chapter represents different approach, in which PSO are used as tool for changing input values of developed predictive model with intention to find optimal customer profile which are willingness to buy specific product.

It is nontrivial task especially in situation when predictive model calculates probability for numerous product / group of products by using numerous input variables.

In that case, PSO algorithm is useful for fast profiling, when numerous combination exists, and when it is time consuming to make profiles manually with uncertain results.

Additional advantage is profile similarity calculation based on given results.

Predictive models based on neural networks are not the only option on which PSO algorithm could be applied for customer profiling. It could be applied on predictive models based on support vector machines, multinomial regression, decision trees, decision trees and Bayesian networks.

Presented methodology has practical value for decision support in business, where information about customer profiles which prefers to buy some product or group products are valuable information for campaign planning.

Also, described methodology could be used frequently (e.g. on quarterly basis) for determination about changes in customer profiles, which implies changes in customer behavior or preferences during certain period of time. This information is valuable source for changes in marketing strategy and in situation when it is automatic process with PSO algorithm, it could be semi-automated process, which is not time consuming.

It is important to keep in mind that presented methodology does not guarantee that it is able to find profiles for each defined product / group of product. As it is seen on results based from empirical data it is not surprising that for some defined product / group of product it is not possible to find reliable customer profile. It depends on data itself, as well as on type of predictive model.

Situation in which for the most of the product / group of product adequate profiles are recognized with certain threshold is acceptable.

REFERENCES

Adhikari, R., & Agrawal, R. K. (2013). Hybridization of Artificial Neural Network and Particle Swarm Optimization Methods for Time Series Forecasting. *International Journal of Applied Evolutionary Computation*, *4*(3), 75–90. doi:10.4018/jaec.2013070107

Adhikari, R., & Agrawal, R. K. (2013). Hybridization of Artificial Neural Network and Particle Swarm Optimization Methods for Time Series Forecasting. *International Journal of Applied Evolutionary Computation*, *4*(3), 75–90. doi:10.4018/jaec.2013070107

Afify, A. (2013). Intelligent Computation for Manufacturing. In Z. Li & A. Al-Ahmari (Eds.), *Formal Methods in Manufacturing Systems: Recent Advances* (pp. 211–246). Hershey, PA: Engineering Science Reference. doi:10.4018/978-1-4666-4034-4.ch009

Aleksander, I., & Morton, H. (1995). *An introduction to neural computing*. International Thompson Computer Press.

Anagnostopoulos, C., & Hadjiefthymiades, S. (2012). Swarm Intelligence in Autonomic Computing: The Particle Swarm Optimization Case. In P. Cong-Vinh (Ed.), *Formal and Practical Aspects of Autonomic Computing and Networking: Specification, Development, and Verification* (pp. 97–117). Hershey, PA: Information Science Reference; doi:10.4018/978-1-60960-845-3.ch004

Arora, V., & Ravi, V. (2013). Data Mining using Advanced Ant Colony Optimization Algorithm and Application to Bankruptcy Prediction. *International Journal of Information Systems and Social Change*, *4*(3), 33–56. doi:10.4018/jissc.2013070103

Babahajyani, P., Habibi, F., & Bevrani, H. (2014). An On-Line PSO-Based Fuzzy Logic Tuning Approach: Microgrid Frequency Control Case Study. In P. Vasant (Ed.), *Handbook of Research on Novel Soft Computing Intelligent Algorithms: Theory and Practical Applications* (pp. 589–616). Hershey, PA: Information Science Reference; doi:10.4018/978-1-4666-4450-2.ch020

Cheng, S., Shi, Y., & Qin, Q. (2013). A Study of Normalized Population Diversity in Particle Swarm Optimization. *International Journal of Swarm Intelligence Research*, *4*(1), 1–34. doi:10.4018/jsir.2013010101

Clerck, M. (2013). *Particle Swarm Optimization*. London: ISTE.

Devi, V. S. (2014). Learning Using Soft Computing Techniques. In B. Tripathy & D. Acharjya (Eds.), *Global Trends in Intelligent Computing Research and Development* (pp. 51–67). Hershey, PA: Information Science Reference. doi:10.4018/978-1-4666-4936-1.ch003

Devi, V. S. (2014). Learning Using Soft Computing Techniques. In B. Tripathy & D. Acharjya (Eds.), *Global Trends in Intelligent Computing Research and Development* (pp. 51–67). Hershey, PA: Information Science Reference. doi:10.4018/978-1-4666-4936-1.ch003

El-Shorbagy. (2013). *Numerical Optimization & Swarm Intelligence for optimization: Trust Region Algorithm & Particle Swarm Optimization*. LAP LAMBERT Academic Publishing.

Giudici, P. (2003). *Applied Data Mining: Statistical Methods for Business and Industry*. John Wiley &Sons Inc.

Giudici, P., & Figini, S. (2009). *Applied Data Mining for Business and Industry (Statistics in Practice)*. Wiley. doi:10.1002/9780470745830

Han, J., & Kamber, M. (2006). *Data Mining: Concepts and Techniques*. Morgan Kaufmann.

Klepac, G. (2010). Preparing for New Competition in the Retail Industry. In A. Syvajarvi & J. Stenvall (Eds.), *Data Mining in Public and Private Sectors: Organizational and Government Applications* (pp. 245–266). Hershey, PA: Information Science Reference. doi:10.4018/978-1-60566-906-9.ch013

Klepac, G. (2014). Data Mining Models as a Tool for Churn Reduction and Custom Product Development in Telecommunication Industries. In P. Vasant (Ed.), *Handbook of Research on Novel Soft Computing Intelligent Algorithms: Theory and Practical Applications* (pp. 511–537). Hershey, PA: Information Science Reference. doi:10.4018/978-1-4666-4450-2.ch017

Klepac, G., Kopal, R., & Mršić, L. (2015). *Developing Churn Models Using Data Mining Techniques and Social Network Analysis*. Hershey, PA: IGI Global. doi:10.4018/978-1-4666-6288-9

Konstantinos, E. P., & Michael, N. V. (2010). Applications in Machine Learning. In K. Parsopoulos & M. Vrahatis (Eds.), *Particle Swarm Optimization and Intelligence: Advances and Applications* (pp. 149–167). Hershey, PA: Information Science Reference. doi:10.4018/978-1-61520-666-7.ch006

Konstantinos, E. P., & Michael, N. V. (2010). Established and Recently Proposed Variants of Particle Swarm Optimization. In K. Parsopoulos & M. Vrahatis (Eds.), *Particle Swarm Optimization and Intelligence: Advances and Applications* (pp. 88–132). Hershey, PA: Information Science Reference. doi:10.4018/978-1-61520-666-7.ch004

Kress, M., Mostaghim, S., & Seese, D. (2010). Intelligent Business Process Execution using Particle Swarm Optimization. In Information Resources Management: Concepts, Methodologies, Tools and Applications (pp. 797-815). Hershey, PA: Information Science Reference. doi:10.4018/978-1-61520-965-1.ch319

Kurbatsky, V., Sidorov, D., Tomin, N., & Spiryaev, V. (2014). Optimal Training of Artificial Neural Networks to Forecast Power System State Variables. *International Journal of Energy Optimization and Engineering*, *3*(1), 65–82. doi:10.4018/ijeoe.2014010104

Larose, D. T. (2005). *Discovering Knowledge in Data: An Introduction to Data Mining*. John Wiley &Sons Inc.

Nguyen, S., & Kachitvichyanukul, V. (2010). Movement Strategies for Multi-Objective Particle Swarm Optimization. *International Journal of Applied Metaheuristic Computing*, *1*(3), 59–79. doi:10.4018/jamc.2010070105

Olson, E. A. (2011). *Particle Swarm Optimization: Theory, Techniques and Applications (Engineering Tools, Techniques and Tables)*. Nova Science Pub Inc.

Rajesh, R., Pugazhendhi, S., & Ganesh, K. (2013). Genetic Algorithm and Particle Swarm Optimization for Solving Balanced Allocation Problem of Third Party Logistics Providers. In J. Wang (Ed.), *Management Innovations for Intelligent Supply Chains* (pp. 184–203). Hershey, PA: Business Science Reference. doi:10.4018/978-1-4666-2461-0.ch010

Russel, C. E., Yuhui, S., & Kennedy, J. (2001). *Swarm Intelligence*. Morgan Kaufmann.

Singh, S., & Singh, J. N. (2012). *Application of Particle Swarm Optimization: In the field of Image Processing*. LAP LAMBERT Academic Publishing.

Taleizadeh, A. A., & Cárdenas-Barrón, L. E. (2013). Metaheuristic Algorithms for Supply Chain Management Problems. In I. Management Association (Ed.), Supply Chain Management: Concepts, Methodologies, Tools, and Applications (pp. 1814-1837). Hershey, PA: Business Science Reference. doi:10.4018/978-1-4666-2625-6.ch106

Tosun, Ö. (2014). Artificial Bee Colony Algorithm. In J. Wang (Ed.), *Encyclopedia of Business Analytics and Optimization* (pp. 179–192). Hershey, PA: Business Science Reference. doi:10.4018/978-1-4666-5202-6.ch018

Xing, B., & Gao, W. (2014). Post-Disassembly Part-Machine Clustering Using Artificial Neural Networks and Ant Colony Systems. In *Computational Intelligence in Remanufacturing* (pp. 135–150). Hershey, PA: Information Science Reference. doi:10.4018/978-1-4666-4908-8.ch008

Xing, B., & Gao, W. (2014a). Overview of Computational Intelligence. In *Computational Intelligence in Remanufacturing* (pp. 18–36). Hershey, PA: Information Science Reference. doi:10.4018/978-1-4666-4908-8.ch002

Yosuf, M. S. (2010). *Nonlinear Predictive Control Using Particle Swarm Optimization: Application to Power Systems. Hidelberg, Germany: VDM Verlag Dr.* Müller.

ADDITIONAL READING

Abbasimehr, H., Tarokh, M. J., & Setak, M. (2011). Determination of Algorithms Making Balance Between Accuracy and Comprehensibility in Churn Prediction Setting. *International Journal of Information Retrieval Research, 1*(2), 39–54. doi:10.4018/IJIRR.2011040103

Agosta, L. (2000). *The Essential Guide to Data Warehousing*. Upper Saddle River, N.J.: Prentice Hall.

Aleksander, I., & Morton, H. (1995). *An introduction to neural computing*. International Thompson Computer Press.

Alippi, C. (2003). A Perturbation Size-Independent Analysis of Robustness in Neural Networks by Randomized Algorithms. In M. Mohammadian, R. Sarker, & X. Yao (Eds.), *Computational Intelligence in Control* (pp. 22–40). Hershey, PA: Idea Group Publishing; doi:10.4018/978-1-59140-037-0.ch002

Almeida, F., & Santos, M. (2014). A Conceptual Framework for Big Data Analysis. In I. Portela & F. Almeida (Eds.), *Organizational, Legal, and Technological Dimensions of Information System Administration* (pp. 199–223). Hershey, PA: Information Science Reference; doi:10.4018/978-1-4666-4526-4.ch011

Bakshi, K. (2014). Technologies for Big Data. In W. Hu & N. Kaabouch (Eds.), *Big Data Management, Technologies, and Applications* (pp. 1–22). Hershey, PA: Information Science Reference; doi:10.4018/978-1-4666-4699-5.ch001

Bang, J., Dholakia, N., Hamel, L., & Shin, S. (2009). Customer Relationship Management and Knowledge Discovery in Database. In J. Erickson (Ed.), *Database Technologies: Concepts, Methodologies, Tools, and Applications* (pp. 1778–1786). Hershey, PA: Information Science Reference; doi:10.4018/978-1-60566-058-5.ch107

Berry, J. A. Michaell, Linoff G., (1997) Data mining techniques for marketing sales and customer support. NY: John Wiley &Sons Inc.

Chen, D., & Mohler, R. R. (2010). Intelligent Control and Optimal Operation of Complex Electric Power Systems Using Hierarchical Neural Networks. In G. Rigatos (Ed.), *Intelligent Industrial Systems: Modeling, Automation and Adaptive Behavior* (pp. 291–320). Hershey, PA: Information Science Reference; doi:10.4018/978-1-61520-849-4.ch011

Dieu, V. N., & Ongsakul, W. (2012). Hopfield Lagrange Network for Economic Load Dispatch. In P. Vasant, N. Barsoum, & J. Webb (Eds.), *Innovation in Power, Control, and Optimization: Emerging Energy Technologies* (pp. 57–94). Hershey, PA: Engineering Science Reference; doi:10.4018/978-1-61350-138-2.ch002

Dresner, H. (2008). *Performance management revolution*. NY: John Wiley &Sons Inc.

Elamvazuthi, I., Vasant, P., & Ganesan, T. (2012). Integration of Fuzzy Logic Techniques into DSS for Profitability Quantification in a Manufacturing Environment. In M. Khan & A. Ansari (Eds.), *Handbook of Research on Industrial Informatics and Manufacturing Intelligence: Innovations and Solutions* (pp. 171–192). Hershey, PA: Information Science Reference; doi:10.4018/978-1-4666-0294-6.ch007

Feng, J., Xu, L., & Ramamurthy, B. (2009). Overlay Construction in Mobile Peer-to-Peer Networks. In B. Seet (Ed.), *Mobile Peer-to-Peer Computing for Next Generation Distributed Environments: Advancing Conceptual and Algorithmic Applications* (pp. 51–67). Hershey, PA: Information Science Reference; doi:10.4018/978-1-60566-715-7.ch003

Garrido, P., & Lemahieu, W. (2008). Collective Intelligence. In G. Putnik & M. Cruz-Cunha (Eds.), *Encyclopedia of Networked and Virtual Organizations* (pp. 280–287). Hershey, PA: Information Science Reference; doi:10.4018/978-1-59904-885-7.ch037

Gavrilova, M. L., & Monwar, M. (2013). Chaotic Neural Networks and Multi-Modal Biometrics. In *Multimodal Biometrics and Intelligent Image Processing for Security Systems* (pp. 130–146). Hershey, PA: Information Science Reference; doi:10.4018/978-1-4666-3646-0.ch009

Hemalatha, M. (2012). A Predictive Modeling of Retail Satisfaction: A Data Mining Approach to Retail Service Industry. In P. Ordóñez de Pablos & M. Lytras (Eds.), *Knowledge Management and Drivers of Innovation in Services Industries* (pp. 175–189). Hershey, PA: Information Science Reference; doi:10.4018/978-1-4666-0948-8.ch014

Hussain, A., & Liatsis, P. (2009). A Novel Recurrent Polynomial Neural Network for Financial Time Series Prediction. In M. Zhang (Ed.), *Artificial Higher Order Neural Networks for Economics and Business* (pp. 190–211). Hershey, PA: Information Science Reference; doi:10.4018/978-1-59904-897-0.ch009

Janecek, A., & Tan, Y. (2011). Swarm Intelligence for Non-Negative Matrix Factorization. [IJSIR]. *International Journal of Swarm Intelligence Research*, *2*(4), 12–34. doi:10.4018/jsir.2011100102

Kawamura, H., & Suzuki, K. (2011). Pheromone-style Communication for Swarm Intelligence. In S. Chen, Y. Kambayashi, & H. Sato (Eds.), *Multi-Agent Applications with Evolutionary Computation and Biologically Inspired Technologies: Intelligent Techniques for Ubiquity and Optimization* (pp. 294–307). Hershey, PA: Medical Information Science Reference; doi:10.4018/978-1-60566-898-7.ch016

Kolomvatsos, K., & Hadjiefthymiades, S. (2012). On the Use of Fuzzy Logic in Electronic Marketplaces. In V. Mago & N. Bhatia (Eds.), *Cross-Disciplinary Applications of Artificial Intelligence and Pattern Recognition: Advancing Technologies* (pp. 609–632). Hershey, PA: Information Science Reference; doi:10.4018/978-1-61350-429-1.ch030

Lee, K., & Paik, T. (2006). A Neural Network Approach to Cost Minimizatin in a Production Scheduling Setting. In J. Rabuñal & J. Dorado (Eds.), *Artificial Neural Networks in Real-Life Applications* (pp. 297–313). Hershey, PA: Idea Group Publishing; doi:10.4018/978-1-59140-902-1.ch014

Lin, D., & Liao, G. (2010). Computational Intelligence Clustering for Dynamic Video Watermarking. In L. Wang & T. Hong (Eds.), *Intelligent Soft Computation and Evolving Data Mining: Integrating Advanced Technologies* (pp. 298–318). Hershey, PA: Information Science Reference; doi:10.4018/978-1-61520-757-2.ch014

Malhotra, R. (2014). SIDE: A Decision Support System Using a Combination of Swarm Intelligence and Data Envelopment Analysis. *International Journal of Strategic Decision Sciences*, *5*(1), 39–58. doi:10.4018/ijsds.2014010103

Michaell, B. J. A., & Gordon, L. (2000). *Mastering data mining*. NY: John Wiley &Sons Inc.

Michaell, B. J. A., & Gordon, L. (2003). *Mining the web*. NY: John Wiley &Sons Inc.

Moein, S. (2014). Optimization Algorithms. In *Medical Diagnosis Using Artificial Neural Networks* (pp. 182–199). Hershey, PA: Medical Information Science Reference; doi:10.4018/978-1-4666-6146-2.ch013

Pacini, E., Mateos, C., & Garino, C. G. (2013). Schedulers Based on Ant Colony Optimization for Parameter Sweep Experiments in Distributed Environments. In S. Bhattacharyya & P. Dutta (Eds.), *Handbook of Research on Computational Intelligence for Engineering, Science, and Business* (pp. 410–448). Hershey, PA: Information Science Reference; doi:10.4018/978-1-4666-2518-1.ch016

Qi, J., Li, Y., Li, C., & Zhang, Y. (2009). Telecommunication Customer Detainment Management. In I. Lee (Ed.), *Handbook of Research on Telecommunications Planning and Management for Business* (pp. 379–399). Hershey, PA: Information Science Reference; doi:10.4018/978-1-60566-194-0.ch024

Sharkey, A. J., & Sharkey, N. (2006). The Application of Swarm Intelligence to Collective Robots. In J. Fulcher (Ed.), *Advances in Applied Artificial Intelligence* (pp. 157–185). Hershey, PA: Idea Group Publishing; doi:10.4018/978-1-59140-827-7.ch006

Shen, Y., Li, Y., Wu, L., Liu, S., & Wen, Q. (2014). Big Data Overview. In Y. Shen, Y. Li, L. Wu, S. Liu, & Q. Wen (Eds.), *Enabling the New Era of Cloud Computing: Data Security, Transfer, and Management* (pp. 156–184). Hershey, PA: Information Science Reference; doi:10.4018/978-1-4666-4801-2.ch008

Shi, Y. (2012). *Innovations and Developments of Swarm Intelligence Applications* (pp. 1–398). Hershey, PA: IGI Global; doi:10.4018/978-1-4666-1592-2

Sirkeci, I., & Mannix, R. (2010). Segmentation Challenges Posed by 'Transnationals' in Mobile Marketing. In K. Pousttchi & D. Wiedemann (Eds.), *Handbook of Research on Mobile Marketing Management* (pp. 94–114). Hershey, PA: Business Science Reference; doi:10.4018/978-1-60566-074-5.ch006

Weiss, G. (2009). Data Mining in the Telecommunications Industry. In J. Wang (Ed.), *Encyclopedia of Data Warehousing and Mining* (2nd ed., pp. 486–491). Hershey, PA: Information Science Reference; doi:10.4018/978-1-60566-010-3.ch076

Werro, N., & Stormer, H. (2012). A Fuzzy Logic Approach for the Assessment of Online Customers. In A. Meier & L. Donzé (Eds.), *Fuzzy Methods for Customer Relationship Management and Marketing: Applications and Classifications* (pp. 252–270). Hershey, PA: Business Science Reference; doi:10.4018/978-1-4666-0095-9.ch011

Willis, R., Serenko, A., & Turel, O. (2007). Contractual Obligations between Mobile Service Providers and Users. In D. Taniar (Ed.), *Encyclopedia of Mobile Computing and Commerce* (pp. 143–148). Hershey, PA: Information Science Reference; doi:10.4018/978-1-59904-002-8.ch025

Willis, R., Serenko, A., & Turel, O. (2009). Contractual Obligations Between Mobile Service Providers and Users. In D. Taniar (Ed.), *Mobile Computing: Concepts, Methodologies, Tools, and Applications* (pp. 1929–1936). Hershey, PA: Information Science Reference; doi:10.4018/978-1-60566-054-7.ch155

Xing, B., & Gao, W. (2014). Overview of Computational Intelligence. In *Computational Intelligence in Remanufacturing* (pp. 18–36). Hershey, PA: Information Science Reference; doi:10.4018/978-1-4666-4908-8.ch002

Yusoff, N., Sporea, I., & Grüning, A. (2012). Neural Networks in Cognitive Science: An Introduction. In P. Lio & D. Verma (Eds.), *Biologically Inspired Networking and Sensing: Algorithms and Architectures* (pp. 58–83). Hershey, PA: Medical Information Science Reference; doi:10.4018/978-1-61350-092-7.ch004

KEY TERMS AND DEFINITIONS

Bayesian Network: Probabilistic graphical model based on conditional probabilities, which contains connected conditional probability tables within chance nodes.

Data Mining: Discipline which reveals useful patterns from huge amount of data.

Decision Tree: Decision support method that uses a tree-like graph with algorithm for partitioning.

Neural Network: Mathematical model-inspired on human neural system, which has ability to learn from data.

Predictive Model: Model, mostly based on data mining methodology and historical data which has purpose to predict some event.

PSO: Particle swarm optimization algorithm based on evolutionary principle and swarm.

Support Vector Machine: Supervised learning models for classification and regression.

Chapter 10
Squeeze Casting Parameter Optimization Using Swarm Intelligence and Evolutionary Algorithms

Manjunath Patel G. C.
Sahyadri College of Engineering and Management, India

Prasad Krishna
National Institute of Technology Karnataka, India

Mahesh B. Parappagoudar
Padre Conceicao College of Engineering, India

Pandu Ranga Vundavilli
Indian Institute of Technology Bhubaneswar, India

S. N. Bharath Bhushan
Sahyadri College of Engineering and Management, India

ABSTRACT

This chapter is focused to locate the optimum squeeze casting conditions using evolutionary swarm intelligence and teaching learning-based algorithms. The evolutionary and swarm intelligent algorithms are used to determine the best set of process variables for the conflicting requirements in multiple objective functions. Four cases are considered with different sets of weight fractions to the objective function based on user requirements. Fitness values are determined for all different cases to evaluate the performance of evolutionary and swarm intelligent methods. Teaching learning-based optimization and multiple-objective particle swarm optimization based on crowing distance have yielded similar results. Experiments have been conducted to test the results obtained. The performance of swarm intelligence is found to be comparable with that of evolutionary genetic algorithm in locating the optimal set of process variables. However, TLBO outperformed GA, PSO, and MOPSO-CD with regard to computation time.

DOI: 10.4018/978-1-5225-5134-8.ch010

INTRODUCTION

The hybrid squeeze casting process was developed by combining the distinct features such as strength, integrity, economic and design flexibility of conventional casting (gravity and die casting) and forging processes (Rajgopal, 1981). The benefits of the squeeze casting process over conventional casting and forging process are near net-shape castability, simpler tooling construction, high productivity, refined structure, improved surface finish, heat-treatability, minimum porosity and segregations, ability to cast ferrous, non-ferrous and wrought alloys (Rajgopal, 1981; Ghomashchi & Vikhrov, 2000). These benefits have helped the squeeze cast parts to find their applications in automobile parts, namely piston, cylinder, clutch housing, brake drum, engine block, connecting rod, wheels, suspension arm, hubbed flanges, barrel heads, truck hubs, and so on (Rajgopal, 1981; Ghomashchi and Vikhrov, 2000; Krishna, 2001).

The diversified applications of squeeze casting process had attracted the researchers' attention toward squeeze casting process across the globe during the 1990s and 2000s. A wide range of research has been reported using analytical, numerical and classical engineering experimental approaches. Yang (2007) determined solidification time using one dimensional analytical model such as Gracias virtual and steady state heat flow models. It should be noted that casting density and mechanical properties improve with low solidification time. Chattopadhyay (2007) carried out the solidification simulation using a numerical approach by solving Navier-Stokes equation coupled with energy equation. The solidification time was found to be inversely proportional to the interfacial heat transfer coefficient. Krishna (2001) had reported that the heat transfer coefficient in metal castings to be dependent mainly on geometry, size, casting shape, mold materials, physical, chemical and interfacial conditions and major interactions among them. You, Wang, Cheng and Jiang (2017) conducted a numerical simulation based on the finite element method using Procast software. They tried to improve the injection mechanism of the squeeze casting process by optimizing the control parameters. Li, Yang and Xing (2017) used Magma software to locate the shrinkage cavity and related defect in the squeeze cast part. The results showed that the shrinkage cavity and its defects were eliminated after adjusting the squeeze cast parameters (casting temperature, filling velocity, and squeeze pressure). However, the cast simulation software uses many assumptions and is difficult to match withthe actual casting practice. Jacob and Michael (2012) had made several assumptions while estimating the heat transfer coefficient during squeeze casting of aluminum alloys. Aweda and Adeyemi (2009) studied the effect of casting temperature and squeeze pressure on heat transfer coefficients using numerical and classical engineering experimental approaches. It is important to note that the experiments were conducted for a fixed pressure duration. Fan et al. (2010) investigated the effect of squeeze pressure variations on density, secondary dendrite arm spacing and mechanical properties without varying pressure duration and temperature influencing parameters during their experiments. They found a steady increase in the properties up to 120 MPa squeeze pressure,thereafter they remained constant. Maleki, Niroumand and Shafyei (2006; 2009) examined the influence of squeeze pressure, die and pouring temperature on density, mechanical, micro and macrostructure properties using the classical approach of varying one factor at a time Wang et al. (2016) and Jahagiri et al. (2017) studied the effect of applied pressure and pouring temperature on the mechanical and microstructure properties of aluminum and magnesium squeeze cast parts using the classical engineering experimental approach. However, the effects of die temperature and applied duration of squeeze pressure were not considered in their research work. Hong, Lee and Shen (2000) analyzed squeeze pressure, waiting time, inoculants, degassing, pouring and die temperature effects on formation of macro-segregation using classical engineering experimental approach. Rajagopal and Altergott (1985) identified many direct squeeze casting defects and suggested a wide scope to determine the appropriate choice of the process parameter combinations to eliminate most of these defects. Further, they also confirmed that casting quality in squeeze casting process is mainly influenced by its process variables. The practical guidelines suggested/followed by authors using analytical, classical engineering experimental and numerical approaches may lead to many sub-optimal solutions that may not meet the global standards. The traditional approaches can only estimate the main process parameter effects and might fail to estimate the interaction factor effects with the minimum number of experiments and computational burden. Process parameters need to be varied simultaneously to estimate the contribution of interaction effect.

In recent years, statistical methods have been used to model, identify, analyze and establish the input-output relationship of the squeeze casting process. The process parameters were varied simultaneously to study and estimate the main, square and interaction factor effects with a minimum number of experiments using statistical Taguchi and conventional regression analysis. Souissi et al. (2014) employed statistical Taguchi method to study the effect of squeeze pressure, die and pouring temperature effects on hardness and tensile strength of cast aluminum alloys. The main drawback of the study is that they had neglected the influence of pressure duration effects in their analysis. Conversely, Vijian and Arunachalam (2007) had investigatedthe impact of die temperature, squeeze pressure and pressure duration on hardness and mechanical strength, but failed to include the influence of waiting time and pouring temperature effects in their analysis. Further, not much literature is available on developing the input-output relations and checking their prediction accuracy.

Predicting response could help the foundry personnel in selecting the appropriate process variable combinations without conducting experiments and without consuming energy and time. Later, research was directed toward addressing the limitations of statistical Taguchi, Response Surface Methodology (RSM) and DOE methods. Sarfraz et al. (2017) conducted experiments with different combinations of squeeze pressure, melt temperature and die temperature as per the design matrices of Box-behnken. The RSM was used for modeling and statistical analysis by utilizing experimental data (i.e., ultimate tensile strength, hardness and percent elongation) of heat-treated squeeze casting Al-Cu alloy. Similarly, Patel, Krishna, Parappagoudar and Vundavilli(2016) employed two non-linear DOE models such as Box-Behnken design (BBD) and central composite design (CCD) to study the influence of squeeze casting process variables on some properties of aluminum based alloys. In the above works, authors had considered pressure duration, squeeze pressure, die and pouring temperature as input parameters, and density, hardness and secondary dendrite arm spacing as outputs. Among the two non-linear regression models, CCD based model was found to be suited for the responses, hardness and secondary dendrite arm spacing predictions, while BBD was found to be suited for casting density.

Improving the casting quality by identifying appropriate process variables combinations is of great relevance to industry. Identifying the optimal process parameter combinations using the above traditional techniques may not be successful, when number of process variables increases and the input-output relations becomes complex with non-linear behavior. In addition, use of traditional optimization methods such as analytical, numerical, classical engineering experimental, statistical design of experiments and RSM may lead to local optimum solutions. Traditional optimization techniques use deterministic search procedure with specific rules that provides one solution at a time and leads to many sub-optimal solutions. Alternatively, global optimum solutions can be obtained using popular non-traditional search techniques such as genetic algorithm (GA), particle swarm optimization (PSO), simulated annealing (SA), ant colony optimization (ACO), differential evolution (DE), harmonic search (HS), bacterial foraging optimization (BFO), artificial bee colony algorithm (ABC), teacher learner base algorithm (TLBO) and so on. According to Rao and Savsani (2012), non-traditional search techniques are stochastic in nature with certain combination of probabilistic transition rules. Process optimization can be performed either for single or multi-responses. In single response optimization, the optimal solutions can be clearly defined based on the problem domain (global minima or maxima). In squeeze casting, identifying the best process variable combinations of all the responses, such as hardness, secondary dendrite arm spacing and density, is difficult due to the conflicting nature of objectives. Patel et al. (2016a) reported that density and hardness had direct relation whereas the response secondary dendrite arm spacing had an inverse relation. This type of situation requires multi-objective optimization. Multi-objective optimization is the process of determining a set of optimum process variables which results in the best combination of responses.

Multi-objective optimization problems can be effectively solved by using heuristic search procedure of evolutionary algorithms. Population based search techniques, namely GA and PSO, have been proved to be cost effective tools in searching near-optimal solution through its heuristic search mechanisms at many distinct locations simultaneously. The early use of evolutionary computational search was first reported by Rosenberg in 1960 (Rosenberg, 1967). Later, Schaffer (1985) proposed multi-objective evolutionary optimization to optimize two or more responses simultaneously. Multi-objective optimization can be solved by using two general approaches. The first approach deals with combining two or more individual objective functions to form a single composite function after assigning suitable weights to each objective function. The second approach deals with generating set of Pareto optimal solutions depending on the trade-offs (weights). In the recent past, weight methods were utilized to determine the optimum process parameters of different manufacturing processes, such as wire electrical discharge machining (Mahapatra & Patnaik, 2007), tube spinning process (Vundavilli, Kumar & Parappagoudar, 2013) and green sand molding process (Surekha et al. 2012). The present research work also focused on the first approach, i.e., multi-response optimization using evolutionary algorithms, namely GA, PSO, MOPSO-CD and TLBO. The heuristic search abilities of GA and PSO will identify the global minima or maxima more quickly through the competitive solutions for potential populations. In recent years, GA and PSO have been used for multi-objective optimization of different problems related to squeeze casting (Vijian & Arunachalam, 2007), green sand molding (Surekha et al. 2012), machining (Mahapatra & Patnaik, 2007), drilling (Ting & Lee, 2012), tube spinning process (Vundavilli, Kumar & Parappagoudar, 2013) and welding (Pashazadeh, Gheisari, & Hamedi, 2014). Multi-objective evolutionary optimization (MEOAs) has been used during recent past in several domains of science and engineering applications (Zhou et al.,2011). Evolutionary algorithm parameters have to be suitably modified using different niching techniques to handle conflicts in multiple objective functions (Das et al., 2011). Therefore major modifications are being made to the simple PSO algorithm to select the best guides for updating the position and velocity based on the non-dominated solutions stored in the external repository through the use of crowding distance (CD) method (Sierra & Coello, 2005). The multi-objective particle swarm optimization based on crowding distance (MOPSO-CD) method outperformed other modification methods such as dynamic niching PSO (DNPSO), cross searching strategy MOPSO (CSS-MOPSO), MOPSO and MOPSO-based crowding distance and local search (MOPSO-CDLS) for solving multi-objective optimization problems (Santana, Pontes & Bastos-Filho, 2009). Vijian and Arunachalam (2007) had used only linear terms in their objective function and had conducted optimization for hardness and ultimate tensile strength which does not have conflicting nature. Swarm intelligence-based PSO and evolutionary GA are the probabilistic algorithms and require common controlling parameters such as population size and generation numbers (Rao2010). Further, the specific tuning algorithm parameters are inertia weight, social and cognitive parameters of PSO,mutation rate and crossover of GA. These parameters critically influence the performance of the GA and PSO in increasing their computational efficiency and optimum solutions (Rao2010; Rao & Savsani, 2012). Unlike GA and PSO, teaching-learning based optimization (TLBO) algorithm does not require algorithm tuning parameters, which enable the finding ofglobal solutions (Rao & Waghmare, 2014a). TLBO locate the global solutions for continuous non-linear functions with high precision and reduced computational time (Rao, Savsani & Vakharia, 2012). TLBO has been proven to have the ability to correctly locate the extreme values of conflicting requirements as compared to other optimization methods (SA, artificial bee colony, etc.) for both the conventional machining processes (i.e., grinding, drilling, and turning) (Rao & Kalyankar, 2012), and non-conventional machining processes (i.e., electrochemical machining processes) (Rao & Kalyankar, 2011). TLBO algorithm reduced the computation time of optimization of the casting parameters in comparison to other optimization techniques (namely, GA, Taguchi and SA) reported by Rao, Kalyankar and Waghmare (2014). Not much research efforts have been made to optimize the parameters having conflicting nature of the responses of squeeze casting process. To the best of the author's knowledge, not much work has been reported on structure to the property (density, hardness, and SDAS) optimization in a squeeze casting process.

In the present work, the non-linear regression equations based on CCD and BBD are used as an objective functions for multi-response optimization (Patel et al., 2016a). GA, PSO, MOPSO-CD and TLBO have been used to determine the best combination of process variables for high values of density and hardness and low values of secondary dendrite arm spacing. Density, hardness and secondary dendrite arm spacing are considered as outputs (objective functions), whereas squeeze pressure, pressure duration, die temperature, and pouring temperatures are treated as inputs (process variables). Using mathematical formulas, all objective functions are suitably modified to form a single objective function. The predicted optimal process parameter combinations using PSO, MOPSO-CD, GA and TLBO are compared among themselves with that of (target) experimental values.

MATHEMATICAL FORMULATION OF THE PROBLEM

In squeeze casting process, the casting properties (density, hardness and secondary dendrite arm spacing) depend mainly on the influence of process variables such as squeeze pressure, pressure duration, die and pouring temperatures. The input-output model of the squeeze casting process is shown in Figure 1.

The selection of process variables and their corresponding levels is of primary importance, since, too narrow range might result in a poor or incomplete information about the process. Conversely, too wide range may lead to an infeasible solution for the response surface (Parappagoudar, Prathihar & Datta, 2007). Hence, squeeze casting process variables and their operating levels were selected after conducting trial experiments in the research laboratory and byreviewing the literature (Refer Table 1).

The experiments were conducted for different process variable combinations and levels using standard matrices of CCD and BBD. For each casting conditions, three replicates were considered and the responses, namely, density, hardness and secondary dendrite arm spacing were measured. The non-linear input-output relations were developed for the responses, namely, density, secondary dendrite arm spacing and hardness, by utilizing RSM. The statistical adequacy and significance were analyzed using ANOVA test. All three non-linear regression (input-output) models were found to be statistically adequate. Prediction performances of the developed non-linear models were tested with the help of 15 test cases. The CCD model performed better for the responses, hardness and secondary dendrite arm spacing prediction;whereas, BBD model outperformed the CCD based model for density (Patel et

Table 1. Squeeze casting process parameters and their respective levels

Description	Notation	Process variables		Levels		
		Units	Symbols	Low	Middle	High
Pressure duration	PD	s	A	20	35	50
Squeeze pressure	SP	MPa	B	40	80	120
Pouring temperature	PT	°C	C	630	675	720
Die temperature	DT	°C	D	150	225	300

Figure 1. Squeeze casting input-output process model

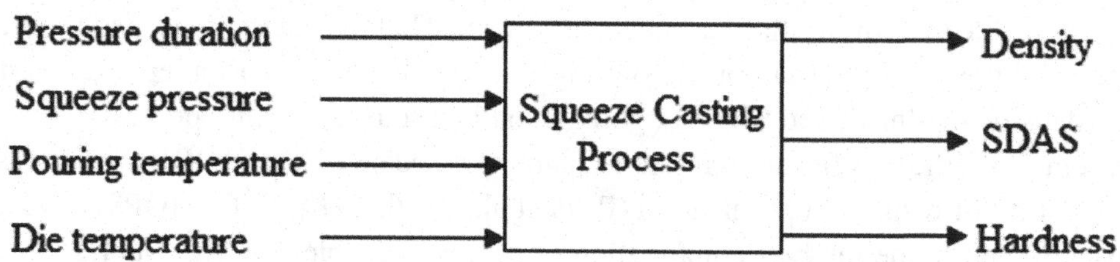

al.,2016a). The best response model was selected for process parameter optimization. The relationship between process variables and the responses are expressed in Equations 1, 2 and 3.

$$Density, \rho_{BBD} = 0.926894 - 0.00162963A + 0.00140417B + 0.00468148C + 0.000867778D - 1.14815 \times 10^{-5} A^2 - 4.19271 \times 10^{-6} B^2 - 3.37449 \times 10^{-6} C^2 - 1.5037 \times 10^{-6} D^2 + 8.33333 \times 10^{-7} AB + 2.59259 \times 10^{-6} AC + 3.11111 \times 10^{-6} AD - 5.55556 \times 10^{-7} BC + 3.33333 \times 10^{-7} BD - 5.92593 \times 10^{-7} CD \quad (1)$$

$$Secondary\ Dendrite\ Arm\ Spacing, SDAS_{CCD} = 558.023 + 0.203851A - 0.186898B - 1.45184C - 0.212065D - 0.00147737A^2 - 3.90046 \times 10^{-5} B^2 + 0.00102844C^2 + 0.000189794D^2 + 7.70833 \times 10^{-5} AB - 8.51852 \times 10^{-5} AC - 3.65556 \times 10^{-4} AD + 0.000168056BC - 1.50417 \times 10^{-4} BD + 0.000252593CD \quad (2)$$

$$Hardness,\ BHN_{CCD} = -380.453 - 0.267973A - 0.219502B + 1.27475C + 0.179611D - 0.00166255A^2 + 0.000766204B^2 - 9.00777 \times 10^{-4} C^2 - 2.20576 \times 10^{-5} D^2 + 0.0005AB + 0.000407407AC + 7.77778 \times 10^{-5} AD + 0.000284722BC + 0.0001BD - 2.88889 \times 10^{-4} CD \quad (3)$$

Density is influenced by internal casting defects such as porosity, voids, segregations, and shrinkages. The internal casting defects decrease the available load area, provoke stress concentration, and initiate crack formation resulting in poor tensile strengths, ductility and hardness. To enhance mechanical properties, finer arm spacing of a casting is desirable. Primary dendrites once developed do not change during or after solidification; whereas, the secondary dendrite arms in the primary dendrites undergo a ripening process. Thus the secondary dendrite arm spacing is of paramount importance to optimize the process variables to enhance microstructure, consequently mechanical properties.

In the present work, attempts were made to optimize the squeeze casting process that could maximize the throughput in improving the casting quality (properties) using evolutionary and swarm intelligent algorithms. For better casting properties, the responses such as density and hardness are to be maximized, while the secondary dendrite arm spacing should be minimized. It is difficult to determine the single optimal combinations of process variables for density, hardness and secondary dendrite arm spacing. Thus, there is a need for multi-objective optimization method to determine optimal solutions for this problem. Therefore, multiple performances of conflicting responses with one to be minimized (refer Equation 5) and rest to be maximized (refer Equations 4 and 6) are converted into a single objective function of maximization using a suitable mathematical formulation (refer Equation 7). The weighted method was adopted for the outputs to form single objective function, similar to the work carried out earlier by Mahapatra and Patnaik (2007), Vundavilli et al. (2013) and Surekha et al. (2012). The formulated weighted objective function for maximization is shown in Equation 7.

$$\text{Objective function } \left(R_1\right) = \text{Density} \tag{4}$$

$$\text{Objective function } \left(R_2\right) = \frac{1}{\text{SDAS}} \tag{5}$$

$$\text{Objective function } \left(R_3\right) = \text{Hardness} \tag{6}$$

$$\text{Maximize } Y = \left(w_1R_1 + w_2R_2 + w_3R_3\right) \tag{7}$$

Subject to constraints:

$$20 \le A \le 50 \tag{8}$$

$$40 \le B \le 120 \tag{9}$$

$$630 \le C \le 720 \tag{10}$$

$$150 \leq D \leq 300 \tag{11}$$

where, R_1, R_2, and $R_3$are the objective functions of responses such as density (ρ), secondary dendrite arm spacing (SDAS) and hardness (BHN), respectively. W_1, W_2 and W_3 are the weights considered for the responses ρ, SDAS and BHN, respectively. Moreover, the terms A, B, C and D are the process variables representing pressure duration, squeeze pressure, pouring temperature, and die temperature, respectively. In multi-objective optimization, there exists a multiple combination of optimal solutions. Selection of a single process variable combination from multiple optimal solutions is a difficult task for foundry personnel. Therefore, four cases have been considered with different combination of weights assigned to the responses by the user. Weighted factors are selected in such a way that their cumulative value is equal to one (Mahapatra & Patnaik,2007; Vundavilli et al.,2013;Surekha et al., 2012). Moreover, higher weight factors indicate that more importance is assigned to the particular objective function. Four different cases have been selected in such a way thatcase 1 deals with equal importance for all the responses ($W_1 = 0.3333$, $W_2 = 0.3333$ and $W_3 = 0.3333$); Case 2 deals with the maximum importance to the response, density ($W_1 = 0.8$, $W_2 = 0.1$ and $W_3 = 0.1$); Case 3 deals with maximum importance to the response, SDAS ($W_1 = 0.1$, $W_2 = 0.8$ and $W_3 = 0.1$); and case 4 deals with maximum importance to the response, hardness ($W_1 = 0.1$, $W_2 = 0.1$ and $W_3 = 0.8$).

METHODOLOGY OF MULTI-OBJECTIVE OPTIMIZATION ALGORITHMS

In the present work, multi-objective evolutionary algorithms such as binary coded PSO, MOPSO-CD, GA and TLBO have been proposed to optimize the squeeze casting process using mathematically formulated single objective function. The working principle of population based optimization techniques of GA, PSO, MOPSO-CD and TLBO algorithms is discussed in the following sections.

Genetic Algorithms

Genetic algorithm was first proposed by Prof. John Holland of the University of Michigan in 1975. GA works with the well known principle of the Charles Darwin theory of survival of the fittest among the individuals over successive generations to simulate the natural system necessary for evolution. GA has been applied in the past to solve various manufacturing related problems (Schaffer, 1985; Mahapatra & Patnaik, 2007; Vundavilli et al., 2013; Pashazadeh et al., 2014). Unlike traditional search techniques, GA searches the optimum solutions at many distinct locations simultaneously. The schematic diagram represents the methodology adopted to optimize the process parameter with the working procedure of evolutionary genetic algorithm (Figure 2). Tournament selection and bit-wise mutations were adopted to avoid local solutions if any.

Particle Swarm Optimization

PSO was introduced by Dr. Russel C. Eberhart and Dr. James Kennedy in 1995. The PSO has gained prime importance in various domains of manufacturing (Vundavilli et al., 2013; Surekha et al. 2012; Ting & Lee, 2012) due to its fewer tuning parameters, easy implementation, and fast convergence rate in comparison to GA. PSO algorithm mimics the movement of foraging behavior of the bird flock. In

PSO, the swarm is a community composed of many individuals referred as particles and all particles fly around in multi-dimensional search space. It is important to note that based on self flying experience and neighboring particles experience, each particle adjusts its own flight path (Sierra & Coello, 2005). The schematic diagram of working cycle of PSO is shown in Figure 3. Unlike evolutionary genetic algorithm parameters such as selection and crossover, PSO utilizes the particles which move individually with a certain velocity and is dynamically adjusted in the search space. The parameters were adjusted by updating the positions and velocity of the particles using Equations 12 and 13.

$$New\ Velocity : V_i^{K+1} = W \times V_i^k + Rand_1 \left[Pbest_i^k - P_i^k \right] + Rand_2 \left[Gbest_i^k - P_i^k \right] \quad (12)$$

$$New\ Position : P_i^{k+1} = P_i^k + V_i^{k+1} \quad (13)$$

where W refers to inertia weight; V_i^k is the current velocity of the individual particle i at iteration k; V_i^{K+1} indicate the modified velocity of the individual i at iteration k+1; $Rand_1$, $Rand_2$ are random numbers that vary in the range of [0 and 1]. $Pbest_i^k$, $Gbest_i^k$ indicate the best positions reached by individual particle *i*and as a group at iteration k. The second term in Equation 12 refers to the cognitive part where the particle changes its velocity based on self-experience, and the third term is the social part where the particle changes its velocity based onthe experience of its neighbor particle.

MULTI-OBJECTIVE PARTICLE SWARM OPTIMIZATION: CROWDING DISTANCE

Multi-objective particle swarm optimization based on crowding distance mechanism coupled with mutation operator is incorporated for simple PSO to keep a variety of non-dominated solutions in an external repository (Raquel & Naval, 2005). The major modifications employed for the basic PSO algorithm are selection process of cognitive leader (*Pbest*) and social leader (*Gbest*) using the Pareto dominance and crowding distance methods. The MOPSO uses the peripheral repository of non-dominated solutions found in earlier iterations and the mutation operator enhance the search capability of the algorithm to prevent premature convergence (local minima) (Raquel & Naval, 2005). The schematic diagram that illustrates the working cycle of the MOPSO-CD is shown in Figure 4. Thus, the MOPSO-CD is considered as an effective tool to handle the complex multi-objective optimization problems which are conflicting in nature.

Teaching-Learning Based Optimization

TLBO algorithm is a new populationbased algorithm based on swarm intelligence inspired from the philosophy of teaching and learning (Rao, Savsani & Vakharia, 2011; 2012). TLBO algorithm works based on the impact of teacher influence on the learners outputs in the class (Rao & Savsani, 2012). There are two paramount elements or modes utilized in teaching and learning based optimization algorithm, namely, teacher phase and learner phase (refer Figure 5). In teacher phase, teachers are considered as highly learned professionals, who share their knowledge, competencies and values with the learners. In the learner phase, the learners interact among themselves. The outcome of learners is evaluated in terms of results or grades and is influenced by the quality of teaching. A good teacher trains learners to gain better results with regard to marks or grades. Further, the results may also improve with the impact of interaction of learners among themselves. There are many solutions in the entire population and the best solution is always referred as a teacher. In TLBO, a set (i.e., team or group) of learners is considered as population and different process or design variables are treated as different subjects offered to the learners. The learner result is the fitness value obtained during task optimization.

Teacher Phase (Rao and Waghmare, 2014b)

In teacher phase, the teachers or trainers always attempt to improve the average student's performance (i.e., result) inthe classroom from any value M_1 for the subject thought by them based on the highest acquired knowledge (i.e. T_A). In actual practice, the teacher always attempts to shift the average performance of the classroom from M_1 to any other better value M_2. Let, M_J corresponds to the mean at any iteration i and T_i refers to the teacher. The function of T_i is to improve the existing mean of M_j and let the new value be selected as M_{new}. The difference of mean between the existing and the new value is determined using the equation given below:

$$Difference\_mean_i = r_i\left(M_{new} - T_F\ M_j\right) \tag{14}$$

where r_i refers to the random number which belongs to the range [0 and 1]; T_F is designated as the teaching factor which corresponds to the value of the mean to be changed. The T_F value in the present work was taken as either 1 or 2, and was decided randomly by maintaining an equal probability after conducting the heuristic search by this algorithm (refer Equation15).

$$T_F = round\left[1 + rand\left(0,1\right)\left\{2-1\right\}\right] \tag{15}$$

If T_F value corresponds to 1,there is no improvement in the knowledge level; whereas, if the T_F value is 2,there is a complete transfer of knowledge. The values between 1 and 2 indicate the level of knowledge transferred. The transfer level of knowledge depends upon the learners' capabilities. The present work also attempted to vary the values of T_F between 1 and 2, which showed no improvement in the results. Hence, T_F values are kept fixed as either 1 or 2 depending on the round up criteria. The solutions are updated based on the mean difference according to the expression given below:

$$X_{new,\ i} = X_{old,\ i} + Difference\_mean\ _i \tag{16}$$

where $X_{new,\ i}$ corresponds to the updated value of $X_{old,\ i}$. $X_{new,\ i}$ value is accepted only if it producesa comparatively better updated function value. The inputs to the learner phase are the accepted function values stored at the end of the teacher phase.

Learner Phase (Rao and Waghmare, 2014)

In the learner phase, the learners could enhance their knowledge or skills using their randomly selected mutual interactions based on the teacher inputs. In some cases, the learner learns new things if the other learner poses comparatively better knowledge or skills. Let n be considered as the size of the population. The learning phase is explained below.

At any iteration i, let X_i and X_j are considered as two different learners under the explicit condition $i \neq j$.

$$X_{new,\ i} = X_{old,\ i} + r_i\left(X_i - X_j\right) \quad if\ f(X_i) < f(X_j) \tag{17}$$

$$X_{new,\ i} = X_{old,\ i} + r_i\left(X_j - X_i\right) \quad if\ f(X_j) < f(X_i) \tag{18}$$

Accept $X_{new,\ i}$, if it produces an improved function value.

RESULTS AND DISCUSSIONS

The results of the parametric study and the optimized process variable combinations for four different cases are discussed in the present section.

Genetic Algorithms

The performance of GA depends mainly on the appropriate choice of algorithm parameters. There are no universal standards available to select the GA parameters such as population size (Pop), probability of mutation (P_M), probability of crossover (P_C) and generation number (Gen). Thus, in the present work, selections are made using parameter study (i.e., varying one parameter at a time and keeping the rest fixed). Selection of weight factor is also of paramount importance in the performance of the casting properties, therefore, was selected based on the requirements of the decision maker.Four different cases were considered after varying the weighing factors based on the importance assigned for objectives. The parametric study was conducted to determine the maximum fitness values of GA. The corresponding parameters responsible for better casting properties are shown in Figure 6. In the first stage, the probability of crossover was varied between 0.5 and 1, after keeping the probability of mutation, population size and number of generations fixed as 0.1, 0.8 and 100, respectively. The probability of crossover (P_C*) with 0.55 showed the best performance in terms of maximum fitness value. Therefore, for the second stage onwards, the probability of crossover was fixed at 0.55. Similarly, the maximum fitness values were determined for P_M, Pop and Gen in successive stages (refer Figure 6). At each stage, the GA parameters responsible for maximum fitness value were identified. The optimum GA parameter values obtained using parametric study are shown below:

Probability of Crossover (P_C*) = 0.55

Figure 2. Methodology followed for process optimization and working cycle of GA (Patel et al. 2016b)

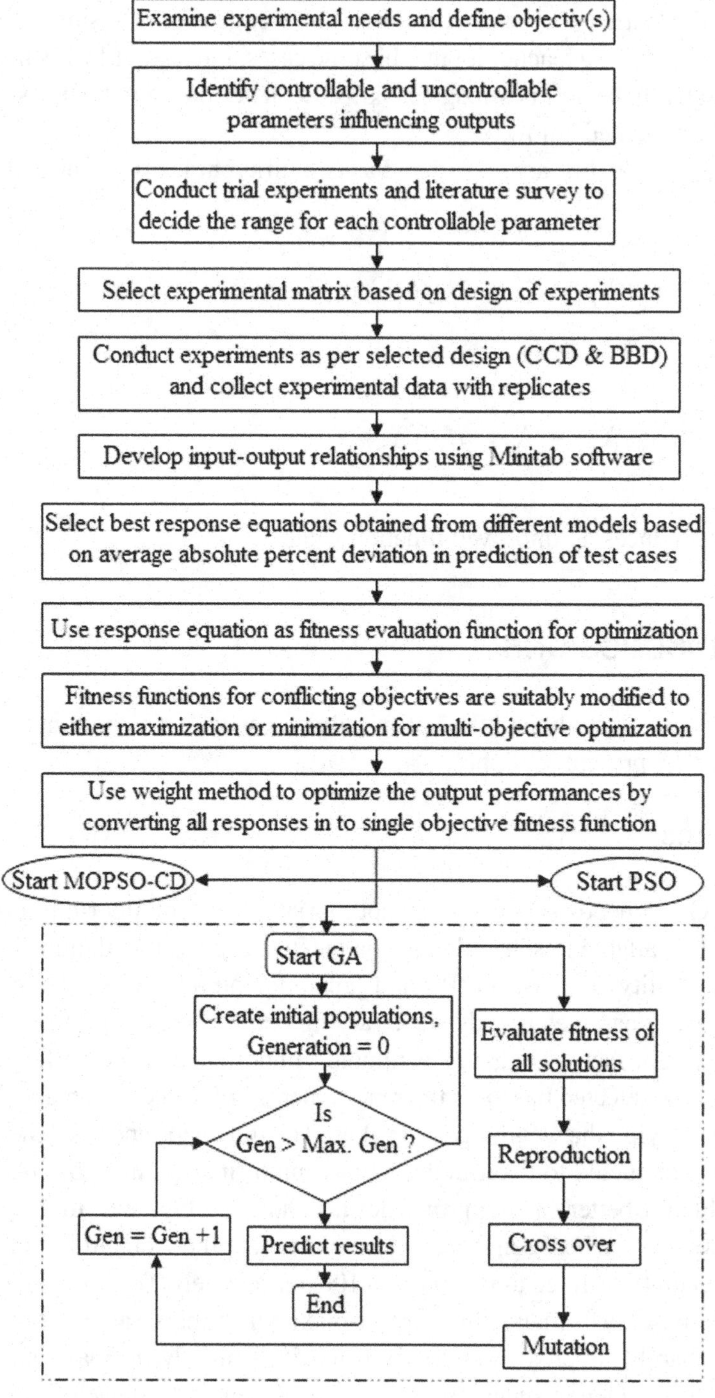

Figure 3. Schematic diagram of working cycle of PSO (Patel et al. 2016b)

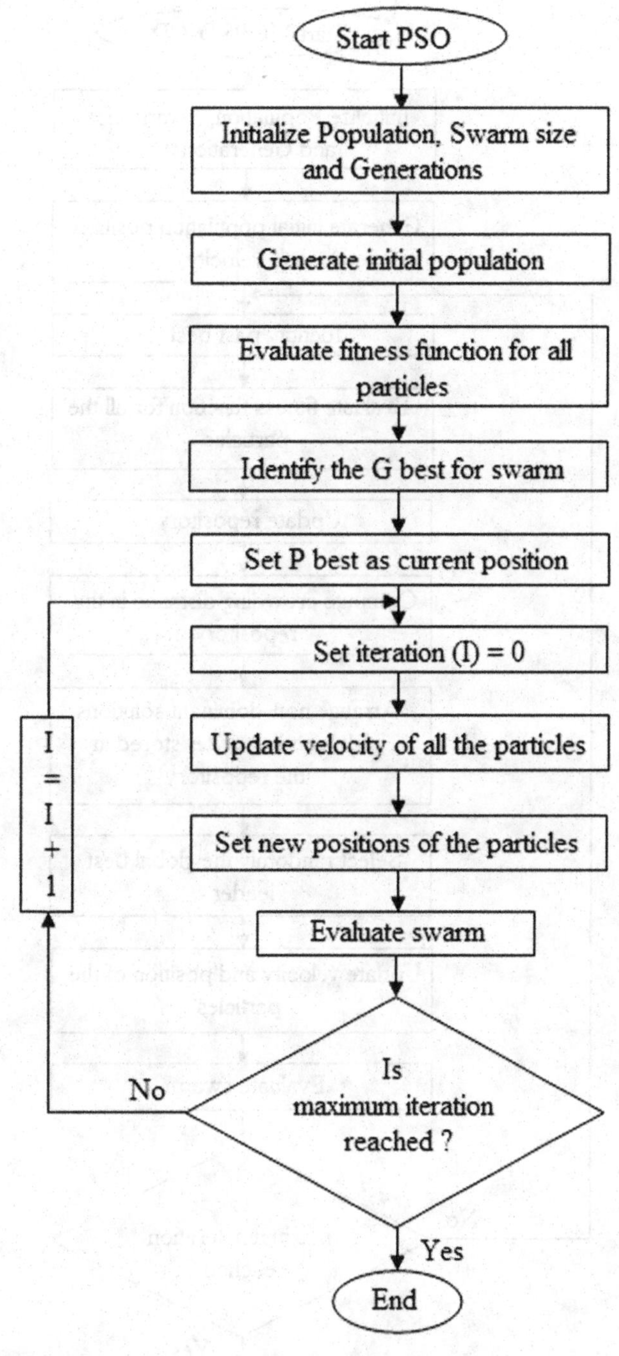

Figure 4. Schematic diagram of working cycle of MOPSO-CD (Patel et al. 2016b)

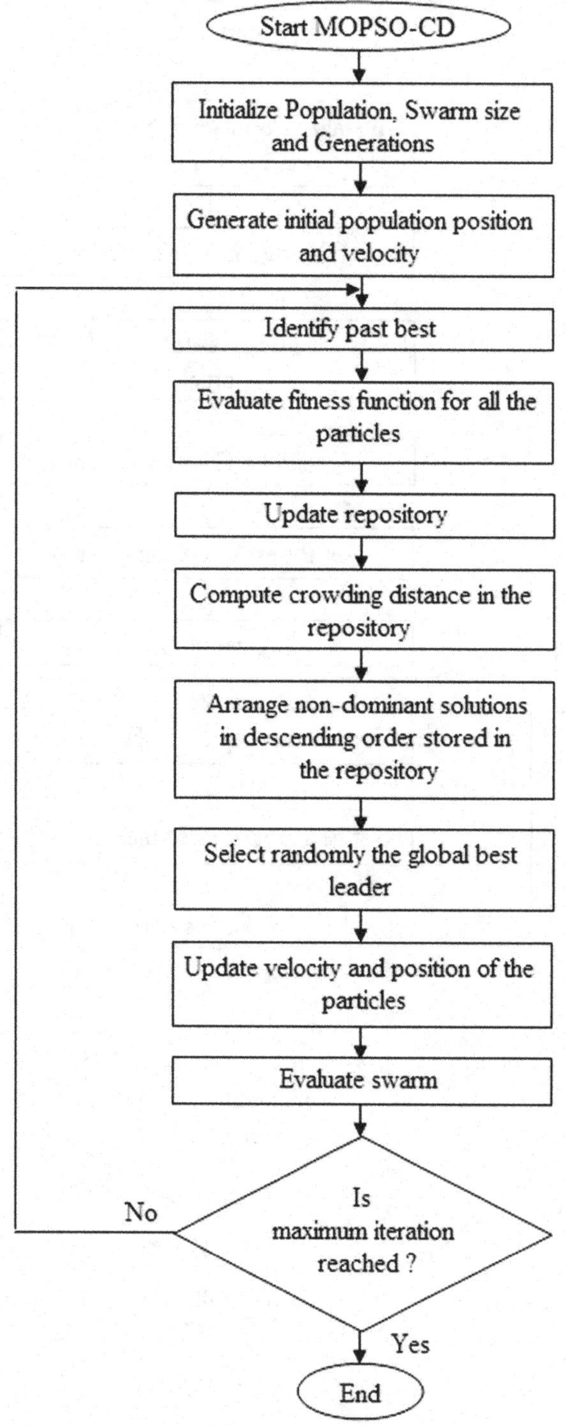

Figure 5. Flowchart of elitist teacher learning based optimization (Rao & Savsani2012)

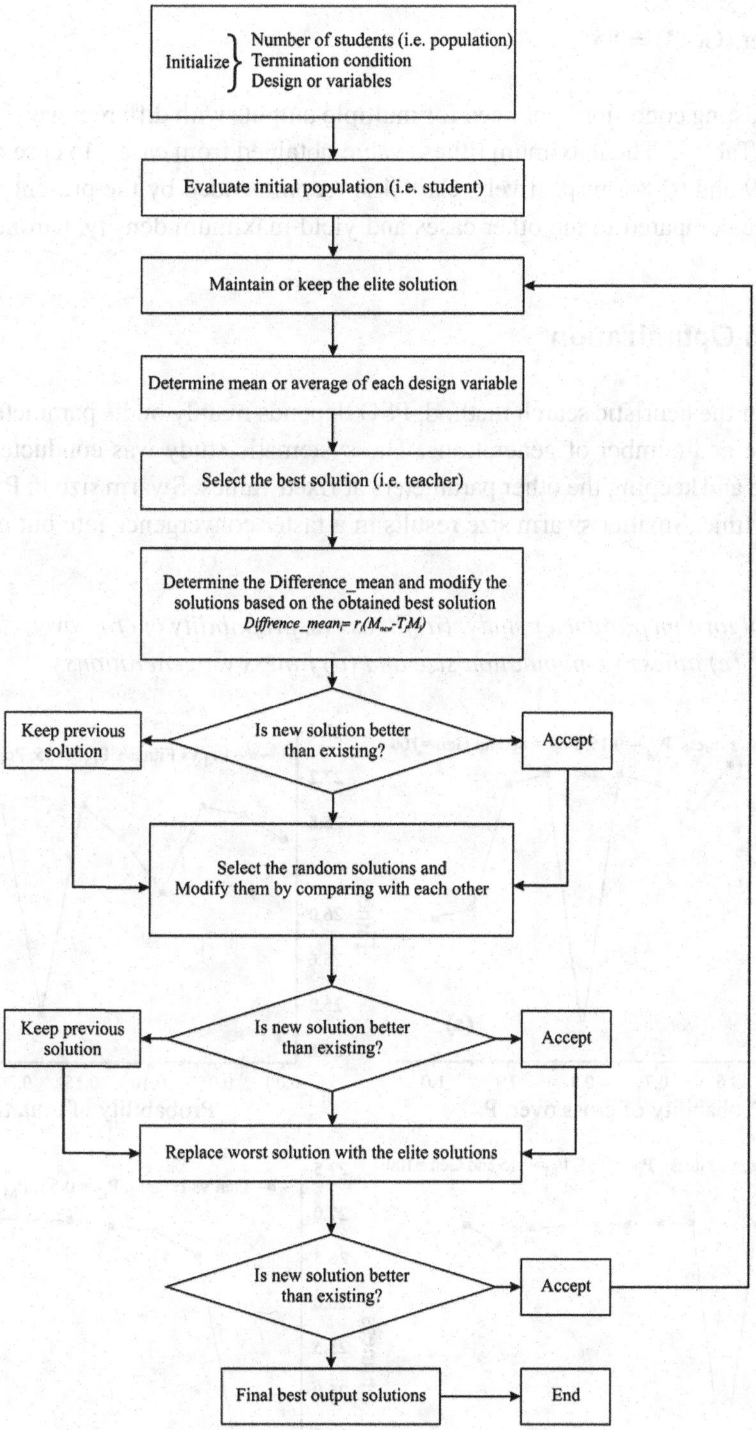

Initialize
Number of students (i.e. population)
Termination condition
Design or variables

Evaluate initial population (i.e. student)

Maintain or keep the elite solution

Determine mean or average of each design variable

Select the best solution (i.e. teacher)

Determine the Difference_mean and modify the solutions based on the obtained best solution
$Diffrence\_mean_i = r_i(M_{new} - T_F M_i)$

Keep previous solution

Is new solution better than existing?

Accept

Select the random solutions and Modify them by comparing with each other

Keep previous solution

Is new solution better than existing?

Accept

Replace worst solution with the elite solutions

Is new solution better than existing?

Accept

Final best output solutions

End

Probability of Mutation (P_M*) = 0.15
Population Size (Pop*) = 80
Generation Number (Gen*) = 85

The optimum casting conditions obtained for multiple outputs with different weight factor combinations are shown in Table 2. The maximum fitness value obtained from case 1 to case 4 werefound to be 26.93, 9.907, 8.089 and 62.88, respectively. Case 4 is recommended by the present work, since it has higher fitness value compared to the other cases and yield maximum density, hardness and minimum values of SDAS.

Particle Swarm Optimization

The performance of the heuristic search method, PSO depends mainly on its parameters such as inertia weight, swarm size and number of generations. The systematic study was conducted by varying one parameter at a time and keeping the other parameters at fixed values. Swarm size in PSO greatly affects the computational time. Smaller swarm size results in a faster convergence rate but may have a higher

Figure 6. Genetic algorithm parameter study: (a) fitness vs. probability of crossover, (b) fitness vs. probability of mutation, (c) fitness vs. population size and (d) fitness vs. generations

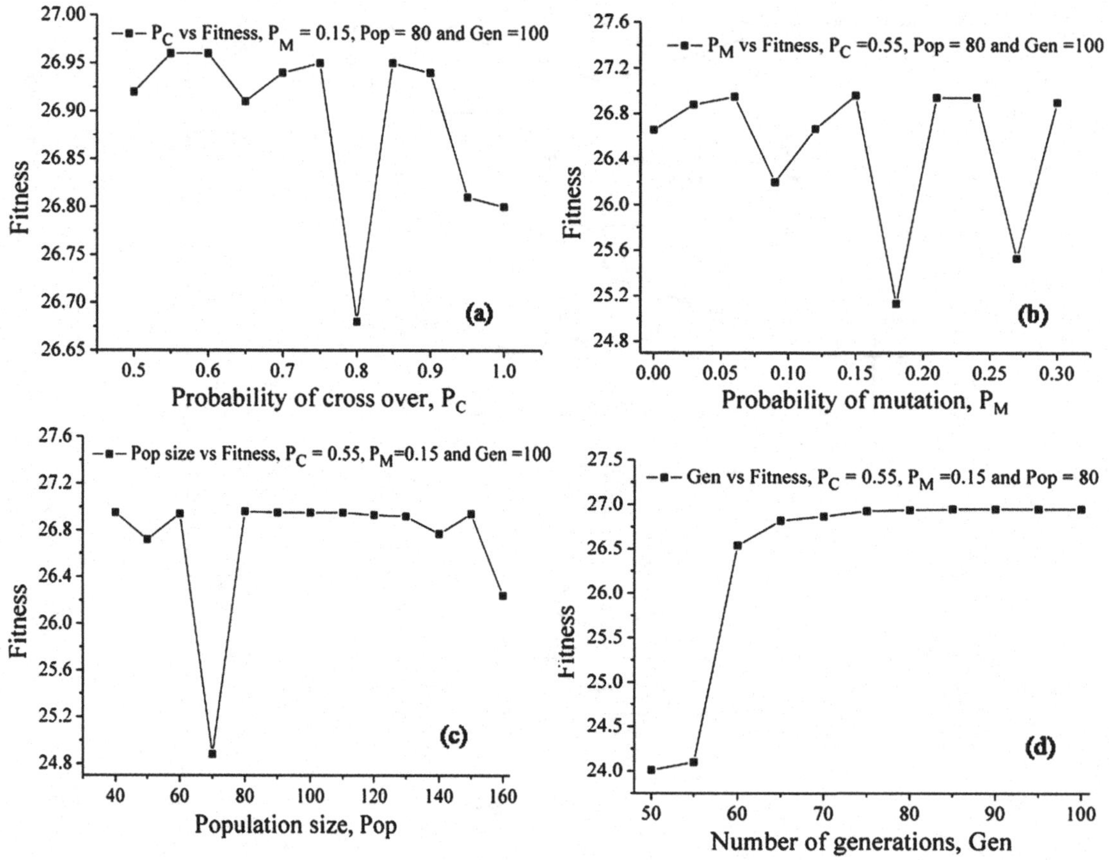

probability of getting trapped inlocal minima. Conversely, improvement in the performance with a large swarm size will be at the cost of computational time. The systematic study has been conducted to determine the maximum fitness of PSO parameters responsible to yield the best casting properties (refer Figure 7). The study was carried out in three stages. In the first stage, the inertia weights were varied between 0 and 1, after keeping both the swarm size and number of generations fixed as 50. The inertia weight (W*) with 0.6 showed the best performance in terms of maximum fitness (see Figure 7 (a)). Hence, from the second stage onwards, the inertia weight was kept fixed at 0.6. Similarly, maximum fitness values were determined for swarm size (SS*) and maximum generation (G*) in the successive stages. Finally the optimized PSO parameters responsible for better performance are as follows:

Inertia Weight (W*) = 0.6
Swarm Size (SS*) = 50
Number of Generations (G*) = 50

Similar to GA, four different cases have been considered to determine the optimal process variable combinations responsible for multiple output performances (refer Table 2). The maximum fitness ob-

Figure 7. Parameter study of PSO: (a) fitness vs. inertia weight, (b) fitness vs. swarm size and (c) fitness vs. generations

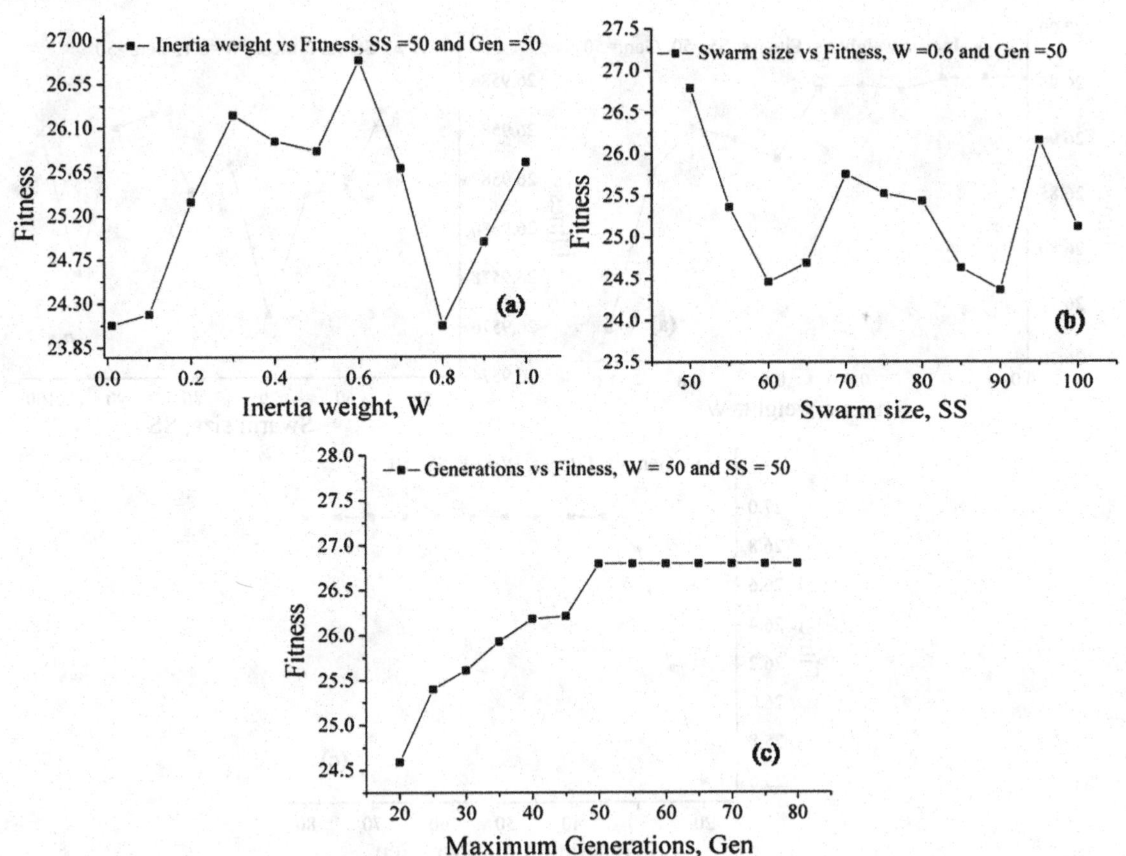

tained from case 1 to case 4 is found to be equal to 26.79, 10.06, 7.78 and 63.16, respectively. Case 4 is recommended for PSO, as it hashigher fitness values and over performed the other cases to yield better casting properties.

Multi-Objective Particle Swarm Optimization – Crowding Distance

In MOPSO-CD also, systematic study has been conducted to determine the optimum PSO parameters (refer Figure 8). The final best set of PSO parameters responsible for the maximum fitness values is determined using the parameter study and listed below.

Inertia Weight (W*) = 0.1
Swarm Size (SS*) = 50
Number of Generations (G*) = 40

The same four different case studies used in the previous approaches were considered to estimate the extreme values of the multiple conflicting responses and their corresponding process variable combina-

Figure 8. Parameter study of MOPSO-CD, (a) fitness vs. inertia weight, (b) fitness vs. swarm size and (c) fitness vs. generations

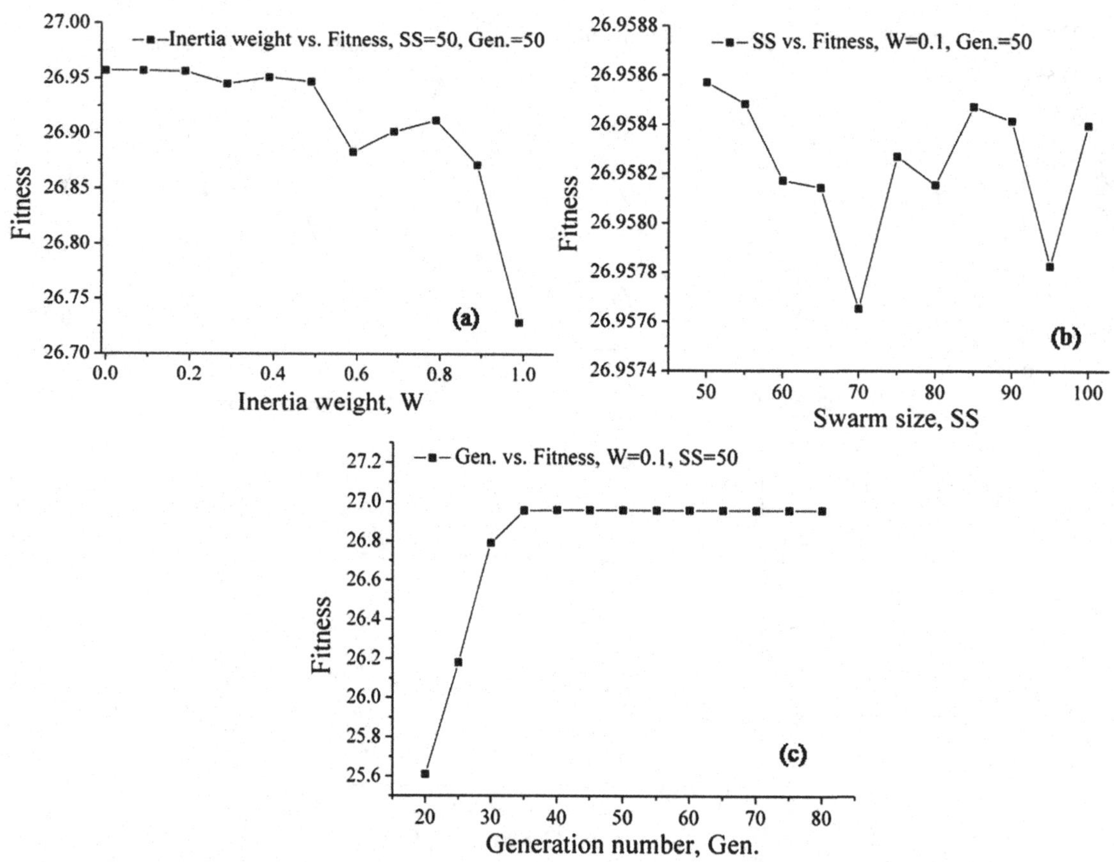

tions (refer Table 2). The fitness values obtained for case 1 to case 4 were found to be 27.04, 10.13, 8.13 and 63.16, respectively. Based on the maximum fitness value, case 4 was selected as the corresponding optimum casting conditions.

Teaching-Learning Based Optimization

TLBO does not require any specific algorithm tuning parameters. Therefore, population size and number of generations were studied individually as common optimization parameters. The optimal parameters responsible for maximum fitness value (refer Figure 9) are as follows:

Number of population = 20
Number of generations = 20

Table 2 presents the summary of the results of input-output variables obtained in four different cases using TLBO. The maximum fitness value corresponding to case 1 to case 4 was found to be 26.94, 10.08, 8.02 and 63.07, respectively. Based on the results, case 4 is recommended as it has the highest fitness value.

Figure 9. Parameter study of TLBO: fitness vs. number of generations

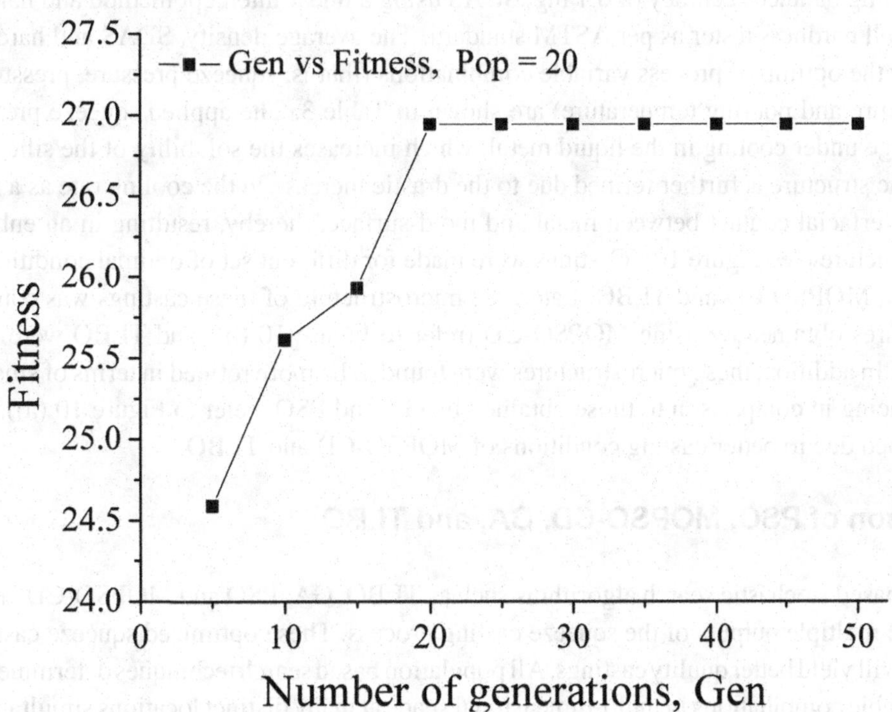

Table 2. Optimum casting conditions for multiple outputs with different combination of weight factors via GA, PSO, MOPSO-CD (Patel et al. 2016b) and TLBO methods

Process variables & Outputs	Optimum Values of Casting Conditions and Casting Properties															
	Case 1 (W_1 = 0.333, W_2 = 0.333 and W_3 =0.333)				Case 2 (W_1 = 0.8, W_2 = 0.1 and W_3 =0.1)				Case 3 (W_1 = 0.1, W_2 = 0.8 and W_3 =0.1)				Case 4 (W_1 = 0.1, W_2 = 0.1 and W_3 =0.8)			
	GA	PSO	MOPSO-CD	TLBO	GA	PSO	MOPSO-CD	TLBO	GA	PSO	MOPSO-CD	TLBO	GA	PSO	MOPSO-CD	TLBO
	Patel et al. (2016b)				Patel et al. (2016b)				Patel et al. (2016b)				Patel et al. (2016b)			
A:PD, sec	27.81	43.24	27.65	26.40	24.07	38.27	38.27	38.04	24.42	45.98	21.34	36.4	27.81	27.88	28.64	30.05
B:SP, MPa	119.6	119.8	120	120.0	119.8	118.1	119.9	120	119.5	117.1	119.99	120.0	120.0	119.9	120	120.0
C:PT, °C	708.6	696.4	708.5	701.4	698.0	698.1	698.4	690.4	705.4	660.8	709.13	668.4	708.4	708.3	705.4	709.3
D:DT, °C	150.3	157.7	150.0	150.8	169.4	222.4	208.5	218.6	158.2	167.7	150.05	155.6	150	150.5	150.1	150.0
ρ, g/cm³	2.663	2.665	2.663	2.664	2.665	2.668	2.668	2.669	2.663	2.663	2.661	2.665	2.663	2.663	2.663	2.663
SDAS, μm	35.16	34.35	35.11	34.70	34.50	35.0	34.64	34.39	34.90	34.33	35.00	34.28	35.14	35.11	34.95	35.20
BHN	78.19	77.52	78.27	78.21	77.72	76.5	77.06	76.82	78.00	74.78	78.20	76.50	78.27	78.26	78.26	78.26

CONFIRMATION TEST

Confirmation tests were conducted with three replicates for the recommended process variable combinations of PSO, GA and TLBO. Confirmation tests were conducted only for case 4, as its fitness value was found to be maximum, compared to other cases. Responses were measured under conditions similar to model developing (CCD and BBD). The density was measured using the Archimedes principle with a weighing balance accuracy of 0.1 mg, SDAS using a linear intercept method and hardness using optical Brinell hardness tester as per ASTM standard. The average density, SDAS and hardness values obtained for the optimized process variable combinations (that is, squeeze pressure, pressure duration, die temperature and pouring temperature) are shown in Table 3. The applied squeeze pressure brings a sudden large under cooling in the liquid metal, which increases the solubility of the silicon particles. The dendritic structure is further refined due to the drastic increase in the cooling rate as a result of the improved interfacial contact between metal and mold surface, thereby, resulting in an enhanced casting microstructure (see Figure 10). Castings were made for different set of optimal conditions obtained by GA, PSO, MOPSO-CD and TLBO. Later, the microstructure of these castings was compared. The microstructures obtained by using MOPSO-CD (refer to Figure 10 (b)) and TLBO were found to be comparable. In addition, these microstructures were found to be more refined in terms of small dendrites and arm spacing in comparison to those obtained by GA and PSO (refer to Figure 10 (a)). This might have happened due to better casting conditions of MOPSO-CD and TLBO.

Comparison of PSO, MOPSO-CD, GA, and TLBO

Population based stochastic search algorithms such as TLBO, GA, PSO and MOPSO-CD are applied to optimize the multiple outputs of the squeeze casting process. These optimized squeeze casting process parameters will yield better quality castings. All population based search techniques determine the optimal process variable combinations in multi-dimensional space at many distinct locations simultaneously. The

Figure 10. Microstructure obtained for optimal squeeze casting condition: (a) GA and PSO and (b) MOPSO-CD

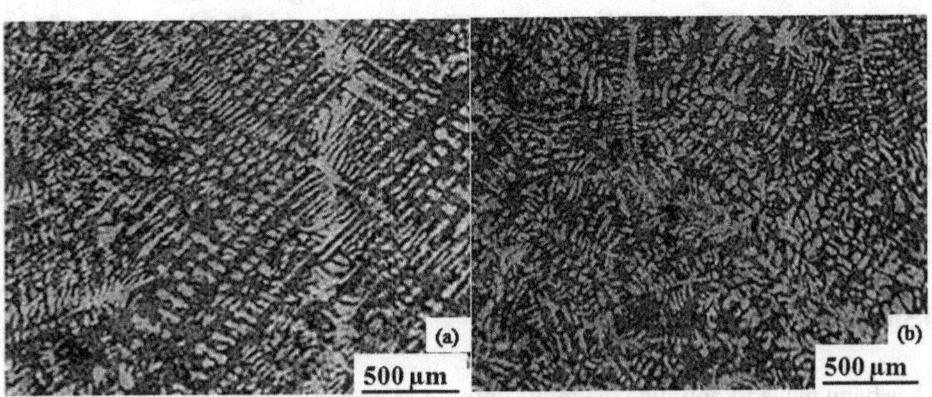

speed of convergence depends mainly on the appropriate choice of algorithm parameters. The optimal GA, PSO and MOPSO-CD parameters are determined after conducting the systematic parametric study by varying one parameter at a time and keeping the rest at a fixed value. It is further observed that optimal GA parameters such as probability of crossover (P_C*), probability of mutation (P_M*), population size (Pop*), and number of generations (Gen*) were found to be 0.55, 0.15, 80, and 85, respectively. Similarly for PSO, the optimal parameters such as inertia weight (W*), swarm size (SS*) and number of generations (G*) were found to be {0.6, 50, 50} and {0.1, 50, 40} for simple PSO and MOPSO-CD, respectively. TLBO does not have any specific algorithm tuning parameters. The best common optimization parameters, namely, number of population (i.e.,the student) and the maximum number of generations are found to be equal to 20. Increase in population and generation number increases the computation time to reach the global fitness (i.e., global solution) values. In the present case, the speed of convergence to reach the maximum fitness value using TLBO is found to be faster than that of evolutionary algorithms (i.e. GA, PSO, and MOPSO-CD). Moreover, the fitness values as obtained for cases 1 to 4 are found to be {26.93, 9.907, 8.089, 62.88}, {26.79, 10.06, 7.78, 63.16}, {27.04, 10.13, 8.13, 63.16} and {26.94, 10.08, 8.02, 63.07} for GA, PSO, MOPSO-CD and TLBO, respectively. It is interesting to note that the performance of TLBO and MOPSO-CD are comparable and outperformedother optimization algorithms (i.e. GA and PSO) in determining the maximum fitness values and yielding better casting conditions. By considering all the different cases,it was found that the casting properties are comparable for density and SDAS; whereas, drastic improvement was observed for the hardness. From Table 2, it can be observed that for case 4, TLBO and MOPSO-CD determined approximately similar outputs for similar combinations of input conditions (i.e., squeeze pressure and die temperature), but slight changes in pouring temperature and pressure duration were observed. Further, no significant change in outputs with small change in pressure duration and pouring temperature was observed (Patel et al.,2016a). Therefore, confirmation tests have been conducted for the different case studies of PSO, MOPSO-CD, GA and TLBO. Case 4 is recommendedas its fitness value was found to be maximum and better for PSO, MOPSO-CD, TLBO and GA. MOPSO-CD and TLBO have yielded the maximum possible values forSDAS and hardness as compared to GA and PSO (refer Table 2).

The determined optimal casting conditions obtained by GA, PSO, MOPSO-CD and TLBO are compared with experimental values. MOPSO-CD and TLBO showed slightly better results for density, hardness and SDAS values. Moreover, the speed of convergence reached the maximum fitness value with 85 generationsfor GA (refer Figure 6 (d)), 50 for PSO (refer Figure 7(c)), 40 for MOPSO-CD (refer Figure 8 (c)) and 20 for TLBO (refer Figure 9 (a)). This indicates that TLBO performed better both in terms of computational time and better set of process variables.It is important to note thatMOPSO-CD and TLBO used approximately similar combination of inputs-outputs based on their exhaustive search mechanisms. Better performance of TLBO algorithm might be due to the exhaustive search carried out in multi-dimensional search space at many distinct locations simultaneously and the lack of specific algorithm tuning parameters.

CONCLUSION

An attempt has been made to optimize the input-output parameters of the squeeze casting process using the popular non-traditional algorithms, namely, PSO, MOPSO-CD, GA and TLBO. The input-output mathematical relationship developed based on central composite and BBD models wasused as the fitness functions for all the optimization algorithms. Three individual objective functions (density, hardness and SDAS) were converted into a single objective function with different combination of weight factors. An exhaustive heuristic search was carried out by non-traditional optimization algorithms in multi-dimensional search space at many distinct locations simultaneously to determine the optimal casting conditions. From the study, it is evident that all algorithms, GA, PSO, MOPSO-CD and TLBO performed effectively to optimize squeeze casting process parameters. TLBO and MOPSO-CD determined approximately similar combination of inputs and outputs. The experiments were conducted to measure the responses, namely, density, secondary arm spacing and hardness for the optimum process parameters obtained after applying GA, PSO, MOPSO-CD and TLBO. Further, microstructure study was also carried out on the castings. The castings obtained with the parameters determined by MOPSO and TLBO showed better microstructure. TLBO was found to perform better than genetic algorithm and PSO in terms of computational efficiency. The improved performance of TLBO might be due to the simple structure with no specific algorithm tuning parameters. The present research work is of great importance to casting industry, since the extreme values of conflicting requirements of the multiple performance outputs are determined. Moreover, the present research work might help to overcome a few shortcomings of the existing traditional approaches (like classical engineering experimental, analytical, numerical, costly simulation, expert reliant try error method and so on) in determining the best process variable combinations, which will result in improved casting quality and reduced computational burden and energy consumption.

Table 3. Results of confirmation test for the optimal casting conditions (Patel et al.,2016b)

Models	Optimal Process Variables				Responses		
	Pressure Duration, s	Squeeze Pressure, MPa	Pouring Temperature, °C	Die Temperature, °C	Density, g/cm^3	SDAS, μm	BHN
GA and PSO	28	120	708	150	2.672	33.12	82.3
MOPSO-CD	29	120	705	150	2.672	32.28	82.6

ACKNOWLEDGMENT

The authors would like to sincerely thank the Department of Applied Mechanics and Hydraulics, National Institute of Technology Karnataka, Surathkal, for providing research facilities.

REFERENCES

Aweda, J. O., & Adeyemi, M. B. (2009). Experimental determination of heat transfer coefficients during squeeze casting of aluminium. *Journal of Materials Processing Technology*, *209*(3), 1477–1483. doi:10.1016/j.jmatprotec.2008.03.071

Chattopadhyay, H. (2007). Simulation of transport processes in squeeze casting. *Journal of Materials Processing Technology*, *186*(1-3), 174–178. doi:10.1016/j.jmatprotec.2006.12.038

Das, S., Maity, S., Qu, B. Y., & Suganthan, P. N. (2011). Real-parameter evolutionary multimodal optimization — A survey of the state-of-the-art. *Swarm and Evolutionary Computation*, *1*(2), 71–88. doi:10.1016/j.swevo.2011.05.005

Fan, C. H., Chen, Z. H., Chen, J. H., & Chen, D. (2010). Effects of applied pressure on density, microstructure and tensile strength of Al–Zn–Mg–Cu alloy prepared by squeeze casting. *International Journal of Cast Metals Research*, *23*(6), 349–353. doi:10.1179/136404610X12693537270253

Ghomashchi, M. R., & Vikhrov, A. (2000). Squeeze casting: An overview. *Journal of Materials Processing Technology*, *101*(1), 1–9. doi:10.1016/S0924-0136(99)00291-5

Hong, C. P., Lee, S. M., & Shen, H. F. (2000). Prevention of macro defects in squeeze casting of an Al-7 wtpct Si alloy. *Metallurgical and Materials Transactions. B, Process Metallurgy and Materials Processing Science*, *31*(2), 297–305. doi:10.1007/s11663-000-0048-5

Jacob, O. A., & Michael, B. A. (2012). Experimental determination of heat transfer coefficients during squeeze casting of aluminium. An overview of heat transfer phenomena. InTech. doi:10.5772/52038

Jahangiri, A., Marashi, S. P. H., Mohammadaliha, M., & Ashofte, V. (2017). The effect of pressure and pouring temperature on the porosity, microstructure, hardness and yield stress of AA2024 aluminum alloy during the squeeze casting process. *Journal of Materials Processing Technology*, *245*, 1–6. doi:10.1016/j.jmatprotec.2017.02.005

Krishna, P. (2001). *A study on interfacial heat transfer and process parameters in squeeze casting and low pressure permanent mold casting* (Ph.D. Thesis). University of Michigan, Ann Arbor, MI.

Li, Y., Yang, H., & Xing, Z. (2017). Numerical simulation and process optimization of squeeze casting process of an automobile control arm. *International Journal of Advanced Manufacturing Technology*, *88*(1-4), 941–947. doi:10.1007/s00170-016-8845-4

Mahapatra, S. S., & Patnaik, A. (2007). Optimization of wire electrical discharge machining (WEDM) process parameters using Taguchi method. *International Journal of Advanced Manufacturing Technology*, *34*(9-10), 911–925. doi:10.1007/s00170-006-0672-6

Maleki, A., Niroumand, B., & Shafyei, A. (2006). Effects of squeeze casting parameters on density, macrostructure and hardness of LM13 alloy. *Materials Science and Engineering A*, *428*(1-2), 135–140. doi:10.1016/j.msea.2006.04.099

Maleki, A., Shafyei, A., & Niroumand, B. (2009). Effects of squeeze casting parameters on the microstructure of LM13 alloy. *Journal of Materials Processing Technology*, *209*(8), 3790–3797. doi:10.1016/j.jmatprotec.2008.08.035

Parappagoudar, M. B., Pratihar, D. K., & Datta, G. L. (2007). Linear and non-linear statistical modelling of green sand mould system. *International Journal of Cast Metals Research*, *20*(1), 1–13. doi:10.1179/136404607X184952

Pashazadeh, H., Gheisari, Y., & Hamedi, M. (2014). Statistical modeling and optimization of resistance spot welding process parameters using neural networks and multi-objective genetic algorithm. *Journal of Intelligent Manufacturing*, 1–11. doi:10.1007/s10845-014-0891-x

Patel, G. C. M., Krishna, P., & Parappagoudar, M. B. (2016a). Modelling of squeeze casting process: Conventional statistical regression analysis approach. *Applied Mathematical Modelling*, *40*(15), 6869–6888. doi:10.1016/j.apm.2016.02.029

Patel, G. C. M., Krishna, P., Parappagoudar, M. B., & Vundavilli, P. R. (2016b). Multi-objective optimization of squeeze casting process using evolutionary algorithms. *International Journal of Swarm Intelligence Research*, *7*(1), 55–74. doi:10.4018/IJSIR.2016010103

Rajagopal, S. (1981). Squeeze casting: A review and update. *Journal of Applied Metalworking*, *14*(4), 3–14. doi:10.1007/BF02834341

Rajagopal, S., & Altergott, W. H. (1985). Quality control in squeeze casting of aluminium. *AFS Transactions*, *93*, 145–154.

Rao, R. V. (2010). *Advanced modeling and optimization of manufacturing processes: international research and development*. Springer Science & Business Media.

Rao, R. V., & Kalyankar, V. D. (2011). Parameters optimization of advanced machining processes using TLBO algorithm. *Proceedings of International Conference on Engineering, Project, and Production Management (EPPM)*, 21-31.

Rao, R. V., & Kalyankar, V. D. (2012). Parameter optimization of machining processes using a new optimization algorithm. *Materials and Manufacturing Processes*, *27*(9), 978–985. doi:10.1080/10426914.2011.602792

Rao, R. V., Kalyankar, V. D., & Waghmare, G. (2014). Parameters optimization of selected casting processes using teaching–learning-based optimization algorithm. *Applied Mathematical Modelling*, *38*(23), 5592–5608. doi:10.1016/j.apm.2014.04.036

Rao, R. V., & Savsani, V. J. (2012). *Mechanical design optimization using advanced optimization techniques*. Springer London Dordrecht Heidelberg New York. doi:10.1007/978-1-4471-2748-2

Rao, R. V., Savsani, V. J., & Vakharia, D. P. (2011). Teaching–learning-based optimization: A novel method for constrained mechanical design optimization problems. *Computer Aided Design*, *43*(3), 303–315. doi:10.1016/j.cad.2010.12.015

Rao, R. V., Savsani, V. J., & Vakharia, D. P. (2012). Teaching–learning based optimization: A novel optimization method for continuous non-linear large scale problems. *Information Sciences*, *183*(1), 1–15. doi:10.1016/j.ins.2011.08.006

Rao, R. V., & Waghmare, G. G. (2014a). A comparative study of a teaching–learning-based optimization algorithm on multi-objective unconstrained and constrained functions. *Journal of King Saud University-Computer and Information Sciences*, *26*(3), 332–346. doi:10.1016/j.jksuci.2013.12.004

Rao, R. V., & Waghmare, G. G. (2014b). Complex constrained design optimisation using an elitist teaching-learning-based optimisation algorithm. *International Journal of Metaheuristics*, *3*(1), 81–102. doi:10.1504/IJMHEUR.2014.058863

Raquel, C. R., & Naval, P. C. Jr. (2005). An effective use of crowding distance in multiobjective particle swarm optimization. In *Proceedings of the 7th conference on Genetic and evolutionary computation (GECCO-05)*. ACM. doi:10.1145/1068009.1068047

Rosenberg, R. S. (1967). *Simulation of genetic populations with biochemical properties* (Ph.D. Thesis). University of Michigan, Ann Arbor, MI.

Santana, R. A., Pontes, M. R., & Bastos-Filho, C. J. A. (2009). A multiple objective particle swarm optimization approach using crowding distance and roulette wheel. *Proceedings of the 2009 Ninth international conference on intelligent systems design and applications (ISDA)*, 93–100, doi:10.1109/ISDA.2009.73

Sarfraz, S., Jahanzaib, M., Wasim, A., Hussain, S., & Aziz, H. (2017). Investigating the effects of as-casted and in situ heat-treated squeeze casting of Al-3.5% Cu alloy. *International Journal of Advanced Manufacturing Technology*, *89*(9-12), 3547–3561. doi:10.1007/s00170-016-9350-5

Schaffer, J. D. (1985). Multiple objective optimization with vector evaluated genetic algorithm. *Proceedings of 1st International Conference on Genetic Algorithms*, 93–100.

Sierra, M. R., & Coello, C. A. C. (2005). Improving PSO-based multi-objective optimization using crowding, mutation and ∈-dominance. *Evolutionary Multi-Criterion Optimization*, 505-519.

Souissi, N., Souissi, S., Niniven, C. L., Amar, M. B., Bradai, C., & Elhalouani, F. (2014). Optimization of squeeze casting parameters for 2017A wrought Al alloy using Taguchi method. *Metals*, *4*(2), 141–154. doi:10.3390/met4020141

Surekha, B., Kaushik, L. K., Panduy, A. K., Vundavilli, P. R., & Parappagoudar, M. B. (2012). Multi-objective optimization of green sand mould system using evolutionary algorithms. *International Journal of Advanced Manufacturing Technology*, *58*(1-4), 9–17. doi:10.1007/s00170-011-3365-8

Ting, T. O., & Lee, T. S. (2012). Drilling optimization via particle swarm optimization. *International Journal of Swarm Intelligence Research*, *3*(1), 43–54. doi:10.4018/jsir.2012010103

Vijian, P., & Arunachalam, V. P. (2007). Modelling and multi objective optimization of LM24 aluminium alloy squeeze cast process parameters using genetic algorithm. *Journal of Materials Processing Technology, 186*(1), 82–86. doi:10.1016/j.jmatprotec.2006.12.019

Vundavilli, P. R., Kumar, J. P., & Parappagoudar, M. B. (2013). Weighted average-based multi-objective optimization of tube spinning process using non-traditional optimization techniques. *International Journal of Swarm Intelligence Research, 4*(3), 42–57. doi:10.4018/ijsir.2013070103

Wang, C., Lavernia, E. J., Wu, G., Liu, W., & Ding, W. (2016). Influence of pressure and temperature on microstructure and mechanical behavior of squeeze cast Mg-10Gd-3Y-0.5Zr alloy. *Metallurgical and Materials Transactions. A, Physical Metallurgy and Materials Science, 47*(8), 4104–4115. doi:10.1007/s11661-016-3546-z

Yang, L. J. (2007). The effect of solidification time in squeeze casting of aluminium and zinc alloy. *Journal of Materials Processing Technology, 192-193*, 114–120. doi:10.1016/j.jmatprotec.2007.04.025

You, D., Wang, X., Cheng, X., & Jiang, X. (2017). Friction modeling and analysis of injection process in squeeze casting. *Journal of Materials Processing Technology, 239*, 42–51. doi:10.1016/j.jmatprotec.2016.08.011

Zhou, A., Qu, B.-Y., Li, H., Zhao, S.-Z., Suganthan, P. N., & Zhang, Q. (2011). Multiobjective evolutionary algorithms: A survey of the state of the art. *Swarm and Evolutionary Computation, 1*(1), 32–49. doi:10.1016/j.swevo.2011.03.001

Chapter 11
Swarm-Intelligence-Based Communication Protocols for Wireless Sensor Networks

Lucia Keleadile Ketshabetswe
Botswana International University of Science and Technology, Botswana

Adamu Murtala Zungeru
Botswana International University of Science and Technology, Botswana

Joseph M. Chuma
Botswana International University of Science and Technology, Botswana

Mmoloki Mangwala
Botswana International University of Science and Technology, Botswana

ABSTRACT

Social insect communities are formed from simple, autonomous, and cooperative organisms that are interdependent for their survival. These communities are able to effectively coordinate themselves to achieve global objectives despite a lack of centralized planning, and the behaviour is referred to as swarm intelligence. This chapter presents a study of communication protocols for wireless sensor networks utilizing nature-inspired systems: social insect-based communities and natural creatures. Three types of insects are used for discussion: ants, termites, and bees. In addition, a study of the social foraging behavior of spider monkeys is presented. The performances of these swarm-intelligence-based algorithms were tested on common routing scenarios. The results were compared with other routing algorithms with varying network density and showed that swarm-intelligence-based routing techniques improved on network energy consumption with a control over best-effort service. The results were strengthened with a model of termite-hill routing algorithm for WSN.

DOI: 10.4018/978-1-5225-5134-8.ch011

INTRODUCTION

Swarm intelligence (SI) is an Artificial Intelligence technique that simulates the behavioural structures of natural creatures to solve complex optimization problems. The techniques demonstrate the desirable characteristics of interpretability, scalability, robustness and efficiency and can be used to achieve better solutions in Wireless Sensor Networks (WSNs) (*Tina Gui* et al, 2016) Bio-inspired systems are tending to be included in new architectures due to the following reasons;

1. Simple to design and interpret with basic rules
2. Adaptive to medium topological change
3. Efficiently manage limited resources

Social insect communities are formed from simple, independent and cooperative organisms that are able to effectively coordinate themselves to achieve global objectives despite a lack of centralized planning. This chapter focuses on simulating and modelling insect-based behaviours in their colony for the problem of routing in wireless sensor networks (WSNs). It also discusses the behavioural patterns of spider monkeys and presents from previous research (*Tina Gui* et al, 2016) a search strategy based on population and aimed to improve the network performance and reduce energy consumption.

A WSN is a distributed infrastructure composed of a large collection of nodes with the ability to instrument and react to events and phenomena in a specific environment (Saleem et al., 2010; Zungeru et al., 2011; Zungeru et al., 2012b; Zungeru et al., 2012c; Sardar et al., 2014; Sensarma et al., 2012; Akyildiz et al., 2002). WSNs are collections of compact-size, relatively inexpensive computational nodes that measure local environmental conditions or other parameters and relay the information to a central point for appropriate processing using wireless communications. Each sensor node is equipped with embedded processors, sensor devices, storage devices and radio transceivers. The critical factor in the design of WSNs is to maximize the lifetime of the sensor nodes which are battery-powered and have a limited energy supply. A key element that determines the lifetime in a WSN is the way that information is transmitted or routed to a destination node (called sink). A node with information to send to the sink does not transmit the information directly to the sink (single-hop network) (a situation when the sink is not a neighbor of the source node) because this will require a very high transmission power. Rather, the node sends the information to a neighboring node which is closer to the sink which in turn sends to its neighbor and so on until the information arrives at the sink (multi-hop network). This process is known as routing. An important problem in WSN is how to design a routing protocol which is not only energy efficient, scalable, robust and adaptable, but also provides the same or better performance than that of existing state-of-the-art routing protocols.

Insects are relatively simple creatures. Their small size and small number of neurons makes them incapable of dealing with complex tasks individually. On the other hand, the insect colony can be seen as an intelligent entity for its high level of self-organization and the complexity of tasks it can perform to achieve global objectives despite a lack of centralized planning and direct communications. One way insects communicate is by secreting chemical agents that will be recognized by receptors on the bodies of other insects. One of the most important of such chemical agents is the pheromone. Pheromones are molecules released from glands on the insect body. Once deposited on the ground they start to evaporate, releasing the chemical agent into the air. Individual insects leave a trail of such scents, which stimulates other insects to follow that trail, dropping pheromones while doing so (Matthews & Mattheus, 1942).

This use of the environment as a medium for indirect communication is called stigmergy. This process will continue until a trail from the colony to the food source is established. While following very basic instincts, insects accomplish complex tasks for their colonies in a demonstration of emergent behaviour. In the foraging example, one of the characteristics of the pheromone trail is that it is highly optimized, tending toward the shortest path between the food source and the insect nest. This trail creation with the shortest distance from the nest to the food source is a side effect of their behaviour, which is not something they have as an *a priori* goal.

This chapter will also focus on how insect colonies use pheromone trails to accomplish complex tasks and show the similarity between the colony behaviors and WSNs. The behaviors which accomplish these tasks are emergent from much simpler behaviors or rules that the individuals are following. In this approach, insect agents are modeled to suit the energy resource constraints in WSNs for the purpose of finding the best paths between sites as a function of the number of visited nodes and the energy of the path. Since communication is an energy expensive function, given a network and a source-destination pair, the problem is to route a packet from the source to the destination node using a minimum number of nodes, low energy, and limited memory space so as to save energy. This implies that when designing a routing protocol for WSN, it is important to consider the path length as well as the energy of the path along which the packet is to traverse before its arrival at the sink, while also maintaining low memory usage at the network nodes. The remainder of this chapter is organized as follows; the next section discusses related work and current research findings for artificial insect-based routing algorithms for WSNs followed by ant, bees and termite-based techniques for routing. Previous research on cluster Spider Monkey Optimization strategy for WSNs is also discussed. The chapter concludes with performance evaluations with other routing protocols and comments for future work.

PREVIOUS WORK ON INSECT-BASED COMMUNICATION PROTOCOLS IN WSN

Researchers have successfully applied ant-based algorithms to the solutions of difficult combinatorial problems such as the travelling salesman problem and the job scheduling problem (Dorigo et al., 1999). In (Ramos & Almeida, 2000) and (Semet et al., 2004), the ant colony approach is used to perform image segmentation. (Heusse et al. 1998) and (Merloti 2004) applied the concepts of ant colonies on routing of network packages. The basic ant-based routing algorithm and its main characteristics (Dorigo & Caro 1998) can be summarized into the following steps:

1. At regular intervals along with the data traffic, a forward ant is launched from the source node towards the sink node.
2. Each agent (forward ant) tries to locate the destination with equal probability by using neighboring nodes with minimum cost (fewer hops) joining its source and sink.
3. Each agent moves step-by-step towards its destination node. At each intermediate node a greedy stochastic policy is applied to choose the next node to move to. The policy makes use of three sources of information: (i) local agent-generated and maintained information, (ii) local problem-dependent heuristic information, and (iii) agent-private information.
4. During the movement, the agents collect information about the time length, the congestion status and the node identifiers of the followed path.

5. Once the destination is reached, a backward ant is created which takes the same path as the forward ant, but in an opposite direction.
6. During this backward travel, local models of the network status and the local routing table of each visited node are modified by the agents as a function of the path they followed and of its goodness.
7. On returning to the source node, the agents die.

In Sensor driven and Cost-aware ant routing (SC) (Zhang et al, 2004), it is assumed that ants have sensors so that they can smell where there is food at the beginning of the routing process so as to increase the possibility of sensing the best direction that the ant will go initially. In addition to the sensing ability, each node stores the probability distribution and the estimates of the cost of destination from each of its neighbors. In another work, Flooded Forward ant routing (FF), (Zhang et al, 2004) argued the fact that ants even augmented with sensors, can be misguided due to the obstacles or moving destinations. This protocol is based on flooding of ants from source node to the sink node. In cases where the destination is not known at the beginning or the cost cannot be estimated, the algorithm simply uses the broadcast method of sensor networks so as to route packets to the destination. The probabilities are updated in the same way as the basic ant routing. Beesensor (Saleem and Farooq, 2007) is an algorithm based on the foraging principles of honey bees with an on-demand route discovery. The algorithm works with three types of agents: packers, scouts and foragers. Packers locate appropriate foragers for the data packets at the source node. Scouts are responsible for discovering the path to a new destination using the broadcasting principle. Foragers are the main workers of Beesensor which follow a point-to-point mode of transmission and carry the data packets to a sink node. When a source node detects an event and does not have a route to the sink node, it launches a forward scout and queues the event. A forward scout is propagated using the broadcasting principle to all neighbors of a node. Each forward scout has a unique identification with the detected event in its payload. Intermediate nodes at a distance of two hops or fewer always broadcast the forward scout while the rest of the nodes stochastically decide whether to broadcast it further or not. The forward scouts do not create a source header in which a complete sequence of the traversed nodes up to the sink node is saved. Hence their size is fixed and is independent of the length of the followed path. The approach is based on the interactions of scouts and source routing in which small forwarding tables are built during the return of a scout.

Ant-Based Communication Protocols in WSNs

The search for food in ants is organized by laying chemical trails while searching for the food source. During foraging for food, ants communicate with the aid of the pheromone laid on their way back to the nest. When food is discovered, ants return to the nest laying a trail to recruit nest mates to the food source. The difference between foraging and recruitment trails is attributed to different quantities of trail pheromone present on the path. Ants have been found to adapt to their environment and always find the most efficient path to their food source (Dorigo and Caro, 1998). Considering Figure 1, the path from the nest to the food source at time $t = 0$, the ants find the food and bring it back efficiently, establishing a pheromone trail to it. At time $t = 1$, when there is an obstacle in their path such that there is one path that is shorter than the other, the ants can choose either path with equal probability, hence having the same number of ants on both sides. The path that is shorter will allow ants to gather food quicker and strengthen the pheromone trail on the way back faster than the ants on the longer path as seen when $t = 2$, causing the other batch of ants to move with higher probability towards the trail that is stronger. As the process continues till time $t = n$, it will be observed that all the ants will use the shortest path towards the food source. The obstacle in this analogy can be congestion, number of nodes on the path to the sink, latency, etc. The following subsections discuss the behavioral pattern of foraging of ants toward food sources.

Positive Feedback

In ant foraging, an ant's attraction along the pheromone site motivates it in adding to where there exist much food piles. If there are many food piles in a place, it is expected that much pheromone will be present in that food pile, that is to say more ants will visit the place due to its pheromone concentration, and as such the ants will add more pheromone to the pile on that path. The greater the biases towards the food source, more ants are also likely to take the path to that food source, which means that pheromone content of the path will be increased.

Negative Feedback

Negative feedback is accomplished by pheromone evaporation. This happens so as to avoid premature convergence among ants (stagnation). For good communication among the ant individuals, pheromone must evaporate over the environment. The evaporation helps to weaken the pheromone, which will bring down the amount of pheromone on that path. The path with lower pheromone concentration will have fewer ants as it will attract fewer ants towards that direction. Though this may seem contrary to the task of collecting all food to the nest, but it is important. Negative feedback is entirely useful in the removal of past or poor solutions for the memory of constituent of any network or system.

Figure 1. Food Search in Ants

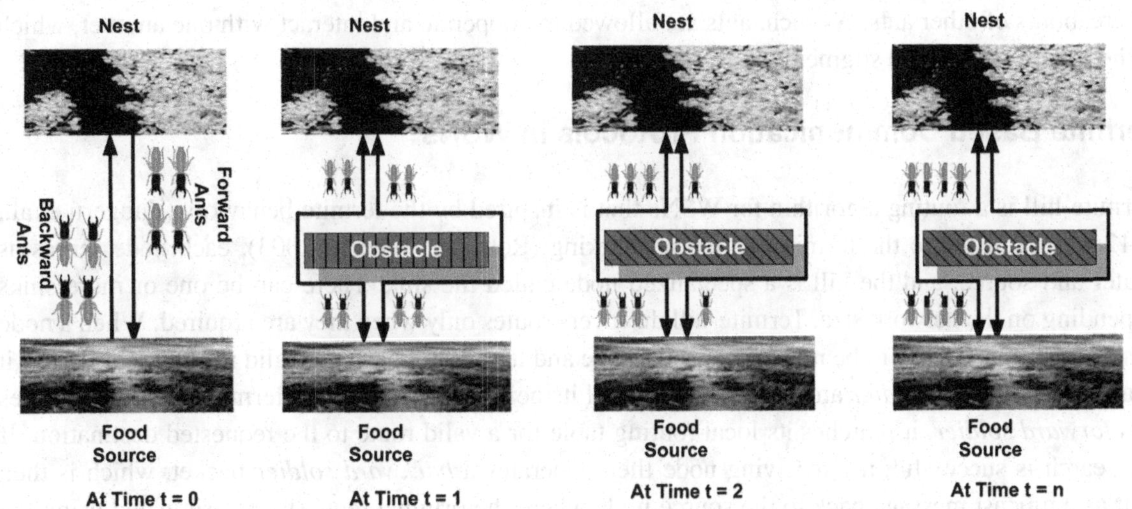

Randomness

The location and path taken by ants towards the food source is determined by chance. A little drift in the behavior of ants will lead to significant effect on the future behavior of the system. Randomness is useful so that new solutions can be built since the network and system under consideration is dynamic.

Multiple Interactions

In the food collection of ants to their nest, it is a necessity that many individuals cooperate and work together to achieve their target. This is in accordance with neighboring nodes of a sensor network acting as routers to other source nodes. If there is insufficient number of ants in a nest, then the pheromone would decay before any more food could be collected at the nest. Also, if we map this to a sensor network, if there are less nodes on the path to the sink node, more packets will be dropped on the way to the sink. This might also be as a result of the low transmission distance (range) of the nodes too. But if there exist more ants in the environment, then more food will be gathered fast to avoid complete pheromone decay in the shortest path, else ants would continue their random walk without building any strong solution as regards to the best paths.

Stigmergy

This is the indirect communications between individuals of the social insect, generally through their environment. Complexity in stigmergic systems is due to the fact that, individuals or constituents of a system do not interact among themselves, but rather they do so with their environment. This behavior or actions lead to changes in the environment where they interact. Due to the changes, there is an advance effect on further behaviors, which give rise to a positive feedback effect where events are dependent on other events. This behavior is similar to the interaction between people in their environment based on their response to other people's comments during conversations. Ants are directed to the path with a high pheromone gradient, it is not necessary for ants to directly interact with themselves or to know the whereabouts of other ants. As such, ants are allowed to cooperate and interact with one another, which is the main issue behind stigmergy.

Termite Based Communication Protocols in WSNs

Termite-hill is a routing algorithm for WSNs that is inspired by the termite behaviors (Zungeru et al., 2012a). Analogous to the termite ad-hoc networking (Roth and Wicker, 2003), each node serves as router and source, and the hill is a specialized node called the sink. There can be one or more sinks depending on the network size. Termite-hill discovers routes only when they are required. When a node has some events or data to be relayed to a sink node and it does not have the valid routing table entry, it generates a *forward soldier* and broadcasts it to all its neighbors. When an intermediate node receives this *forward soldier*, it searches its local routing table for a valid route to the requested destination. If the search is successful, the receiving node then generates a *backward soldier* packet, which is then sent as a unicast message back to the source node where the original request was originated using the reverse links. If the node has no valid route to the destination, it sets up a reverse link to the node from which the *forward soldier* was received and further broadcasts the *forward soldier* packet. When the destination node receives the *forward soldier* packet, it generates a *backward soldier* packet which is also unicast back to the source node. On reception of the *backward soldier* packet, each intermediate node updates its routing table to set up a forward pointer and relays the *backward soldier* message to the next hop using the reverse pointer. The process continues till the *backward soldier* is received by the original source node. The algorithm does not use *HELLO* packets to detect link failures. Rather it uses feedback from the link layer (MAC) to achieve the same objective. Intermediate nodes do not generate *backward soldier* packets even if they have a valid route which avoids the overhead of multiple replies. It also employs cross layer techniques to avoid paths which have high packet loss. In the course of the algorithm design, the following assumptions were also made:

1. Each node is linked to one or more nodes in the network (neighbors).
2. A node may act as a source, a destination or a router for a communication between different pair of nodes.
3. Neither network configuration nor adjacency information is known beforehand.
4. The same amount of power is required for sending a message between any pair of adjacent nodes throughout the network.

The Pheromone Table

The pheromone table keeps the information gathered by the forward soldier. Each node maintains a table keeping the amount of pheromone on each neighbor path. The node has a distinct pheromone scent, and the table is in the form of a matrix with destination nodes listed along the side and neighbor nodes listed across the top. Rows correspond to destinations and columns to neighbors. An entry in the pheromone table is referenced by $T_{n,d}$ where *n* is the neighbor index and *d* denotes the destination index. The values in the pheromone table are used to calculate the selecting probabilities of each neighbor. From Figure 2, when a packet arrives at node *G* from previous hop *S*, i.e. the source, the source pheromone decay, and pheromone are added to link $\overrightarrow{SG}$. A *backward soldier* on its way back from the sink node is more likely to take the path through *G*, since it is the shortest path to the destination i.e. $\overrightarrow{SGED}$. The pheromone table of node *G* is shown in Figure 2 with nodes A, S, F, and E as its neighbors. It is worth noting that all neighbors are potential destinations. At node G, the total probability of selecting links $\overrightarrow{ED}$, $\overrightarrow{FE}$, $\overrightarrow{AC}$ or $\overrightarrow{SB}$ to the destination node is equal to unity (1) i.e. $\sum T_{ED} + T_{SD} + T_{AD} + T_{FD} = 1$. It will then be observed that, since link $\overrightarrow{GED}$ is shorter to the destination for a packet at node G, more pheromone will be present on it and hence, soldiers are more likely to take that path.

Pheromone Update

When a packet arrives at a node, the pheromone for the source of the packet is incremented by γ, where γ is the reward. Only packets addressed to a node will be processed. A node is said to be addressed if it is the intended next hop recipient of the packet. Equation (1) describes the pheromone update procedure when a packet from source *s* is delivered from previous hop *r*. A T-prime indicates the updated value.

Figure 2. Description of pheromone table of node G

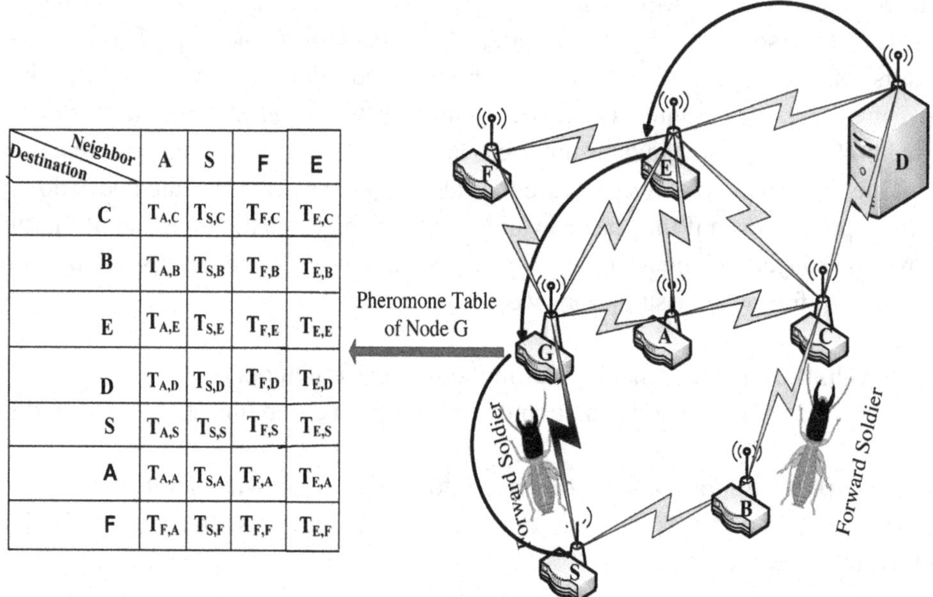

Destination \ Neighbor	A	S	F	E
C	$T_{A,C}$	$T_{S,C}$	$T_{F,C}$	$T_{E,C}$
B	$T_{A,B}$	$T_{S,B}$	$T_{F,B}$	$T_{E,B}$
E	$T_{A,E}$	$T_{S,E}$	$T_{F,E}$	$T_{E,E}$
D	$T_{A,D}$	$T_{S,D}$	$T_{F,D}$	$T_{E,D}$
S	$T_{A,S}$	$T_{S,S}$	$T_{F,S}$	$T_{E,S}$
A	$T_{A,A}$	$T_{S,A}$	$T_{F,A}$	$T_{E,A}$
F	$T_{F,A}$	$T_{S,F}$	$T_{F,F}$	$T_{E,F}$

$$T'_{r,s} = T_{r,s} + \gamma \tag{1}$$

and

$$\gamma = \frac{N}{E - \left(\dfrac{E_{min} - N_j}{E_{av} - N_j} \right)} \tag{2}$$

where E is the initial energy of the nodes and, E_{min}, E_{av} are the minimum and average energy respectively of the path traversed by the forward soldier as it moves towards the hill. The values of E_{min} and E_{av}, depends on the number of nodes on the path and the energy consumed by the nodes on the path during the transmission and reception of packets. The minimum energy of the path (E_{min}) can be less than the number of nodes visited by the forward soldier, but the average energy of the path (E_{av}) can never be less than the number of visited nodes. N_j represents the number of nodes that the forward soldier has visited, and N is the total number of network nodes.

Pheromone Evaporation

Pheromone is evaporated so as to build a good solution in the network. Each value in the pheromone table is periodically multiplied by the evaporation factor $e^{-\rho}$. The evaporation rate is $\rho \geq 0$. A high evaporation rate will quickly reduce the amount of remaining pheromone, while a low value will degrade the pheromone slowly. The pheromone evaporation interval is one second; this is called the decay period. Equation (3) describes the pheromone decay.

$$T'_{n,d} = T'_{n,d} * e^{-\rho} \tag{3}$$

Applications requiring robustness and flexibility need a slow decay rate, and some applications like security and target tracking applications need a fast decay process. The value of ρ and x in equation (4) depends on the application area. To account for the pheromone decay each value in the pheromone table is periodically subtracted by a percentage of the original value as shown in equation (4).

$$T'_{n,d} = \left(1 - x\right)T'_{n,d} \tag{4}$$

where $0 \leq x \leq 1$. If all of the pheromone for a particular node has been removed, then the corresponding row and/or column are removed from the pheromone table. The removal of an entry from the pheromone table indicates that no packet has been received from that node for quite some time. It has likely become irrelevant and no route information needs to be maintained.

A column (destination) is considered decayed if all of the pheromone in that column is equal to a minimum value. If that particular destination is also a neighbor then it cannot be removed unless all entries in the neighbor row are also decayed. A row is considered decayed if all of the pheromone values on the row are equal to the pheromone floor. Neighbor nodes must be specially handled because they can forward packets as well as originate packets. A decayed column indicates that no traffic has been seen which was sourced by that node. Since neighbors can also forward traffic, their role as traffic sources may become secondary to their role as traffic relays. Thus, the neighbor row must be declared decayed before the neighbor node can be removed from the pheromone table. If a neighbor is determined to be lost by means of communications failure (the neighbor has left communications range), the neighbor row is simply removed from the pheromone table.

Pheromone Limits

The limit of the pheromone table is bounded by three values which are: (1) the *upper pheromone*, (2) the *lower pheromone*, and (3) the *initial pheromone*. When a data packet is received at a node from the node that is not known to it, an entry for it is created in that receiving node pheromone table. The entries consist of a column and a row. If the information received about the node tells that it is a neighbor, a column in addition to a row is created for it, otherwise, only a row is created in the case that it is not a neighbor. The cells created will be initialized with the initial pheromone values. When pheromone is to be evaporated, the value is never allowed to enter the critical value which is normally the lowest pheromone value. This is done to make sure that nodes that are hardly used are detected. Also, no value is permitted to be more than the upper value. These limits help in safeguarding the pheromone difference from affecting the calculation of the probabilities of the next hop selection. Each parameter may be chosen based on the network environments and requirements.

Route Selection

Each of the routing tables of the nodes is initialized with a uniform probability distribution given as

$$P_{s,d} = \frac{1}{N} \tag{5}$$

where $P_{s,d}$ is the initial probability of each source node, and represents the probability by which an agent at source node s will take to get to node d (destination), and N is the total number of nodes in the network. Equation (6) details the transformation of pheromone for d on link s $T_{s,\,d}$ into the probability $P_{s,\,d}$ that the packet will be forwarded to d.

$$P_{s,\,d} = \frac{(T_{s,\,d} + \alpha)^{\beta}}{\sum_{i=1}^{N}(T_{i,\,d} + \alpha)^{\beta}} \tag{6}$$

As shown in Figure 2 and further explained in Figure 3 as a routing example, the summation of the probabilities of taking all paths leading to the destination node is unity (1). The parameters α and β are used to fine tune the routing behavior of Termite-hill. The value of α determines the sensitivity of the probability calculations to small amounts of pheromone, $\alpha \geq 0$ and the real value of α is zero. Similarly, $0 \leq \beta \leq 2$ is used to modulate the differences between pheromone amounts, and the real

Figure 3. An example of route selection based on pheromone concentration

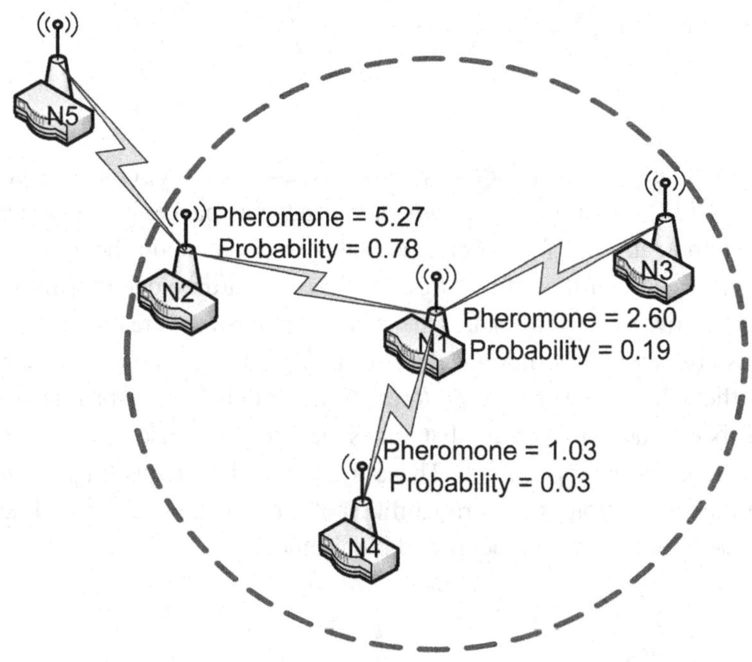

value of β is two. For each of the N entries in the node k routing table, it will be N_k (where N_k represents neighboring nodes of node k) values of $P_{s,d}$ subject to the condition:

$$\sum_{s \in N_k} P_{s,d} = 1;\ d = 1, \ldots, N \tag{7}$$

Taking for example, if a packet is expected to be forwarded from N1 to N5, assuming $\alpha = 0$ $\beta = 2$. Analysing Figure 3, Destination address = N5, Neighbor address = N2, Pheromone on link N1-N2 = 5.27 (using Equation 6). Also, if Neighbor address = N3, using the same equation, Pheromone on link N1-N3 = 2.60. For Neighbor address = N4, Pheromone on link N1-N4 = 1.03

As further illustration of route selection, we present Figure 4. In this figure, route is discovered using forward and backward soldiers. In route selection, the stronger the pheromone concentration on path, the better the path, leading to its selection.

Bees Based Communication Protocol in WSNs

Bees are insects that live in a colony which is divided into a single breeding female (queen), a few thousands males (drones), a several thousands of sterile females (workers) and many young bee larvae (broods). Their communication language is based on dances which are performed by the worker called ''Scout'' when if finds food. The dance recruits others by transmitting the distance, direction and quantity of found food with a visual, tangible and olfactory perception. Recruited bees then become "foragers". Their number is proportional to the quantity of food found. This is the exploration phase. A bee collects food and calculates its quantity to make a new decision. Either, it continues collecting by memorizing this best location or it leaves the food and returns to the beehive as a simple bee. This completes the exploitation step (Salim Bitam and Abdelhamid Mellouk, 2011)

Figure 4. Route selection with route discovery using forward and backward soldiers

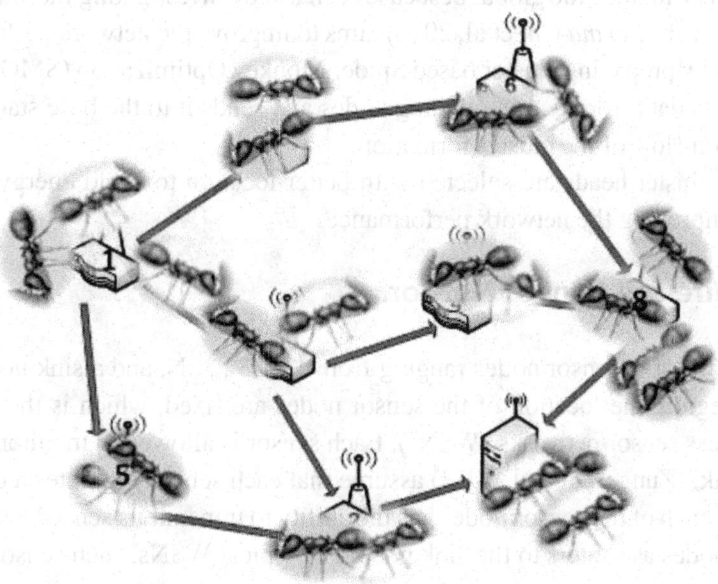

Honeybees are typically real social insects. Direct and indirect communication among workers provides cooperation in collecting nectar. Honeybees learn about their environment. When any worker has learned and remembered information about food, it transmits this information to other bees in the hive by means of a set of signal. Foraging behavior in honeybees is a good example of self-organization. Honeybee colony must discover nectar regions and exploit them in an efficient way. When a honeybee forages for nectar within an environment with highly variable conditions, learning becomes important for hive productivity. Honeybees employ a 'trial and error' learning approach in their foraging activity. In a decentralized and parallel way, each bee obeys a set of simple rules based on some metrics (e.g. nectar concentration, location of the source, travel time to the source, etc.). All of the metrics that includes inner parameters (number of food storer bees) in the hive determine profitability of a nectar source. If colony encounters with more than one sources of nectar, highest profitable source is preferred by foragers relative to other source with less profitability. Most well-known model was developed by Seeley in 1991.

In the foraging, honeybees use positive and negative feedback mechanisms to adjust their capacities to varying sources. These feedback mechanisms allow colony to be adaptive to changes in environmental conditions (Albayrak1 Z and Zengin A, 2014).

Spider Monkey Based Communication Protocol in WSNs

Monkeys are known as 'dry nosed' primates in zoology. They normally move in a group. Spider monkeys are a new species that add to the New World monkeys. In order to update the position of female monkeys during the foraging phase, (Kumar S et al, 2015) proposed a strategy that incorporates the fitness of the individual monkeys. Spider monkey optimization is a simple, yet powerful and well-organized algorithm that has been proved to be efficient and reliable. It is a search strategy based on population. (*Tina Gui* et al, 2016)

Major Steps of Spider Monkey Optimization are Population Initialization Phase (PIP), Local Leader Phase (LLP), Global Leader Phase (GLP), Global Leader Learning (GLL) Phase, Local Leader Learning (LLL) Phase, Local Leader Decision (LLD) Phase and Global Leader Decision (GLD) Phase

Exploration and exploitation are primary factors of the population based optimization strategies and they indicate the ability to trace the global best case scenario by investigating the variety of unidentified solutions in the search area. (*Tina Gui* et al, 2016) aims to improve the network performance and reduce energy consumption by proposing cluster based Spider Monkey Optimization (SMO-C). In this protocol a cluster head collects data from its surrounding nodes and sends it to the base station (sink). Figure 5 presents the execution flow of the cluster formation.

In this approach cluster heads are selected with better location to avoid energy loss and minimize dead nodes hence improving the network performance.

Modeling the Wireless Sensor Network

Considering a network of N sensor nodes ranging from 1, 2, 3 . . . N, and a sink node (base station) D, distributed over a region, the location of the sensor nodes are fixed, which is the case in most of the application of wireless sensor networks (WSNs). Each sensor is allowed to monitor the vicinity or area of interest of the sink. (Zungeru, et, al, 2013) assume that each sensor generates a data packet per time with size n-bits, and each of the sensor nodes has the ability to transmit its sensed event either directly or using other sensor nodes as routers to the sink node. For typical WSNs, each sensor node has a battery

Figure 5. Execution of the cluster formation in SMO-C

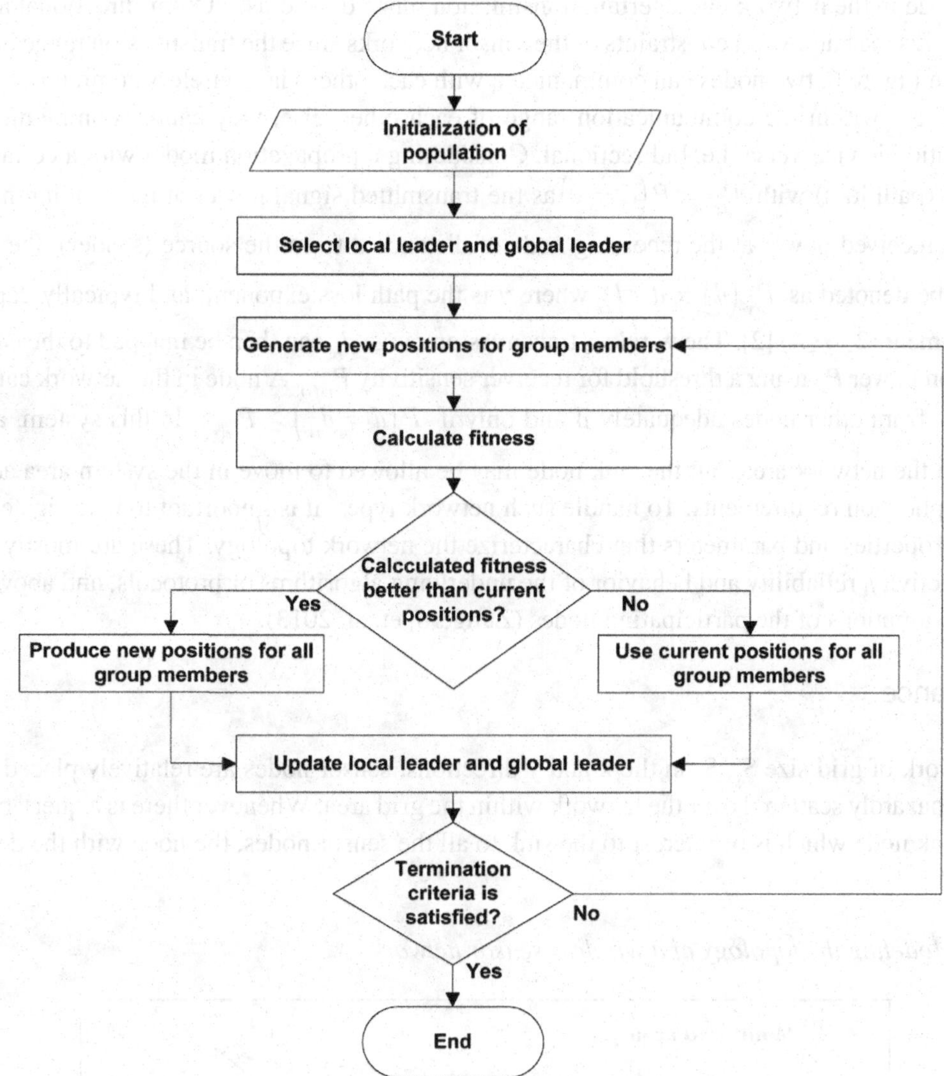

with finite and non-rechargeable energy. When an event is received or transmitted by a sensor node, part of its energy is utilized on the process. In this model, it is assumed that the sink node has an unlimited amount of energy available to it. A grid based network and a randomly distributed network in a ring is also assumed. To represent and describe the bandwidth and limited energy constraints in WSNs, some basic fundamental models are needed to actually describe the system. 1. Mathematical analysis (model) for node distribution and connectivity. 2. A model for network lifetime using the energy consumption of the network nodes. 3. A model for reliability of the system.

With this network of N sensor nodes independently and randomly distributed on a two dimensional simulation area A, if a uniform random distribution is used such that for a large number of nodes N and a wide space area A, the node density in the network can be given as $\rho = N / A$. This represents the expected number of nodes at a given area.

To analyse the connectivity between nodes in the network, a simple radio link model is assumed such that each node in the network has a certain transmission range d_{tx} and uses Omni-directional antennas. This represents the bandwidth constraints of the sensor networks since the transmission range is limited. As shown in Figure 6, two nodes can communicate with each other via a wireless communication link, only if they are within the communication range of each other, else, they cannot communicate. The communication is vice-versa, i.e. bidirectional. Considering a propagation model with a certain signal attenuation (path loss) with $P_{tx} = P\left(d = 0\right)$ as the transmitted signal power at the sending node, and $P_{rx}\left(d\right)$ the received power at the receiving node of distance d from the source (sender), the received power can be denoted as $P_{rx}\left(d\right) \propto d^{-\gamma} P_{tx}$ where γ is the path loss exponent, and typically depends on the environment (2≤γ≤4) [2]. The wireless transmission range d_{tx} can then be mapped to the equivalent transmission power P_{tx} using a threshold for receiver sensitivity $P_{rx(s)}$. A node in the network can receive information from other nodes adequately if and only if $P\left(d = d_{tx}\right) \geq P_{rx(s)}$. In this system, all nodes are static in the network area, but the sink node may be allowed to move in the system area according to some application requirements. To handle such network types, it is important to investigate the fundamental properties and parameters that characterize the network topology. These are mostly the possible connectivity, reliability and behavior of the underlying algorithms or protocols, and above all, the energy consumptions of the participating nodes (Zungeru, et, al, 2013).

Grid Distance

In the network of grid size S_x, S_y in the x and y directions, sensor nodes are relatively placed over the area or haphazardly scattered over the network within the grid area. Whenever there is a query broadcast from the sink node which is of interest to the sink to all the sensor nodes, the node with the desired in-

Figure 6. Modeling the topology of a wireless sensor network

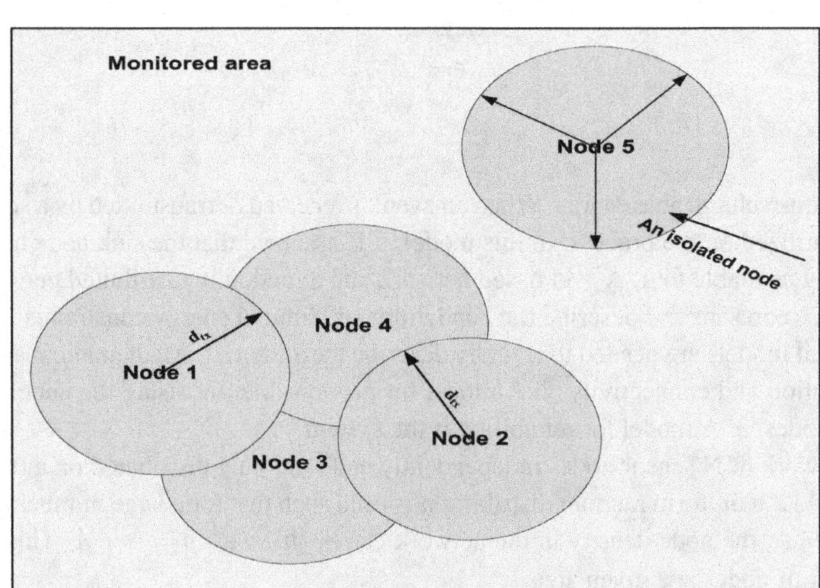

formation upon receiving the query, relay the information to the sink. The information relaying process can be directed to the sink node using just one hop or relayed using other intermediate nodes (using multiple hops). This node with the interested information by the sink node is called the source node. Or, in some cases, when nodes are placed within a monitored area of the grid, any of the sensor nodes that has information to send to the sink node at any point in time, is the source of the information, hence termed as the source node.

In a grid based approach, a grid topology is constructed with grid nodes from source nodes to sink node for event forwarding or relaying. A typical example of a grid topology is shown in Figure 7.

If a grid topology is constructed with sensor nodes placed randomly on each grid point as shown in Figure 7, to determine the distance between two neighbouring nodes for the construction of a grid topology, a trade-off between distance and energy consumption is required. If the distance selected between two consecutive neighbouring nodes is too short, the number of forwarding hops to the sink node increases with a corresponding increase in energy consumption. On the other hand, if the distance selected is too long, more energy will be required for the node in the grid to forward the intended information to its neighbours. Also, the amount of transmission energy needed to forward a packet of information between nodes of the same communication range is proportional to the volume of information, measured in bits, and the square of the distance between them. The energy (E_p) required by a grid node for event forwarding using a single hop, involves the energy consumption by the sensor node for transmitting a packet of information E_{tx} and the energy consumption for receiving the packet by the receiver, E_{rx} (Zungeru, et, al, 2013). That is:

Figure 7. A rectangular x-y grid topology in wireless sensor network

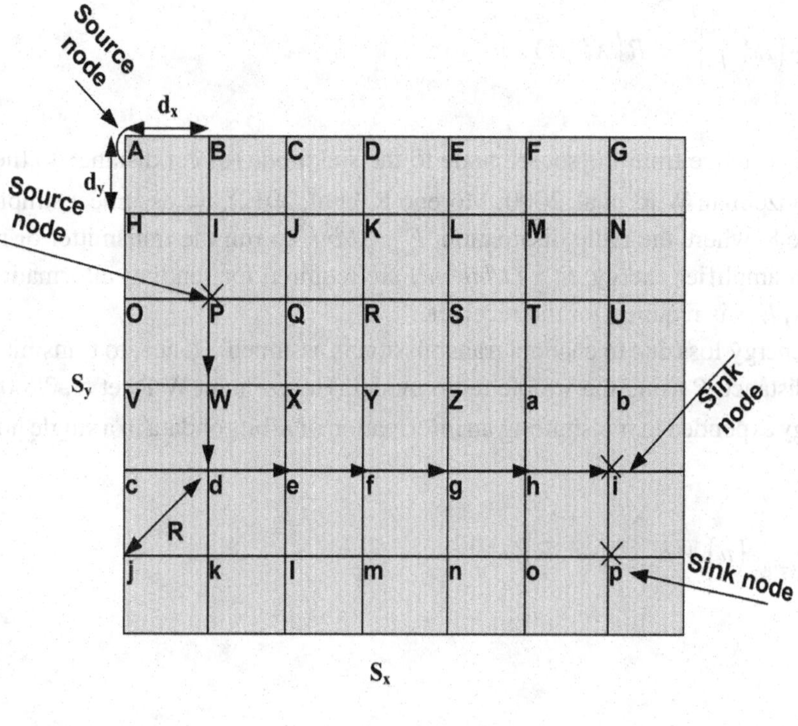

$$E_p = E_{tx} + E_{rx} \tag{8}$$

In a typical grid based topology where the source node is at an extreme end of the grid topology, and the sink node is also at the other corner end of the grid topology, the number of horizontal and vertical hops for any path from the source node to the sink node are the same. That is, for source node at point *A*, and sink node at point *p*, the path hops for any direction is 11. Now, assuming that the source node is at point *P*, and sink node at point *i*, taking the grid distance coordinate as d_x and d_y respectively for *x* and *y* direction. For two consecutive grid nodes, the distance between them *R* is:

$$R = ((d_{x1} - d_{x2})^2 + \left(d_{y1} - d_{y2}\right)^2)^{\frac{1}{2}} \tag{9}$$

For a grid topology of width S_x and height S_y, the number of horizontal hops *X* and vertical hops *Y* from the source node to the sink node will be $\frac{S_x}{R}$ and $\frac{S_y}{R}$ respectively. For appropriate grid distance selection, the average transmission cost, T_{cav}, is defined in such a way as to indicate the average energy consumed per unit distance as:

$$T_{cav} = \frac{\sum_{(X+Y)hops}\left(E_{tx} + E_{rx}\right)}{R_d} \tag{10}$$

and,

$$R_d = \left((RX)^2 + \left(RY\right)^2\right)^{\frac{1}{2}} = R\left(X^2 + Y^2\right)^{\frac{1}{2}} \tag{11}$$

where R_d is the distance from the source node to the sink node (direct distance to the sink). In accordance with (Heinzelman W R, et al, 2000; Moreno R, et al, 2012), we assume a simple radio model as shown in Figure 8, where the radio dissipation, E_{elec} *(J/bit)* to run the transmitter or receiver circuitry and the transmit amplifier energy, E_{amp} *(J/bit*m²)* are required for sending information. Though, only the radio energy, E_{elec} is required for the receiver.

Also, an R^2 energy loss due to channel transmission is assumed. Hence, to transmit an n-bit of information over a distance *R* using the simple radio model (Heinzelman W R, et al, 2000; Panda M, et al, 2010), the energy expended in transmitting an information of n-bits of data in a single hop is $\left(E_{tx} + E_{rx}\right)$, and

$$E_{tx}\left(n, R\right) = E_{tx-elec}\left(n\right) + E_{tx-amp}\left(n, R\right) \tag{12}$$

or

Figure 8. First order radio model (single hop transmission)

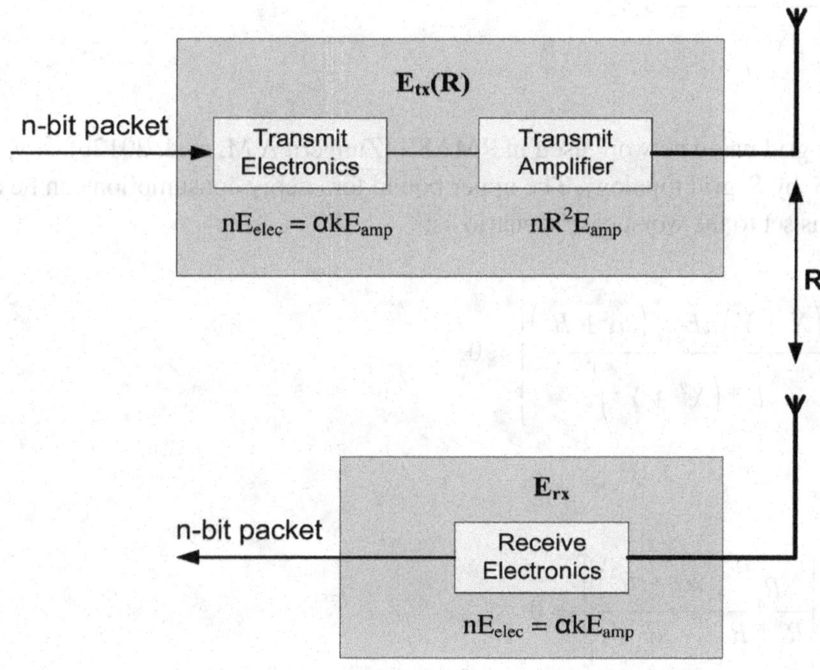

$$E_{tx}\left(n,R\right)=nE_{elec}+nR^{\lambda}E_{amp}=n\alpha E_{amp}+nR^{\lambda}E_{amp} \tag{13}$$

where λ is the path-loss exponent such that $\left(2\leq\lambda\leq 4\right)$. If we assumed $\lambda=2$ for a single hop transmission (minimum loss) or minimum transmission cost,

$$E_{tx}\left(n,R\right)=nE_{amp}\left(\alpha+R^{2}\right) \tag{14}$$

where α is an amplification factor such that $\alpha=\frac{E_{elec}}{E_{amp}}$. And to receive the *n*-bit of message, the radio energy expended is:

$$E_{rx}\left(n\right)=E_{rx-elec}\left(n\right)=nE_{elec}=\alpha nE_{amp} \tag{15}$$

But the average energy consumed per unit distance in (10), can then be re-arranged as:

$$T_{cav}=\frac{\sum_{(X+Y)hops}\left(E_{tx}+E_{rx}\right)}{R_{d}}=\frac{\left(X+Y\right)\left[\alpha nE_{amp}+nR^{2}E_{amp}+\alpha nE_{amp}\right]}{R*\left(X^{2}+Y^{2}\right)^{\frac{1}{2}}} \tag{16}$$

$$= \frac{\left(X+Y\right)nE_{amp}\left(2\alpha+R^2\right)}{R*\left(X^2+Y^2\right)^{\frac{1}{2}}} \tag{17}$$

For the static grid based network used in RMASE (Zungeru A M, et al, 2012b), x, y, n, and E_{amp} are constant in the S_x by S_y grid topology. The upper bound for energy consumption can be achieved if the expression (17) is set to the worst case scenario as:

$$T'_{cav} = \frac{R_d}{R_d * R}\left[\frac{\left(X+Y\right)nE_{amp}\left(2\alpha+R^2\right)}{R*\left(X^2+Y^2\right)^{\frac{1}{2}}}\right] = 0 \tag{18}$$

That is

$$\frac{\left(X+Y\right)nE_{amp}}{\left(X^2+Y^2\right)^{\frac{1}{2}}}\left[\frac{R_d}{R_d * R}\left[\frac{\left(2\alpha+R^2\right)}{R}\right]\right] = 0$$

or

$$\frac{R_d}{R_d * R}\left[2\alpha R^{-1} + R\right] = 0$$

and

$$-2\alpha R^{-2} + 1 = 0 \tag{19}$$

$$\rightarrow \qquad -2\alpha = -R^2$$

$$\therefore R = \left(2\alpha\right)^{1/2} \tag{20}$$

It then implies that, the average transmission cost occurred when $R = \left(2\alpha\right)^{1/2}$.

Performance Evaluation of Ant-Based Routing Algorithm

This section discusses the comparison of experimental results for three ant-based routing algorithms (IEEABR, SC, EEABR). The comparison with Beesensor is also discussed. Routing Modeling Application Simulation Environment (RMASE) (PARC, 2006; Zhang et al., 2006; Zhang, 2005) was used. The simulation parameters used are as shown in Table 1. The following metrics were used to evaluate the performance.

- **Success Rate:** It is a ratio of total number of events received at the destination to the total number of events generated by the nodes in the sensor network (%).
- **Energy Consumption:** It is the total energy consumed by the nodes in the network during the period of the experiment (Joules).
- **Energy Utilization Efficiency:** It is a measure of the ratio of total packet delivered at the destination to the total energy consumed by the network's sensor nodes (Kbits/Joules).

The algorithms were tested using two well-known application scenarios of WSN (converge-cast and target tracking). In the converge-cast scenario, sensor nodes were distributed in a random fashion with the main aims of monitoring a static event. All sources and sink are fixed, while the center of the circle is randomly selected at the start of the experiment. In this scenario, the location of the event and the position of the end node are assumed to be unknown, and each node is responsible to monitor its own vicinity and send the relevant sensed information to the destination node. The results of the experiments are shown Figure 9(a-c) for three parameters (energy consumption, energy efficiency, and success rates). In this scenario of fixed sensor nodes, nodes near the sink are more likely to use up their energy as they serve as sources and the same time as routers for the other source nodes. Hence, they will be forced to periodically transmit information on behalf of other nodes.

Figure 10 shows the simulation results using the target-tracking scenario. In the target-tracking scenario, a sensor node within the coverage of a moving target generates a random sequence of information to be able to track the target, and as the target drifts away from the coverage or transmission range of that particular node, it stops generating the random information, and this is taken up by another node within the coverage of the target/event. The sink node moves randomly in the monitored area, hence

Table 1. Simulation Parameters

Parameters	Values
Routing Protocol	Termite-hill, SC, FF, AODV, EEABR, IEEABR, Bees
Size of Topology (A)	100 x 100
Nodes Distribution	Random distribution
Maximum number of Retransmission (n)	3
Transmission distance (R)	35 m
Data Traffic	Constant Bit Rate (CBR)
Data Rate	250 kbps
Propagation model	Probabilistic
Energy consumption	Waspmote-802.15.4
Time of topology change	2 s
Simulation Time, Average Simulation times	360s, 10
Number of Nodes (N)	100

Figure 9. Performance evaluation for ant-based algorithm in converge-cast scenario: (a) Energy consumption (b) Energy efficiency (c) Success rates

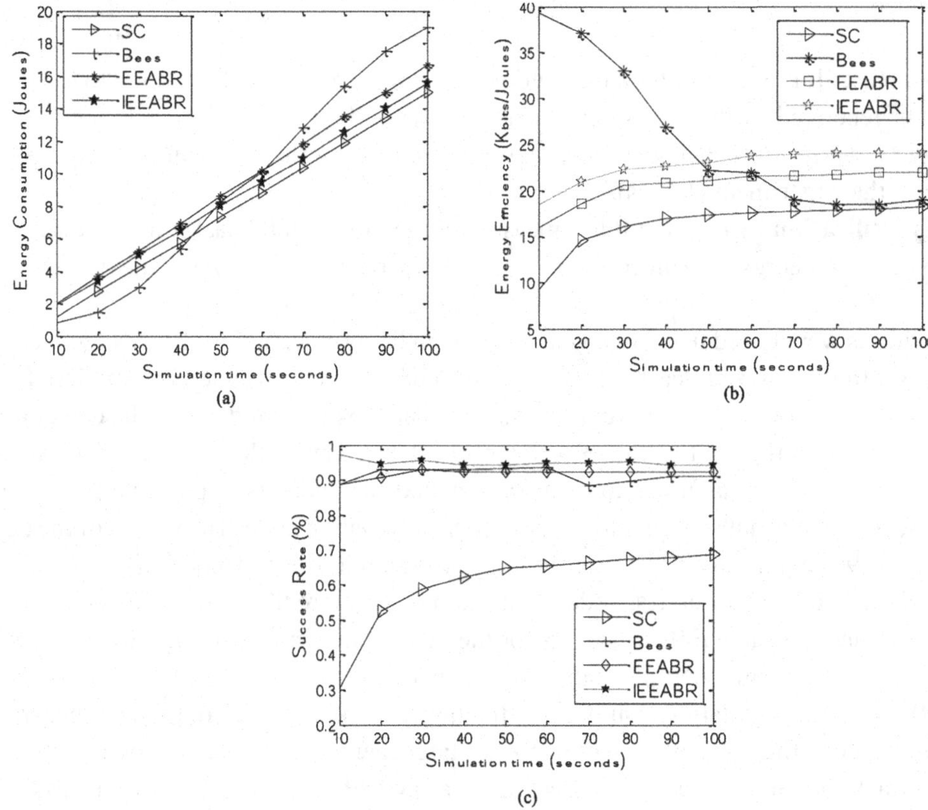

some broken paths are taken up by other paths so that the event can be delivered to the sink node via other alternate available paths.

Computational and Simulation Experiments Based on Termite Hill Protocol

Throughout the experiments, two different types of network topologies have been considered, that is; the rectangular randomly distributed grid based sensor network and the line based sensor network topologies. In the first and second part of the analytical experiment, parameters in (Saleem M, et al, 2008; Torres C E, et al, 2010; Hsu L-H and Lin C-H, 2009) were used. While in the last part of the experiment, the analytical results were compared with the simulation results, and the energy model of Waspmote (Zungeru A M, et al, 2011; Wang G, et al, 2009) sensor nodes was also used. The change in the parameters is to aid in fair comparison between the analytical results and simulation results. For each pair of communication, both the current drawn in reception and transmission, data rate, minimum supply voltage are given in the literature. RMASE simulation environment is used. In the line topology, it was assumed that all sensor nodes lie uniformly distributed in a line of sensor network of length L, and each pairs of nodes are separated with a distance R, and the sink node is at a distance nR from the source, where n represents the number of hops or nodes in-between the source and the sink node. The

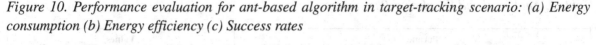

Figure 10. Performance evaluation for ant-based algorithm in target-tracking scenario: (a) Energy consumption (b) Energy efficiency (c) Success rates

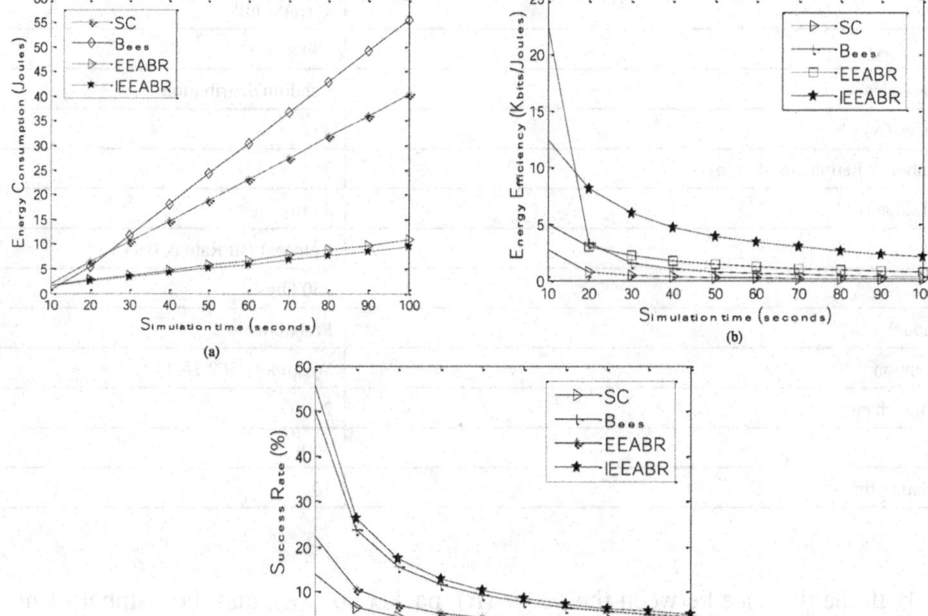

grid topology consider a rectangular grid network where nodes are randomly distributed on a grid sensor network of size S_x, S_y in the *x* and *y* directions, and each nodes are also separated by a distance *R* equal to their transmission range.

In our experiments comprising of computation as well as simulation, different possible models are illustrated to analyse transmission cost, energy consumption for both direct communication and multi-hop communication with variable packet size in bits, network size, and transmission distance. The analysis is further strengthened by modelling the energy consumption of a typical reactive routing protocol for wireless sensor network with respect to network size, topology change rate and packet arrival rate (light traffic load and heavy traffic load). The analytical results were then compared with the simulation results. The parameters used in the first part of the analytical results in accordance with (Saleem M, et al, 2008; Torres C E, et al, 2010) where $E_{elec} = 100nJ / bit$, $E_{amp} = 500\mu J / \left(bit * m^2\right)$, transmission distance, packet size, and number of nodes used in the experiments where varied accordingly as shown in Figure 11 and Figure 12. In Table 2 are the analytical and simulation parameters settings for the last part of the experiment.

Average Transmission Cost of a Grid Based Sensor Network

In this section, the average transmission cost of a grid based wireless sensor network is analysed. From the computational results, it is found that the transmission cost in joules per unit meter, is directly pro-

Table 2. Analytical and Simulation Parameters

Parameters	Values
Routing Protocol	Termite-hill
Size of Topology (A)	100 x 100
Distribution of Nodes	Random distribution
Number of Nodes (N)	441
Maximum number of Retransmission (n)	3
Transmission Range (R)	35 m
Data Traffic	Constant Bit Rate (CBR)
Data Rate	250 kbps
Propagation model	Probabilistic
Energy consumption	Waspmote-802.15.4
Time of topology change	2 s
Simulation Time	360s
Average Simulation times	10

portional to both the distance between the nodes (R), packet size (n), and the number of nodes (hops) in the X and Y directions. Figure 11(a) is a representation of the effect of transmission distance on the average cost of transmission. As it is seen, for every increase in transmission distance (R), there is a high rise in energy consumption per node. The rise in transmission cost is as a result of the proportionality between the transmission cost and the transmission distance (R) as described in Eqn. (17). The high rise in transmission cost is not favourable for sensor network, since the sensor nodes have limited energy as well as limited bandwidth. For a typical wireless sensor node of the Libelium (Waspmote) as described in (Zhang Y, et al, 2004), each sensor node can transmit at a maximum distance of 500m, Crossbow MICAz for 100m, and Intel IMote2 for 30m. Even the ones that can transmit at a long distance have limited available energy, hence it is encouraged to adopt to the multi-hop means of communication to evenly distribute the energy cost and also limit the transmission distance. Shown in Figure 11(b) is the variation of transmission cost with packet size. There is also an increase in transmission cost for every increase in number of bits transmitted on the wireless link. The increase in transmission cost is as a result of increase in packet size. The transmission cost is a function of the number of bits transmitted (n). Also, a typical sensor node has low memory and storage capacity, and a sensor frame occupies an average of approximate 100bytes (800bits) of information. With the low memory of 8KB SRAM of Waspmote, it then becomes necessary to limit the overhead cost of transmission so as to save space for data transmission. As can be seen, the transmission cost is computed to a maximum of 900bits of information, of which every increase in bits also corresponds to an increase in transmission cost. In Figure 11(c), the relationship between the transmission cost of grid based sensor network and the number of nodes in the network in the form of number of X and Y hops is shown. Also, the figure shows an increase in the transmission cost with corresponding increase in the network density. This is true because as shown, the average transmission cost is proportional to the number of hops in the X and Y directions.

Figure 11. Effect of (a) Transmission distance (b) Packet Size, and (c) Number of Nodes on the Transmission cost for a grid based sensor network

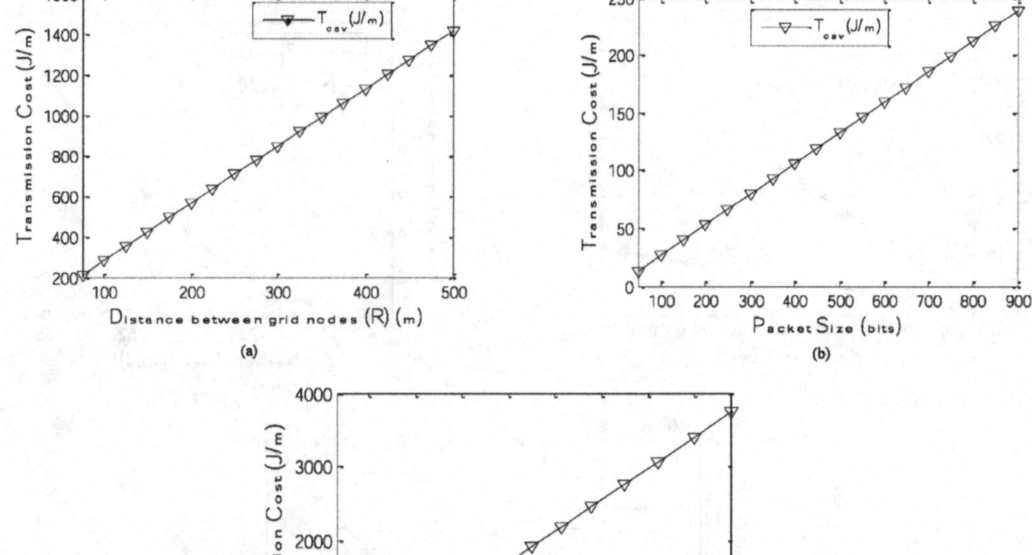

Energy Consumption of a Direct and Multi-Hop Communication in WSN

In this section, the reaction of the energy consumption for multi-hop and direct communication with increase in packet size, network size, and transmission distance between source nodes and sink node in a wireless sensor network is explored. The behaviour of the network in terms of increase in energy consumption for the direct communications as against the multi-hop communication due to variable packet size is expected, as shown in Figure 12(a). This is because, the energy consumed in direct transmission is proportional to the square of the number of bits transmitted, and it is measured in joules per bits. This then means that, for multi-hop communications, the number of bits transmitted is at a short distance between nodes, hence saving more energy. It can be seen that, as the packet size increases up to a value of 900bits, the energy consumed per node for the direct communication rises up to the value of 450, while it is 113 for multi-hop. This is a high difference when compared to the energy available per node for network lifetime. Also, as can be seen in Figure 12(b), even with an increase in number of nodes in the network, the energy consumed by the multi-hop communication tends to remain the same as the initial consumption in the fewer nodes, whereas, it increases sharply and higher in the case of direct communication per node. This is expected since as the network size increase, the transmission range increases, which is not favourable for direct communication. As for multi-hop, as the network size increases with increase in number of nodes, it has less effect as neighbouring nodes serve as routers and

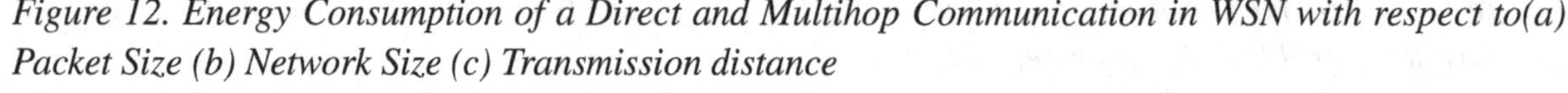

Figure 12. Energy Consumption of a Direct and Multihop Communication in WSN with respect to(a) Packet Size (b) Network Size (c) Transmission distance

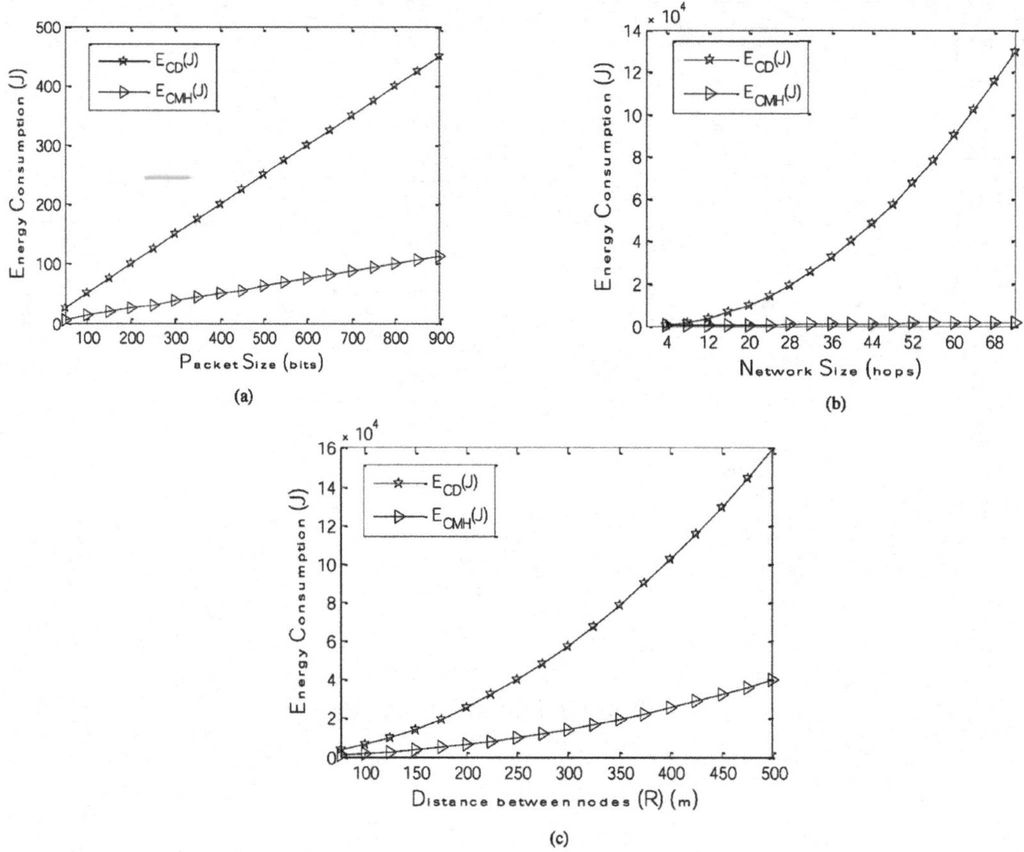

hence, same or equivalent energy is expected to be consumed. Figure 12(c) shows the effect of transmission distance on energy consumption of grid based sensor network. As can be seen, though, there is a little increase in energy consumption of multi-hop communication, but the increase in that of the direct communication is much higher. The increase in node pair distance is an indirect way of increasing the network area. The increase in network area means that much energy will be required per node for transmitting a bit of information as the energy consumption is a function of transmission distance (R) between nodes as shown.

Energy Consumption of a Termite-Hill Routing Protocol in WSN

In this section, the computational results and the simulation results of Termite-hill routing algorithm in terms of energy consumption with respect to network size, topology change rate, and packet arrival rate is compared. Figure 13(a)-(c) show the effect of high number of retransmissions on the energy consumption of Termite-hill routing algorithm. As shown in Figure 13(a), as the mobility is varied from 0.05 to 0.9 for every step of 0.05, the total energy consumption increases, also, at the point of high network density of about 289 nodes corresponding to high mobility of 0.6, we have the energy consumed due to

Figure 13. Effect of high number of retransmission on Energy Consumption of termite-hill in WSN with respect to (a) Number of nodes (b) Packet arrival rate (c) Mobility

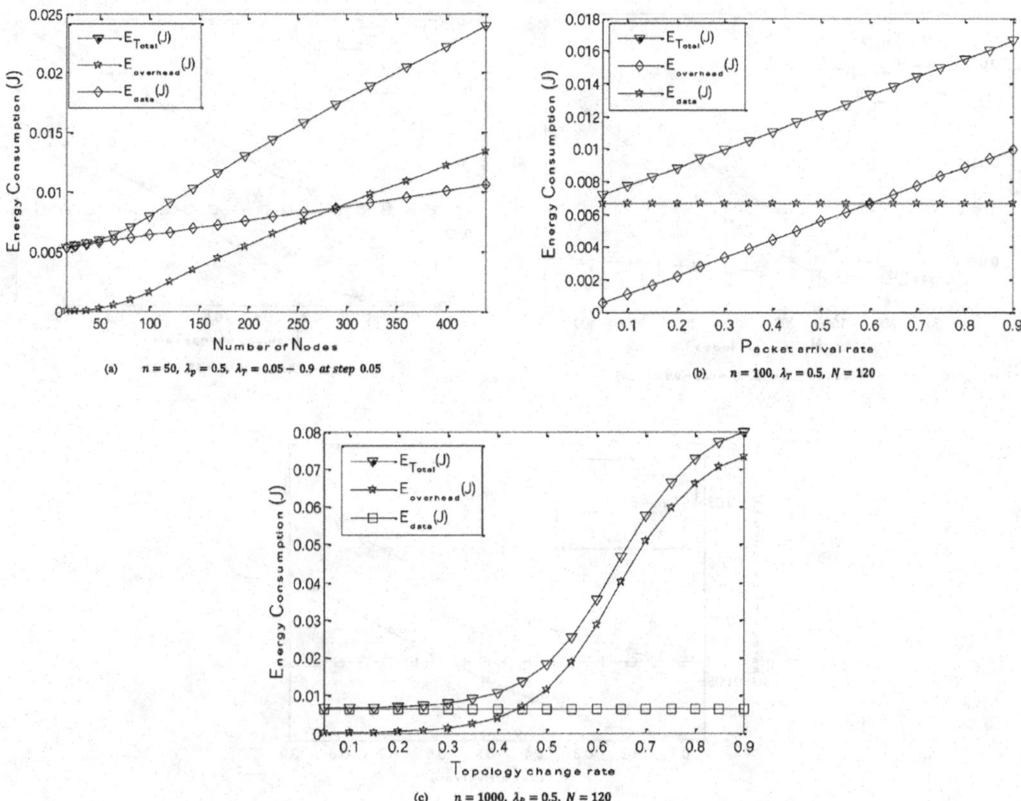

control traffic equals the energy consumed in transmitting the data packets. After that point, the energy consumption as a result of control traffic grows above that of the data, hence, many packets were dropped and the system encounters unnecessary and wasted energy. Also shown in Figure 13(b) and (c), there is a point at which the energy consumption due to control packets becomes higher than energy used to transmit the data packets. But in (c), with very high number of retransmission of about 1000, the energy consumption of the system due to control packets approaches the total energy consumed in the system, and at that instance, it then shows that it is necessary to limit the number of retransmission so as to save energy for transmitting the real information (data packets). Figure 14(a)-(c) shows a similar behaviour to that of Figure 13, but the main difference here is that, the number of retransmission was varied for each variation of number of nodes, mobility and traffic load. Most important observation is in Figure 14(a), which shows that, for high network density, the energy consumption due to control traffic approaches the total energy consumption as we increase the number of retransmission of the control packets. Figure 15(a) shows the relationship between the total energy consumed in the network using the analytical method, overhead energy consumption, energy consumption for data transmission, and energy consumed by the termite-hill using the RMASE simulation environment with respect to variation of network density. Figure 15(a) shows that the total energy consumption is comparable with the energy consumed in data transmission since the overhead energy consumption by the termite-hill protocol is negligible. This is the point at which the retransmission was reduced to optimal value (three). It is also worth noting that,

Figure 14. Effect of varying number of retransmission on Energy Consumption of termite-hill in WSN with respect to (a) Number of nodes (b) Mobility (c) Packet arrival rate

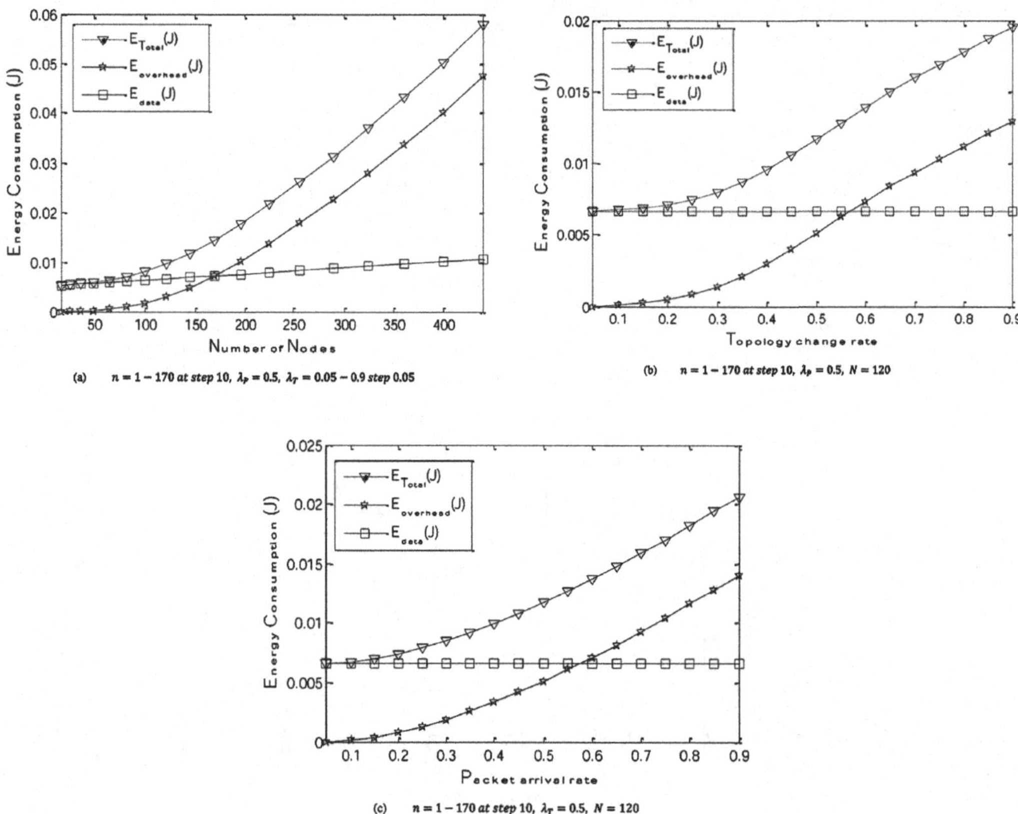

the analytical results varied slightly with the simulation results due to the environment of simulation and other simulation parameters which are prone to errors and the limitation of retransmission of *forward soldiers* and data packets. Though, our main goal is to evaluate the effect of overhead cost on the total energy consumption of Termite-hill algorithm. As shown in Figure 15(b), and 15(c), the topology change rate as well as packet arrival rate has less effect on the energy consumption when the number of retransmission is reduced to minimal. Though for high traffic load and at high mobility, the energy consumption tends to increase slowly, but the increase is minimal.

(a) $n = 50,\ \lambda_p = 0.5,\ \ \lambda_T = 0.05 - 0.9\ at\,step\ 0.05$

(b) $n = 100,\ \lambda_T = 0.5,\ N = 120$

Figure 15. Analytical and Simulation Energy Consumption of termite-hill in WSN with respect to (a) Number of nodes (b) Mobility (c) Packet arrival rate

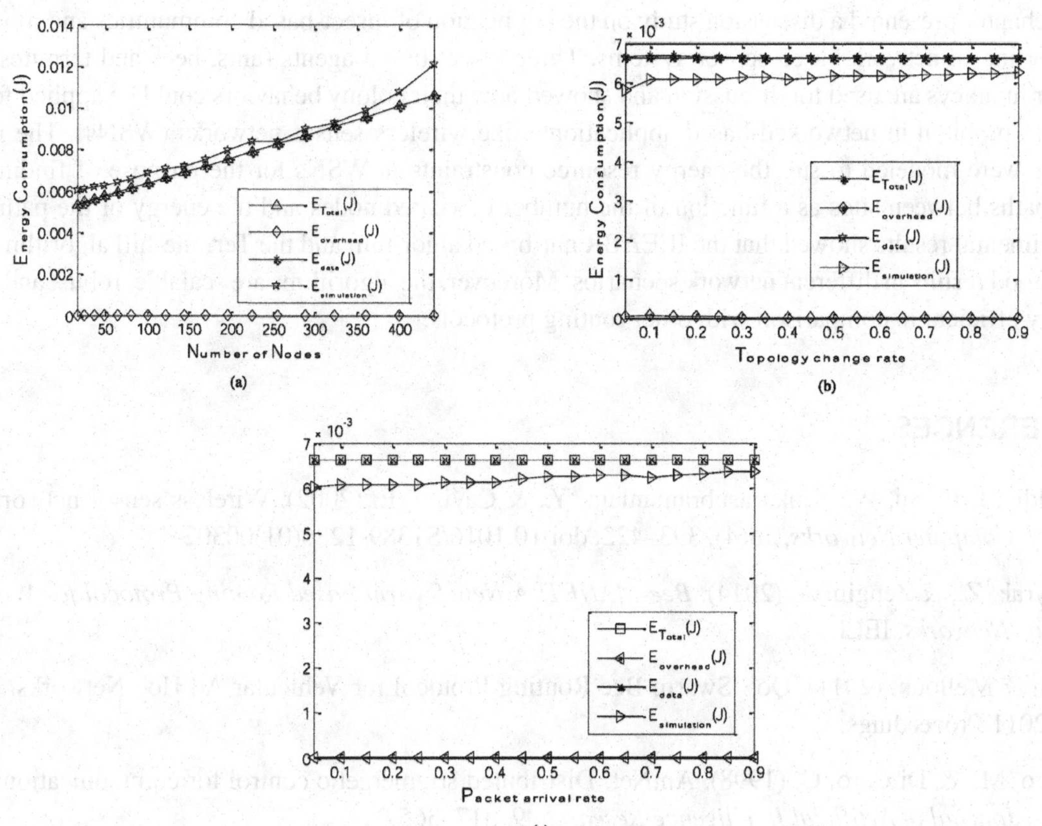

(c) $n = 1000,\ \lambda_P = 0.5,\ N = 120$

(a) $n = 1 - 170 at\, step 10,\ \lambda_P = 0.5,\ \lambda_T = 0.05 - 0.9 step 0.05$

(b) $n = 1 - 170 at\, step 10,\ \lambda_P = 0.5,\ N = 120$

(c) $n = 1 - 170 at\, step 10,\ \lambda_T = 0.5,\ N = 120$

CONCLUSION

This chapter presented a discussion study on the application of insect-based communities and monkeys for routing in network-based sensor systems. Three insect-based agents (ants, bees and termites) and spider monkeys are used for discussion and showed how their colony behaviors could be applied for the routing problem in networked-based applications, like wireless sensor networks (WSNs). The insect agents were modeled to suit the energy resource constraints in WSNs for the purpose of finding the best paths between sites as a function of the number of visited nodes and the energy of the path. The experimental results showed that the IEEABR ant-based algorithm and the Termite-hill algorithm gave very good results in different network scenarios. Moreover, the algorithms are scalable, robust and more energy efficient in comparison with other routing protocols.

REFERENCES

Akyildiz, I. F., Su, W., Sankarasubramaniam, Y., & Cayirci, E. (2002). Wireless sensor networks: A survey. *Computer Networks*, *38*(4), 393–422. doi:10.1016/S1389-1286(01)00302-4

Albayrak, Z., & Zengin, A. (2014). *Bee-MANET: A New Swarm-based Routing Protocol for Wireless Ad Hoc Networks*. IEEE.

Bitam & Mellouk. (2011). QoS Swarm Bee Routing Protocol for Vehicular Ad Hoc Networks. IEEE ICC 2011 Proceedings.

Dorigo, M., & Di Caro, G. (1998). AntNet: Distributed stigmergetic control for communications networks. *Journal of Artificial Intelligence Research*, *9*, 317–365.

Dorigo, M., Di Caro, G., & Gambardella, L. M. (1999). Ant Algorithms for Discrete Optimization. *Artificial Life*, *5*(3), 137–172. doi:10.1162/106454699568728 PMID:10633574

Gui, Man, Wang, Li, & Wilkins. (2016). A novel Cluster-based Routing Protocol Wireless Sensor Networks using Spider Monkey Optimization. *Industrial Electronics Society, IECON 2016-42nd Annual Conference of the IEEE.*

Heinzelman, W. R., Chandrakasan, A., & Balakrishnan, H. (2000). Energy efficient communication protocol for wireless microsensor network. *Proceedings of the 33rd annual Hawaii international conference on systems science*, 2, 3005-3014. doi:10.1109/HICSS.2000.926982

Heusse, S., Guérin, Snyers, D., & Kuntz, P. (1998). *Adaptive Agent-driven Routing and Load Balancing. Communication Networks*. Technical Report RR-98001-IASC. Department Intelligence Artificielle et Sciences Cognitives, ENST Bretagne.

Hsu, L.-H., & Lin, C.-H. (2009). *Graph theory and interconnection networks. CRC Press.*

Kumar, S., Kumari, R., & Sharma, V. K. (2015). Fitness Based Position Update in Spider Monkey Optimization Algorithm. *Procedia Computer Science*, *62*, 442–449. doi:10.1016/j.procs.2015.08.504

Kumar, S. E., & Kusuma, S. M. (2014). Clustering protocol for wireless sensor networks based on Rhesus Macaque (Macaca mulatta) animal's social behavior. *International Journal of Computer Applications, 87*(8).

Matthews, R. W., & Mattheus, J. R. (1942). *Insect Behavior.* New York: Wiley-Interscience.

Merloti, P. E. (2004). Optimization Algorithms Inspired by Biological Ants and Swarm Behavior. San Diego State University, Artificial Intelligence Technical Report, CS550.

Moreno, R., Antonio, R.-G., Aurelio, B., & Rafael, C. (2012). SensGrid: modeling and simulation for wireless sensor grids. Simulation: Transactions of the society for modeling and simulation international, 1-16.

Panda, M., & Patra, M. R. (2010). Modeling radio channels for CSMA-MAC based wireless sensor networks. *International Journal of Computers and Applications*, *9*(6), 6–11. doi:10.5120/1392-1876

PARC. (2006). *RMASE: Routing Modeling Application Simulation Environment.* Available at: http://webs.cs.berkeley.edu/related.html

Ramos, V., & Almeida, F. (2000). Artificial Ant Colonies in Digital Image Habitats – A Mass Behavior Effect Study on Pattern Recognition. *Proceedings of ANTS'2000, 2nd International Workshop on Ant Algorithms*, 113-116.

Roth, M., & Wicker, S. (2003). Termite: ad-hoc networking with stigmergy. *GLOBECOM '03, IEEE Global Telecommunications Conference*, 5, 2937-2941.

Saleem, M., Di Caro, G. A., & Farooq, M. (2010). Swarm intelligence based routing protocol for wireless sensor networks: Survey and future directions. *Information Sciences*, *181*(20), 4597–4624. doi:10.1016/j.ins.2010.07.005

Saleem, M., & Farooq, M. (2005). Beesensor: A bee-inspired power aware routing algorithms. Proceedings EvoCOMNET, 136-146.

Saleem, M., Khayam, S., & Farooq, M. (2008). Formal modeling of bee ad-hoc: a bio-inspired mobile ad-hoc network routing protocol. *6th international conference on ant colony optimization and swarm intelligence*, 315–322.

Sardar, A., Singh, A., Sahoo, R., Majumder, R., Sing, R., & Sarkar, R. (2014). An efficient ant colony based routing algorithm for better quality of services in MANET. In *ICT & CI* (pp. 233–240). Springer. doi:10.1007/978-3-319-03107-1_26

Semet, Y., O'Reilly, U., & Durand, F. (2004). An Interactive Artificial Ant Approach to Non-Photorealistic Rendering. Springer-Verlag.

Sensarma, D., & Majumder, K. (2012). A comparative analysis of the ant based systems for QoS routing in MANET. In *International Conference, SNDS,* (pp. 485–496). Springer. doi:10.1007/978-3-642-34135-9_47

Torres, C. E., Rossi, L. F., Keffer, J., Li, K., & Shen, C.-C. (2010). Modeling, analysis and simulation of ant-based network routing protocols. *Swarm Intelligence*, *4*(3), 221–244. doi:10.1007/s11721-010-0043-7

Wang, G., Wang, Y., & Tao, X. (2009). An ant colony clustering routing algorithm for wireless sensor networks. *Third international conference on genetic and evolutionary computing,* 670–73. doi:10.1109/WGEC.2009.22

Zhang, Y. (2005). *Routing Modeling Application Simulation Environment (RMASE).* Available at: https://docs.google.com/file/d/0B-29IhEITY3bbGY2VVo2SGxxRFE/edit

Zhang, Y., Kuhn, L. D., & Fromherz, M. P. J. (2004). Improvements on Ant Routing for Sensor Networks. In *ANTS 2004, LNCS 3172* (pp. 289–313). doi:10.1007/978-3-540-28646-2_14

Zhang, Y., Simon, G., & Balogh, G. (2006). High-Level Sensor Network Simulations for Routing Performance Evaluations. *Proceedings of 3rd International Conference on Networked Sensing Systems,* 1-4.

Zungeru, Ang, & Seng. (2013). A formal mathematical framework for modeling and simulation of wireless sensor network environments utilizing the hill-building behavior of termites. *Simulation: transactions of the Society for Modeling and Simulation International, 89*(5), 589-615.

Zungeru, A. M., Ang, L.-M., & Prabaharan, S. R. S. (2011). Improved energy-efficient ant-based routing algorithm in wireless sensor networks. In K. Ragab, A. B. Abdullah, & N. Zaman (Eds.), *Wireless sensor networks and energy efficiency: protocols, routing and management* (pp. 420–444). Hershey, PA: IGI Global.

Zungeru, A. M., Ang, L.-M., & Seng, K. P. (2011). Ant Based Routing Protocol for Visual Sensors. *Communications in Computer and Information Science, Springer, 252*(3), 250–264. doi:10.1007/978-3-642-25453-6_23

Zungeru, A. M., Ang, L.-M., & Seng, K. P. (2012a). Performance of Termite-hill Routing Algorithm on Sink Mobility in Wireless Sensor Networks. In Advances in Swarm Intelligence (pp. 334-343). Springer. doi:10.1007/978-3-642-31020-1_39

Zungeru, A. M., Ang, L.-M., & Seng, K. P. (2012b). Classical and swarm intelligence based routing protocols for wireless sensor networks. *Journal of Network and Computer Applications, 35*(5), 1508–1536. doi:10.1016/j.jnca.2012.03.004

Zungeru, A. M., Ang, L.-M., & Seng, K. P. (2012c). Performance Evaluation of Ant Based Routing Protocols for Wireless Sensor Networks. *International Journal of Computer Science Issues, 9*(3), 388–397.

Chapter 12
Image Reconstruction of Electrical Impedance Tomography Using Fish School Search and Differential Evolution

Valter Augusto de Freitas Barbosa
Universidade Federal de Pernambuco, Brazil

Wellington Pinheiro dos Santos
Universidade Federal de Pernambuco, Brazil

Ricardo Emmanuel de Souza
Universidade Federal de Pernambuco, Brazil

Reiga Ramalho Ribeiro
Universidade Federal de Pernambuco, Brazil

Allan Rivalles Souza Feitosa
Universidade Federal de Pernambuco, Brazil

Victor Luiz Bezerra Araújo da Silva
Escola Politécnica da Universidade de Pernambuco, Brazil

David Edson Ribeiro
Universidade Federal de Pernambuco, Brazil

Rafaela Covello Freitas
Escola Politécnica da Universidade de Pernambuco, Brazil

Manoela Paschoal
Universidade Federal de Pernambuco, Brazil

Natália Souza Soares
Universidade Federal de Pernambuco, Brazil

Rodrigo Beltrão Valença
Universidade Federal de Pernambuco, Brazil

Rodrigo Luiz Tomio Ogava
Universidade Federal de Pernambuco, Brazil

Ítalo José do Nascimento Silva Araújo Dias
Universidade Federal de Pernambuco, Brazil

ABSTRACT

Electrical impedance tomography (EIT) is a noninvasive imaging technique that does not use ionizing radiation with application both in environmental sciences and in health. Image reconstruction is performed by solving an inverse problem and ill-posed. Evolutionary and bioinspired computation have

DOI: 10.4018/978-1-5225-5134-8.ch012

become a source of methods for solving inverse problems. In this chapter, the authors investigate the performance of fish school search (FSS) and differential evolution (DE) using non-blind search (NBS) considering meshes of 415, 3190, and 9990 finite elements. The methods were evaluated using numerical phantoms consisting of electrical conductivity images with objects in the center, between the center and the edge, and on the edge of a circular section. Twenty simulations were performed for each configuration. Results showed that both FSS and DE are able to perform EIT image reconstruction with large meshes and converge faster by using non-blind search.

INTRODUCTION

The most commonly medical image machines, such as Mammography, Positron Emission Tomography and X-Rays, use ionizing radiation in their process. Using those electromagnetic waves may provide benefits to the quality of the image obtained from these methods, however there are many associated risks to whom operates those machines or is submitted to these kind of exams. In addition to that, the prolonged exposition to ionizing radiation may cause many diseases, such as cancer (Rolnik & Seleghim Jr, 2006). Given the importance of this issue to Public Health throughout the world, the search for imaging technologies that are efficient, low-cost, simple and safe to those that uses them becomes of the utmost importance.

Within these circumstances, Electric Impedance Tomography (EIT) has earmarks of being a promising imaging technique, considering that it does not uses ionizing radiation (Bera & Nagaraju, 2014; Rolnik & Seleghim Jr, 2006). EIT consist in a non-invasive technique that builds images of inside a body (or any object), using electrical properties, measured over the surface of interest. Applying a low amplitude current through some electrodos disposed around the transverse section of interest induces an electric potential, known as "border potential". This low-voltage signal is measured from these same electrodos and conveyed to a computer that uses them in a reconstruction algorithm to rebuilds the image of this region of interest. (Rasteiro, Silva, Garcia & Faia, 2011; Tehrani, Jin, McEwan & van Schaik, 2010; Brown, Barber & Seagar, 1985).

EIT has many applications in several fields of knowledge, such as medical sciences, botanic, industry and geology. In medical science, it is utilized to detect pulmonary embolism or blood clots in the lungs (Cheney, Isaacson & Newell, 1999), pulmonary ventilation monitoring (Alves, Amato, Terra, Vargas & Caruso, 2014), and also to detect breast cancer (Cherepenin et al., 2001). Examples of its application in other fields are: generating images of the trees' trunks' insides, allowing the knowledge of its biological conditions without damaging it (Filipowicz & Rymarczyk, 2012); monitoring multiphasic outflow in pipes (Rolnik & Seleghim Jr, 2006) and find underground storage of mineral and different geological formations (Cheney et al., 1999).

Considering that Electrical Impedance Tomography requires only an equipment able to generate and measure current and electrical potential and a computer able to rebuild the image, look as though it is an advantageous method due to it relatively low cost when compared to other methods like Magnetic Resonance, Tomography or X-Rays (Tehrani et al, 2010). Another benefit of this imaging method is that it uses only the electrical properties (conductivity and permittivity) of the body, it does not use ionizing radiation, in such manner that there is no associated risk to its use.

However, image reconstruction in EIT is something that still needs to be improved, since that it has a low resolution and undefined borders, which harms its popularity and diffusion among the imaging field

(Rolnik & Seleghim Jr, 2006). The image acquisition of EIT consist on the resolution of a mathematical problem ill-posed and ill-conditioned, i.e., there are not only one solution (image) for a given potential border distribution. In order to improve this aspect, researchers of EIT search for new algorithms of image reconstruction that are able to create images with good resolution and definition with a low computational cost. Thereby, this method would be a reliable and easy tool to diagnostic imaging.

A further way of trying to solve the EIT problem is managing it as an optimization problem. In this case, the problem is solved iteratively and with the objective to minimize the relative error between the measured border potential of an object and the calculated border potential of a solution candidate (Feitosa, Ribeiro, Barbosa, de Souza & dos Santos, 2014; Ribeiro, Feitosa, de Souza & dos Santos, 2014a, 2014b, 2014c).

A heuristic that provides good results and solve this as an optimization problem is the Fish School Search (FSS) (Bastos-Filho, de Lima Neto, Lins, Nascimento & Lima, 2008; Bastos-Filho & Guimarães, 2015). This technique is inspired in fish schools' behavior on food search. The search process on FSS is made by a population which its individuals (the fishes) has a limited memory. Each school represents a possible solution for the system. The fishes interact among each other and with the environment that surrounds them, and, by influence of the collective and individual movement's operator and food operator, the school increases the possibility of convergence to the food surroundings, which means the best position and solution to that problem (Lins, Bastos-Filho, Nascimento, Junior & de Lima-Neto, 2012).

The aim of this work is to propose a relatively simple approach to image reconstruction problem of EIT using Fish School Search (FSS). Two ways of solution candidates (fish) initialization are presenting: one completely random and other that select, among the random candidates, one solution candidate. This second initialization method is derived from the Gauss-Newton reconstruction method (Sasha & Bandyopadhyay, 2008) and was called Non-Blind Search.

This work is organized as following: in section Materials and Methods is presented a brief on the theoretical foundations of Electrical Impedance Tomography, Finite Element Method, Fish School Search, Genetic Algorithm, Differential Evolution, Non-Blind Search and presents the Proposed Method and Experiments used in this work. In section Results and Discussion is showed the experimental results and detailed discussion about them. The chapter ending with Conclusion section where is given an overall coverage of the chapter and some highlights of future developments.

LITERATURE REVIEW

Several works have shown the field of Electrical Impedance Tomography, since the electrodes configurations, most of them inspired on the electrocardiogram (ECG) (McAdams et al., 1994), until the recent Artificial Intelligence techniques (Feitosa et al., 2014; Ribeiro et al., 2014; Martin & Charles, 2016; Barbosa et al., 2017) to perform image reconstruction.

In the decade of 1990, (McAdams et al., 1994) described several ways of EIT electrodes usage. They related electrodes attachment techniques, some methods of rapidly and accurately locating electrodes and methods of enabling inter-electrode movement. They have shown that the set of electrodes to be used depends on the EIT specific application, like one 1988 breast EIT imaging example pointed by them among others approaches.

(Jin et al., 2012) Proposed an EIT reconstruction technique based on Sparsity Regularization. They have based their approach in a Tikhonov functional incorporating a sparsity-promoting L1-penalty term.

They have made the internal conductivity reconstruction by assuming a priori, the inhomogeneity sparsity. The qualitative results generation occurs when this a priori assumption is valid.

An image reconstruction method with locally-refined mesh using the adaptive Kaczmarz method was developed by (Li et al., 2014). In their technique, the mesh becomes more refined in the sites where there are the resistant searched objects.

In their work, (Zhou et al., 2015) have shown a comparison among several EIT reconstruction techniques based on Total Variation. They have investigated the noise, resolution, the convergence and convergence time of some techniques, such Primal Dual Interior Point Method, the Linearised Alternating Direction Method of Multipliers and the Split Bregman technique.

In a Neural Network based, EIT image reconstruction technique, (Martin & Choi, 2016), have shown that the use of Particle Swarm Optimization to the training of the net can significantly improve the performance of the algorithm. They have trained a NN based on the position error of the object and the resolution distances to the ground truth image for the presented potential pattern.

The EIT image reconstruction also has been made by modeling the problem as a search and optimization problem (Feitosa et al., 2014; Ribeiro et al., 2014; Barbosa et al., 2017). In these works, the image is generated by optimizing an objective function that measures a relative error. This is calculated by the distance between the border potential of the solution candidate, and the border potential whose image is intended to be reconstructed.

MATERIALS AND METHODS

Electrical Impedance Tomography

In EIT the estimate of the electrical conductivity distribution, inside a heterogeneous body or object, is made by the resolution of a partial differential equation named Poisson's Equation (Borcea, 2002; Cheney et al., 1999). The process to obtain the Poisson's Equation is originated from the Maxwell's Equations, it is starting from the Gauss's law in point form (Tombe, 2012):

$$\nabla \cdot \vec{D} = \rho \tag{1}$$

where $\nabla \cdot$ is the divergent operator, ρ is the free electric charge in the interest region, and $\vec{D}$ is the electric elasticity given by the multiplication of the electrical conductive distribution $\sigma\left(\vec{u}\right)$ in the point $\vec{u} = \left(x, y, z\right)$ and the Electrical field $\vec{E}$, as a follow:

$$\vec{D} = \sigma\left(\vec{u}\right)\vec{E} \tag{2}$$

Knowing that the electrical field $\vec{E}$ is determined by the negative gradient (denoted by the nabla symbol - ∇) of the electrical potentials ($\phi\left(\vec{u}\right)$), we have that:

$$\vec{E} = -\nabla\phi\left(\vec{u}\right) \tag{3}$$

In the reconstruction problem of EIT images we consider that there is no free electric charge in the interest region (i.e. $\rho = 0$). Taking that into account and replacing the Equations (2) and (3) in (1) we get the Poisson's Equation (Borcea, 2002; Cheney et al., 1999) as given below:

$$\nabla \cdot \left[\sigma\left(\vec{u}\right)\nabla\phi\left(\vec{u}\right)\right] = 0 \quad (4)$$

Besides, we also need to consider the following boundary conditions (Borcea, 2002):

$$\phi_{ext}\left(\vec{u}\right) = \phi\left(\vec{u}\right), \forall \vec{u} \in \partial\Omega \quad (5)$$

$$I\left(\vec{u}\right) = -\sigma\left(\vec{u}\right)\nabla\phi\left(\vec{u}\right)\cdot\hat{n}\left(\vec{u}\right), \forall \vec{u} \in \partial\Omega \quad (6)$$

where $\vec{u} = \left(x, y, z\right)$ is the position of a given object, $\phi\left(\vec{u}\right)$ is the potentials' global distribution, $\phi_{ext}\left(\vec{u}\right)$ is the electric potentials distribution on the surface electrodes, $I\left(\vec{u}\right)$ is the electric current applied on the interest region's surface, $\sigma\left(\vec{u}\right)$ is the electric conductivity distribution (i.e., the goal image), Ω is the interest volume, $\partial\Omega$ is the volume border and $\hat{n}\left(\vec{u}\right)$ is the border's normal vector on $\vec{u} \in \partial\Omega$ position.

Finding the electric potential of the surface electrodes $\phi_{ext}\left(\vec{u}\right)$, given the electric currents $I\left(\vec{u}\right)$ and the conductivity distribution $\sigma\left(\vec{u}\right)$ is named EIT's Direct Problem, and modeled by the following relation:

$$\phi_{ext}\left(\vec{u}\right) = f\left(I\left(\vec{u}\right), \sigma\left(\vec{u}\right)\right), \forall \vec{u} \in \partial\Omega \wedge \vec{u} \in \Omega \quad (7)$$

In Direct Problem's situation, the surface electric potentials estimative, when the internal conductivity distribution is already known, is calculated using the Poisson's equation, shown in (4). Considering the contour condition, given by the following equation:

$$\sigma\frac{\partial\phi}{\partial\hat{n}} = J \quad (8)$$

where $\hat{n}$ is the surface's normal vector and J corresponds to the electric current density (Baker, 1989). It is important to emphasize that there are no analytical solutions to (4) and (8), for an arbitrary given domain Ω.

Nevertheless, an approximate solution to the border's potentials may be obtained by the Finite Elements Method (FEM), which converts the nonlinear system in (4) and (8) in the following linear equation's system (Bathe, 2006; Castro Martins, Camargo, Lima, Amato, & Tsuzuki, 2012):

$$K(\sigma)\cdot\Phi - C = 0 \quad (9)$$

where $K(\sigma)$ is a conductivity-dependent (σ) coefficients matrix and C is a constant's values vector. In this way, it is possible to obtain an approximated value for the border potentials Φ, known as conductivity distribution σ.

While the conductivity distribution determination problem $\sigma(\vec{u})$ (tomographic image), given $I(\vec{u})$ and $\phi_{ext}(\vec{u})$ is known as EIT Inverse Problem, modeled as follows:

$$\sigma(\vec{u}) = f^{-1}\left(I(\vec{u}), \phi_{ext}(\vec{u})\right), \forall \vec{u} \in \partial\Omega \wedge \vec{u} \in \Omega \quad (10)$$

In this situation it is possible to obtain the conductivity distribution $\sigma(\vec{u})$ by Poisson's equation solution (4), considering the contour conditions, mentioned in Equations (5) and (6).

Finite Element Method

In engineering field, several physical phenomena can be described from partial differential equations. Due to the great complexity in the resolution of this type of equation, the Finite Element Method was developed (FEM) (BATHE, 2006) as a numerical method capable of discretizing the geometry in the domain under analysis, in order to approximate the desired solution by a function defined under a subdomain, also called the finite element mesh.

In most cases, it's not possible to solve the direct problem analytically (Menin, 2009; Ribeiro, 2016), thus, it is necessary to discrete the domain to be reconstructed, where, through numerical methods, it is possible to find an approximate solution of the problem. One of the most used discretization methods for the direct problem of EIT is the Finite Element Method.

In this method, the domain to be imaged is divided in geometrical forms (such as triangles) called finite elements, where each element in FEM has a specific value of conductivity. Therefore, the conductivity distribution, which was previously given by a finite set of points within the domain, is transformed into a finite element distribution given by the elements. In the FEM, Poisson's Equation and its boundary conditions are transformed in a system of linear equations, which can be solved through linear methods (Momenté, Peixoto, Tsuzuki & Martins, 2013). The number of finite elements in the mesh (as is called the way in which the domain is divided by the elements) defines the refinement of the solution, that is, the greater the number of elements in the mesh, the greater the refinement. This leads to a solution that is more faithful to reality and of better quality, but, as a result, there is an increase of the linear equation system, and, consequently, an increase in the computational cost to solve the problem. According to Menin (2009), the FEM has the advantage of accepting domains with complex geometry, besides allowing a greater refinement of the mesh only in certain critical regions, however, the method can generate large systems, which depend on the desired refinement.

About the field of applications of FEM in engineering, we can mention:

- Thermal, vibration and voltage analysis, in industrial and automotive devices;
- Simulation of technological processes aiming at the prediction of physical phenomena;
- Ballistic impact, cars, trains and airplanes simulations.

To implement the FEM in order to solve a generic partial linear differential equation, it is necessary to follow the following steps:

1. **Discretization:** This step consists of the division of the domain under analysis in finite elements, where the finite element is divided by the "nodes", it can be uni, bi or tridimensional.
2. **Finite Elements Formulation:** This step consists of the definition of the approximation function which represents the solution for every finite element or subdomain. Such a function must contain unknown coefficients that must be obtained in order to minimize the error in the solution. These coefficients are defined in function of the nodal values of the magnitude under study.
3. **Elaboration of the Matrix System for Finite Elements:** This step consists of the definition of the matrix system which represents all the domain under study, being the coefficients of this system dependent of the approximation function for each finite element.
4. **Boundary Conditions:** After the elaboration of the global matrix system, it is necessary to modify it through the application of the boundary conditions of the domain.
5. **Matrix System Solution:** This step consists of the resolution of the linear matrix system from direct or iterative methods. These approximate solutions correspond to the nodal values of the domain that must be organized in order to allow their interpretation, such as in the form of tables, graphs, etc.

EIT Reconstruction as an Optimization Problem

In the literature, there are several studies where the reconstruction of electrical impedance tomography images is approached as an optimization problem (Cheng, Chen & Tong, 1996; Rolnik & Seleghim-Jr, 2006; Herentry, 2007), Momenté, Peixoto, Tsuzuki & Martins, 2013). For this, it is necessary to use a function that represents as accurately as possible the problem of reconstruction of electrical impedance tomography. The reconstruction is obtained by optimizing this function, which is achieved, by finding the maximum or minimum value of the function. Whether the optimization will be by finding a maximum value or a minimum value will depend on how the function is representing the problem in question.

The function considered for EIT reconstruction in this chapter was the Relative Quadratic Error, which is the function that has been used by the research group of Electric Impedance Tomography of the UFPE (Ribeiro, Feitosa, Souza & Santos, 2014; Feitosa, Ribeiro, Barbosa, Souza & Santos, 2014). In the function, the edge potentials measured in the domain to be imaged and the edge potentials calculated by simulation of an artificially generated image are compared. The closer the error is to zero, the closer the artificial image of the section of the domain in Question, then the objective is to obtain an artificial image with the lowest possible value for the relative quadratic error, thus characterizing a minimization problem. The error function in the optimization method is called the objective function or fitness function ($f_0(x)$) its expression is given in the following equation:

$$f_0(x) = \left[\frac{\sum_{i=1}^{n_e} \left(U_{i(x)} - V_i \right)^2}{\sum_{i=1}^{n_e} \left(V_i \right)^2} \right]^{\frac{1}{2}} \quad (11)$$

$$V = \left(V_1, V_2, \ldots, V_{n_e} \right)^T \quad (12)$$

$$U(x) = \left(U_1(x), U_2(x), \ldots, U_{n_e}(x) \right)^T \quad (13)$$

where represents the generated artificial image, the distribution of measured electrical potentials, the distribution of electrical potentials of edges calculated for the artificial image, and the number of electrodes considered.

The first step in the simulation of EIT image reconstruction is to construct a ground-truth image which we will try to reconstruct through the optimization of the objective function ($f_0(x)$). Then, the direct problem is solved in this image, obtaining the electrical potential values of edge. Current data and electrical potentials are the input parameters of the optimization algorithm, which is responsible for generating a set of artificial images and solving the direct problem in each of the input parameters. The evaluation of the objective function is accomplished for each artificial image generated when comparing its values of electrical potentials with the ground-truth image potential values. Following the concepts of the evolutionary or bio-inspired algorithm, new artificial images will be generated in an iterative process with the objective of obtaining a lower value in the objective function and, consequently, an artificial image closer to the ground-truth image.

Fish School Search

Fish School Search (FSS) algorithm is a meta-heuristic based on fish behavior for food search, developed by Bastos Filho e Lima Neto, in 2007 (Bastos-Filho et al., 2008; Bastos-Filho & Guimarães, 2015). The search process on FSS is made by a population which its individuals (the fishes) have limited memory. Also, each fish in the school represents a point on fitness function domain. The FSS algorithm has four operators that can be classified in two classes: food and swimming.

Food Operator

Aiming to find more food, the fish on the school may move. Therefore, accordingly to its positions, each fish can be heavier or lighter (increase or decrease its weight), depending on how close they are from food (Lins et al., 2012). The food operator, then, quantifies how successful a fish is, due its fitness function variation. The fish weight is given by Equation 14, below:

$$W_i(t+1) = W_i(t) + \frac{f[x_i(t+1)] - f[x_i(t)]}{\max\{|f[x_i(t+1)] - f[x_i(t)]|\}} \tag{14}$$

where $W_i(t)$, $f[x_i(t)]$ represents the fish 'i' weight and its fitness function value at $x_i(t)$, respectively. According to Bastos-Filho et al (2008) the concept of food is related to the fitness function, i.e., in a minimization problem the amount of food in a region is inversely proportional to the function evaluation in this region. Thus, in this case, the fish weight is given by the following expression:

$$W_i(t+1) = W_i(t) + \frac{f[x_i(t)] - f[x_i(t+1)]}{\max\{|f[x_i(t)] - f[x_i(t+1)]|\}} \tag{15}$$

Swimming Operators

The swimming operators are responsible for the fish movements when they are in the food search, and are named as: individual movement operator, collective-instinctive movement operator and collective-volitive movement operator, explained in details as below.

The first swimming operator is the individual movement executed at the beginning of each algorithm's iteration, where each fish is displaced to a random position of its surroundings. An important characteristic of this movement is that the fish only executes the individual movement if the new position, randomly determined, is better than the previous one, meaning that it only occurs if the new position provides a better fitness function value. Otherwise, the fish will not execute the movement.

The individual movement of each fish is given in Equation (16), $rand[-1,1]$ is a vector composed by several numbers randomly generated with values between $[-1,1]$, and $step_{ind}$ is a parameter that represents the fish ability of exploration on the individual movement. After the individual movement's calculus, the fish position is updated by Equation (17).

$$\Delta x_{ind_i}(t+1) = step_{ind} \cdot rand[-1,1] \tag{16}$$

$$x_{ind_i}(t+1) = x_{ind_i}(t) + \Delta x_{ind_i}(t+1) \tag{17}$$

This movement can be understood as a disturbance in the fish position, to guarantee a wider way to explore the search space. Therefore, to assure convergence at the end of the algorithm's operation, the value of $step_{ind}$ linearly decays, accordingly to Equation (18), where $step_{ind_{init}}$ and $step_{ind_{end}}$ are the initial and final values of $step_{ind}$, and, $iterations$ is the maximum iterations possible value of the algorithm.

$$step_{ind}(t+1) = step_{ind}(t+1) - \frac{step_{ind_{init}} - step_{ind_{end}}}{iterations} \quad (18)$$

The second swimming operator of the FSS is the collective-instinctive movement. Is the one where the most well succeeded fishes on their individual movements attracts to themselves other fishes. To execute this movement, it is considered the resultant direction vector, $I(t)$, given by the weighted average of all individual movements of each fish, having as weight, its fitness value variation, given in Equation (19), where N is the total of fishes in the school. In the same way of the feeding operator, in minimization problems the fitness variation in Equation (19) must be inverted. After the direction vector calculation, the fish position is updated, as shown in Equation (20).

$$I(t) = \frac{\sum_{i=1}^{N} \Delta x_{ind_i} f[x_i(t+1)] - f[x_i(t)]}{\sum_{i=1}^{N} f[x_i(t+1)] - f[x_i(t)]} \quad (19)$$

$$x_i(t+1) = x_i(t) + I(t) \quad (20)$$

The collective-volitive movement (the third and the last swimming operator) is based on the school's global performance (Lins et al., 2012). The collective-volitive movement is the tool that provides to the algorithm the ability to adjust the search space radius. Therefore, if the fish global weight increases, the search is characterized as well-succeeded and the fish radius search must diminish; otherwise, the same given search radius must increase, in order to enlarge the fish exploration, aiming to find better regions. In this movement, the fish's position is updated in relation to the school's mass center, as showed in (21).

$$Bary(t) = \frac{\sum_{i=1}^{N} x_i(t) W_i(t)}{\sum_{i=1}^{N} W_i(t)} \quad (21)$$

Still, each fish's movement is made by (22), if the school's weight is increasing, or by Equation (22), if the school's weight is decreasing. Also, in the same equations, mentioned above, $rand[0,1]$ is a vector which values are randomly generated between $[0,1]$, and $step_{vol}$ is the parameter that represents the intensity of the fish search adjust intensity.

$$x(t+1) = x(t) - step_{vol} \cdot rand[0,1](x(t) - Bary(t)) \quad (21)$$

$$x(t+1) = x(t) + step_{vol} \cdot rand[0,1](x(t) - Bary(t)) \quad (22)$$

Fish School Search algorithm's pseudocode is given in Algorithm 1.

Genetic Algorithm

According to Cintra (2007), around 1960 the researcher John Henry Holland created the genetic algorithm (GA) for the study of natural phenomena based on the adaptation of species and natural selection. Such algorithms consist of iterative procedures with potential to obtain good solutions for problems at a time considered acceptable.

The basic structure of the genetic algorithms is formed by genetic operators that follow the biological foundations of Mendel's theories, being these: crossover, mutation and inversion. Implementation of these genetic operators are able to obtain a new generation of individuals (Lopes, 2006; Rolnik & Seleghim, 2006; Carosio et al., 2007; Eberhart & Shi, 2011).

The GA pseudocode is given in Algorithm 2.

The basic concepts of genetic algorithms (GA) are:

1. **Generation of the Initial Population:** According to the literature, the initial population is generated, in its simplest form, by a random model based on the randomness of genes that make up the individual. It is of paramount importance to combat the ambiguity of solutions, avoiding the repeated representation of a same value for individuals (Michalewicz, 1996);
2. **Selection:** The methods used to obtain the intermediate population of individuals, that is, possible solutions of problem under analysis that have been modified by genetic operators, are described below (Michalewicz, 1996):

Table 1. Finish School Search

Algorithm 1: Fish School Search			
1.	Initialize all the fish in random positions		
2.	Repeat the following (a) to (f) until some stopping criterion is met		
	a.	For each fish do:	
		i.	Execute the individual movement
		ii.	Evaluate the fitness function
		iii.	Execute the feeding operator
	b.	Calculate the resulting direction vector - I(t).	
	c.	For each fish do:	
		i.	Execute the collective-instinctive movement
	d.	Calculate the barycenter.	
	e.	For each fish do:	
		i.	Execute the collective-volitive movement
	f.	Update the values of individual and collective-volitive step	
3.	Select the fish in the final school that has better fitness.		

Table 2. Genetic Algorithm

Algorithm 2: Genetic Algorithm		
1.	Initialize a random initial population	
2.	Repeat the following (a) to (e) until the stopping criterion is met	
	a.	Evaluate the fitness function to each individual
	b.	Parent selection: Using Roulette Wheel individuals are selected to be recombined
	c.	Recombination: New individuals are generated through 2-points crossover
	d.	Mutation: gene of descendants is randomly selected and modified.
	e.	Survivor selection: individuals of the next generation are selected using elitism and roulette wheel.
3.	Select the individual's final population that has better fitness	

a. **Roulette:** This method uses the principle of draw to select the individual from the population to compose the next generation, based on the analysis of their aptitude index. Thus, individuals with higher performance will have a greater chance of being chosen for the next generation;

b. **Tournament:** This method seeks to select the individuals to compose the intermediate population through repeated draws until it is filled, where these draws consist of the choice of the individual with the highest aptitude index among n individuals of the population randomly chosen with the same probability (usually $n = 3$);

3. **Crossover**: The crossover is the genetic operator capable of generating one or two children individuals obtained from the exchange of genetic material between parents (Michalewicz, 1996);
4. **Mutation**: The mutation is the genetic operator capable of generating new individuals by modifying one or more genes that compose the individual from the previously chosen population (Michalewicz, 1996);
5. **Stop Criterion**: This operation is a condition used to finalize the convergence of the algorithm, which can be: execution time, number of generations or minimum, average and/or maximum aptitude value (Michalewicz, 1996).

Differential Evolution

The differential Evolution is dedicated to the non-linear functions and non-differential (Price, Storn & Lampinen, 2006). It was created in 1995, when Storn and Price published the article "New Heuristic Approach for Minimizing Possibly Nonlinear and Non-Differentiable Continuous Space Functions" describing the major concepts of differential Evolution (Eiben & Smith, 2015).

To understand the operation of the algorithm, consider a general minimization problem: Be the objective function $f : X \subseteq \mathbb{R}^D \rightarrow \mathbb{R}$, where the subset $X \neq \varnothing$, the resolution objective to find is $x^* \epsilon X$, such that $f\left(x^{*}\right) \leq f\left(x\right) \forall x \leq X$, where $f\left(x^{*}\right) \neq -\infty$. The main steps of the method are: Initialization, Mutation, Recombination and Selection, described below:

- **Initialization:** On this step, we create a set of NP vectors $x_i \epsilon X$ as in the following way:

$$x_{i,G} = \left[x_{1,i,G}, x_{2,i,G}, \ldots, x_{D,i,G}\right] \tag{23}$$

where $i = 1,2,\ldots NP$ and G represents the generation number (the algorithm's iteration number), where, in the initialization we have $G = 1$. The NP number is also known as the population's size. Each vector's component x_i represents a parameter of the addressed problem, in the initialization, these parameters are randomly and uniformly selected within a specific range, as given below:

$$X_j^{Inferior\ Limit} \leq x_{j,i,1} \leq x_j^{Upper\ Limit} \tag{24}$$

where $j = 1,2,\ldots D$, and D is the problem dimension. The values of the lower and upper limits depend on the addressed problem and delimit the space where the algorithm will consider the vectors in their iterations, this space is called search space.

- **Mutation:** for each vector $x_{i,G}$ (called target vector) three vectors are randomly chosen $x_{r1,G}$, $x_{r2,G}$ and $x_{r3,G}$, where $r1, r2, r3 \epsilon \left[0, NP\right]$ are integers and $r1 \neq r2 \neq r3 \neq i$. Then the donor vector, $v_{i,G+1}$, is calculated as given in the Equation (25) (Liu & Sun, 2011):

$$v_{i,G+1} = r_{r1,G} + F\left(r_{r2,G} - r_{r3,G}\right) \tag{25}$$

where F, mutation rate, is a real and constant value, defined before the execution of the algorithm. This parameter controls the amplification of differential variation $\left(r_{r2,G} - r_{r3,G}\right)$. Usually, $F \epsilon \left[0,1\right]$ (Liu & Sun, 2011).

- **Recombination:** With the goal of increasing the vectors diversity within the population, we create the trial vector, $u_{j,i,G+1}$, where we combine the vectors $x_{i,G}$ and $v_{i,G+1}$, as shown in Equation 26.

$$u_{j,i,G+1} = \begin{cases} v_{j,i,G+1}, \text{if } rand_j \leq CR \text{ ou } j = rnbr\left(i\right) \\ x_{j,i,G}, \text{if } rand_j > CR \text{ ou } j \neq rnbr\left(i\right) \end{cases} \tag{26}$$

where $j = 1,2,...,D$, $CR \epsilon \left[0,1\right]$ is the recombination rate defined by the user, $rand_j$ is a random number generated within range $\left[0,1\right]$, $rnbr\left(i\right)$ is a value randomly chosen between $\left[1,D\right]$ which guarantees that $u_{j,i,G+1}$ receives values from the parameters of both vectors (Liu & Sun, 2011).

- **Selection:** to decide if the vector $u_{j,i,G+1}$ will become member of the next generation's population $\left(G+1\right)$ it will be compared with the vector $x_{i,G}$. If $u_{j,i,G+1}$ provides us with a value, in the objective function, smaller than $x_{i,G}$, then, $x_{i,G+1}$ will receive the trial vector, otherwise, it will receive the generation G vector (Liu & Sun, 2011), mathematically, we have this comparison in the equation below:

$$x_{i,G+1} = \begin{cases} u_{i,G+1}, \text{if } f\left(u_{i,G+1}\right) \leq f\left(x_{i,G}\right) \\ x_{i,G}, \quad \text{otherwise} \end{cases} \tag{27}$$

It is important to remember that the trial vector is compared with $x_{i,G}$, as shown in Equation (27), for it is a minimization problem. In case of a maximization problem, the comparison is done as shown in Equation (28).

$$x_{i,G+1} = \begin{cases} u_{i,G+1}, \text{if } f\left(u_{i,G+1}\right) \geq f\left(x_{i,G}\right) \\ x_{i,G}, \quad \text{otherwise} \end{cases} \tag{28}$$

Mutation, recombination and selection will continue until a stopping criteria is reached. In Algorithm 3 is given the pseudocode of the Differential Evolution.

Non-Blind Search

According to Saha and Bandyopadhyay (2008), it is possible to accelerate the process of convergence of optimization algorithms and to avoid very random search, from the inclusion of solutions obtained from simple and direct imprecise methods to the initial population of candidate solutions, this method is known as non-blind search.

The use of Evolutionary Computing and Swarm Intelligence techniques to solve the misaligned inverse problem of TIE can obtain reasonable solutions using a small number of iterations when the initial population involves a candidate solution constructed using noisy versions of the solution obtained by Gauss-Newton method (Feitosa et al., 2014; Ribeiro et al., 2014; Barbosa et al., 2017).

Gauss-Newton method is considered the most efficient method known to solve nonlinear least squares problems (Gonçalves, 2011) (Adler et al., 2007). Let X and Y be real or complex spaces of Hibert, $\Omega \epsilon X$ an open set and $F : \Omega \rightarrow Y$ a differentiable Fréchet. The problem can be considered as a nonlinear least squares.

Table 3. Differential Evolution

Algorithm 3: Differential Evolution			
1.	Generate vectors with real numbers to create the initial set		
2.	Evaluate the objective function for all the vectors		
3.	Repeat until a stopping criteria is reached		
	a.	For each vector of the set, do	
		i.	Mutation: choose three vectors for the calculation of the donor vector
		ii.	Recombination: combination of the target vector and the donor vector to generate the trial vector
		iii.	Evaluate the objective function for the trial vector
		iv.	Selection: choose the best vector between the target vector and the trial vector
4.	Choose the best vector in the final set as a solution		

$$minF\left(x\right)^2 \tag{29}$$

If $F'\left(x\right)$ is an injective function and has closed image for every $x \epsilon$ ©, the Gauss-Newton method finds stationary points for problem (29), i.e., the solution for the system of linear equations given by:

$$F'\left(x\right) * F\left(x\right) = 0 \tag{30}$$

where $B*$ corresponds to the adjacent matrix of operator B. Formally the Gauss-Newton method is described as $x_0 \epsilon$ ©. Given then:

$$x_{k+1} = x_k + S_k,\ \ F'\left(x_k\right) * F'\left(x_k\right) S_k = -F'\left(x_k\right) * F'\left(x_k\right),\ \ k = 0,1,\ldots \tag{31}$$

It is important to note that x^* is the solution of (29). On the other hand, note that each step of the Gauss-Newton method consists of solving a system of linear equations, which can be computationally very "expensive" if the number of unknowns is too large. An alternative is to directly solve a linear reconstruction matrix that describes the problem (Adler et al., 2007), which gives rise to a new class of iterative Gauss-Newton process known as Gauss-Newton One-Step. This method tries to solve the problem of the least squares in a single step, in case the inverse problem of the EIT is defined as

$$y - J\hat{x}^2_{\underset{n}{\Sigma}^{-1}} + y - Jx^{o2}_{\underset{n}{\Sigma}^{-1}} \tag{32}$$

$$y = Jx + n \tag{33}$$

where x^o is the expected value of conductivity of the element, $\sum_n \epsilon\, \mathbb{R}^{n_M X n_M}$ is the covariance matrix of the measured noise n, $\sum_x \epsilon\, \mathbb{R}^{n_M X n_M}$ is the covariance of the expected image, $J \epsilon\, \mathbb{R}^{n_M X n_M}$ is the Jacobian matrix, x is the conductivity change vector, y is the potential change vector is the solution of the inverse problem of EIT.

Solving problem (32), the inverse solution of Gauss-newton One-Step is obtained as

$$\hat{x} = \left(J^T \frac{1}{\sigma_n^2} WJ + \frac{1}{\sigma_x^2} R \right)^{-1} J^T \frac{1}{\sigma_n^2} Wy \tag{34}$$

where $W = \sigma_n^2 \sum_n^{-1}$, $W = \sigma_x^2 \sum_x^{-1}$, σ_n is the measure of the amplitude of the noise and σ_n is the amplitude of the conductivity.

Electrical Impedance Tomography and Diffuse Optical Tomography Reconstruction Software

Electrical Impedance Tomography and Diffuse Optical Tomography Reconstruction Software (EIDORS) is an open source software developed for MATLAB/Octave that has as goal to solve the direct and inverse problems of the electrical impedance tomography and diffuse optical tomography (Adler & Lionheart, 2006; Vauhkonen, Lionheart, Heikkinen, Vauhkonen, & Kaipio, 2001). This software allows its free modification, thus, we can easily adapt it to the problem of this work.

This software contains a several public access algorithms that can be used to solve the inverse problem of EIT, how is described in GREIT (Adler et al., 2009), Gauss-Newton (Adler et al., 2007), NOSER (Cheney et al., 1990) e Backprojection (Santosa and Vogelius, 1990). With EIDORS it is possible to simulate different kinds of meshes of finite elements that represents computationally one cross-section of an object as well as its internal conductivity distribution in the form of colors.

Proposed Method and Experiments

Using EIDORS, three ground-truth images were created with meshes of 415, 3190 and 9990 finite elements. The goal was detecting irregular objects isolated in three positions: in the center, between the center and the edge and on the edge of the circular domain. The EIDORS parameters to create these images were: 16 electrodes, two-dimensional mesh (2D) with elements density 'b', 'd' and 'g', for meshes with 415, 3190 and 9990 finite elements and electrode refinement level '2'. Figure 1 shows the nine ground-truth images considered in this work.

Each ground-truth image were reconstructed by the methods described in this chapter (Fish School Search, Genetic Algorithm and Differential Evolution), to observe the main behavior of the methods, the authors performed twenty (20) simulations for each image and each method considered. The relative squared error was used between the distribution of electrical potentials measured and calculated at the edge as fitness function for the heuristics considered in this work. Solution candidates are real-valued vectors utilized as theoretical abstractions for possible distributions conductivity, where each dimension of the vector corresponds to a particular finite element on the mesh.

For the simulations using Fish School Search, 100 fishes (solution candidates) were set as the school's population, and the following parameters were defined: $W_0 = 100$, $step_{ind_{init}} = 0.01$, $step_{ind_{init}} = 0.0001$ and $step_{vol} = 2step_{ind}$. Whereas for the genetic algorithm we used a population with 100 individuals, selection for the 10 best evaluated individuals, probability of recombination and mutation in 100% and elitism of 10 individuals. Finally, for differential evolution it was used a set of 100 vectors, $F=0.5$ and $CR=0.9$. The stop criterion for all methods was the number of iterations in 500 iterations.

RESULTS AND DISCUSSION

In this section it will be presented the obtained results of EIT image reconstruction by executing the following search and optimization methods: Genetic Algorithms, Simple Differential Evolution, non-blind search Differential Evolution, simple Fish School Search and non-blind Fish School Search. The obtained results are evaluated under quali and quantitative analysis. From the qualitative perspective, the reconstructed images are visually compared with their ground-truth images. This is done to confirm if the generated images are, really, similar to their ground-truth ones. On the other hand, the qualitative analysis is performed by the observation of the decreasing of the relative error of the best solution candidate along the iterations of the evaluated techniques. They are calculated by the same objective function, independent of the search technique implemented.

Firstly, it will be analysed the quali and quantitative results regarding the mesh containing 415 elements. The first results to be presented, are the images which were reconstructed by the methods. These images are shown in the Figures 2, 3, 4 and 5. They show the reconstructed images using Fish School Search and Non-Blind Fish School Search, Genetic Algorithms, and Differential Evolution, respectively. For each ground-truth image, it were obtained partial generated images at 50 and 300 iterations of the used search algorithm as well as the reconstructed image at 500 iterations. These images are the image generated from the candidate solution with the best objective function evaluation at determined number of iterations. The objective of extracting the partial best solution is to evaluate the performance of the algorithm along the convergence process.

The organization of the Figures 2, 3, 4 and 5 is done as follows: the obtained images aiming to reconstruct the ground-truth center image have the subindex (a); the ones related to the ground-truth between the center and the border have the subindex (b); and the ones related to the border ground-truth have the subindex (c). Regarding the iteration number, the obtained images at 50, 300 and 500 iterations, are identified by the numbers 1, 2 and 3, respectively. For instance, the image located at (c2) is the reconstructed image at 300 iterations for the object placed at the border of the circular domain.

By considering the reconstructed images, it is possible to notice that for the 415 element mesh, all the methods could generate anatomically consistent images at 500 iterations. However, for 50 iterations, despite of its low resolution, the FSS+NBS could identify the objects from the ground-truth images. At the same iteration number, the FSS could get only one satisfactory result. This one was regarding the border ground-truth. This technique, on the other cases (between the center and the border and at the center), could not identify the object. Thus, it can be observed that the implementation of the Non-Blind search could accelerate the search process. For the other techniques, the obtained images at 50 iterations were noisy and anatomically less expressives.

Figure 1. Ground-truth images for the object placed in the center, between the center and the edge and on the edge of the circular domain with a mesh with (a) 415 (b) 3190 and (c) 9990 finite elements

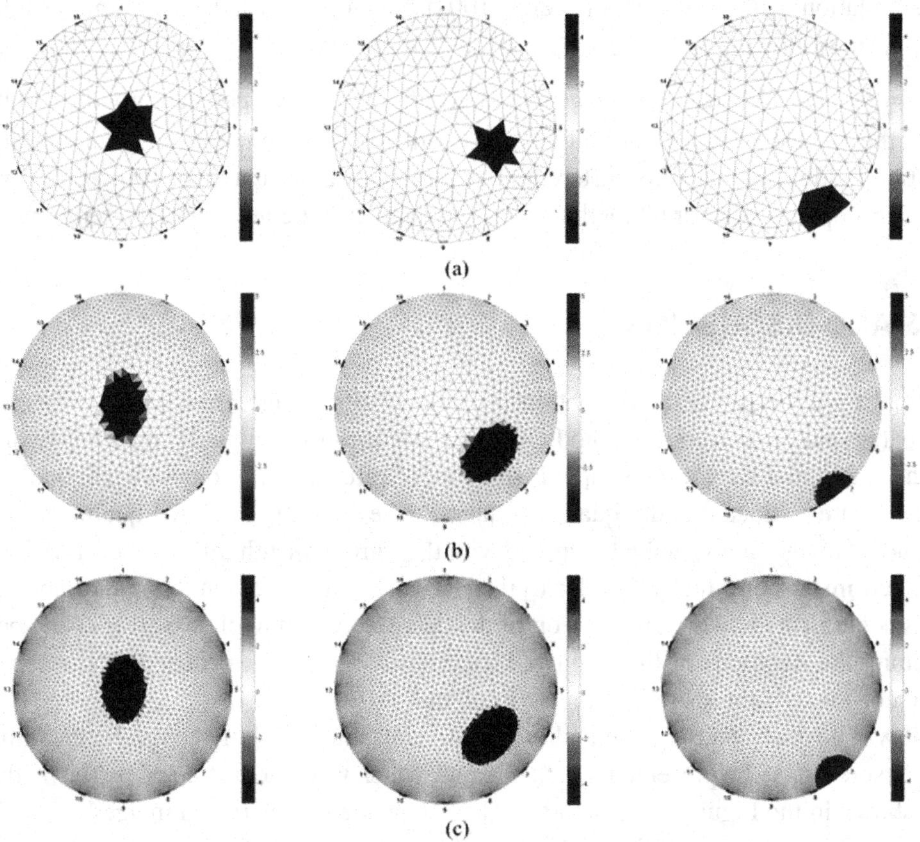

**For a more accurate representation see the electronic version.*

In the case of 300 iterations, all the methods could locate the objects in their reconstructed images. The main differences among the 300 iterations images, were the noise level (the blur around the objects) present in the reconstructed images, and the size of the objects. Among results for this iterations number, the obtained image by using FSS+NBS, in which the size of the objects is close to the real size (ground-truth) and there is a low noise level. Other good results were obtained by using FSS and dFSS, however, the obtained objects were bigger than the real and the obtained images by using FSS-NBS. The GA and DE have obtained deformed objects and with varied sizes when related to the ground-truth images. Those images were, also, more noisy when compared with the other techniques.

Finally, at 500 iterations, it can be noticed that the GA and the FSS+NBS outperformed the others by obtaining low noise and real size close images. The FSS also could get low noise images when compared to the FSS+NBS images, however, it has obtained objects which were bigger than the real size. While that the DE obtained images were noisy and with anatomically deformed objects when searched the center and the between the center and the border ground-truth. At the search of the border ground truth the DE was successful. Besides that, it can be observed that the FSS and FSS+NBS methods could obtain images at 500 iterations, which are shortly different from the ones obtained at 300 iterations, in other words, the generated images at 300 and 5000 iterations are similar.

Figure 2. Results using FSS for an object placed in the center (a1, a2 and a3), between the center and the edge (b1, b2 and b3) and on the edge (c1, c2 and c3) of the circular domain for 50, 300 and 500 iterations for a mesh with 415 finite elements

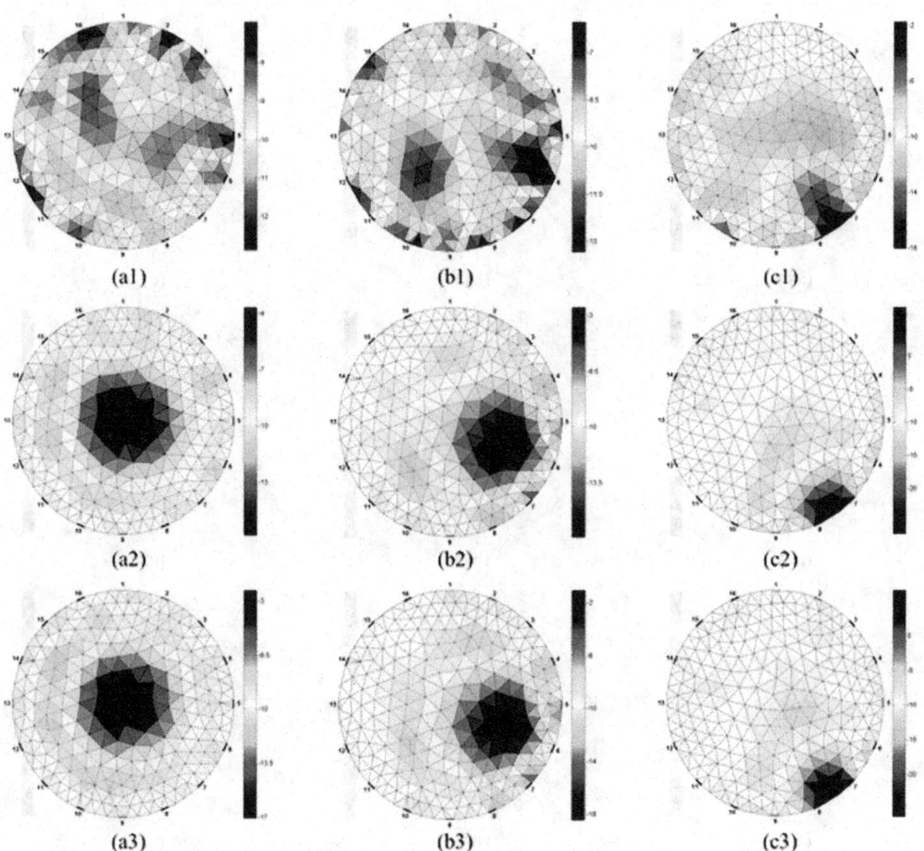

**For a more accurate representation see the electronic version.*

Quantitatively, the algorithm performance could be evaluated through the graphs of objective function value (the mean square error) as a function of number of iterations considered.

To accomplish these graphs, 20 simulations were performed for each method and for each gold standard image, so the generated graphs show the average behavior of the algorithms in 20 simulations. Figures 6, 7 and 8 show the graphs of relative error drop as a function of the number of iterations. In these graphs, the average fall of the relative error for genetic GA is given by the black curve, the DE is represented by the red curve, the search for FSS is given by the green curve And with local search (FSS + NBS) for the blue curve.

The graphs given in Figures 6, 7 and 8 allow us to evaluate the behavior of these methods according to the search process convergence. From the graphs, it can be observed that the convergence of methods resemble to an exponential decay. In addition, the curves for FSS and FSS + NBS overlap in some iterations, however, at the beginning of the search process, the FSS + NBS curve obtained slightly lower values than the FSS. Actually, FSS and FSS + NBS were the methods that achieved the lowest values of the objective function with a smaller number of iterations, followed by DE and GA. However, among the evaluated methods, GA was the method with more pronounced decrease of the relative error, and with

Figure 3. Results using FSS+NBS for an object placed in the center (a1, a2 and a3), between the center and the edge (b1, b2 and b3) and on the edge (c1, c2 and c3) of the circular domain for 50, 300 and 500 iterations for a mesh with 415 finite elements

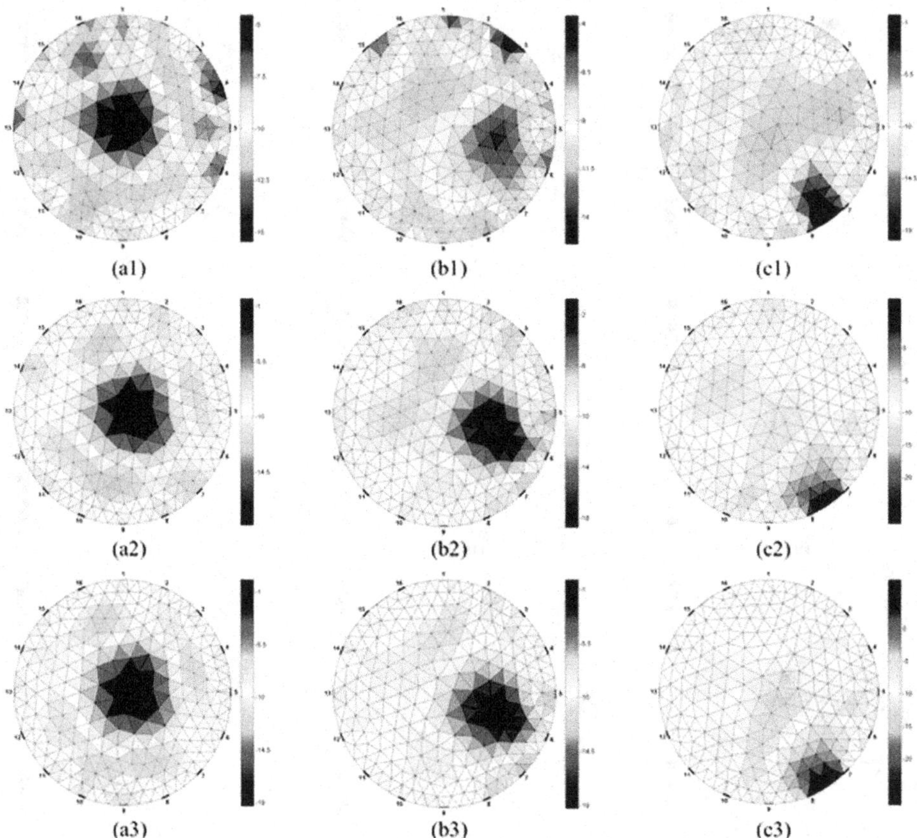

**For a more accurate representation see the electronic version.*

the advancement of the search process, the results for GA surpassed the results of DE and equated to the results of FSS and FSS + NBS. Furthermore, through the graphs, it can be observed that between 300 and 500 iterations for the FSS and FSS + NBS methods. The relative error drop is slightly accentuated and significant, which confirms what was observed by the images reconstructed by these methods. The images in 500 iterations are not very different from the images obtained in 300 iterations.

Table 4 shows some data referring to the 20 simulations made by the FSS, FSS + NBS, GA and DE methods using the 415 finite element mesh. These data represent, regard to the objective function value, the best and worst candidate for the solution, and also from the 20 simulations the average of all candidates for the solution and the average time (in minutes) for all reconstructions considered. From the table, it can be observed that GA and FSS with non-blind search obtained the lowest individual value in the objective function, GA for the object on the edge and FSS + NBS for the object positioned in the center and between the center and the edge of the domain.When analyzing the worst individuals for the FSS + NBS, it can be observed that there were discrepancies during the search process, being these values obtained precisely by the solution candidates that were inserted into the set resulting from the Gauss-Newton method. The reason for this is still unknown to the authors. On the reconstruction time,

Figure 4. Results using GA for an object placed in the center (a1, a2 and a3), between the center and the edge (b1, b2 and b3) and on the edge (c1, c2 and c3) of the circular domain for 50, 300 and 500 iterations for a mesh with 415 finite elements.

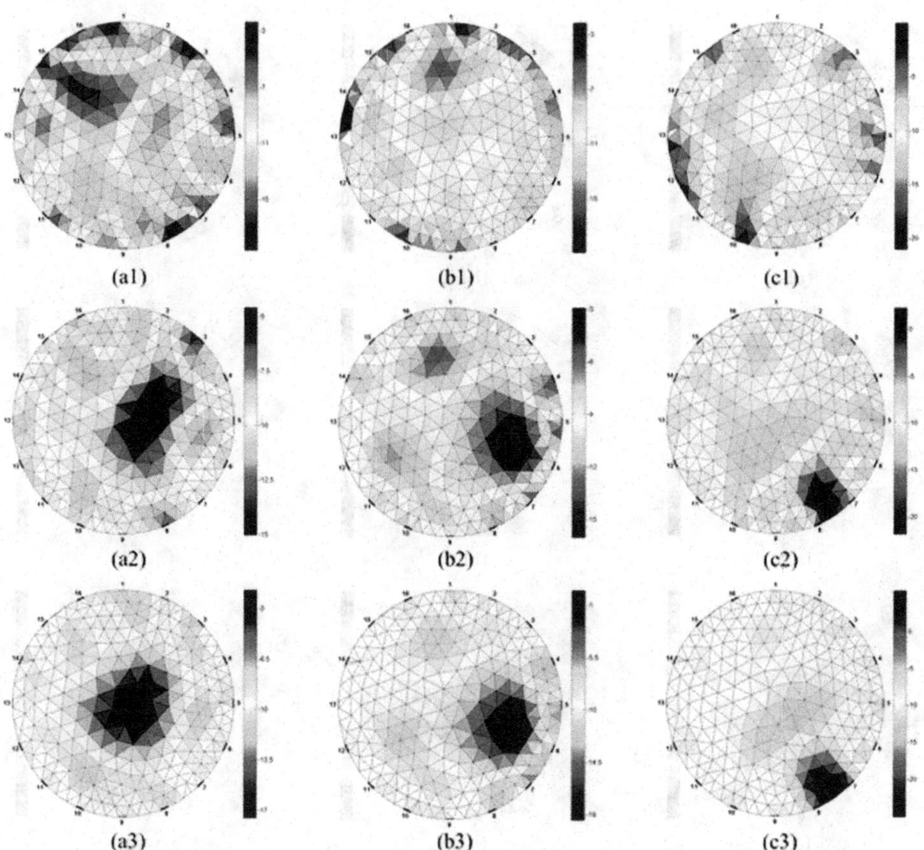

**For a more accurate representation see the electronic version.*

it can be observed that the differential evolution was the technique which had the minor reconstruction time, with values between 48 and 49 minutes. The second method with minor time was the Genetic Algorithm, with times between 64 and 65 minutes. FSS and FSS+NBS were the slowest methods with execution times between 83 and 87 minutes.

Following the same organization of the images for the mesh with 415 elements, the obtained reconstructed images using the mesh of 3190 elements are shown in the Figures 9, 10, 11, 12 and 13 using the Fish School Search without (FSS) and with (FSS + NBS) non-blind search, genetic algorithms (GA), differential evolution without (DE) and with (DE + NBS) non-blind search, respectively.

When analyzing the reconstructed images, it is observed that, for 50 iterations, also for the mesh of 415 elements, the FSS+NBS method stood out for being able to identify the objects, along with images of better resolution, therefore, the FSS also could identify all objects, although, deformed and larger than the actual size. For the image with the object in the boundary, the DE method also achieved satisfactory results, yet it failed for other settings. Meanwhile, GA got noisy and anatomically unexpressive images.

At 300 iterations, excepting the Genetic Algorithm, the other techniques could identity the objects located at the three places. The GA could identify only the border placed ground-truth object. The

Figure 5. Results using DE for an object placed in the center (a1, a2 and a3), between the center and the edge (b1, b2 and b3) and on the edge (c1, c2 and c3) of the circular domain for 50, 300 and 500 iterations for a mesh with 415 finite elements.

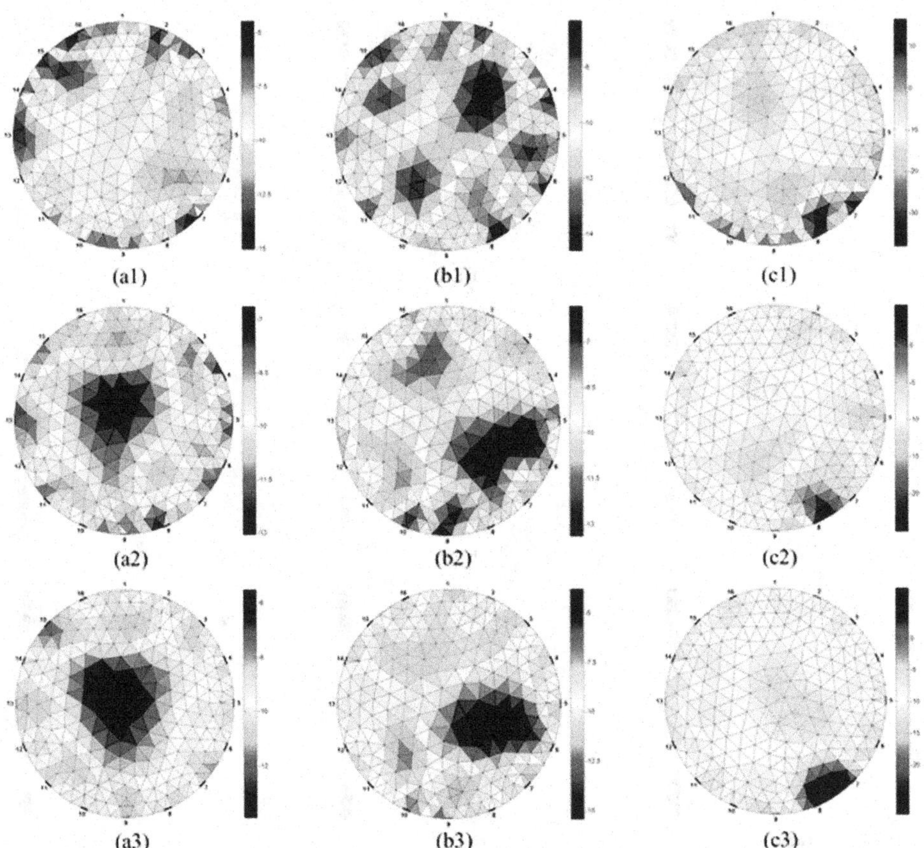

**For a more accurate representation see the electronic version.*

FSS+NBS overperformed the other techniques by generating images with approximated size to the ground-truth objects. The DE and FSS results were also satisfactory, different among themselves regarding the size and noise of the generated objects. Besides, it can be noticed that at the object between the center and the border, the FSS generated a bigger object, almost reaching the border of the domain.

Finally, in 500 iterations, the genetic algorithm was able to reconstruct only the image for the object at the edge and failing for other two images. For the other methods, the images obtained in 500 iterations are slight modifications of the images obtained in 300 iterations, being satisfactory images. Again FSS+NBS excelled at obtaining images with good resolution, anatomically consistent with the shape and size of the objects. The method also excelled by achieving images, for the standards with the object in the edge and in between the center and edge, with the size of the object close to the real. With respect to the FSS, the method obtained a object with good size to the center and edge standards, however, for the object between the center and edge the reconstruction was of an object of greater size. What can be concluded from the fact that GA has achieved good results for the mesh of 415 finite elements and have obtained poor results for the mesh of 3190 elements is that the operators considered in GA method are not dedicated to problems of this order of complexity, that is, with real vectors of high dimension. This

Figure 6. Average error of 20 simulations in function of the number of iterations for the object in the center of the domain using FSS, FSS+NBS, AG, DE and DE+NBS

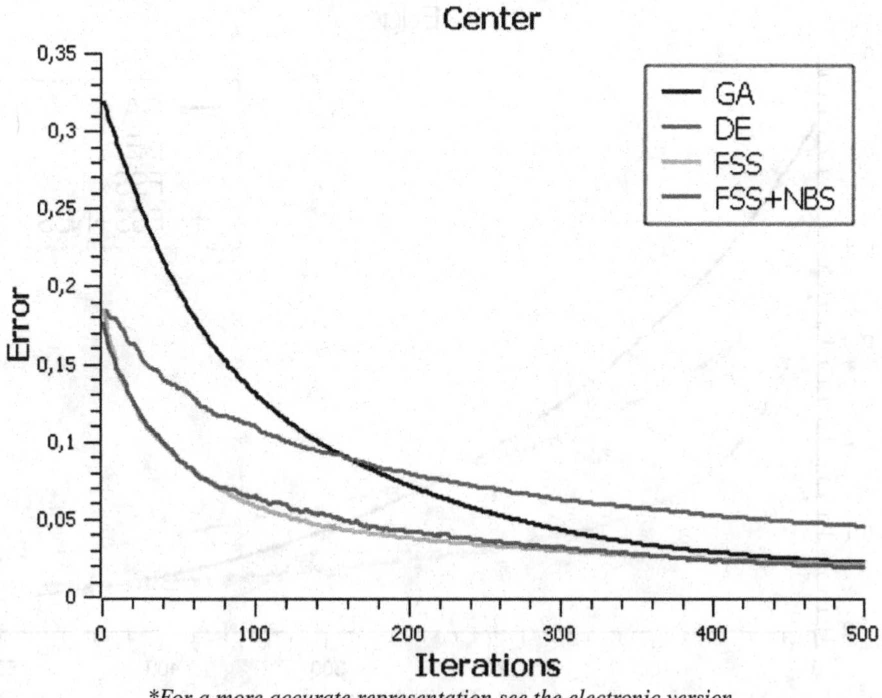

**For a more accurate representation see the electronic version.*

Figure 7. Average error of 20 simulations in function of the number of iterations for the object between the center and the edge of the domain using FSS, FSS+NBS, AG, DE and DE+NBS

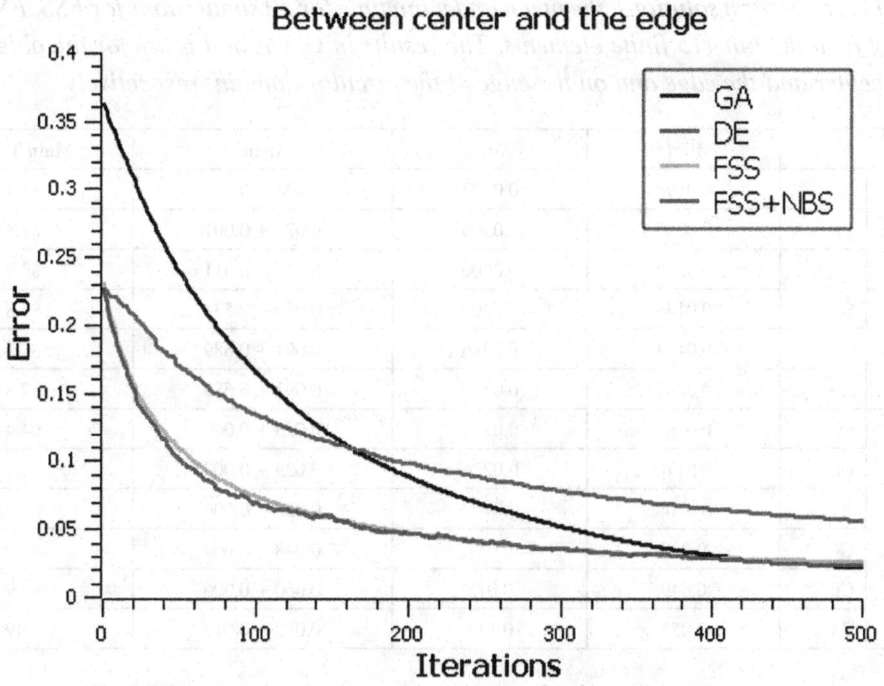

Between center and the edge

GA
DE
FSS
FSS+NBS

Error

0.4
0.35
0.3
0.25
0.2
0.15
0.1
0.05
0

0
100
200
300
400
500

Iterations

**For a more accurate representation see the electronic version.*

Figure 8. Average error of 20 simulations in function of the number of iterations for the object on the edge of the domain using FSS, FSS+NBS, AG, DE and DE+NBS

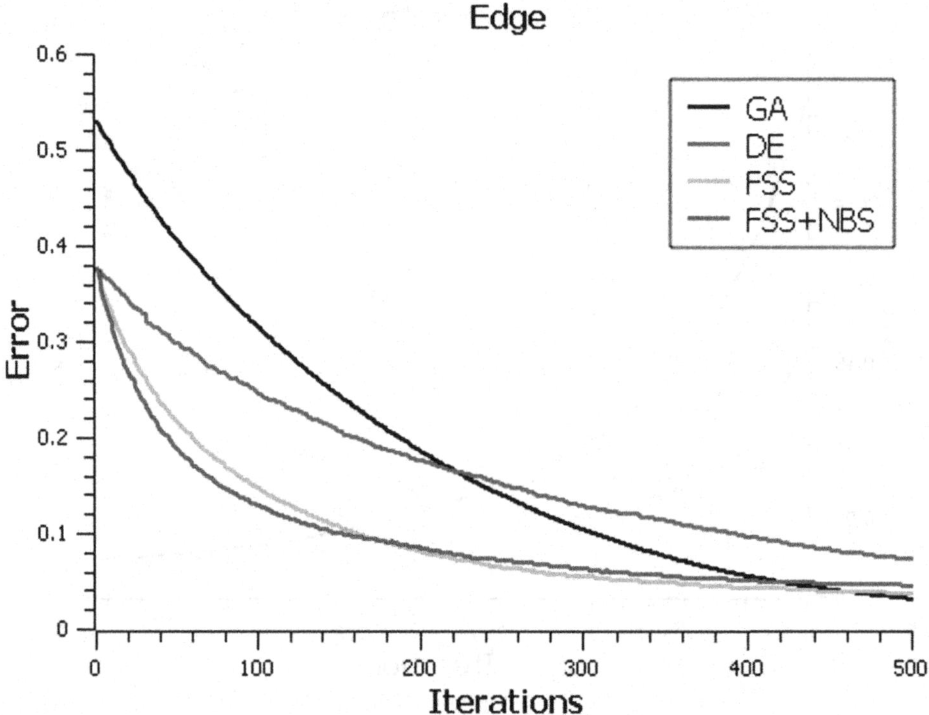

*For a more accurate representation see the electronic version.

Table 4. The best and worst solutions, the mean and main time for 20 simulations for FSS, FSS+NBS, GA and DE using a mesh with 415 finite elements. The results in C, CE and E are for the object in center, between the center and the edge and on the edge of the circular domain, respectively

		Best	Worst	Mean	Main Time (min)
FSS	C	0.0198	0.0242	0.023 ± 0.001	83.1 ± 1.5
	CE	0.0245	0.0306	0.027 ± 0.001	87.3 ± 1.2
	E	0.0242	0.0600	0.045 ± 0.011	83.7 ± 1.4
FSS+NBS	C	0.0148	0.0308	0.055 ± 0.538	85.8 ± 1.7
	CE	0.0174	0.0286	0.091 ± 0.689	87.1 ± 2.2
	E	0.0376	0.0590	0.091 ± 0.689	87.8 ± 1.6
GA	C	0.0182	0.0279	0.023 ± 0.003	64.4 ± 2.9
	CE	0.0176	0.0276	0.023 ± 0.003	65.1 ± 2.2
	E	0.0208	0.0467	0.032 ± 0.006	64.3 ± 3.1
DE	C	0.038	0.057	0.048 ± 0.004	48.2 ± 2.3
	CE	0.049	0.075	0.060 ± 0.006	48.9 ± 1.7
	E	0.053	0.115	0.082 ± 0.013	49 ± 2

Figure 9. Results using FSS for an object placed in the center (a1, a2 and a3), between the center and the edge (b1, b2 and b3) and on the edge (c1, c2 and c3) of the circular domain with 3190 finite elements for 50, 300 and 500 iterations for a mesh with 3190 finite elements

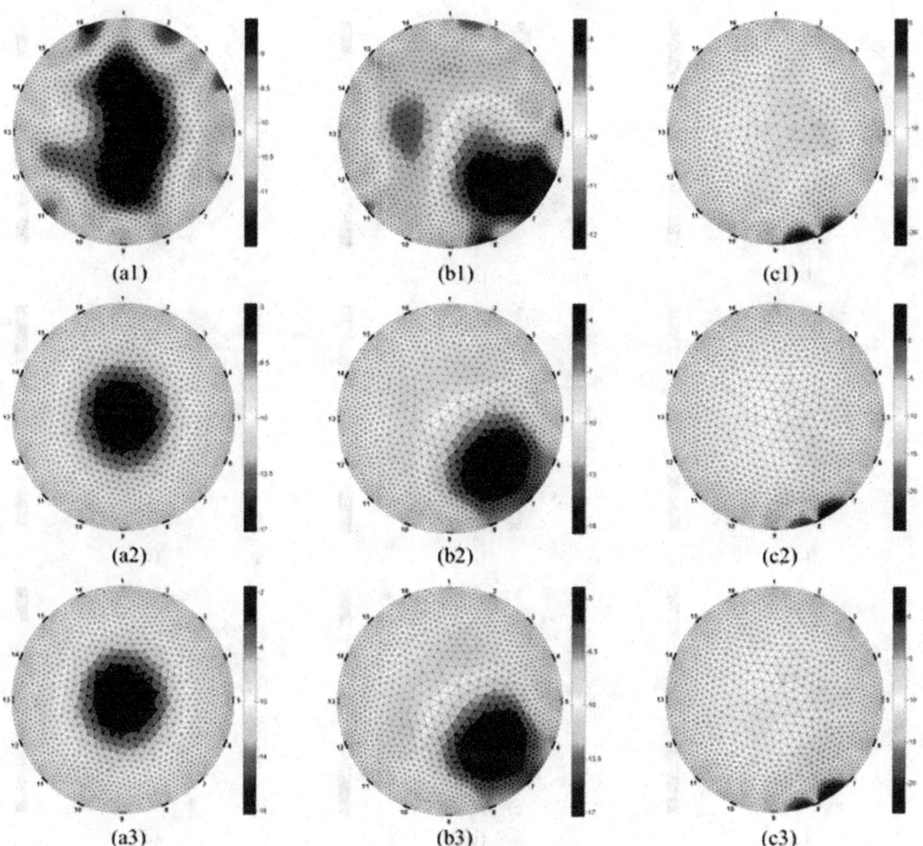

**For a more accurate representation see the electronic version.*

is because by increasing the number of finite elements there is consequently an increase in the complexity of the problem. However, the the Differential Evolution method obtained better results using a 3910 mesh than one of 415 finite elements. Because of this, the authors decided to investigate the behavior of the method with the non-blind search. Figure 13 shows the reconstructed images using Differential Evolution with non-blind search (DE + NBS). Comparing the results presented in Figures 12 and 13 (results for DE and DE + NBS), it can be observed that the implementation of the non-blind search made the differential evolution method achieve better results for the object in the edge and in between the center and the edge. For, in these cases, the obtained objects have sizes closer to the original size.

Quantitatively, the results of algorithms can be analyzed by the graphs given in Figures 14, 15 and 16. In the same way for the mesh with 415 finite elements, 20 simulations were executed for each method and for each gold standard image and the curves shown in the graphs are the mean values obtained for the error as a function of the number of iterations. For all graphs, the avarage decay of the relative error for genetic algorithms (GA) is given by the black curve, the pure differential evolution (DE) is represented by the red curve and with local search (DE+NBS) by the cyan curve, the pure fish school search (FSS) is given by the green curve and with local search (FSS+NBS) by the blue curve.

Figure 10. Results using FSS+NBS for an object placed in the center (a1, a2 and a3), between the center and the edge (b1, b2 and b3) and on the edge (c1, c2 and c3) of the circular domain with 3190 finite elements for 50, 300 and 500 iterations for a mesh with 3190 finite elements

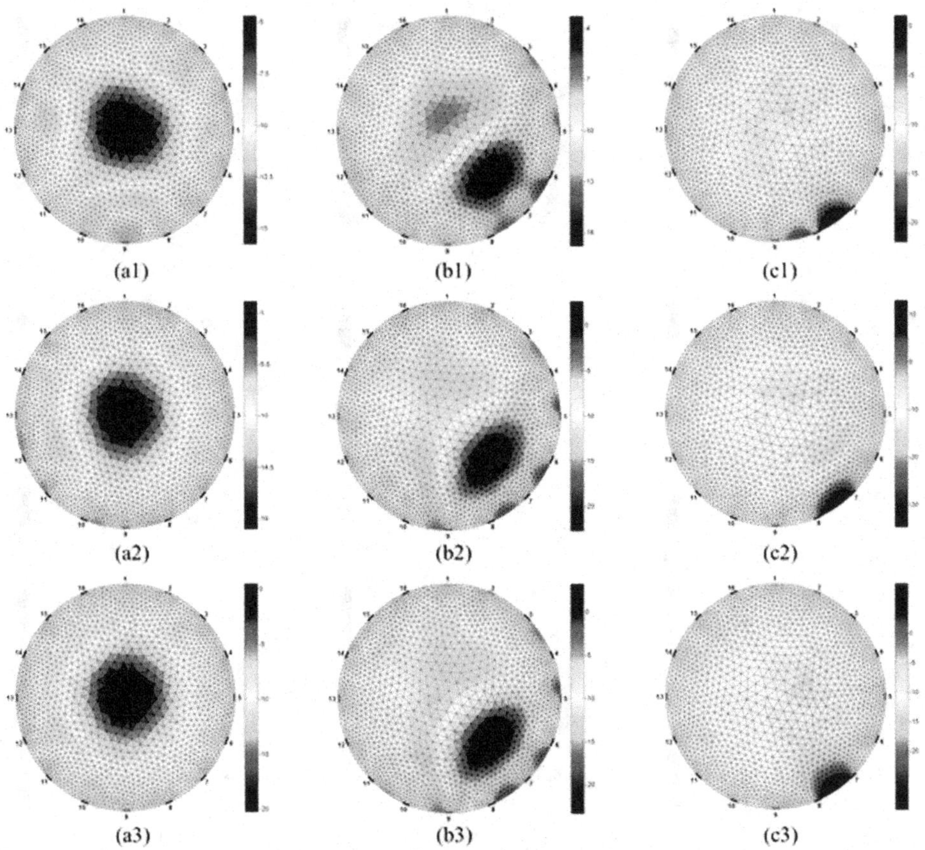

For a more accurate representation see the electronic version.

Analyzing the graphs is notorious the high values and the low decay rate of the curves obtains by GA, corroborating with the images obtained shown in Figure 11 and indicating that the method was not able to reconstruct the gold standard images using the mesh of 3190 elements. Considering that the curve is decreasing, one hypothesis to be considered is that 500 iterations are not enough for the method to reconstruct the EIT images with the finite elements mesh of that size. In contrast to the results for 415 elements, it can be observed that some curves obtained by the methods, such as GA and FSS+NBS, are not similar to an decreasing exponential, however, the curves obtained by FSS, DE, and DE+NBS are similar to an exponential. In the same way as seen for the mesh with fewer elements, the method FSS+NBS was able to obtain lower results in initial iterations. The lowest values, on average, were obtained by the DE (object at the edge) and FSS (object in the center and object in between center and edge). It is interesting to observe that for the object at the edge the decay rate of the curve for DE method in initial iterations of reconstruction is not very expressive, but with the passing of process the rate increases and DE is able to surpass the results of FSS and FSS+NBS. On the overlap of the FSS and FSS+NBS curves seen for the graphs with 415 elements, for the graphs with 3190 elements this overlap is not observed anymore, existing a more significant distance between the curves.

Figure 11. Results using GA for an object placed in the center (a1, a2 and a3), between the center and the edge (b1, b2 and b3) and on the edge (c1, c2 and c3) of the circular domain with 3190 finite elements for 50, 300 and 500 iterations for a mesh with 3190 finite elements

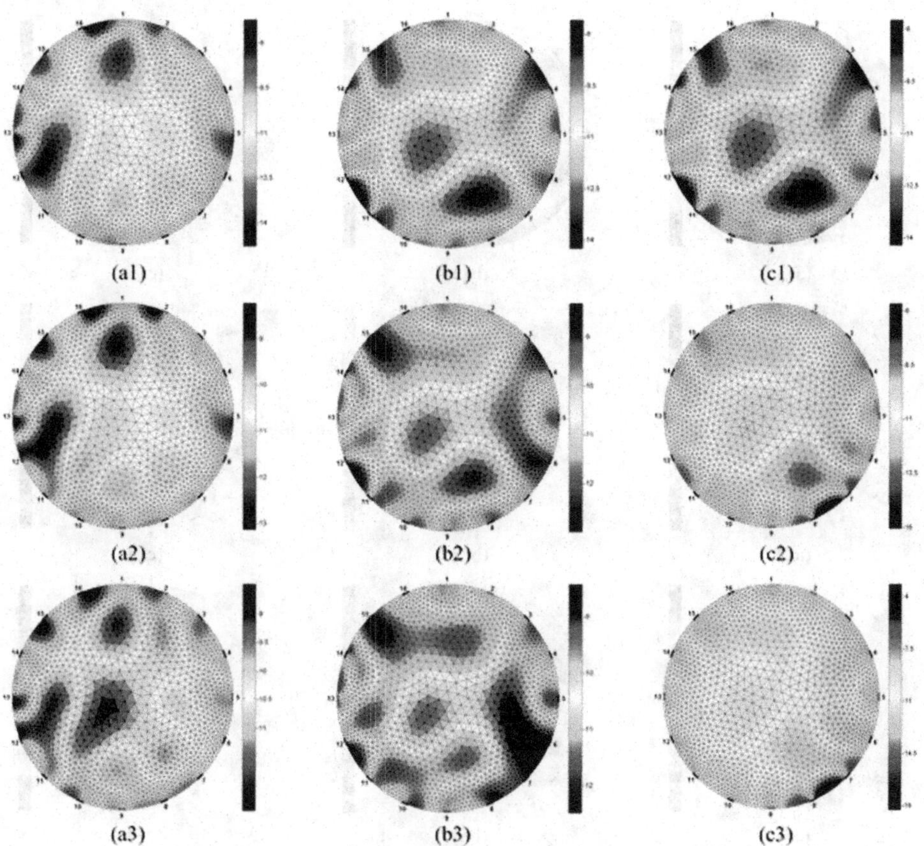

**For a more accurate representation see the electronic version.*

In the Table 5, similarly to Table 4, are shown the the best and worst solution candidates, the average error and and the average time (minutes). Those data are regarding the 20 executions made for each technique (FSS, FSS+NBS, GA, DE e DE+NBS) using the 3190 element mesh. It can be observed that the Differential Evolution and the Fish School Search, when implemented with non-blind search, generated solutions with best objective function values, being the DE+NBS to the border ground-truth, and the FSS+NBS to the center and between the center and the border placed object. Similarly to the Table 1, there were discrepancies during the search process of the FSS+NBS, which resulted in solutions with worse objective function values. Therefore, the worst considered values were resulted from FSS+NBS.

Regarding the reconstruction time, by increasing the quantity of elements in the mesh, it was expected that the reconstruction time also increases. By comparing the reconstruction times shown in the Tables 1 and 2, it can be observed that did not happened. Actually, the reconstruction times of the techniques in a mesh with 3190 elements, remained very close to the reconstruction times in a mesh with 415 elements. The GA, DE and DE+NBS reconstructed in less time, while FSS and FSS+NBS reconstructed in more time.

Figure 12. Results using DE for an object placed in the center (a1, a2 and a3), between the center and the edge (b1, b2 and b3) and on the edge (c1, c2 and c3) of the circular domain with 3190 finite elements for 50, 300 and 500 iterations for a mesh with 3190 finite elements

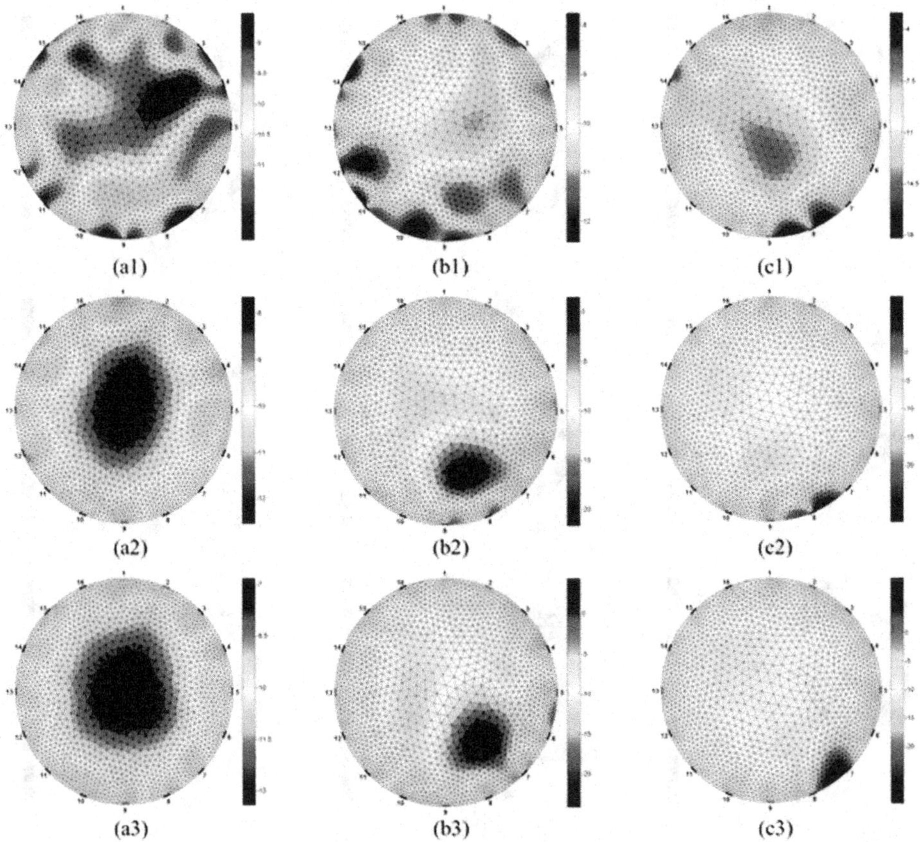

**For a more accurate representation see the electronic version.*

Finally, it was evaluated the performance of the techniques FSS+NBS and DE+NBS when using an elements mesh of size bigger than the other cases. Those experiments have shown that the image reconstruction time was also bigger than the others. That was the reason why those two methods were additionally evaluated. The Figures 17 and 18 show the reconstructed images by using FSS+NBS and DE+NBS, respectively, using a 9990 elements mesh. Comparing those images, it is possible to notice the capacity of the Fish School Search of handling high dimensional problems. This was verified since the obtained images from FSS+NBS were better in terms of object size and noise level, from the DE+NBS images.

The quantitative results, from the simulations using a higher mesh, are shown in the Figure 19. From the graphic, it is possible to notice that the significant increasing of the finite elements, resulted

Figure 13. Results using DE+NBS for an object placed in the center (a1, a2 and a3), between the center and the edge (b1, b2 and b3) and on the edge (c1, c2 and c3) of the circular domain with 3190 finite elements for 50, 300 and 500 iterations for a mesh with 3190 finite elements

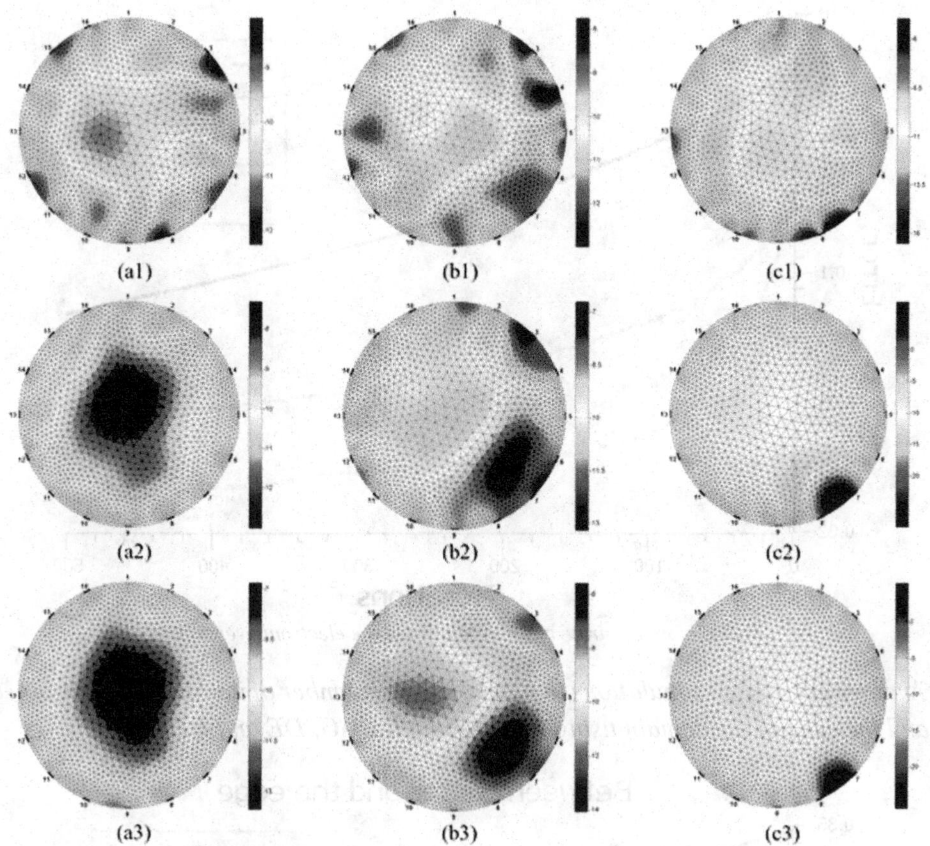

**For a more accurate representation see the electronic version.*

in bigger error rates. Regarding the curve shapes, they are similar to the curves obtained by using the 3190 element mesh. It is important to notice that FSS+NBS had an increasing error fall during the first iterations, but is at the 100th iteration (approximately), that the method starts to diverge. On the other hand, the DE+NBS has a minor error fall, but this fall remains along all the search process.

Regarding the best and worst obtained solution, the average relative error of the solution as well as the average simulation time by using a 9990 elements mesh are shown in the Table 6. These results show that the FSS+NBS kept the same behavior shown when using the 3190 mesh and diverged. Regarding the reconstruction time, the significant increasing of finite elements resulted in a considerable increasing of the simulations duration. By analyzing the data in the table, it is possible to notice that the simulations, when using DE+NBS lasted between 117 and 119 minutes, while the FSS+NBS lasted between 234 and 238 minutes.

Figure 14. Average error of 20 simulations in function of the number of iterations for the object in the center of the domain using FSS, FSS+NBS, AG, DE and DE+NBS

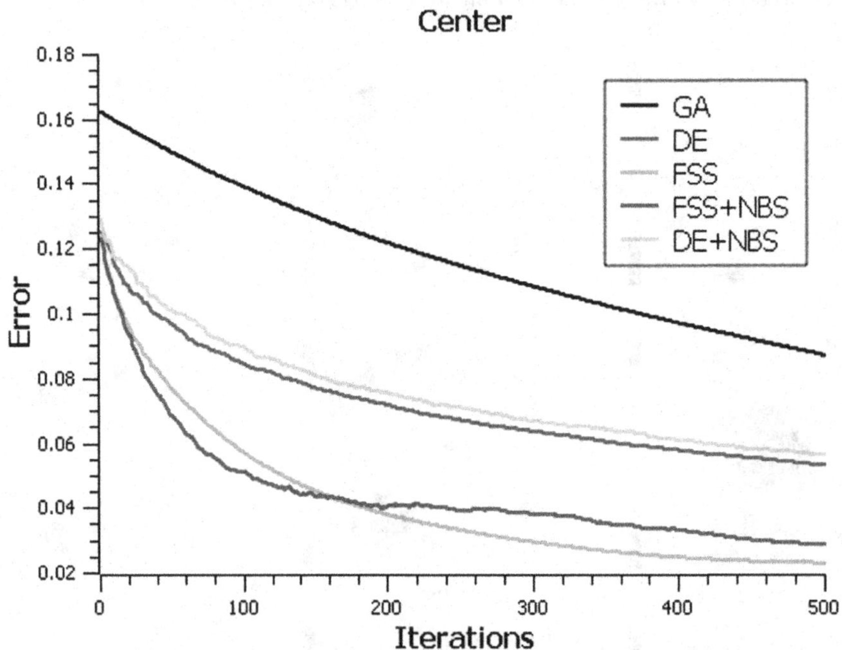

**For a more accurate representation see the electronic version.*

Figure 15. Average error of 20 simulations in function of the number of iterations for the object between the center and the edge of the domain using FSS, FSS+NBS, AG, DE and DE+NBS

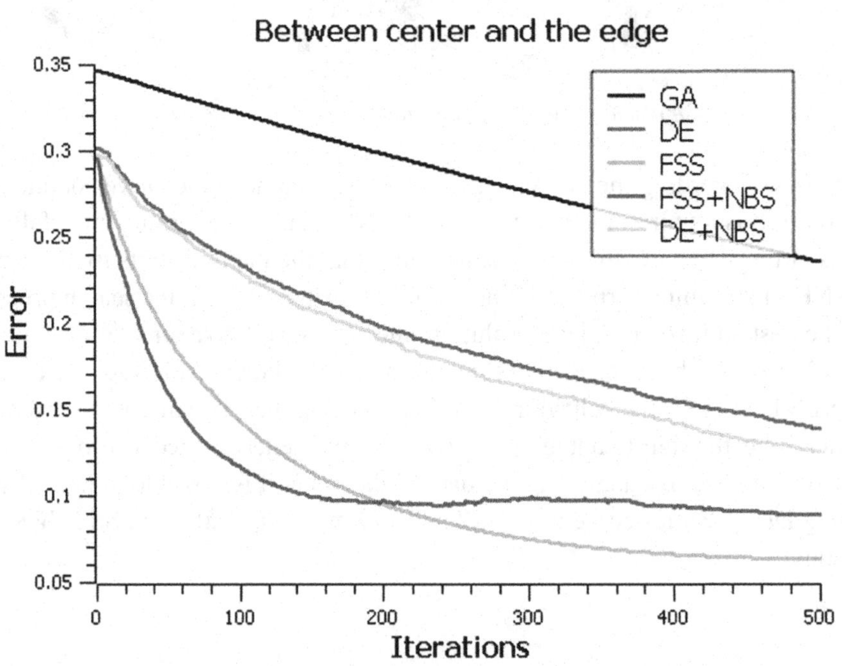

**For a more accurate representation see the electronic version.*

Figure 16. Average error of 20 simulations in function of the number of iterations for the object on the edge of the domain using FSS, FSS+NBS, AG, DE and DE+NBS

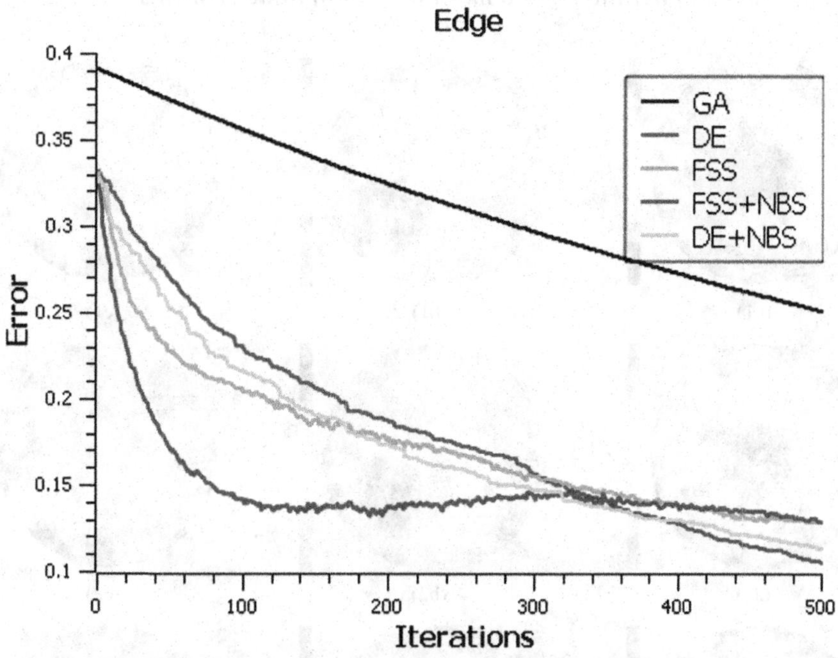

**For a more accurate representation see the electronic version.*

Table 5. The best and worst solutions, the mean and main time for 20 simulations for FSS, FSS+NBS, GA, DE and DE+NBS using a mesh with 3190 finite elements. The results in C, CE and E are for the object in center, between the center and the edge and on the edge of the circular domain, respectively

		Best	Worst	Mean	Main Time (min)
FSS	C	0.0223	0.0246	0.0236 ± 0.0004	84.1 ± 1.6
	CE	0.0626	0.0663	0.0641 ± 0.0006	85.5 ± 1.8
	E	0.0866	0.2198	0.1380 ± 0.0285	85.7 ± 1.7
FSS+NBS	C	0.0165	44.693	0.1727 ± 1,799	88 ± 3
	CE	0.0439	537.691	0.6552 ± 13.849	88.5 ± 2.7
	E	0.0991	57.067	0.2404 ± 1.378	89.2 ± 2.6
GA	C	0.0771	0.0976	0.0873 ± 0.0061	56.8 ± 0.8
	CE	0.2165	0.2652	0.2356 ± 0.0122	55.3 ± 0.9
	E	0.2224	0.2872	0.2514 ± 0.0199	54 ± 2
DE	C	0.0503	0.0591	0.0546 ± 0.0018	47.3 ± 1.1
	CE	0.1056	0.1619	0.1447 ± 0.0101	46.9 ± 0.9
	E	0.0626	0.1867	0.1237 ± 0.0247	47.3 ± 1.1
DE+NBS	C	0,0412	0,0623	0,0576 ± 0,0036	50,4 ± 0,9
	CE	0,0851	0,1681	0,1316 ± 0,0197	50,5 ± 0,7
	E	0,0218	0,1882	0,1261 ± 0,0447	50,7 ± 0,7

Figure 17. Results using FSS+NBS for an object placed in the center (a1, a2 and a3), between the center and the edge (b1, b2 and b3) and on the edge (c1, c2 and c3) of the circular domain with 3190 finite elements for 50, 300 and 500 iterations for a mesh with 9990 finite elements

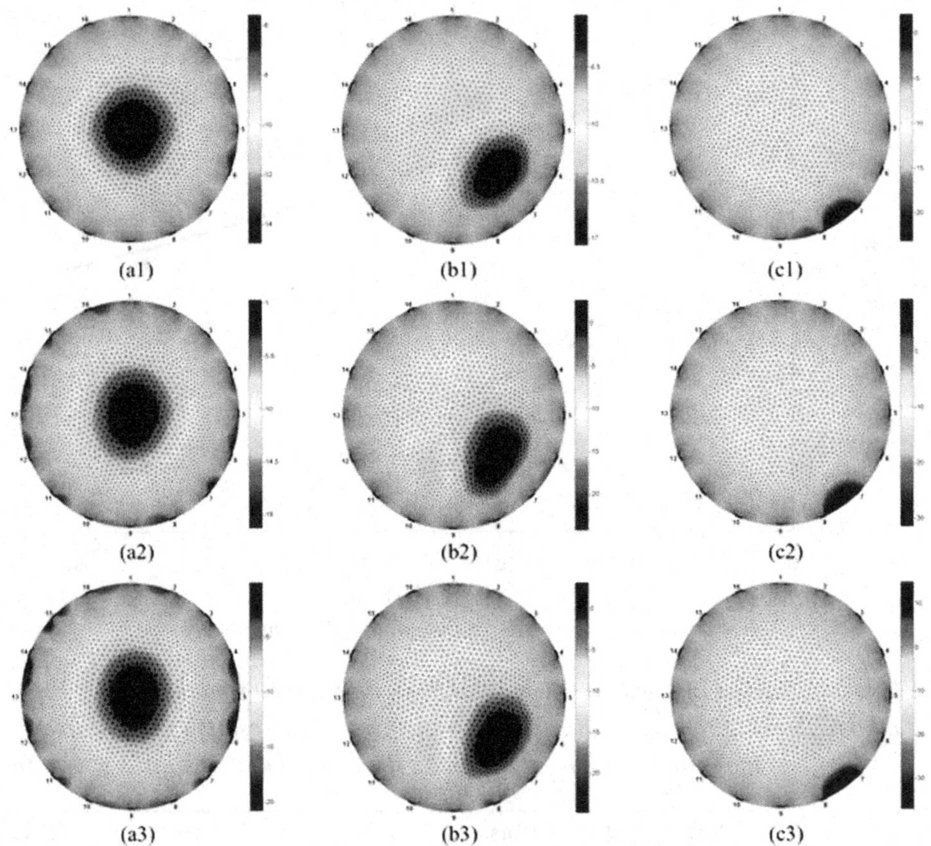

**For a more accurate representation see the electronic version.*

CONCLUSION

Electric impedance tomography is a promising imaging technique, that has applications on engineering, sciences and medical sciences fields. Nowadays, the technique still presents low resolution images, which explains the researchers' efforts in this area. This work investigated the performance of evolutionary and bioinspired algorithms applied to EIT image reconstruction using ground-truth images with meshes of differents size. It was also investigated the implementation of the Non-Blind Search based on Saha and Bandyopadhyay's Criterion (Saha & Bandyopadhyay, 2008) to theses algorithms. In general perspective, we can conclude that Fish School Search and Differential Evolution are well-succeed methods to perform the EIT reconstruction, as an optimization problem, of high dimension, in other words, to lead the reconstruction in meshes of large size (with 3190 or 9990 finite elements). In this perspective, Genetic Algorithm obtained good results in a mesh with 415 finite elements, nevertheless, the method was not able to handle with larger meshes. Considering the Non-Blind Search method, the using of this technique in Fish School Search and Differential Evolution accelerated the search process, obtaining good images with a smaller number of iterations when compared to the simple methods' results.

Figure 18. Results using DE+NBS for an object placed in the center (a1, a2 and a3), between the center and the edge (b1, b2 and b3) and on the edge (c1, c2 and c3) of the circular domain with 3190 finite elements for 50, 300 and 500 iterations for a mesh with 9990 finite elements

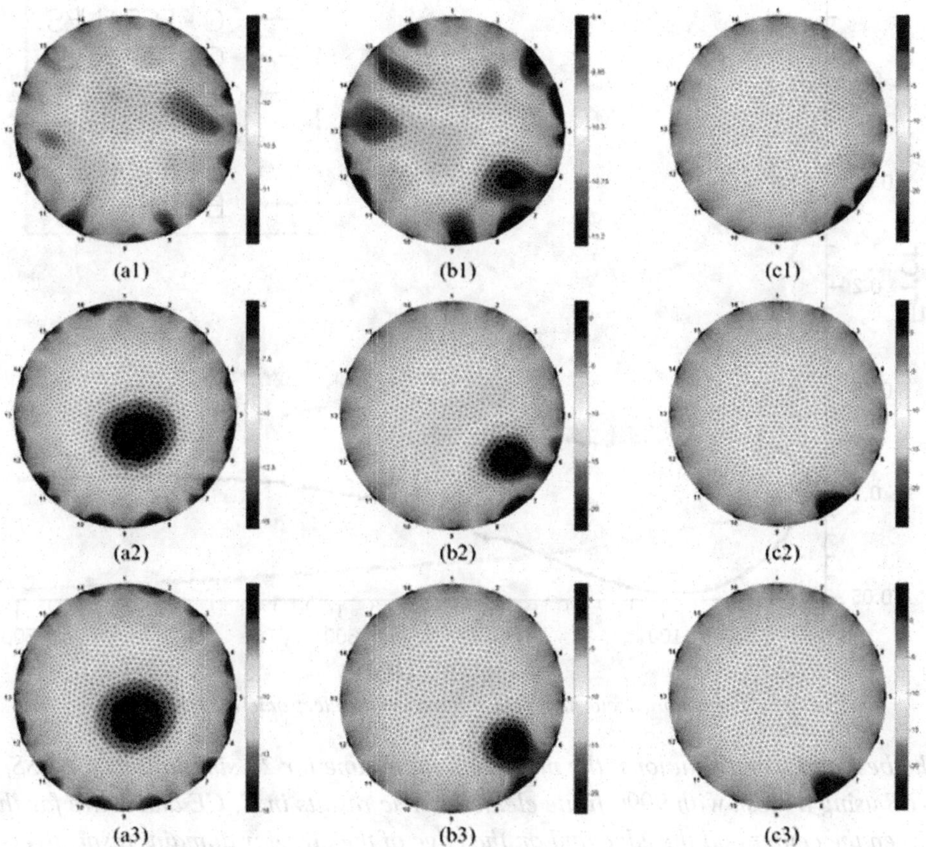

**For a more accurate representation see the electronic version.*

For future works, looking forward to solve problems related to software, we propose the investigation of FSS' algorithm's hybridization with other methods, in order to improve EIT's image reconstruction, and to compare it with other methods in the actual Evolutionary Computing state of Art, including the hybridization with NBS. This research group will also focus on the migration of EIDORS from Matlab/Octave to a compiled or, at least, precompiled language, that supports experiments with parallel techniques and architecture, investigating software infrastructure and programming languages to achieve this goal.

From the hardware point of view, parallel architectures will be investigated, such as GPUs and clusters as and parallelism techniques, all of them to reduce the execution time of those algorithms. Evolutionary algorithms tend to load in its definitions a high parallelism level, and, with FSS, this situation is not different, explaining why it is important to invest in researches on the fields mentioned above.

Figure 19. Average error of 20 simulations in function of the number of iterations using FSS+NBS and DE+NBS

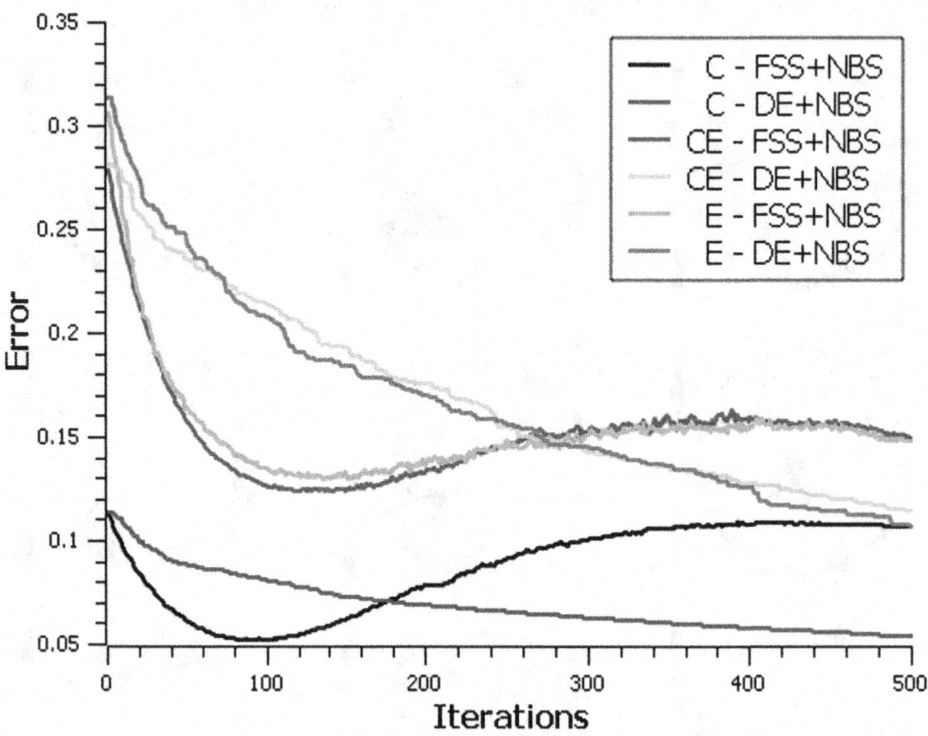

**For a more accurate representation see the electronic version.*

Table 6. The best and worst solutions, the mean and main time for 20 simulations for FSS, FSS+NBS and DE+NBS using a mesh with 9990 finite elements. The results in C, CE and E are for the object in center, between the center and the edge and on the edge of the circular domain, respectively

		Best	Worst	Mean	Main Time (min)
FSS+NBS	C	0.078	17091.201	9.721 ± 82.604	237.5 ± 4.6
	CE	0.117	38.512	0.338 ± 1.701	234.4 ± 3.1
	E	0.129	140.692	0.447 ± 4.182	238.8 ± 2.9
DE+NBS	C	0.028	0.064	0.055 ± 0.008	117.151 ± 1.1
	CE	0.074	0.181	0.129 ± 0.023	117.985 ± 1.2
	E	0.062	0.224	0.135 ± 0.034	118.980 ± 1.7

ACKNOWLEDGMENT

The authors are grateful to the Brazilian scientific agencies CAPES and FACEPE, for the partial financial support of this work.

REFERENCES

Adler, A., Arnold, J. H., Bayford, R., Borsic, A., Brown, B., Dixon, P., & Wolf, G. K. et al. (2009). GREIT: A unified approach to 2D linear EIT reconstruction of lung images. *Physiological Measurement*, *30*(6), S35–S55. doi:10.1088/0967-3334/30/6/S03 PMID:19491438

Adler, A., & Lionheart, W. R. (2006). Uses and abuses of EIDORS: An extensible software base for EIT. *Physiological Measurement*, *27*(5), S25–S42. doi:10.1088/0967-3334/27/5/S03 PMID:16636416

Adler, A., Dai, T., & Lionheart, W. R. B. (2007). Temporal image reconstruction in electrical impedance tomography. *Physiological Measurement, 28*, S1-S11.

Alves, S. H., Amato, M. B., Terra, R. M., Vargas, F. S., & Caruso, P. (2014). Lung reaeration and reventilation after aspiration of pleural effusions. a study using electrical impedance tomography. *Annals of the American Thoracic Society*, *11*(2), 186–191. doi:10.1513/AnnalsATS.201306-142OC PMID:24308560

Baker, L. E. (1989). Principles of the impedance technique. *IEEE Engineering in Medicine and Biology Magazine: The Quarterly Magazine of the Engineering in Medicine & Biology Society*, *8*(1), 11–15. doi:10.1109/51.32398 PMID:18238298

Barbosa, V. A., Ribeiro, R. R., Feitosa, A. R., Silva, V. L., Rocha, A. D., Freitas, R. C., & Santos, W. P. et al. (2017). Reconstruction of Electrical Impedance Tomography Using Fish School Search, Non-Blind Search, and Genetic Algorithm. *International Journal of Swarm Intelligence Research*, *8*(2), 17–33. doi:10.4018/IJSIR.2017040102

Bastos-Filho, C. J., de Lima Neto, F. B., Lins, A. J., Nascimento, A. I., & Lima, M. P. (2008). A novel search algorithm based on fish school behavior. In *Systems, Man and Cybernetics, 2008. SMC 2008. IEEE International Conference on* (pp. 2646–2651). Academic Press. doi:10.1109/ICSMC.2008.4811695

Bastos-Filho, C. J. A., & Guimarães, A. C. S. (2015). Multi-objective fish school search. International Journal of Swarm Intelligence Research, 23–40.

Bathe, K.-J. (2006). *Finite element procedures*. Klaus-Jurgen Bathe.

Bera, T. K., & Nagaraju, J. (2014). Electrical impedance tomography (EIT): a harmless medical imaging modality. In Research Developments in Computer Vision and Image Processing: Methodologies and Applications. IGI Global.

Borcea, L. (2002). Electrical impedance tomography. *Inverse Problems*, *18*(6), R99–R136. doi:10.1088/0266-5611/18/6/201

Brown, B., Barber, D., & Seagar, A. (1985). Applied potential tomography: Possible clinical applications. *Clinical Physics and Physiological Measurement*, *6*(2), 109–121. doi:10.1088/0143-0815/6/2/002 PMID:4017442

Carosio, G. L. C., Rolnik, V., & Seleghim, P. (2007). Improving efficiency in electrical impedance tomography problem by hybrid parallel genetic algorithm and a priori information. *Proceedings of the XXX Congresso Nacional de Matemática Aplicada e Computacional.*

Castro Martins, T., Camargo, E. D. L. B., Lima, R. G., Amato, M. B. P., & Tsuzuki, M. S. G. (2012). Image reconstruction using interval simulated annealing in electrical impedance tomography. *IEEE Transactions on Biomedical Engineering*, *59*(7), 1861–1870. doi:10.1109/TBME.2012.2188398 PMID:22361655

Cheney, M., Isaacson, D., & Newell, J. C. (1999). Electrical impedance tomography. *SIAM Review*, *41*(1), 85–101. doi:10.1137/S0036144598333613

Cheney, M., Isaacson, D., Newell, J. C., Simske, S., & Goble, J. (1990). NOSER: An algorithm for solving the inverse conductivity problem. *International Journal of Imaging Systems and Technology*, *2*(2), 66–75. doi:10.1002/ima.1850020203

Cheng, K. S., Chen, B. H., & Tong, H. S. Electrical impedance image reconstruction using the genetic algorithm. In *IEEE. Engineering in Medicine and Biology Society, 1996. Bridging Disciplines for Biomedicine. Proceedings of the 18th Annual International Conference of the IEEE.* IEEE.

Cherepenin, V., Karpov, A., Korjenevsky, A., Kornienko, V., Mazaletskaya, A., Mazourov, D., & Meister, D. (2001). A 3D electrical impedance tomography (EIT) system for breast cancer detection. *Physiological Measurement*, *22*(1), 9–18. doi:10.1088/0967-3334/22/1/302 PMID:11236894

CINTRA. (2007). *M. E. Geração genética de regras fuzzy com pré-seleção de regras candidatas. Tese (Mestrado).* Universidade Federal de São Carlos.

Eberhart, R. C., & Shi, Y. (2011). *Computational intelligence: concepts to implementations*. Elsevier.

Eiben, A. E., & Smith, J. E. (2015). *Introduction to evolutionary computing* (Vol. 2). Springer. doi:10.1007/978-3-662-44874-8

Feitosa, A. R., Ribeiro, R. R., Barbosa, V. A., de Souza, R. E., & dos Santos, W. P. (2014). Reconstruction of electrical impedance tomography images using particle swarm optimization, genetic algorithms and non-blind search. In 5th *ISSNIP-IEEE Biosignals and Biorobotics Conference (2014): Biosignals and Robotics for Better and Safer Living (BRC)* (pp. 1–6). IEEE. doi:10.1109/BRC.2014.6880996

Filipowicz, S. F., & Rymarczyk, T. (2012). Measurement methods and image reconstruction in electrical impedance tomography. *Przegląd Elektrotechniczny*, *88*(6), 247–250.

Gonçalves, M. L. N. (2011). *Análise de Convergência dos Métodos de Gauss-Newton do Ponto de Vista do Princípio Majorante.* Tese (Doutorado), COPPE da Universidade Federal do Rio de Janeiro.

Herrera, C. N. L. (2007). *Algoritmo de tomografia por impedância elétrica baseado em Simulated Annealing. Dissertação (Mestrado)*. Universidade de São Paulo.

Jin, B., Khan, T., & Maass, P. (2012). A reconstruction algorithm for electrical impedance tomography based on sparsity regularization. *International Journal for Numerical Methods in Engineering, 89*(3), 337-353.

Li, T., Isaacson, D., Newell, J. C., & Saulnier, G. J. (2014). Adaptive techniques in electrical impedance tomography reconstruction. *Physiological Measurement, 35*(6), 1111–1124. doi:10.1088/0967-3334/35/6/1111 PMID:24845260

Lins, A., Bastos-Filho, C. J., Nascimento, D. N., Junior, M. A. O., & de Lima-Neto, F. B. (2012). Analysis of the performance of the fish school search algorithm running in graphic processing units. *Theory and New Applications of Swarm Intelligence*, 17–32.

Liu, Y., & Sun, F. (2011). A fast differential evolution algorithm using K-nearest neighbour predictor. *Expert Systems with Applications, Elsevier, 38*(4), 4254–4258. doi:10.1016/j.eswa.2010.09.092

LOPES. (2006). H. S. Fundamentos de computação evolucionária e aplicações. In *Escola Regional de Informática da SBC – Paraná.* Anais, Bandeirantes. SBC.

Martin, S., & Choi, C. T. M. (2016). Nonlinear Electrical Impedance Tomography Reconstruction Using Artificial Neural Networks and Particle Swarm Optimization. *IEEE Transactions on Magnetics, 52*(3), 1–4. doi:10.1109/TMAG.2015.2488901

McAdams, E. T., McLaughlin, J. A., & Anderson, J. McC. (1994). Multi-electrode systems for electrical impedance tomography. *Physiological Measurement, 15*(2A), A101–AI06. doi:10.1088/0967-3334/15/2A/014 PMID:8087031

Menin, O. H. (2009). *Método dos elementos de contorno para tomografia de impedância elétrica. Dissertação (Mestrado).* Faculdade de Filosofia, Ciências e Letras de Ribeirão Preto da Universidade de São Paulo.

Michalewicz. (1996). *Z. Genetic Algorithms + Data Structures = Evolution Programs* (3rd ed.). Springer.

Momenté, G. V., Peixoto, B. H. L. N., Tsuzuki, M. S. G., & Martins, T. D. C. (2013). New objective function for electrical image tomography reconstruction. *ABCM Symposium Series in Mechatronics.*

Price, K., Storn, R. M., & Lampinen, J. A. (2006). *Differential evolution: a practical approach to global optimization*. Springer Science & Business Media.

Rasteiro, M. G., Silva, R. C., Garcia, F. A., & Faia, P. M. (2011). Electrical tomography: A review of configurations and applications to particulate processes. *Kona Powder and Particle Journal, 29*(0), 67–80. doi:10.14356/kona.2011010

Ribeiro, R. R. (2016). *Reconstrução de imagens de tomografia por impedância elétrica usando evolução diferencial. Dissertação (Mestrado).* Universidade Federal de Pernambuco.

Ribeiro, R. R., Feitosa, A. R., de Souza, R. E., & dos Santos, W. P. (2014a). A modified differential evolution algorithm for the reconstruction of electrical impedance tomography images. In 5th *ISSNIP-IEEE Biosignals and Biorobotics Conference (2014): Biosignals and Robotics for Better and Safer Living (BRC)* (pp. 1–6). IEEE. doi:10.1109/BRC.2014.6880982

Ribeiro, R. R., Feitosa, A. R., de Souza, R. E., & dos Santos, W. P. (2014b). Reconstruction of electrical impedance tomography images using chaotic self adaptive ring-topology differential evolution and genetic algorithms. In *2014 IEEE International Conference on Systems, Man, and Cybernetics (SMC)* (pp. 2605–2610). IEEE. doi:10.1109/SMC.2014.6974320

Ribeiro, R. R., Feitosa, A. R., de Souza, R. E., & dos Santos, W. P. (2014c). Reconstruction of electrical impedance tomography images using genetic algorithms and non-blind search. In *2014 IEEE 11th International Symposium on Biomedical Imaging (ISBI)* (pp. 153–156). IEEE. doi:10.1109/ISBI.2014.6867832

Rolnik, V. P., & Seleghim, P. Jr. (2006). A specialized genetic algorithm for the electrical impedance tomography of two-phase flows. *Journal of the Brazilian Society of Mechanical Sciences and Engineering*, *28*(4), 378–389. doi:10.1590/S1678-58782006000400002

Saha, S., & Bandyopadhyay, S. (2008). Application of a new symmetry-based cluster validity index for satellite image segmentation. *IEEE Geoscience and Remote Sensing Letters*, *5*(2), 166–170. doi:10.1109/LGRS.2008.915595

Santosa, F., & Vogelius, M. A. (1990). Backprojection Algorithm for Electrical Impedance Imaging. *SIAM Journal on Applied Mathematics*, *50*(1), 216–243. doi:10.1137/0150014

Tehrani, J. N., Jin, C., McEwan, A., & van Schaik, A. (2010). A comparison between compressed sensing algorithms in electrical impedance tomography. In *2010 Annual International Conference of the IEEE Engineering in Medicine and Biology* (pp. 3109–3112). IEEE. doi:10.1109/IEMBS.2010.5627165

Tombe, F. D. (2012). *Maxwell's original equations*. The General Science Journal.

Vauhkonen, M., Lionheart, W. R., Heikkinen, L. M., Vauhkonen, P. J., & Kaipio, J. P. (2001). A MATLAB package for the EIDORS project to reconstruct two-dimensional EIT images. *Physiological Measurement*, *22*(1), 107–111. doi:10.1088/0967-3334/22/1/314 PMID:11236871

Zhou, Z., dos Santos, G. S., Dowrick, T., Avery, J., Sun, Z., Xu, H., & Holder, D. S. (2015). Comparison of total variation algorithms for electrical impedance tomography. *Physiological Measurement*, *36*(6), 1193–1209. doi:10.1088/0967-3334/36/6/1193 PMID:26008768

Chapter 13
Multi-Thresholding of Histopathological Images Using Fuzzy Entropy and Parameterless Cuckoo Search

Krishna Gopal Gopal Dhal
Midnapore College (Autonomous), India

Mandira Sen
Tata Consultancy Services, India

Sanjoy Das
University of Kalyani, India

ABSTRACT

This chapter presents a multi-level histopathological image thresholding approach based on fuzzy entropy theory. This entropy measure is maximized to obtain the optimal thresholds of the image. In order to solve this problem, one self-adaptive and parameter-less cuckoo search (CS) algorithm has been employed, which leads to an accurate convergence towards the optima within less computational time. The performance of the proposed CS is also compared with traditional CS (TCS) algorithm and particle swarm optimization (PSO). The outcomes of the proposed fuzzy entropy-based model are compared with Shannon entropy-based model both visually and statistically in order to establish the perceptible difference in image.

INTRODUCTION

Image thresholding, which is the most significant and highly complicated task in low-level image analysis, is the process of extracting the objects from its background based on threshold levels. Several image segmentation processes, such as gray level thresholding, interactive pixel classification, neural network based approaches, edge detection and fuzzy based segmentation, etc.are reported in literature (Riseman, E.M.,

DOI: 10.4018/978-1-5225-5134-8.ch013

Arbib, M.A. (1977), Weszka, J.S. (1978), Fu, K.S., Mui, J.K. (1981), Haralharick, R.M., Shapiro, L.G. (1985), Borisenko, V.I., Zlatotol, A.A., Muchnik, I.B. (1987), Sahoo, P.K., Soltani, S., Wong, A.K.C., Chen, Y.C. (1988), Pal, N.R., Pal, S.K. (1993)).Global thresholding based segmentation for graylevel image is the well-known technique. Entropy based global thresholding techniques are reported in literature such as Kapur's entropy (Kapur, J.N., Sahoo, P.K., Wong, A.K.C. (1985)), Sahoo et.al. (Wong, A.K.C., Sahoo, P.K. (1989)), Pun et. al. (T. Pun (1981)), Pal et.al.(Pal, N.R. (1996)), Li et.al.(Li, C.H., Lee, C.K. (1993)), Rosin et.al.(Rosin, P.L. (2001)), Reyni's entropy (Sarkar S., Das S., Chaudhuri S. S., (2016.)), Tsallis entropy (Bhandari A. K., Kumar A., Singh G. K.(2015)). Multi-thresholding based image segmentation represents the splitting the image into different regions by selecting multiple threshold points. Otsu developed one multi-level image segmentation method based on region variance. Kapur et. al. proposed entropy based method for segmentation where the sum of the class entropy was maximized to find the optimal threshold (Kapur, J.N., Sahoo, P.K., Wong, A.K.C. (1985)). But the majority of the said techniques do not consider the inexactness of the gray levels i.e. if there is no clear boundary among different region leads to some ambiguity. In order to overcome the ambiguity problem, fuzzy theory is introduced in entropy based segmentation.Luca and Termini (Luca, A.D., Termini, S.(1972)) introduced a fuzzy partition technique for image segmentation.Bloch et. al. Employed fuzzy spatial relationship in image processing andimage interpretation area (Bloch, I.(2005)). Notably, application of fuzzy multi-level thresholding approach was performed by Zhao et. al. where three membership functions for 3-level thresholding i.e. dark, medium and bright was employed (Zhao, M.S., Fu, A.M.N., Yan, H.(2001)). Based on this paper, Tao et. al. developed one 3-level fuzzy entropy based segmentation technique by using Z-function, F-function and S-function as membership functions (Tao, W.B., Tian, J.W., Liu, J.(2003)). A thresholding approach based on the maximum fuzzy entropy principal over two dimensional histogram had been discussed by Cheng et. al. (H.D. Cheng, Y.H. Chen, and X.H Jiang.(2000)) where inter pixel relationship was taken into account. The threshold levels of the multi-thresholding problem were computed by employing metaheuristic algorithms as it helps to reduce the computational time (Olive, D., Cuevas, E., Pajares, G., Zaldivar, D., Perez-Cisneros, M.(2013), Krishna Priya,R., Thangaraj, C., Kesavadas, C., Kannan, S.(2013)). One Modified Particle Swarm Optimization (MPSO) was employed with fuzzy entropy in the MRI image segmentation field and the proposed model gave promising result in terms of visual analysis, statistical analysis and computational time (Krishna Priya,R., Thangaraj, C., Kesavadas, C., Kannan, S.(2013)). Sarkar et. al. proposed one Differential Evolution (DE) with fuzzy entropy based segmentation model which outperforms Shannon's entropy based model visually and statistically (Sarkar, S., Paul, S., Burman, R., Das, S., Chaudhuri, S.S.(2015)). DE helped to find the optimal threshold values within less computational time. In this study, fuzzy entropy based multi-thresholding model is used to segment the histopathological images which is an untouched area as per best of our knowledge. One modified CS algorithm is employed for finding the fuzzy parameters and one comparative study among traditional CS, PSO and proposed CS algorithm has been performed in this study in terms of different statistical test and computational time. The fuzzy entropy based model is also compared with Shannon entropy based model. The visual and statistical results proved that the proposed model outperforms the Shannon entropy model in the histopathological image segmentation field. The chapter is composed of mainly four section. First section demonstrates the concept of multi-level fuzzy entropy. Second section represents the methodology behind the development of modified CS. In third section, discussion about the experimental results has been performed. The chapter is concluded in the last section.

CONCEPT OF MULTI-LEVEL FUZZY ENTROPY

The discussion about multi level fuzzy entropy has been done as follows.

Multi-Level Shannon Entropy (SE)

Let

$$P = \left(p_1, p_2, p_3, \ldots\ldots\ldots\ldots, p_n\right) \in \Delta_n$$

where

$$\Delta_n = \left\{\left(p_1, p_2, \ldots\ldots\ldots\ldots, p_n\right) \mid p_i \geq 0, i = 1, 2, \ldots\ldots, n, n \geq 2, \sum_{i=1}^{n} p_i = 1\right\}$$

is a set of discrete finite n -ary probability distributions. Then entropy of the total image can be defined as (Sarkar, S., Paul, S., Burman, R., Das, S., Chaudhuri, S.S.(2015)):

$$H\left(P\right) = -\sum_{i=1}^{n} p_i \log_2 p_i \tag{1}$$

I denote a 8 bit gray level digital image of dimension $M \times N$. P is the normalizedhistogram for image with $L = 256$ gray levels. Now, if there are $n-1$ thresholds$\left(t\right)$, partitioning the normalized histogram into n classes, then the entropy for each class may be computed as,

$$H_1\left(t\right) = -\sum_{i=0}^{t_1} \frac{p_i}{P_1} \ln \frac{p_i}{P_1},$$

$$H_2\left(t\right) = -\sum_{i=t_1+1}^{t_2} \frac{p_i}{P_2} \ln \frac{p_i}{P_2},$$

$$H_n\left(t\right) = -\sum_{i=t_{n-1}+1}^{L-1} \frac{p_i}{P_n} \ln \frac{p_i}{P_n}. \tag{2}$$

where,

$$P_1(t) = \sum_{i=0}^{t_1} p_i, P_2(t) = \sum_{i=t_1+1}^{t_2} p_i, \ldots\ldots\ldots, P_n(t) = -\sum_{i=t_{n-1}+1}^{L-1} p_i \quad (3)$$

where, For ease of computation, two dummy thresholds $t_0 = 0,\ t_n = L - 1$ are introduced with $t_0 < t_1 < \ldots < t_{n-1} < t_n$. Then the optimum threshold value can be found by

$$Æ(t_1, t_2, \ldots\ldots, t_n) = \text{Arg max}\left(\left[H_1(t) + H_2(t) + \ldots + H_n(t)\right]\right) \quad (4)$$

In the next sub-section, discussion about the fuzzy entropy has been done.

Multi-Level Fuzzy Entropy (FE)

A classical set A can be defined as a collection of element that can either belong to ornot belongs to set A. Whereas according to fuzzy set, which is a generalization of classical set, an element can partially belongs to a set A. A can be defined as(Sarkar, S., Paul, S., Burman, R., Das, S., Chaudhuri, S.S.(2015)):

$$A = \left\{\left(x, \mu_A(x)\right) \mid x \in X\right\} \quad (5)$$

where, $0 \le \mu_A(x) \le 1$ and $\mu_A(x)$ is called the membership function, which measures the closeness of x to A. For simplicity trapezoidal membership function is used in this paper to estimate the membership of n segmented regions, $\mu_1, \mu_2, \ldots\ldots\ldots, \mu_n$ by using $2 \times (n-1)$ unknown fuzzy parameters, namely $a_1, c_1 \ldots a_{n-1}, c_{n-1}$ where $0 \le a_1 \le c_1 \le \ldots \le a_{n-1}, c_{n-1} \le L - 1$ Then the following membership function can be derived for n level thresholding

$$\mu_1(k) = \begin{cases} 1 & k \le a_1 \\ \dfrac{k - c_1}{a_1 - c_1} & a_1 \le k \le c_1 \\ 0 & k > c_1 \end{cases}$$

$$\mu_{n-1}(k) = \begin{cases} 0 & k \le a_{n-2} \\ \dfrac{k - a_{n-2}}{c_{n-2} - a_{n-2}} & a_{n-2} < k \le c_{n-2} \\ 1 & c_{n-2} < k \le a_{n-2}. \\ \dfrac{k - c_{n-1}}{a_{n-1} - c_{n-1}} & a_{n-1} < k \le c_{n-1} \\ 0 & k > c_{n-1} \end{cases} \quad (6)$$

The maximum fuzzy entropy for each segment of $n-$ level segments can be defined by

$$H_1 = -\sum_{i=0}^{L-1} \frac{p_i * \mu_1(i)}{P_1} * \ln\left(\frac{p_i * \mu_1(i)}{P_1}\right),$$

$$H_2 = -\sum_{i=0}^{L-1} \frac{p_i * \mu_2(i)}{P_2} * \ln\left(\frac{p_i * \mu_2(i)}{P_2}\right),$$

$$H_n = -\sum_{i=0}^{L-1} \frac{p_i * \mu_n(i)}{P_n} * \ln\left(\frac{p_i * \mu_n(i)}{P_n}\right). \quad (7)$$

where,

$$P_1(t) = \sum_{i=0}^{L-1} p_i * \mu_1(i),\ P_2(t) = \sum_{i=0}^{L-1} p_i * \mu_2(i), \ldots\ldots\ldots\ldots\ldots\ldots,\ P_n(t) = \sum_{i=0}^{L-1} p_i * \mu_n(i), \quad (8)$$

The optimum value of parameters can be obtained by maximizing the total entropy,

$$\mathrm{Fit}(a_1, c_1 \ldots a_{n-1}, c_{n-1}) = \mathrm{Arg\ max}\left(\left[H_1(t) + H_2(t) + \ldots + H_n(t)\right]\right) \quad (9)$$

A global optimization technique is needed to optimize Eq.(9) efficiently and also to reduce the time complexity of the proposed method. The $(n-1)$ number of threshold values can obtained using the fuzzy parameters in the following way:

$$t_1 = \frac{(a_1 + c_1)}{2},\ t_2 = \frac{(a_2 + c_2)}{2}, \ldots\ldots. t_{n-1} = \frac{(a_{n-1} + c_{n-1})}{2} \quad (10)$$

PROPOSED MODIFIED CUCKOO SEARCH (CS)

The aforementioned parasitic behavior among cuckoo birds refers to the aggressive and highly successful reproduction strategy of certain species of cuckoo birds based on an evolutionary predisposition to put down their eggs in the nests of the host birds (Yang, X.S.(2010)). This behavior aided in the propagation of their species. This natural observation is applied in the computational field by treating the host bird eggs as the initial solutions and the cuckoo eggs as the alternative solutions with the aim of reaching a near-optimal solution by successful iterations involving the replacement of weaker solutions with better ones.

Three idealize rules are based on which Cuckoo Search (CS) Algorithm was proposed are as follows:

1. One egg at a time has been laid by each cuckoo and then it chooses a random nest to put its egg into the nest.
2. The finest nests having high class eggs will move to the subsequent generation.
3. There are fixed numbers of accessible host nests. There is a probability p∈ [0, 1] that the host bird finds out the eggs. As a result, the egg either has been thrown by host bird or abandoned (Yang, X.S.(2010)).

Cuckoo Search (CS) algorithm has already proved its supreme performance in image processing field (Dhal, K. G., Sen, M., Das, S.(2017), Dhal, K.G, Quraishi, I. M., Das, S.(2015), Dhal, K. G., Das, S.(2017)). However, it may possible to increase its efficiency when solving complex optimization problems. The traditional CS algorithm is very simple algorithm in terms of number of parameters. But there are some demerits of traditional CS algorithm which are given below (Dhal, K.G, Quraishi, I. M., Das, S.(2017)):

1. There is no communication between solutions. No solution share information to the other solution unlike particle swarm optimization (PSO). So, there is no guidanceof direction on which direction the new solution has been generated.
2. Only lévy flight with a fixed step size has been used to generate new solutions, which is not so good. It does not show ergodocity behavior. Fixed step size used for diversification as well as for intensification. To choose an appropriate step size for diversification step and intensification step plays a great role in any metaheuristic algorithm.

In this study, one modified CS algorithmhas been proposed based on communication between solutions, Lévy flight, chaotic sequence and one novel step size. The developed step size helps to reduce the problem of the fixed step size of Lévy flight. The discussions about these are as follows:

Step Size

In this study one new step size has been employed to control the Lévy flight based solution generation. The methodology behind this step size has been discussed below

$$Step\ Size\left(SS_i^t\right) = \left|\frac{Fit\left(X_{gbest}\right) - Fit^t\left(X_i\right)}{\max\left(Fit\left(X_{gbest}\right),\ Fit^t\left(X_i\right)\right)}\right| \tag{11}$$

where, $\mathrm{Fit}\left(\mathrm{X}_{\mathrm{gbest}}\right)$ is the fitness value of the global best solution up to generation number *t*. $\mathrm{Fit}^{\mathrm{t}}\left(\mathrm{X}_{\mathrm{i}}\right)$ is the fitness value of ith individual at generation number *t*. It is easily understood that $\left(0 \le \mathrm{SS} \le 1\right)$. It is also clear that *SS* performs the main criteria of any metaheuristic algorithm that the step size be decreased or increased depending upon whether the solution is good or bad very well. Hence *SS* may be called as *Fitness-based Step-size* (Dhal, K. G., Das, S.(2017), K. G. Dhal, S. Das.(2017)).

Chaotic Sequence

The complex behavior of non-linear deterministic system is defined by chaos (Dhal, K.G, Quraishi, I. M., Das, S.(2017)). Chaos has non-repetition property and for this it searches best solution faster than any searching strategy that depends upon the probability distribution (Dhal, K.G, Quraishi, I. M., Das, S.(2017)). Recently, chaotic sequence has been incorporated with nature inspired algorithms to enhance their capability(Dhal, K.G, Quraishi, I. M., Das, S.(2015), Dhal, K.G, Quraishi, I. M., Das, S.(2015), Dhal, K., G., Das, S(2015), Dhal, K.G, Quraishi, I. M., Das, S.(2015), Coelho, L. d. S., Mariani, V. C.(2008)). Chaotic sequences are used in metaheuristic algorithms for three purposes 1. To generate random numbers 2.To generate inertia weight 3.To perform the local search. In this study the chaotic sequence has been successfully applied to update the mutation factor and crossover rate of the DE algorithm which are responsible for controlling the trade-off between exploration and exploitation. There are several chaotic generators like logistic map, tent map, gauss map, sinusoidal iterator, lozi map, chua's oscillator etc (Dhal, K.G, Quraishi, I. M., Das, S.(2017)). Among those logistic equation is used in this paper as it carries greater variance and outperforms others (Dhal, K.G, Quraishi, I. M., Das, S.(2017), Dhal, K., G., Das, S(2015)). The equation of logistic map is given below:

$$L_{m+1} = aL_m\left(1 - L_m\right) \quad (12)$$

a is a control parameter and $0<a \leq 4$, L_m is the chaotic value at m^{th} iteration. The behaviour of the system mostly depends on the variation of a. Value of a is set to 4 and L_0 does not belong to {0, 0.25, 0.5, 0.75, 1} otherwise the logistic equation does not show chaotic behaviour (H.D. Cheng, Y.H. Chen, and X.H Jiang.(2000)).

Lévy flight

Lévy Flight has been used to generate random walk which plays a great role in metaheuristic algorithms. A random walk is a mathematical method of representing a series of consecutive random steps. It has wide applications in the fields of computer science, physics, statistics, economics and engineering (Yang, X.S.(2010)).It can be expressed by the formula

$$S_N = \sum_{i=1}^{N} X_i \quad (13)$$

where, X_i is a random step size drawn from a random distribution and S_N is the sum of each of these consecutive random steps. Lévy Flight is a random walk whose step length is determined from the lévy distribution. It is capable of exploring large amount of search space. Lévy Flight can be produced using different algorithms which include Rejection algorithm, McCulloch's algorithm, Mantegna's algorithm etc. In this study, Mantegna's algorithm has been used. It produces random numbers according to a symmetric Lévy stable distribution as described below—

$$\sigma = \left[\Gamma\left(1+\alpha\right)\sin\left(\pi\alpha / 2\right) / \Gamma(\left(1+\alpha\right) / 2\alpha 2^{(\alpha-1)/2}\right)]^{1/\alpha} \tag{14}$$

where, Γ is the gamma function, $0<\alpha \leq 2$ (Yang, X.S.(2010)), in this study it is taken as 1.5. σ is the standard deviation.

As per Mantegna's algorithm the step length v can be calculated as,

$$\mathrm{v} = \mathrm{x} / \mathrm{y}^{1/\alpha} \tag{15}$$

Here, x and y are taken from normal distribution and $\sigma_x = \sigma, \sigma_y = 1$ (Dhal, K.G, Quraishi, I. M., Das, S.(2015)). Where σ is the standard deviation.The resulting distribution has the same behavior of Lévy distribution for large values of the random variables [34]. Mantegna's algorithm is preferred in this study for generating Lévy distribution because of its simple calculation steps than McCulloch's algorithm and its faster computational speed in the range $0.75 \leq \alpha \leq 1.95$.

Lévy Flight is used for the diversification as well as intensification in stochastic optimization algorithm (Yang, X.S.(2010)). For the case of diversification the step size has been taken larger than in the case of intensification. The developed step size (SS_i^t) is employed to reduce the step size selection problem as it increases or decreases depending on the considered solution. The repetition of the same position in its space by lévy Flight is less than the Brownian motion (Dhal, K.G, Quraishi, I. M., Das, S.(2015), Dhal, K, G., Namtirtha, A., Quraishi, I. M., Das, S.(2016)).

Creation of Initial Population

The initial population is usually created randomly in the most nature-inspired optimization algorithms by knowing the lower and upper bound of the search space of the objective function. The equation for intializing the initial solutions randomly is given below:

$$\mathrm{x_i} = \mathrm{low} + \left(\mathrm{up} - \mathrm{low}\right) \times \partial \tag{16}$$

$\mathrm{x_i}$ is the ith individual. up $\&low$ are the upper and lower bound of the search space of objective function. ∂ is the random variable that belongs to [0,1].

If the initial population carries a great variance then it helps to restrict the premature convergence of the algorithm. Average population diversity is good when ∂ is generated using logistic equation (H. D. Cheng, Y. H. Chen, and X. H Jiang.(2000), Dhal, K.G, Quraishi, I. M., Das, S.(2015)). In this study, logistic equation based initial population has been used.

Based on the above discussed methodology, one modified CS algorithm has been proposed . The pseudo-code of the proposed CS is as follows:

Step 1: Objective function has been taken as per Eq. (9).

Step 2: Initialize the population of cuckoos $X = \{X_i \mid i = 1,2,3,\dots n\}$ where, n is the number of cuckoo and X_i is the ith cuckoo.

Step 3: Evaluate quality or fitness value (Fit_i) of X_i

Step 4: Sort all solutions according to their fitness value i.e. Fit_i.

Step 5: Sort out the abandoned solutions depend upon the fitness value.

Step 6: For all abandoned solutions new solutions are generated using Lévy flight and step size. Find new solution X_j around the abandoned solution X_i by the following equation:

$$X_j = X_i + SS_i^t.Sign\left[rand - \frac{1}{2}\right] \otimes Levy$$

Sign function gives the direction, *rand* is a random number within [0, 1], $\otimes$ is the entry-wise multiplication.

If $Fit_i > Fit_j$ then replace X_j by X_i

Otherwise do nothing.

Step 7: For the all nests with higher fitness value do the following steps:

Suppose, current position is X_i.

Calculate $\Delta X = \left|X_i - X_{globalbest}\right| \otimes \left(SS_i^t \times L_m\right)$

$L_m \in \left[-1,1\right]$

Move the nest X_i towards the global best nest $X_{globalbest}$ with distance ΔX to find X_k.

$$X_k = X_i + \Delta X$$

If ($Fit_k > Fit_i$) then replace X_i by X_k

Otherwise, do nothing.

Step 8: Find the global best solution.

Step 9: Repeat the steps 3-8 until the stopping criterion.

In this modified CS algorithm, Lévy flight is used to update the abandoned solutions as Lévy flight is better to explore the larger area which is beneficial for diversification. The rage of chaotic sequence is by-default [0, 1], but, in this study, it converts to [-1, 1] to perform the intensification around best solutions. SS_i^t is used to control the Lévy flight and as well as chaotic sequence based modification. Here, 30 numbers of individuals are taken as initial population. All the major parameters of this proposed CS algorithm are adaptive i.e. no human interaction is needed during running of the algorithm and that's why this algorithm may be called *adaptive and parameter less CS* algorithm.

Stopping Conditions

Find the optimal stopping condition is a challenging matter in nature-inspired algorithms based optimization field. It has been chosen experimentally in this chapter. The stopping conditions are given as follows:

1. When the fitness value of the global best solution does not change for continuous 20 times for a specific image.
2. But the maximum number of function evaluation is 1000xD. Where D denoting the search space dimensionality. Note that for a n levels segmentation problem the dimensionality of the search space is D = (n-1) for Shannon entropy and D = 2x(n-1) for Fuzzy entropy as number of unknown fuzzy parameters are 2.

EXPERIMENTAL RESULTS

The experiment has been performed over 50 histopathological images with Matlab R2012b with x64-based PC, Intel(R) Core(TM) i3-CPU with 4 GB RAM with Windows 7 ulitimate operating system. Among these, the five images are given as Figure 1. The effectiveness of the fuzzy entropy based approach is established by comparing the results with Shannon entropy in terms of both visual and statistical analysis. Performance of proposed method is tested with the help of two well-known image quality assessment matrices such as Feature similarity (FSIM) index (Sarkar, S., Paul, S., Burman, R., Das, S., Chaudhuri, S.S.(2015)), Quality Index based on Local Variance (QILV) (Sarkar, S., Paul, S., Burman, R., Das, S., Chaudhuri, S.S.(2015), Dhal, K. G., Das, S.(2017)). The thresolded images corresponding to Figure 1 are presented as Figure 2 and 3. The performance of the proposed CS, traditional CS and PSO are evaluated in terms of Computational time (*CT*), Mean Fitness value (Fit_m) and Standard Deviation (Fit_{std}) which are given in Table 1. Proposed CS proves that it has a better convergence rate with the better ability of finding global optima within less computational time compares to traditional CS and PSO. The obtained threshold values and fuzzy parameters of SE and FE for 2nd, 3rd and 4th level thresholding are displayed in table 2. The qualitative based results have been given in table 3 and 4. Table 3 and 4 represent the values of the FSIM and QILV for segmented images respectively. FE reveals better segmentation in comparison with SE for most of the test images. This findingis also established by examining the outcomes SE and FE by deploying quality parameters, i.e. FSIM (Table 3) and QILV (Table 4). In significantly majority cases FE gives better results than SE.

CONCLUSION

It can be concluded from the above discussion that Fuzzy entropy based thresholding methods for multilevel segmentation performs significantly better than Shannon based methods in the histopathological image segmentation field. Fuzzy entropy based thresholding techniques delivers satisfactory results in the case of visual comparison. These claims are doubtlessly established via state-of-art image quality as-

Figure 1. (a) -(e) Original gray level histopathological images

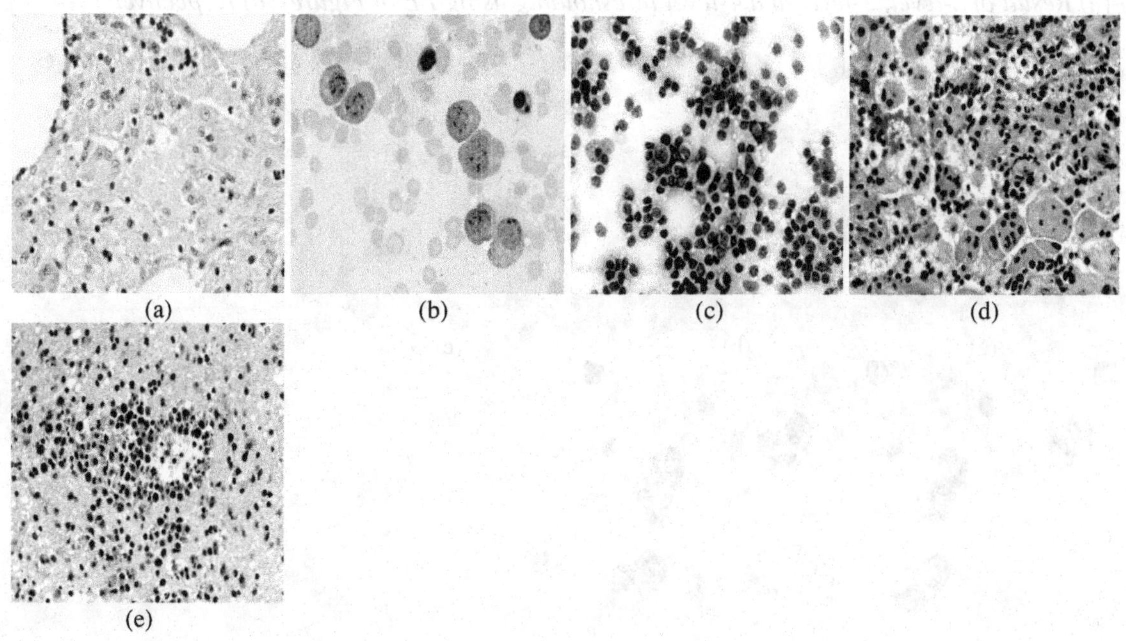

Figure 2. (a)-(c) Result of 2-level, 3-level and 4-level thresholding using SE of Figure 1(a)respectively(d)-(e) Result of 2-level, 3-level and 4-level thresholding using FE of Figure1(a) respectively

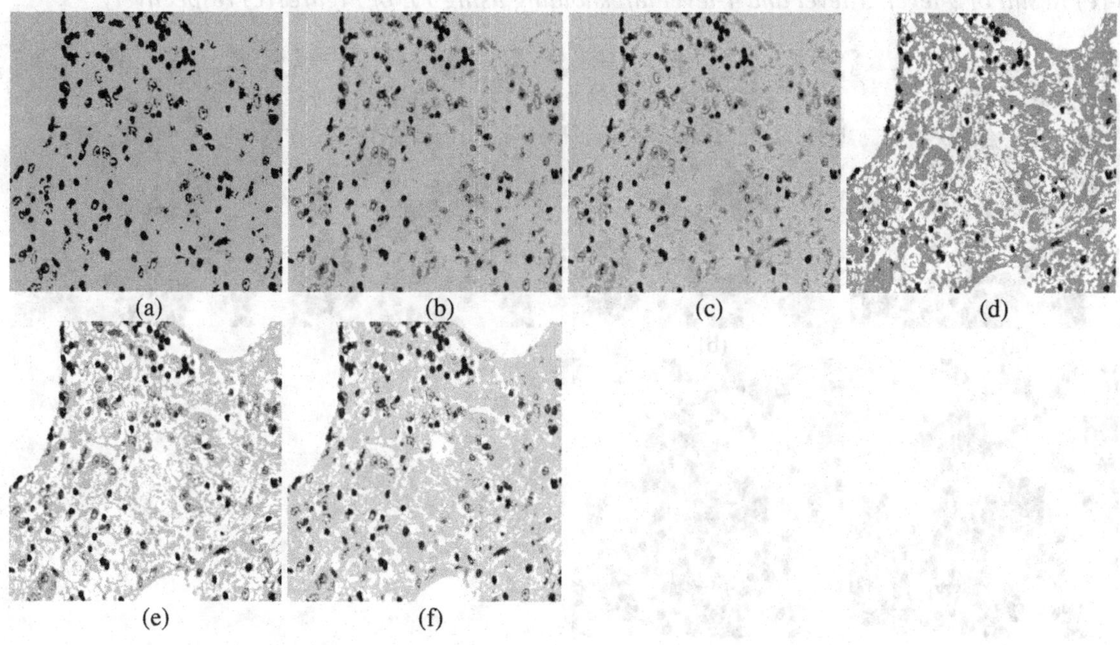

Figure 3. (a)-(c) Result of 2-level, 3-level and 4-level thresholding using SE of Figure 1(b) respectively (d)-(e) Result of 2-level, 3-level and 4-level thresholding using FE of Figure1(b) respectively

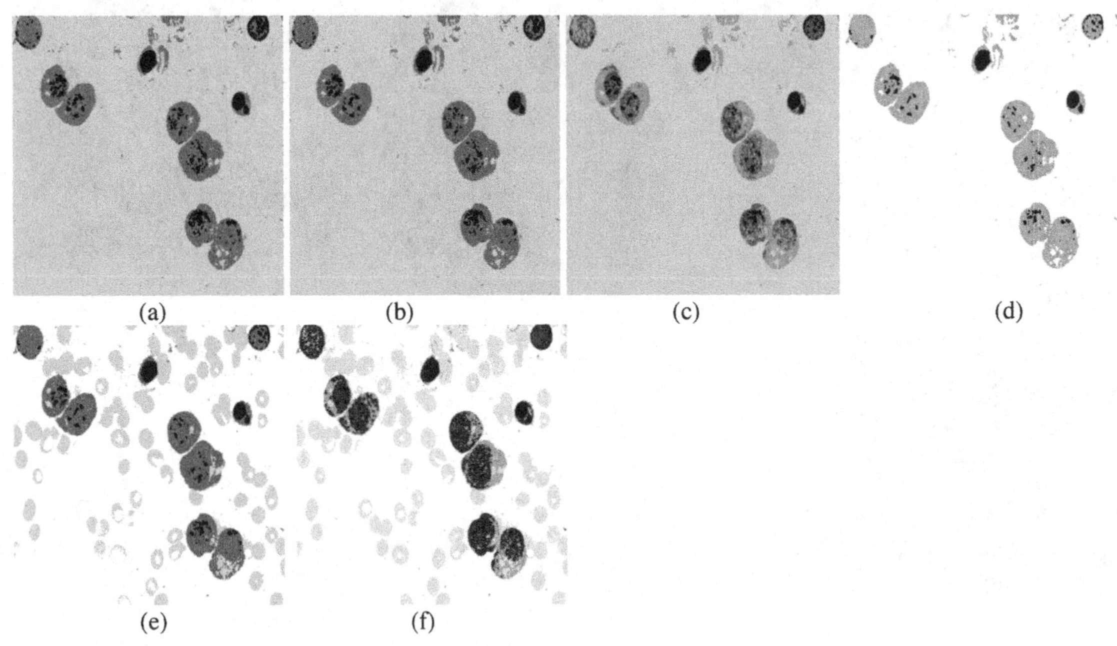

Figure 4. (a)-(c) Result of 2-level, 3-level and 4-level thresholding using SE of Figure 1(c) respectively (d)-(e) Result of 2-level, 3-level and 4-level thresholding using FE of Figure1(c) respectively

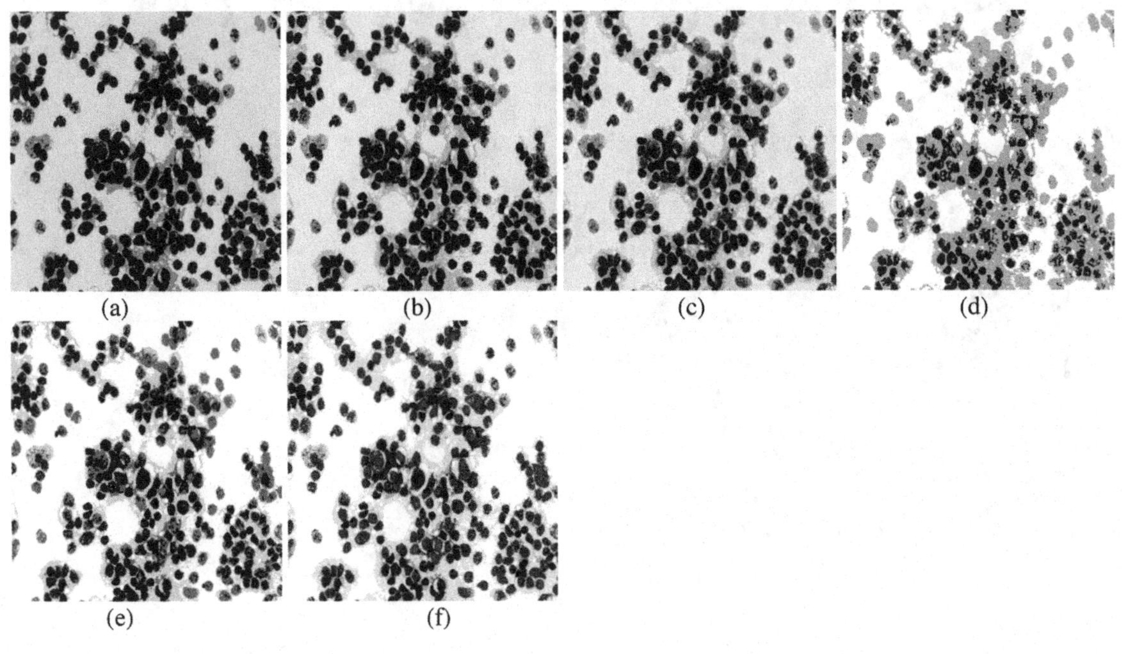

Figure 5. (a)-(c) Result of 2-level, 3-level and 4-level thresholding using SE of Figure 1(d) respectively (d)-(e) Result of 2-level, 3-level and 4-level thresholding using FE of Figure1(d) respectively

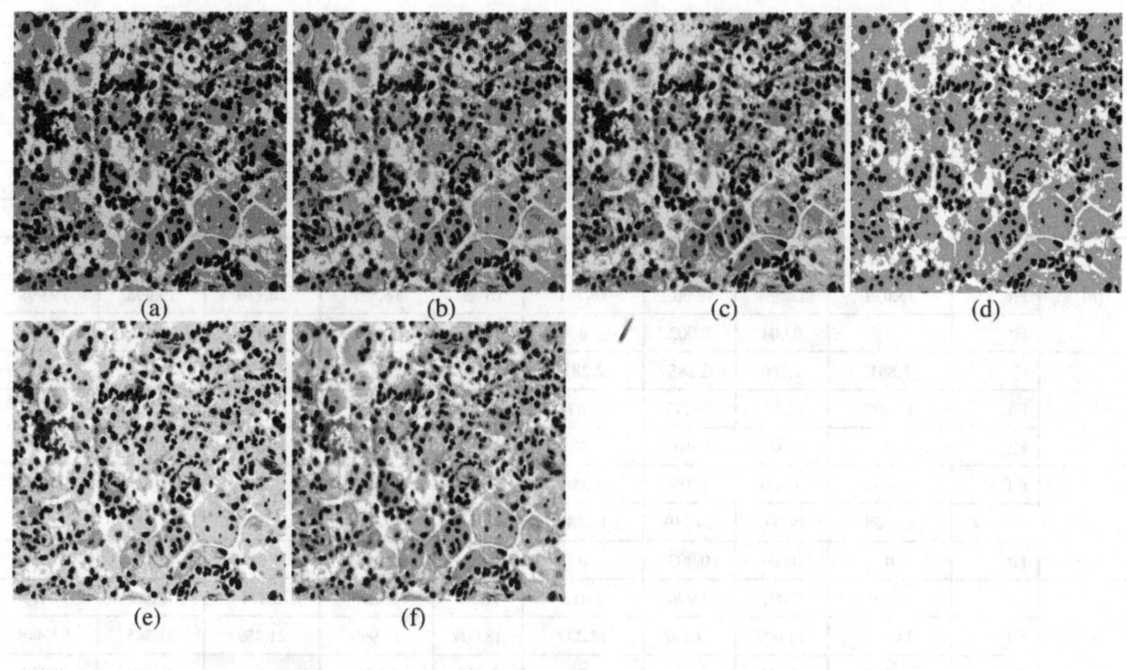

Figure 6. (a)-(c) Result of 2-level, 3-level and 4-level thresholding using SE of Figure 1(e) respectively. (d)-(e) Result of 2-level, 3-level and 4-level thresholding using FE of Figure1(e) respectively

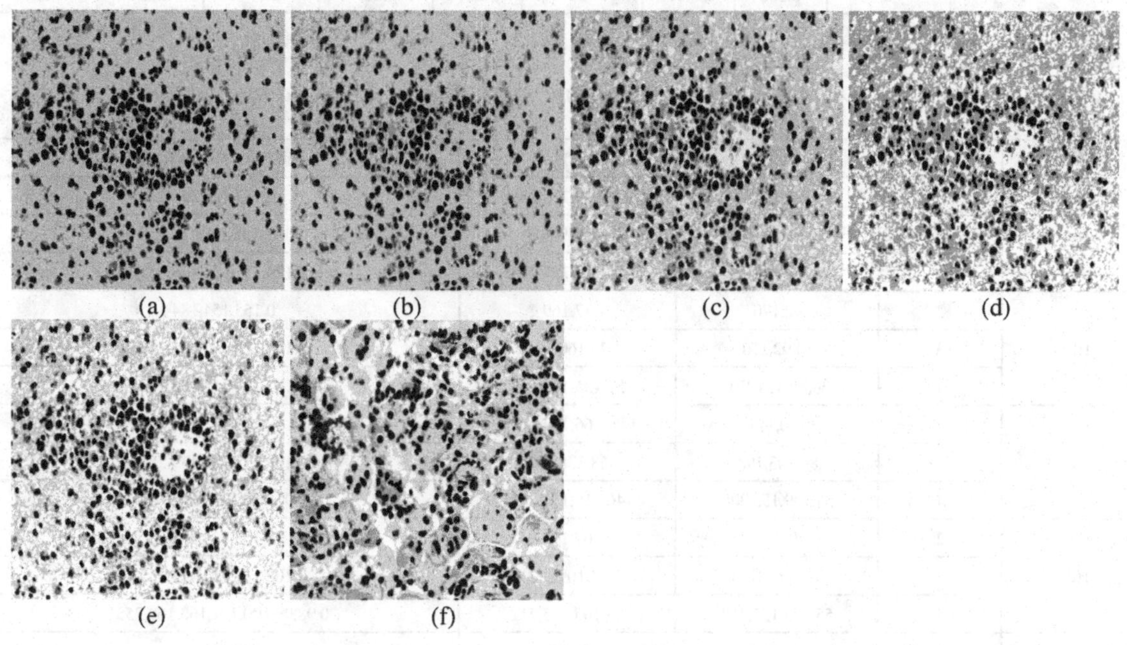

Table 1. Comparison of Computational time (CT), Mean Fitness value (Fit_m) and Standard Deviation (Fit_{std}) between Proposed CS, traditional CS (TCS) and PSO.

Image		2-Level Thresholding			3-Level Thresholding			4-Level Thresholding		
		Proposed CS	TCS	PSO	Proposed CS	TCS	PSO	Proposed CS	TCS	PSO
1(a)	CT	**1.702**	1.892	1.996	**2.579**	2.875	3.012	**3.488**	3.980	4.101
	Fit_m	**13.402**	13.023	13.123	**17.402**	17.233	17.233	**20.557**	20.146	20.121
	Fit_{std}	**0**	0.004	0.003	**0**	0.023	0.188	**0**	0.024	0.021
1(b)	CT	**1.406**	1.678	1.564	**2.316**	2.876	2.855	**3.626**	4.325	4.287
	Fit_m	**13.079**	12.564	12.668	**16.731**	16.551	16.551	**20.120**	19.998	19.998
	Fit_{std}	**0**	0.004	0.002	**0**	0.035	0.030	**0**	0.27	0.22
1(c)	CT	**1.801**	2.266	2.285	**2.281**	2.985	3.001	**3.357**	3.989	4.001
	Fit_m	**13.892**	13.776	13.777	**17.877**	17.786	17.788	**21.184**	21.001	21.001
	Fit_{std}	**0**	0.007	0.010	**0**	0.009	0.005	**0**	0.018	0.011
1(d)	CT	**1.646**	1.900	1.912	**2.380**	2.448	2.459	**3.347**	3.990	4.187
	Fit_m	**14.389**	14.009	14.119	**18.289**	17.998	17.998	**21.6774**	21.223	21.238
	Fit_{std}	**0**	0.004	0.003	**0**	0.009	0.004	**0**	0.005	0.006
1(e)	CT	**1.699**	2.001	1.996	**2.413**	3.001	2.984	**3.894**	4.221	4.019
	Fit_m	**14.281**	14.002	14.101	**18.339**	18.009	17.999	**21.759**	21.345	21.448
	Fit_{std}	**0**	0.004	0.003	**0**	0.045	0.055	**0**	0.055	0.048
Average Over 50 images	CT	**1.559**	1.875	1.879	**2.403**	2.986	2.984	**3.678**	4.222	4.211
	Fit_m	**13.879**	13.554	13.605	**18.202**	18.100	18.107	**21.243**	21.190	21.221
	Fit_{std}	**0**	0.002	0.001	**0**	0.031	0.027	**0**	0.034	0.33

Table 2. Threshold values obtained by CS and variant for 2–4 level thresholding

Image	Level	SE	FE	Parameters Values for FE
1(a)	2	33,150	79,203	0,157,158,248
	3	33, 107,164	74,149,203	0, 147,148,149,150,255
	4	33,89,133,175	60,129,157,215	0,119,120,137,138,176,175,255
1(b)	2	92,170	77,169	0,153,154,184
	3	30,92,170	79,160,194	0,158,159,160,161,226
	4	30,81,124,171	52,135,165,198	0,104,105,164,165,166,167,228
1(c)	2	100,177	66,194	0,131,132,255
	3	86,143,198	68,138,197	0,136,137,138,139,255
	4	64,109,158,206	46,115,152,212	0,92,93,136,137,167,168,255
1(d)	2	101,181	67,195	0,133,134,255
	3	61,117,186	54,109,183	0,108,109,110,111,255
	4	55,105,155,202	49,100,135,212	0,98,99,100,101,168,169,255
1(e)	2	88,159	70,198	0,140,141,255
	3	67,118,169	69,139,198	0,137,138,139,140,255
	4	63,112,160,213	52,115,153,218	0,103,104,125,126,179,180,255

Table 3. Results of IQA matrices FSIM using Proposed CS

Image	2-Level		3-Level		4-Level	
	SE	FE	SE	FE	SE	FE
1(a)	0.6126	**0.6356**	0.7181	**0.7694**	0.8018	**0.7895**
1(b)	0.7495	**0.7583**	0.7618	**0.7831**	0.7757	**0.8152**
1(c)	0.6737	**0.7669**	0.7787	**0.8101**	0.8156	**0.8487**
1(d)	0.7276	**0.7721**	0.8051	**0.8498**	0.8425	**0.8969**
1(e)	0.7109	**0.7707**	0.8302	**0.8241**	0.8727	**0.9067**
Average Over 50 images	0.6979	**0.7203**	0.7718	**0.8110**	0.8425	**0.8869**

Table 4. Results of IQA matrices QILV using Proposed CS

Image	2-Level		3-Level		4-Level	
	SE	FE	SE	FE	SE	FE
1(a)	0.5175	**0.7502**	0.6111	**0.8643**	0.7098	**0.9204**
1(b)	0.7598	**0.7337**	0.7553	**0.7455**	0.7381	**0.7837**
1(c)	0.7099	**0.9475**	0.8536	**0.9607**	0.8944	**0.9784**
1(d)	0.7642	**0.9257**	0.8221	**0.9079**	0.9104	**0.9388**
1(e)	0.7259	**0.8878**	0.7979	**0.9345**	0.9248	**0.9775**
Average Over 50 images	0.6987	**0.7754**	0.8021	**0.8743**	0.8854	**0.9204**

sessments metrics FSIM and QILV. Undoubtedly, CS and its modified variant adds speed to the proposed multi-thresholding model. The proposed self adaptive and parameter less CS algorithm outperforms the traditional CS and PSO algorithms in this multi-thresholding domain in terms of computational time, consistency and convergence rate. However, in future more metaheuristic algorithms could be compared with the proposed CS algorithm in this domain and other also. Several other fuzzy membership functions may be used for further experiment and other well-established quality assessment metrics could be employed to prove the competence of the segmentation algorithms. Lastly and most importantly, the 2-D histogram based approach could be implemented in order to get improved outcomes.

REFERENCES

Bhandari, A. K., Kumar, A., & Singh, G. K. (2015). Tsallis entropy based multi-level thresholding image segmentation using evolutionary algorithms. *Expert System with Applications, 42*, 8707-8730.

Bloch, I. (2005). Fuzzy spatial relationships for image processing and interpretation: A review. *Image and Vision Computing*, *23*(2), 89–110. doi:10.1016/j.imavis.2004.06.013

Borisenko, V. I., Zlatotol, A. A., & Muchnik, I. B. (1987). Image segmentation (state of the art survey). *Automation and Remote Control, 48*, 837–879.

Cheng, H. D., Chen, Y. H., & Jiang, X. H. (2000). Thresholding using two dimensional histogram and fuzzy entropy principle. *IEEE Transactions on Image Processing*, *9*(4), 732–735. doi:10.1109/83.841949 PMID:18255445

Coelho, L. S., & Mariani, V. C. (2008). Use of chaotic sequences in a biologically inspired algorithm for engineering design optimization. *Expert Systems with Applications*, *34*(3), 1905–1913. doi:10.1016/j.eswa.2007.02.002

Dhal & Das. (2017). Colour Retinal images enhancement using Modified Histogram Equalization methods and Firefly Algorithm. *Int. Jr. of Biomedical Engineering and Technology*. (in press)

Dhal, K. G., & Das, S. (2015). Diversity Conserved Chaotic Artificial Bee Colony Algorithm based Brightness Preserved Histogram Equalization and Contrast Stretching Method. *International Journal of Natural Computing Research, 5*, 45-73.

Dhal, K. G., & Das, S. (2017). Cuckoo search with search strategies and proper objective function for brightness preserving image enhancement. *Pattern Recognition and Image Analysis*. (in press)

Dhal, K. G., Namtirtha, A., Quraishi, I. M., & Das, S. (2016). Grey level image enhancement using Particle Swarm Optimization with Lévy Flight: An Eagle Strategy Approach. *Int. Conf. on Emerging Trends in Computer Sc. and Information (ETCSIT-2015)*.

Dhal, K.G, Quraishi, I. M., & Das, S. (2015). Performance Analysis of Chaotic Lévy Bat Algorithm and Chaotic Cuckoo Search Algorithm for Gray Level Image Enhancement. *Information Systems Design and Intelligent Applications*, 233-244.

Dhal, K. G., Quraishi, I. M., & Das, S. (2015). *Development of firefly algorithm via chaotic sequence and population diversity to enhance the image contrast. Natural Computing* , 15, 1–12.

Dhal, K.G., Quraishi, I. M., & Das, S. (2015). A Chaotic Lévy flight Approach in Bat and Firefly Algorithm for Gray level image Enhancement. *I. J. Image, Graphics and Signal Processing, 7*, 69-76.

Dhal, K.G., Quraishi, I. M., & Das, S. (2015). Performance Enhancement of Differential Evolution by Incorporating Lévy Flight and Chaotic Sequence for the Cases of Satellite Images. *Int. J. of Applied Metaheuristic Computing, 6*, 69-81.

Dhal, K.G., Quraishi, I. M., & Das, S. (2017). An improved cuckoo search based optimal ranged brightness preserved histogram equalization and contrast stretching method. *Int. Jr. of Swarm intelligence Research, 8*, 1-29.

Dhal, K. G., Sen, M., & Das, S. (2017). Cuckoo search based modified Bi-Histogram Equalization-method to enhance the cancerous tissues in Mammography images. *International Journal of Medical Engineering and Informatics*.

Fu, K. S., & Mui, J. K. (1981). A survey on image segmentation. *Pattern Recognition, 13*(1), 3–16. doi:10.1016/0031-3203(81)90028-5

Haralharick, R. M., & Shapiro, L. G. (1985). Survey: Image segmentation techniques. *CVGIP, 29*, 100–132.

Kapur, J. N., Sahoo, P. K., & Wong, A. K. C. (1985). A new method for gray-level picture thresholding using the entropy of the histogram. *Computer Vision Graphics and Image Processing, 29*(3), 273–285. doi:10.1016/0734-189X(85)90125-2

Krishna Priya, R., Thangaraj, C., Kesavadas, C., & Kannan, S. (2013). Fuzzy Entropy-Based MR Brain Image Segmentation Using Modified Particle Swarm Optimization. *Int J Imaging Syst Technol., 23*, 281-288.

Li, C. H., & Lee, C. K. (1993). Minimum cross entropy thresholding. *Pattern Recognition, 26*(4), 617–625. doi:10.1016/0031-3203(93)90115-D

Luca, A.D., & Termini, S. (1972). Definition of a non probabilistic entropy in the setting of fuzzy sets theory. *Inf. Contr., 20*, 301–315.

Olive, D., Cuevas, E., Pajares, G., Zaldivar, D., & Perez-Cisneros, M. (2013). Multilevel Thresholding Segmentation Based on Harmony Search Optimization. *Journal of Applied Mathematics, 2013*, 1–24. doi:10.1155/2013/575414

Pal, N. R. (1996). On minimum cross entropy thresholding. *Pattern Recognition, 29*(4), 575–580. doi:10.1016/0031-3203(95)00111-5

Pal, N. R., & Pal, S. K. (1993). A review on image segmentation. *Pattern Recognition, 26*(9), 1277–1294. doi:10.1016/0031-3203(93)90135-J

Pun, T. (1981). Entropic thresholding, a new approach. *Computer Graphics and Image Processing, 16*(3), 210–239. doi:10.1016/0146-664X(81)90038-1

Riseman, E. M., & Arbib, M. A. (1977). Survey: Computational techniques in the visual segmentation of static scenes. *Computer Vision Graphics and Image Processing, 6*(3), 221–276. doi:10.1016/S0146-664X(77)80028-2

Rosin, P. L. (2001). Unimodal thresholding. *Pattern Recognition, 34*(11), 2083–2096. doi:10.1016/S0031-3203(00)00136-9

Sahoo, P. K., Soltani, S., Wong, A. K. C., & Chen, Y. C. (1988). A survey of thresholding techniques. *CVGIP, 41*, 233–260.

Sarkar, S., Paul, S., Burman, R., Das, S., & Chaudhuri, S. S. (2015). A Fuzzy Entropy Based Multi-Level Image Thresholding Using Differential Evolution. *SEMCCO, 2014*, 386–395.

Sarkar, S., Das, S., & Chaudhuri, S. (2016). Hyper-Spectral image segmentation Renyi entropy based multi-level thresholding aided with differential evolution. *Expert System with Applications, 50*, 120-129.

Tao, W. B., Tian, J. W., & Liu, J. (2003). Image segmentation by three-level thresholding based on maximum fuzzy entropy and genetic algorithm. *Pattern Recognition Letters*, *24*(16), 3069–3078. doi:10.1016/S0167-8655(03)00166-1

Weszka, J. S. (1978). A survey of threshold selection techniques. *CGIP*, *7*(2), 259–265.

Wong, A. K. C., & Sahoo, P. K. (1989). A gray-level threshold selection method based on maximum entropy principle. *IEEE Transactions on Systems, Man, and Cybernetics*, *19*(4), 866–871. doi:10.1109/21.35351

Yang, X. S. (2010). *Nature-Inspired Metaheuristic Algorithms* (2nd ed.). Luniver Press.

Zhao, M. S., Fu, A. M. N., & Yan, H. (2001). A technique of three level thresholding based on probability partition and fuzzy 3-partition. *IEEE Transactions on Fuzzy Systems*, *9*(3), 469–479. doi:10.1109/91.928743

KEY TERMS AND DEFINITIONS:

Chaotic Sequence: Chaos defines the complex behavior of non-linear deterministic system which has ergodicity property.

Entropy: Shannon defined the entropy as a function of probability of occurrence of states of the system.

Lévy Flight: Lévy flight is a random walk whose step length is determined from the Lévy distribution. A random walk is a mathematical method of representing a series of consecutive random steps.

Segmentation: Image segmentation is a process which sub-divides the image in the non-overlapping subset containing similar property, color, intensity, etc.

Chapter 14
Optimized Base Station Sleeping and Smart Grid Energy Procurement Scheme to Improve Energy Efficiency

Qiang Wang
Yulin Normal University, China

Hai-Lin Liu
Guangdong University of Technology, China

ABSTRACT

In this chapter, the authors propose a joint BS sleeping strategy, resource allocation, and energy procurement scheme to maximize the profit of the network operators and minimize the carbon emission. Then, a joint optimization problem is formulated, which is a mixed-integer programming problem. To solve it, they adopt the bi-velocity discrete particle swarm optimization (BVDPSO) algorithm to optimize the BS sleeping strategy. When the BS sleeping strategy is fixed, the authors propose an optimal algorithm based on Lagrange dual domain method to optimize the power allocation, subcarrier assignment, and energy procurement. Numerical results illustrate the effectiveness of the proposed scheme and algorithm.

INTRODUCTION

With the exponential increasing of the number of the mobile terminals and traffic demands, reducing the power consumption of the cellular radio networks becomes more and more urgent to reduce the cost of the transmission and the pollution on the environment. Indeed, the carbon emission caused by the information and communication technologies (ICT) accounts for more than 2%. Meanwhile, the energy cost constitutes a significant portion of the expenditure of the operators. Thus, the technologies of green communication becomes more and more popular in industry and academia. Especially, base station (BS) sleeping strategy is a well known technique to improve the energy efficiency. Indeed, for the wireless communication system, over 70%-80% power is consumed by base stations, and an active base station

DOI: 10.4018/978-1-5225-5134-8.ch014

in idle status expends more than 50% of the energy because of circuit processing and air conditioning (Wu, Zhou & Niu, 2013; Marsan, Chiaraviglio, Ciullo, & Meo, 2013). Therefore, switching off redundant BSs is an efficient technology to decrease the energy consumption of the wireless networks. BS sleeping can enable the BS in light sleep mode in the low-load time slot to decrease the energy consumption.

On the other hand, the integration of the wireless networks and smart grids is also investigated to decrease the carbon emission (Huang, Crow, Heydt, Zheng, & Dale, 2011; Yu, Zhang, Xiao, & Choudhury, 2011; Erol-Kantarci and Mouftah, 2011; Lu, Wang, & Ma, 2013; Bu, Yu, Cai, & Liu, 2012; Ghazzai, Yaacoub, Alouini, & Abudayya, 2014). Smart grids are new generation electricity grids, and they can significantly improve the energy efficiency of the wireless network since smart grids can enhance energy savings and reduce carbon emission to achieve the green goals of consumers through using the massive renewable energy (wind energy, solar energy and conventional energy, etc.). Furthermore, smart grids make customers have more feasible procurement strategy due to the intelligent scheduling. Due to the limited availability and the uncertainty about the timing and the quantity of renewable energy (e.g., the solar energy can be used only in the daytime.), the smart grid should determine to sell power to each BS from which energy retailers and sell how much power from each energy retailer, which is called smart grid procurement strategy in this paper. Besides BS sleeping and the smart grid procurement, the energy efficient for the OFDMA cellular networks is also important to improve the system energy efficiency since suitable subcarrier and power allocation can significantly enhance the system throughput with the same energy consumption (Ghazzai et al., 2014).

As aforementioned, obviously, it will create a lot of advantages to jointly consider the BS sleeping, resource allocation and smart grid procurement decision to decrease the system energy consumption. It is worth nothing that these issues are not independent but have strong correlation. In fact, the smart grid procurement decision is dependent on the radio resource allocation and power control which determines the energy consumption of the cellular network. Meanwhile, the BS sleeping strategy is dependent on the smart grid procurement decision, resource allocation and power control. Therefore, joint optimization is necessary to achieve high system energy efficiency. Nonetheless, to the best of our knowledge, there are no paper which consider these issues at the same time, and most of the relation works only consider the subset of the above issues.

Evolutionary algorithm (EA) is a strong optimization approach which can be used to solve a lot of complicated optimization problems (Wenyong, & MengChu, 2017). Due to its simpler implementation, faster convergence speed and strong global search ability, EA has been wildly adopted in engineering field, such as(Junzhi, Zhengxing, Ming, & Min, 2016; Nataraj, Tanuj, & Vivek, 2017; Rui, Yuzhou, & Liuqing, 2017; Safdar, Hazlie, Hamzah, Kanendra, Javed, Anis, & Mohd, 2016; Santosh, & Sanjay. 2016; Shuangxin, Guibin, Dingli, & Yijiang, 2015; Zhao-Hua, Hua-Liang, Qing-Chang, Kan, Xiao-Shi, & Liang-Hong, 2017). Rui, et al. (2017) consider the multiple constrained quality-of-service (QoS) routing in named data networking which is a representation and implementation of an information centric network. Then, a particle swarm optimisation-forwarding information base (PSO-FIB) algorithm which uses the forwarding experiences of particles to maintain the forwarding probability of each entry in the FIB is proposed to solve the problem.

In this chapter, we combine the BS sleeping with subcarrier assignment and power allocation to decrease the cellular network's energy consumption due to their strong complementarity. Meanwhile, we consider the scenario in which the cellular network is powered by the distributed smart grid, and there are some different retailers in the smart grid to provide power with different prices and pollutant levels depending on the nature of the generated energy. As already noted, the cellular network should determine to procure power form which retailers and procure how much power from each retailer to obtain a good trade-off between the revenue and carbon emission. To maximize the system energy efficiency, our objective is to give an optimal scheme which can determine the BS should be turned into BS sleeping mode in which time slots to maximize the profit of network operators and minimize the carbon emission at the same time. Unfortunately, the more profits the network operators gain, the more carbon dioxide is emitted. Thus, we should achieve a good trade-off between the system throughput and energy consumption. To this end, we propose a joint optimization problem involving the BS sleeping mode selection, smart grid procurement, power allocation as well as subcarrier assignment. In the distributed smart grid, the renewable energy is more green but more expensive than the traditional energy, therefore it is important to optimize the energy procurement of the smart grid to achieve a good trade-off between the profit and the carbon emission. The joint optimization problem is formulated as a mixed integer programming problem in which there are both integer variables (BS sleeping mode selection and subcarrier assignment) and continuous variables (power allocation and procurement decision). In general, the mixed-integer programming problem becomes more and more intractable with the increase of the number of users, subcarriers and BSs due to the computational nature of the subcarrier assignment and BS sleeping mode selection. PSO is a famous and efficient swarm intelligence algorithm to tackle the engineering problem. In this chapter, we adopt the bi-velocity discrete particle swarm optimization (BVDPSO) algorithm to solve the BS sleeping strategy, and then the original optimization problem only consists of the power allocation, subcarrier assignment and energy procurement which is still difficult to solve due to the combinatorial nature of the subcarrier assignment. Finally, a mixed algorithm is proposed based on Lagrange dual domain algorithm to solve the power allocation, subcarrier assignment and energy procurement.

The rest of the chapter is organized as follows. The related work is described in section II. In section III, the system model is presented. Section IV introduces the BVDPSO briefly. In section V, we describe the iterative algorithm based on Lagrange dual domain method to solve the resource allocation and energy procurement. In section VI, simulation results are provided to evaluate the performance of the proposed algorithm. Finally, we conclude this paper in section VII.

RELATED WORK

With the exponential increase in mobile internet traffic, the technology of green communication attracts more and more attentions. Energy efficient resource allocation, BS sleeping and the integration of the smart grid and mobile networks are promising green communication technologies, and there are enormous amount works which investigate these two issues to decrease the energy consumption of the wireless networks. In this section, we review the previous works related to the above issues.

Energy efficient resource allocation is an effective technique to improve the energy efficiency of wireless communication system since suitable resource allocation can not only improve the system throughput but also reduce energy consumption (Loodaricheh, Mallick, & Bhargava, 2014; Héliot, 2014; Xu et al., 2014; Li et al., 2014). Loodaricheh et al. (2014) consider the energy efficient resource allocation for orthogonal frequency-division multiple-access (OFDMA) cellular networks with multiuser cooperation and QoS constraint. They jointly optimize the subcarrier pairing, relay selection, subcarrier allocation as well as power allocation to maximize the system energy efficiency. The joint optimization problem is a mixed-integer programming problem, which is generally difficult to solve. Next, they reformulate the mixed-integer programming problem into a convex optimization problem by relaxing the integer variables, and then propose an optimal algorithm to tackle this problem. Héliot (2014) considers the energy efficient resource allocation problem for cooperative multiple-input-multiple-output-amplify forward (MIMO-AF) system. Then, a low-complexity energy efficient resource allocation method is proposed to solve the problem. Meanwhile, Héliot (2014) shows that the usage of one relay is only energy efficient when the quality of the direct link is very poor. In the work of Li et al. (2014), the joint resource allocation problem for multicell networks is considered. Li et al. (2014) jointly optimize the power control, subcarrier assignment and user association, and the joint optimization problem is formulated as a max-min cell throughput problem. Then, an alternating-optimization-based algorithm based on branch-and-bound and simulated annealing (SA) is proposed to solve it.

BS sleeping can significantly decrease the energy cost and carbon emission by switch-off the light load BSs and draws a lot of attention. In the work of Wu et al. (2013), two types of BS sleeping schemes, user number based and vacation time based sleeping schemes, are proposed with the aim of improving the energy efficiency. The conditions for incorporating these different types of sleeping control into the power matching energy efficiently are obtained. Then, the optimal energy-delay tradeoffs are provided by jointly optimizing the service rate and the sleeping parameter. The various BS sleeping modes are also considered by the work of Marsan et al. (2013). In their work, an analytical framework to identify the optimal scheduling of low-power network configurations (including how many BSs should be put into sleep mode and when) is proposed. Besides, the sleep scheme for the heterogeneous networks is also investigated by the work of Marsan et al. (2013). Marsan et al. (2013) show that in a realistic heterogeneous network with real traffic profiles, large savings can be achieved by putting BSs to sleep, starting from the least loaded to the most loaded. Yong et al. (2013) and Peng et al. (2014) also consider the BS sleeping scheme for the heterogeneous network. In the work of Yong et al. (2013), the authors derive the success probability and energy efficiency in homogeneous macrocell (single-tier) and heterogeneous K-tier wireless networks under different sleeping policies using stochastic geometry. In addition, the power consumption minimization and energy efficiency maximization problems are formulated, and the optimal operating regimes for macrocell base stations is determined. In the work of Peng et al. (2014), the optimal BS density for both homogeneous and heterogeneous cellular networks to minimize network energy cost is studied. Peng et al. (2014) show that if the ratio between the micro BS cost and the macro BS cost is lower than a threshold then the optimal strategy is to deploy micro BSs for capacity extension or to switch off macro BSs for energy saving with higher priority.

After BS sleeping, the remaining active users in the sleeping cell also need service. Thus, cell zooming, which can adaptively change the coverage of the neighboring active BS, is proposed to meet the requirement. Tabassum et al. (2014) develop a tractable framework to characterize the performance of cellular systems with BS sleeping and then propose a user association scheme in which a user of sleeping cell selects an active BS with the maximum mean channel access probability. After the BS sleeping, the rest of the active users in the cell still need the service. Cao et al. (2013) study the spectrum-energy efficiency optimization problem where BSs are with the ability to perform cell zooming, sleep mode, and user migration. Furthermore, in their work, revenue is regarded as efficiency in spectrum use, the cost as energy consumption, and then the revenue-to-cost ratio is interpreted as spectrum-energy efficiency. They formulate the problem as an integer linear programming problem and solve the problem using CPLEX. In the work of Yang et al. (2013), the authors propose a dynamic scheme that reduces energy consumption in relay-assisted cellular networks by switching light-loaded BSs into sleeping mode, and then transfer the users in the sleeping cells to neighboring cells using dynamic relay-station-BS (RS-

BS) associations. Hsu et al. (2014) study the spectrum-energy efficiency optimization problem where BSs are with the ability to perform cell zooming, sleep mode, and user migration. They formulate the problem into an integer linear program.

However, all the previous works consider the large-time scale BS sleeping, which have many disadvantages in some cases. For example, the cellular network load and channel condition may be changing rapidly, on the contrary the sleeping BS cannot be waken up in sufficient short time. Therefore, it is not available for the case of small-time scale. Based on this, Discontinuous Transmission (DTX) is proposed which enable the deactivation of some components of the base station and can wake up the BS in sufficient short time, and has attracted much attention recently(Tombaz, Han, Sung, & Zander, 2014; Ashraf, Boccardi, & Ho, 2011; Holtkamp, Auer, Bazzi, & Haas, 2013; Cui, Lau, & Wu, (2012). Tombaz et al. (2014) analyze the maximum achievable energy saving with cell DTX and obtain the optimum BS density that minimizes the daily average area power consumption under certain coverage and quality of service constraints. Ashraf et al. (2011) introduce energy-efficient sleep mode algorithms for small cell base stations in a bid to reduce cellular networks' power consumption.

In order to reduce the carbon emission, there is increasing interest in integrating renewable resources into the power grid (Huang et al., 2011; Yu et al., 2011; Erol-Kantarci and Mouftah, 2011; Lu et al., 2013; Bu et al., 2012; Ghazzai et al., 2014). One of the difficulties for integrating renewable resources into the power grid is the intermittent nature of the renewable energy. Yu et al. (2011) present some solutions adopting the advance sensing, communication and control functionalities for grid integration of renewable energy resources. Bu et al. (2012) and Ghazzai et al. (2014) investigate the scenario that the mobile communication system powered by the smart grid. In the work of Erol-Kantarci and Mouftah (2011), sleeping mode is considered, and coordinated multipoint (CoMP) is used to ensure acceptable service quality in the cells whose base stations have been shut down. Bu et al. (2012) consider how the dynamic operation of cellular base stations based on the traffic arrival rate, real time price provided by the smart grid, and pollutant levels of electricity retailers can reduce operational expenditure and greenhouse gas emission in green wireless cellular networks. Finally, a Stackelberg game is formulated to solve the problem. A similar problem is investigated by Ghazzai et al. (2014). Specially, both the DL and UL directions are investigated where orthogonal frequency-division multiple access (OFDMA) and single carrier frequency-domain multiple access (SC-FDMA) are adopted in the work of Ghazzai et al. (2014), respectively. Then, evolutionary algorithm based methods for implementing the BS sleeping strategy are proposed to solve the formulated problem.

SYSTEM MODEL AND PROBLEM FORMULATION

System Model

In this chapter, we consider a downlink OFDMA cellular network consisting of M BSs. To simplify the expression, we assume that each BS equips a single omnidirectional antenna (i.e., each BS corresponds to one cell). Without loss of generality, we assume there are K users and N subcarriers in each cell. Besides, the wireless cellular network is powered by the smart grid where the renewable resource is integrated into. The wireless cellular network purchases energy from the S retailers of the smart grid with different prices since the energy sources of each retailer are different, such as solar energy, wind energy or conventional energy, and so on.

Although inter-cell interference is the major interference for the OFDMA system, we ignore the inter-cell interference since we assume the inter-cell interference is managed efficiently with the inter-cell interference control mechanism. In this paper, our goal is to determine that which BSs should be switched off and determine each BS should purchase energy from which energy retailers and how much energy should be purchased from each retailer to maximize the operator's profit and minimize the carbon emission at the same time.

Problem Formulation

We denote the achievable rate of user *k* associated with the *m*th BS over subcarrier *n* as $R^{m}_{n,k}$. Then, the achievable rate $R^{m}_{n,k}$ can be given as:

$$R^{m}_{n,k} = \log_2(1 + \left|h_{m,n,k}\right|^2 p_{m,n,k}) \tag{1}$$

where $h^{t}_{m,n,k}$ denotes the channel coefficient from the *m*th BS to the *k*th user over subcarrier *n*; The average rate of the *k*th user in the *m*th cell in the frame can be represented as:

$$R_{m,k} = \sum_{n=1}^{N} u_{mnk} R^{m}_{n,k} \tag{2}$$

where u_{mnk} is the subchannel assignment indicator, $\forall$ *m*, *n*, *k*. $u_{mnk} = 1$, if subcarrier *n* is assigned to user *k* in the *m*th cell; otherwise, $u_{mnk} = 0$;

Thus, the overall throughput of the *m*th cell can be given as:

$$R^{m} = \rho_m \sum_{n=1}^{N} \sum_{k=1}^{K} u_{mnk} R^{m}_{n,k} \tag{3}$$

where ρ_m is the BS sleeping indicator $\forall$ *m*. If the *m*th BS is active, $\rho_m = 1$; otherwise, $\rho_m = 0$.

Finally, the overall system throughput can be given as follows

$$R = \sum_{m=1}^{M} R^{m} \tag{4}$$

Clearly, when the *m*th BS is put into DTX mode, the throughput of the *m*th cell is zero. In this case, the network operator has no revenue from the *m*th cell.

Let ψ denote the price of the unit throughput. The overall revenue of the network operator can be given as:

$$E = \psi R = \psi \sum_{m=1}^{M} R^m \quad (5)$$

Intuitively, the network operators should pay more energy cost and pollutant emission cost to obtain more revenue. It can be readily explained that more throughput consumes more energy, and then more carbon emission is created. Next, we introduce the cost of energy consumption and pollutant emission function. The total cost of the energy consumption of the network is expressed as:

$$C(\rho,\mathrm{q}) = \sum_{m=1}^{M} \sum_{r=1}^{S} \rho_m \pi_r q_m^r \quad (6)$$

where π_r is the cost of one unit of energy provided by energy retailer *r*, q_m^r indicates the amount of energy procured by the *m*th BS from retailer *r*, $\rho = \left\{\rho_m\right\}_{1\times M}$, and $\mathrm{q} = \left\{q_m^r\right\}_{M\times S}$.

The pollutant emission function is modeled as follows (Ghazzai et al., 2014).

$$F(q_m^r) = \alpha_r (q_m^r)^2 + \beta_r q_m^r \quad (7)$$

where α_r and β_r are the emission coefficient costs of retailer *r*. For instance, if the retailer's energy source is renewable energy, the corresponding emission coefficient costs are small; otherwise, if the retailer's energy source is conventional energy, the corresponding emission coefficient costs are large.

Thus, the carbon emission cost function of the network *I* can be given as follows:

$$I(\rho,\mathrm{q}) = \sum_{m=1}^{M} \sum_{r=1}^{S} \rho_m F\left(q_m^r\right) \quad (8)$$

$I(\rho,\mathrm{q})$ can be regarded as the cost of the carbon emission. To reduce the impact on the environment, the network operators should procure more renewable energy. However, since the renewable energy is more expensive and limited, operators should pay more to procure the clean energy; and when the renewable energy is not enough to cover the need of operators, the operators should procure energy from another retailers owning the conventional energy.

As aforementioned, the operators should achieve a good tradeoff between the revenue of the network operators and the carbon emission. To this end, the operators should carefully adjust their attitude toward the revenue and the environment to maximize their profits and minimize the carbon emission. Then, the optimization problem can be formulated as

$$\mathrm{P1} \max_{\mathrm{p},\mathrm{u},\rho,\mathrm{q}} w(E(\rho,\mathrm{q}) - C(\rho,\mathrm{q})) + (1-w)I(\rho,\mathrm{q}) \quad (9)$$

$$s.t.\ \sum_{m=1}^{M} \rho_m q_m^r \le Q_{\max}^r, \forall r \tag{10}$$

$$\sum_{r=1}^{S} q_m^r = \sum_{n=1}^{N} \sum_{k=1}^{K} p_{m,n,k} + P_0, \forall m \tag{11}$$

$$\sum_{n=1}^{N} \sum_{k=1}^{K} p_{m,n,k} \le P_m, \forall m \tag{12}$$

$$\sum_{k=1}^{K} u_{mnk} = 1, \forall m, n, k \tag{13}$$

$$\rho_m \in \{0,1\}, \forall m \tag{14}$$

$$u_{mnk} \in \{0,1\}, \forall m, n, k \tag{15}$$

where **u**= $\{u_{mnk}\}_{M \times N \times K}$ and **p**= $\{p_{m,n,k}\}_{M \times N \times K}$; w is the weight parameter to be defined and P_m is the peak power of the *m*th BS; constraints (10) and (12) mean the joint energy procurement constraint and joint power constraint, respectively; constraint (11) indicates that the energy procured by a BS from all retailers should be equal to the overall power consumption of the BS; constraint (13) indicates that each subcarrier can be only assigned to one user in each cell.

BVDPSO FOR BASE STATION SLEEPING

The optimization problem **P1** is a mixed integer programming problem because of the combinatorial nature of the BS sleeping strategy and subcarrier assignment. In the first, we adopt the BVDPSO proposed by Shen et al. (2014) to solve the BS sleeping strategy variables, and then an optimal algorithm based on Lagrange dual domain method is proposed to jointly optimize the subcarrier assignment, power allocation and energy procurement. Next, we intend to introduce the BVDPSO.

For the scenario with *M* BSs, the position code for each particle *i* is defined as

$$X_i = [x_{i1}, x_{i2}, \cdots, x_{iM}]$$

where x_{im} = 0 or 1. If x_{im} = 1, BS *m* is active; otherwise, BS *m* is inactive.

In BVDPSO, the velocity of particle *i* is coded by a bi-velocity fashion as

$$V_i = \begin{bmatrix} v_{i1}^0 & v_{i2}^0 & \cdots & v_{iM}^0 \\ v_{i1}^1 & v_{i2}^1 & \cdots & v_{iM}^1 \end{bmatrix} \tag{16}$$

where $0 \le v_{im}^0 \le 1$, and $0 \le v_{im}^1 \le 1$.

The *m*th dimension of V_i is associated with bi-values, where v_{im}^0 is the possibility of x_{im} being 0, and v_{im}^1 is the possibility of x_{im} being 1.

Let $B_i = [b_{i,1}, \cdots, b_{i,M}]$ denote the personal historical best position vector of the *i*th particle, and the best position of all B_i is denoted as $L_i = [l_{i,1}, \cdots, l_{i,M}]$. V_i and X_i are updated in each generation by the guidance of B_i and L_i as follows

$$v_{i,m} = w \times v_{im} \oplus c_1 \times \left(b_{i,m} - x_{i,m}\right) \oplus c_2 \times \left(l_{i,m} - x_{i,m}\right) \tag{17}$$

$$x_{im} = x_{im} \otimes v_{im} \tag{18}$$

where *w* is the inertia weight, c_1 and c_2 are the acceleration coefficients; "$\otimes$" is the position update operator.

Velocity Update

There are three steps to update the particle's velocity in BVDPSO. The details are described as follows.

Velocity= *Position*1 − *Position*2: Suppose that *Position1* is X_1 and *Position2* is X_2. $V_i = X_1 - X_2$ means that if x_{1m} is **b** but x_{2m} is not **b** (**b** is 0 or 1), $v_{im}^b = 1$ and $v_{im}^{b-1} = 0$.

Velocity= *Coefficient*× *Velocity*: *Coefficient*× *Velocity* means to multiply c_1 or c_2 with each entry of the current *Velocity* to obtain each entry of the final *Velocity*. If any dimension of the final *Velocity* is larger than 1, this value is set to 1.

Velocity = *Velocity1* ⊕ *Velocity2*: Assume *Velocity1* and *Velocity2* are V_1 and V_2, and then $V_i = V_1 \oplus V_2$ is the final *Velocity*. According to [12], the *m*th dimension v_{im}^b in V_i is equal to the larger one between v_{1m}^b and v_{2m}^b (**b** is 0 or 1).

Position Update

In BVDPSO, the position is updated by using the strategy as follows:

$$x_{im} = \begin{cases} rand\{0,1\}, if\left(v_{im}^{0} > \alpha \text{and} v_{im}^{1} > \alpha\right) \\ 0, \qquad if\left(v_{im}^{0} > \alpha \text{and} v_{im}^{1} \leq \alpha\right) \\ 1, \qquad if\left(v_{im}^{0} \leq \alpha \text{and} v_{im}^{1} > \alpha\right) \\ x_{im}, \qquad if\left(v_{im}^{0} \leq \alpha \text{and} v_{im}^{1} \leq \alpha\right) \end{cases} \tag{19}$$

ITERATIVE ALGORITHM FOR ENERGY PROCUREMENT AND RESOURCE ALLOCATION

In the above section, we solve the BS sleeping strategy variables using BVDPSO. In fact, as A is known, there are only subcarrier assignment variable **u**, power allocation variable **p** and energy procurement variable **q** in the original optimization problem. Without loss generality, we let the price of unit throughput ψ be 1. Therefore, the original problem becomes as follows

$$\textbf{P2} \max_{\text{p,u,q}} U = w\text{P}(\text{p,u,q})\text{-}(1\text{-}w)I(\text{q}) \tag{20}$$

$$s.t.\ (10),(11),(12),(13),(15)$$

The problem **P2** is still a mixed integer programming problem which is also difficult to tackle in general. In this section, we introduce an optimal algorithm based on Lagrange dual domain method to solve problem **P2**.

Optimizing Resource Allocation and Energy Procurement

In the first, let $p_{m,n,k} = \frac{p_{m,n,k}}{u_{mnk}}$, $\forall m,n,k$. Clearly, it dose not change the problem **P2**. Indeed, if u_{mnk} = 0, the *n*th subcarrier is not allocated to user *k* in the *m*th cell. Then, $R_{n,k}^{m}$ can be rewritten as:

$$R_{n,k}^{m} = \log_2(1 + \frac{p_{m,n,k}}{u_{mnk}}\left|h_{m,n,k}\right|^2)$$

Next, we relax the subcarrier assignment variable **u** into continuous variable $\tilde{u}$. Therefore, problem **P2** can be converted into the form as follows:

$$\textbf{P3} \max_{\text{p,u,q}} U = w\text{P}(\text{p,u,q})\text{-}(1\text{-}w)I(\text{q}) \tag{21}$$

$$s.t. \sum_{k=1}^{K} \tilde{u}_{mnk} = 1, \forall m, n \tag{22}$$

$$0 \leq \tilde{u}_{mnk} \leq 1, \forall m, n, k \tag{23}$$

$$, (11), (12) \tag{10}$$

It is easy to prove that $\mathrm{P(p,\tilde{u},q)}$, **q** is concave in $\mathrm{(p,\tilde{u},q)}$, since $\tilde{u}_{mnk} \log_2(1 + \frac{p_{m,n,k}}{\tilde{u}_{mnk}} \left|h_{m,n,k}\right|^2)$ is the perspective function of $\log_2(1 + p_{m,n,k} \left|h_{m,n,k}\right|^2)$, and ***I(q)*** is convex in **q** through computing its Hessian matrix. Moreover, all constraints are linear functions. Therefore, problem **P3** is a convex optimization problem without duality gap which can be solved by Lagrange dual domain method.

Then, we introduce three Lagrange multiplier vectors $\vec{\eta} = [\eta_1, \cdots, \eta_S]$, $\vec{\mu} = [\mu_1, \cdots, \mu_S]$ and $\vec{\lambda} = [\lambda_1, \cdots, \lambda_S]$ associated with (10), (11) and (12), respectively.

Finally, the Lagrangian function of (20) is given by

$$L(\vec{\eta}, \vec{\mu}, \vec{\lambda}, \mathrm{p,u,q}) = F(\vec{\lambda}) + D(\vec{\eta}, \vec{\mu},) + (\sum_{m=1}^{M} (\mu_m + \lambda_m) P_m + \sum_{r=1}^{S} \eta_r Q_{\max}^r) \tag{24}$$

where

$$F(\vec{\lambda}) = \max_{\mathrm{\tilde{u},p}} w \sum_{m=1}^{M} \sum_{n=1}^{N} \sum_{k=1}^{K} \tilde{u}_{mnk} \log_2(1 + \frac{p_{mnk}}{\tilde{u}_{mnk}} \left|h_{m,n,k}\right|^2) - \sum_{m=1}^{M} \lambda_m \rho_m \sum_{n=1}^{N} \sum_{k=1}^{K} p_{m,n,k} \tag{25}$$

$$D(\eta, \mu) = \max_{\mathrm{q}} (w-1) \sum_{\mathrm{m}=1}^{\mathrm{M}} \sum_{\mathrm{r}=1}^{\mathrm{S}} F(q_m^r) - wC(\rho, \mathrm{q}) - \sum_{r=1}^{S} \eta_r \sum_{m=1}^{M} \rho_m q_m^r - \sum_{m=1}^{M} \rho_m \mu_m \sum_{r=1}^{S} q_m^r \tag{26}$$

Then, we can obtain the dual problem as follows

$$g(\vec{\eta}, \vec{\mu}, \vec{\lambda}) = \max_{\mathrm{\tilde{u},p,q}} L(\vec{\eta}, \vec{\mu}, \vec{\lambda}, \mathrm{p,\tilde{u},q}) \tag{27}$$

$$s.t. \;\; (22),(23)$$

Differentiating (24) with respect to **p** and **q** for fixed $\tilde{u}$, we can obtain the optimal power allocation **p*** and energy procurement **q***:

$$p^{*}_{m,n,k} = \rho_m \left[\frac{w}{\beta\lambda_m} - \frac{1}{\left|h_{m,n,k}\right|^2} \right]^{+} \tilde{u}_{mnk} \tag{28}$$

$$q^{r*}_{m} = \left[\frac{(w\pi_r + \eta_r + \mu_m)\rho_m - (w-1)\beta_r}{2(w-1)\alpha_r} \right]^{+} \tag{29}$$

where $\beta = 2\ln 2$, $\left[a\right]^{+} = \max\left\{0, a\right\}$. It can be observed that $p^{*}_{m,n,k}$ is dependent of $\tilde{u}_{mnk}$. Next, we continue to optimize $\tilde{u}_{mnk}$, $\forall m, n, k$.

Substituting **p*** into (25), the power allocation variables are eliminated. We define

$$A_{mnk} = \log_2(1 + \frac{p^{*}_{m,n,k}}{\tilde{u}_{mnk}} \left|h_{m,n,k}\right|^2) - \sum_{m=1}^{M} \lambda_m \sum_{n=1}^{N} \sum_{k=1}^{K} p^{*}_{m,n,k}$$

It is clear that A_{mnk} is independent of $\tilde{u}_{mnk}$.

Then, (25) can be rewritten as:

$$\max_{\tilde{\mathrm{u}}} \sum_{m=1}^{M} \sum_{k=1}^{K} \sum_{n=1}^{N} \tilde{u}_{mnk} A_{mnk} \tag{30}$$

$$s.t. \sum_{k=1}^{K} \tilde{u}_{mnk} = 1, \forall m, n \tag{31}$$

In this work, we ignore the inter-cell interference so that we can allocate the radio resources for each cell independently. For the *m*th cell, the corresponding resource allocation problem is given by

$$\max_{\tilde{\mathrm{u}}} \sum_{k=1}^{K} \sum_{n=1}^{N} \tilde{u}_{mnk} A_{mnk} \tag{32}$$

$$s.t. \sum_{k=1}^{K} \tilde{u}_{mnk} = 1, \forall n \tag{33}$$

Problem (32) is a linear programming problem, and there always exists a binary optimal solution. In fact, A_{mnk} can be regarded as the coefficient of $\tilde{u}_{mnk}$ since A_{mnk} is a constant with given λ_m. If there is no tie, there is only one optimal solution, which is that the variable with maximal coefficient is equal to 1, and all another variables are equal to 0. If there is tie, there are infinite optimal solutions. Since we are only interest in the binary optimal solution, arbitrary tie-breaking can be performed which is that a variable with maximal coefficient is randomly selected to be 1, and all another variables are equal to 0. The optimal solution for problem (32) is:

$$\tilde{u}_{mnk}^{*} = \begin{cases} 1, & if\, k = \arg\max_{1 \le l \le K} A_{mnl} \\ 0, & otherwise \end{cases} \quad (34)$$

Optimizing the Dual Problem

In the previous subsection, we have optimized the power allocation, subcarrier assignment and energy procurement with given $\vec{\eta}$, $\vec{\mu}$ and $\vec{\lambda}$. In this subsection, we optimize the standard dual problem as follows:

$$\min_{\vec{\eta},\vec{\mu},\vec{\lambda}} g(\vec{\eta},\vec{\mu},\vec{\lambda}) = \max_{\mathrm{p},\tilde{\mathrm{u}},\mathrm{q}} L(\vec{\eta},\vec{\mu},\vec{\lambda},\mathrm{p},\tilde{\mathrm{u}},\mathrm{q}) \quad (35)$$

$$s.t.\ \vec{\eta} \succ 0, \vec{\mu} \succ 0, \vec{\lambda} \succ 0,$$

The subgradient-based algorithm can be adopted to optimize the dual problem. The subgradient at point $(\vec{\eta},\vec{\mu},\vec{\lambda})$ can be given by

$$\Delta\eta_r = Q_{\max}^{r} - \sum_{m=1}^{M} \rho_m q_m^r,\ r = 1,2,\cdots,S \quad (36)$$

$$\Delta\mu_m = P_m - \rho_m \sum_{r=1}^{S} q_m^r,\ m = 1,2,\cdots,M \quad (37)$$

$$\Delta\lambda_m = P_m - \sum_{n=1}^{N}\sum_{k=1}^{K} p_{m,n,k},\ m = 1,2,\cdots,M \quad (38)$$

Now, we give the details of the subgradient algorithm.

Algorithm 1. The Subgradient Algorithm

Initialize Lagrange multiplier $\vec{\eta}^0$, $\vec{\mu}^0$ and $\vec{\lambda}^0$
repeat
set t←t+1
Given $\vec{\eta}^t$, $\vec{\mu}^t$ and $\vec{\lambda}^t$, obtain the optimal $p(\vec{\lambda}^t)$, $\tilde{u}(\vec{\lambda}^{(t)})$ and $q(\vec{\eta}^t,\vec{\mu}^t)$ according to (28), (29) and (34), respectively.
Update $\vec{\eta}$, $\vec{\mu}$ and $\vec{\lambda}$ through $\vec{\eta}^{t+1}=\left[\vec{\eta}^t-\Delta\vec{\eta}v^t\right]^+$, $\vec{\mu}^{t+1}=\left[\vec{\mu}^t-\Delta\vec{\mu}v^t\right]^+$ and $\vec{\lambda}^{t+1}=\left[\vec{\lambda}^t-\Delta\vec{\lambda}v^t\right]^+$, where $\Delta\vec{\eta}=\left(\Delta\eta_1,\Delta\eta_2,\cdots,\Delta\eta_S\right)$, $\Delta\vec{\mu}=\left(\Delta\mu_1,\Delta\mu_2,\cdots,\Delta\mu_M\right)$, $\Delta\vec{\lambda}=\left(\Delta\lambda_1,\Delta\lambda_2,\cdots,\Delta\lambda_M\right)$ and v^t is the step size at the tth iteration.
Until The convergence of $\min_t g\left(\vec{\eta}^t,\vec{\mu}^t,\vec{\lambda}^t\right)$.

The Framework of The Proposed Algorithm

As aforementioned, the formulated problem is a mixed integer programming problem due to the combinatorial nature of the BS sleeping strategy and subcarrier assignment. We adopt the BVDPSO to solve the binary variables. In fact, each particle corresponds to one BS sleeping strategy. When the BS sleeping strategy is fixed, there are only power allocation, subcarrier assignment and energy procurement variables in the original optimization problem, which is also difficult to tackle since the subcarrier assignment variables are also binary. We propose an optimal algorithm based on Lagrange dual domain method to optimize the remaining variables. Thus, for each particle, we can obtain the corresponding optimal power allocation, subcarrier assignment and energy procurement, and compute the corresponding objective function value which can be regarded as this particle's fitness value. In the following, we give the details of the proposed algorithm in Algorithm 2.

SIMULATION RESULTS

In this section, we evaluate the performance of the proposed BS sleeping scheme and algorithm using simulations. In the first, we introduce the simulation setup. In the simulation, the number of the BSs is set to M=4, and the radius of each cell is 1 km. Without loss of generality, we assume that all cells have the same number of the users and subcarriers. The unit price of the throughput is set to 1. At the smart grid side, we assume that there are S=3 retailers with 3 different energy source, respectively, and the cost of unit energy of each retailer are different.

The maximum energy supply for the renewable energy retailer and traditional energy is 1500J and infinite, respectively. The price of the renewable energy is higher than the traditional energy. Further system parameters in this paper is detailed in TableI. In this work, 3GPP path loss model is adopted, and the small scale fading is modeled as Rayleigh fading.

Algorithm 2 The Algorithm to Optimize Problem P1

General an initial population G composed of L random particles ρ^l, $l=1,2,\cdots,L$;
Initialize the iteration index $g=0$;
while Not Converged **do**
    for $l=1,2,\cdots,L$ **do**
        Compute the optimal p^l, q^l and u^l corresponding to the particle $\rho^l \in G$ //Algorithm 1
        Substituting ρ^l, p^l, q^l and u^l into (7), compute the corresponding fitness value $U_l(g)$
end for
Find $\left(l_m, g_m\right) = \arg\max_{l,g} U_l(g)$, i.e., $\rho^{l_m}(g_m)$ is the historical best position of all particles. Set $\rho^{\max} = \rho^{l_m}(g_m)$.
Find $g_l = \arg\max_g U_l(g)$ for each particle l, i.e., $\rho^l(g_l)$ is the personal historical best position of particle l. Set $\rho^{(l,local)} = \rho^l(g_l)$
Adjust the velocities and positions of all particles using BVDPSO
g=g+1.
end while

Table 1. Simulation parameters

Similation Parameter	Value
Cell radius	1 Km
Inner boundary radius	0.6 Km
Subcarrier bandwidth	15 KHz
Number of retailers	3
Noise power spectral density	-174 dBm/Hz
Path loss coefficient	4
Peak power of BS	30 dBm
price of the unit throughput	1
price of the wind energy	0.02
price of the solar energy	0.03
price of the traditional energy	0.01

Comparing With Benchmarks

To evaluate the performance gain of the proposed algorithm, we consider some schemes with simple configurations as benchmarks:

1. **Maximum Power Consumption:** In this case, each BS transmit signals at maximum power, and each subcarrier is allocated to equal power. We only consider the BS sleeping scheme, subcarrier assignment and the energy procurement.
2. **No BS Sleeping:** In this scheme, the BS sleeping technology is not considered, and we only consider the subcarrier assignment, power allocation and energy procurement.
3. **Uniform Energy Procurement:** In this case, each energy retailer sells energy to each BS uniformly. We only consider the BS sleeping scheme, subcarrier assignment and power allocation.

In the following, we compare the performance of the scheme proposed in this chapter with the aforementioned benchmarks. It is shown by Figure 1 that the operator can obtain more and more profits with the increase of the number of users. This result comes from the fact that the subcarriers have higher probability to be allocated to the users with higher channel gain, which can also be called user diversity. The proposed scheme achieves 15 to 30 percent profit improvement than these above benchmarks. It can be seen that the performance of *Maximum Power Consumption* scheme is superior to *No BS Sleeping* and *Uniform Energy Procurement*. This result shows that the BS sleeping strategy can efficiently decrease the running costs. The result that the *No BS Sleeping* scheme outperforms the *Uniform Energy Procurement* scheme illustrates the necessity of resource allocation. From Figure 1, It can also be seen that the energy procurement is conducive to obtain a good trade-off between the revenue and carbon emission.

Figure 1. Operator's profit vs different number of users. N = 32, M = 4

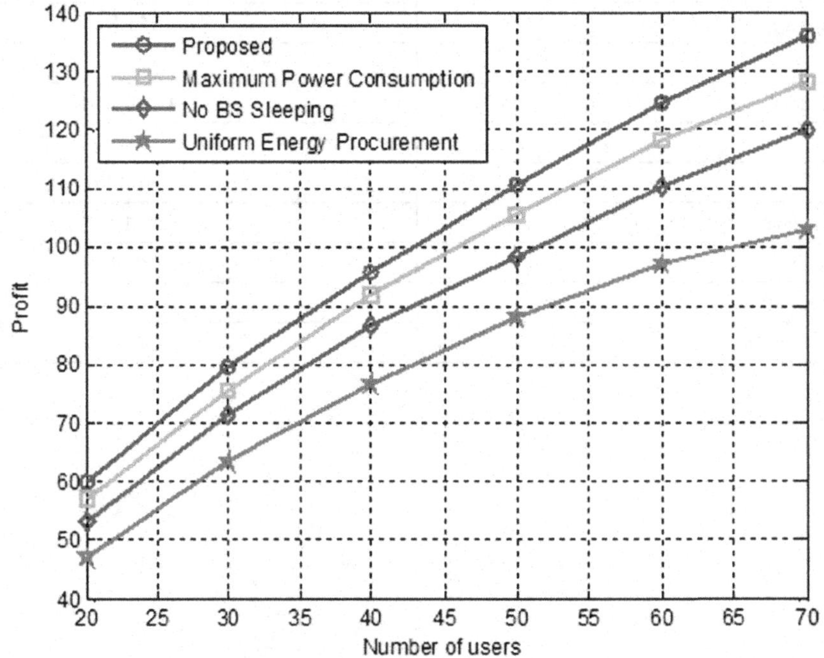

**For a more accurate representation see the electronic version.*

Figure 2 shows the carbon emission performance of the proposed algorithm in comparison to the benchmarks. From Figure 2, it can be observed that the overall carbon emission becomes more and more with the increase of the number of users. The result comes from the fact that more users causes more power consumption which result in the more carbon emission. We can observe that the proposed scheme outperforms the other benchmarks to reduce the carbon emission. This result shows that the BS sleeping can significantly decrease the energy consumption by turning off the redundant BSs. Furthermore, the increasing rate of the curve of the proposed algorithm goes slower and slower with the increase of the number of the users. For *Uniform Energy Procurement*, since the retailers sell the power to operators randomly, it is probable that cellular network procures more traditional energy while the carbon emission's weight is larger, *vice verse*.

Figure 3 shows the different carbon emission versus different weight (operator attitude). From Figure 3, it can be observed that the carbon emission decreases with the increase of the weight. The result indicates that the operators' attitude towards to environment can impact the carbon emission significantly. It also can be observed that when the weight is the same, the carbon emission obtained by the proposed algorithm is less than the other benchmarks. In fact, the power allocation and the subcarrier assignment can effectively improve the system sum rate by increasing the energy and spectrum efficiency. BS sleeping scheme can reduce the energy consumption by switching off redundant BSs whose traffic load is light. The energy procurement scheme can optimize the energy purchase of cellular network according to the weight between the revenue and carbon cost. Thus, the combination of these issues can decrease the carbon emission and increase the operator's profit more effectively.

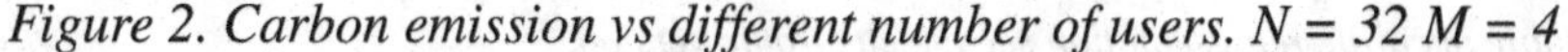

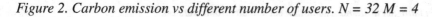

Figure 2. Carbon emission vs different number of users. N = 32 M = 4

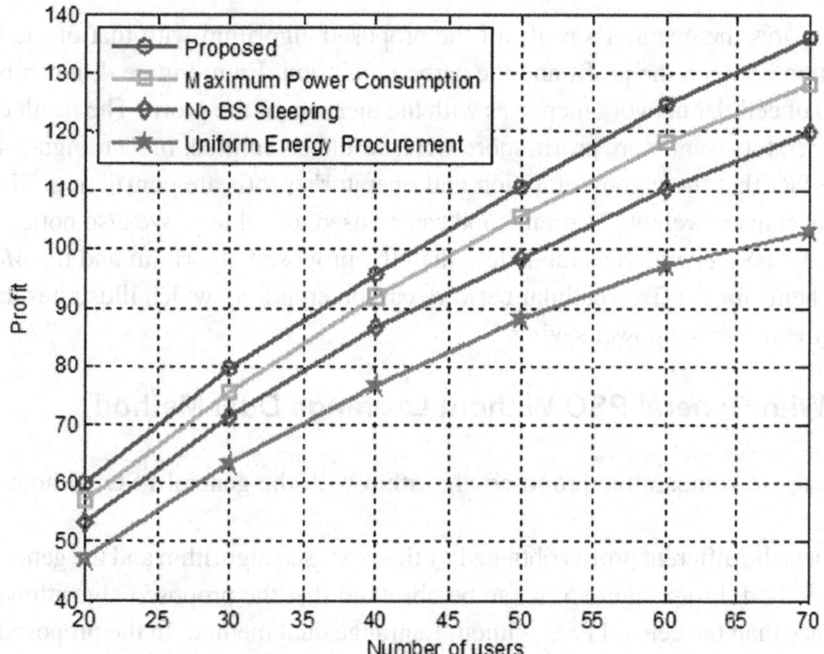

**For a more accurate representation see the electronic version.*

Figure 3. Carbon emission vs different attitude toward environment. N = 32, M = 4, K = 16

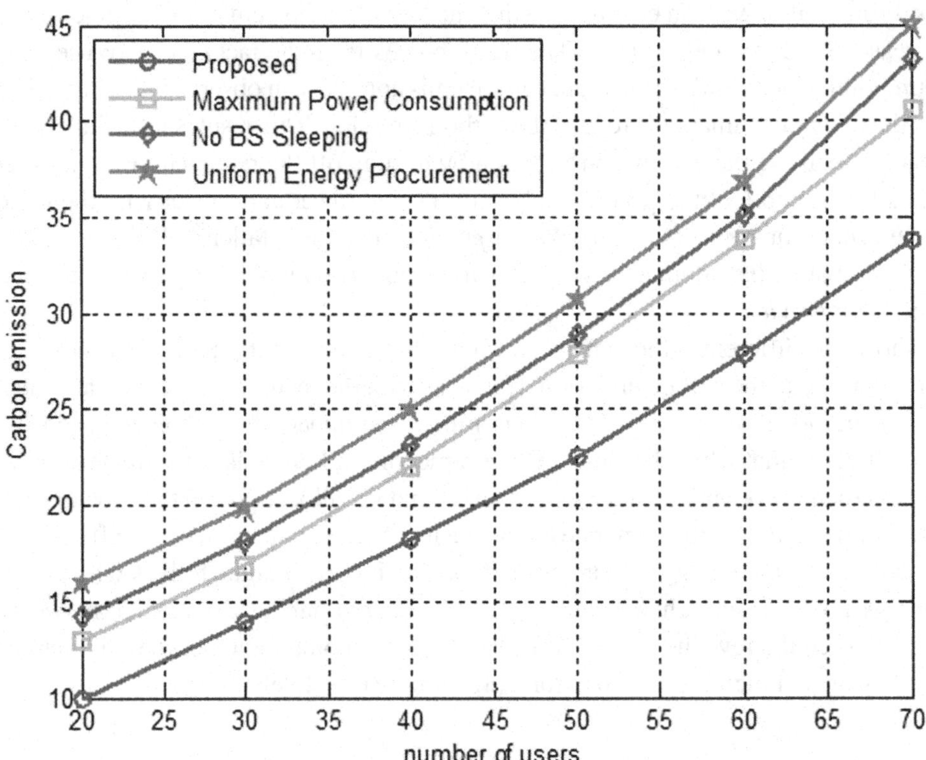

For a more accurate representation see the electronic version.

Figure 4 compares the operator's profit of the proposed algorithm with that of the benchmarks. It depicts the relation between the profit and the carbon emission. From Figure 4, it can be seen that the carbon emission of cellular network increases with the increase of the profit. The result comes from the fact that if the operators want more profit, more GHG would be emitted. In fact, Figure 4 plots a Pareto front due to the fact that the carbon emission and operator's profit are conflicting. Since both of the two functions are convex, weighted sum method can be used to tackle it. We also notice that the profits obtained by the *No BS sleeping* Scheme is less than the proposed algorithm and the *Maximum Power Consumption* scheme for the fixed cellular network carbon emission, which illustrates that BS sleeping can significantly enhance the power saving.

Comparing With General PSO Without Lagrange Dual Method

In this subsection, we compare the proposed algorithm with the general PSO without Lagrange dual method.

Figure 5 depicts the different profits obtained by the proposed algorithm and the general PSO without Lagrange dual method. From Figure 5, it can be observed that the proposed algorithm achieves better profit performance than the general PSO without Lagrange dual method. In the proposed algorithm, we use the PSO to optimize the BS sleeping variables, and solve the power allocation as well as subcarrier

Figure 4. Operators' profit vs different carbon emission. N = 32, M = 4, K = 16

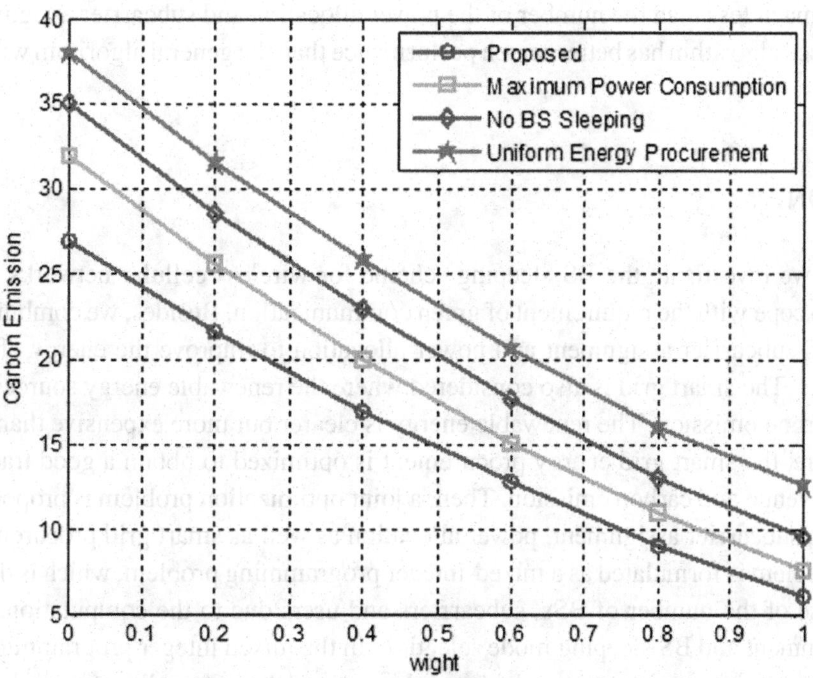

**For a more accurate representation see the electronic version.*

Figure 5. Operators' profits obtained by different algorithms vs different number of users. N = 32, M = 4

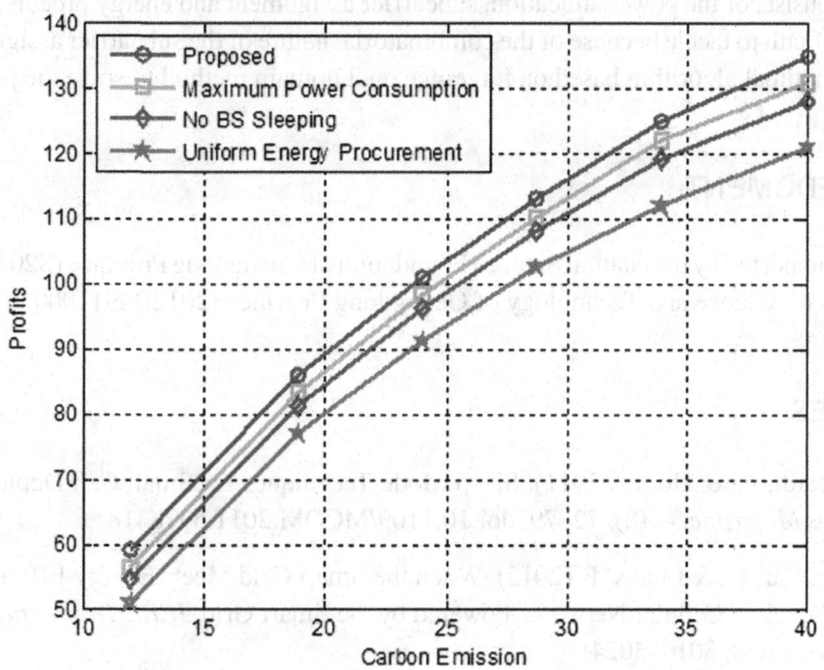

**For a more accurate representation see the electronic version.*

assignment using the Lagrange dual method. In fact, in the proposed problem, the number of BS sleeping variables is much less than the number of the power allocation and subcarrier assignment variables. Thus, the proposed algorithm has better search performance than the general algorithm without Lagrange dual method.

CONCLUSION

In this chapter, we investigate the BS sleeping scheme for wireless cellular networks to enhance the energy saving to cope with the requirement of green communication. Besides, we combine the BS sleeping scheme with subcarrier assignment and power allocation to improve the energy efficiency of the cellular networks. The smart grid is also considered where the renewable energy sources are integrated to reduce the carbon emission. The renewable energy is clearer but more expensive than the traditional energy. Therefore, the smart grid energy procurement is optimized to obtain a good trade-off between the operator's revenue and carbon emission. Then, a joint optimization problem is proposed to optimize the BS sleeping, subcarrier assignment, power allocation as well as smart grid procurement. This joint optimization problem is formulated as a mixed-integer programming problem, which is difficult to solve with the increase of the number of BSs, subcarriers and users due to the computational nature of the subcarrier assignment and BS sleeping mode selection. In the mixed integer programming problem, the BS sleeping and subcarrier assignment variables are binary, and the power allocation and energy procurement variables are continuous. Then, the BVDPSO, which is a current PSO to solve the combinatorial optimization problem, is introduced to solve the BS sleeping variables. Thus, the original optimization problem only consists of the power allocation, subcarrier assignment and energy procurement variables which is still difficult to tackle because of the combinatorial nature of the subcarrier assignment. Finally, we propose an optimal algorithm based on Lagrange dual domain method to solve the problem.

ACKNOWLEDGMENT

This work was supported by the Natural Science Foundation of Guangdong Province (S2011030002886), and the projects of Science and Technology of Guangdong Province (2012B091100033).

REFERENCES

Ashraf, I., Boccardi, F., & Ho, L. (2011). Sleep Mode Techniques for Small Cell Deployments. *IEEE Communications Magazine*, *49*(8), 72–79. doi:10.1109/MCOM.2011.5978418

Bu, S., Yu, F. R., Cai, Y., & Liu, X. P. (2012). When the Smart Grid Meets Energy-Efficient Communications: Green Wireless Cellular Networks Powered by the Smart Grid. *IEEE Transactions on Wireless Communications*, *11*(8), 3014–3024.

Cao, D., Zhou, S., & Niu, Z. (2013). Optimal Combination of Base Station Densities for Energy-Efficient Two-Tier Heterogeneous Cellular Networks. *IEEE Transactions on Wireless Communications*, *12*(9), 4350–4362. doi:10.1109/TWC.2013.080113.121280

Cui, Y., Lau, V. K. N., & Wu, Y. (2012). Delay-aware Bs Discontinuous Transmission Control and User Scheduling for Energy Harvesting Downlink Coordinated MIMO Systems. *IEEE Transactions on Signal Processing*, *60*(7), 3786–3795. doi:10.1109/TSP.2012.2194291

Erol-Kantarci, M., & Mouftah, H. T. (2011). Wireless Multimedia Sensor and Actor Networks for the Next Generation Power Grid. *Ad Hoc Networks*, *9*(4), 542–551. doi:10.1016/j.adhoc.2010.08.005

Ghazzai, H., Yaacoub, E., Alouini, M., & Abudayya, A. (2014). Optimized Smart Grid Energy Procurement for LTE Networks using Evolutionary Algorithms. *IEEE Transactions on Vehicular Technology*, *63*(9), 4508–4519. doi:10.1109/TVT.2014.2312380

Héliot, F. (2014). Low-complexity Energy-efficient Joint Resource Allocation for Two-Hop MIMO-AF Systems. *IEEE Transactions on Wireless Communications*, *13*(6), 3088–3099. doi:10.1109/TWC.2014.042814.130898

Holtkamp, H., Auer, G., Bazzi, S., & Haas, H. (2013). Minimizing Base Station Power Consumption. *IEEE Journal on Selected Areas in Communications*, *32*(2), 297–306. doi:10.1109/JSAC.2014.141210

Hsu, C. C., Chang, J. M., Chou, Z. T., & Abichar, Z. (2014). Optimizing Spectrum-Energy Efficiency in Downlink Cellular Networks. *IEEE Transactions on Mobile Computing*, *13*(9), 2100–2112. doi:10.1109/TMC.2013.99

Huang, A. Q., Crow, M. L., Heydt, G. T., Zheng, J. P., & Dale, S. J. (2011). The Future Renewable Electric Energy Delivery and Management (FREEDM) System: The Energy Internet. *Proceedings of the IEEE*, *99*(1), 133–148. doi:10.1109/JPROC.2010.2081330

Junzhi, Y., Zhengxing, W., Ming, W., & Min, T. (2016). CPG Network Optimization for a Biomimetic Robotic Fish via PSO. *IEEE Transactions on Neural Networks and Learning Systems*, *27*(9), 1962–1968. doi:10.1109/TNNLS.2015.2459913 PMID:26259223

Loodaricheh, R. A., Mallick, S., & Bhargava, V. K. (2014). Energy-efficient Resource Allocation for OFDMA Cellular Networks with User Cooperation and QoS Provisioning. *IEEE Transactions on Wireless Communications*, *13*(11), 6132–6146. doi:10.1109/TWC.2014.2329877

Lu, X., Wang, W., & Ma, J. (2013). An Empirical Study of Communication Infrastructures Towards the Smart Grid: Design, Implementation, and Evaluation. *IEEE Transactions on Smart Grid*, *4*(1), 170–183. doi:10.1109/TSG.2012.2225453

Marsan, M. A., Chiaraviglio, L., Ciullo, D., & Meo, M. (2013). On the Effectiveness of Single and Multiple Base Station Sleep Modes in Cellular Networks. *Computer Networks*, *57*(17), 3276–3290. doi:10.1016/j.comnet.2013.07.016

Nataraj, P., Tanuj, S., & Vivek, A. (2017). Adaptive Velocity PSO for Global Maximum Power Control of a PV Array Under Nonuniform Irradiation Conditions. *IEEE Journal of Photovoltaics*, *7*(2), 624–639. doi:10.1109/JPHOTOV.2016.2629844

Peng, J., Hong, P., & Xue, K. (2014). Stochastic Analysis of Optimal Base Station Energy Saving in Cellular Networks with Sleep Mode. *IEEE Communications Letters*, *18*(4), 612–615. doi:10.1109/LCOMM.2014.030114.140241

Rui, H., Yuzhou, C., & Liuqing, Y. (2017). Multi-constrained QoS routing based on PSO for named data networking. Multi-constrained QoS routing based on PSO, for named data networking. *IET Communications*, *11*(8), 1251–1255. doi:10.1049/iet-com.2016.0783

Safdar, R., Hazlie, M., Hamzah, A., Kanendra, N., Javed, A. L., Anis, S., & Mohd, K. (2016). Minimum-features-based ANN-PSO approach for islanding detection in distribution system. *IET Renewable Power Generation*, *10*(9), 1255–1263. doi:10.1049/iet-rpg.2016.0080

Santosh, K., & Sanjay, K. S. (2016). Hybrid BFO and PSO Swarm Intelligence Approach for Biometric Feature Optimization. *International Journal of Swarm Intelligence Research*, *7*(2), 36–62. doi:10.4018/IJSIR.2016040103

Shen, M., Zhan, Z. H., Chen, W. N., Gong, Y. J., Zhang, J., & Li, Y. (2014). Bi-Velocity Discrete Particle Swarm Optimization and its Application to Multicast Routing Problem in Communication Networks. *IEEE Transactions on Industrial Electronics*, *61*(12), 7141–7151. doi:10.1109/TIE.2014.2314075

Shuangxin, W., Guibin, T., Dingli, Y., & Yijiang, L. (2015). Dynamic Particle Swarm Optimization with Any Irregular Initial Small-World Topology. *International Journal of Swarm Intelligence Research*, *6*(4), 1–23. doi:10.4018/IJSIR.2015100101

Tabassum, H., Siddique, U., Hossain, E., & Hossain, M. J. (2014). Downlink Performance of Cellular System with Base Station Sleeping, User Association ans Scheduling. *IEEE Transactions on Wireless Communications*, *13*(10), 5752–5767. doi:10.1109/TWC.2014.2336249

Tombaz, S., Han, S. W., Sung, K. W., & Zander, J. (2014). Energy Efficient Network Deployment with Cell DTX. *IEEE Communications Letters*, *18*(6), 977–980. doi:10.1109/LCOMM.2014.2323960

Wenyong, D. (2017). A Supervised Learning and Control Method to Improve Particle Swarm Optimization Algorithms. *IEEE Transactions on Systems, Man, and Cybernetics. Systems*, *47*(7), 1135–1148. doi:10.1109/TSMC.2016.2560128

Wu, J., Zhou, S., & Niu, Z. (2013). Traffic-aware Base Station Sleeping Control and Power Matching for Energy-delay Tradeoffs in Green Cellular Networks. *IEEE Transactions on Wireless Communications*, *12*(8), 4196–4209. doi:10.1109/TWC.2013.071613.122092

Yang, Z., & Niu, Z. (2013). Energy Saving in Cellular Networks by Dynamic RS–BS Association and BS Switching. *IEEE Transactions on Vehicular Technology*, *62*(9), 4602–4614. doi:10.1109/TVT.2013.2265403

Yong, S. S., Quek, T. Q. S., Kountouris, M., & Shin, H. (2013). Energy Efficient Heterogeneous Cellular Networks. *IEEE Journal on Selected Areas in Communications*, *31*(5), 840–850. doi:10.1109/JSAC.2013.130503

Yu, F., Zhang, P., Xiao, W., & Choudhury, P. (2011). Communication Systems for Grid Integration of Renewable Energy Resources. *IEEE Network the Magazine of Global Internetworking*, *25*(5), 22–29. doi:10.1109/MNET.2011.6033032

Zhao-Hua, L., Hua-Liang, W., Qing-Chang, Z., Kan, L., Xiao-Shi, X., & Liang-Hong, W. (2017). Parameter Estimation for VSI-Fed PMSM Based on a Dynamic PSO With Learning Strategies. *IEEE Transactions on Power Electronics*, *32*(4), 3154–3165. doi:10.1109/TPEL.2016.2572186

Chapter 15
Using Cuckoo Search Algorithm for Hybrid Flow Shop Scheduling Problems Under Makespan Criterion

M. K. Marichelvam
Mepco Schlenk Engineering College, India

Ömür Tosun
Akdeniz University, Turkey

ABSTRACT

In this chapter, cuckoo search algorithm (CSA) is used to solve the multistage hybrid flow shop (HFS) scheduling problems with parallel machines. The objective is the minimization of makespan. The HFS scheduling problems are proved to be strongly non-deterministic polynomial time-hard (NP-hard). Proposed CSA algorithm has been tested on benchmark problems addressed in the literature against other well-known algorithms. The results are presented in terms of percentage deviation (PD) of the solution from the lower bound. The results indicate that the proposed CSA algorithm is quite effective in reducing makespan because average PD is observed as 1.531, whereas the next best algorithm has result of average PD of 2.295, which is, in general, nearly 50% worse, and other algorithms start from 2.645.

INTRODUCTION

Scheduling is one of the most important decision making process in production and operation management. The hybrid flow shop (HFS) environment is a combination of parallel machine and flow shop environments. The HFS scheduling problem was first addressed by Arthanari and Ramamurthy (Arthanari & Ramamurthy, 1971). The HFS scheduling problems are NP-hard type combinatorial optimization problems (Gupta 1988; Hoogeveen et al. 1996). The HFS is also called as flow shop with multiple processors (machines), flexible flow shop (FFS), multiprocessor flow shop, or flow shop with parallel machines (Ribas et al. 2010).

DOI: 10.4018/978-1-5225-5134-8.ch015

Cuckoo search algorithm is a population based meta-heuristic algorithm based on the obligate brood parasitic behavior of some cuckoo species in combination with the Lévy flight behavior of some birds and flies in the nature (Yand & Deb, 2009). Yang and Deb (Yang & Deb, 2010) solved various optimization problems using the CSA. CSA has been proposed for solving knapsack problems (Layeb, 2011; Gherboudj, 2012), steel structure optimization problems (Kaveh et al. 2012; Gandomi et al. 2013), scheduling problems (Marichelvam, 2012; Marichelvam et al. 2014), multimodal optimization problems (Jamil & Zepernick, 2013), travelling salesman problems (Ouyang et al. 2013), reliability optimization problems (Valian et al. 2013) and machining parameters optimization problems (Yildiz, 2013). Cuckoo search and tabu search algorithms are hybridized to solve the quadratic assignment problems (Dejam et al. 2012). Detailed review on cuckoo search algorithm can be found in (Fister et al. 2013). Also there are new promising algorithms like neighborhood field and contour gradient optimization which initially designed for continuous optimization but soon to be adapted for scheduling problems (Wu et al., 2013).

Though wide variety of heuristics and meta-heuristics has been applied to solve HFS scheduling problems, the applications of recently developed bio-inspired meta-heuristic algorithms are very limited. Hence, in this paper, we propose the recently developed metaheuristic cuckoo search algorithm (CSA) for solving the multistage HFS scheduling problems with makespan objective. Its results will be compared against another recent algorithm (Bat algorithm) and others from the literature. The rest of the paper is organized as follows. Section 2 presents the problem definition. Section 3 will describe the proposed meta-heuristic algorithms in detail. An overview of the computational experiments and results are given in Section 4. In Section 5, overall conclusions are drawn and future research paths are briefly highlighted.

PROBLEM DEFINITION

In a HFS scheduling problem, a set of *n* jobs are available simultaneously to be processed sequentially on different stages. Each job *j* has its fixed processing time for every stage *s*, $s\epsilon \left\{1,2,\ldots,\boldsymbol{M}\right\}$ and at each stage there is a set of identical parallel machines $\boldsymbol{m}\epsilon \left\{1,2,\ldots,\boldsymbol{m}_s\right\}$ where some production stages may have only one machine, but at least one production stage must have multiple machines. Each job may consist of different operations. These operations will be performed by any one of the machines at different stages. The jobs arrive at first stage where the corresponding operations are to be performed and the jobs are delivered to the next stage for the completion of succeeding operations. The jobs have to pass through all the stages sequentially. The objective of scheduling is to assign jobs to the machines at the corresponding stages and determine the processing sequences on the machines so that the makespan (Cmax), i.e., the maximum completion time is minimized.

The HFS problem is known as NP-hard. In the basic model where HFS restricted to two processing stages, even in the case when one stage contains two machines and the other one a single machine, it's proved that the HFS is NP-hard based on the results of Gupta (1988). Moreover, the special case where there is a single machine per stage, known as the flow shop, and the case where there is a single stage with several machines, known as the parallel machines environment, are also NP-hard (Ruiz and Vazquez-Rodriguez, 2010).

The HFS problem has attracted a lot of attention and found in all kinds of real world scenarios including the electronics, paper and textile industries. Examples are also found in the production of concrete, the manufacturing of photographic film, civil engineering, internet service architectures and container handling systems (Ruiz and Vazquez-Rodriguez, 2010).

Researchers applied branch and bound method (Brah & Hunsuchker, 1991; Moursli & Pochet, 2000) and heuristics (Haouari & M'Hallah, 1997; Riane et al. 1998; Oguz et al. 2003; Wang & Liu, 2013) to solve the problems.

Ding & Kittichartphayak (1994) presented three heuristics to solve the flexible flow line scheduling problems. They considered parallel machines in each stage. Hunsucker & Shah (1994) evaluated the performance of different dispatching rules for a constrained HFS scheduling environment. A two-stage flexible flow shop (FFS) with a single machine at the first stage and several identical machines at the second stage was addressed to minimize the makespan (Li 1997). He considered the independent setup times in his work. A three-stage HFS scheduling problem with one machine in the first and third stage and two identical machines in the second stage was addressed by Riane et al (1998). Linn & Zhang (1999) conducted a survey of scheduling literature in the HFS environment. Carlier & Néron (2000) proposed a branch-and-bound algorithm to solve the multiprocessor flow shop scheduling problems. A new mixed integer programming (MIP) model was proposed by Sawik (2000) to solve the flexible flow line scheduling problems with blocking. He considered the identical machines in each stage. He also applied the basic MIP formulation to solve the reentrant HFS scheduling problems. Mixed integer programming formulations were proposed for serial batch scheduling in flexible flow lines with limited intermediate buffers (Sawik 2002). He considered identical processing times for jobs belong to the same batch. Allaoui & Artiba (2004) integrated the simulation and the optimization techniques to solve the HFS scheduling problems with maintenance constraints. They considered the setup, cleaning and transportation times in their research. Xie & Wang (2005) considered the two-stage FFS scheduling problems with availability constraints. They proposed some approximation algorithms to solve the problems. Allaoui & Artiba (2006) proposed a branch-and-bound algorithm to minimize the makespan in the two-stage HFS scheduling problem with one machine in the first stage and m identical parallel machines in the second stage. They considered that each machine is subject to at most one unavailability period and the start time and the end time of each period are known in advance. Low et al (2008) addressed a two-stage HFS scheduling problem with unrelated alternative machines. They considered m unrelated alternative machines at the first machine center, followed by a single machine at the second center. The objective was to minimize the makespan. A mixed integer programming mathematical model was formulated by Ruiz et al (2008) for solving the realistic hybrid FFS scheduling problems. They considered several realistic characteristics including release dates for machines, existence of unrelated parallel machines at each stage of the flowshop, machine eligibility, possibility for jobs to skip stages, sequence dependent setup times, possibility for setup times to be both anticipatory as well as non-anticipatory, positive and/or negative time lags between operations and generalized precedence relationships between jobs. They addressed some heuristics to solve the problems.

Most of the researchers assumed that all jobs are processed in all stages in solving the HFS scheduling problems. But, in real-life industries, all jobs are not being processed in all stages. For instance, there may be some missing operations. Tseng et al (2008) considered the two-stage HFS scheduling problems with missing operations to minimize the makespan. They proposed a three phase heuristic algorithm to generate a non-permutation schedule for the problem. They addressed a stainless steel factory with two stages in which the first stage consists of one machine and the second stage consists of two machines. They applied the heuristic to some random problem instances and compared the results to the dispatching rules and constructive heuristics addressed in the literature. However, the two-stage HFS scheduling problems are practically insignificant. The HFS scheduling problems with unrelated parallel machines at each stage were addressed by Jungwattanakit et al (2008). They considered both sequence and machine-dependent setup times. The objective was to determine a schedule that minimizes a convex combination of makespan and the number of tardy jobs. They formulated a 0–1 mixed integer program of the problem. They developed heuristic algorithms to solve the problems. Amin-Naseri & Beheshti-Nia (2009) addressed the parallel batch scheduling problems in a HFS environment to minimize the makespan. They assumed that the machines in some stages can perform a several operations simultaneously.

As the HFS scheduling problems are NP-hard, exact methods cannot be used to solve the problems. Hence, researchers proposed many meta-heuristics to solve the problems. Many metaheuristics such as genetic algorithm (GA) (Hou et al. 1994; Serifoglu & Ulusoy, 2004; Oguz & Ercan, 2005; Shenassa & Mahmoodi, 2006; Shiau et al. 2008; Kahraman et al. 2008; Engin et al. 2011), simulated annealing (SA) algorithm (Serifoglu & Tiryaki, 2002; Low 2005; Naderi et al. 2009; Wang et al. 2010), ant colony optimization (ACO) algorithm (Ying & Lin, 2006; Alaykiran et al. 2007), artificial immune system (AIS) algorithm (Alisantoso et al. 2003; Engin & Döyen, 2004; Niu et al. 2009; Ying 2012), harmony search algorithm (Marichelvam & Geetha, 2016) and particle swarm optimization (PSO) algorithm (Liao et al. 2012; Chou 2013; Li et al. 2014) are utilized by the researchers to solve the HFS problems. Tabu search (TS) algorithm (Bozejko et al. 2013), greedy algorithm (Kahraman et al. 2010) and water flow algorithm (Tran & Ng, 2013) are also applied to solve the HFS scheduling problems.

Apart from the minimization of makespan, different objectives are also considered. Haouari & M'Hallah (1997) considered a two-stage HFS scheduling problem with several parallel machines in each stage and n jobs to be processed on at most one machine per stage. The objective was to minimize the maximum completion time. They developed two two-phase methods based on SA and TS. By comparing the results from heuristics with a newly derived lower bound, they showed the superiority of the derived lower bound and the efficiency and effectiveness of the proposed heuristic. Gupta & Tunc (1998) developed several heuristic algorithms to find optimal or near optimal schedule for solving the two-stage HFS scheduling problems with one machine in the first stage and m identical-parallel machines in the second stage with the objective of minimizing the total number of tardy jobs. Brah & Loo (1999) proposed several heuristics to minimize the makespan and flow time in HFS scheduling problems. They performed the regression analysis to examine the effects of problem characteristics and the performance of heuristics. They proved that the NEH heuristics proposed by Nawaz et al (1983) was providing better results. Several heuristics were developed for solving the HFS scheduling problems with parallel identical machines in each stage to minimize the maximum lateness (Botta-Genoulaz 2000). He considered the positive time lags between the stages and precedence constraints between jobs as well as sequence-independent setup and removal times. Lin & Liao (2003) addressed the scheduling problem of a label sticker manufacturing company that resembles a two-stage HFS. The objective was to schedule one day's mix of label stickers through the shop such that the weighted maximal tardiness is minimized. They developed a heuristic algorithm to find the near-optimal schedule to solve the problem. The performance of the proposed heuristic algorithm was evaluated by comparing its solution with both the optimal solution for small-size problems and the solution obtained by the scheduling method currently used in the shop and a branch-and-bound algorithm. Lee & Kim (2004) addressed the two-stage HFS scheduling problems with the objective of minimizing total tardiness of jobs. They considered one machine at the first stage and multiple identical-parallel machines at the second stage. They developed a branch-and-bound algorithm that can find optimal solutions for problems with up to 15 jobs in a reasonable amount of central processing unit

(CPU) time. Choi et al (2005) focused on HFS scheduling problems with identical-parallel machines to minimize the total tardiness. They developed heuristic algorithms. Flowshop scheduling problems with multiple unrelated machines and independent setup and dependent removal times with the objective of minimizing the total flow time were considered (Low 2005). He proposed a SA based meta-heuristic to solve the problem. He has also applied the dispatching rules based on shortest processing time (SPT) and longest processing time (LPT) to generate the initial solutions. Al-Anzi & Allahverdi (2006) addressed the two-stage assembly scheduling problems to minimize the total completion time. They considered m machines at the first stage and an assembly machine at the second stage. They proposed an SA heuristic, a TS heuristic, and a hybrid TS heuristic algorithm. They proved that the proposed hybrid TS heuristic outperforms the TS and SA heuristics. Tang et al (2006) investigated the multistage HFS problems with parallel-identical machines at each stage. An integer programming formulation was constructed and a new Lagrangian relaxation algorithm based on the stage decomposition method was presented to minimize the sum of weighted completion times of the jobs. The PSO algorithm was applied for minimizing the makespan and total flow time for the permutation flow shop sequencing problems by Tasgetiren et al (2007). They tested the performance of the proposed algorithm with the benchmark problems addressed in the literature. Allahverdi & Al-Anzi (2009) developed heuristic algorithms to minimize the total completion time in the two-stage assembly scheduling problems with m machines at the first stage and an assembly machine at the second stage with setup times. A three-phase multi-objective method was developed by Behnamian et al (2009) to solve the HFS scheduling problems with sequence-dependent setup time to minimize the makespan and sum of the earliness and tardiness of jobs. Choi & Lee (2009) proposed a branch-and-bound algorithm to minimize the number of tardy jobs in a two-stage HFS. They also proposed two-phase heuristic algorithms to obtain good solutions for large-size problems within a reasonable amount of computational time. In the first phase, the ready time of each job at the first stage is obtained using a backward schedule, and then in the second phase, it changes to a better schedule if any of the ready times is negative. They addressed six heuristic algorithms according to the methods used in the second phase. Computational experiments are carried out on a number of randomly generated test problems, and the test results are compared with other heuristic algorithms addressed in the literature. Davoudpour & Ashrafi (2009) proposed a Greedy Randomized Adaptive Search Procedure (GRASP) algorithm to solve the HFS scheduling problems with sequence-dependent setup times with a non-regular optimization criterion based on due dates. They considered different release date for each job. Heuristic algorithms based on the SPT, LPT dispatching rules, Johnson's rule and two meta-heuristic algorithms based on GA and SA were proposed to minimize the makespan for HFS scheduling problems by Jabbarizadeh et al (2009). They considered the sequence-dependent setup times and machine availability constraints in their work.

Some authors also studied multi-objective scheduling problems. Sha & Lin (2009) presented a PSO based multi-objective algorithm for solving the flow shop scheduling problems to minimize the makespan, mean flow time, and machine idle time. They applied a mutation operator with the PSO algorithm. A bi-objective GA was applied to solve the hybrid FFS group scheduling problems with sequence-dependent setup times to minimize the makespan and total weighted tardiness by Karimi et al (2010). Behnamian & Fatemi Ghomi (2011) proposed a hybrid meta-heuristic to minimize the makespan and total resource allocation costs in HFS scheduling problems with sequence-dependent setup times. They combined the GA and variable neighborhood search. They considered the machine and resource dependent processing time of each job for their research. They tested the performance with the benchmark problems addressed in the literature. Han et al (2012) considered the HFS scheduling problems with the earliness-tardiness criterion. They proposed a scheduling strategy based on the differential evolution (DE) algorithm and factor space multi-rule decision method to solve the problems. A multi-objective electromagnetism algorithm is addressed to minimize both makespan and total tardiness in no-wait HFS scheduling problems (Khalili 2012). Syam & Al-Harkan (2012) compared the performance of three meta-heuristics namely GA, SA and TS to minimize the makespan for FFS scheduling problems. They considered parallel machines in each stage. They tested the algorithms with the benchmark problems. Experimental results illustrated that the TS was effective and efficient to solve the HFS scheduling problems. The HFS scheduling problems with sequence-dependent setup times to minimize the makespan and total tardiness were addressed by Mousavi et al (2013). They proposed a bi-objective heuristic (BOH) for obtaining the Pareto-optimal frontier. They compared the performance of the proposed BOH with the MOSA algorithm and a variable neighborhood search algorithm. They proved that the proposed algorithm was efficient and effective.

The detailed review on HFS scheduling problems and comparison of different algorithms can be found in (Ruiz & Vazquez-Rodriguez, 2010; Jungwattanakit et al., 2009; Syam & Al-Harkan, 2012, respectively).

The layout of a HFS environment is shown in Figure 1.

The problem is formulated as below (Marichelvam & Prabaharan, 2014):

$$\text{Minimise } \boldsymbol{C}_{max} \tag{1}$$

Subject to:

$$\boldsymbol{C}_{max} \geq \boldsymbol{C}_{js}, \textit{ for all } s = 1,2,\ldots,\boldsymbol{M}, \boldsymbol{j} = 1,2,\ldots,\boldsymbol{n} \tag{2}$$

$$\boldsymbol{C}_{js} = \boldsymbol{S}_{js} + \boldsymbol{P}_{sj} \tag{3}$$

$$\sum_{i=1}^{m_i} \boldsymbol{Y}_{jis} = 1, \textit{ for all } s = 1,2,\ldots \boldsymbol{M}, \boldsymbol{j} = 1,2,\ldots,\boldsymbol{n} \tag{4}$$

Figure 1. Layout of a HFS

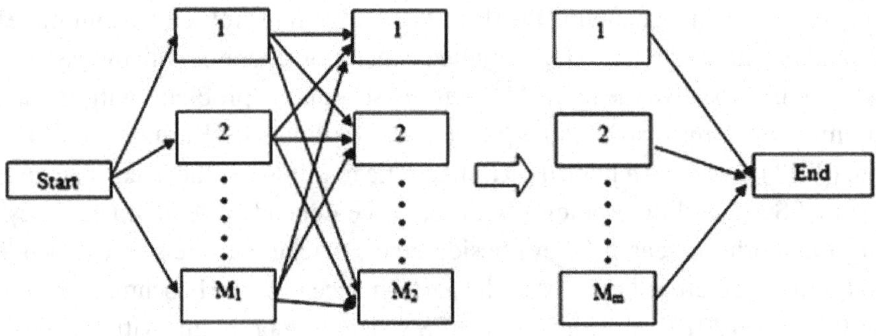

$$C_{js} \leq S_{j(s+1)},\ \boldsymbol{for}\ s = 1, 2, \ldots, M - 1 \tag{5}$$

$$S_{hs} \geq C_{js} - KW_{hjs},\ \boldsymbol{for\ all\ job\ pairs}\left(h, j\right) \tag{6}$$

$$S_{js} \geq C_{hs} + K - 1,\ \boldsymbol{for\ all\ job\ pairs}\left(h, j\right) \tag{7}$$

$$S_{j1} \geq R_j,\ \boldsymbol{for\ all}\ j = 1, 2, \ldots, n \tag{8}$$

$$Y_{jis} \in \left\{0, 1\right\}, W_{hjs} \in \left\{0, 1\right\},\ \boldsymbol{for\ all}\ j = 1, 2, \ldots n, i = 1, 2, \ldots, m_s, s = 1, 2, \ldots, M \tag{9}$$

$$C_{js} \geq 0,\ \boldsymbol{for\ all}\ s = 1, 2, \ldots, M, j = 1, 2, \ldots, n \tag{10}$$

The objective function is the minimization of the makespan. The constraint (2) ensures that the makespan is at least equal to the completion times of the last job. Because the objective is to minimize the makespan, constraints in this set will be tight at optimality whenever Cmax is positive. Eq. (3) is the computation of the completion time of job *j* at stage *s*. Eq. (4) ensures that each job is assigned to exactly one machine at each stage. Eq. (5) forces to start the processing of each job only when it has been completed at the precedent stage. The set of constraints (5) and (6) ensure that only one job is on a machine of a stage at any one time. When $W_{hjs} = 1$, and job *h* is before job *j*, the constraint in (6) is satisfied. Eq. (7) requires that the starting time of job *j* at stage *s* must be after the completion time for job *h*. When $W_{hjs} = 0$, indicating that job *j* is before job *h*, the constraint in (7) is satisfied and the starting time of job *h* at stage *s* must be the completion time for job *j* at stage *s* to satisfy (6). The constraint (8) bound the job starting times to be after job release times in the system. The constraint (9) forces both variable Y_{jis} and W_{hjs} to assume binary values 0 or 1. Eq. (10) represents the non-negative constraints.

For solving this problem, we consider the following assumptions.

1. The number of stages and the number of machines at each stage are known in advance.
2. The numbers of jobs, their processing times are known in advance and are fixed.
3. All the jobs and the machines are available at time zero.
4. No preemption is allowed.
5. The setup and transportation times of the jobs are independent of the sequence and are included in the processing times.
6. Each machine can process only one job at a time.
7. All the machines are available for the entire period of scheduling. (No machine breakdown)

METAHEURISTICS ALGORİTHMS

Sometimes there exists an optimization problem that is impossible to solve, to find the best strategy or even not exist any good solution. For this kind of problems, researchers proposed new methods called metaheuristic algorithms to find near optimal solutions under an acceptable run-time (Tosun, 2014).

The metaheuristic algorithms based on two basic strategies searching for the global optimum. These strategies are known as exploration and exploitation. The exploration process focused on enabling the algorithm to reach the best local solutions within the search space, while the exploitation process is the ability to reach the global optimum solution which is likely to exist around the local solutions obtained. The efficiency of any algorithm is depends on these two characteristics. A metaheuristic algorithm must be able to rapidly converge to the global optimum solution with the given objective function. Furthermore, the run-time required by a metaheuristic algorithm to reach to global minimum and the total calculation amount must be at acceptable levels for practical applications. Too short running time leads to missing some better local solutions whereas too long running time is the waste of resources and decreases the designed efficiency. The algorithmic structure of any metaheuristic algorithm is desired to be simple enough to enable for its easy adaptation to different problems. Also, it is desired that the metaheuristic algorithm has no or very few algorithmic control parameters except the general ones (i.e., size of population, total number of iterations, problem dimension) of the population based optimization algorithms (Civicioglu and Besdok, 2011).

The increasing popularity of metaheuristics and swarm intelligence has attracted a great deal of attention from researchers and practitioners. One of the reasons for this popularity is that nature inspired metaheuristics are versatile and efficient, and such simple algorithms can deal with very complex optimization problems. Metaheuristic algorithms form an important part of contemporary global optimization algorithms, computational intelligence and soft computing. Nature-inspired algorithms often use multiple interacting agents. A subset of metaheuristics are often referred to as swarm intelligence based algorithms, and these algorithms have been developed by inspiring from the swarm intelligence characteristics of biological agents such as insects, birds, fish, humans and others. For example, particle swarm optimization was based on the swarming behavior of birds and fish, while the firefly algorithm was based on the flashing pattern of tropical fireflies, and cuckoo search algorithm was inspired by the brood parasitism of some cuckoo species (Yang, 2012).

CUCKOO SEARCH ALGORITHM

Cuckoo Behavior

Modern metaheuristic algorithms have been developed with the purpose of efficient global search with three main objectives: solving problems faster, solving large problems, and obtaining robust algorithms. The efficiency of any metaheuristic algorithms can be attributed to the fact that they imitate the best features in nature, especially the selection of the fittest in biological systems which have evolved by natural selection over millions of years (Tosun, 2014).

Cuckoo search algorithm is a nature inspired search algorithm based on the obligate brood parasitism of some cuckoo species by laying their eggs in the nests of host birds and was developed by Yang and Deb (Yang & Deb, 2009). Some cuckoos have evolved in such a way that female parasitic cuckoos can imitate the colors and patterns of the eggs of a few chosen host species. This reduces the probability of the eggs being abandoned and, therefore, increases the chance of productivity. It is known that several host birds engage direct conflict with intruding cuckoos. In this case, if host birds discover the eggs are not their own, they will either throw them away or simply abandon their nests and build new ones elsewhere. Parasitic cuckoos often choose a nest where the host bird just laid its own eggs. In general, the cuckoo eggs hatch slightly earlier than their host eggs. Once the first cuckoo chick is hatched, his first instinct action is to evict the host eggs by blindly propelling the eggs out of the nest. This action results in increasing the cuckoo chick's share of food provided by its host bird (Yang & Deb, 2013; Tosun, 2014).

An important component of a CSA is the Lévy flights used for both local and global searching. This process, which has previously been used by Pavlyukevich (Pavlyukevich, 2007), is a random walk that is characterized by a series of instantaneous jumps chosen from a probability density function which has a power law tail. This process represents the optimum random search pattern and is frequently found in nature. When generating a new egg in CSA, a Lévy flight is performed starting at the position of a randomly selected egg, if the objective function value at these new coordinates is better than another randomly selected egg then that egg is moved to this new position. The scale of this random search is controlled by multiplying the generated Lévy flight by a step size α (Walton et al., 2013).

Lévy Flight

In nature, animals search for food in a random or quasi-random manner. Foraging path of an animal is mostly a random walk because the next move is based on the current location/state and the transition probability to the next location. Which direction it chooses depends implicitly on a probability which can be modeled mathematically. While flying, some animals and insects follow the path of long trajectories with sudden 90^0 turns combined with short, random movements. This random walk is called Lévy flight and it describes foraging patterns in natural systems, such as systems of ants, bees and bumbles. Mathematical formulation of Lévy flight relates to chaos theory and it is widely used in stochastic simulations of random and pseudo-random phenomena in nature. (Yang & Deb, 2013; Tosun 2014).

Assume $x_i^{(t)}$ is the solution of the ith cuckoo at iteration t. A new solution $x^{(t+1)}$ for cuckoo i is generated by using a Lévy flight according to the following equation:

$$x_i^{(t+1)} = x_i^{(t)} + \alpha \otimes Levy(\lambda) \tag{11}$$

where α (α > 0) represents a step scaling size. This parameter should be related to the scales of problem the algorithm is trying to solve. In most cases, α can be set to the value of 1 or some other constant. The product ⊗ represents entry-wise multiplications which is the multiplication of element by element of the each given matrix.

Equation (11) states that described random walk is a Markov chain, whose next location depends on two elements: current location (first term in the equation) and transition probability (second term in the equation). The random step length comes from a Lévy distribution which has an infinite variance with an infinite mean:

$$Levy \sim u = t^{-\lambda} \quad (12)$$

where $\lambda \epsilon \left(1,3\right]$ (Yang & Deb, 2013; Tosun 2014).

The consecutive jumps of a cuckoo essentially form a random walk process which obeys a power-law step-length distribution with a heavy tail. In the real world, if a cuckoo's egg is very similar to a host's eggs, then this cuckoo's egg is less likely to be discovered, thus the fitness should be related to the difference in solutions. Therefore, it is a good idea to do a random walk in a biased way with some random step sizes (Yang & Deb, 2013; Tosun 2014). Some of the new solutions would be generated by Lévy walk around the best solution obtained so far, which will speed up the local search. To prevent the search system trapped in a local optimum, a substantial fraction of the new solutions would be generated by far field randomization and whose locations should be far enough from the current best solution (Yang & Deb, 2009).

Proposed Algorithm

The following three idealized rules are considered for describing the CSA.

1. Each cuckoo lays one egg (solution) at a time, and dumps its egg in a randomly chosen nest.
2. The best nests with high-quality eggs (solutions) will carry out to the next generation.
3. The egg laid by a cuckoo can be discovered by the host bird with a probability Pa and a nest will then be built.

For minimization problems the quality or fitness function value is the reciprocal of the objective function. Each egg in a nest represents a solution and the Cuckoo egg represents a new solution. The better solutions replace the worse solutions. The Pseudo code of the CSA was given by Yang and Deb (Yang & Deb, 2009). The Pseudo code is depicted below.

Pseudo Code of the Cuckoo Search (CS)

Start
Objective function f(x), $x = (x_1, ..., x_d)^T$
Generate initial population of n host nests x_i ($i = 1, 2,..., n$)
While (t < MaxGeneration) or (stop criterion)
Get a cuckoo randomly by Lévy flights
Evaluate its quality/fitness F_i
Choose a nest among n (say, j) randomly
if ($F_i > F_j$),
replace j by the new solution;
End
A fraction (Pa) of worse nests are abandoned and new ones are built;
Keep the best solutions (or nests with quality solutions);
Rank the solutions and find the current best

end while
Post process results and visualization
End

Solution Representation

Each egg in a nest represents a solution and the cuckoo egg represents a new solution. Therefore, there is no difference between an egg, a nest, and a solution. Hence, the cuckoo search algorithm will be directly used to the scheduling problems.

Computational Results

This section describes the computational experiments that have been conducted to compare the performance of the proposed algorithm against other algorithms. The algorithms are implemented in the C++ language.

We considered the benchmark problems studied by Singh and Mahapatra (Singh & Mahapatra, 2011). The size of the problem ranges from five jobs and two stages to 100 jobs and eight stages. The processing times are generated randomly in the range (1, 100). There are two types of problem namely, P and Q types. In type P problems, the number of processors available at various stages is randomly selected from the set (ms = 2,…,5), whereas in type Q problems, it is fixed with ms = 5 for all stages. The P10S2T03 problem is a P-type problem defined as ten jobs, two stages, and 03 problem index. In P1HS2T05 problems, 1HS represents 100 jobs. In this paper, only P type problems are considered.

CSA algorithm consists of three parameters Pa, α, and λ. Among them the parameters Pa and α are very important to obtain better solutions. The impact of the values of these parameters was discussed in (Valian et al., 2011). In the literature these parameters of the CSA algorithm are kept constant. The parameters Pa and α are defined in the initial step and the values cannot be changed (Marichelvam, 2012). The parameters are given in Table 1.

We selected 90 problems randomly and compared the performance of different algorithms. The performance of the proposed CSA for the benchmark problems is compared with the results reported in the literature GA_1 (Oguz & Ercan, 2005), PGA (Kahraman et al., 2010), GA_2 (Engin et al., 2011), PSO (Singh & Mahapatra, 2011), BA (Marichelvam et al 2013), SS (Scatter search algorithm; Saravan et al., 2008) and IHGSS (Improved hybrid genetic scatter search algorithm; Marichelvam & Prabaharan, 2014).

Table 1. Parameters of the CSA

Factors	Levels
discovery rate of alien eggs Pa	0.01 (low) 0.10 (medium) 0.50 (high)
step size α	0.05 (low) 0.50 (medium) 1.00 (high)
exponent from Lévy flights λ	1.50 (low) 2.00 (medium) 3.00 (high)

Table 2. Performance comparison of the proposed algorithm

Problems	PD							
	GA_1	PGA	GA_2	PSO	BA	SS	IHGSS	CSA
P10S2T03	5.96	5.96	5.96	8.7	5.96	5.96	5.96	4.86
P10S2T08	0	0	0	10	0	0	0	0
P20S2T01	1.997	1.69	2.611	8.089	1.58	3.40	1.80	1.46
P20S2T02	2.368	1.275	1.639	6.98	1.24	4.20	1.26	1.16
P20S2T04	0	0	0	6.80	0	0.20	0	0
P20S2T06	0	0	0	8.577	0	0	0	0
P20S2T07	0.341	0.341	0.341	0	0	0.46	0.28	0
P20S2T08	0.278	0.278	0.278	4.02	0	0.72	0.24	0
P50S2T01	1.753	1.088	0.605	1.046	0.52	2.64	0.68	0.40
P50S2T03	0.59	0.215	0	17.20	0	1.24	0.21	0
P50S2T04	1.238	1.423	0.681	12.027	0.646	1.80	0.86	0.56
P50S2T05	0.353	0.588	0.235	3.166	0.19	0.92	0.22	0.16
P50S2T07	2.716	2.13	0.692	19.87	0.64	3.68	1.34	0.56
P50S2T10	0.262	0.052	0.052	3.36	0.052	0.72	0.18	0.04
P1HS2T01	0.534	0.507	0.721	0	0	0.62	0	0
P1HS2T03	0.814	0.603	0.693	2.84	0.59	1.24	0.56	0.46
P1HS2T07	0.926	0.538	0.657	0.81	0.62	1.37	0.48	0.56
P1HS2T09	0.105	0.394	0.683	0.116	0.10	0.20	0.08	0
P1HS2T10	0.097	0.242	0.097	0	0	0.12	0	0
P10S8T01	21.268	23.662	21.268	9.59	13.58	19.32	13.62	9.46
P10S8T02	26.179	28.455	31.87	0	11.24	28.16	14.28	8.56
P10S8T03	20.027	21.786	20.027	12.71	14.12	18.28	13.26	12.46
P10S8T04	13.091	14.038	17.35	7.57	8.94	14.54	8.28	7.37
P10S8T05	1.902	4.212	4.212	0	0	1.96	0.80	0
P10S8T06	0.409	0.409	0.409	0	0	0.51	0.32	0
P10S8T07	24.757	26.214	30.097	0.91	5.86	26.12	12.42	4.32
P10S8T08	19.479	21.933	19.479	8.282	10.26	16.40	12.34	8.28
P10S8T09	0.83	2.075	2.075	0	0	0.92	0	0
P10S8T10	19.589	20	19.589	12.876	14.57	20.12	13.42	11.28
P20S8T01	8.163	9.448	9.599	0	2.68	8.80	4.82	0
P20S8T03	2.573	4.117	2.573	0	0	2.68	0	0
P20S8T04	1.593	3.805	7.08	0	1.08	2.04	1.28	0
P20S8T05	3.152	2.641	2.3	2.214	2.28	3.28	2.48	2.20
P20S8T06	8.163	9.675	4.913	0	3.46	8.40	4.08	0
P20S8T07	23.795	27.487	28.821	0	12.87	24.22	14.24	0
P20S8T08	3.791	2.729	3.791	0	1.32	3.64	1.26	0
P20S8T10	4.117	4.803	3.945	0	2.24	4.08	3.12	0

continued on following page

Table 2. Continued

Problems	PD							
	GA_1	PGA	GA_2	PSO	BA	SS	IHGSS	CSA
P10S5T01	4.53	4.878	4.53	1.744	2.20	4.42	2.42	1.64
P10S5T02	6.022	6.022	6.022	1.748	1.42	6.26	2.88	1.72
P10S5T03	7.54	7.54	7.54	2.673	3.84	7.58	4.12	2.62
P10S5T04	8.609	11.755	11.755	17.79	7.64	8.46	7.20	6.80
P10S5T05	3.684	3.684	3.684	2.636	2.84	4.07	3.28	2.52
P10S5T07	8.21	8.21	8.21	32.7	14.42	9.02	7.12	6.82
P10S5T08	2.742	2.258	2.258	28.065	3.54	2.80	2.14	2.20
P10S5T09	9.076	9.076	9.076	3.81	4.89	8.92	4.56	3.62
P10S5T10	10.417	12.179	12.66	11.2	10.12	10.12	9.24	9.08
P20S5T01	1.567	1.567	1.567	0	0	1.18	0	0
P20S5T02	7.165	6.858	7.165	0	3.45	7.12	5.82	3.14
P20S5T03	2.561	6.17	2.561	10.50	3.62	2.78	2.46	2.40
P20S5T04	2.268	0.113	0	0	0	1.82	0.92	0
P20S5T05	2.313	3.049	1.682	8.014	1.64	2.62	2.08	1.56
P20S5T06	2.65	2.479	1.88	0	0	2.74	1.68	0
P20S5T07	0	0	0	1.434	0	0.04	0	0
P20S5T08	3.519	3.519	3.128	14.33	3.08	3.62	3.12	2.67
P20S5T10	7.165	7.165	6.858	0	4.12	6.80	5.42	0
P50S5T01	0.911	0.835	0.911	0	0	1.02	0.46	0
P50S5T02	4.539	0.532	1.099	0	0	4.38	1.02	0
P50S5T03	0.998	0.998	0.998	0	0	1.02	0	0
P50S5T04	0.618	4.325	2.523	17.507	0.52	0.72	0.49	0.34
P50S5T07	1.1	0.477	0.513	0	0	0.98	0.46	0
P50S5T08	2.447	0.745	1.099	0	0	2.26	0.94	0
P50S5T09	5.096	0.668	0	0	0	4.62	2.14	0
P50S5T10	0.271	1.264	0.587	3.324	0.26	0.56	0.28	0.24
P1HS5T01	3.493	0.056	0	0	0	3.20	0.82	0
P1HS5T02	1.543	0	0	11.76	0	1.12	0.24	0
P1HS5T03	3.819	2.272	0.674	1.8	0.66	4.20	2.56	0.42
P1HS5T04	1.425	1.548	1.13	2.994	1.08	1.32	1.04	0.95
P1HS5T05	2.347	0	0	0	0	2.42	0.62	0
P1HS5T06	3.591	4.488	2.924	5.56	2.26	3.54	2.62	1.86
P1HS5T10	3.248	3.389	2.994	3.5019	2.49	3.18	2.62	2.06
P50S8T01	2.709	6.578	5.288	0	2.27	2.56	1.82	1.63
P50S8T02	2.75	2.75	0	1.72	0	2.52	0.81	0
P50S8T03	0.936	1.161	0.787	0	0	0.86	0.24	0
P50S8T04	4.76	3.917	2.696	0	2.46	4.24	2.26	1.68

continued on following page

Table 2. Continued

Problems	PD							
	GA_1	PGA	GA_2	PSO	BA	SS	IHGSS	CSA
P50S8T05	3.639	2.691	0.986	0	0	3.64	0.94	0
P50S8T06	1.875	1.641	0.313	0.351	0.31	1.54	0.34	0.26
P50S8T07	5.436	3.701	2.544	0.1126	1.24	5.20	2.42	0.15
P50S8T08	2.434	1.917	1.881	1.659	1.72	2.38	1.68	1.42
P50S8T09	4.76	4.465	3.412	0	1.42	4.80	1.84	0.98
P50S8T10	5.371	4.726	3.187	6.4804	3.08	5.44	3.24	3.12
P1HS8T01	2.877	1.509	0	0	0	1.17	0.46	0
P1HS8T02	3.568	0.801	0.157	1.461	0.18	3.12	0.62	0.17
P1HS8T03	1.987	1.472	0.644	0	0	1.83	0.38	0
P1HS8T04	2.149	0.498	0.103	0	0	2.24	0.46	0
P1HS8T05	1.944	0.731	0.019	0	0	2.02	0.12	0
P1HS8T06	3.422	2.907	1.104	4.839	0.98	2.87	1.26	0.84
P1HS8T07	2.426	1.203	0.019	1.6806	0.02	2.12	1.02	0.02
P1HS8T08	7.294	8.451	5.584	0	1.28	5.87	2.42	0.26
P1HS8T09	1.951	1.334	0.02	0.11	0.02	1.29	0.62	0
P1HS8T10	3.838	0.985	0.185	0	0.86	3.24	0.22	0.46
Average	*4.609*	*4.626*	*4.225*	*3.833*	*2.295*	*4.631*	*2.645*	*1.531*

The performance of the algorithms is represented in terms of percentage deviation (PD) from the lower bound (LB). The LB of the makespan was proposed by Oguz et al. (Oguz et al., 2004). All the results are taken from the related papers. The PD is defined as follows:

$$PD = \frac{Best\ C_{max} - LB}{LB} * 100$$

The result comparison of different algorithms on the basis of PD is presented in Table 2.

From the Table 2, it can be easily concluded that the CSA is better than other tested algorithms. In 78 of the 90 test instances, proposed CSA algorithm finds the best known solution or at least a better solution than the other algorithms. This number is 41 in PSO and 32 in BA. Also CSA has the minimum average PD results against the other algorithms.

CONCLUSION

In this paper, we presented a recently developed bio-inspired meta-heuristic algorithms for solving the multistage HFS scheduling problems to minimize the makespan. To the best of our knowledge, this is the first attempt to compare the performance of the cuckoo search algorithm against bat algorithm and others from the literature to solve the HFS scheduling problems. Extensive computational experiments proved that the CSA would yield more efficient solutions than other meta-heuristic algorithms. The hybridization of the proposed meta-heuristic algorithms with constructive heuristics would be another interesting future research work. Parameter optimization and comparison is another important research scope.

REFERENCES

Al-Anzi, F. S., & Allahverdi, A. (2006). A hybrid tabu search heuristic for the two-stage assembly scheduling problem. *International Journal of Operations Research*, *3*(2), 109–119.

Alaykiran, K., Engin, O., & Döyen, A. (2007). Using ant colony optimization to solve hybrid flow shop scheduling problems. *International Journal of Advanced Manufacturing Technology*, *35*(5-6), 541–550. doi:10.1007/s00170-007-1048-2

Alisantoso, D., Khoo, L. P., & Jiang, P. Y. (2003). An immune algorithm approach to the scheduling of a flexible PCB flow shop. *International Journal of Advanced Manufacturing Technology*, *22*(11-12), 819–827. doi:10.1007/s00170-002-1498-5

Allahverdi, A., & Al-Anzi, F. S. (2009). The two-stage assembly scheduling problem to minimize total completion time with setup times. *Computers & Operations Research*, *36*(10), 2740–2747. doi:10.1016/j.cor.2008.12.001

Allaoui, H., & Artiba, A. (2004). Integrating simulation and optimization to schedule a hybrid flow shop with maintenance constraints. *Computers & Industrial Engineering*, *47*(4), 431–450. doi:10.1016/j.cie.2004.09.002

Allaoui, H., & Artiba, A. (2006). Scheduling two stage hybrid flow shop with availability constraints. *Computers & Operations Research*, *33*(5), 1399–1419. doi:10.1016/j.cor.2004.09.034

Amin-Naseri, M. R., & Beheshti-Nia, M. A. (2009). Hybrid flow shop scheduling with parallel batching. *International Journal of Production Economics*, *117*(1), 185–196. doi:10.1016/j.ijpe.2008.10.009

Arthanari, T. S., & Ramamurthy, K. G. (1971). An extension of two machines sequencing problem. *Operations Research*, *8*, 10–22.

Behnamian, J., & Fatemi Ghomi, S. M. T. (2011). Hybrid flowshop scheduling with machine and resource-dependent processing times. *Applied Mathematical Modelling*, *35*(3), 1107–1123. doi:10.1016/j.apm.2010.07.057

Behnamian, J., Fatemi Ghomi, S. M. T., & Zandieh, M. (2009). A multi-phase covering Pareto-optimal front method to multi-objective scheduling in a realistic hybrid flowshop using a hybrid metaheuristic. *Expert Systems with Applications*, *36*(8), 11057–11069. doi:10.1016/j.eswa.2009.02.080

Botta-Genoulaz, V. (2000). Hybrid flow shop scheduling with precedence constraints and time lags to minimize maximum lateness. *International Journal of Production Economics*, *64*(1-3), 1–3, 101–111. doi:10.1016/S0925-5273(99)00048-1

Bożejko, W., Pempera, J., & Smutnicki, C. (2013). Parallel tabu search algorithm for the hybrid flow shop problem. *Computers & Industrial Engineering*, *65*(3), 466–474. doi:10.1016/j.cie.2013.04.007

Brah, S. A., & Hunsuchker, J. L. (1991). Branch and bound algorithm for the flow shop with multiple processors. *European Journal of Operational Research*, *51*(1), 88–99. doi:10.1016/0377-2217(91)90148-O

Brah, S. A., & Loo, L. L. (1999). Heuristics for scheduling in a flow shop with multiple processors. *European Journal of Operational Research*, *113*(1), 113–122. doi:10.1016/S0377-2217(97)00423-2

Carlier, J., & Néron, E. (2000). An exact method for solving the multi-processor flow-shop. *Operations Research*, *34*(1), 1–25. doi:10.1051/ro:2000103

Choi, H. S., & Lee, D. H. (2009). Scheduling algorithms to minimize the number of tardy jobs in two-stage hybrid flow shops. *Computers & Industrial Engineering*, *56*(1), 113–120. doi:10.1016/j.cie.2008.04.005

Choi, S. W., Kim, Y. D., & Lee, G. C. (2005). Minimizing total tardiness of orders with reentrant lots in a hybrid flowshop. *International Journal of Production Research*, *43*(11), 2149–2167. doi:10.1080/00207540500050071

Chou, F. D. (2013). Particle swarm optimization with cocktail decoding method for hybrid flow shop scheduling problems with multiprocessor tasks. *International Journal of Production Economics*, *141*(1), 137–145. doi:10.1016/j.ijpe.2012.05.015

Chung, T. P., & Liao, C. J. (2013). An immunoglobulin-based artificial immune system for solving the hybrid flow shop problem. *Applied Soft Computing*, *13*(8), 3729–3736. doi:10.1016/j.asoc.2013.03.006

Civicioglu, P., & Besdok, E. (2011). A conceptual comparison of the Cuckoo-search, particle swarm optimization, differential evolution and artificial bee colony algorithms. *Artificial Intelligence Review*. doi:10.1007/s10462-011-9276-0

Davoudpour, H., & Ashrafi, M. (2009). Solving multi-objective SDST flexible flow shop using GRASP algorithm. *International Journal of Advanced Manufacturing Technology*, *44*(7-8), 7–8, 737–747. doi:10.1007/s00170-008-1887-5

Dejam, S., Sadeghzadeh, M., & Mirabedini, S. J. (2012). Combining cuckoo and tabu algorithms for solving quadratic assignment problems. *Journal of Academic and Applied Studies*, *2*, 1–8.

Ding, F. Y., & Kittichartphayak, D. (1994). Heuristics for scheduling flexible flow lines. *Computers & Industrial Engineering*, *26*(1), 27–34. doi:10.1016/0360-8352(94)90025-6

Engin, O., Ceran, G., & Yilmaz, M. K. (2011). An efficient genetic algorithm for hybrid flow shop scheduling with multiprocessor task problems. *Applied Soft Computing*, *11*(3), 3056–3065. doi:10.1016/j.asoc.2010.12.006

Engin, O., & Döyen, A. (2004). A new approach to solve hybrid flow shop scheduling problems by artificial immune system. *Future Generation Computer Systems*, *20*(6), 1083–1095. doi:10.1016/j.future.2004.03.014

Fister, I., Fister, D., & Fister, I. (2013). A comprehensive review of cuckoo search: Variants and hybrids. *International Journal of Mathematical Modelling and Numerical Optimisation*, *4*, 387–409. doi:10.1504/IJMMNO.2013.059205

Gandomi, A. H., Yang, X. S., & Alavi, A. H. (2013). Cuckoo search algorithm: A metaheuristic approach to solve structural optimization problems. *Engineering with Computers*, *29*(1), 17–35. doi:10.1007/s00366-011-0241-y

Gherboudj, A., Layeb, A., & Chikhi, S. (2012). Solving 0–1 knapsack problems by a discrete binary version of cuckoo search algorithm. *International Journal of Bio-inspired Computation*, *4*(4), 229–236. doi:10.1504/IJBIC.2012.048063

Gupta, J. N. D. (1988). Two-stage, hybrid flowshop scheduling problem. *The Journal of the Operational Research Society*, *39*(4), 359–364. doi:10.1057/jors.1988.63

Gupta, J. N. D., & Tunc, E. A. (1998). Minimizing tardy jobs in a two-stage hybrid flowshop. *International Journal of Production Research*, *36*(9), 2397–2417. doi:10.1080/002075498192599

Han, Z., Shi, H., Qiao, F., & Yue, L. (2012). Multiple rules decision-based DE solution for the earliness-tardiness case of hybrid flow-shop scheduling problem. *International Journal of Modelling. Identification and Control*, *16*(2), 97–107. doi:10.1504/IJMIC.2012.047118

Haouari, M., & M'Hallah, R. (1997). Heuristic algorithm for two stage hybrid flow shop. *Operations Research Letters*, *21*(1), 43–53. doi:10.1016/S0167-6377(97)00004-7

Hoogeveen, J. A., Lenstra, J. K., & Vettman, B. (1996). Preemptive scheduling in a two-stage multiprocessor flow shop is NP-hard. *European Journal of Operational Research*, *89*(1), 172–175. doi:10.1016/S0377-2217(96)90070-3

Hou, E. S. H., Ansari, N., & Ren, H. (1994). A genetic algorithm for multiprocessor scheduling. *IEEE Transactions on Parallel and Distributed Systems*, *5*(2), 113–120. doi:10.1109/71.265940

Hunsucker, J. L., & Shah, J. R. (1994). Comparative performance analysis of priority rules in a constrained flow shop with multiple processors environment. *European Journal of Operational Research*, *72*(1), 102–114. doi:10.1016/0377-2217(94)90333-6

Jabbarizadeh, F., Zandieh, M., & Talebi, D. (2009). Hybrid flexible flowshops with sequence-dependent setup times and machine availability constraints. *Computers & Industrial Engineering*, *57*(3), 949–957. doi:10.1016/j.cie.2009.03.012

Jamil, M., & Zepernick, H. (2013). Multimodal function optimisation with cuckoo search algorithm. *International Journal of Bio-inspired Computation*, *5*(2), 73–83. doi:10.1504/IJBIC.2013.053509

Jungwattanakit, J., Reodecha, M., Chaovalitwongse, P., & Werner, F. (2008). Algorithms for flexible flow shop problems with unrelated parallel machines, setup times, and dual criteria. *International Journal of Advanced Manufacturing Technology*, *37*(3-4), 3–4, 354–370. doi:10.1007/s00170-007-0977-0

Jungwattanakit, J., Reodecha, M., Chaovalitwongse, P., & Werner, F. (2009). A comparison of scheduling algorithms for flexible flow shop problems with unrelated parallel machines, setup times, and dual criteria. *Computers & Operations Research*, *36*(2), 358–378. doi:10.1016/j.cor.2007.10.004

Kahraman, C., Engin, O., Kaya, I., & Öztürk, R. E. (2010). Multiprocessor task scheduling in multistage hybrid flow-shops: A parallel greedy algorithm approach. *Applied Soft Computing*, *10*(4), 1293–1300. doi:10.1016/j.asoc.2010.03.008

Kahraman, C., Engin, O., Kaya, I., & Yilmaz, M. K. (2008). An application of effective genetic algorithm for solving hybrid flowshop scheduling problems. *International Journal of Computational Intelligence Systems*, *1*(2), 134–147. doi:10.1080/18756891.2008.9727611

Karimi, N., Zandieh, M., & Karamooz, H. R. (2010). Bi-objective group scheduling in hybrid flexible flowshop: A multi-phase approach. *Expert Systems with Applications*, *37*(6), 4024–4032. doi:10.1016/j.eswa.2009.09.005

Kaveh, A., Bakhshpoori, T., & Ashoory, M. (2012). An efficient optimization procedure based on cuckoo search algorithm for practical design of steel structures. *International Journal of Optimization in Civil Engineering*, *2*, 1–14.

Khalili, M. (2012). Multi-objective no-wait hybrid flowshop scheduling problem with transportation times. *International Journal on Computer Science and Engineering*, *7*(2), 147–154. doi:10.1504/IJCSE.2012.048094

Layeb, A. (2011). A novel quantum inspired cuckoo search for knapsack problems. *International Journal of Bio-inspired Computation*, *3*(5), 297–305. doi:10.1504/IJBIC.2011.042260

Lee, G. C., & Kim, Y. D. (2004). A branch-and-bound algorithm for a two-stage hybrid flowshop scheduling problem minimizing total tardiness. *International Journal of Production Research*, *42*(22), 4731–4743. doi:10.1080/0020754041233127044

Li, J. K., Pan, Q. K., & Mao, K. (2014). Hybrid particle swarm optimization for hybrid flowshop scheduling problem with maintenance activities. *The Scientific World Journal*. doi:10.1155/2014/596850 PMID:24883414

Li, S. (1997). A hybrid two-stage flowshop with part family, batch production, major and minor set-ups. *European Journal of Operational Research*, *102*(1), 142–156. doi:10.1016/S0377-2217(96)00213-5

Liao, C. J., Tjandradjaja, E., & Chung, T. P. (2012). An approach using particle swarm optimization and bottleneck heuristic to solve hybrid flow shop scheduling problem. *Applied Soft Computing*, *12*(6), 1755–1764. doi:10.1016/j.asoc.2012.01.011

Lin, H. T., & Liao, C. J. (2003). A case study in a two-stage hybrid flow shop with setup time and dedicated machines. *International Journal of Production Economics*, *86*(2), 133–143. doi:10.1016/S0925-5273(03)00011-2

Linn, R., & Zhang, W. (1999). Hybrid flow shop schedule: A survey. *Computers & Industrial Engineering*, *37*(1-2), 1–2, 57–61. doi:10.1016/S0360-8352(99)00023-6

Low, C. (2005). Simulated annealing heuristic for flow shop scheduling problems with unrelated parallel machines. *Computers & Operations Research*, *32*(8), 2013–2025. doi:10.1016/j.cor.2004.01.003

Low, C., Hsu, C. J., & Su, C. T. (2008). A two-stage hybrid flowshop scheduling problem with a function constraint and unrelated alternative machines. *Computers & Operations Research*, *35*(3), 845–853. doi:10.1016/j.cor.2006.04.004

Marichelvam, M. K. (2012). An improved hybrid cuckoo search (IHCS) metaheuristics algorithm for permutation flow shop scheduling problems. *International Journal of Bio-inspired Computation*, *4*(4), 200–205. doi:10.1504/IJBIC.2012.048061

Marichelvam, M. K., & Geetha, M. (2016). Application of novel harmony search algorithm for solving hybrid flow shop scheduling problems to minimize makespan. *International Journal of Industrial and Systems Engineering*, *23*(4), 467–481. doi:10.1504/IJISE.2016.077698

Marichelvam, M. K., & Prabaharan, T. (2014). Performance evaluation of an improved hybrid genetic scatter search algorithm for multistage hybrid flow shop scheduling problems with missing operations. *International Journal of Industrial and System Engineering*, *16*(1), 120–141. doi:10.1504/IJISE.2014.057946

Marichelvam, M. K., Prabaharan, T., & Yang, X. S. (2014). Improved cuckoo search algorithm for hybrid flow shop scheduling problems to minimize makespan. *Applied Soft Computing*, *19*, 93–101. doi:10.1016/j.asoc.2014.02.005

Marichelvam, M. K., Prabaharan, T., Yang, X. S., & Geetha, M. (2013). Solving hybrid flow shop scheduling problems using bat algorithm. *International Journal of Logistics Economics and Globalisation*, *5*(1), 15–29. doi:10.1504/IJLEG.2013.054428

Moursli, O., & Pochet, Y. (2000). A branch and bound algorithm for the hybrid flow shop. *International Journal of Production Economics*, *64*(1-3), 113–125. doi:10.1016/S0925-5273(99)00051-1

Naderi, B., Zandieh, M., Ghoshe, A. K., & Roshanaei, V. (2009). An improved simulated annealing for hybrid flowshops with sequence-dependent setup and transportation times to minimize total completion time and total tardiness. *Expert Systems with Applications*, *36*(6), 9625–9633. doi:10.1016/j.eswa.2008.09.063

Niu, Q., Zhou, T., & Ma, S. (2009). A quantum-inspired immune algorithm for hybrid flow shop with makespan criterion. *Journal of Universal Computer Science*, *15*, 765–785.

Oguz, C., & Ercan, M. F. (2005). A genetic algorithm for hybrid flow shop scheduling with multiprocessor tasks. *Journal of Scheduling*, *8*(4), 323–351. doi:10.1007/s10951-005-1640-y

Oguz, C., Ercan, M. F., Cheng, T. C. E., & Fung, Y. F. (2003). Heuristic algorithms for multiprocessor task scheduling in a two-stage hybrid flow-shop. *European Journal of Operational Research*, *149*(2), 390–403. doi:10.1016/S0377-2217(02)00766-X

Ouyang, X., Zhou, Y., Luo, Q., & Chen, H. (2013). A Novel Discrete Cuckoo Search Algorithm for Spherical Traveling Salesman Problem. *Applied Mathematics & Information Sciences*, *7*(2), 777–784. doi:10.12785/amis/070248

Riane, F., Artiba, A., & Elmaghraby, S. E. (1998). A hybrid three stage flow shop problem: Efficient heuristics to minimize makespan. *European Journal of Operational Research*, *109*, 321–329. doi:10.1016/S0377-2217(98)00060-5

Ribas, I., Leisten, R., & Framiñan, J. M. (2010). Review and classification of hybrid flow shop scheduling problems from a production system and a solutions procedure perspective. *Computers & Operations Research*, *37*(8), 1439–1454. doi:10.1016/j.cor.2009.11.001

Ruiz, R., Serifoğlu, F. S., & Urlings, T. (2008). Modeling realistic hybrid flexible flowshop scheduling problems. *Computers & Operations Research*, *35*(4), 1151–1175. doi:10.1016/j.cor.2006.07.014

Ruiz, R., & Vazquez-Rodriguez, J. A. (2010). The hybrid flow shop scheduling problem. *European Journal of Operational Research*, *205*(1), 1–18. doi:10.1016/j.ejor.2009.09.024

Saravanan, M., Haq, A. N., Vivekraj, A. R., & Prasad, T. (2008). Performance evaluation of the scatter search method for permutation flowshop sequencing problems. *International Journal of Advanced Manufacturing Technology*, *37*(11/12), 1200–1208. doi:10.1007/s00170-007-1053-5

Sawik, T. (2000). Mixed integer programming for scheduling flexible flow lines with limited intermediate buffers. *Mathematical and Computer Modelling*, *31*(13), 39–52. doi:10.1016/S0895-7177(00)00110-2

Sawik, T. (2002). An exact approach for batch scheduling in flexible flow lines with limited intermediate buffers. *Mathematical and Computer Modelling*, *36*(4), 461–471. doi:10.1016/S0895-7177(02)00176-0

Serifoğlu, S. F. S., & Tiryaki, I. U. (2002). Multiprocessor task scheduling in multistage hybrid flowshops: a simulated annealing approach. *Proceedings of the 2nd International Conference on Responsive Manufacturing*, 270–274.

Serifoğlu, S. F. S., & Ulusoy, G. (2004). Multiprocessor task scheduling in multistage hybrid flow shops: A genetic algorithm approach. *The Journal of the Operational Research Society*, *55*(5), 504–512. doi:10.1057/palgrave.jors.2601716

Sha, D. Y., & Lin, H. H. (2010). A multi-objective PSO for job-shop scheduling problems. *Expert Systems with Applications*, *37*(2), 1065–1070. doi:10.1016/j.eswa.2009.06.041

Shenassa, M. H., & Mahmoodi, M. (2006). A novel intelligent method for task scheduling in multiprocessor systems using genetic algorithm. *Journal of the Franklin Institute*, *343*(4-5), 361–371. doi:10.1016/j.jfranklin.2006.02.022

Shiau, D. F., Cheng, S. C., & Huang, Y. M. (2008). Proportionate flexible flow shop scheduling via a hybrid constructive genetic algorithm. *Expert Systems with Applications*, *34*(2), 1133–1143. doi:10.1016/j.eswa.2006.12.002

Singh, M. R., & Mahapatra, S. S. (2011). A swarm optimization approach for flexible flow shop scheduling with multiprocessor tasks. *International Journal of Advanced Manufacturing Technology*, *62*(1-4), 267–277. doi:10.1007/s00170-011-3807-3

Syam, W. P., & Al-Harkan, I. M. (2012). Improvement and comparison of three metaheuristics to optimize flexible flow-shop scheduling problems. *International Journal of Engineering Science and Technology*, *4*, 373–383.

Tang, L., Xuan, H., & Liu, J. (2006). A new Lagrangian relaxation algorithm for hybrid flowshop scheduling to minimize total weighted completion time. *Computers & Operations Research*, *33*(11), 3344–3359. doi:10.1016/j.cor.2005.03.028

Tasgetiren, M. F., Liang, Y. C., Sevkli, M., & Gencyilmaz, G. (2007). A particle swarm optimization algorithm for makespan and total flowtime minimization in the permutation flowshop sequencing problem. *European Journal of Operational Research*, *177*(3), 1930–1947. doi:10.1016/j.ejor.2005.12.024

Tosun, Ö. (2014). Cuckoo Search Algorithm. In J. Wang (Ed.), *Encylopedia of Business Analytics and Optimization* (pp. 558–564). IGI Global. doi:10.4018/978-1-4666-5202-6.ch050

Tran, T. H., & Ng, K. M. (2013). A hybrid water flow algorithm for multi-objective flexible flow shop scheduling problems. *Engineering Optimization*, *45*(4), 483–502. doi:10.1080/0305215X.2012.685072

Tseng, C. T., Liao, C. J., & Liao, T. X. (2008). A note on two-stage hybrid flowshop scheduling with missing operations. *Computers & Industrial Engineering*, *54*(3), 695–704. doi:10.1016/j.cie.2007.09.005

Valian, E., Mohanna, S., & Tavakoli, S. (2011). Improved cuckoo search algorithm for feed forward neural network training. *International Journal of Artificial Intelligence and Applications*, *2*(3), 36–43. doi:10.5121/ijaia.2011.2304

Valian, E., Tavakoli, S., Mohanna, S., & Haghi, A. (2013). Improved cuckoo search for reliability optimization problems. *Computers & Industrial Engineering*, *64*(1), 459–468. doi:10.1016/j.cie.2012.07.011

Walton, S., Hassan, O., & Morgan, K. (2013). Reduced order mesh optimization using proper orthogonal decomposition and a modified cuckoo search. *International Journal for Numerical Methods in Engineering*, *93*(5), 527–550. doi:10.1002/nme.4400

Wang, H. M., Chou, F. D., & Wu, F. C. (2010). A simulated annealing for hybrid flow shop scheduling with multiprocessor tasks to minimize makespan. *International Journal of Advanced Manufacturing Technology*, *53*(5-8), 761–776. doi:10.1007/s00170-010-2868-z

Wang, S., & Liu, M. (2013). A heuristic method for two-stage hybrid flow shop with dedicated machines. *Computers & Operations Research*, *40*(1), 438–450. doi:10.1016/j.cor.2012.07.015

Wu, Z., Chow, T. W. S., Cheng, S., & Shi, Y. (2013). Contour gradient optimization. *International Journal of Swarm Intelligence Research*, *2*(2), 1–28. doi:10.4018/jsir.2013040101

Xie, J., & Wang, X. (2005). Complexity and algorithms for two-stage flexible flowshop scheduling with availability constraints. *Computers & Mathematics with Applications (Oxford, England)*, *50*(10), 1629–1638. doi:10.1016/j.camwa.2005.07.008

Yang, X. S. (2012). Nature-Inspired Metaheuristic Algorithms: Success and New Challenges. *Journal of Computer Engineering & Information Technology*, *1*(1). doi:10.4172/2324-9307.1000e101

Yang, X. S., & Deb, S. (2009). Cuckoo search via Lévy flights. *NaBIC 2009: Proceedings of the World Congress on Nature & Biologically Inspired Computing*, 210-214.

Yang, X. S., & Deb, S. (2010). Engineering Optimisation by Cuckoo Search. *International Journal of Mathematical Modelling and Numerical Optimisation*, *1*(4), 330–343. doi:10.1504/IJMMNO.2010.035430

Yang, X. S., & Deb, S. (2013). Multiobjective cuckoo search for design optimization. *Computers & Operations Research*, *40*(6), 1616–1624. doi:10.1016/j.cor.2011.09.026

Yildiz, A. R. (2013). Cuckoo search algorithm for the selection of optimal machining parameters in milling operations. *International Journal of Advanced Manufacturing Technology*, *64*(1-4), 55–61. doi:10.1007/s00170-012-4013-7

Ying, K. C., & Lin, S. W. (2006). Multiprocessor task scheduling in multistage hybrid flowshops: An ant colony system approach. *International Journal of Production Economics*, *44*(16), 3161–3177. doi:10.1080/00207540500536939

Chapter 16
Particle Swarm Optimization for Model Predictive Control in Reinforcement Learning Environments

Daniel Hein
Technische Universität München, Germany

Alexander Hentschel
AxiomZen, Canada

Thomas A. Runkler
Siemens AG, Germany

Steffen Udluft
Siemens AG, Germany

ABSTRACT

This chapter introduces a model-based reinforcement learning (RL) approach for continuous state and action spaces. While most RL methods try to find closed-form policies, the approach taken here employs numerical online optimization of control action sequences following the strategy of nonlinear model predictive control. First, a general method for reformulating RL problems as optimization tasks is provided. Subsequently, particle swarm optimization (PSO) is applied to search for optimal solutions. This PSO policy (PSO-P) is effective for high dimensional state spaces and does not require a priori assumptions about adequate policy representations. Furthermore, by translating RL problems into optimization tasks, the rich collection of real-world-inspired RL benchmarks is made available for benchmarking numerical optimization techniques. The effectiveness of PSO-P is demonstrated on two standard benchmarks mountain car and cart-pole swing-up and a new industry-inspired benchmark, the so-called industrial benchmark.

DOI: 10.4018/978-1-5225-5134-8.ch016

INTRODUCTION

This chapter focuses on a general reinforcement learning (RL) setting with continuous state and action spaces. In this domain, the policy performance often strongly depends on the algorithms for policy generation and the chosen policy representation (Sutton & Barto, 1998). In the authors' experience, tuning the policy learning process is generally challenging for industrial RL problems. Specifically, it is hard to assess whether a trained policy has unsatisfactory performance due to inadequate training data, unsuitable policy representation, or an unfitting training algorithm. Determining the best problem-specific RL approach often requires time-intensive trials with various policy configurations and training algorithms. In contrast, it is often significantly easier to train a well-performing system model from observational data, compared to directly learning a policy and assessing its performance.

The main purpose of the present contribution is to provide a heuristic for solving RL problems which employs numerical online optimization of control action sequences. As an initial step, a neural system model is trained from observational data with standard methods. However, the presented method also works with any other model type, e.g., Gaussian process or first principal models. The resulting problem of finding optimal control action sequences based on model predictions is solved with particle swarm optimization (PSO), because PSO is an established algorithm for non-convex optimization. Specifically, the presented heuristic iterates over the following steps. (1) PSO is employed to search for an action sequence that maximizes the expected return when applied to the current system state by simulating its effects using the system model. (2) The first action of the sequence with the highest expected return is applied to the real-world system. (3) The system transitions to the subsequent state and the optimization process are repeated based on the new state (go to step 1).

As this approach can generate control actions for any system state, it formally constitutes an RL policy. This PSO policy (PSO-P) deviates fundamentally from common RL approaches. Most methods for solving RL problems try to learn a closed-form policy (Sutton & Barto, 1998). The most significant advantages of PSO-P are the following. (1) Closed-form policy learners generally select a policy from a user-parameterized (potentially infinite) set of candidate policies. For example, when learning an RL policy based on tile coding (Sutton, 1996), the user must specify partitions of the state space. The partition's characteristics directly influence how well the resulting policy can differentiate the effect of different actions. For complex RL problems, policy performances usually vary drastically depending on the chosen partitions. In contrast, PSO-P does not require a priori assumptions about problem-specific policy representations, because it directly optimizes action sequences. (2) Closed-form RL policies operate on the state space and are generally affected by the *curse of dimensionality* (Bellman, Adaptive Control Processes: A Guided Tour, 1962). Simply put, the number of data points required for a representative coverage of the state space grows exponentially with the state space's dimensionality. Common RL methods, such as tile coding, quickly become computationally intractable with increasing dimensionality. Moreover, for industrial RL problems it is often very expensive to obtain adequate training data prohibiting data-intensive RL methods. In comparison, PSO-P is not affected by the state space dimensionality because it operates in the space of action sequences.

From a strictly mathematical standpoint, PSO-P follows a known strategy from nonlinear model predictive control (MPC): employing online numerical optimization in search for the best action sequences. While MPC and RL target almost the same class of control optimization problems with different methods, the mathematical formalisms in both communities are drastically different. Particularly, the authors find that the presented approach is rarely considered in the RL community. The main contribution of this chapter is to provide a hands-on guide for employing online optimization of action sequences in the mathematical RL framework and demonstrate its effectiveness for solving RL problems. On the one hand, PSO-P generally requires significantly more computation time to determine an action for a given system state compared to closed-form RL policies. On the other hand, the authors found PSO-P particularly useful for determining the optimization potential of various industrial control optimization problems and for benchmarking other RL methods.

In the Sections 'Formulation of Reinforcement Learning as Optimization Problem' and 'The PSO-Policy Framework', the methodology is developed, starting by formulating RL as a non-convex optimization problem and subsequently employing PSO as a solver. The results of the conducted benchmark experiments are presented in the Section 'Experiments, Results, and Analysis'. Future research opportunities are proposed in Section 'Future Research Directions' followed by the discussion of the experimental results and current limitations of PSO-P in the final Section 'Conclusion'.

BACKGROUND

RL is an area of machine learning inspired by biological learning. Formally, a software agent interacts with a system in discrete time steps. At each time step, the agent observes the system's state s and applies an action a. Depending on s and a, the system transitions into a new state and the agent receives a real-valued reward $r \in \mathbb{R}$. The agent's goal is to maximize its expected cumulative reward, called return $\mathcal{R}$. The solution to an RL problem is a policy, i.e., a map that generates an action for any given state. (Sutton & Barto, Reinforcement learning: An introduction, 1998)

To bypass the challenges of learning a closed-form RL policy, the authors adapted an approach from MPC (Rawlings & Mayne, 2009; Camacho & Alba, 2007), which employs only a system model. The general idea behind MPC is deceptively simple: given a reliable system model, one can predict the future evolution of the system and determine a control strategy that results in the desired system behavior. However, complex industry systems and plants commonly exhibit nonlinear system dynamics (Schaefer, Schneegass, Sterzing, & Udluft, 2007; Piche, et al., 2000). In such cases, closed-form solutions to the optimal control problem often do not exist or are computationally hard to find (Findeisen & Allgoewer, 2002; Magni & Scattolini, 2004). Therefore, MPC tasks for nonlinear systems are typically solved by numerical online optimization of sequences of control actions (Gruene & Pannek, 2011). Unfortunately, the resulting optimization problems are generally non-convex (Johansen, 2011) and no universal method for tackling nonlinear MPC tasks has yet been found (Findeisen, Allgoewer, & Biegler, 2007; Rawlings, Tutorial overview of model predictive control, 2000). Moreover, one might argue, based on theoretical considerations, that such a universal optimization algorithm does not exist (Wolpert & Macready, 1997).

PSO and evolutionary algorithms are established heuristics for solving non-convex optimization problems. Both have been applied in the context of RL, however, almost exclusively to optimize policies directly. Moriarty, Schultz, & Grefenstette (1999) give a comprehensive overview of the various approaches, using evolutionary algorithms to tackle RL problems. Methods, which apply PSO to generate policies for specific system control problems, were studied in (Feng, 2005), (Solihin & Akmeliawati, 2010), and (Montazeri-Gh, Jafari, & Ilkhani, 2012).

Recently, several combinations of swarm optimization and MPC have been proposed in the literature. In (Van Heerden, Fujimoto, & Kawamura, 2014) the nonlinear and underactuated Acrobot problem was solved by adapting PSO to run in parallel on graphics hardware, yielding a real-time MPC controller. Ou,

Kang, Kim, & Julius (2015) investigated the use of a single control signal and a PSO-MPC algorithm for controlling the movement of multiple magnetized cells while avoiding obstacles. In (Xu, Chen, Gong, & Mei, 2016) the authors tackled the problem of real-time application of nonlinear MPC by implementing it on a field-programmable gate array that employs a PSO algorithm. By using a parallelized PSO implementation, good computational performance and satisfactory control performance were achieved. Lee & Myung (2015) significantly reduced the computational cost of collision avoidance for a class of mobile robots. By applying PSO instead of traditional optimization techniques, such as sequential quadratic programming, they achieved a significant speedup during the optimization phase. They also verified the effectiveness of the proposed RHPSO-based formation control by means of numerical simulations.

However, none of the reviewed approaches generalizes to RL, as expert-designed objective functions, that already contain detailed knowledge about the optimal solution to the respective control problem, are used. In contrast, in the present chapter, the general RL problem is reformulated as an optimization problem. This representation allows searching for optimal action sequences on a system model, even if no expert knowledge about the underlying problem dynamics is available.

FORMULATION OF REINFORCEMENT LEARNING AS OPTIMIZATION PROBLEM

In this chapter, the problem of optimizing the behavior of a physical system, that is observed in discrete, equally spaced time steps $t \in \mathbb{Z}$, is considered. The current time is denoted as $t = 0$. Hence, $t = 1$ and $t = -1$ represent one step into the future and one step into the past, respectively. At each time step t, the system is described by its Markovian state $s_t \in \mathcal{S}$, from the state space $\mathcal{S}$. The agent's action a_t is represented by a vector of I different control parameters, i.e., $a_t \in \mathcal{A} \subset \mathbb{R}^I$. Based on the system's state and the applied action, the system transitions into the state s_{t+1} and the agent receives the reward r_t.

In the following, deterministic systems, which are described by a state transition function $m : \mathcal{S} \times \mathcal{A} \rightarrow \mathcal{S} \times \mathbb{R}$ with $m(s_t, a_t) = (s_{t+1}, r_t)$, are considered.

The goal is to find an action sequence $\mathbf{x} = (a_t, a_{t+1}, \ldots, a_{t+T-1})$ that maximizes the expected return $\mathcal{R}$. The search space is bounded by $\mathbf{x}_{\min}$ and $\mathbf{x}_{\max}$ which are defined as:

$$\mathbf{x}_{\min_j} = a_{\min_{(j \bmod I)}} \quad \forall j = 0, \ldots, I \cdot T - 1 \tag{1}$$

and

$$\mathbf{x}_{\max_j} = a_{\max_{(j \bmod I)}} \quad \forall j = 0, \ldots, I \cdot T - 1, \tag{2}$$

where $a_{\min}$ ($a_{\max}$) are the lower (upper) bounds of the control parameters.

To incorporate the increasing uncertainty when planning actions further and further into the future, the simulated reward r_{t+k} for k time steps into the future is weighted by γ^k, where $\gamma \in [0,1]$ is referred to as the discount factor.

A common strategy is to simulate the system evolution only for a finite number of $T \geq 1$ steps. The return is (Sutton & Barto, 1998)

$$\mathcal{R}(s_t, \mathbf{x}) = \sum_{k=0}^{T-1} \gamma^k r_{t+k}, \quad \text{with } (s_{t+k+1}, r_{t+k}) = m(s_{t+k}, a_{t+k}). \tag{3}$$

The authors chose γ such that at the end of the time horizon T, the last reward accounted for is weighted by the user-defined constant $q \in [0,1]$, which implies $\gamma = q^{1/(T-1)}$.

Solving the RL problem corresponds to finding the optimal action sequence $\mathbf{x}$ by maximizing

$$\hat{\mathbf{x}} \in \operatorname*{argmax}_{\mathbf{x} \in \mathcal{A}^T} f_{s_t}(\mathbf{x}), \tag{4}$$

with respect to the fitness function $f_{s_t} : \mathbb{R}^{I \cdot T} \to \mathbb{R}$ with $f_{s_t}(\mathbf{x}) = \mathcal{R}(s_t, \mathbf{x})$. Figure 1 illustrates the process of computing $f_{s_t}(\mathbf{x})$.

Figure 1. Model-based computation of the fitness function, i.e., return function, from the system's current state s_t and an action sequence $\mathbf{x}$. The accumulated rewards, predicted by the model, yield the fitness value f_{s_t}, which is then used to drive the optimization.

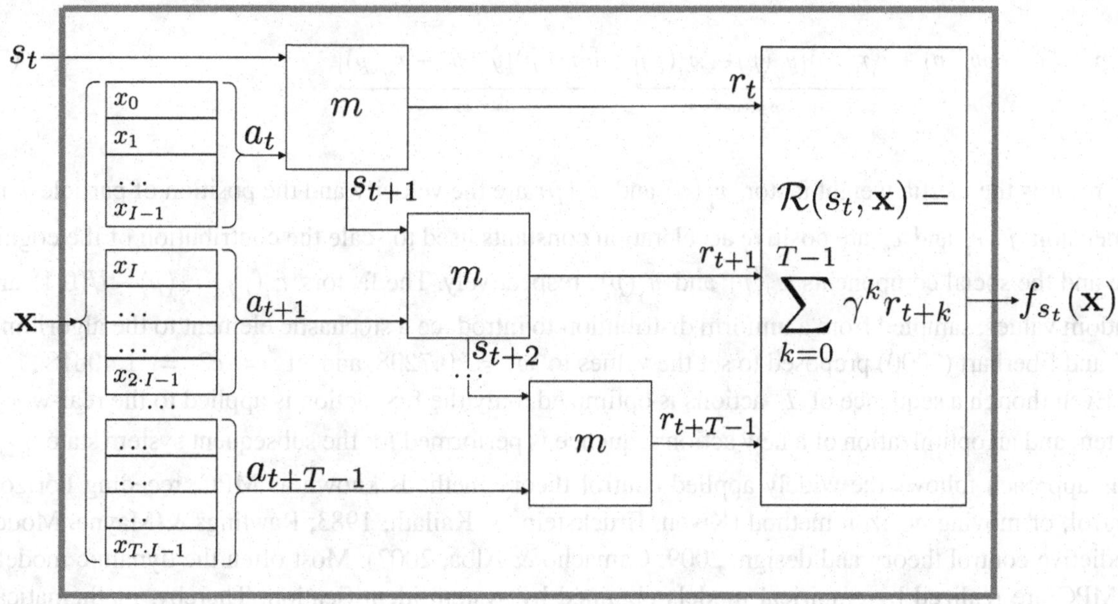

THE PSO-POLICY FRAMEWORK

The PSO algorithm is a population-based, stochastic optimization heuristic for solving non-convex optimization problems (Kennedy & Eberhart, 1995). Generally, PSO can operate on any search space that is a bounded sub-space of a finite-dimensional vector space (Engelbrecht, 2005). The PSO algorithm performs a search using a population (swarm) of individuals (particles) that are updated from iteration to iteration.

In this chapter, PSO is used to solve Eq. (4), i.e., the particles move through the search space of action sequences $\mathcal{A}^T$. Consequently, a particle's position represents a candidate action sequence $\mathbf{x} = (a_t, a_{t+1}, \ldots, a_{t+T-1})$, which is initially chosen at random.

At each iteration, particle i remembers its local best position $\mathbf{y}_i$ that it has visited so far (including its current position). Furthermore, particle i also knows the neighborhood best position

$$\hat{\mathbf{y}}_i(p+1) \in \underset{\mathbf{z}\in\{\mathbf{y}_j(p)|j\in\mathcal{N}_i\}}{\operatorname{argmax}} f(\mathbf{z}), \tag{5}$$

found so far by any particle in its neighborhood $\mathcal{N}_i$ (including itself). The neighborhood relations between particles are determined by the swarm's population topology and are generally fixed, irrespective of the particles' positions.

In the experiments presented in Section 'Experiments, Results, and Analysis' the authors use the ring topology (Eberhart, Simpson, & Dobbins, 1996).

From iteration p to $p+1$ the particle position update rule is

$$\mathbf{x}_i(p+1) = \mathbf{x}_i(p) + \mathbf{v}_i(p+1). \tag{6}$$

The components of the velocity vector $\mathbf{v}$ are calculated as

$$v_{ij}(p+1) = wv_{ij}(p) + \underbrace{c_1 r_{1j}(p)[y_{ij}(p) - x_{ij}(p)]}_{\text{cognitive component}} + \underbrace{c_2 r_{2j}(p)[\hat{y}_{ij}(p) - x_{ij}(p)]}_{\text{social component}}, \tag{7}$$

where w is the inertia weight factor, $v_{ij}(p)$ and $x_{ij}(p)$ are the velocity and the position of particle i in dimension j, c_1 and c_2 are positive acceleration constants used to scale the contribution of the cognitive and the social components $y_{ij}(p)$ and $\hat{y}_{ij}(p)$, respectively. The factors $r_{1j}(p)$, $r_{2j}(p) \sim U(0,1)$ are random values, sampled from a uniform distribution to introduce a stochastic element to the algorithm. Shi and Eberhart (2000) proposed to set the values to $w = 0.7298$ and $c1 = c2 = 1.49618$.

Even though a sequence of T actions is optimized, only the first action is applied to the real-world system and an optimization of a new action sequence is performed for the subsequent system state s_{t+1}. This approach follows the widely applied control theory methods known as MPC, receding horizon control, or moving horizon method (Kwon, Bruckstein, & Kailath, 1983; Rawlings & Mayne, Model predictive control theory and design, 2009; Camacho & Alba, 2007). Most often the dynamic models in MPC are realized by empirical models obtained by system identification. Thereby, mathematical models $\tilde{m}$ are learned by measured data from the real dynamical system m. Since this data is already available in batch RL problems considered herein, applying an MPC-like approach like PSO-P appears likely to succeed for such problems, too.

Despite the fact that empirical models $\tilde{m}$ are likely to be inaccurate in their predictions, i.e., $\tilde{m}(s_t, a_t) = (\tilde{s}_{t+1}, \tilde{r}_t) \neq (s_{t+1}, r_t) = m(s_t, a_t)$ in Eq. (3), the experiments presented in Section 'Experiments, Results, and Analysis' verify that very stable control results can still be achieved. The reason for this advantageous behavior lies in the fact, that applying only the first action of the optimized action trajectory to the system, and subsequently initializing PSO-P with the resulting real system state s_{t+1}, resets the agent to the underlying true environmental conditions after each time step. Subsequently, the optimization starts with the correct initialization from scratch.

Implementation details can be found in Appendix 2.

EXPERIMENTS, RESULTS, AND ANALYSIS

The authors applied the PSO-P framework to three different RL problems. Two standard problems are the mountain car (MC) (Sutton & Barto, 1998) and the cart-pole (CP) swing-up benchmark (Fantoni & Lozano, 2002), which are used to illustrate the framework's capability of solving RL problems in general. The third problem is an industry inspired benchmark, the so-called industrial benchmarks (IB) (Hein, et al., 2017b), which evaluates the framework's performance on high-dimensional and stochastic dynamics.

For each benchmark, a neural network (NN) has been trained as the system model m using standard techniques (Montavon, Orr, & Müller, 2012). NNs are well suited for data-driven black-box models as they are universal approximators (Hornik, Stinchcombe, & White, 1989). In addition, the authors found that the resulting models generalize well to new data in many real-world applications.

The authors have chosen this approach instead of working directly with benchmark simulations because in many real-world scenarios physical simulations are either unavailable or strongly idealized. However, PSO-P works with other model types as well, such as first principle or Gaussian process models (Rasmussen & Williams, 2006).

Mountain Car Benchmark

In the MC benchmark an underpowered car is driven up to the top of a hill (Figure 2). This is done by building up momentum with the help of driving in the opposite direction to gain enough potential energy.

In the present implementation, the hill landscape is equivalent to $\sin(3\rho)$. The task for the RL agent is to find a sequence of force actions $a_t, a_{t+1}, a_{t+2}, \ldots \in [-1,1]$ that drive the car up the hill, which is achieved when reaching a position $\rho > \pi/6$.

At the start of each episode the car's state is $(\rho, \dot{\rho}) = (-\pi / 6, 0.0)$. The agent receives a reward of $r(\rho) = \sin(3\rho) - 1$ after every action-state update. When the car reaches the goal position, the car's position is fixed, and the agent receives the maximum reward in every following time step, regardless of the applied actions.

Using the parameters given in Table 1, PSO-P is able to solve this RL problem. Details of the algorithm and the determination of suitable algorithmic parameters are summarized in Appendix 1.

Figure 2. Mountain car task. The system can be described completely by its Markov state variables ρ and $\dot{\rho}$, which represent the car's position and velocity, respectively (Sutton & Barto, 1998)

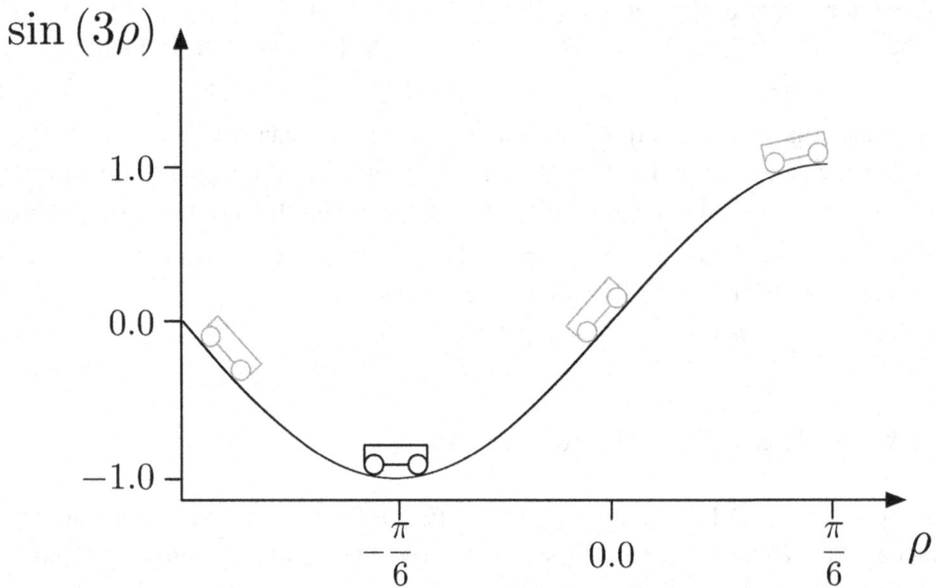

Table 1. PSO-P setup parameters and achieved experiment results for the MC benchmark

Particles	100
Iterations	100
Topology	(each particle with 5 neighbors, including itself)
(w, c_1, c_2)	(0.72981, 1.49618, 1.49618)
(T, q)	(100, 0.05)
Model approximation m	RNN trained with 10,000 randomly generated state transitions
Benchmark start states	100 times $s = (\rho, \dot{\rho}) = (-\pi / 6, 0.0)$
Return (1,000 steps)	median: -350, min: -644, max: -197

To confirm that finding the optimal way of driving the car up the mountain is represented as a non-convex optimization problem, the performance of PSO has been compared with a standard simplex algorithm (NM) published by (Nelder & Mead, 1965) applied to Eq. (4). The NM algorithm was allowed to utilize the exact same number of fitness evaluations during the optimization as the PSO (100 particles and 100 PSO iterations corresponding to 10,000 fitness evaluations).

The results presented in Figure 3 show that on average PSO yields a significantly better control performance than NM. This result was expected, since the problem is assumed to be highly non-convex and NM is likely to get stuck in local optima. Nevertheless, the majority of runs using NM managed to drive the car up the hill in less than 1,000 time steps, even though it took NM significantly more time steps on average (Figure 4).

Figure 3. Visualization of the average return of PSO and NM computed from 100 experiments per setup. Applying the exact same number of fitness function evaluations, PSO outperforms NM on the MC benchmark. On each box, the central mark is the median, the box edges are the 25th and 75th percentiles, and the whiskers extend to the most extreme data points not considered outliers. An average return point g is categorized as an outlier (+) if $g > q_3 + 1.5(q_3 - q_1)$ or $g < q_1 - 1.5(q_3 - q_1)$, for q_1 the 25th and q_3 the 75th percentile.

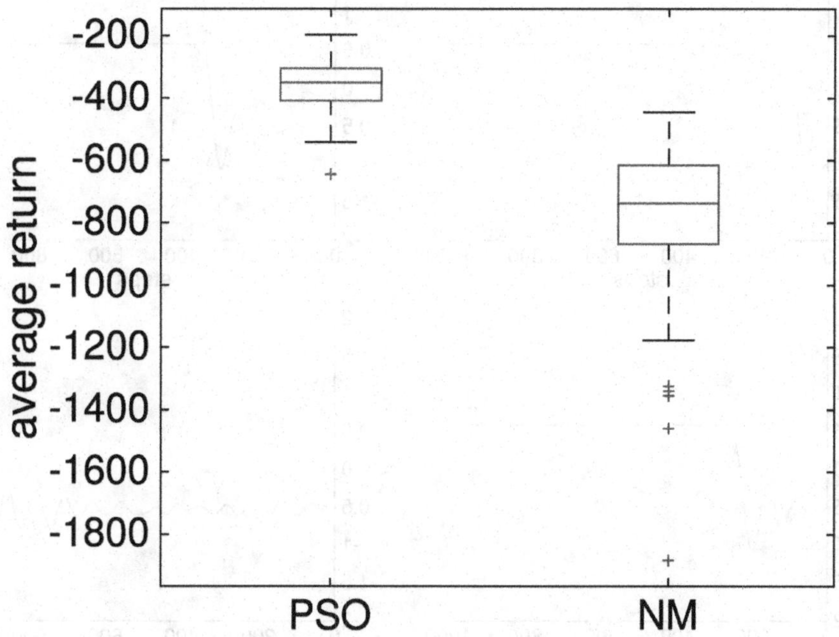

Cart-Pole Swing-Up Benchmark

The objective of the CP benchmark is to apply forces to a cart moving on a one-dimensional track to bring a pole hinged to the cart in an upright position (Fantoni & Lozano, 2002). The four Markov state variables are the pole's angle θ, the pole's angular velocity $\dot{\theta}$, the cart's position ρ, and the cart's velocity $\dot{\rho}$, as illustrated in Figure 5.

The start settings for the experiments are: $\theta = \pi$, $\dot{\theta} = 0$, $\rho = 0$, and $\dot{\rho} = 0$, i.e., the pole is hanging down with the cart at rest. The goal is to find force actions $a_t, a_{t+1}, a_{t+2}, \ldots \in [-1,1]$, that swing the pole up and subsequently prevent the pole from falling over while keeping the cart close to $\rho = 0$ for a possibly infinite period of time. The closer the CP gets to the desired position ($\theta = 0, \rho = 0$) the higher are the rewards $r(\rho,\theta) = -\sqrt{(\rho / 1.4)^2 + (\theta / 0.3)^2}$ for the corresponding transitions.

Using the parameters given in Table 2, the authors show that PSO-P is able to solve this RL problem. To find the best setting for the user-defined parameters, the authors again followed their recipe from Appendix 1.

Similar to the MC benchmark, the authors compared the resulting performance of PSO to NM when solving Eq. (4). While the MC optimization problem is simple enough for NM to solve it in less than 1,000 time steps, NM completely failed to stabilize the cart's pole in 1,000 time steps. In Figure 6 the

Figure 4. Mountain car experiments. Applying PSO always resulted in well-performing and successful action trajectories, while using NM sometimes did not generate action sequences driving the car up the hill in less than 1,000 time steps.

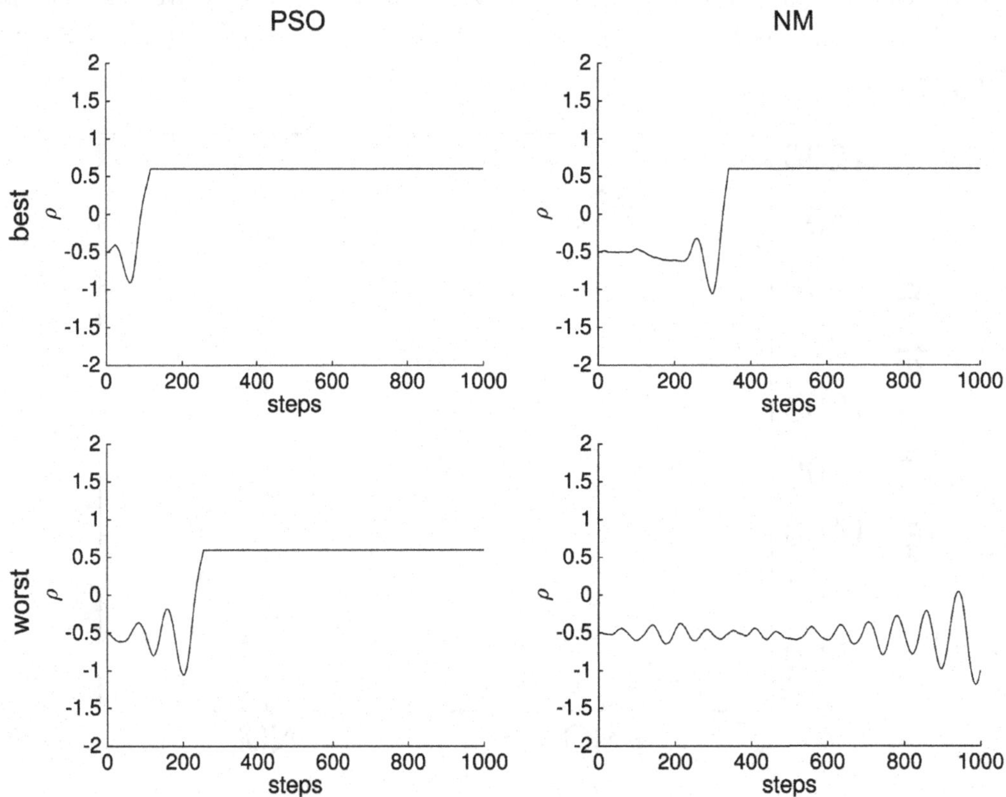

average return values of PSO and NM are compared. The best and worst out of 100 generated trajectories with PSO and NM optimizations are compared in Figure 7. It is evident that PSO significantly outperforms NM, which indicates that solving CP is a hard optimization problem for deterministic algorithms such as NM.

Industrial Benchmark

The (Hein, et al., 2017a; Hein, et al., 2017b) (source code available at http://github.com/siemens/industrialbenchmark) was designed to emulate several challenging aspects eminent in many industrial applications. It is not designed to be an approximation of any specific real-world system, but to pose a comparable hardness and complexity found in many industrial applications.

State and action spaces are continuous. Moreover, the state space is high-dimensional and only partially observable. The actions consist of three continuous components and affect three control inputs. Moreover, the IB includes stochastic and delayed effects. The optimization task is multi-criterial in the sense that there are two reward components that show opposite dependencies on the actions. The dynamical behavior is heteroscedastic with state-dependent observation noise and state-dependent probability

Figure 5. Cart-pole system

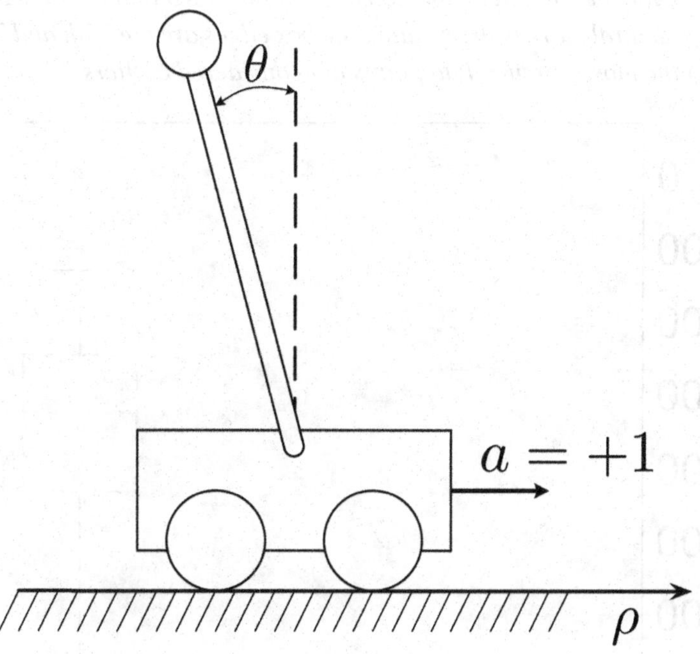

Table 2.PSO-P setup parameters and achieved experiment results for the CP benchmark

Particles	100
Iterations	100
Topology	(each particle with 5 neighbors, including itself)
(w, c_1, c_2)	(0.72981, 1.49618, 1.49618)
(T, q)	(150, 0.05)
Model approximation m	RNN trained with 10,000 randomly generated state transitions
Benchmark start states	100 times $s = (\theta, \dot{\theta}, \rho, \dot{\rho}) = (\pi, 0, 0, 0)$
Return (1,000 steps)	median: -860, min: -918, max: -823

distributions, based on latent variables. Furthermore, it depends on an external driver that cannot be influenced by the actions.

The IB is designed such that the optimal policy will not approach a fixed operation point in the three control inputs, i.e., constantly changing the control inputs with regard to past observations, resulting in significantly higher return. Note that any specific design choice is driven by experience with industrial challenges.

At any time step t the RL agent can influence the IB via actions a_t that are three dimensional vectors in $[-1,1]^3$. Each action can be interpreted as three proposed changes to three observable state

Figure 6. Visualization of the average return of PSO and NM computed from 100 experiments per setup. Applying the exact same number of fitness function evaluations, PSO outperforms NM on the CP benchmark. On each box, the central mark is the median, the box edges are the 25th and 75th percentiles, and the whiskers extend to the most extreme data points not considered outliers.

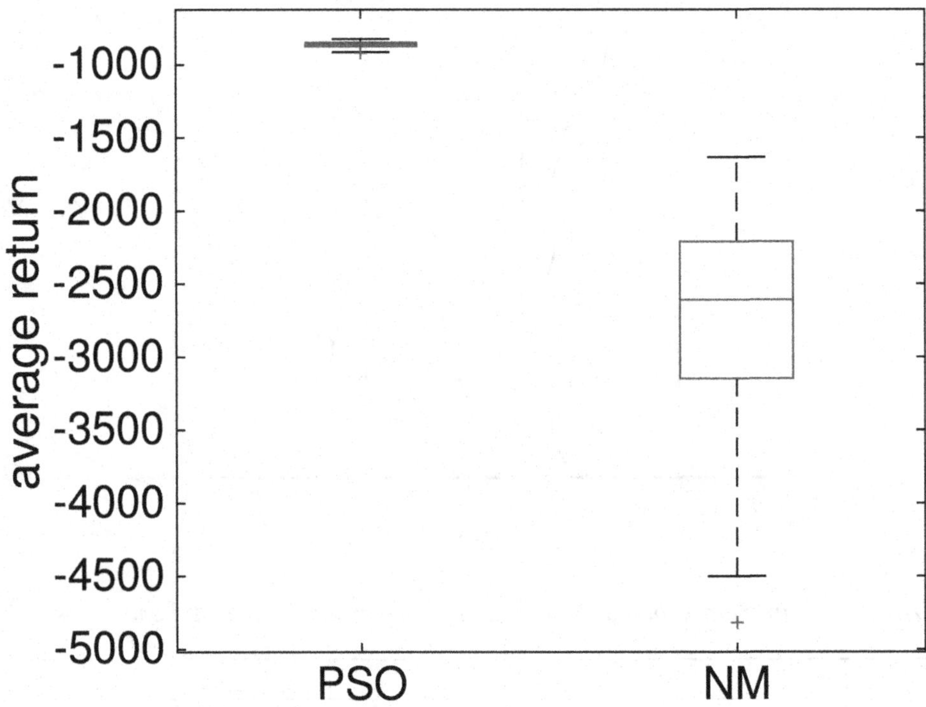

control variables. Those variables are: velocity v, gain g, and shift h. Each variable is limited to $[0,100]$ and calculated as follows:

$$a_t = (\Delta v_t, \Delta g_t, \Delta h_t), \tag{8}$$

$$v_{t+1} = \max(0, \min(100, v_t + d^{\mathrm{v}} \Delta v_t)), \tag{9}$$

$$g_{t+1} = \max(0, \min(100, g_t + d^{\mathrm{g}} \Delta g_t)), \tag{10}$$

$$h_{t+1} = \max(0, \min(100, h_t + d^{\mathrm{h}} \Delta h_t)), \tag{11}$$

with scaling factors $d^{\mathrm{v}} = 1$, $d^{\mathrm{g}} = 10$, and $d^{\mathrm{h}} = 5.75$.

Figure 7. Cart-pole experiments. Even the worst PSO runs produced action sequences, capable of swinging up the pole and balancing it upright. In contrary the best NM sequences still yielded an overall unstable system control policy.

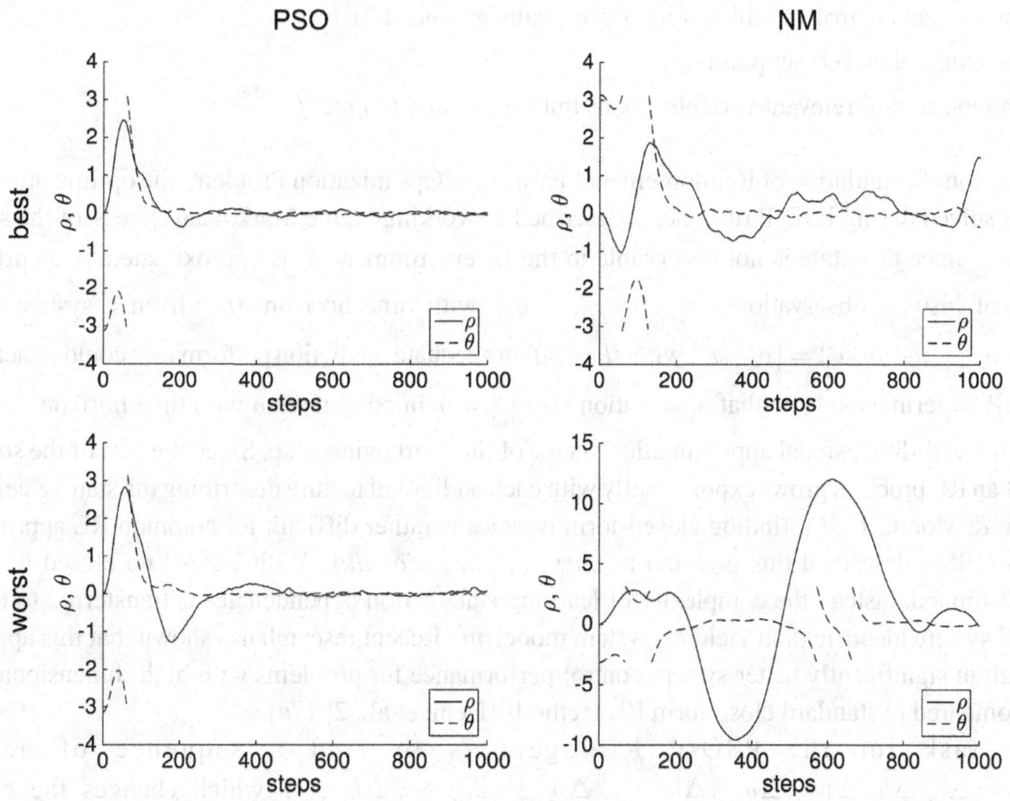

After applying the action a_t, the environment transitions to the next time step $t+1$, yielding the internal state s_{t+1}. State s_t and successor state s_{t+1} are the Markovian states of the environment, which are only partially observable by the agent. In addition to the three control variables velocity v, gain g, and shift h, an operator defined load p_t is applied to the system. Load p_t simulates an external force like the demanded load in a power plant or the wind speed actuating a wind turbine, which cannot be controlled by the agent, but still has a major influence on the system's dynamics. Depending on load p_t and the control values a_t, the system suffers from detrimental fatigue f_t and consumes resources such as power, fuel, etc., represented by consumption c_t. Both, p_t and a_t, are external drivers for the IB dynamics. In response, the IB generates output values for c_{t+1} and f_{t+1}, which are part of the internal state s_{t+1}. The reward is solely determined by s_{t+1} as follows:

$$r_t = -c_{t+1} - 3f_{t+1} \tag{12}$$

In the real-world tasks that motivated the design of the IB, the reward function has always been known explicitly. Therefore, it is assumed that the reward function of the IB is also known and consumption and fatigue are observable. However, except for the values of the steerings, the remaining part of the Markov state s_t remains unobservable. This yields an observation vector $o_t \subset s_t$ consisting of:

- The current control variables: velocity v_t, gain g_t, and shift h_t,
- The external driver: set point p_t,
- And the reward relevant variables: consumption c_t and fatigue f_t.

In Section 'Formulation of Reinforcement Learning as Optimization Problem' the optimization task, which is solved during PSO-P runtime, is described as working on the Markovian state s of the system dynamics. Since this state is not observable in the IB environment s_t is approximated by a sufficient amount of historic observations $\left(o_{t-H,} o_{t-H+1}, \ldots, o_t\right)$ with time horizon H. Given a system model $m(o_{t-H}, o_{t-H+1}, \ldots, o_t, a_t) = \left(o_{t+1}, r_t\right)$ with $H = 30$ an adequate prediction performance could be achieved during IB experiments. Note that observation size $\left|o\right| = 6$ in combination with time horizon $H = 30$ results in a 180-dimensional approximation vector of the Markovian state. Since the size of the solution space of an RL problem grows exponentially with each additional feature describing the state (Kaelbling, Littman, & Moore, 1996), finding closed-form policies is rather difficult for common RL approaches. Belman (1957) described this problem as *curse of dimensionality*. With PSO-P no closed-form RL policy is trained, instead the complexity of learning state-action dependencies is transferred to the supervised system identification yielding system model m. Recent research has shown that this approach can result in significantly better system control performance for problems with high-dimensional state space compared to standard close-form RL methods (Hein, et al., 2017a).

The task for the PSO-P RL agent is to find a sequence of actions $\mathbf{x} = (\Delta v_t, \Delta g_t, \Delta h_t, \Delta v_{t+1}, \Delta g_{t+1}, \Delta h_{t+1}, \ldots, \Delta v_{t+T-1}, \Delta g_{t+T-1}, \Delta h_{t+T-1})$ which changes the control variables in a way that return $\mathcal{R}$ is as high as possible for a given time horizon T.

Using the parameters given in Table 3, the authors were able to produce excellent control results on the IB task in terms of average per-step-rewards. Moreover, PSO-P has shown that the policy performance is robust even against highly stochastic benchmark dynamics as present in the IB. Figure 8 compares the average per-step-reward-values of 10 independent IB runs on set point $p = 100$. Even though NM performed the exact same number of function evaluations during the optimization phase, it produced a far less satisfying average performance. In Figure 9 the best and worst trajectories of PSO and NM optimization runs are depicted.

FUTURE RESEARCH DIRECTIONS

The experiments with the IB demonstrate that there are stochastic systems which PSO-P can successfully control using a deterministic system model. It is expected that this is not possible in general for stochastic RL environments. To overcome this problem, modeling techniques that can provide a measure of uncertainty along with their predictions are a very promising area of research. Possible modeling candidates are Bayesian NNs, which are approximators with prior distributions on their network weights (Depeweg, Hernández-Lobato, Doshi-Velez, & Udluft, 2016; Neal, 1996), or Gaussian processes (Ras-

Table 3. PSO-P setup parameters and achieved experiment results for the IB benchmark

Particles	100
Iterations	100
Topology	(each particle with 5 neighbors, including itself)
(w, c_1, c_2)	(0.72981, 1.49618, 1.49618)
(T, q)	(100, 0.05)
Model approximation m	RNN trained with 100,000 state transitions generated by random trajectories
Benchmark start states	10 times IB initialized with set point $p = 100$
Return (1,000 steps)	median: -223, min: -224, max: -222

Figure 8. Visualization of the average reward of PSO and NM computed from 10 experiments per setup. Applying the exact same number of fitness function evaluations, PSO outperforms NM on the IB benchmark. On each box, the central mark is the median, the box edges are the 25th and 75th percentiles, and the whiskers extend to the most extreme data points not considered outliers.

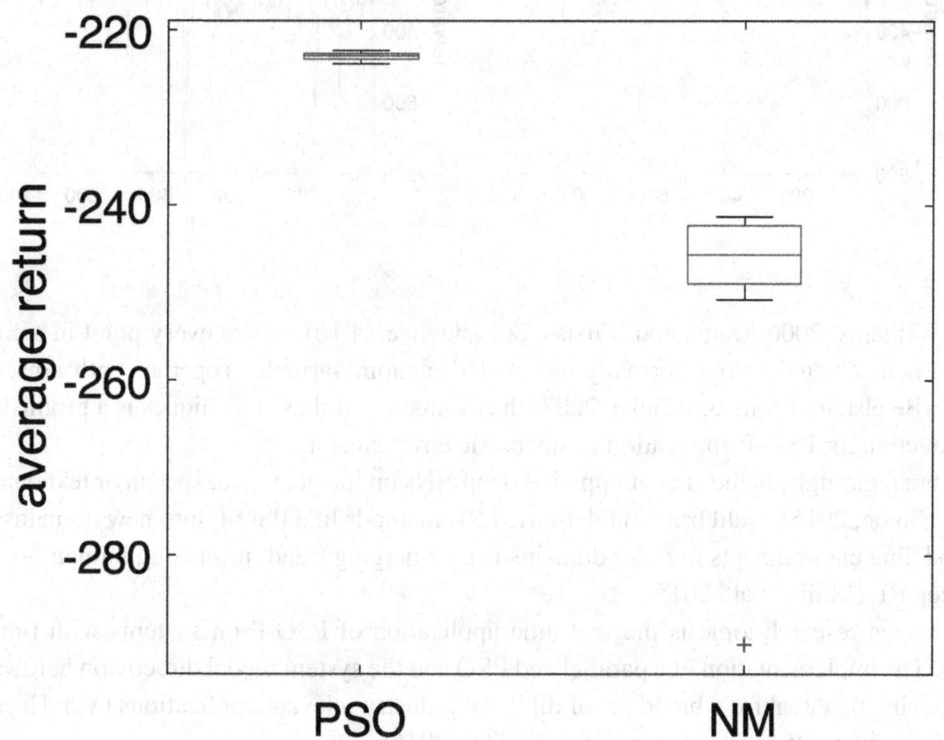

Figure 9. Industrial benchmark experiments. Depicted are the best and the worst performing trajectories for PSO and NM. Note that the performance can easily break down in the IB if suboptimal actions are applied. On the other hand, applying PSO shows clearly that it is possible to find well performing actions even under the presence of latent stochastic effects and state-dependent observation noise.

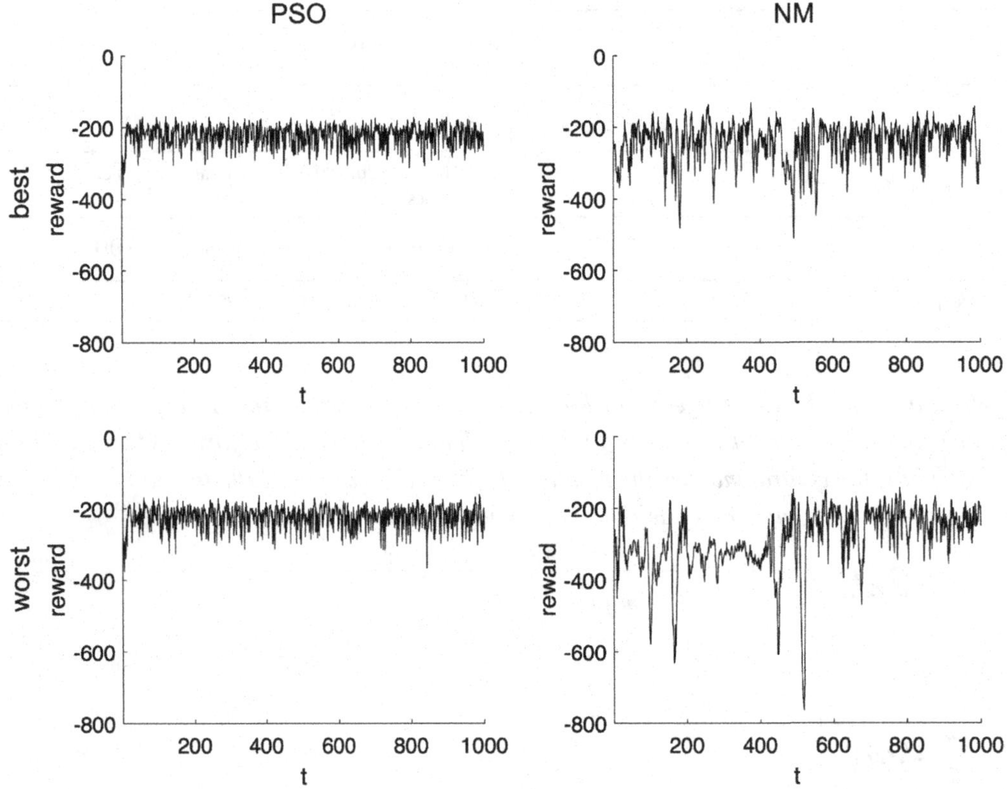

mussen & Williams, 2006; Damianou, Titsias, & Lawrence, 2016), where every point in a continuous input space is associated with a normally distributed random variable. Together with noise-resistant PSO (Bartz-Beielstein, Blum, & Branke, 2007) the evaluation of these techniques is a promising future research direction for PSO-P application in stochastic environments.

Recent breakthroughs in the area of applying deep NNs on image, video, speech or text data (Lecun, Bengio, & Hinton, 2015) could bring model-based RL methods like PSO-P into new domains of application. Modeling environments in these domains is an emerging trend, promising human-level control through deep RL (Mnih, et al., 2015).

Another open research topic is the real-time application of PSO-P on systems with time-critical constraints. The implementation of a parallelized PSO and the system model directly on hardware could enable achieving this goal for a broad set of different industry relevant applications (Van Heerden, Fujimoto, & Kawamura, 2014; Xu, Chen, Gong, & Mei, 2016).

CONCLUSION

The presented results show that PSO-P is capable of providing RL agents with high-quality state-to-action mappings. In essence, PSO-P performs an online optimization of an action sequence, each time an action for a given system state is requested. Compared to learning a functional policy representation, whose actions are recalled later on, PSO-P has the following advantages:

- PSO-P does not require a priori assumptions about adequate policy representations. Hence, no bias with respect to a specific policy behavior is introduced.
- PSO-P is effective for high-dimensional state spaces, as the optimization runs in the space of action sequences, which are independent of the state space's dimensionality.
- The reward function can be changed after each system transition, as the optimization process starts from scratch for each new system state.

The drawback compared to closed-form policies is the significantly higher computational load for computing actions using PSO-P. Implementing parallelized PSO on hardware or using cloud-based computational resources will enable MPC policy solutions like PSO-P to become feasible for more and more applications. Furthermore, in many real-world industrial applications high-level system control is implemented by changing control parameters in terms of seconds or minutes which, in many cases, is a sufficient amount of time to compute the next action using PSO-P.

PSO-P is a complementary approach for solving RL because it searches in the action space, while established RL methods generally work in the value function space or the policy space (Sutton & Barto, 1998). Therefore, a promising application is to use PSO-P for benchmarking other RL methods. Moreover, PSO-P can be used for reward function design or tuning, i.e., for the process of designing a reward function that induces a desired policy behavior.

Furthermore, the presented method for formulating RL problems as optimization tasks makes the rich class of real-world inspired RL benchmarks accessible for benchmarking gradient-free optimization algorithms. The fitness landscapes of RL problems are generally non-convex and high-dimensional. Since each point in this space corresponds to an action trajectory, the optimization process can be visualized as a sequence of such action trajectories, which may be used to interpret the behavior of different optimization algorithms.

ACKNOWLEDGMENT

The project this report is based on was supported with funds from the German Federal Ministry of Education and Research under project number 01IB15001. The sole responsibility for the report's contents lies with the authors.

REFERENCES

Bartz-Beielstein, T., Blum, D., & Branke, J. (2007). Particle swarm optimization and sequential sampling in noisy environments. In K. F. Doerner, M. Gendreau, P. Greistorfer, W. Gutjahr, R. F. Hartl, & M. Reimann (Eds.), *Metaheuristics: Progress in Complex Systems Optimization* (pp. 261–273). Boston, MA: Springer US. doi:10.1007/978-0-387-71921-4_14

Bellman, R. E. (1957). *Dynamic Programming*. Princeton University Press.

Bellman, R. E. (1962). *Adaptive Control Processes: A Guided Tour*. Princeton University Press.

Camacho, F., & Alba, C. (2007). *Model predictive control*. London: Springer. doi:10.1007/978-0-85729-398-5

Damianou, A. C., Titsias, M. K., & Lawrence, N. D. (2016). Variational inference for latent variables and uncertain inputs in Gaussian processes. *Journal of Machine Learning Research*, *17*(1), 1425–1486.

Depeweg, S., Hernández-Lobato, J. M., Doshi-Velez, F., & Udluft, S. (2016). *Learning and policy search in stochastic dynamical systems with Bayesian neural networks*. arXiv preprint arXiv:1605.07127

Eberhart, R., & Shi, Y. (2000). Comparing inertia weigths and constriction factors in particle swarm optimization. *Proceedings of the IEEE Congress on Evolutionary Computation*, (1), 84–88.

Eberhart, R., Simpson, P., & Dobbins, R. (1996). *Computational intelligence PC tools*. San Diego, CA: Academic Press Professional, Inc.

Engelbrecht, A. (2005). *Fundamentals of computational swarm intelligence*. Wiley.

Fantoni, I., & Lozano, R. (2002). *Non-linear control for underactuated mechanical systems*. London: Springer. doi:10.1007/978-1-4471-0177-2

Feng, H.-M. (2005). Particle swarm optimization learning fuzzy systems design. *Third International Conference on Information Technology and Applications*, 1, 363-366. doi:10.1109/ICITA.2005.206

Findeisen, R., & Allgoewer, F. (2002). An introduction to nonlinear model predictive control. *21st Benelux Meeting on Systems and Control*, 1-23.

Findeisen, R., Allgoewer, F., & Biegler, L. (2007). *Assessment and future directions of nonlinear model predictive control*. Berlin: Springer-Verlag. doi:10.1007/978-3-540-72699-9

Gruene, L., & Pannek, J. (2011). *Nonlinear model predictive control*. London: Springer. doi:10.1007/978-0-85729-501-9

Hein, D., Depeweg, S., Tokic, M., Udluft, S., Hentschel, A., Runkler, T. A., & Sterzing, V. (2017b). *A benchmark environment motivated by industrial control problems*. arXiv preprint arXiv:1709.09480

Hein, D., Udluft, S., Tokic, M., Hentschel, A., Runkler, T. A., & Sterzing, V. (2017a). Batch reinforcement learning on the industrial benchmark: First experiences. *Proceedings of the IEEE International Joint Conference on Neural Networks*, 4214-4221. doi:10.1109/IJCNN.2017.7966389

Hornik, K., Stinchcombe, M., & White, H. (1989). Multilayer feedforward networks are universal approximators. *Neural Networks*, *2*(5), 359–366. doi:10.1016/0893-6080(89)90020-8

Johansen, T. (2011). Introduction to nonlinear model predictive control and moving horizon estimation. In *Selected Topics on Constrained and Nonlinear Control*. Bratislava: STU Bratislava/NTNU Trondheim.

Kaelbling, L. P., Littman, M. L., & Moore, A. W. (1996). Reinforcement Learning: A Survey. *Journal of Artificial Intelligence Research*, *4*(1), 237–285.

Kennedy, J., & Eberhart, R. (1995). Particle swarm optimization. *Proceedings of IEEE International Conference on Neural Networks*, 1942–1948. doi:10.1109/ICNN.1995.488968

Kwon, W. H., Bruckstein, A. M., & Kailath, T. (1983). Stabilizing state-feedback design via the moving horizon method. *International Journal of Control*, *37*(3), 631–643. doi:10.1080/00207178308932998

Lecun, Y., Bengio, Y., & Hinton, G. (2015). Deep learning. *Nature*, *521*(7553), 436–444. doi:10.1038/nature14539 PMID:26017442

Lee, S.-M., & Myung, H. (2015). Receding horizon particle swarm optimisation-based formation control with collision avoidance for non-holonomic mobile robots. *IET Control Theory & Applications*, *9*(14), 2075–2083. doi:10.1049/iet-cta.2015.0071

Magni, L., & Scattolini, R. (2004). Stabilizing model predictive control of nonlinear continuous time systems. *Annual Reviews in Control*, *28*(1), 1–11. doi:10.1016/j.arcontrol.2004.01.001

Mnih, V., Kavukcuoglu, K., Silver, D., Rusu, A. A., Veness, J., Bellemare, M. G., & Hassabis, D. et al. (2015). Human-level control through deep reinforcement learning. *Nature*, *518*(7540), 529–533. doi:10.1038/nature14236 PMID:25719670

Montavon, G., Orr, G., & Müller, K. (2012). *Neural networks: Tricks of the trade*. Berlin: Springer. doi:10.1007/978-3-642-35289-8

Montazeri-Gh, M., Jafari, S., & Ilkhani, M. (2012). Application of particle swarm optimization in gas turbine engine fuel controller gain tuning. *Engineering Optimization*, *44*(2), 225–240. doi:10.1080/0305215X.2011.576760

Moriarty, D., Schultz, A., & Grefenstette, J. (1999). Evolutionary algorithms for reinforcement learning. *Journal of Artificial Intelligence Research*, *11*, 241–276.

Neal, R. M. (1996). *Bayesian learning for neural networks* (Vol. 118). New York: Springer-Verlag. doi:10.1007/978-1-4612-0745-0

Nelder, J., & Mead, R. (1965). A simplex method for function minimization. *The Computer Journal*, *7*(4), 308–313. doi:10.1093/comjnl/7.4.308

Ou, Y., Kang, P., Jun, K. M., & Julius, A. A. (2015). Algorithms for simultaneous motion control of multiple T. pyriformis cells: Model predictive control and particle swarm optimization. *2015 IEEE International Conference on Robotics and Automation (ICRA)*, 3507-3512. doi:10.1109/ICRA.2015.7139684

Piche, S., Keeler, J., Martin, G., Boe, G., Johnson, D., & Gerules, M. (2000). Neural network based model predictive control. *Advances in Neural Information Processing Systems*, 1029–1035.

Rasmussen, C., & Williams, C. (2006). *Gaussian processes for machine learning*. MIT Press.

Rawlings, J. (2000). Tutorial overview of model predictive control. *IEEE Control Systems Magazine*, *20*(3), 38–52. doi:10.1109/37.845037

Rawlings, J., & Mayne, D. (2009). *Model predictive control theory and design*. Nob Hill Publishing.

Schaefer, A., Schneegass, D., Sterzing, V., & Udluft, S. (2007). A neural reinforcement learning approach to gas turbine control. *IEEE International Conference on Neural Networks - Conference Proceedings*, 1691-1696. doi:10.1109/IJCNN.2007.4371212

Solihin, M., & Akmeliawati, R. (2010). Particle swam optimization for stabilizing controller of a self-erecting linear inverted pendulum. *International Journal of Electrical and Electronic Systems Research*, *2*, 13–23.

Sutton, R. (1996). Generalization in reinforcement learning: Successful examples using sparse coarse coding. *Advances in Neural Information Processing Systems*, *8*, 1038–1044.

Sutton, R., & Barto, A. (1998). *Reinforcement learning: An introduction*. Cambridge, MA: MIT Press.

Van Heerden, K., Fujimoto, Y., & Kawamura, A. (2014). A combination of particle swarm optimization and model predictive control on graphics hardware for real-time trajectory planning of the under-actuated nonlinear acrobot. *2014 IEEE 13th International Workshop on Advanced Motion Control (AMC)*, 464-469.

Wolpert, D., & Macready, W. (1997). No free lunch theorems for optimization. *IEEE Transactions on Evolutionary Computation*, *1*(1), 67–82. doi:10.1109/4235.585893

Xu, F., Chen, H., Gong, X., & Mei, Q. (2016). Fast nonlinear model predictive control on FPGA using particle swarm optimization. *IEEE Transactions on Industrial Electronics*, *63*(1), 310–321. doi:10.1109/TIE.2015.2464171

KEY TERMS AND DEFINITIONS

Benchmark: A computer program used to assess the performance of different methods.

Model Predictive Control: A method of process control using a system model with finite time-horizon, where at each time step only the next control action is applied to the real system.

Neural Network: A technical computing system inspired by biological brains. It consists of connected nodes (neurons) arranged in layers, where the output of each neuron is computed from the inputs using activation functions.

Policy: A mapping from state to action space, which is the result of a reinforcement learning training.

Reinforcement Learning: Software agents are trained to take optimal actions in a given environment in order to maximize a cumulative reward.

System Model: An approximation of the input-to-output behavior of a real system trained from observational data by supervised machine learning. It may be used for policy evaluation or selection.

Trajectory: A time-ordered set of states or actions.

APPENDIX 1

Given a sufficiently trained model of the real system, the conducted experiments show that the following recipe successfully finds appropriate parameters for the PSO-P:

0. Start with the ring topology and an initial guess of the swarm size, depending on the intended computational effort.
1. Evaluate the problem dependent *time horizon* T.
2. Compare different *topologies* for both convergence properties; speed and quality of the found solutions.
3. Determine the *number of particles* which leads to the best rewards, given a fixed level of computational effort.

In the following, an exemplary PSO-P parameter evaluation for the CP benchmark is described. The first step is to find a suitable time horizon for the RL problem. On the one hand, this horizon should be as short as possible to keep computational effort low. On the other hand, it has to be long enough to recognize all possible future effects of the current action. Figure 10 shows the results for time horizons of length 100, 150, 200 and 250 time steps. A time horizon length of 100 yields a relatively low average return compared to the horizon lengths 150, 200 and 250. The reason for this is that it is much harder for the

Figure 10. The data has been produced evaluating 100 independent trial runs with the goal of swinging up and stabilizing the cart-pole. Each trial contains 1,000 applied actions

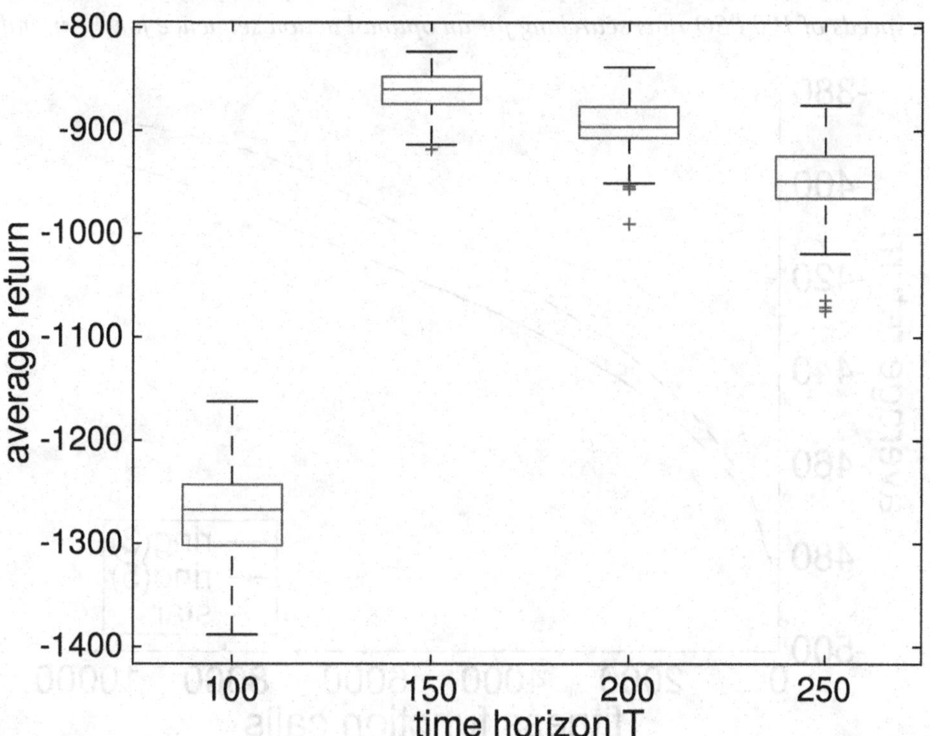

PSO-P to determine whether an action sequence leads to constantly good results in the future if the time horizon is below 150 in the CP benchmark. The increase of the horizon above 150 did not yield better results, so the horizon of 150 seems to be a good compromise between stable results and fast computing.
In the second step, the influence of the PSO topology on the CP task is evaluated. Three topologies have been tested: star (global PSO), ring with three neighbors, and ring with five neighbors (including the particle itself). While the two ring topologies produced similar results, the global PSO performed slightly worse. Probably, the swarm prematurely collapses to suboptimal solutions. In Figure 11 - Figure 12 the average performance of 100 PSO optimizations on the CP start state is shown in relation to the number of function calls. A smaller neighborhood seems to be a much better approach to the CP task, which in essence limits the communication of good positions through the swarm. Thereby, a smaller neighborhood size favors exploration over exploitation. Since the topology ring with five neighbors produced the best median result the experiments are continued using this topology.
In the last step, the influences of the number of particles and PSO iterations are investigated. In the experiments, the runtime of the optimization has been fixed by limiting the PSO to a total of 10,000 fitness evaluations. Consequently, a swarm of 200 particles can run 50 PSO iterations, while a swarm of 100 Particles can perform 100 iterations using the same computation time. The results in Figure 13 - Figure 14 show that a swarm of size 100 particles finds better solutions in 100 PSO iteration steps than 50 particles in 200 iterations, or 200 particles in 50 iterations. However, if the time frame allowed only 5000 fitness function calls to compute the next action, it would be significantly better to use the combination of 50 particles in 200 PSO iterations than any other ratio evaluated in the experiment.

Figure 11. Results of the comparison of the three PSO topologies, ring with three neighbors for each particle, ring with five neighbors for each particle, and the star topology. Illustrated are the average convergence speeds of 100 PSO runs searching for an optimal action sequence for the initial state.

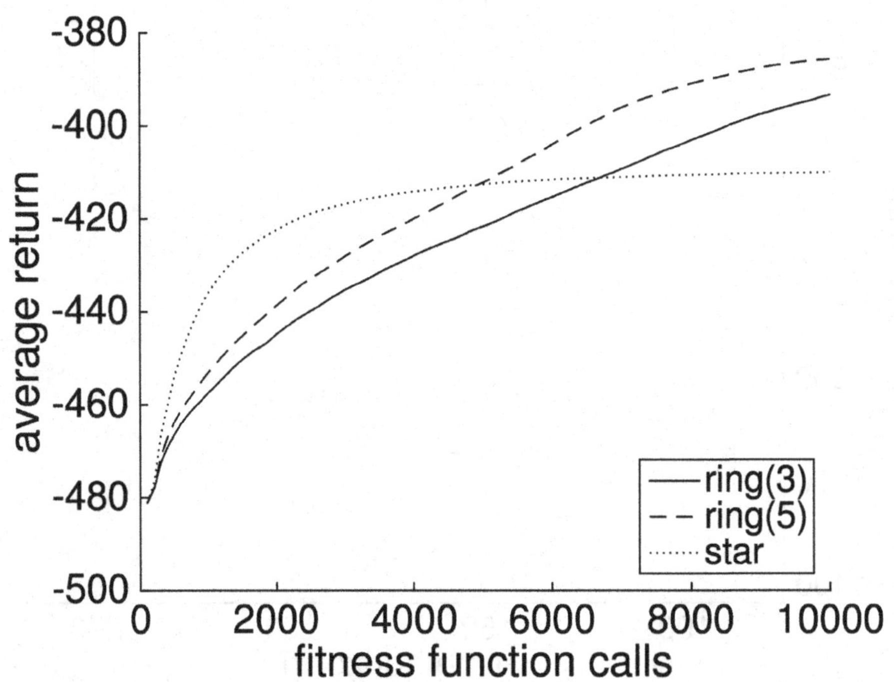

Figure 12. Depicted are the average results on a complete PSO-P run of 1,000 steps

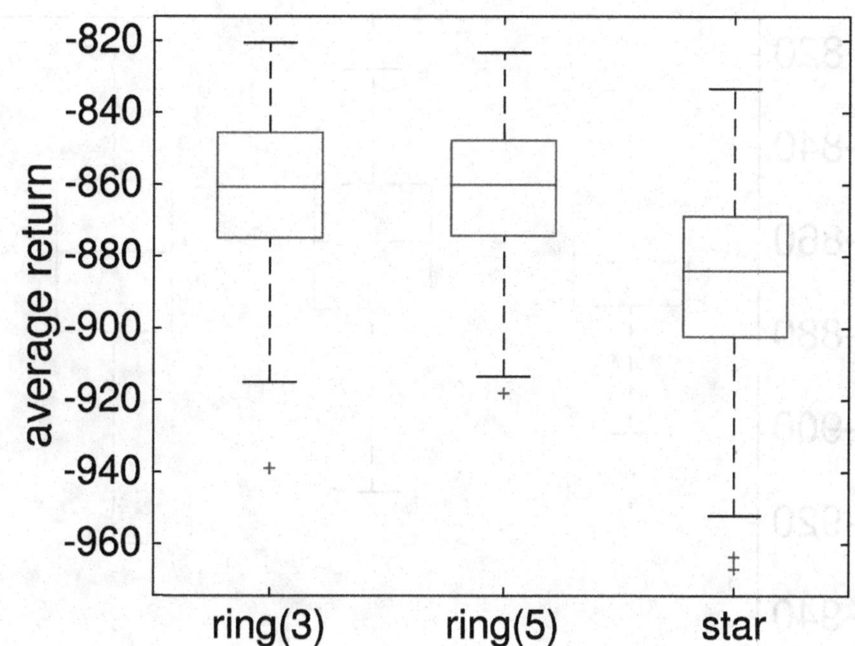

Figure 13. Results of the comparison of three numbers of particles to PSO iteration ratios. The graphs illustrate the average convergence speed of 100 PSO runs searching for an optimal action sequence for the initial state

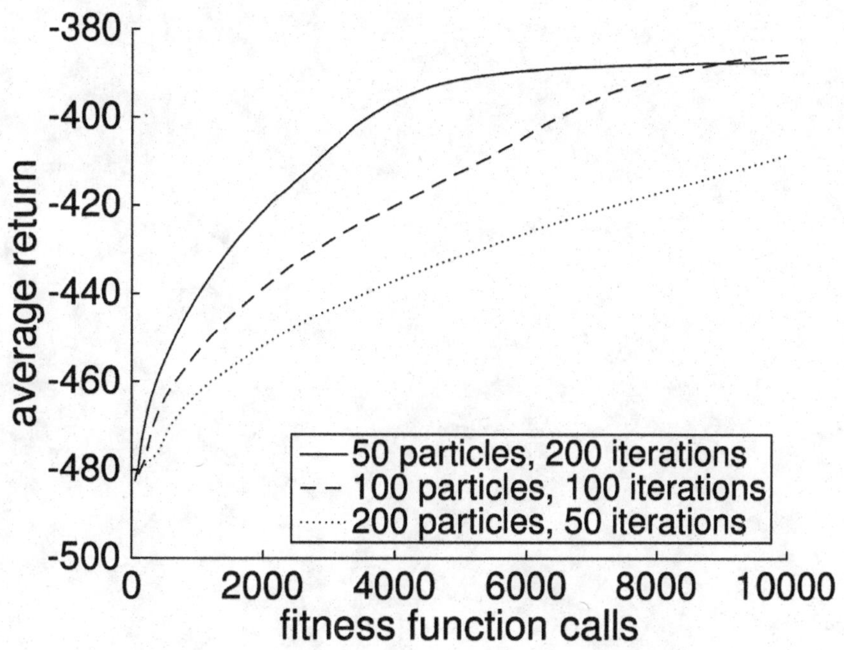

Figure 14. Depicted are the average results on a complete PSO-P run of 1,000 steps

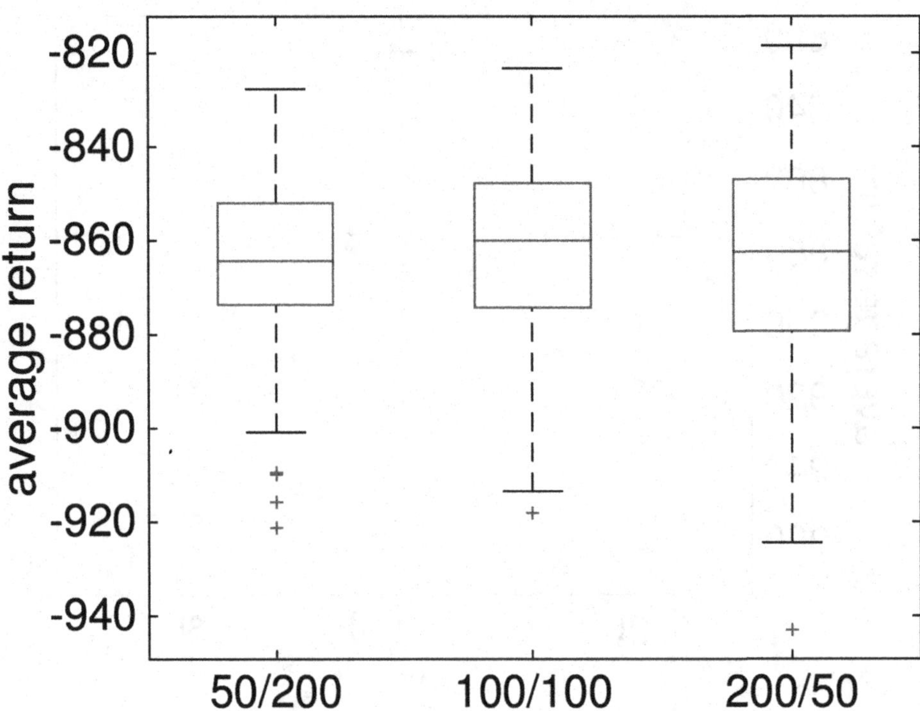

APPENDIX 2

Table 4.

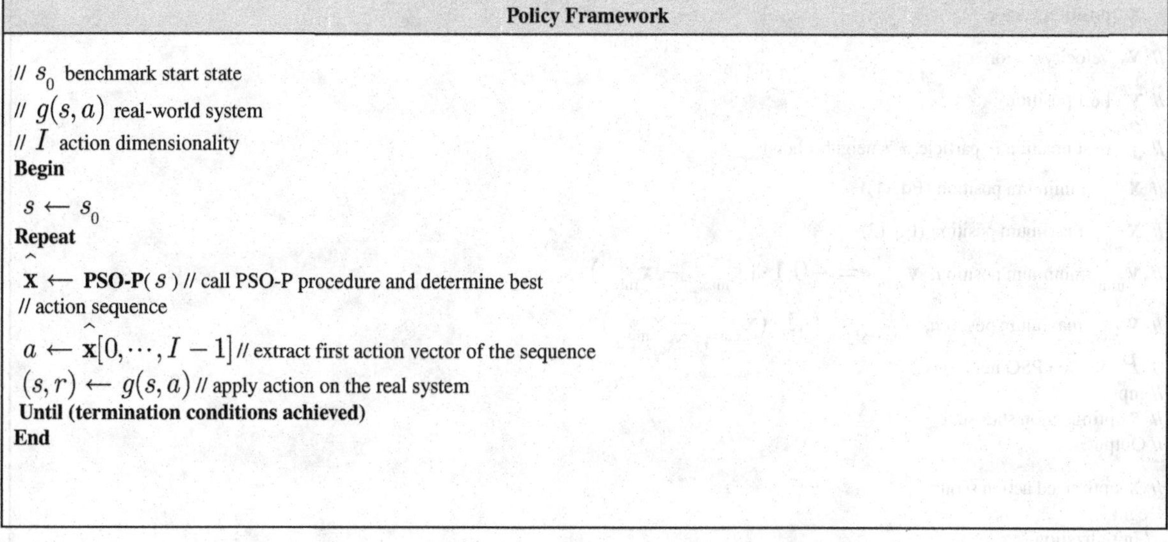

Policy Framework

// s_0 benchmark start state
// $g(s, a)$ real-world system
// I action dimensionality
Begin
$s \leftarrow s_0$
Repeat
$\hat{\mathbf{x}} \leftarrow$ **PSO-P**(s) // call PSO-P procedure and determine best
// action sequence
$a \leftarrow \hat{\mathbf{x}}[0, \cdots, I-1]$ // extract first action vector of the sequence
$(s, r) \leftarrow g(s, a)$ // apply action on the real system
Until (termination conditions achieved)
End

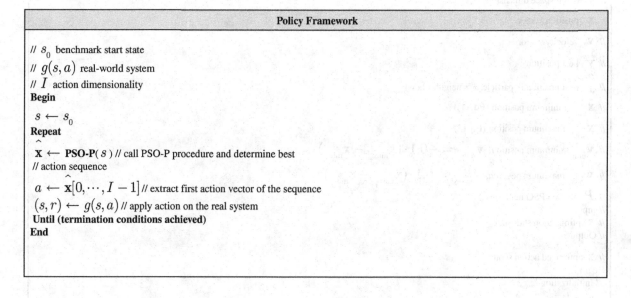

Table 5.

PSO-P

// i particle index
// j search space dimension
// $\mathbf{x}_i$ position vector
// $\mathbf{v}_i$ velocity vector
// $\mathbf{y}_i$ best position
// $\hat{\mathbf{y}}_i$ best position in particle i 's neighborhood
// $\mathbf{x}_{\min}$ minimum position (Eq. (1))
// $\mathbf{x}_{\max}$ maximum position (Eq. (2))
// $\mathbf{v}_{\min}$ minimum position, $\mathbf{v}_{\min_j} = -0.1 \cdot (\mathbf{x}_{\max_j} - \mathbf{x}_{\min_j})$
// $\mathbf{v}_{\max}$ maximum position, $\mathbf{v}_{\max_j} = 0.1 \cdot (\mathbf{x}_{\max_j} - \mathbf{x}_{\min_j})$
// P applied PSO iterations
// Input:
// s optimization start state
// Output:
// $\hat{\mathbf{x}}$ optimized action sequence
Begin
// Initialization
$p \leftarrow 0$
$\mathbf{x}_i(p) \sim U(\mathbf{x}_{\min}, \mathbf{x}_{\max})$ // set random positions
$\mathbf{v}_i(p) \sim U(\mathbf{v}_{\min}, \mathbf{v}_{\max})$ // set random velocities
// Iteration
For $p < P$
$f(\mathbf{x}_i(p)) \leftarrow \mathbf{mbc}(s, \mathbf{x}_i(p))$ // compute fitness of all particles
Update best positions $\mathbf{y}_i(p)$
Update best neighborhood positions $\hat{\mathbf{y}}_i(p)$ // Eq. (5)
Update velocity vectors $\mathbf{v}_i(p+1)$ // Eq. (7)
Bound velocity vectors in between $\mathbf{v}_{\min}$ and $\mathbf{v}_{\min}$
Update positions $\mathbf{x}_i(p+1)$ // Eq. (6)
Bound positions in between $\mathbf{x}_{\min}$ and $\mathbf{x}_{\max}$
$p \leftarrow p + 1$
End
$\hat{\mathbf{x}} \leftarrow$ best overall particle position // Eq. (4)
End

Table 6.

mbc - Model-Based Computation

// $m(s,a)$ model approximation of the real-world system $g(s,a)$
// γ discount factor
// I action dimensionality
// Input:
// s model start state
// $\mathbf{x}$ action sequence
// Output:
// $\mathcal{R}$ return prediction
Begin
$\mathcal{R} \leftarrow 0$
$s \leftarrow s_t$
$k \leftarrow 0$
For $k < T$
$a \leftarrow \mathbf{x}[k \cdot I, \cdots, k \cdot I + I - 1]$ // extract action
$(s,r) \leftarrow m(s,a)$ // perform one step on the model
$\mathcal{R} \leftarrow \mathcal{R} + \gamma^k \cdot r$ // discount reward and accumulate
$k \leftarrow k+1$
End
End

Compilation of References

Adhikari, R., & Agrawal, R. K. (2013). Hybridization of Artificial Neural Network and Particle Swarm Optimization Methods for Time Series Forecasting. *International Journal of Applied Evolutionary Computation, 4*(3), 75–90. doi:10.4018/jaec.2013070107

Adler, A., Dai, T., & Lionheart, W. R. B. (2007). Temporal image reconstruction in electrical impedance tomography. *Physiological Measurement, 28*, S1-S11.

Adler, A., Arnold, J. H., Bayford, R., Borsic, A., Brown, B., Dixon, P., & Wolf, G. K. et al. (2009). GREIT: A unified approach to 2D linear EIT reconstruction of lung images. *Physiological Measurement, 30*(6), S35–S55. doi:10.1088/0967-3334/30/6/S03 PMID:19491438

Adler, A., & Lionheart, W. R. (2006). Uses and abuses of EIDORS: An extensible software base for EIT. *Physiological Measurement, 27*(5), S25–S42. doi:10.1088/0967-3334/27/5/S03 PMID:16636416

Adra, S. F., Dodd, T. J., Griffin, I. A., & Fleming, P. J. (2009). Convergence acceleration operator for multiobjective optimization. *IEEE Transactions on Evolutionary Computation, 12*(4), 825–847. doi:10.1109/TEVC.2008.2011743

Adra, S. F., & Fleming, P. J. (2011). Diversity management in evolutionary many-objective optimization. *IEEE Transactions on Evolutionary Computation, 15*(2), 183–195. doi:10.1109/TEVC.2010.2058117

Afify, A. (2013). Intelligent Computation for Manufacturing. In Z. Li & A. Al-Ahmari (Eds.), *Formal Methods in Manufacturing Systems: Recent Advances* (pp. 211–246). Hershey, PA: Engineering Science Reference. doi:10.4018/978-1-4666-4034-4.ch009

Akyildiz, I. F., Su, W., Sankarasubramaniam, Y., & Cayirci, E. (2002). Wireless sensor networks: A survey. *Computer Networks, 38*(4), 393–422. doi:10.1016/S1389-1286(01)00302-4

Alamaniotis, M., & Tsoukalas, L. H. (2015, November). Developing Intelligent Radiation Analysis Systems: A Hybrid Wave-Fuzzy Methodology for Analysis of Radiation Spectra. In *Tools with Artificial Intelligence (ICTAI), 2015 IEEE 27th International Conference on* (pp. 1114-1121). IEEE. doi:10.1109/ICTAI.2015.158

Alamaniotis, M., Young, J., & Tsoukalas, L. H. (2010). An insight in wavelet denoising of nuclear resonance fluorescence spectra for identification of hazardous materials. *1st National Conference on Advanced Tools and Solutions for Nuclear Material Detection*, (pp. 1-6), Salt Lake City, UT: Academic Press.

Alamaniotis, M., Young, J., & Tsoukalas, L. H. (2015). Assessment of fuzzy logic radioisotopic pattern identifier on gamma-ray signals with application to security. In Research Methods: Concepts, Methodologies, Tools, and Applications (pp. 1052-1071). IGI Global. doi:10.4018/978-1-4666-7456-1.ch046

Alamaniotis, M., Choi, C. K., & Tsoukalas, L. H. (2015). Application of fireworks algorithm in gamma-ray spectrum fitting for radioisotope identification. *International Journal of Swarm Intelligence Research*, *6*(2), 102–125. doi:10.4018/IJSIR.2015040105

Alamaniotis, M., Gao, R., Tsoukalas, L. H., & Jevremovic, T. (2009). Intelligent Order-based Method for Synthesis of NRF Spectra and Detection of Hazardous Materials. In *21st IEEE International Conference on Tools with Artificial Intelligence*, (pp. 658-665). Newark, NJ: IEEE. doi:10.1109/ICTAI.2009.96

Alamaniotis, M., Heifetz, A., Raptis, A. C., & Tsoukalas, L. H. (2013). Fuzzy-logic radioisotope identifier for gamma spectroscopy in source search. *IEEE Transactions on Nuclear Science*, *60*(4), 3014–3024. doi:10.1109/TNS.2013.2265307

Alamaniotis, M., Ikonomopoulos, A., Jevremovic, T., & Tsoukalas, L. H. (2011). Intelligent recognition of signature patterns in NRF spectra. *Nuclear Technology*, *175*(2), 480–497. doi:10.13182/NT11-A12319

Alamaniotis, M., Ikonomopoulos, A., & Tsoukalas, L. H. (2012). *Swarm Intelligence Optimization: Applications of Particle Swarms in Industrial Engineering and Nuclear Power Plants.* In C. Kahraman (Ed.), *Computational Intelligence Systems in Industrial Engineering* (pp. 181–202). Springer & Atlantis Press.

Alamaniotis, M., & Jevremovic, T. (2015). Hybrid fuzzy-genetic approach integrating peak identification and spectrum fitting for complex gamma-ray spectra analysis. *IEEE Transactions on Nuclear Science*, *62*(3), 1262–1277. doi:10.1109/TNS.2015.2432098

Alamaniotis, M., Mattingly, J., & Tsoukalas, L. H. (2013a). Kernel-Based Machine Learning for Background Estimation of NaI Low-Count Gamma-Ray Spectra. *IEEE Transactions on Nuclear Science*, *60*(3), 2209–2221. doi:10.1109/TNS.2013.2260868

Alamaniotis, M., Mattingly, J., & Tsoukalas, L. H. (2013b). Pareto-Optimal gamma spectroscopic radionuclide identification using evolutionary computing. *IEEE Transactions on Nuclear Science*, *60*(3), 2222–2231. doi:10.1109/TNS.2013.2260869

Al-Anzi, F. S., & Allahverdi, A. (2006). A hybrid tabu search heuristic for the two-stage assembly scheduling problem. *International Journal of Operations Research*, *3*(2), 109–119.

Alatas, B. (2010). Chaotic bee colony algorithms for global numerical optimization. *Expert Systems with Applications*, *37*(8), 5682–5687. doi:10.1016/j.eswa.2010.02.042

Alaykiran, K., Engin, O., & Döyen, A. (2007). Using ant colony optimization to solve hybrid flow shop scheduling problems. *International Journal of Advanced Manufacturing Technology*, *35*(5-6), 541–550. doi:10.1007/s00170-007-1048-2

Albayrak, Z., & Zengin, A. (2014). *Bee-MANET: A New Swarm-based Routing Protocol for Wireless Ad Hoc Networks.* IEEE.

Aleksander, I., & Morton, H. (1995). *An introduction to neural computing*. International Thompson Computer Press.

Alisantoso, D., Khoo, L. P., & Jiang, P. Y. (2003). An immune algorithm approach to the scheduling of a flexible PCB flow shop. *International Journal of Advanced Manufacturing Technology*, *22*(11-12), 819–827. doi:10.1007/s00170-002-1498-5

Allahverdi, A., & Al-Anzi, F. S. (2009). The two-stage assembly scheduling problem to minimize total completion time with setup times. *Computers & Operations Research*, *36*(10), 2740–2747. doi:10.1016/j.cor.2008.12.001

Allaoui, H., & Artiba, A. (2004). Integrating simulation and optimization to schedule a hybrid flow shop with maintenance constraints. *Computers & Industrial Engineering*, *47*(4), 431–450. doi:10.1016/j.cie.2004.09.002

Allaoui, H., & Artiba, A. (2006). Scheduling two stage hybrid flow shop with availability constraints. *Computers & Operations Research*, *33*(5), 1399–1419. doi:10.1016/j.cor.2004.09.034

Alves, S. H., Amato, M. B., Terra, R. M., Vargas, F. S., & Caruso, P. (2014). Lung reaeration and reventilation after aspiration of pleural effusions. a study using electrical impedance tomography. *Annals of the American Thoracic Society*, *11*(2), 186–191. doi:10.1513/AnnalsATS.201306-142OC PMID:24308560

Am briz-Perez, Acha, Fuerte-Esquivel, & De la Torre. (1998). Incorporation of a UPFC model in an Optimal Power Flow Using Newton's method. *IEE Proceedings. Generation, Transmission and Distribution*, *145*(3).

Amin-Naseri, M. R., & Beheshti-Nia, M. A. (2009). Hybrid flow shop scheduling with parallel batching. *International Journal of Production Economics*, *117*(1), 185–196. doi:10.1016/j.ijpe.2008.10.009

Anagnostopoulos, C., & Hadjiefthymiades, S. (2012). Swarm Intelligence in Autonomic Computing: The Particle Swarm Optimization Case. In P. Cong-Vinh (Ed.), *Formal and Practical Aspects of Autonomic Computing and Networking: Specification, Development, and Verification* (pp. 97–117). Hershey, PA: Information Science Reference; doi:10.4018/978-1-60960-845-3.ch004

Aparna, R. R. (2016). Swarm Intelligence for Automatic Video Image Contrast Adjustment. *International Journal of Rough Sets and Data Analysis*, *3*(3), 21–37. doi:10.4018/IJRSDA.2016070102

Ara, Kazemi, & NabaviNiaki. (2012). Multi objective Optimal Location of FACTS Shunt-Series Controllers for Power System Operation Planning. *IEEE Transactions on Power Delivery*, *27*(2), 481-490.

Argyris, N., Figueira, J. R., & Morton, A. (2011). Identifying preferred solutions to Multi-Objective Binary Optimisation problems, with an application to the Multi-Objective Knapsack Problem. *Journal of Global Optimization*, *49*(2), 213–235. doi:10.1007/s10898-010-9541-9

Arora, V., & Ravi, V. (2013). Data Mining using Advanced Ant Colony Optimization Algorithm and Application to Bankruptcy Prediction. *International Journal of Information Systems and Social Change*, *4*(3), 33–56. doi:10.4018/jissc.2013070103

Arsic, A., Tuba, M., & Jordanski, M. (2016). Fireworks algorithm applied to wireless sensor networks localization problem. In *Evolutionary Computation (CEC), 2016 IEEE Congress on* (pp. 4038-4044). IEEE. doi:10.1109/CEC.2016.7744302

Arthanari, T. S., & Ramamurthy, K. G. (1971). An extension of two machines sequencing problem. *Operations Research*, *8*, 10–22.

Ashraf, I., Boccardi, F., & Ho, L. (2011). Sleep Mode Techniques for Small Cell Deployments. *IEEE Communications Magazine*, *49*(8), 72–79. doi:10.1109/MCOM.2011.5978418

Aweda, J. O., & Adeyemi, M. B. (2009). Experimental determination of heat transfer coefficients during squeeze casting of aluminium. *Journal of Materials Processing Technology*, *209*(3), 1477–1483. doi:10.1016/j.jmatprotec.2008.03.071

Babahajyani, P., Habibi, F., & Bevrani, H. (2014). An On-Line PSO-Based Fuzzy Logic Tuning Approach: Microgrid Frequency Control Case Study. In P. Vasant (Ed.), *Handbook of Research on Novel Soft Computing Intelligent Algorithms: Theory and Practical Applications* (pp. 589–616). Hershey, PA: Information Science Reference; doi:10.4018/978-1-4666-4450-2.ch020

Bacanin, N., & Tuba, M. (2015, May). Fireworks algorithm applied to constrained portfolio optimization problem. In *Evolutionary Computation (CEC), 2015 IEEE Congress on* (pp. 1242-1249). IEEE. doi:10.1109/CEC.2015.7257031

Back, T. (1996). *Evolutionary Algorithms in Theory and Practice*. Oxford, UK: Oxford Univ. Press.

Baker, L. E. (1989). Principles of the impedance technique. *IEEE Engineering in Medicine and Biology Magazine: The Quarterly Magazine of the Engineering in Medicine & Biology Society*, *8*(1), 11–15. doi:10.1109/51.32398 PMID:18238298

Barbosa, V. A., Ribeiro, R. R., Feitosa, A. R., Silva, V. L., Rocha, A. D., Freitas, R. C., & Santos, W. P. et al. (2017). Reconstruction of Electrical Impedance Tomography Using Fish School Search, Non-Blind Search, and Genetic Algorithm. *International Journal of Swarm Intelligence Research*, *8*(2), 17–33. doi:10.4018/IJSIR.2017040102

Barnard, C., & Sibly, R. (1981). Producers and scroungers: A general model and its application to captive flocks of house sparrows. *Animal Behaviour*, *29*(2), 543–550. doi:10.1016/S0003-3472(81)80117-0

Bartz-Beielstein, T., Blum, D., & Branke, J. (2007). Particle swarm optimization and sequential sampling in noisy environments. In K. F. Doerner, M. Gendreau, P. Greistorfer, W. Gutjahr, R. F. Hartl, & M. Reimann (Eds.), *Metaheuristics: Progress in Complex Systems Optimization* (pp. 261–273). Boston, MA: Springer US. doi:10.1007/978-0-387-71921-4_14

Bastos-Filho, C. J. A., & Guimarães, A. C. S. (2015). Multi-objective fish school search. International Journal of Swarm Intelligence Research, 23–40.

Bastos-Filho, C. J. A., & Nascimento, D. O. (2013, September). An enhanced fish school search algorithm. In *Computational Intelligence and 11th Brazilian Congress on Computational Intelligence (BRICS-CCI & CBIC), 2013 BRICS Congress on* (pp. 152-157). IEEE. doi:10.1109/BRICS-CCI-CBIC.2013.34

Bastos-Filho, C. J. A., Lima-Neto, F. B., Lins Sousa, M. F. C., Pontes, M. R., & Madeiro, S. S. (2009). On the influence of the swimming operators in the fish school search algorithm. *2009 IEEE International Conference on Systems, Man and Cybernetics*, 5012–5017. doi:10.1109/ICSMC.2009.5346377

Bastos-Filho, C. J. A., Lima-Neto, F. B., Lins, A. J. C. C., Nascimento, A. I. S., & Lima, M. P. (2008). A novel search algorithm based on fish school behavior. *IEEE International Conference on Systems, Man and Cybernetics*, 2646–2651. doi:10.1109/ICSMC.2008.4811695

Bastos-Filho, C. J., & Guimarães, A. C. (2015). Multi-objective fish school search. *International Journal of Swarm Intelligence Research*, *6*(1), 23–40. doi:10.4018/ijsir.2015010102

Bathe, K.-J. (2006). *Finite element procedures*. Klaus-Jurgen Bathe.

Battiti, R. (1992). First-and second-order methods for learning: Between steepest descent and Newton's method. *Neural Computation*, *4*(2), 141–166. doi:10.1162/neco.1992.4.2.141

Behnamian, J., & Fatemi Ghomi, S. M. T. (2011). Hybrid flowshop scheduling with machine and resource-dependent processing times. *Applied Mathematical Modelling*, *35*(3), 1107–1123. doi:10.1016/j.apm.2010.07.057

Behnamian, J., Fatemi Ghomi, S. M. T., & Zandieh, M. (2009). A multi-phase covering Pareto-optimal front method to multi-objective scheduling in a realistic hybrid flowshop using a hybrid metaheuristic. *Expert Systems with Applications*, *36*(8), 11057–11069. doi:10.1016/j.eswa.2009.02.080

Bellman, R. E. (1957). *Dynamic Programming*. Princeton University Press.

Bellman, R. E. (1962). *Adaptive Control Processes: A Guided Tour*. Princeton University Press.

Bera, T. K., & Nagaraju, J. (2014). Electrical impedance tomography (EIT): a harmless medical imaging modality. In Research Developments in Computer Vision and Image Processing: Methodologies and Applications. IGI Global.

Berkovitch, E., & Khanna, N. (1990). How target shareholders benefit from value-reducing defensive strategies in takeovers. *The Journal of Finance*, *45*(1), 137–156. doi:10.1111/j.1540-6261.1990.tb05084.x

Bhandari, A. K., Kumar, A., & Singh, G. K. (2015). Tsallis entropy based multi-level thresholding image segmentation using evolutionary algorithms. *Expert System with Applications, 42*, 8707-8730.

Bitam & Mellouk. (2011). QoS Swarm Bee Routing Protocol for Vehicular Ad Hoc Networks. IEEE ICC 2011 Proceedings.

Bloch, I. (2005). Fuzzy spatial relationships for image processing and interpretation: A review. *Image and Vision Computing, 23*(2), 89–110. doi:10.1016/j.imavis.2004.06.013

Bonabeau, E., Dorigo, M., & Theraulaz, G. (2000). Inspiration for optimization from social insect behavior. *Nature, 406*(6791), 39–42. doi:10.1038/35017500 PMID:10894532

Bonyadi, M. R., & Michalewicz, Z. (2017). Particle Swarm Optimization for Single Objective Continuous Space Problems: A Review. *Evolutionary Computation, 25*(1), 1–54. doi:10.1162/EVCO_r_00180 PMID:26953883

Borcea, L. (2002). Electrical impedance tomography. *Inverse Problems, 18*(6), R99–R136. doi:10.1088/0266-5611/18/6/201

Borisenko, V. I., Zlatotol, A. A., & Muchnik, I. B. (1987). Image segmentation (state of the art survey). *Automation and Remote Control, 48*, 837–879.

Botta-Genoulaz, V. (2000). Hybrid flow shop scheduling with precedence constraints and time lags to minimize maximum lateness. *International Journal of Production Economics, 64*(1-3), 1–3, 101–111. doi:10.1016/S0925-5273(99)00048-1

Bouarara, H. A., Hamou, R. M., Amine, A., & Rahmani, A. (2015). A fireworks algorithm for modern web information retrieval with visual results mining. *International Journal of Swarm Intelligence Research, 6*(3), 1–23. doi:10.4018/IJSIR.2015070101

Bourbakis, N., Pantelopoulos, A., & Kannavara, R. (2008). A NRF Spectra Signature Detection Model using loca- global graphs. In *20st International Conference on Tools with Artificial Intelligence*, (pp. 547-550), Dayton, OH: Academic Press. doi:10.1109/ICTAI.2008.125

Bożejko, W., Pempera, J., & Smutnicki, C. (2013). Parallel tabu search algorithm for the hybrid flow shop problem. *Computers & Industrial Engineering, 65*(3), 466–474. doi:10.1016/j.cie.2013.04.007

Brah, S. A., & Hunsuchker, J. L. (1991). Branch and bound algorithm for the flow shop with multiple processors. *European Journal of Operational Research, 51*(1), 88–99. doi:10.1016/0377-2217(91)90148-O

Brah, S. A., & Loo, L. L. (1999). Heuristics for scheduling in a flow shop with multiple processors. *European Journal of Operational Research, 113*(1), 113–122. doi:10.1016/S0377-2217(97)00423-2

Brown, B., Barber, D., & Seagar, A. (1985). Applied potential tomography: Possible clinical applications. *Clinical Physics and Physiological Measurement, 6*(2), 109–121. doi:10.1088/0143-0815/6/2/002 PMID:4017442

Bunn, G. (2003). The Nuclear Nonproliferation Treaty: History and Current Problems. *Arms Control Today, 33*(10), 4.

Burke, E. K., Gustafson, S., & Kendall, G. (2002). A survey and analysis of diversity measures in genetic programming. In *Proceedings of the Genetic and Evolutionary Computation Conference (GECCO 2002)*. San Francisco, CA: Morgan Kaufmann Publishers Inc. (pp. 716-723).

Burr, T., & Hamada, M. (2009). Radio-isotope identification algorithms for NaI γ spectra. *Algorithms, 2*(1), 339–360. doi:10.3390/a2010339

Bu, S., Yu, F. R., Cai, Y., & Liu, X. P. (2012). When the Smart Grid Meets Energy-Efficient Communications: Green Wireless Cellular Networks Powered by the Smart Grid. *IEEE Transactions on Wireless Communications, 11*(8), 3014–3024.

Camacho, F., & Alba, C. (2007). *Model predictive control*. London: Springer. doi:10.1007/978-0-85729-398-5

Cao, D., Zhou, S., & Niu, Z. (2013). Optimal Combination of Base Station Densities for Energy-Efficient Two-Tier Heterogeneous Cellular Networks. *IEEE Transactions on Wireless Communications, 12*(9), 4350–4362. doi:10.1109/TWC.2013.080113.121280

Carlevaro, C. M., Wilkinson, M.V., & Barrios, L.A. (2008). A genetic algorithm approach to routine gamma spectra analysis. *Journal of Instrumentation, 3.*

Carlier, J., & Néron, E. (2000). An exact method for solving the multi-processor flow-shop. *Operations Research, 34*(1), 1–25. doi:10.1051/ro:2000103

Carneiro, R. F., & Bastos-Filho, C. J. (2016, November). Improving the Binary Fish School Search Algorithm for feature selection. In *Computational Intelligence (LA-CCI), 2016 IEEE Latin American Conference on* (pp. 1-6). IEEE. doi:10.1109/LA-CCI.2016.7885708

Carosio, G. L. C., Rolnik, V., & Seleghim, P. (2007). Improving efficiency in electrical impedance tomography problem by hybrid parallel genetic algorithm and a priori information. *Proceedings of the XXX Congresso Nacional de Matemática Aplicada e Computacional.*

Carpentier. (1979). Optimal Power Flows. *Electrical Power and Energy Systems, 1*, 959-972.

Castro Martins, T., Camargo, E. D. L. B., Lima, R. G., Amato, M. B. P., & Tsuzuki, M. S. G. (2012). Image reconstruction using interval simulated annealing in electrical impedance tomography. *IEEE Transactions on Biomedical Engineering, 59*(7), 1861–1870. doi:10.1109/TBME.2012.2188398 PMID:22361655

Chattopadhyay, H. (2007). Simulation of transport processes in squeeze casting. *Journal of Materials Processing Technology, 186*(1-3), 174–178. doi:10.1016/j.jmatprotec.2006.12.038

Cheney, M., Isaacson, D., & Newell, J. C. (1999). Electrical impedance tomography. *SIAM Review, 41*(1), 85–101. doi:10.1137/S0036144598333613

Cheney, M., Isaacson, D., Newell, J. C., Simske, S., & Goble, J. (1990). NOSER: An algorithm for solving the inverse conductivity problem. *International Journal of Imaging Systems and Technology, 2*(2), 66–75. doi:10.1002/ima.1850020203

Cheng, K. S., Chen, B. H., & Tong, H. S. Electrical impedance image reconstruction using the genetic algorithm. In *IEEE. Engineering in Medicine and Biology Society, 1996. Bridging Disciplines for Biomedicine. Proceedings of the 18th Annual International Conference of the IEEE.* IEEE.

Cheng, S. (2013). *Population diversity in particle swarm optimization: Definition, observation, control, and application* (Ph.D. dissertation). Department of Electrical Engineering and Electronics, University of Liverpool.

Cheng, H. D., Chen, Y. H., & Jiang, X. H. (2000). Thresholding using two dimensional histogram and fuzzy entropy principle. *IEEE Transactions on Image Processing, 9*(4), 732–735. doi:10.1109/83.841949 PMID:18255445

Cheng, S., Qin, Q., Chen, J., & Shi, Y. (2016). Brain storm optimization algorithm: A review. *Artificial Intelligence Review, 46*(4), 445–458. doi:10.1007/s10462-016-9471-0

Cheng, S., & Shi, Y. (2011). Diversity control in particle swarm optimization. In *Proceedings of 2011 IEEE Symposium on Swarm Intelligence (SIS 2011)* (pp. 110-118). IEEE.

Cheng, S., Shi, Y., & Qin, Q. (2011). Experimental study on boundary constraints handling in particle swarm optimization: From population diversity perspective. *International Journal of Swarm Intelligence Research, 2*(3), 43–69. doi:10.4018/jsir.2011070104

Cheng, S., Shi, Y., & Qin, Q. (2012). Population diversity of particle swarm optimizer solving single and multi-objective problems. *International Journal of Swarm Intelligence Research*, *3*(4), 23–60. doi:10.4018/jsir.2012100102

Cheng, S., Shi, Y., & Qin, Q. (2013). A study of normalized population diversity in particle swarm optimization. *International Journal of Swarm Intelligence Research*, *4*(1), 1–34. doi:10.4018/jsir.2013010101

Cheng, S., Shi, Y., Qin, Q., & Gao, S. (2013). Solution clustering analysis in brain storm optimization algorithm. In *Proceedings of The 2013 IEEE Symposium on Swarm Intelligence, (SIS 2013)*. Singapore: IEEE. doi:10.1109/SIS.2013.6615167

Cheng, S., Shi, Y., Qin, Q., Zhang, Q., & Bai, R. (2014). Population diversity maintenance in brain storm optimization algorithm. *Journal of Artificial Intelligence and Soft Computing Research*, *4*(2), 83–97. doi:10.1515/jaiscr-2015-0001

Chen, W. N., Zhang, J., Lin, Y., Chen, N., Zhan, Z. H., Chung, H. S. H., & Shi, Y. H. et al. (2013). Particle swarm optimization with an aging leader and challengers. *IEEE Transactions on Evolutionary Computation*, *17*(2), 241–258. doi:10.1109/TEVC.2011.2173577

Cherepenin, V., Karpov, A., Korjenevsky, A., Kornienko, V., Mazaletskaya, A., Mazourov, D., & Meister, D. (2001). A 3D electrical impedance tomography (EIT) system for breast cancer detection. *Physiological Measurement*, *22*(1), 9–18. doi:10.1088/0967-3334/22/1/302 PMID:11236894

Choi, H. S., & Lee, D. H. (2009). Scheduling algorithms to minimize the number of tardy jobs in two-stage hybrid flow shops. *Computers & Industrial Engineering*, *56*(1), 113–120. doi:10.1016/j.cie.2008.04.005

Choi, S. W., Kim, Y. D., & Lee, G. C. (2005). Minimizing total tardiness of orders with reentrant lots in a hybrid flowshop. *International Journal of Production Research*, *43*(11), 2149–2167. doi:10.1080/00207540500050071

Chou, F. D. (2013). Particle swarm optimization with cocktail decoding method for hybrid flow shop scheduling problems with multiprocessor tasks. *International Journal of Production Economics*, *141*(1), 137–145. doi:10.1016/j.ijpe.2012.05.015

Chudler, E. H. (2012). Brain development. *Neuroscience For Kids*. Retrieved from http://faculty.washington.edu/chudler/dev.html

Chung, T. P., & Liao, C. J. (2013). An immunoglobulin-based artificial immune system for solving the hybrid flow shop problem. *Applied Soft Computing*, *13*(8), 3729–3736. doi:10.1016/j.asoc.2013.03.006

Chu, W., Gao, X., & Sorooshian, S. (2011). Handling boundary constraints for particle swarm optimization in high-dimensional search space. *Information Sciences*, *181*(20), 4569–4581. doi:10.1016/j.ins.2010.11.030

CINTRA. (2007). *M. E. Geração genética de regras fuzzy com pré-seleção de regras candidatas. Tese (Mestrado)*. Universidade Federal de São Carlos.

Civicioglu, P., & Besdok, E. (2011). A conceptual comparison of the Cuckoo-search, particle swarm optimization, differential evolution and artificial bee colony algorithms. *Artificial Intelligence Review*. doi:10.1007/s10462-011-9276-0

Clark, C. W., & Mangel, M. (1984). Foraging and flocking strategies: Information in an uncertain environment. *American Naturalist*, *123*(5), 626–641. doi:10.1086/284228

Clerck, M. (2013). *Particle Swarm Optimization*. London: ISTE.

Clerc, M. (2010). *Particle swarm optimization*. John Wiley & Sons.

Clerc, M., & Kennedy, J. (2002). The particle swarm-explosion, stability, and convergence in a multidimensional complex space. *IEEE Transactions on Evolutionary Computation*, *6*(1), 58–73. doi:10.1109/4235.985692

Coelho, L. S., & Mariani, V. C. (2008). Use of chaotic sequences in a biologically inspired algorithm for engineering design optimization. *Expert Systems with Applications, 34*(3), 1905–1913. doi:10.1016/j.eswa.2007.02.002

Coello Coello, C. A., Lamont, G. B., & Veldhuizen, D. A. V. (2007). *Evolutionary Algorithms for Solving Multi-Objectives Problems*. Springer.

Coello Coello, C. A., Pulido, G., & Lechuga, M. S. (2004). Handling multiple objectives with particles swarm optimization. *IEEE Transactions on Evolutionary Computation, 8*(3), 256–279. doi:10.1109/TEVC.2004.826067

Collette, Y., & Siarry, P. (2003). *Multiobjective Optimization - Principles and Case Studies*. Springer.

Cui, Y., Lau, V. K. N., & Wu, Y. (2012). Delay-aware Bs Discontinuous Transmission Control and User Scheduling for Energy Harvesting Downlink Coordinated MIMO Systems. *IEEE Transactions on Signal Processing, 60*(7), 3786–3795. doi:10.1109/TSP.2012.2194291

Damianou, A. C., Titsias, M. K., & Lawrence, N. D. (2016). Variational inference for latent variables and uncertain inputs in Gaussian processes. *Journal of Machine Learning Research, 17*(1), 1425–1486.

Das, S., Maity, S., Qu, B. Y., & Suganthan, P. N. (2011). Real-parameter evolutionary multimodal optimization — A survey of the state-of-the-art. *Swarm and Evolutionary Computation, 1*(2), 71–88. doi:10.1016/j.swevo.2011.05.005

Davoudpour, H., & Ashrafi, M. (2009). Solving multi-objective SDST flexible flow shop using GRASP algorithm. *International Journal of Advanced Manufacturing Technology, 44*(7-8), 7–8, 737–747. doi:10.1007/s00170-008-1887-5

De Castro, L. N. (2006). *Fundamentals of Natural Computing*. Champman & Hall/CRC.

de Souza, L. S., de Miranda, P. B., Prudencio, R. B., & Barros, F. D. A. (2011, November). A multi-objective particle swarm optimization for test case selection based on functional requirements coverage and execution effort. In *Tools with Artificial Intelligence (ICTAI), 2011 23rd IEEE International Conference on* (pp. 245-252). IEEE. doi:10.1109/ICTAI.2011.45

de Souza, L. S., Prudêncio, R. B., & Barros, F. D. A. (2014, October). A hybrid binary multi-objective particle swarm optimization with local search for test case selection. In *Intelligent Systems (BRACIS), 2014 Brazilian Conference on* (pp. 414-419). IEEE.

Deb, K., Pratap, A., Agarwal, S., & Meyarivan, T. (2002). A fast and elitist multiobjective genetic algorithm: NSGA-II. *IEEE Transactions on Evolutionary Computation, 6*(2), 182–197. doi:10.1109/4235.996017

Deb, K., Thiele, L., Laumanns, M., & Zitzler, E. (2001). *Scalable Test Problems for Evolutionary Multi-Objective Optimization. TIK Report 112, Computer Engineering and Networks Laboratory (TIK)*. ETH Zurich.

Deb, K., Thiele, L., Laumanns, M., & Zitzler, E. (2002). Scalable Multi-Objective Optimization Test Problems. *IEEE Congress on Evolutionary Computation*, 825–830.

Deb, K., Thiele, L., Laumanns, M., & Zitzler, E. (2005). Scalable Test Problems for Evolutionary Multi-Objective Optimization. In A. Abraham, R. Jain, & R. Goldberg (Eds.), *Evolutionary Multiobjective Optimization: Theoretical Advances and Applications* (pp. 105–145). Springer. doi:10.1007/1-84628-137-7_6

Dejam, S., Sadeghzadeh, M., & Mirabedini, S. J. (2012). Combining cuckoo and tabu algorithms for solving quadratic assignment problems. *Journal of Academic and Applied Studies, 2*, 1–8.

Delgarm, N., Sajadi, B., Kowsary, F., & Delgarm, S. (2016). Multi-objective optimization of the building energy performance: A simulation-based approach by means of particle swarm optimization (PSO). *Applied Energy, 170*, 293–303. doi:10.1016/j.apenergy.2016.02.141

Depeweg, S., Hernández-Lobato, J. M., Doshi-Velez, F., & Udluft, S. (2016). *Learning and policy search in stochastic dynamical systems with Bayesian neural networks.* arXiv preprint arXiv:1605.07127

Devi, V. S. (2014). Learning Using Soft Computing Techniques. In B. Tripathy & D. Acharjya (Eds.), *Global Trends in Intelligent Computing Research and Development* (pp. 51–67). Hershey, PA: Information Science Reference. doi:10.4018/978-1-4666-4936-1.ch003

Dhal & Das. (2017). Colour Retinal images enhancement using Modified Histogram Equalization methods and Firefly Algorithm. *Int. Jr. of Biomedical Engineering and Technology*. (in press)

Dhal, K. G., & Das, S. (2015). Diversity Conserved Chaotic Artificial Bee Colony Algorithm based Brightness Preserved Histogram Equalization and Contrast Stretching Method. *International Journal of Natural Computing Research, 5*, 45-73.

Dhal, K. G., & Das, S. (2017). Cuckoo search with search strategies and proper objective function for brightness preserving image enhancement. *Pattern Recognition and Image Analysis*. (in press)

Dhal, K. G., Namtirtha, A., Quraishi, I. M., & Das, S. (2016). Grey level image enhancement using Particle Swarm Optimization with Lévy Flight: An Eagle Strategy Approach. *Int. Conf. on Emerging Trends in Computer Sc. and Information (ETCSIT-2015).*

Dhal, K.G, Quraishi, I. M., & Das, S. (2015). Performance Analysis of Chaotic Lévy Bat Algorithm and Chaotic Cuckoo Search Algorithm for Gray Level Image Enhancement. *Information Systems Design and Intelligent Applications*, 233-244.

Dhal, K.G., Quraishi, I. M., & Das, S. (2015). A Chaotic Lévy flight Approach in Bat and Firefly Algorithm for Gray level image Enhancement. *I. J. Image, Graphics and Signal Processing, 7*, 69-76.

Dhal, K.G., Quraishi, I. M., & Das, S. (2015). Performance Enhancement of Differential Evolution by Incorporating Lévy Flight and Chaotic Sequence for the Cases of Satellite Images. *Int. J. of Applied Metaheuristic Computing, 6*, 69-81.

Dhal, K.G., Quraishi, I. M., & Das, S. (2017). An improved cuckoo search based optimal ranged brightness preserved histogram equalization and contrast stretching method. *Int. Jr. of Swarm intelligence Research, 8*, 1-29.

Dhal, K. G., Quraishi, I. M., & Das, S. (2015). *Development of firefly algorithm via chaotic sequence and population diversity to enhance the image contrast. Natural Computing* , 15, 1–12.

Dhal, K. G., Sen, M., & Das, S. (2017). Cuckoo search based modified Bi-Histogram Equalizationmethod to enhance the cancerous tissues in Mammography images. *International Journal of Medical Engineering and Informatics*.

Ding, F. Y., & Kittichartphayak, D. (1994). Heuristics for scheduling flexible flow lines. *Computers & Industrial Engineering*, *26*(1), 27–34. doi:10.1016/0360-8352(94)90025-6

Dong, W., & Zhou, M. (2017). A Supervised Learning and Control Method to Improve Particle Swarm Optimization Algorithms. *IEEE Transactions on Systems, Man, and Cybernetics. Systems*, *47*(7), 1135–1148. doi:10.1109/TSMC.2016.2560128

Dorigo, M., & Di Caro, G. (1998). AntNet: Distributed stigmergetic control for communications networks. *Journal of Artificial Intelligence Research*, *9*, 317–365.

Dorigo, M., Di Caro, G., & Gambardella, L. M. (1999). Ant Algorithms for Discrete Optimization. *Artificial Life*, *5*(3), 137–172. doi:10.1162/106454699568728 PMID:10633574

Dorigo, M., & Gambardella, L. M. (1997). Ant colony system: A cooperative learning approach to the traveling salesman problem. *IEEE Transactions on Evolutionary Computation*, *1*(1), 53–66. doi:10.1109/4235.585892

Dorigo, M., Maniezzo, V., & Colorni, A. (1996). Ant system: Optimization by a colony of cooperating agents. *IEEE Transactions on Systems, Man, and Cybernetics. Part B, Cybernetics*, *26*(1), 29–41. doi:10.1109/3477.484436 PMID:18263004

Duan, H. B., Yu., Y. X., & Zhou, R. (2008). UCAV path planning based on ant colony optimization and satisficing decision algorithm. In *Proceedings of IEEE Congress on Evolutionary Computation.* (pp. 957–962). IEEE. doi:10.1109/CEC.2008.4630912

Duan, H. B., & Li, J. N. (2014). Gaussian harmony search algorithm: A novel method for loney's solenoid problem. *IEEE Transactions on Magnetics*, *50*(3), 83–87. doi:10.1109/TMAG.2013.2284764

Duan, H. B., Luo, Q. N., Ma, G. J., & Shi, Y. H. (2013). Hybrid particle swarm optimization and genetic algorithm for multi-UAVs formation reconfiguration. *IEEE Computational Intelligence Magazine*, *8*(3), 16–27. doi:10.1109/MCI.2013.2264577

Duan, H. B., & Qiao, P. X. (2014). Pigeon-inspired optimization: A new swarm intelligence optimizer for air robot path planning. *International Journal of Intelligent Computing and Cybernetics.*, *7*(1), 24–37. doi:10.1108/IJICC-02-2014-0005

Duan, H., Li, S., & Shi, Y. (2013). Predator-Prey Based Brain Storm Optimization for DC Brushless Motor. *IEEE Transactions on Magnetics*, *49*(3), 5336–5240. doi:10.1109/TMAG.2013.2262296

Duin-Borkowski, R., McCartney, M. R., & Frankel, R. B. (1998). Magnetic Microstructure of magnetotactic bacteria by electron holography. *Science*, *282*(5395), 1868–1870. doi:10.1126/science.282.5395.1868 PMID:9836632

Durillo, J. J., & Nebro, A. J. (2011). jmetal: A java framework for multi-objective optimization. *Advances in Engineering Software*, *42*(10), 760–771. doi:10.1016/j.advengsoft.2011.05.014

Durillo, J., Nebro, A., & Alba, E. (2010). The jmetal framework for multi-objective optimization: Design and architecture. *IEEE Congress on Evolutionary Computation*, 4138–4325. doi:10.1109/CEC.2010.5586354

Dutta, S., Roy, P. K., & Nandi, D. (2016). Optimal Allocation of Static Synchronous Series Compensator Controllers using Chemical Reaction Optimization for Reactive Power Dispatch. *International Journal of Energy Optimization and Engineering*, *5*(3), 43–62. doi:10.4018/IJEOE.2016070103

Du, W. B., Ying, W., Yan, G., Zhu, Y. B., & Cao, X. B. (2017). Heterogeneous Strategy Particle Swarm Optimization. *IEEE Transactions on Circuits and Wystems. II, Express Briefs*, *64*(4), 467–471. doi:10.1109/TCSII.2016.2595597

Ebenezer, H. (2010). *Garden Cities of Tomorrow*. Nabu Press.

Eberhart, R. C., & Shi, Y. (2011). *Computational intelligence: concepts to implementations*. Elsevier.

Eberhart, R., & Kennedy, J. (1995). A new optimizer using particle swarm theory. *Proceedings of the Sixth International Symposium on Micro Machine and Human Science*, 39--43. doi:10.1109/MHS.1995.494215

Eberhart, R., & Shi, Y. (2000). Comparing inertia weigths and constriction factors in particle swarm optimization. *Proceedings of the IEEE Congress on Evolutionary Computation,* (1), 84–88.

Eberhart, R., & Shi, Y. (2007). *Computational Intelligence, Concepts to Implementation* (1st ed.). Morgan Kaufmann Publishers.

Eberhart, R., & Shi, Y. (2007). *Computational Intelligence: Concepts to Implementations*. Morgan Kaufmann Publisher. doi:10.1016/B978-155860759-0/50002-0

Eberhart, R., Simpson, P., & Dobbins, R. (1996). *Computational intelligence PC tools.* San Diego, CA: Academic Press Professional, Inc.

Eiben, A. E., & Smith, J. E. (2015). *Introduction to evolutionary computing* (Vol. 2). Springer. doi:10.1007/978-3-662-44874-8

El-Shorbagy. (2013). *Numerical Optimization & Swarm Intelligence for optimization: Trust Region Algorithm & Particle Swarm Optimization*. LAP LAMBERT Academic Publishing.

Engelbrecht, A. (2005). *Fundamentals of computational swarm intelligence*. Wiley.

Engelbrecht, A. P. (2007). *Computational Intelligence: An Introduction*. John Wiley and Sons. doi:10.1002/9780470512517

Engin, O., Ceran, G., & Yilmaz, M. K. (2011). An efficient genetic algorithm for hybrid flow shop scheduling with multiprocessor task problems. *Applied Soft Computing*, *11*(3), 3056–3065. doi:10.1016/j.asoc.2010.12.006

Engin, O., & Döyen, A. (2004). A new approach to solve hybrid flow shop scheduling problems by artificial immune system. *Future Generation Computer Systems*, *20*(6), 1083–1095. doi:10.1016/j.future.2004.03.014

Enriquez, N., & Sabot, C. (2006). Random walks in a Dirichlet environment. *Electronic Journal of Probability*, *11*(31), 802–817.

Erol-Kantarci, M., & Mouftah, H. T. (2011). Wireless Multimedia Sensor and Actor Networks for the Next Generation Power Grid. *Ad Hoc Networks*, *9*(4), 542–551. doi:10.1016/j.adhoc.2010.08.005

Faivre, D., & Schuler, D. (2008). Magnetotactic bacteria and magnetosomes. *Chemical Reviews*, *108*(11), 4875–4898. doi:10.1021/cr078258w PMID:18855486

Fan, C. H., Chen, Z. H., Chen, J. H., & Chen, D. (2010). Effects of applied pressure on density, microstructure and tensile strength of Al–Zn–Mg–Cu alloy prepared by squeeze casting. *International Journal of Cast Metals Research*, *23*(6), 349–353. doi:10.1179/136404610X12693537270253

Fantoni, I., & Lozano, R. (2002). *Non-linear control for underactuated mechanical systems*. London: Springer. doi:10.1007/978-1-4471-0177-2

Fatah, A. H., & Ahmed, A. H. (2011). Analysis of gamma-ray spectra using Levenberg-Marquardt method. *Engineering Technologies*, *73*, 269–274.

Feitosa, A. R., Ribeiro, R. R., Barbosa, V. A., de Souza, R. E., & dos Santos, W. P. (2014). Reconstruction of electrical impedance tomography images using particle swarm optimization, genetic algorithms and non-blind search. In 5th *ISSNIP-IEEE Biosignals and Biorobotics Conference (2014): Biosignals and Robotics for Better and Safer Living (BRC)* (pp. 1–6). IEEE. doi:10.1109/BRC.2014.6880996

Feng, H.-M. (2005). Particle swarm optimization learning fuzzy systems design. *Third International Conference on Information Technology and Applications,* 1, 363-366. doi:10.1109/ICITA.2005.206

Ficici, S. G. (2005). Monotonic solution concepts in coevolution. In *Genetic and Evolutionary Computation Conference (GECCO 2005)*, (pp. 499-506). Academic Press.

Filipowicz, S. F., & Rymarczyk, T. (2012). Measurement methods and image reconstruction in electrical impedance tomography. *Przegląd Elektrotechniczny*, *88*(6), 247–250.

Findeisen, R., & Allgoewer, F. (2002). An introduction to nonlinear model predictive control. *21st Benelux Meeting on Systems and Control*, 1-23.

Findeisen, R., Allgoewer, F., & Biegler, L. (2007). *Assessment and future directions of nonlinear model predictive control*. Berlin: Springer-Verlag. doi:10.1007/978-3-540-72699-9

Fister, I., Fister, D., & Fister, I. (2013). A comprehensive review of cuckoo search: Variants and hybrids. *International Journal of Mathematical Modelling and Numerical Optimisation*, *4*, 387–409. doi:10.1504/IJMMNO.2013.059205

Fogel, L. J. (1962). Autonomous automata. *Industrial Research*, *4*, 14–19.

Forman, G. (2003). An extensive empirical study of feature selection metrics for text classification. *Journal of Machine Learning Research*, *3*(Mar), 1289–1305.

Forsberg, P., Agarwal, V., Gao, R., Tsoukalas, L. H., & Jevremovic, T. (November 2009). Peakseek: A statistical processing algorithm for radiation spectrum peak identification. In *21th IEEE International Conference on Tools with Artificial Intelligence*, (pp. 674-678). Newark, NJ: IEEE. doi:10.1109/ICTAI.2009.97

Frankel, R. B. (1984). Magnetic guidance of organisms. Ann. Reo. *Biophys. Bioeng.*, *13*(1), 85–10. doi:10.1146/annurev.bb.13.060184.000505 PMID:6378076

Fu, K. S., & Mui, J. K. (1981). A survey on image segmentation. *Pattern Recognition*, *13*(1), 3–16. doi:10.1016/0031-3203(81)90028-5

Gandomi, A. H., Yang, X. S., & Alavi, A. H. (2013). Cuckoo search algorithm: A metaheuristic approach to solve structural optimization problems. *Engineering with Computers*, *29*(1), 17–35. doi:10.1007/s00366-011-0241-y

Gao, H., & Diao, M. (2011). Cultural firework algorithm and its application for digital filters design. *International Journal of Modelling. Identification and Control*, *14*(4), 324–331. doi:10.1504/IJMIC.2011.043157

Gao, Morison, & Kundur. (1992). Voltage Stability Evaluation using Modal Analysis. *IEEE Transactions on Power Systems*, *7*(4), 1529–1542.

Gao, W. F., & Liu, S. Y. (2011). Improved artificial bee colony algorithm for global optimization. *Information Processing Letters*, *111*(17), 871–882. doi:10.1016/j.ipl.2011.06.002

García-Nieto, J., & Alba, E. (2011). Restart particle swarm optimization with velocity modulation: A scalability test. *Soft Computing*, *15*(11), 2221–2232. doi:10.1007/s00500-010-0648-1

Garcia-Talavera, M., & Ulicny, B. (2003). A genetic algorithm approach for multiplet deconvolution in γ-ray spectra. *Nuclear Instruments & Methods in Physics Research. Section A, Accelerators, Spectrometers, Detectors and Associated Equipment*, *512*(3), 585–594. doi:10.1016/S0168-9002(03)02052-7

Gardner, W. A. (1984). Learning characteristics of stochastic-gradient-descent algorithms: A general study, analysis, and critique. *Signal Processing*, *6*(2), 113–133. doi:10.1016/0165-1684(84)90013-6

Ghahremani, E., & Kamwa, I. (2013, May). Optimal Placement of Multiple-Type FACTS Devices to Maximize Power System Loadability Using a Generic Graphical User Interface. *IEEE Transactions on Power Systems*, *28*(2), 764–778. doi:10.1109/TPWRS.2012.2210253

Ghazzai, H., Yaacoub, E., Alouini, M., & Abudayya, A. (2014). Optimized Smart Grid Energy Procurement for LTE Networks using Evolutionary Algorithms. *IEEE Transactions on Vehicular Technology*, *63*(9), 4508–4519. doi:10.1109/TVT.2014.2312380

Gherboudj, A., Layeb, A., & Chikhi, S. (2012). Solving 0–1 knapsack problems by a discrete binary version of cuckoo search algorithm. *International Journal of Bio-inspired Computation*, *4*(4), 229–236. doi:10.1504/IJBIC.2012.048063

Ghomashchi, M. R., & Vikhrov, A. (2000). Squeeze casting: An overview. *Journal of Materials Processing Technology*, *101*(1), 1–9. doi:10.1016/S0924-0136(99)00291-5

Giudici, P. (2003). *Applied Data Mining: Statistical Methods for Business and Industry*. John Wiley &Sons Inc.

Giudici, P., & Figini, S. (2009). *Applied Data Mining for Business and Industry (Statistics in Practice)*. Wiley. doi:10.1002/9780470745830

Goel, S., Sharma, A., & Panchal, V. K. (2014). Multiobjective Cuckoo Search for Anticipating the Enemy's Movements in the Battleground. *International Journal of Applied Metaheuristic Computing*, *5*(4), 26–46. doi:10.4018/ijamc.2014100102

Gonçalves, M. L. N. (2011). *Análise de Convergência dos Métodos de Gauss-Newton do Ponto de Vista do Princípio Majorante*. Tese (Doutorado), COPPE da Universidade Federal do Rio de Janeiro.

Goswami, D., & Chakraborty, S. (2015b). A study on the optimization performance of fireworks and cuckoo search algorithms in laser machining processes. *Journal of The Institution of Engineers (India): Series C, 96*(3), 215-229.

Goswami, D., & Chakraborty, S. (2015a). Parametric optimization of ultrasonic machining process using gravitational search and fireworks algorithms. *Ain Shams Engineering Journal*, *6*(1), 315–331. doi:10.1016/j.asej.2014.10.009

Grady, L. (2006). Random walks for image segmentation. *IEEE Transactions on Pattern Analysis and Machine Intelligence*, *28*(11), 1768–1783. doi:10.1109/TPAMI.2006.233 PMID:17063682

Gregory, S. (2002). *Urban Sprawl: Causes, Consequences and Policy Responses*. Washington, DC: The Urban Institute Press.

Gruene, L., & Pannek, J. (2011). *Nonlinear model predictive control*. London: Springer. doi:10.1007/978-0-85729-501-9

Guendouz, M., Amine, A., & Hamou, R. M. (2017). A discrete modified fireworks algorithm for community detection in complex networks. *Applied Intelligence*, *46*(2), 373–385. doi:10.1007/s10489-016-0840-9

Gui, Man, Wang, Li, & Wilkins. (2016). A novel Cluster-based Routing Protocol Wireless Sensor Networks using Spider Monkey Optimization. *Industrial Electronics Society, IECON 2016-42nd Annual Conference of the IEEE.*

Gupta, J. N. D. (1988). Two-stage, hybrid flowshop scheduling problem. *The Journal of the Operational Research Society*, *39*(4), 359–364. doi:10.1057/jors.1988.63

Gupta, J. N. D., & Tunc, E. A. (1998). Minimizing tardy jobs in a two-stage hybrid flowshop. *International Journal of Production Research*, *36*(9), 2397–2417. doi:10.1080/002075498192599

Guyon, I., & Elisseeff, A. (2003). An introduction to variable and feature selection. *Journal of Machine Learning Research*, *3*(Mar), 1157–1182.

Gyugyi, Schauder, Williams, Rictman, Torgerson, & Edris. (1995). The Unified Power Flow Controller; A New Approach to Power Transmission Control. *IEEE Trans on Power Delivery, 10*(2), 1085-1097.

Hall, M., Frank, E., Holmes, G., Pfahringer, B., Reutemann, P., & Witten, I. H. (2009). The WEKA data mining software: An update. *SIGKDD Explorations*, *11*(1), 10–18. doi:10.1145/1656274.1656278

Han, J., & Kamber, M. (2006). *Data Mining: Concepts and Techniques*. Morgan Kaufmann.

Han, Z., Shi, H., Qiao, F., & Yue, L. (2012). Multiple rules decision-based DE solution for the earliness-tardiness case of hybrid flow-shop scheduling problem. *International Journal of Modelling. Identification and Control*, *16*(2), 97–107. doi:10.1504/IJMIC.2012.047118

Haouari, M., & M'Hallah, R. (1997). Heuristic algorithm for two stage hybrid flow shop. *Operations Research Letters*, *21*(1), 43–53. doi:10.1016/S0167-6377(97)00004-7

Haralharick, R. M., & Shapiro, L. G. (1985). Survey: Image segmentation techniques. *CVGIP*, *29*, 100–132.

Hearst, M. A., Dumais, S. T., Osuna, E., Platt, J., & Scholkopf, B. (1998). Support vector machines. *IEEE Intelligent Systems & their Applications*, *13*(4), 18–28. doi:10.1109/5254.708428

Hein, D., Depeweg, S., Tokic, M., Udluft, S., Hentschel, A., Runkler, T. A., & Sterzing, V. (2017b). *A benchmark environment motivated by industrial control problems.* arXiv preprint arXiv:1709.09480

Hein, D., Udluft, S., Tokic, M., Hentschel, A., Runkler, T. A., & Sterzing, V. (2017a). Batch reinforcement learning on the industrial benchmark: First experiences. *Proceedings of the IEEE International Joint Conference on Neural Networks*, 4214-4221. doi:10.1109/IJCNN.2017.7966389

Heinzelman, W. R., Chandrakasan, A., & Balakrishnan, H. (2000). Energy efficient communication protocol for wireless microsensor network. *Proceedings of the 33rd annual Hawaii international conference on systems science*, 2, 3005-3014. doi:10.1109/HICSS.2000.926982

Héliot, F. (2014). Low-complexity Energy-efficient Joint Resource Allocation for Two-Hop MIMO-AF Systems. *IEEE Transactions on Wireless Communications*, *13*(6), 3088–3099. doi:10.1109/TWC.2014.042814.130898

Herrera, C. N. L. (2007). *Algoritmo de tomografia por impedância elétrica baseado em Simulated Annealing. Dissertação (Mestrado)*. Universidade de São Paulo.

He, S., Wu, Q. H., & Saunders, J. R. (2009). Group search optimizer: An optimization algorithm inspired by animal searching behavior. *IEEE Transactions on Evolutionary Computation*, *13*(5), 973–990. doi:10.1109/TEVC.2009.2011992

Heusse, S., Guérin, Snyers, D., & Kuntz, P. (1998). *Adaptive Agent-driven Routing and Load Balancing. Communication Networks*. Technical Report RR-98001-IASC. Department Intelligence Artificielle et Sciences Cognitives, ENST Bretagne.

He, W., Mi, G., & Tan, Y. (2013). Parameter optimization of local-concentration model for spam detection by using fireworks algorithm. In *Advances in swarm intelligence* (pp. 439–450). Springer Berlin Heidelberg. doi:10.1007/978-3-642-38703-6_52

Hingorani, N. G., & Gyugyi, L. (2000). *Understanding FACTS: Concepts and Technology of Flexible AC Transmission System*. IEEE Press.

Hogan, M. A., Yamamoto, S., Covell, D. F., & Brown, M. (1970). Multiple linear regression analysis of scintillation gamma-ray spectra: Automatic candidate selection. *Nuclear Instruments and Methods*, *80*(1), 61–68. doi:10.1016/0029-554X(70)90298-3

Holland, J. H. (1975). *Adaptation in natural and artificial systems*. Ann Arbor, MI: Univ. of Michigan Press.

Holland, J. H. (1975). *Adaptation in Natural and Artificial Systems*. University of Michigan Press.

Holtkamp, H., Auer, G., Bazzi, S., & Haas, H. (2013). Minimizing Base Station Power Consumption. *IEEE Journal on Selected Areas in Communications*, *32*(2), 297–306. doi:10.1109/JSAC.2014.141210

Hong, C. P., Lee, S. M., & Shen, H. F. (2000). Prevention of macro defects in squeeze casting of an Al-7 wtpct Si alloy. *Metallurgical and Materials Transactions. B, Process Metallurgy and Materials Processing Science*, *31*(2), 297–305. doi:10.1007/s11663-000-0048-5

Hoogeveen, J. A., Lenstra, J. K., & Vettman, B. (1996). Preemptive scheduling in a two-stage multiprocessor flow shop is NP-hard. *European Journal of Operational Research*, *89*(1), 172–175. doi:10.1016/S0377-2217(96)90070-3

Hoos, H. H., & Stutzle, T. (2005). *Stochastic Local Search: Foundations and Applications*. Morgan Kaufmann.

Hornik, K., Stinchcombe, M., & White, H. (1989). Multilayer feedforward networks are universal approximators. *Neural Networks*, *2*(5), 359–366. doi:10.1016/0893-6080(89)90020-8

Hou, E. S. H., Ansari, N., & Ren, H. (1994). A genetic algorithm for multiprocessor scheduling. *IEEE Transactions on Parallel and Distributed Systems*, *5*(2), 113–120. doi:10.1109/71.265940

Ho, Y.-C., & Pepyne, D. L. (2002). Simple explanation of the no-free-lunch theorem and its implications. *Journal of Optimization Theory and Applications*, *115*(3), 549–570. doi:10.1023/A:1021251113462

Hsu, C. C., Chang, J. M., Chou, Z. T., & Abichar, Z. (2014). Optimizing Spectrum-Energy Efficiency in Downlink Cellular Networks. *IEEE Transactions on Mobile Computing*, *13*(9), 2100–2112. doi:10.1109/TMC.2013.99

Hsu, L.-H., & Lin, C.-H. (2009). *Graph theory and interconnection networks. CRC Press.*

Huang, A. Q., Crow, M. L., Heydt, G. T., Zheng, J. P., & Dale, S. J. (2011). The Future Renewable Electric Energy Delivery and Management (FREEDM) System: The Energy Internet. *Proceedings of the IEEE*, *99*(1), 133–148. doi:10.1109/JPROC.2010.2081330

Huang, H., Pasquier, M., & Quek, C. (2011). Decision Support System based on hierarchical co-evolutionary fuzzy approach: A case study in detecting gamma ray signals. *Expert Systems with Applications*, *38*(9), 10719–10729. doi:10.1016/j.eswa.2010.10.011

Hunsucker, J. L., & Shah, J. R. (1994). Comparative performance analysis of priority rules in a constrained flow shop with multiple processors environment. *European Journal of Operational Research*, *72*(1), 102–114. doi:10.1016/0377-2217(94)90333-6

Imran, A. M., & Kowsalya, M. (2014). A new power system reconfiguration scheme for power loss minimization and voltage profile enhancement using Fireworks Algorithm. *International Journal of Electrical Power & Energy Systems*, *62*, 312–322. doi:10.1016/j.ijepes.2014.04.034

Imran, A. M., Kowsalya, M., & Kothari, D. P. (2014). A novel integration technique for optimal network reconfiguration and distributed generation placement in power distribution networks. *International Journal of Electrical Power & Energy Systems*, *63*, 461–472. doi:10.1016/j.ijepes.2014.06.011

Jabbarizadeh, F., Zandieh, M., & Talebi, D. (2009). Hybrid flexible flowshops with sequence-dependent setup times and machine availability constraints. *Computers & Industrial Engineering*, *57*(3), 949–957. doi:10.1016/j.cie.2009.03.012

Jacob, O. A., & Michael, B. A. (2012). Experimental determination of heat transfer coefficients during squeeze casting of aluminium. An overview of heat transfer phenomena. InTech. doi:10.5772/52038

Jadhav, H. T., Sharma, U., Patel, J., & Roy, R. (2012). Brain storm optimization algorithm based economic dispatch considering wind power. *2012 IEEE International Conference on Power and Energy (PECon)*, 588-593. doi:10.1109/PECon.2012.6450282

Jahangiri, A., Marashi, S. P. H., Mohammadaliha, M., & Ashofte, V. (2017). The effect of pressure and pouring temperature on the porosity, microstructure, hardness and yield stress of AA2024 aluminum alloy during the squeeze casting process. *Journal of Materials Processing Technology*, *245*, 1–6. doi:10.1016/j.jmatprotec.2017.02.005

Jamil, M., & Zepernick, H. (2013). Multimodal function optimisation with cuckoo search algorithm. *International Journal of Bio-inspired Computation*, *5*(2), 73–83. doi:10.1504/IJBIC.2013.053509

Janecek, A., & Tan, Y. (2011, July). Iterative improvement of the multiplicative update nmf algorithm using nature-inspired optimization. In *Natural Computation (ICNC), 2011 Seventh International Conference on* (Vol. 3, pp. 1668-1672). IEEE. doi:10.1109/ICNC.2011.6022356

Janecek, A., & Tan, Y. (2011). Using population based algorithms for initializing nonnegative matrix factorization. In *Advances in swarm intelligence* (pp. 307–316). Springer Berlin Heidelberg. doi:10.1007/978-3-642-21524-7_37

Jiaqin, Z. (2011). Fireworks Algorithm for Solving 0/1 Knapsack Problem. *Journal of Wuhan Engineering Institute, 3*, 21.

Jin, B., Khan, T., & Maass, P. (2012). A reconstruction algorithm for electrical impedance tomography based on sparsity regularization. *International Journal for Numerical Methods in Engineering, 89*(3), 337-353.

Jin, Y., & Sendhoff, B. (2009). A systems approach to evolutionary multiobjective structural optimization and beyond. *IEEE Computational Intelligence Magazine, 4*(3), 62–76. doi:10.1109/MCI.2009.933094

Johansen, T. (2011). Introduction to nonlinear model predictive control and moving horizon estimation. In *Selected Topics on Constrained and Nonlinear Control.* Bratislava: STU Bratislava/NTNU Trondheim.

Jungwattanakit, J., Reodecha, M., Chaovalitwongse, P., & Werner, F. (2008). Algorithms for flexible flow shop problems with unrelated parallel machines, setup times, and dual criteria. *International Journal of Advanced Manufacturing Technology, 37*(3-4), 3–4, 354–370. doi:10.1007/s00170-007-0977-0

Jungwattanakit, J., Reodecha, M., Chaovalitwongse, P., & Werner, F. (2009). A comparison of scheduling algorithms for flexible flow shop problems with unrelated parallel machines, setup times, and dual criteria. *Computers & Operations Research, 36*(2), 358–378. doi:10.1016/j.cor.2007.10.004

Junzhi, Y., Zhengxing, W., Ming, W., & Min, T. (2016). CPG Network Optimization for a Biomimetic Robotic Fish via PSO. *IEEE Transactions on Neural Networks and Learning Systems, 27*(9), 1962–1968. doi:10.1109/TNNLS.2015.2459913 PMID:26259223

Kaelbling, L. P., Littman, M. L., & Moore, A. W. (1996). Reinforcement Learning: A Survey. *Journal of Artificial Intelligence Research, 4*(1), 237–285.

Kahraman, C., Engin, O., Kaya, I., & Öztürk, R. E. (2010). Multiprocessor task scheduling in multistage hybrid flowshops: A parallel greedy algorithm approach. *Applied Soft Computing, 10*(4), 1293–1300. doi:10.1016/j.asoc.2010.03.008

Kahraman, C., Engin, O., Kaya, I., & Yilmaz, M. K. (2008). An application of effective genetic algorithm for solving hybrid flowshop scheduling problems. *International Journal of Computational Intelligence Systems, 1*(2), 134–147. doi:10.1080/18756891.2008.9727611

Kamuda, M., Stinnett, J., & Sullivan, C. (2017). Automated Isotope Identification Algorithm Using Artificial Neural Networks. *IEEE Transactions on Nuclear Science, 64*(7), 1858–1864. doi:10.1109/TNS.2017.2693152

Kangas, L. J., Keller, P. E., Siciliano, E. R., Kouzes, R. T., & Ely, J. H. (2008). The use of artificial neural networks in PVT-based radiation portal monitors. *Nuclear Instruments & Methods in Physics Research. Section A, Accelerators, Spectrometers, Detectors and Associated Equipment, 587*(2), 398–412. doi:10.1016/j.nima.2008.01.065

Kang, F., Li, J. J., & Ma, Z. Y. (2011). Rosenbrock artificial bee colony algorithm for accurate global optimization of numerical functions. *Inform. Sci., 12*(16), 3508–3531. doi:10.1016/j.ins.2011.04.024

Kapur, J. N., Sahoo, P. K., & Wong, A. K. C. (1985). A new method for gray-level picture thresholding using the entropy of the histogram. *Computer Vision Graphics and Image Processing, 29*(3), 273–285. doi:10.1016/0734-189X(85)90125-2

Karaboga, D. (n.d.). *Artificial bee colony homepage.* Available: http://mf.erciyes.edu.tr/abc/

Karaboga, D., & Gorkemli, B. (2011). A combinatorial artificial bee colony algorithm for traveling salesman problem. In *Proceedings of International Symposium on INnovations in Intelligent SysTems and Applications.* (pp. 50–53). Academic Press. doi:10.1109/INISTA.2011.5946125

Karaboga, D., & Akay, B. (2009). A comparative study of Artificial Bee Colony algorithm. *Applied Mathematics and Computation, 214*(1), 108–132. doi:10.1016/j.amc.2009.03.090

Karaboga, D., & Basturk, B. (2007). A powerful and efficient algorithm for numerical function optimization: Artificial bee colony. *Journal of Global Optimization*, *39*(3), 459–471. doi:10.1007/s10898-007-9149-x

Karaboga, D., & Basturk, B. (2008). On the performance of artificial bee colony algorithm. *Applied Soft Computing*, *8*(1), 687–697. doi:10.1016/j.asoc.2007.05.007

Karimi, N., Zandieh, M., & Karamooz, H. R. (2010). Bi-objective group scheduling in hybrid flexible flowshop: A multi-phase approach. *Expert Systems with Applications*, *37*(6), 4024–4032. doi:10.1016/j.eswa.2009.09.005

Kaveh, A., Bakhshpoori, T., & Ashoory, M. (2012). An efficient optimization procedure based on cuckoo search algorithm for practical design of steel structures. *International Journal of Optimization in Civil Engineering*, *2*, 1–14.

Kennedy, J., & Mendes, R. (2002). *Population structure and particle swarm performance*. Paper presented at the IEEE Congress on Evolutionary Computation.

Kennedy, J., Eberhart, R., & Shi, Y. (2001). Swarm Intelligence. Morgan Kaufmann Publisher.

Kennedy, J., & Eberhart, R. (1995). Particle swarm optimization. *IEEE International Conference on Neural Networks*, 1942-1948.

Kennedy, J., & Eberhart, R. (1995). Particle swarm optimization. *Proceedings of IEEE International Conference on Neural Networks*, 1942–1948. doi:10.1109/ICNN.1995.488968

Kennedy, J., & Eberhart, R. C. (1995). Particle swarm optimization. In *Proceedings of the 1995 IEEE International Conference on Neural Networks. Part 1 (of 6)*. (pp. 1942–1948). IEEE.

Kennedy, J., & Eberhart, R. C. (1997). A discrete binary version of the particle swarm algorithm. In *Proceedings of the IEEE International Conference on Systems, Man and Cybernetics* (pp. 4104–4108). IEEE. doi:10.1109/ICSMC.1997.637339

Kennedy, J., & Eberhart, R. C. (2001). *Swarm Intelligence*. Morgan Kaufmann Publishers.

Kennedy, J., & Mendes, R. (2002). Population structure and particle swarm performance. *Proceedings of The Fourth Congress on Evolutionary Computation (CEC 2002)*, 1671-1676.

Khalili, M. (2012). Multi-objective no-wait hybrid flowshop scheduling problem with transportation times. *International Journal on Computer Science and Engineering*, *7*(2), 147–154. doi:10.1504/IJCSE.2012.048094

Klepac, G. (2010). Preparing for New Competition in the Retail Industry. In A. Syvajarvi & J. Stenvall (Eds.), *Data Mining in Public and Private Sectors: Organizational and Government Applications* (pp. 245–266). Hershey, PA: Information Science Reference. doi:10.4018/978-1-60566-906-9.ch013

Klepac, G. (2014). Data Mining Models as a Tool for Churn Reduction and Custom Product Development in Telecommunication Industries. In P. Vasant (Ed.), *Handbook of Research on Novel Soft Computing Intelligent Algorithms: Theory and Practical Applications* (pp. 511–537). Hershey, PA: Information Science Reference. doi:10.4018/978-1-4666-4450-2.ch017

Klepac, G., Kopal, R., & Mršić, L. (2015). *Developing Churn Models Using Data Mining Techniques and Social Network Analysis*. Hershey, PA: IGI Global. doi:10.4018/978-1-4666-6288-9

Konstantinos, E. P., & Michael, N. V. (2010). Applications in Machine Learning. In K. Parsopoulos & M. Vrahatis (Eds.), *Particle Swarm Optimization and Intelligence: Advances and Applications* (pp. 149–167). Hershey, PA: Information Science Reference. doi:10.4018/978-1-61520-666-7.ch006

Konstantinos, E. P., & Michael, N. V. (2010). Established and Recently Proposed Variants of Particle Swarm Optimization. In K. Parsopoulos & M. Vrahatis (Eds.), *Particle Swarm Optimization and Intelligence: Advances and Applications* (pp. 88–132). Hershey, PA: Information Science Reference. doi:10.4018/978-1-61520-666-7.ch004

Koza, J. R. (1992). *Genetic Programming: On the Programming of Computers by Means of Natural Selection*. MIT Press.

Kress, M., Mostaghim, S., & Seese, D. (2010). Intelligent Business Process Execution using Particle Swarm Optimization. In Information Resources Management: Concepts, Methodologies, Tools and Applications (pp. 797-815). Hershey, PA: Information Science Reference. doi:10.4018/978-1-61520-965-1.ch319

Krishna Priya, R., Thangaraj, C., Kesavadas, C., & Kannan, S. (2013). Fuzzy Entropy-Based MR Brain Image Segmentation Using Modified Particle Swarm Optimization. *Int J Imaging Syst Technol., 23*, 281-288.

Krishna, P. (2001). *A study on interfacial heat transfer and process parameters in squeeze casting and low pressure permanent mold casting* (Ph.D. Thesis). University of Michigan, Ann Arbor, MI.

Krishnanand, K. N., & Ghose, D. (2009). Glowworm swarm optimization for simultaneous capture of multiple local optima of multimodal functions. *Swarm Intelligence, 3*(2), 87–124. doi:10.1007/s11721-008-0021-5

Krishnanand, K. R., Hasani, S. M. F., Panigrahi, B. K., & Panda, S. K. (2013). Optimal Power Flow Solution Using Self–Evolving Brain–Storming Inclusive Teaching–Learning–Based Algorithm. In *Advances in Swarm Intelligence* (pp. 338–345). Springer Berlin Heidelberg. doi:10.1007/978-3-642-38703-6_40

Kumar, S. E., & Kusuma, S. M. (2014). Clustering protocol for wireless sensor networks based on Rhesus Macaque (Macaca mulatta) animal's social behavior. *International Journal of Computer Applications, 87*(8).

Kumar, S., Kumari, R., & Sharma, V. K. (2015). Fitness Based Position Update in Spider Monkey Optimization Algorithm. *Procedia Computer Science, 62*, 442–449. doi:10.1016/j.procs.2015.08.504

Kundur, P. (1993). *Power System Stability and Control*. New York: McGraw-Hill, Inc.

Kurbatsky, V., Sidorov, D., Tomin, N., & Spiryaev, V. (2014). Optimal Training of Artificial Neural Networks to Forecast Power System State Variables. *International Journal of Energy Optimization and Engineering, 3*(1), 65–82. doi:10.4018/ijeoe.2014010104

Kwon, W. H., Bruckstein, A. M., & Kailath, T. (1983). Stabilizing state-feedback design via the moving horizon method. *International Journal of Control, 37*(3), 631–643. doi:10.1080/00207178308932998

Lam, A. Y. S., & Li, V. O. K. (2010). Chemical-reaction-inspired metaheuristic for optimization. *IEEE Transactions on Evolutionary Computation, 14*(3), 381–399. doi:10.1109/TEVC.2009.2033580

Larose, D. T. (2005). *Discovering Knowledge in Data: An Introduction to Data Mining*. John Wiley &Sons Inc.

Layeb, A. (2011). A novel quantum inspired cuckoo search for knapsack problems. *International Journal of Bio-inspired Computation, 3*(5), 297–305. doi:10.1504/IJBIC.2011.042260

Lecun, Y., Bengio, Y., & Hinton, G. (2015). Deep learning. *Nature, 521*(7553), 436–444. doi:10.1038/nature14539 PMID:26017442

Le, D. A., & Vo, D. N. (2016). Cuckoo Search Algorithm for Minimization of Power Loss and Voltage Deviation. *International Journal of Energy Optimization and Engineering, 5*(1), 23–34. doi:10.4018/IJEOE.2016010102

Lee, G. C., & Kim, Y. D. (2004). A branch-and-bound algorithm for a two-stage hybrid flowshop scheduling problem minimizing total tardiness. *International Journal of Production Research, 42*(22), 4731–4743. doi:10.1080/0020754041233127044

Lee, S.-M., & Myung, H. (2015). Receding horizon particle swarm optimisation-based formation control with collision avoidance for non-holonomic mobile robots. *IET Control Theory & Applications*, *9*(14), 2075–2083. doi:10.1049/iet-cta.2015.0071

Li, J., Zheng, S., & Tan, Y. (2014, July). Adaptive Fireworks Algorithm. In *Evolutionary Computation (CEC), 2014 IEEE Congress on* (pp. 3214-3221). IEEE. doi:10.1109/CEC.2014.6900418

Liang, J., Suganthan, P., & Deb, K. (2005). *Novel composition test functions for numerical global optimization*. Paper presented at the IEEE Swarm Intelligence Symposium. doi:10.1109/SIS.2005.1501604

Liang, J., Qin, A. K., Suganthan, P. N., & Baskar, S. (2006). Comprehensive learning particle swarm optimizer for global optimization of multimodal functions. *IEEE Transactions on Evolutionary Computation*, *10*(3), 281–295. doi:10.1109/TEVC.2005.857610

Liao, C. J., Tjandradjaja, E., & Chung, T. P. (2012). An approach using particle swarm optimization and bottleneck heuristic to solve hybrid flow shop scheduling problem. *Applied Soft Computing*, *12*(6), 1755–1764. doi:10.1016/j.asoc.2012.01.011

Li, C. H., & Lee, C. K. (1993). Minimum cross entropy thresholding. *Pattern Recognition*, *26*(4), 617–625. doi:10.1016/0031-3203(93)90115-D

Lihu, A., & Holban, Ş. (2015). De novo motif prediction using the fireworks algorithm. *International Journal of Swarm Intelligence Research*, *6*(3), 24–40. doi:10.4018/IJSIR.2015070102

Li, J. K., Pan, Q. K., & Mao, K. (2014). Hybrid particle swarm optimization for hybrid flowshop scheduling problem with maintenance activities. *The Scientific World Journal*. doi:10.1155/2014/596850 PMID:24883414

Li, J., Zheng, S., & Tan, Y. (2017). The effect of information utilization: Introducing a novel guiding spark in the fireworks algorithm. *IEEE Transactions on Evolutionary Computation*, *21*(1), 153–166. doi:10.1109/TEVC.2016.2589821

Lin, H. T., & Liao, C. J. (2003). A case study in a two-stage hybrid flow shop with setup time and dedicated machines. *International Journal of Production Economics*, *86*(2), 133–143. doi:10.1016/S0925-5273(03)00011-2

Linn, R., & Zhang, W. (1999). Hybrid flow shop schedule: A survey. *Computers & Industrial Engineering*, *37*(1-2), 1–2, 57–61. doi:10.1016/S0360-8352(99)00023-6

Lins, A., Bastos-Filho, C. J., Nascimento, D. N., Junior, M. A. O., & de Lima-Neto, F. B. (2012). Analysis of the performance of the fish school search algorithm running in graphic processing units. *Theory and New Applications of Swarm Intelligence*, 17–32.

Li, S. (1997). A hybrid two-stage flowshop with part family, batch production, major and minor set-ups. *European Journal of Operational Research*, *102*(1), 142–156. doi:10.1016/S0377-2217(96)00213-5

Li, T., Isaacson, D., Newell, J. C., & Saulnier, G. J. (2014). Adaptive techniques in electrical impedance tomography reconstruction. *Physiological Measurement*, *35*(6), 1111–1124. doi:10.1088/0967-3334/35/6/1111 PMID:24845260

Liu, Z., Feng, Z., & Ke, L. (2015, May). Fireworks algorithm for the multi-satellite control resource scheduling problem. In *Evolutionary Computation (CEC), 2015 IEEE Congress on* (pp. 1280-1286). IEEE. doi:10.1109/CEC.2015.7257036

Liu, J., Zheng, S., & Tan, Y. (2013). The improvement on controlling exploration and exploitation of firework algorithm. In *Advances in Swarm Intelligence* (Vol. 7923, pp. 11–23). Springer Berlin Heidelberg. doi:10.1007/978-3-642-38703-6_2

Liu, Y., & Sun, F. (2011). A fast differential evolution algorithm using K-nearest neighbour predictor. *Expert Systems with Applications, Elsevier*, *38*(4), 4254–4258. doi:10.1016/j.eswa.2010.09.092

Li, Y., Yang, H., & Xing, Z. (2017). Numerical simulation and process optimization of squeeze casting process of an automobile control arm. *International Journal of Advanced Manufacturing Technology*, *88*(1-4), 941–947. doi:10.1007/s00170-016-8845-4

Loodaricheh, R. A., Mallick, S., & Bhargava, V. K. (2014). Energy-efficient Resource Allocation for OFDMA Cellular Networks with User Cooperation and QoS Provisioning. *IEEE Transactions on Wireless Communications*, *13*(11), 6132–6146. doi:10.1109/TWC.2014.2329877

LOPES. (2006). H. S. Fundamentos de computação evolucionária e aplicações. In *Escola Regional de Informática da SBC – Paraná*. Anais, Bandeirantes. SBC.

Lovbjerg, M., & Krink, T. (2002). *Extending particle swarm optimisers with self-organized criticality.* Paper presented at the IEEE World on Congress on Computational Intelligence. doi:10.1109/CEC.2002.1004479

Low, C. (2005). Simulated annealing heuristic for flow shop scheduling problems with unrelated parallel machines. *Computers & Operations Research*, *32*(8), 2013–2025. doi:10.1016/j.cor.2004.01.003

Low, C., Hsu, C. J., & Su, C. T. (2008). A two-stage hybrid flowshop scheduling problem with a function constraint and unrelated alternative machines. *Computers & Operations Research*, *35*(3), 845–853. doi:10.1016/j.cor.2006.04.004

Lu, G., Tan, D., & Zhao, H. (November 2002). Improvement on regulating definition of antibody density of immune algorithm. In *Neural Information Processing 2002. ICONIP'02. Proceedings of the 9th International Conference on* (*vol. 5*, pp. 2669-2672). IEEE.

Luca, A.D., & Termini, S. (1972). Definition of a non probabilistic entropy in the setting of fuzzy sets theory. *Inf. Contr.*, *20*, 301–315.

Lu, X., Wang, W., & Ma, J. (2013). An Empirical Study of Communication Infrastructures Towards the Smart Grid: Design, Implementation, and Evaluation. *IEEE Transactions on Smart Grid*, *4*(1), 170–183. doi:10.1109/TSG.2012.2225453

Magni, L., & Scattolini, R. (2004). Stabilizing model predictive control of nonlinear continuous time systems. *Annual Reviews in Control*, *28*(1), 1–11. doi:10.1016/j.arcontrol.2004.01.001

Mahapatra, S. S., & Patnaik, A. (2007). Optimization of wire electrical discharge machining (WEDM) process parameters using Taguchi method. *International Journal of Advanced Manufacturing Technology*, *34*(9-10), 911–925. doi:10.1007/s00170-006-0672-6

Maleki, A., Niroumand, B., & Shafyei, A. (2006). Effects of squeeze casting parameters on density, macrostructure and hardness of LM13 alloy. *Materials Science and Engineering A*, *428*(1-2), 135–140. doi:10.1016/j.msea.2006.04.099

Maleki, A., Shafyei, A., & Niroumand, B. (2009). Effects of squeeze casting parameters on the microstructure of LM13 alloy. *Journal of Materials Processing Technology*, *209*(8), 3790–3797. doi:10.1016/j.jmatprotec.2008.08.035

Mansour, Xu, Alvarado, & Chhewangrinzin. (1994). SVC placement using Critical Modes of voltage stability. *IEEE Transactions on Power Systems*, *9*(2), 757–763.

Marichelvam, M. K. (2012). An improved hybrid cuckoo search (IHCS) metaheuristics algorithm for permutation flow shop scheduling problems. *International Journal of Bio-inspired Computation*, *4*(4), 200–205. doi:10.1504/IJBIC.2012.048061

Marichelvam, M. K., & Geetha, M. (2016). Application of novel harmony search algorithm for solving hybrid flow shop scheduling problems to minimize makespan. *International Journal of Industrial and Systems Engineering*, *23*(4), 467–481. doi:10.1504/IJISE.2016.077698

Marichelvam, M. K., & Prabaharan, T. (2014). Performance evaluation of an improved hybrid genetic scatter search algorithm for multistage hybrid flow shop scheduling problems with missing operations. *International Journal of Industrial and System Engineering, 16*(1), 120–141. doi:10.1504/IJISE.2014.057946

Marichelvam, M. K., Prabaharan, T., & Yang, X. S. (2014). Improved cuckoo search algorithm for hybrid flow shop scheduling problems to minimize makespan. *Applied Soft Computing, 19*, 93–101. doi:10.1016/j.asoc.2014.02.005

Marichelvam, M. K., Prabaharan, T., Yang, X. S., & Geetha, M. (2013). Solving hybrid flow shop scheduling problems using bat algorithm. *International Journal of Logistics Economics and Globalisation, 5*(1), 15–29. doi:10.1504/IJLEG.2013.054428

Marsan, M. A., Chiaraviglio, L., Ciullo, D., & Meo, M. (2013). On the Effectiveness of Single and Multiple Base Station Sleep Modes in Cellular Networks. *Computer Networks, 57*(17), 3276–3290. doi:10.1016/j.comnet.2013.07.016

Martin, S., & Choi, C. T. M. (2016). Nonlinear Electrical Impedance Tomography Reconstruction Using Artificial Neural Networks and Particle Swarm Optimization. *IEEE Transactions on Magnetics, 52*(3), 1–4. doi:10.1109/TMAG.2015.2488901

Ma, T., & Niu, D. (2016). Icing forecasting of high voltage transmission line using weighted least square support vector machine with fireworks algorithm for feature selection. *Applied Sciences, 6*(12), 438. doi:10.3390/app6120438

Matthews, R. W., & Mattheus, J. R. (1942). *Insect Behavior.* New York: Wiley-Interscience.

Mattingly, J., & Mitchell, D. J. (2010). A framework for the solution of inverse radiation transport problems. *IEEE Transactions on Nuclear Science, 57*(6), 3734–3743.

Mauldin, M. L. (1984). Maintaining diversity in genetic search. In *Proceedings of the National Conference on Artificial Intelligence (AAAI 1984).* (pp. 247-250). Academic Press.

McAdams, E. T., McLaughlin, J. A., & Anderson, J. McC. (1994). Multi-electrode systems for electrical impedance tomography. *Physiological Measurement, 15*(2A), A101–AI06. doi:10.1088/0967-3334/15/2A/014 PMID:8087031

Mehrabian, A. R., & Lucas, C. (2006). A novel numerical optimization algorithm inspired from weed colonization. *Ecological Informatics, 1*(4), 355–366. doi:10.1016/j.ecoinf.2006.07.003

Menin, O. H. (2009). *Método dos elementos de contorno para tomografia de impedância elétrica. Dissertação (Mestrado).* Faculdade de Filosofia, Ciências e Letras de Ribeirão Preto da Universidade de São Paulo.

Merloti, P. E. (2004). Optimization Algorithms Inspired by Biological Ants and Swarm Behavior. San Diego State University, Artificial Intelligence Technical Report, CS550.

Michael, W., Leida, G. A., & Alfonso, F. D. (2007). Barros magnetic optimization in a multicellular magnetotactic organism. *Biophysical Journal, 92*(2), 661–670. doi:10.1529/biophysj.106.093823 PMID:17071652

Michalewicz. (1996). *Z. Genetic Algorithms + Data Structures = Evolution Programs* (3rd ed.). Springer.

Mihalie, Zunko, & Povh. (1994). Improvement of Transient using Unified Power Flow Controller. *IEEE Trans.*

Mitchell, D. J., Sanger, H. M., & Marlow, K. W. (1989). Gamma-ray response functions for scintillation and semiconductor detectors. *Nuclear Instruments & Methods in Physics Research. Section A, Accelerators, Spectrometers, Detectors and Associated Equipment, 276*(3), 547–556. doi:10.1016/0168-9002(89)90582-2

Mitchell, J. G., & Kogure, K. (2006). Bacterial motility: Links to the environment and a driving force for microbial physics. *FEMS Microbiology Ecology, 55*(1), 3–16. doi:10.1111/j.1574-6941.2005.00003.x PMID:16420610

Mnih, V., Kavukcuoglu, K., Silver, D., Rusu, A. A., Veness, J., Bellemare, M. G., & Hassabis, D. et al. (2015). Human-level control through deep reinforcement learning. *Nature, 518*(7540), 529–533. doi:10.1038/nature14236 PMID:25719670

Mo, H. W., & Geng, M. J. (2014). Magnetotactic bacteria optimization algorithm based on best-rand scheme. The 6th Naturei and Biologically Inspired Computing, 59-64.

Mo, H. W., & Xu, L. F. (2013). Magnetotactic bacteria optimization algorithm for multimodal optimization. *Swarm Intelligence (SIS), IEEE Symposium on,* 240-247.

Mock, W. B. (2011). Treaty of Westphalia. In *Encyclopedia of Global Justice* (pp. 1095–1096). Springer Netherlands. doi:10.1007/978-1-4020-9160-5_660

Modiri, A., Gu, X., Hagan, A. M., & Sawant, A. (2017). Radiotherapy Planning Using an Improved Search Strategy in Particle Swarm Optimization. *IEEE Transactions on Biomedical Engineering, 64*(5), 980–989. doi:10.1109/TBME.2016.2585114 PMID:27362755

Mo, H. W. (2012). Research on magnetotactic bacteria optimization algorithm. *The Fifth International Conference on Advanced Computational Intelligence*, 423-428.

Mo, H. W., & Liu, L. L. (2014). Magnetotactic bacteria optimization algorithm based on best-target scheme. *International Conference on Nature Computing and Fuzzy Knowledge*, 103-114. doi:10.1109/ICNC.2014.6975877

Mo, H. W., Liu, L. L., & Geng, M. J. (2014). A new magnetotactic bacteria optimization algorithm based on moment migration. *International Conference on Swarm Intelligence*, 103-114. doi:10.1007/978-3-319-11857-4_12

Mo, H. W., Liu, L. L., & Xu, L. F. (2014). A power spectrum optimization algorithm inspired by magnetotactic bacteria. *Neural Computing & Applications, 25*(7), 1823–1844. doi:10.1007/s00521-014-1672-3

Mo, H. W., Liu, L. L., Xu, L. F., & Zhao, Y. Y. (2014). Research on magnetotactic bacteria optimizationalgorithm based on the best individual. *The Sixth International Conference on Bio-inspired Computing*, 318-322.

Mo, H. W., Liu, L. L., & Zhao, J. (2015). Performance research on Magnetotactic Bacteria Optimization Algorithm with the Best Individual-guided Differential Interaction Energy. *Journal of Computer and Communications., 03*(05), 127–136. doi:10.4236/jcc.2015.35016

Mo, H. W., Liu, L. L., & Zhao, J. (2017). A new magnetotactic bacteria optimization algorithm based on moment migration. *IEEE/ACM Transactions on Computational Biology and Bioinformatics, 14*(1), 15–26. doi:10.1109/TCBB.2015.2453949 PMID:28182541

Momenté, G. V., Peixoto, B. H. L. N., Tsuzuki, M. S. G., & Martins, T. D. C. (2013). New objective function for electrical image tomography reconstruction. *ABCM Symposium Series in Mechatronics*.

Montavon, G., Orr, G., & Müller, K. (2012). *Neural networks: Tricks of the trade*. Berlin: Springer. doi:10.1007/978-3-642-35289-8

Montazeri-Gh, M., Jafari, S., & Ilkhani, M. (2012). Application of particle swarm optimization in gas turbine engine fuel controller gain tuning. *Engineering Optimization, 44*(2), 225–240. doi:10.1080/0305215X.2011.576760

Moreno, R., Antonio, R.-G., Aurelio, B., & Rafael, C. (2012). SensGrid: modeling and simulation for wireless sensor grids. Simulation: Transactions of the society for modeling and simulation international, 1-16.

Moriarty, D., Schultz, A., & Grefenstette, J. (1999). Evolutionary algorithms for reinforcement learning. *Journal of Artificial Intelligence Research, 11*, 241–276.

Moscato, P., & Cotta, C. (2002). Memetic algorithms. Handbook of Applied Optimization, 157-167.

Moursli, O., & Pochet, Y. (2000). A branch and bound algorithm for the hybrid flow shop. *International Journal of Production Economics*, *64*(1-3), 113–125. doi:10.1016/S0925-5273(99)00051-1

Mucherino, A. & Seref, O. (2007). Monkey search: A novel metaheuristic search for global optimization. *Proceedings of Data Mining, Systems Analysis and Optimization in Biomedicine,* 162-173.

Müeller, S., Marchetto, J., Airaghi, S., & Koumoutsakos, P. (2002). Optimization based on bacterial chemotaxis. *IEEE Transactions on Evolutionary Computation*, *6*(1), 16–29. doi:10.1109/4235.985689

Mukherjee, A., Paul, S., & Roy, P. K. (2015). Transient Stability Constrained Optimal Power Flow Using Teaching Learning Based Optimization. *International Journal of Energy Optimization and Engineering*, *4*(1), 18–35. doi:10.4018/ijeoe.2015010102

Murray, W. S., Butterfield, K. B., & Baird, W. (2000). Automated radioisotope identification using fuzzy logic and portable CZT detectors. In *Nuclear Science Symposium Conference Record*, 2000 *IEEE* (*Vol.* 2, pp. 9-129). IEEE. doi:10.1109/NSSMIC.2000.949884

Naderi, B., Zandieh, M., Ghoshe, A. K., & Roshanaei, V. (2009). An improved simulated annealing for hybrid flowshops with sequence-dependent setup and transportation times to minimize total completion time and total tardiness. *Expert Systems with Applications*, *36*(6), 9625–9633. doi:10.1016/j.eswa.2008.09.063

Nataraj, P., Tanuj, S., & Vivek, A. (2017). Adaptive Velocity PSO for Global Maximum Power Control of a PV Array Under Nonuniform Irradiation Conditions. *IEEE Journal of Photovoltaics*, *7*(2), 624–639. doi:10.1109/JPHOTOV.2016.2629844

Neal, R. M. (1996). *Bayesian learning for neural networks* (Vol. 118). New York: Springer-Verlag. doi:10.1007/978-1-4612-0745-0

Nebro, A. J., Durillo, J. J., Garça-Nieto, J., Coello Coello, C. A., Luna, F., & Alba, E. (2009). SMPSO: A new PSO-based metaheuristic for multi-objective optimization. *IEEE Symposium on Computational Intelligence in Multicriteria Decision-Making*, 66–73. doi:10.1109/MCDM.2009.4938830

Nelder, J., & Mead, R. (1965). A simplex method for function minimization. *The Computer Journal*, *7*(4), 308–313. doi:10.1093/comjnl/7.4.308

Neri, F., & Cotta, C. (2012). Memetic algorithms and memetic computing optimization: A literature review. *Swarm and Evolutionary Computation*, *2*, 1–14. doi:10.1016/j.swevo.2011.11.003

Nguyen, Q. H., Ong, Y.-S., & Lim, M. H. (2009). A probabilistic memetic framework. *IEEE Transactions on Evolutionary Computation*, *13*(3), 604–623. doi:10.1109/TEVC.2008.2009460

Nguyen, S., & Kachitvichyanukul, V. (2010). Movement Strategies for Multi-Objective Particle Swarm Optimization. *International Journal of Applied Metaheuristic Computing*, *1*(3), 59–79. doi:10.4018/jamc.2010070105

Niu, Q., Zhou, T., & Ma, S. (2009). A quantum-inspired immune algorithm for hybrid flow shop with makespan criterion. *Journal of Universal Computer Science*, *15*, 765–785.

Oguz, C., & Ercan, M. F. (2005). A genetic algorithm for hybrid flow shop scheduling with multiprocessor tasks. *Journal of Scheduling*, *8*(4), 323–351. doi:10.1007/s10951-005-1640-y

Oguz, C., Ercan, M. F., Cheng, T. C. E., & Fung, Y. F. (2003). Heuristic algorithms for multiprocessor task scheduling in a two-stage hybrid flow-shop. *European Journal of Operational Research*, *149*(2), 390–403. doi:10.1016/S0377-2217(02)00766-X

Olive, D., Cuevas, E., Pajares, G., Zaldivar, D., & Perez-Cisneros, M. (2013). Multilevel Thresholding Segmentation Based on Harmony Search Optimization. *Journal of Applied Mathematics*, *2013*, 1–24. doi:10.1155/2013/575414

Olson, E. A. (2011). *Particle Swarm Optimization: Theory, Techniques and Applications (Engineering Tools, Techniques and Tables)*. Nova Science Pub Inc.

Osborn, A. F. (1963). *Applied imagination: Principles and procedures of creative problem solving* (3rd ed.). New York, NY: Charles Scribner's Son.

Ou, Y., Kang, P., Jun, K. M., & Julius, A. A. (2015). Algorithms for simultaneous motion control of multiple T. pyriformis cells: Model predictive control and particle swarm optimization. *2015 IEEE International Conference on Robotics and Automation (ICRA)*, 3507-3512. doi:10.1109/ICRA.2015.7139684

Ouyang, X., Zhou, Y., Luo, Q., & Chen, H. (2013). A Novel Discrete Cuckoo Search Algorithm for Spherical Traveling Salesman Problem. *Applied Mathematics & Information Sciences*, *7*(2), 777–784. doi:10.12785/amis/070248

Padiyar, K.R., & Uma Rao, K. (1999). Modeling and Control of Unified Power Flow Controller For Transient Stability. *Electrical Power and Energy Systems, 21.*

Padiyar, K. R., & Kulakarni, A. M. (1998). Control design and simulation of unified power flow controller. *IEEE Transactions on Power Delivery*, *13*(4), 1348–1354. doi:10.1109/61.714507

Pal, N. R. (1996). On minimum cross entropy thresholding. *Pattern Recognition*, *29*(4), 575–580. doi:10.1016/0031-3203(95)00111-5

Pal, N. R., & Pal, S. K. (1993). A review on image segmentation. *Pattern Recognition*, *26*(9), 1277–1294. doi:10.1016/0031-3203(93)90135-J

Panda, M., & Patra, M. R. (2010). Modeling radio channels for CSMA-MAC based wireless sensor networks. *International Journal of Computers and Applications*, *9*(6), 6–11. doi:10.5120/1392-1876

Pantelopoulos, A., Alamaniotis, M., Jevremovic, T., Park, S. M., Chung, S. M., & Bourbakis, N. (2009, November). LG-graph based detection of NRF spectrum signatures: Initial results and comparison. In *Tools with Artificial Intelligence, 2009. ICTAI'09. 21st International Conference on* (pp. 683-686). IEEE.

Panwar, L. K., Reddy, S., & Kumar, R. (2015). Binary fireworks algorithm based thermal unit commitment. *International Journal of Swarm Intelligence Research*, *6*(2), 87–101. doi:10.4018/IJSIR.2015040104

Parappagoudar, M. B., Pratihar, D. K., & Datta, G. L. (2007). Linear and non-linear statistical modelling of green sand mould system. *International Journal of Cast Metals Research*, *20*(1), 1–13. doi:10.1179/136404607X184952

PARC. (2006). *RMASE: Routing Modeling Application Simulation Environment.* Available at: http://webs.cs.berkeley.edu/related.html

Parpinelli, R. S., & Lopes, H. S. (2011). New inspirations in swarm intelligence: A survey. *International Journal of Bio-inspired Computation*, *3*(1), 1–16. doi:10.1504/IJBIC.2011.038700

Pashazadeh, H., Gheisari, Y., & Hamedi, M. (2014). Statistical modeling and optimization of resistance spot welding process parameters using neural networks and multi-objective genetic algorithm. *Journal of Intelligent Manufacturing*, 1–11. doi:10.1007/s10845-014-0891-x

Patel, G. C. M., Krishna, P., & Parappagoudar, M. B. (2016a). Modelling of squeeze casting process: Conventional statistical regression analysis approach. *Applied Mathematical Modelling*, *40*(15), 6869–6888. doi:10.1016/j.apm.2016.02.029

Patel, G. C. M., Krishna, P., Parappagoudar, M. B., & Vundavilli, P. R. (2016b). Multi-objective optimization of squeeze casting process using evolutionary algorithms. *International Journal of Swarm Intelligence Research, 7*(1), 55–74. doi:10.4018/IJSIR.2016010103

Patrick, G. (1968). *Cities in Evolution*. New York: Harper & Row.

Peer, E. S., van den Bergh, F., & Engelbrecht, A. P. (2003). *Using neighborhoods with the guaranteed convergence PSO*. Paper presented at the IEEE Swarm Intelligence Symposium.

Pei, Y., Zheng, S., Tan, Y., & Takagi, H. (2012). An empirical study on influence of approximation approaches on enhancing fireworks algorithm. In *Systems, Man, and Cybernetics (SMC), 2012 Conference on,* (pp.1322-1327). IEEE.

Peng, H., Long, F., & Ding, C. (2005). Feature selection based on mutual information criteria of max-dependency, max-relevance, and min-redundancy. *IEEE Transactions on Pattern Analysis and Machine Intelligence, 27*(8), 1226–1238. doi:10.1109/TPAMI.2005.159 PMID:16119262

Peng, J., Hong, P., & Xue, K. (2014). Stochastic Analysis of Optimal Base Station Energy Saving in Cellular Networks with Sleep Mode. *IEEE Communications Letters, 18*(4), 612–615. doi:10.1109/LCOMM.2014.030114.140241

Peter, H., & Kathy, P. (2006). *The Polycentric Metropolis: Learning from Mega-city Regions in Europe*. London: Earthscan Press.

Philipse, A. P., & Maas, D. (2002). Magnetic colloids from magnetotactic bacteria: Chain formation and colloidal stability. *Langmuir, 18*(25), 9977–9984. doi:10.1021/la0205811

Piche, S., Keeler, J., Martin, G., Boe, G., Johnson, D., & Gerules, M. (2000). Neural network based model predictive control. *Advances in Neural Information Processing Systems*, 1029–1035.

Powell, M. J. D. (1964). An efficient method for finding the minimum of a function of several variables without calculating derivatives. *The Computer Journal, 7*(2), 155–162. doi:10.1093/comjnl/7.2.155

Prabhneetkaur & Taranjotkaur. (2014). A Comparative Study of Various Metaheuristic Algorithms. *International Journal of Computer Science and Information Technologies, 5*(5), 6701–6704.

Price, K., Storn, R. M., & Lampinen, J. A. (2006). *Differential evolution: a practical approach to global optimization*. Springer Science & Business Media.

Pun, T. (1981). Entropic thresholding, a new approach. *Computer Graphics and Image Processing, 16*(3), 210–239. doi:10.1016/0146-664X(81)90038-1

Qin, Q., Cheng, S., Zhang, Q., Li, L., & Shi, Y. (2016). Particle Swarm Optimization With Interswarm Interactive Learning Strategy. *IEEE Transactions on Cybernetics, 46*(10), 2238–2251. doi:10.1109/TCYB.2015.2474153 PMID:26357418

Qu, B. Y., Suganthan, P. N., & Das, S. (2013). A distance-based locally informed particle swarm model for multimodal optimization. *IEEE Transactions on Evolutionary Computation, 17*(3), 387–402. doi:10.1109/TEVC.2012.2203138

Radakrishnan, K. K. (2013). Optimal Power Flow Solution Using Self-Evolving Brain-Storming Inclusive Teaching-Learning-Based Algorithm. *4th International Conference on Swarm Intelligence*.

Rahmani, A., Amine, A., Hamou, R. M., Rahmani, M. E., & Bouarara, H. A. (2015). Privacy preserving through fireworks algorithm based model for image perturbation in big data. *International Journal of Swarm Intelligence Research, 6*(3), 41–58. doi:10.4018/IJSIR.2015070103

Rahul Khandelwal, J. (2016). A Novel Multiobjective Optimization for Cement Stabilized Soft Soil based on Artificial Bee Colony. *International Journal of Applied Metaheuristic Computing, 7*(4), 1–17. doi:10.4018/IJAMC.2016100101

Rajagopal, S. (1981). Squeeze casting: A review and update. *Journal of Applied Metalworking*, *14*(4), 3–14. doi:10.1007/BF02834341

Rajagopal, S., & Altergott, W. H. (1985). Quality control in squeeze casting of aluminium. *AFS Transactions*, *93*, 145–154.

Rajaram, R., Palanisamy, K., Ramasamy, S., & Ramanathan, P. (2014). Selective harmonic elimination in PWM inverter using fire fly and fire works algorithm. *International Journal of Innovative Research in Advanced Engineering*, *1*, 55–62.

Rajesh, R., Pugazhendhi, S., & Ganesh, K. (2013). Genetic Algorithm and Particle Swarm Optimization for Solving Balanced Allocation Problem of Third Party Logistics Providers. In J. Wang (Ed.), *Management Innovations for Intelligent Supply Chains* (pp. 184–203). Hershey, PA: Business Science Reference. doi:10.4018/978-1-4666-2461-0.ch010

Ramanand, K. R., Krishnanand, K. R., Panigrahi, B. K., & Mallick, M. K. (2012). Brain Storming Incorporated Teaching–Learning–Based Algorithm with Application to Electric Power Dispatch. In Swarm, Evolutionary, and Memetic Computing, (pp. 476-483). Springer Berlin Heidelberg. doi:10.1007/978-3-642-35380-2_56

Ramasamy, V. & ZainalAbidin. (2009). A study on FVSI index as an indicator for under voltage load shedding (UVLS). *Proceedings of ICEE 2009 3rd International Conference on Energy and Environment*, 84-88. doi:10.1109/POWERI.2006.1632526

Ramos, V., & Almeida, F. (2000). Artificial Ant Colonies in Digital Image Habitats – A Mass Behavior Effect Study on Pattern Recognition. *Proceedings of ANTS'2000, 2nd International Workshop on Ant Algorithms*, 113-116.

Rao, R. V. (2010). *Advanced modeling and optimization of manufacturing processes: international research and development*. Springer Science & Business Media.

Rao, R. V., & Kalyankar, V. D. (2011). Parameters optimization of advanced machining processes using TLBO algorithm. *Proceedings of International Conference on Engineering, Project, and Production Management (EPPM)*, 21-31.

Rao, R. V., & Kalyankar, V. D. (2012). Parameter optimization of machining processes using a new optimization algorithm. *Materials and Manufacturing Processes*, *27*(9), 978–985. doi:10.1080/10426914.2011.602792

Rao, R. V., Kalyankar, V. D., & Waghmare, G. (2014). Parameters optimization of selected casting processes using teaching–learning-based optimization algorithm. *Applied Mathematical Modelling*, *38*(23), 5592–5608. doi:10.1016/j.apm.2014.04.036

Rao, R. V., & Savsani, V. J. (2012). *Mechanical design optimization using advanced optimization techniques*. Springer London Dordrecht Heidelberg New York. doi:10.1007/978-1-4471-2748-2

Rao, R. V., Savsani, V. J., & Vakharia, D. P. (2011). Teaching–learning-based optimization: A novel method for constrained mechanical design optimization problems. *Computer Aided Design*, *43*(3), 303–315. doi:10.1016/j.cad.2010.12.015

Rao, R. V., Savsani, V. J., & Vakharia, D. P. (2012). Teaching–learning based optimization: A novel optimization method for continuous non-linear large scale problems. *Information Sciences*, *183*(1), 1–15. doi:10.1016/j.ins.2011.08.006

Rao, R. V., & Waghmare, G. G. (2014a). A comparative study of a teaching–learning-based optimization algorithm on multi-objective unconstrained and constrained functions. *Journal of King Saud University-Computer and Information Sciences*, *26*(3), 332–346. doi:10.1016/j.jksuci.2013.12.004

Rao, R. V., & Waghmare, G. G. (2014b). Complex constrained design optimisation using an elitist teaching-learning-based optimisation algorithm. *International Journal of Metaheuristics*, *3*(1), 81–102. doi:10.1504/IJMHEUR.2014.058863

Raquel, C. R., & Naval, P. C. Jr. (2005). An effective use of crowding distance in multiobjective particle swarm optimization. In *Proceedings of the 7th conference on Genetic and evolutionary computation (GECCO-05)*. ACM. doi:10.1145/1068009.1068047

Rasmussen, C., & Williams, C. (2006). *Gaussian processes for machine learning*. MIT Press.

Rasteiro, M. G., Silva, R. C., Garcia, F. A., & Faia, P. M. (2011). Electrical tomography: A review of configurations and applications to particulate processes. *Kona Powder and Particle Journal*, *29*(0), 67–80. doi:10.14356/kona.2011010

Ratnaweera, A., Halgamuge, S., & Watson, H. (2004). Self-organizing hierarchical particle swarm optimizer with time-varying acceleration coefficients. *IEEE Transactions on Evolutionary Computation*, *8*(3), 240–255. doi:10.1109/TEVC.2004.826071

Ratniyomcha, T., & Kulworawanichpong, T. (2009). Evaluation of voltage stability indices by using Monte Carlo simulation. *Proceedings of the 4th IASME / WSEAS International Conference on Energy & Environment (EE'09)*, 297-302.

Rawlings, J. (2000). Tutorial overview of model predictive control. *IEEE Control Systems Magazine*, *20*(3), 38–52. doi:10.1109/37.845037

Rawlings, J., & Mayne, D. (2009). *Model predictive control theory and design*. Nob Hill Publishing.

Rechenberg, I. (1973). *Evolutionsstrategie: Optimierung technischer Systeme nach Prinzipien der biologischen Evolution*. Stuttgart, Germany: Frommann-Holzboog.

Reddy, K. S., Panwar, L. K., Kumar, R., & Panigrahi, B. K. (2016). Distributed resource scheduling in smart grid with electric vehicle deployment using fireworks algorithm. *Journal of Modern Power Systems and Clean Energy*, *4*(2), 188–199. doi:10.1007/s40565-016-0195-6

Reynolds, R. G. (1994). An introduction to cultural algorithms. *Proceedings of the Third Annual Conference on Evolutionary Programming*, 131-139.

Riane, F., Artiba, A., & Elmaghraby, S. E. (1998). A hybrid three stage flow shop problem: Efficient heuristics to minimize makespan. *European Journal of Operational Research*, *109*, 321–329. doi:10.1016/S0377-2217(98)00060-5

Ribas, I., Leisten, R., & Framiñan, J. M. (2010). Review and classification of hybrid flow shop scheduling problems from a production system and a solutions procedure perspective. *Computers & Operations Research*, *37*(8), 1439–1454. doi:10.1016/j.cor.2009.11.001

Ribeiro, R. R., Feitosa, A. R., de Souza, R. E., & dos Santos, W. P. (2014a). A modified differential evolution algorithm for the reconstruction of electrical impedance tomography images. In 5th *ISSNIP-IEEE Biosignals and Biorobotics Conference (2014): Biosignals and Robotics for Better and Safer Living (BRC)* (pp. 1–6). IEEE. doi:10.1109/BRC.2014.6880982

Ribeiro, R. R., Feitosa, A. R., de Souza, R. E., & dos Santos, W. P. (2014c). Reconstruction of electrical impedance tomography images using genetic algorithms and non-blind search. In *2014 IEEE 11th International Symposium on Biomedical Imaging (ISBI)* (pp. 153–156). IEEE. doi:10.1109/ISBI.2014.6867832

Ribeiro, R. R. (2016). *Reconstrução de imagens de tomografia por impedância elétrica usando evolução diferencial. Dissertação (Mestrado)*. Universidade Federal de Pernambuco.

Ribeiro, R. R., Feitosa, A. R., de Souza, R. E., & dos Santos, W. P. (2014b). Reconstruction of electrical impedance tomography images using chaotic self adaptive ring-topology differential evolution and genetic algorithms. In *2014 IEEE International Conference on Systems, Man, and Cybernetics (SMC)* (pp. 2605–2610). IEEE. doi:10.1109/SMC.2014.6974320

Riseman, E. M., & Arbib, M. A. (1977). Survey: Computational techniques in the visual segmentation of static scenes. *Computer Vision Graphics and Image Processing*, *6*(3), 221–276. doi:10.1016/S0146-664X(77)80028-2

Rolnik, V. P., & Seleghim, P. Jr. (2006). A specialized genetic algorithm for the electrical impedance tomography of two-phase flows. *Journal of the Brazilian Society of Mechanical Sciences and Engineering*, *28*(4), 378–389. doi:10.1590/S1678-58782006000400002

Rosenberg, R. S. (1967). *Simulation of genetic populations with biochemical properties* (Ph.D. Thesis). University of Michigan, Ann Arbor, MI.

Rosin, P. L. (2001). Unimodal thresholding. *Pattern Recognition*, *34*(11), 2083–2096. doi:10.1016/S0031-3203(00)00136-9

Roth, M., & Wicker, S. (2003). Termite: ad-hoc networking with stigmergy. *GLOBECOM '03, IEEE Global Telecommunications Conference*, 5, 2937-2941.

Rui, H., Yuzhou, C., & Liuqing, Y. (2017). Multi-constrained QoS routing based on PSO for named data networking. Multi-constrained QoS routing based on PSO, for named data networking. *IET Communications*, *11*(8), 1251–1255. doi:10.1049/iet-com.2016.0783

Ruiz, R., Serifoğlu, F. S., & Urlings, T. (2008). Modeling realistic hybrid flexible flowshop scheduling problems. *Computers & Operations Research*, *35*(4), 1151–1175. doi:10.1016/j.cor.2006.07.014

Ruiz, R., & Vazquez-Rodriguez, J. A. (2010). The hybrid flow shop scheduling problem. *European Journal of Operational Research*, *205*(1), 1–18. doi:10.1016/j.ejor.2009.09.024

Runkle, R. C., Bernstein, A., & Vanier, P. E. (2010). Securing special nuclear material: Recent advances in neutron detection and their role in nonproliferation. *Journal of Applied Physics*, *108*(11), 13. doi:10.1063/1.3503495

Russell, S. J., & Norvig, P. (2002). Artificial intelligence: a modern approach (International Edition). Academic Press.

Safdar, R., Hazlie, M., Hamzah, A., Kanendra, N., Javed, A. L., Anis, S., & Mohd, K. (2016). Minimum-features-based ANN-PSO approach for islanding detection in distribution system. *IET Renewable Power Generation*, *10*(9), 1255–1263. doi:10.1049/iet-rpg.2016.0080

Saha, S., & Bandyopadhyay, S. (2008). Application of a new symmetry-based cluster validity index for satellite image segmentation. *IEEE Geoscience and Remote Sensing Letters*, *5*(2), 166–170. doi:10.1109/LGRS.2008.915595

Sahoo, P. K., Soltani, S., Wong, A. K. C., & Chen, Y. C. (1988). A survey of thresholding techniques. *CVGIP*, *41*, 233–260.

Saleem, M., & Farooq, M. (2005). Beesensor: A bee-inspired power aware routing algorithms. Proceedings EvoCOMNET, 136-146.

Saleem, M., Khayam, S., & Farooq, M. (2008). Formal modeling of bee ad-hoc: a bio-inspired mobile ad-hoc network routing protocol. *6th international conference on ant colony optimization and swarm intelligence*, 315–322.

Saleem, M., Di Caro, G. A., & Farooq, M. (2010). Swarm intelligence based routing protocol for wireless sensor networks: Survey and future directions. *Information Sciences*, *181*(20), 4597–4624. doi:10.1016/j.ins.2010.07.005

Sangeetha, K., Babu, T. S., & Rajasekar, N. (2016). Fireworks algorithm-based maximum power point tracking for uniform irradiation as well as under partial shading condition. In *Artificial Intelligence and Evolutionary Computations in Engineering Systems* (pp. 79–88). New Delhi: Springer. doi:10.1007/978-81-322-2656-7_8

Sankaran, A., Jain, A., Vashisth, T., Vatsa, M., & Singh, R. (2017). Adaptive latent fingerprint segmentation using feature selection and random decision forest classification. *Information Fusion*, *34*, 1–15. doi:10.1016/j.inffus.2016.05.002

Santana, R. A., Pontes, M. R., & Bastos-Filho, C. J. A. (2009). A multiple objective particle swarm optimization approach using crowding distance and roulette wheel. *Ninth International Conference on Intelligent Systems Design and Applications*, 237–242. doi:10.1109/ISDA.2009.73

Santosa, F., & Vogelius, M. A. (1990). Backprojection Algorithm for Electrical Impedance Imaging. *SIAM Journal on Applied Mathematics*, *50*(1), 216–243. doi:10.1137/0150014

Santosh, K., & Sanjay, K. S. (2016). Hybrid BFO and PSO Swarm Intelligence Approach for Biometric Feature Optimization. *International Journal of Swarm Intelligence Research*, *7*(2), 36–62. doi:10.4018/IJSIR.2016040103

Saravanan, M., Haq, A. N., Vivekraj, A. R., & Prasad, T. (2008). Performance evaluation of the scatter search method for permutation flowshop sequencing problems. *International Journal of Advanced Manufacturing Technology*, *37*(11/12), 1200–1208. doi:10.1007/s00170-007-1053-5

Sardar, A., Singh, A., Sahoo, R., Majumder, R., Sing, R., & Sarkar, R. (2014). An efficient ant colony based routing algorithm for better quality of services in MANET. In *ICT & CI* (pp. 233–240). Springer. doi:10.1007/978-3-319-03107-1_26

Sarfi, V., Niazazari, I., & Livani, H. (2016, September). Multiobjective fireworks optimization framework for economic emission dispatch in microgrids. In *North American Power Symposium (NAPS)*, 2016 (pp. 1-6). IEEE. doi:10.1109/NAPS.2016.7747896

Sarfraz, S., Jahanzaib, M., Wasim, A., Hussain, S., & Aziz, H. (2017). Investigating the effects of as-casted and in situ heat-treated squeeze casting of Al-3.5% Cu alloy. *International Journal of Advanced Manufacturing Technology*, *89*(9-12), 3547–3561. doi:10.1007/s00170-016-9350-5

Sargo, J. A. G. (2013). *Binary Fish School Search applied to Feature Selection*. Academic Press.

Sargo, J. A., Vieira, S. M., Sousa, J. M., & Bastos Filho, C. J. (2014, July). Binary Fish School Search applied to feature selection: Application to ICU readmissions. In *Fuzzy Systems (FUZZ-IEEE), 2014 IEEE International Conference on* (pp. 1366-1373). IEEE.

Sarkar, S., Das, S., & Chaudhuri, S. (2016). Hyper-Spectral image segmentation Renyi entropy based multi-level thresholding aided with differential evolution. *Expert System with Applications, 50*, 120-129.

Sarkar, S., Paul, S., Burman, R., Das, S., & Chaudhuri, S. S. (2015). A Fuzzy Entropy Based Multi-Level Image Thresholding Using Differential Evolution. *SEMCCO*, *2014*, 386–395.

Sawik, T. (2000). Mixed integer programming for scheduling flexible flow lines with limited intermediate buffers. *Mathematical and Computer Modelling*, *31*(13), 39–52. doi:10.1016/S0895-7177(00)00110-2

Sawik, T. (2002). An exact approach for batch scheduling in flexible flow lines with limited intermediate buffers. *Mathematical and Computer Modelling*, *36*(4), 461–471. doi:10.1016/S0895-7177(02)00176-0

Schachner, E. (2013). How Has the Human Brain Evolved? *Scientific American Mind*, *24*(3). Retrieved from http://www.scientificamerican.com/article/how-has-human-brain-evolved/

Schaefer, A., Schneegass, D., Sterzing, V., & Udluft, S. (2007). A neural reinforcement learning approach to gas turbine control. *IEEE International Conference on Neural Networks - Conference Proceedings*, 1691-1696. doi:10.1109/IJCNN.2007.4371212

Schaffer, J. D. (1985). Multiple objective optimization with vector evaluated genetic algorithm. *Proceedings of 1st International Conference on Genetic Algorithms*, 93–100.

Semet, Y., O'Reilly, U., & Durand, F. (2004). An Interactive Artificial Ant Approach to Non-Photorealistic Rendering. Springer-Verlag.

Sensarma, D., & Majumder, K. (2012). A comparative analysis of the ant based systems for QoS routing in MANET. In *International Conference, SNDS,* (pp. 485–496). Springer. doi:10.1007/978-3-642-34135-9_47

Serifoğlu, S. F. S., & Tiryaki, I. U. (2002). Multiprocessor task scheduling in multistage hybrid flow-shops: a simulated annealing approach. *Proceedings of the 2nd International Conference on Responsive Manufacturing*, 270–274.

Serifoğlu, S. F. S., & Ulusoy, G. (2004). Multiprocessor task scheduling in multistage hybrid flow shops: A genetic algorithm approach. *The Journal of the Operational Research Society, 55*(5), 504–512. doi:10.1057/palgrave.jors.2601716

Sha, D. Y., & Lin, H. H. (2010). A multi-objective PSO for job-shop scheduling problems. *Expert Systems with Applications, 37*(2), 1065–1070. doi:10.1016/j.eswa.2009.06.041

Sheikhpour, R., Sarram, M. A., & Sheikhpour, R. (2016). Particle swarm optimization for bandwidth determination and feature selection of kernel density estimation based classifiers in diagnosis of breast cancer. *Applied Soft Computing, 40,* 113–131. doi:10.1016/j.asoc.2015.10.005

Shenassa, M. H., & Mahmoodi, M. (2006). A novel intelligent method for task scheduling in multiprocessor systems using genetic algorithm. *Journal of the Franklin Institute, 343*(4-5), 361–371. doi:10.1016/j.jfranklin.2006.02.022

Shenfield, A., & Rostami, S. (2015, August). A multi objective approach to evolving artificial neural networks for coronary heart disease classification. In *Computational Intelligence in Bioinformatics and Computational Biology (CIBCB), 2015 IEEE Conference on* (pp. 1-8). IEEE. doi:10.1109/CIBCB.2015.7300294

Shen, M., Zhan, Z. H., Chen, W. N., Gong, Y. J., Zhang, J., & Li, Y. (2014). Bi-Velocity Discrete Particle Swarm Optimization and its Application to Multicast Routing Problem in Communication Networks. *IEEE Transactions on Industrial Electronics, 61*(12), 7141–7151. doi:10.1109/TIE.2014.2314075

Shi, Y. (2011). *Brain storm optimization algorithm.* Academic Press.

Shi, Y. H. (2011). Brain storm optimization algorithm. Advances in Swarm Intelligence in Lecture Notes in Computer Science, 728, 303-309.

Shi, Y. H. (2011). Brain storm optimization algorithm. In Y. Tan, Y. Shi, Y. Chai, & G. Wang (Eds.), *Proceedings of the Second International Conference On Advances in Swarm Intelligence, Chongqing, China* (LNCS 6728, pp. 303-309). Springer. doi:10.1007/978-3-642-21515-5_36

Shi, Y., & Eberhart, R. (1998). *A modified particle swarm optimizer.* Paper presented at the IEEE International Congress on Evolutionary Computation.

Shi, Y., & Eberhart, R. (2008). Population diversity of particle swarms. In *Proceedings of the 2008 Congress on Evolutionary Computation (CEC 2008)* (pp. 1063-1067). Academic Press. doi:10.1109/CEC.2008.4630928

Shiau, D. F., Cheng, S. C., & Huang, Y. M. (2008). Proportionate flexible flow shop scheduling via a hybrid constructive genetic algorithm. *Expert Systems with Applications, 34*(2), 1133–1143. doi:10.1016/j.eswa.2006.12.002

Shi, Y. (2014). Developmental Swarm Intelligence: Developmental Learning Perspective of Swarm Intelligence Algorithms. *International Journal of Swarm Intelligence Research, 5*(1), 36–54. doi:10.4018/ijsir.2014010102

Shi, Y. H. (2011). An optimization algorithm based on brainstorming process. *International Journal of Swarm Intelligence Research,* 2(4), 35–62. doi:10.4018/IJSIR.2011100103

Shi, Y., & Eberhart, R. (1998). A modified particle swarm optimizer. *Proceedings of the 1998 Congress on Evolutionary Computation (CEC1998)*, 69-73. doi:10.1109/ICEC.1998.699146

Shi, Y., & Eberhart, R. (2009). Monitoring of particle swarm optimization. *Frontiers of Computer Science*, *3*(1), 31–37. doi:10.1007/s11704-009-0008-4

Shi, Y., Xue, J., & Wu, Y. (2013). Multi-Objective Optimization Based on Brain Storm Optimization Algorithm. *International Journal of Swarm Intelligence Research*, *4*(3), 1–21. doi:10.4018/ijsir.2013070101

Shuangxin, W., Guibin, T., Dingli, Y., & Yijiang, L. (2015). Dynamic Particle Swarm Optimization with Any Irregular Initial Small-World Topology. *International Journal of Swarm Intelligence Research*, *6*(4), 1–23. doi:10.4018/IJSIR.2015100101

Sierra, M. R., & Coello, C. A. C. (2005). Improving PSO-based multi-objective optimization using crowding, mutation and ∈-dominance. *Evolutionary Multi-Criterion Optimization*, 505-519.

Simon, D. (2008). Biogeography-based optimization. *IEEE Transactions on Evolutionary Computation*, *12*(6), 702–713. doi:10.1109/TEVC.2008.919004

Singh, J. G., Singh, S. N., & Srivastava, S. C. (2006). Placement of FACTS controllers for enhancing power system loadability. In *Power India Conference*. IEEE.

Singh, M. R., & Mahapatra, S. S. (2011). A swarm optimization approach for flexible flow shop scheduling with multiprocessor tasks. *International Journal of Advanced Manufacturing Technology*, *62*(1-4), 267–277. doi:10.1007/s00170-011-3807-3

Singh, S., & Singh, J. N. (2012). *Application of Particle Swarm Optimization: In the field of Image Processing*. LAP LAMBERT Academic Publishing.

Sjoden, G. E., Detwiler, R., LaVigne, E., & Baciak, J. E. Jr. (2009). Positive SNM gamma detection achieved through synthetic enhancement of sodium iodide detector spectra. *IEEE Transactions on Nuclear Science*, *56*(3), 1329–1339. doi:10.1109/TNS.2009.2014757

Sjoden, G. E., Maniscalco, J., & Chapman, M. (2012). Recent advances in the use of ASEDRA in post processing scintillator spectra for resolution enhancement. *Journal of Radioanalytical and Nuclear Chemistry*, *291*(2), 365–371. doi:10.1007/s10967-011-1335-0

Smith, R. (2002). *The 7 Levels of Change* (2nd ed.). Tapeslry Press.

Solihin, M., & Akmeliawati, R. (2010). Particle swam optimization for stabilizing controller of a self-erecting linear inverted pendulum. *International Journal of Electrical and Electronic Systems Research*, *2*, 13–23.

Solis, F. J., & Wets, R. J. B. (1981). Minimization by random search techniques. *Mathematics of Operations Research*, *6*(1), 19–30. doi:10.1287/moor.6.1.19

Souissi, N., Souissi, S., Niniven, C. L., Amar, M. B., Bradai, C., & Elhalouani, F. (2014). Optimization of squeeze casting parameters for 2017A wrought Al alloy using Taguchi method. *Metals*, *4*(2), 141–154. doi:10.3390/met4020141

Souza, L. S., de Miranda, P. B., Prudencio, R. B., & Barros, F. D. A. (2011, November). A multi-objective particle swarm optimization for test case selection based on functional requirements coverage and execution effort. In *Tools with UCI Machine Learning Repository: Data Sets*. Retrieved 21 June 2017, from https://archive.ics.uci.edu/ml/datasets.html

Spears, W. M., De Jong, K. A., Bäck, T., Fogel, D. B., & De Garis, H. (1993). *An overview of evolutionary computation*. Academic Press.

Stinnett, J., & Sullivan, C. J. (2013). An automated isotope identification algorithm using Bayesian statistics. *IEEE Nuclear Science Symposium Conference Record.*

Storn, R., & Price, K. (1997). Differential evolution-a simple and efficient heuristic for global optimization over continuous spaces. *Journal of Global Optimization, 11*(4), 341–359. doi:10.1023/A:1008202821328

Suganthan, P. N., Hansen, N., Liang, J. J., Deb, K., Chen, Y., Auger, A., & Tiwari, S. (2005). *Problem definitions and evaluation criteria for the CEC 2005 special session on real-parameter optimization.* KanGAL Report, 2005005.

Suganthan, P.N., Hansen, N., Liang, J.J., Deb, K., Chen, Y.-P., Auger, A., & Tiwari, S. (2005). *Problem definitions and evolution criteria for the CEC 2005 special session on real-parameter optimization.* Nanyang Technol. Univ., Singapore, Tech. Rep. and KanGAL Rep. 2005005.

Sullivan, C. J., Martinez, M. E., & Garner, S. E. (2006). Wavelet analysis of sodium iodide spectra. *IEEE Transactions on Nuclear Science, 53*(5), 2916–2922. doi:10.1109/TNS.2006.881909

Sullivan, C. J., & Stinnett, J. (2015). Validation of a Bayesian-based isotope identification algorithm. *Nuclear Instruments & Methods in Physics Research. Section A, Accelerators, Spectrometers, Detectors and Associated Equipment, 784*, 298–305. doi:10.1016/j.nima.2014.11.113

Sun, C., Duan, H., & Shi, Y. (2013). Optimal Satellite Formation Reconfiguration Based on Closed-Loop Brain Storm Optimization. *Computational Intelligence Magazine, IEEE, 8*(4), 39–51. doi:10.1109/MCI.2013.2279560

Sundaram, R. K. (1996). *A First Course in Optimization Theory.* Cambridge University Press. doi:10.1017/CBO9780511804526

Surekha, B., Kaushik, L. K., Panduy, A. K., Vundavilli, P. R., & Parappagoudar, M. B. (2012). Multi-objective optimization of green sand mould system using evolutionary algorithms. *International Journal of Advanced Manufacturing Technology, 58*(1-4), 9–17. doi:10.1007/s00170-011-3365-8

Sutton, R. (1996). Generalization in reinforcement learning: Successful examples using sparse coarse coding. *Advances in Neural Information Processing Systems, 8*, 1038–1044.

Sutton, R., & Barto, A. (1998). *Reinforcement learning: An introduction.* Cambridge, MA: MIT Press.

Swann, W. H. (1964). *Report on the development of a new direct search method of optimization.* Research Note (64).

Syam, W. P., & Al-Harkan, I. M. (2012). Improvement and comparison of three metaheuristics to optimize flexible flowshop scheduling problems. *International Journal of Engineering Science and Technology, 4*, 373–383.

Tabassum, H., Siddique, U., Hossain, E., & Hossain, M. J. (2014). Downlink Performance of Cellular System with Base Station Sleeping, User Association ans Scheduling. *IEEE Transactions on Wireless Communications, 13*(10), 5752–5767. doi:10.1109/TWC.2014.2336249

Taleizadeh, A. A., & Cárdenas-Barrón, L. E. (2013). Metaheuristic Algorithms for Supply Chain Management Problems. In I. Management Association (Ed.), Supply Chain Management: Concepts, Methodologies, Tools, and Applications (pp. 1814-1837). Hershey, PA: Business Science Reference. doi:10.4018/978-1-4666-2625-6.ch106

Tang, L., Xuan, H., & Liu, J. (2006). A new Lagrangian relaxation algorithm for hybrid flowshop scheduling to minimize total weighted completion time. *Computers & Operations Research, 33*(11), 3344–3359. doi:10.1016/j.cor.2005.03.028

Tan, Y. (2010). Particle Swarm Optimization Algorithms Inspired by Immunity-Clonal Mechanism and Their Applications to Spam Detection. *International Journal of Swarm Intelligence Research, 1*(1), 64–86. doi:10.4018/jsir.2010010104

Tan, Y. (2015). Fireworks Algorithm with Dynamic Search. In *Fireworks Algorithm* (pp. 103–117). Springer Berlin Heidelberg. doi:10.1007/978-3-662-46353-6_7

Tan, Y. (2015). *Fireworks Algorithm: A Novel Swarm Intelligence Optimization Method.* Springer. doi:10.1007/978-3-662-46353-6

Tan, Y. (2015a). Adaptive Fireworks Algorithm. In *Fireworks Algorithm* (pp. 119–131). Springer Berlin Heidelberg. doi:10.1007/978-3-662-46353-6_8

Tan, Y. (2015b). Cooperative Fireworks Algorithm. In *Fireworks Algorithm* (pp. 133–149). Springer Berlin Heidelberg. doi:10.1007/978-3-662-46353-6_9

Tan, Y., Yu, C., Zheng, S., & Ding, K. (2013). Introduction to fireworks algorithm. *International Journal of Swarm Intelligence Research, 4*(4), 39–70. doi:10.4018/ijsir.2013100103

Tan, Y., & Zhu, Y. (2010). Fireworks algorithm for optimization. In *Advances in Swarm Intelligence* (Vol. 6145, pp. 355–364). Springer Berlin Heidelberg. doi:10.1007/978-3-642-13495-1_44

Tao, W. B., Tian, J. W., & Liu, J. (2003). Image segmentation by three-level thresholding based on maximum fuzzy entropy and genetic algorithm. *Pattern Recognition Letters, 24*(16), 3069–3078. doi:10.1016/S0167-8655(03)00166-1

Tasca, M., Plastino, A., Ribeiro, C., & Zadrozny, B. (2017). A Fast and Effective Strategy for Feature Selection in High-dimensional Datasets. *Journal of Information and Data Management, 7*(2), 155.

Tasgetiren, M. F., Liang, Y. C., Sevkli, M., & Gencyilmaz, G. (2007). A particle swarm optimization algorithm for makespan and total flowtime minimization in the permutation flowshop sequencing problem. *European Journal of Operational Research, 177*(3), 1930–1947. doi:10.1016/j.ejor.2005.12.024

Tehrani, J. N., Jin, C., McEwan, A., & van Schaik, A. (2010). A comparison between compressed sensing algorithms in electrical impedance tomography. In *2010 Annual International Conference of the IEEE Engineering in Medicine and Biology* (pp. 3109–3112). IEEE. doi:10.1109/IEMBS.2010.5627165

Ting, T. O., & Lee, T. S. (2012). Drilling optimization via particle swarm optimization. *International Journal of Swarm Intelligence Research, 3*(1), 43–54. doi:10.4018/jsir.2012010103

Tinney, W. F., & Hart, C. E. (1967, November). Power Flow- Solution by Newton's Method. *IEEE Transactions, 86*, 1449.

Tiwari, P. K., & Sood, Y. R. (2012). Efficient and optimal approach for location and parameter setting of multiple unified power flow controllers for a deregulated power sector. *IET Generation, Transmission & Distribution, 6*(10), 958–967. doi:10.1049/iet-gtd.2011.0722

Tombaz, S., Han, S. W., Sung, K. W., & Zander, J. (2014). Energy Efficient Network Deployment with Cell DTX. *IEEE Communications Letters, 18*(6), 977–980. doi:10.1109/LCOMM.2014.2323960

Tombe, F. D. (2012). *Maxwell's original equations.* The General Science Journal.

Torres, C. E., Rossi, L. F., Keffer, J., Li, K., & Shen, C.-C. (2010). Modeling, analysis and simulation of ant-based network routing protocols. *Swarm Intelligence, 4*(3), 221–244. doi:10.1007/s11721-010-0043-7

Tosun, Ö. (2014). Artificial Bee Colony Algorithm. In J. Wang (Ed.), *Encyclopedia of Business Analytics and Optimization* (pp. 179–192). Hershey, PA: Business Science Reference. doi:10.4018/978-1-4666-5202-6.ch018

Tosun, Ö. (2014). Cuckoo Search Algorithm. In J. Wang (Ed.), *Encylopedia of Business Analytics and Optimization* (pp. 558–564). IGI Global. doi:10.4018/978-1-4666-5202-6.ch050

Tran, T. H., & Ng, K. M. (2013). A hybrid water flow algorithm for multi-objective flexible flow shop scheduling problems. *Engineering Optimization*, *45*(4), 483–502. doi:10.1080/0305215X.2012.685072

Tseng, C. T., Liao, C. J., & Liao, T. X. (2008). A note on two-stage hybrid flowshop scheduling with missing operations. *Computers & Industrial Engineering*, *54*(3), 695–704. doi:10.1016/j.cie.2007.09.005

Tsoukalas, L. H., & Uhring, R. E. (1997). *Fuzzy and Neural Approaches in Engineering*. John Wiley and Sons.

Tsoulfanidis, N., & Landsberger, S. (2013). *Measurement and detection of radiation.* CRC press.

Tuba, M., Bacanin, N., & Alihodzic, A. (2015a, April). Multilevel image thresholding by fireworks algorithm. In *Radioelektronika (RADIOELEKTRONIKA), 2015 25th international conference* (pp. 326-330). IEEE. doi:10.1109/RADIOELEK.2015.7129057

Tuba, M., Bacanin, N., & Beko, M. (2015b, April). Fireworks algorithm for RFID network planning problem. In *Radioelektronika (RADIOELEKTRONIKA), 2015 25th International Conference* (pp. 440-444). IEEE. doi:10.1109/RADIOELEK.2015.7129049

Tuba, E., Tuba, M., & Beko, M. (2016, June). Support vector machine parameters optimization by enhanced fireworks algorithm. In *International Conference in Swarm Intelligence* (pp. 526-534). Springer International Publishing. doi:10.1007/978-3-319-41000-5_52

Valian, E., Mohanna, S., & Tavakoli, S. (2011). Improved cuckoo search algorithm for feed forward neural network training. *International Journal of Artificial Intelligence and Applications*, *2*(3), 36–43. doi:10.5121/ijaia.2011.2304

Valian, E., Tavakoli, S., Mohanna, S., & Haghi, A. (2013). Improved cuckoo search for reliability optimization problems. *Computers & Industrial Engineering*, *64*(1), 459–468. doi:10.1016/j.cie.2012.07.011

Van Heerden, K., Fujimoto, Y., & Kawamura, A. (2014). A combination of particle swarm optimization and model predictive control on graphics hardware for real-time trajectory planning of the under-actuated nonlinear acrobot. *2014 IEEE 13th International Workshop on Advanced Motion Control (AMC)*, 464-469.

Vauhkonen, M., Lionheart, W. R., Heikkinen, L. M., Vauhkonen, P. J., & Kaipio, J. P. (2001). A MATLAB package for the EIDORS project to reconstruct two-dimensional EIT images. *Physiological Measurement*, *22*(1), 107–111. doi:10.1088/0967-3334/22/1/314 PMID:11236871

VenkateswaraRao, B., & Nagesh Kumar, G. V. (2014). Optimal Location of Thyristor Controlled Series Capacitor for reduction of Transmission Line losses using bat Search Algorithm. *WSEAS Transactions on Power Systems, 9*, 459-470.

Vesterstroem, J., & Thomsen, R. (2004). A comparative study of differential evolution, particle swarmoptimization, and evolutionary algorithms on numerical benchmark problems. *Proc. IEEE Congr. Evolutionary Computation,* 1980–1987.

Vijian, P., & Arunachalam, V. P. (2007). Modelling and multi objective optimization of LM24 aluminium alloy squeeze cast process parameters using genetic algorithm. *Journal of Materials Processing Technology, 186*(1), 82–86. doi:10.1016/j.jmatprotec.2006.12.019

Vundavilli, P. R., Kumar, J. P., & Parappagoudar, M. B. (2013). Weighted average-based multi-objective optimization of tube spinning process using non-traditional optimization techniques. *International Journal of Swarm Intelligence Research*, *4*(3), 42–57. doi:10.4018/ijsir.2013070103

Walton, S., Hassan, O., & Morgan, K. (2013). Reduced order mesh optimization using proper orthogonal decomposition and a modified cuckoo search. *International Journal for Numerical Methods in Engineering*, *93*(5), 527–550. doi:10.1002/nme.4400

Wang, G., Wang, Y., & Tao, X. (2009). An ant colony clustering routing algorithm for wireless sensor networks. *Third international conference on genetic and evolutionary computing*, 670–73. doi:10.1109/WGEC.2009.22

Wang, C., Lavernia, E. J., Wu, G., Liu, W., & Ding, W. (2016). Influence of pressure and temperature on microstructure and mechanical behavior of squeeze cast Mg-10Gd-3Y-0.5Zr alloy. *Metallurgical and Materials Transactions. A, Physical Metallurgy and Materials Science*, *47*(8), 4104–4115. doi:10.1007/s11661-016-3546-z

Wang, G.-G., Gandomi, A. H., Alavi, A. H., & Deb, S. (2016). A hybrid method based on krill herd and quantum-behaved particle swarm optimization. *Neural Computing & Applications*, *27*(4), 989–1006. doi:10.1007/s00521-015-1914-z

Wang, H. M., Chou, F. D., & Wu, F. C. (2010). A simulated annealing for hybrid flow shop scheduling with multiprocessor tasks to minimize makespan. *International Journal of Advanced Manufacturing Technology*, *53*(5-8), 761–776. doi:10.1007/s00170-010-2868-z

Wang, S., & Liu, M. (2013). A heuristic method for two-stage hybrid flow shop with dedicated machines. *Computers & Operations Research*, *40*(1), 438–450. doi:10.1016/j.cor.2012.07.015

Weszka, J. S. (1978). A survey of threshold selection techniques. *CGIP*, *7*(2), 259–265.

Wolpert, D. H., & Macready, W. G. (1997). No free lunch theorems for optimization. *IEEE Transactions on Evolutionary Computation*, *1*(1), 67–82. doi:10.1109/4235.585893

Wong, A. K. C., & Sahoo, P. K. (1989). A gray-level threshold selection method based on maximum entropy principle. *IEEE Transactions on Systems, Man, and Cybernetics*, *19*(4), 866–871. doi:10.1109/21.35351

Wu, J., Zhou, S., & Niu, Z. (2013). Traffic-aware Base Station Sleeping Control and Power Matching for Energy-delay Tradeoffs in Green Cellular Networks. *IEEE Transactions on Wireless Communications*, *12*(8), 4196–4209. doi:10.1109/TWC.2013.071613.122092

Wu, Z., Chow, T. W. S., Cheng, S., & Shi, Y. (2013). Contour gradient optimization. *International Journal of Swarm Intelligence Research*, *2*(2), 1–28. doi:10.4018/jsir.2013040101

Xie, J., & Wang, X. (2005). Complexity and algorithms for two-stage flexible flowshop scheduling with availability constraints. *Computers & Mathematics with Applications (Oxford, England)*, *50*(10), 1629–1638. doi:10.1016/j.camwa.2005.07.008

Xing, B., & Gao, W. (2014). Post-Disassembly Part-Machine Clustering Using Artificial Neural Networks and Ant Colony Systems. In *Computational Intelligence in Remanufacturing* (pp. 135–150). Hershey, PA: Information Science Reference. doi:10.4018/978-1-4666-4908-8.ch008

Xing, B., & Gao, W. (2014a). Overview of Computational Intelligence. In *Computational Intelligence in Remanufacturing* (pp. 18–36). Hershey, PA: Information Science Reference. doi:10.4018/978-1-4666-4908-8.ch002

Xue, B., Zhang, M., & Browne, W. N. (2013a). Particle swarm optimization for feature selection in classification: A multi-objective approach. *IEEE Transactions on Cybernetics, 43*(6), 1656-1671. doi:10.1109/TSMCB.2012.2227469

Xue, B., Cervante, L., Shang, L., Browne, W. N., & Zhang, M. (2014). Binary PSO and rough set theory for feature selection: A multi-objective filter based approach. *International Journal of Computational Intelligence and Applications*, *13*(2). doi:10.1142/S1469026814500096

Xue, B., Zhang, M., & Browne, W. N. (2015). A comprehensive comparison on evolutionary feature selection approaches to classification. *International Journal of Computational Intelligence and Applications*, *14*(2). doi:10.1142/S146902681550008X

Xue, B., Zhang, M., Browne, W. N., & Yao, X. (2016). A survey on evolutionary computation approaches to feature selection. *IEEE Transactions on Evolutionary Computation*, *20*(4), 606–626. doi:10.1109/TEVC.2015.2504420

Xue, J., Wu, Y., Shi, Y., & Cheng, S. (2012). Brain storm optimization algorithm for multi-objective optimization problems. In *Advances in Swarm Intelligence* (pp. 513–519). Springer Berlin Heidelberg. doi:10.1007/978-3-642-30976-2_62

Xu, F., Chen, H., Gong, X., & Mei, Q. (2016). Fast nonlinear model predictive control on FPGA using particle swarm optimization. *IEEE Transactions on Industrial Electronics*, *63*(1), 310–321. doi:10.1109/TIE.2015.2464171

Yang, X. S. (2010). A New Metaheuristic bat Inspired Algorithm. Nature Inspired Cooperative Strategies for Optimization (NISCO 2010), Studies in Computational Intelligence. Springer. doi:10.1007/978-3-642-12538-6_6

Yang, L. J. (2007). The effect of solidification time in squeeze casting of aluminium and zinc alloy. *Journal of Materials Processing Technology*, *192-193*, 114–120. doi:10.1016/j.jmatprotec.2007.04.025

Yang, X. S. (2008). *Nature-Inspired Metaheuristic Algorithms*. Luniver Press.

Yang, X. S. (2010). *Firefly algorithm, Levy flights and global optimization. In Research and Development in Intelligent Systems XXVI* (pp. 209–218). London, UK: Springer. doi:10.1007/978-1-84882-983-1_15

Yang, X. S. (2010). Firefly algorithm, stochastic test functions and design optimisation. *International Journal of Bio-inspired Computation*, *2*(2), 78–84. doi:10.1504/IJBIC.2010.032124

Yang, X. S. (2011). Bat Algorithm for Multi objective Optimization. *International Journal of Bio-inspired Computation*, *3*(5), 267–274. doi:10.1504/IJBIC.2011.042259

Yang, X. S. (2011). Chaos-Enhanced Firefly Algorithm with Automatic Parameter Tuning. *International Journal of Swarm Intelligence Research*, *2*(4), 1–11. doi:10.4018/jsir.2011100101

Yang, X. S. (2012). Nature-Inspired Metaheuristic Algorithms: Success and New Challenges. *Journal of Computer Engineering & Information Technology*, *1*(1). doi:10.4172/2324-9307.1000e101

Yang, X. S., & Deb, S. (2009). Cuckoo search via Lévy flights. *NaBIC 2009: Proceedings of the World Congress on Nature & Biologically Inspired Computing*, 210-214.

Yang, X. S., & Deb, S. (2010). Engineering Optimisation by Cuckoo Search. *International Journal of Mathematical Modelling and Numerical Optimisation*, *1*(4), 330–343. doi:10.1504/IJMMNO.2010.035430

Yang, X. S., & Deb, S. (2013). Multiobjective cuckoo search for design optimization. *Computers & Operations Research*, *40*(6), 1616–1624. doi:10.1016/j.cor.2011.09.026

Yang, X.-S. (2009). Firefly algorithms for multimodal optimization. *Stochastic Algorithms: Foundation and Applications SAGA*, *5792*, 169–178. doi:10.1007/978-3-642-04944-6_14

Yang, Y., Shi, Y., & Xia, S. (2013). Discussion mechanism based brain storm optimization algorithm. *Journal of Zhejiang University (Engineering Science)*, *47*(10), 1705–1711. doi:10.3785/j.issn.1008-973X.2013.10.002

Yang, Z., & Niu, Z. (2013). Energy Saving in Cellular Networks by Dynamic RS–BS Association and BS Switching. *IEEE Transactions on Vehicular Technology*, *62*(9), 4602–4614. doi:10.1109/TVT.2013.2265403

Yao, S. M., Chen, Z. G., & Zhu, Y. M. (2006). *The Urban Agglomerations of China*. Hefei, China: Univ. Science and Technology of China Press.

Yao, X., Liu, Y., & Lin, G. M. (1999). Evolutionary programming made faster. *IEEE Transactions on Evolutionary Computation*, *3*(2), 82–102. doi:10.1109/4235.771163

Yildiz, A. R. (2013). Cuckoo search algorithm for the selection of optimal machining parameters in milling operations. *International Journal of Advanced Manufacturing Technology*, *64*(1-4), 55–61. doi:10.1007/s00170-012-4013-7

Ying, K. C., & Lin, S. W. (2006). Multiprocessor task scheduling in multistage hybrid flowshops: An ant colony system approach. *International Journal of Production Economics*, *44*(16), 3161–3177. doi:10.1080/00207540500536939

Yin, T. (2015). *Firefly Algorithm*. Science Publisher.

Yong, S. S., Quek, T. Q. S., Kountouris, M., & Shin, H. (2013). Energy Efficient Heterogeneous Cellular Networks. *IEEE Journal on Selected Areas in Communications*, *31*(5), 840–850. doi:10.1109/JSAC.2013.130503

Yoshida, E., Shizuma, K., Endo, S., & Oka, T. (2003). Application of neural networks for the analysis of gamma-ray spectra measured with a Ge spectrometer. *Nuclear Instruments & Methods in Physics Research. Section A, Accelerators, Spectrometers, Detectors and Associated Equipment*, *484*(1-3), 557–563. doi:10.1016/S0168-9002(01)01962-3

Yosuf, M. S. (2010). *Nonlinear Predictive Control Using Particle Swarm Optimization: Application to Power Systems. Hidelberg, Germany: VDM Verlag Dr.* Müller.

You, D., Wang, X., Cheng, X., & Jiang, X. (2017). Friction modeling and analysis of injection process in squeeze casting. *Journal of Materials Processing Technology*, *239*, 42–51. doi:10.1016/j.jmatprotec.2016.08.011

Yu, C., Li, J., & Tan, Y. (2014, October). Improve enhanced fireworks algorithm with differential mutation. In *Systems, Man and Cybernetics (SMC), 2014 IEEE International Conference on* (pp. 264-269). IEEE. doi:10.1109/SMC.2014.6973918

Yu, F., Zhang, P., Xiao, W., & Choudhury, P. (2011). Communication Systems for Grid Integration of Renewable Energy Resources. *IEEE Network the Magazine of Global Internetworking*, *25*(5), 22–29. doi:10.1109/MNET.2011.6033032

Zaharis, Z. D., Gravas, I. P., Yioultsis, T. V., Lazaridis, P. I., Glover, I. A., Skeberis, C., & Xenos, T. D. (2017). Exponential Log-Periodic Antenna Design Using Improved Particle Swarm Optimization With Velocity Mutation. *IEEE Transactions on Magnetics*, *53*(6), 1–4. doi:10.1109/TMAG.2017.2660061

Zhan, Z., Zhang, J., Shi, Y., & Liu, H. (2012). A modified brain storm optimization. *Evolutionary Computation (CEC), 2012 IEEE Congress on,* 1-8. doi:10.1109/CEC.2012.6256594

Zhang, W., Xie, X.-F., & Bi, D.-C. (2004). Handling boundary constraints for numerical optimization by particle swarm flying in periodic search space. In *Proceedings of the 2004 Congress on Evolutionary Computation*, (pp. 2307-2311). Academic Press. doi:10.1109/CEC.2004.1331185

Zhang, Y. (2005). *Routing Modeling Application Simulation Environment (RMASE).* Available at: https://docs.google.com/file/d/0B-29IhEITY3bbGY2VVo2SGxxRFE/edit

Zhang, B., Zhang, M., & Zheng, Y. J. (2014). Improving Enhanced Fireworks Algorithm with New Gaussian Explosion and Population Selection Strategies. In *Advances in Swarm Intelligence* (pp. 53–63). Springer International Publishing. doi:10.1007/978-3-319-11857-4_7

Zhang, X. Y., Duan, H. B., & Jin, J. Q. (2008). DEACO: hybrid ant colony optimization with differential evolution. In *Proceedings of IEEE Congress on Evolutionary Computation.* (pp. 921–927). IEEE.

Zhang, X. Y., Duan, H. B., & Yu, Y. X. (2010). Receding horizon control for Multi-UAVs close formation control based on differential evolution. *Science China. Information Sciences*, *53*(2), 223–235. doi:10.1007/s11432-010-0036-6

Zhang, Y., Kuhn, L. D., & Fromherz, M. P. J. (2004). Improvements on Ant Routing for Sensor Networks. In *ANTS 2004, LNCS 3172* (pp. 289–313). doi:10.1007/978-3-540-28646-2_14

Zhang, Y., Simon, G., & Balogh, G. (2006). High-Level Sensor Network Simulations for Routing Performance Evaluations. *Proceedings of 3rd International Conference on Networked Sensing Systems*, 1-4.

Zhang, Y., Wang, S., & Ji, G. (2015). A comprehensive survey on particle swarm optimization algorithm and its applications. *Mathematical Problems in Engineering*.

Zhan, Z. H., Zhang, J., Li, Y., & Chung, S. H. (2009). Adaptive particle swarm optimization. *IEEE Transactions on Systems, Man, and Cybernetics. Part B, Cybernetics*, *39*(6), 1362–1381. doi:10.1109/TSMCB.2009.2015956 PMID:19362911

Zhan, Z., Zhang, J., Li, Y., & Chung, H. S. (2009). Adaptive particle swarm optimization. *IEEE Trans. Syst., Man, Cybern. Part-B. Appl. Rev.*, *39*(6), 1362–1381.

Zhan, Z., Zhang, J., Li, Y., & Shi, Y. (2011). Orthogonal learning particle swarm optimization. *IEEE Transactions on Evolutionary Computation*, *15*(6), 832–847. doi:10.1109/TEVC.2010.2052054

Zhao-Hua, L., Hua-Liang, W., Qing-Chang, Z., Kan, L., Xiao-Shi, X., & Liang-Hong, W. (2017). Parameter Estimation for VSI-Fed PMSM Based on a Dynamic PSO With Learning Strategies. *IEEE Transactions on Power Electronics*, *32*(4), 3154–3165. doi:10.1109/TPEL.2016.2572186

Zhao, M. S., Fu, A. M. N., & Yan, H. (2001). A technique of three level thresholding based on probability partition and fuzzy 3-partition. *IEEE Transactions on Fuzzy Systems*, *9*(3), 469–479. doi:10.1109/91.928743

Zheng, S., & Tan, Y. (2013, March). A unified distance measure scheme for orientation coding in identification. In *Information Science and Technology (ICIST), 2013 International Conference on* (pp. 979-985). IEEE. doi:10.1109/ICIST.2013.6747701

Zheng, S., Janecek, A., & Tan, Y. (2013). Enhanced fireworks algorithm. In *Proceedings of 2013 IEEE Congress on Evolutionary Computation, (CEC 2013)*. Cancun, Mexico: IEEE. doi:10.1109/CEC.2013.6557813

Zheng, Y. J., Song, Q., & Chen, S. Y. (2013). Multiobjective fireworks optimization for variable-rate fertilization in oil crop production. *Applied Soft Computing*, *13*(11), 4253–4263. doi:10.1016/j.asoc.2013.07.004

Zheng, Y. J., Xu, X. L., Ling, H. F., & Chen, S. Y. (2015). A hybrid fireworks optimization method with differential evolution operators. *Neurocomputing*, *148*, 75–82. doi:10.1016/j.neucom.2012.08.075

Zheng, Y., Janecek, A., & Tan, Y. (2013). Enhanced fireworks algorithm. In *IEEE Congress on Evolutionary Computation* (pp. 2069-2077). IEEE.

Zhen-xin, D. U. (2013). Fireworks Algorithm for Solving Nonlinear Equation and System. *Modern Computer*, *4*, 6.

Zhou, A., Qu, B.-Y., Li, H., Zhao, S.-Z., Suganthan, P. N., & Zhang, Q. (2011). Multiobjective evolutionary algorithms: A survey of the state of the art. *Swarm and Evolutionary Computation*, *1*(1), 32–49. doi:10.1016/j.swevo.2011.03.001

Zhou, D., Shi, Y., & Cheng, S. (2012). Brain storm optimization algorithm with modified step-size and individual generation. In *Advances in Swarm Intelligence* (pp. 243–252). Springer Berlin Heidelberg. doi:10.1007/978-3-642-30976-2_29

Zhou, Z., dos Santos, G. S., Dowrick, T., Avery, J., Sun, Z., Xu, H., & Holder, D. S. (2015). Comparison of total variation algorithms for electrical impedance tomography. *Physiological Measurement*, *36*(6), 1193–1209. doi:10.1088/0967-3334/36/6/1193 PMID:26008768

Zhu, G. P., & Kwong, S. (2010). Gbest-guided artificial bee colony algorithm for numerical function optimization. *Applied Mathematics and Computation*, *217*(7), 3166–3173. doi:10.1016/j.amc.2010.08.049

Zhu, M. H., Liu, L. G., Qi, D. X., You, Z., & Xu, A. A. (2009). Least square fitting of low resolution gamma ray spectra with cubic B-spline basis functions. *Chinese Phys. C.*, *33*(1), 24–29. doi:10.1088/1674-1137/33/1/006

Zhu, Z., Zhou, J., Ji, Z., & Shi, Y. (2011). DNA Sequence Compression Using Adaptive Particle Swarm Optimization Based Memetic Algorithm. *IEEE Transactions on Evolutionary Computation*, *15*(5), 643–658. doi:10.1109/TEVC.2011.2160399

Zitzler, E., Deb, K., & Thiele, L. (2000). Comparison of multiobjective evolutionary algorithms: Empirical results. *Evolutionary Computation*, *8*(2), 173–195. doi:10.1162/106365600568202 PMID:10843520

Zitzler, E., Laumanns, M., & Thiele, L. (2001). *SPEA2: Improving the strength Pareto evolutionary algorithm for multiobjective optimization*. Evolutionary Methods for Design Optimization and Control with Applications to Industrial Problems.

Zitzler, E., & Thiele, L. (1999). Multiobjective evolutionary algorithms: A comparative case study and the strength pareto approach. *IEEE Transactions on Evolutionary Computation*, *3*(4), 257–271. doi:10.1109/4235.797969

Zungeru, A. M., Ang, L.-M., & Seng, K. P. (2012a). Performance of Termite-hill Routing Algorithm on Sink Mobility in Wireless Sensor Networks. In Advances in Swarm Intelligence (pp. 334-343). Springer. doi:10.1007/978-3-642-31020-1_39

Zungeru, Ang, & Seng. (2013). A formal mathematical framework for modeling and simulation of wireless sensor network environments utilizing the hill-building behavior of termites. *Simulation: transactions of the Society for Modeling and Simulation International*, *89*(5), 589-615.

Zungeru, A. M., Ang, L.-M., & Prabaharan, S. R. S. (2011). Improved energy-efficient ant-based routing algorithm in wireless sensor networks. In K. Ragab, A. B. Abdullah, & N. Zaman (Eds.), *Wireless sensor networks and energy efficiency: protocols, routing and management* (pp. 420–444). Hershey, PA: IGI Global.

Zungeru, A. M., Ang, L.-M., & Seng, K. P. (2011). Ant Based Routing Protocol for Visual Sensors. *Communications in Computer and Information Science, Springer*, *252*(3), 250–264. doi:10.1007/978-3-642-25453-6_23

Zungeru, A. M., Ang, L.-M., & Seng, K. P. (2012b). Classical and swarm intelligence based routing protocols for wireless sensor networks. *Journal of Network and Computer Applications*, *35*(5), 1508–1536. doi:10.1016/j.jnca.2012.03.004

Zungeru, A. M., Ang, L.-M., & Seng, K. P. (2012c). Performance Evaluation of Ant Based Routing Protocols for Wireless Sensor Networks. *International Journal of Computer Science Issues*, *9*(3), 388–397.

About the Contributors

Miltiadis Alamaniotis received the Dipl-Ing. degree in electrical and computer engineering from the University of Thessaly, Volos, Greece, in 2005, and the M.S. and Ph.D. degrees in nuclear engineering from Purdue University, West Lafayette, IN, USA, in 2010 and 2012, respectively. His research interests include development of intelligent systems and machine learning approaches for radiation detection, signal processing, smart energy systems, smart grids, and nuclear power plant controls and instrumentation. He has been a Research Assistant Professor with the School of Nuclear Engineering, Purdue University, since 2014. Dr. Alamaniotis has served as a reviewer for several journals in the areas of nuclear science, instrumentation, artificial intelligence, and smart grids. He is an active member of the American Nuclear Society.

Valter A. F. Barbosa is a mechanical engineer's Ph.D. candidate. He received the M.Sc. degree in biomedical engineering from Federal University of Pernambuco, Recife, BRA, in 2017. His research interests include image reconstruction algorithms applied to electrical impedance tomography, and evolutionary and bioinspired computation, and neural artificial network.

Carmelo J. A. Bastos-Filho was born in Recife, Brazil, in 1978. He received the B.Sc. in electronics engineering and the M.Sc. and Ph.D. degrees in electrical engineering from Federal University of Pernambuco (UFPE) in 2000, 2003, and 2005, respectively. In 2006, he received the best Brazilian thesis award in electrical engineering. His interests are related to optical networks, swarm intelligence, evolutionary computation, multiobjective optimization, and biomedical applications. He is currently an Associate Professor at the Polytechnic School of the University of Pernambuco. He is the head of the research division of the Polytechnic School of Pernambuco and coordinates the masters course on systems engineering. He is an IEEE senior member and a Research fellow of the National Research Council of Brazil (CNPq). More information at http://scholar.google.com/citations?user=t3A96agAAAAJ&hl=en.

S. N. Bharath Bhushan is member of Core Research Group, Karnataka Government Research Centre of Sahyadri College of Engineering and Management, Mangalore, Karnataka. He completed his B.Sc from Kuvempu University, Shimoga, Karnataka and M.S. from Mysore University, Mysore, Karnataka. Currently pursuing Ph.D under VTU Belguam, on the topic "Design and Analysis of Supervised Machine Learning Algorithms for Automatic Text Mining" under the supervision of Dr. Ajit Danti, Professor and Director, Department of MCA, JNNCE, Shimoga.

Junfeng Chen received the PhD degree in control science and engineering from Zhejiang University, Hangzhou, China, in 2011. Currently, she is an associate professor in the College of IOT Engineering, Hohai University, Changzhou, China. Her research interests include swarm intelligence, artificial intelligence with uncertainty and big data analytics.

Shi Cheng received the Bachelor's degree in Mechanical and Electrical Engineering from Xiamen University, Xiamen, the Master's degree in Software Engineering from Beihang University (BUAA), Beijing, China, the Ph.D. degree in Electrical Engineering and Electronics from Liverpool University, Liverpool, United Kingdom, the Ph.D. degree in Electrical and Electronic Engineering from Xi'an Jiaotong-Liverpool University, Suzhou, China in 2005, 2008, and 2013, respectively. He is currently a lecturer with School of Computer Science, Shaanxi Normal University, Xi'an, China. His current research interests include swarm intelligence, multiobjective optimization, and data mining techniques and their applications.

D. DeepakChowdary was born in srikakulam, India in 1978. He received his Bachelor degree in Electrical and Electronics Engineering from College of Engineering, Gandhi Institute of Technology And Management (GITAM) Visakapatnam, Andhra Pradesh, India in 2000, the Master degree in Electrical Power Engineering from the College of Engineering, JNTU, Hyderabad in 2007 and He received his Doctoral degree from Jawaharlal Nehru Technological University, Hyderabad in 2014. He is presently working as Professor & Principal, Dr.L.Bullayya College of Engineering (for Women), Resapuvanipalem, Visakhapatnam. His research interests include gas insulated substations, FACTS devices, Power System Stability analysis, fuzzy logic and neural network applications, distributed generation, Partial Discharge Studies and Bearing less drives. He has published several research papers in national and international conferences and journals. He is a member of ISTE and IE.

Joseph M. Chuma is an associate professor of Telecommunication and Wireless Communications at the Botswana International University of Science and Technology. He received his PhD in Electronic Systems Engineering and MSc from University of Essex in UK and BEng from University of Nottingham UK. He has served as the Dean of the Faculty of Engineering and Technology at University of Botswana. He is serving as a board member in the Parastatals Organization in Botswana. He has also served as a postgraduate and undergraduate external examiner in a number of universities. He has authored 3 academic books and over 50 Journals and conference publications. His research interests are in the design and fabrication of Microwave components including filters and antennas for mobile and satellite communications, wireless communications and Electromagnetic field problems.

Krishna Gopal Dhal completed his B.Tech and M. Tech from Kalyani Government Engineering College. Currently he is working as Assistant Professor in Midnapore College (Autonomous). His research interests are image Processing and Nature inspired Metaheuristics.

Ítalo Dias is an undergraduate researcher in biomedical engineering at Universidade Federal de Pernambuco (UFPE) and also undergraduate student in mechanical engineering at UFPE.

Wellington Pinheiro dos Santos received a bachelor's degree in Electrical Electronics Engineering (2001) and MS in Electrical Engineering (2003) from the Federal University of Pernambuco, and Ph.D. in Electrical Engineering from the Federal University of Campina Grande (2009). He is currently a Professor (exclusive devotion) of the Department of Biomedical Engineering at the Center of Technology and Geosciences - Engineering School of Pernambuco, Federal University of Pernambuco, acting in Undergraduate Biomedical Engineering and Graduate Program in Biomedical Engineering, which was one of the founders (2011). He founded the Center for Social Technologies and Bioengineering, at the Federal University of Pernambuco, NETBio-UFPE (2012). He is member of the Graduate Program in Computer Engineering from the Polytechnic School of Pernambuco, University of Pernambuco, since 2009. He also has experience in the area of Computer Science, with an emphasis on Graphic Processing (Graphics), acting on the following themes: digital image processing, pattern recognition, computer vision, evolutionary computation, numerical methods of optimization, computational intelligence, computer graphics, virtual reality, game design and applications of Computing and Engineering in Medicine and Biology. He is a member of the Brazilian Society of Biomedical Engineering (SBEB), the Brazilian Society of Computational Intelligence, and the International Federation of Medical and Biological Engineering (IFMBE).

Mariana Gomes da Motta Macedo is studying the Master degree in Computer Engineering at the University of Pernambuco (2016). She worked in the research area of Swarm Intelligence and Multi-Objective Problems. She graduated in Computer Engineering at the University of Pernambuco (2016). Worked at Artics Mobile developing apps and websites (2015-2016). She studied the research area of Educational Data Mining. She worked at the University of Pernambuco as Laboratory Assistant (2013-2014). She studied extra courses at Pace University (2014-2015). She studied in the research area of coordination of aerial vehicles using swarm intelligence for two years (2012-2014).

Daniel Hein received his BSc degree in Computer Sciences from the University of Applied Sciences Zwickau, Germany, in 2011 and the MSc degree in Informatics from the Technische Universität München, Germany, in 2014. He is currently pursuing a PhD in Informatics at Technische Universität München, Germany, and is conducting his research in partnership with Siemens Corporate Technology. His research interests include evolutionary algorithms, like particle swarm optimization or genetic programming, interpretable reinforcement learning, and industrial application of machine learning approaches.

Alexander Hentschel graduated with a diploma degree in Physics (2007) and a diploma in Computer Science (2010) from the Humboldt-Universität zu Berlin, Germany. He did his doctorate research in the interdisciplinary field of quantum computing and quantum information science at the University of Calgary, Canada. There, he developed machine learning algorithms for quantum-enhanced measurement procedures. In 2011, Alexander continued his research in the area of applied machine learning as a Research Scientist at Siemens Corporate Technology. His current focus is interpretable reinforcement learning and swarm algorithms. In 2017, Alexander moved to Axiom Zen in Vancouver as a Senior Machine Learning Engineer.

Lucia Keleadile Ketshabetswe is a Technician in the Electronics Laboratory and an MSc student at the Botswana International University of Science and Technology (BIUST). She possesses a Telecommunications BEng (Hons) from the University of Essex in England. She was an Electronics Engineer from 2000 to 2013 at Botswana Technology Centre (BOTEC), a Research, Design and Development Organisation that has now been changed into a new entity called Botswana Institute for Technology, Research and Innovation (BITRI). Before working with BOTEC, she worked as a Telecommunications Officer for five years at the Department of Civil Aviation responsible for maintenance and repair of Telecommunications and Navigational Aids equipment.

Goran Klepac, Ph.D., works as a head of Stretegic unit in Sector of credit risk in Raiffeisenbank Austria d.d., Croatia. In several universities in Croatia, he lectures subjects in domain of data mining, predictive analyitics, decision support system, banking risk, risk evaluation models, expert system, database marketing and business intelligence. As a team leader, he successfully finished many data mining projects in different domanins like retail, finance, insurance, hospitality, telecommunications, and productions. He is an author/coauthor of several books published in Croatian and English in domain of data mining.

Prasad Krishna obtained his Bachelor Degree in Mechanical Engineering from NITK, Surathkal, India in 1983, Master's Degree in Manufacturing from IIT Madras, India and Doctoral Degree in Manufacturing (Eng Manufacturing) from the University of Michigan, Ann Arbor, USA. Prof. Krishna has more than thirty-one years of professional experience in manufacturing, precision machine tool design & development and teaching a variety of courses in the field of manufacturing and materials engineering. His research interests are in the areas of Metal Casting, Additive Manufacturing and CNC Machine Tools. Currently, Prof. Krishna is working as Professor of Mechanical Engineering and Dean (Alumni Affairs and Institutional Relations) at NITK Surathkal, India.

G. V. Nagesh Kumar was born in Visakhapatnam, India in 1977. He graduated College of Engineering, Gandhi Institute of Technology and Management, Visakhapatnam, India, Masters Degree from the College of Engineering, Andhra University, Visakhapatnam. He received his Doctoral degree from Jawaharlal Nehru Technological University, Hyderabad. He is presently working as Professor in the Department of Electrical and Electronics Engineering, Vignans Institute of Information Technology, Visakhapatnam. His research interests include gas insulated substations, FACTS devices, Power System Stability analysis, fuzzy logic and neural network applications, distributed generation, Partial Discharge Studies and Bearing less drives. He has published more than 250 research papers in national and international conferences and journals. He received "Sastra Award", "Best Paper Award" and "Best Researcher Award". He is a member of various societies, ISTE, IEEE, IE and System Society of India. He is also a reviewer for IEEE Transactions on Dielectrics and Electrical Insulation, Power Systems and a member on Board of several conferences and journals.

Ling Lin was a postgraduate student in Shenzhen University during 2010 - 2013.

Hai-Lin Liu is currently a Professor of School of applied mathematics at the Guangdong University of Technology. He received the B.S. degree in mathematics from Henan Normal University, Xinxiang, China, the M.S degree in applied mathematics from Xidian University, Xi' an, China, the Ph.D. degree in control theory and engineering from South China University of Technology, Guangzhou, China, and Post-doctor in the Institute of Electronic and Information, South China University of Technology, Guangzhou, China. His research interests include evolutionary computation and optimization, wireless network planning and optimization,and their applications.

Lili Liu has obtained the Ph.D. degree in the College of Automation, Harbin Engineering University, Harbin, China. Her research interesting includes nature inspired computing, magnetotactic bacteria optimization algorithm, DE and other computational intelligence techniques, as well as their applications in real-world problems.

Mmoloki Mangwala is a lecturer of Computer Engineering in the College of Engineering and Acting Director of Research, Development and Innovation at Botswana International University of Science and Technology (BIUST). He received his BSc degree in Computer Engineering from University of KwaZulu Natal, South Africa, MSc degree in Computer Science and PhD in Computer Science from North West University in South Africa specializing in All-Optical Switching. He has been involved in teaching Computer Systems Programming, Computer Organization and Architecture, Analogue Electronics, Operating Systems, Digital Electronics among others. Prior to joining BIUST, he was a Computer Systems Engineering lecturer at Botswana Accountancy College.

M. K. Marichelvam is working as an Assistant Professor in the Department of Mechanical Engineering, Mepco Schlenk Engineering College, Sivakasi, Tamilnadu, India. He received his BE in Mechanical Engineering from Madurai Kamaraj University in 2000 and ME in Industrial Engineering from Madurai Kamaraj University, Madurai, India in 2002 and PhD from Anna University, Chennai, Tamilnadu, India in 2015. His area of interest is manufacturing scheduling, multi-objective optimisation, heuristics, and hybrid metaheuristics. He has published more than twenty papers in the referred international journals.

Hongwei Mo is a professor in Automation College of Harbin Engineering University. He got Ph.D degree in the same University in 2005. His main research interests include natural computing, artificial immune system, datamining, intelligent system, and artificial intelligence. He had published 60 papers on artificial immune systems and nature inspired computing in international Journals and conferences. He was the Guest Editor of Special issue on Nature inspired computing and applications of Journal of Information Technology Research. He was the author of 4 books. He is the editor of 'Handbook of Artificial Immune Systems and Nature inspired computing: Applying Complex Adaptive Technologies. And he is a member of IEEE Computing Intelligence Society, IEEE Robotics and Automaton Society. He was also the program committee member of over 30 International Conferences. He serves as the member of editorial review board of the Journal of Information Technology Research, Journal of Man, Machine and Technology, Progress in Intelligent Computing and Applications and International Journal of immunocomputing and so on.

Rodrigo Ogava is an undergraduate student in biomedical engineering at Universidade Federal de Pernambuco, a research student in the area of electrical impedance tomography involved in health technology, health computing and entrepreneurship projects.

Mahesh B. Parappagoudar completed his engineering graduation in Industrial & Production Engineering from B.V. Bhoomaraddi College of Engineering and Technology, Hubli, affiliated to Karnataka University, Dharwad. He obtained his Master of Engineering degree in Production Management from Gogte Institute of Technology, affiliated to Karnataka University, Dharwad, India, in 1996. He joined Indian Institute of Technology, Kharagpur in 2004 as a research scholar, in the mechanical engineering department under the quality improvement program funded by MHRD, Govt. of India. Further, he obtained his PhD degree in Mechanical Engineering from Indian Institute of Technology, Kharagpur - 721302, India in 2008. Presently he is working as the principal and professor in Padre Conceicao College of Engineering, Verna, Goa 403722, India. He has published around 50 papers in reputed international Journals. His total experience (Industry, Teaching, Research, and Administration) extends over a period of 27 years. His biography (distinguished personality) is published in the 30th edition of Marquis Who's Who in the world 2013. His research interests include application of statistical and soft computing tools in manufacturing and industrial engineering.

Manjunath Patel G. C. received his Bachelor Degree in Mechanical Engineering from Jawaharlal Nehru National College of Engineering, Shimoga, and his MTech in Production Management from Gogte Institute of Technology, Belgaum, affiliated to Visvesvaraya Technological University, Belgaum, India, in 2009 and 2011 respectively. He has obtained his PhD in Mechanical Engineering from National Institute of Technology Karnataka, Surathkal, India. His area of interests includes Casting and Solidification, Modelling and Optimization of Manufacturing Processes.

Quande Qin received PhD degree in Management Science and Engineering from School of Business Administration, South China University of Technology, Guangzhou, China. Currently, he is a lecturer in the College of Management, Shenzhen University, Shenzhen, China. His current research interests include swarm intelligence, evolutionary optimization and their applications in management and economics.

David Ribeiro is a Computer Engineer and received his MSc in biomedical engineering from the Federal University of Pernambuco, Brazil.

Reiga R. Ribeiro graduated in Biomedical Engineering, Master Degree in Biomedical Engineering and PhD Candidate in Materials Science by the Federal University of Pernambuco. His research interests include electrical impedance tomography images reconstruction algorithms based on evolutionary and swarm optimization, image processing and biomedical instrumentation.

Thomas Runkler received his MSc and PhD in electrical engineering from the Technical University of Darmstadt, Germany, in 1992 and 1995, respectively, and was a postdoctoral researcher at the University of West Florida from 1996-1997. He has been teaching computer science at the Technische Universität München, Germany, since 1999, and was appointed adjunct professor in 2011. Since 1997 he has been working for Siemens Corporate Technology in various expert and management functions, currently as a Principal Research Scientist. His main research interests include machine learning, data analysis, pattern recognition, and optimization.

Natália Soares is an undergraduate researcher in biomedical engineering at Universidade Federal de Pernambuco (UFPE) and also undergraduate student in electronic engineering at UFPE.

Polamraju V. S. Sobhan was born in Ongole, A.P, India in 1977. He received his B.Tech. in Electrical and Electrical Engineering from SVH COE, Nagarjuna University, India in 1999 and M.E degree in Control Systems from College of Engineering, Andhra University, India in 2002. He is pursuing Ph.D. from JNT University, Kakinada, India. Presently he is working as an Associate Professor in the Department of Electrical and Electrical Engineering, VFSTR University, Guntur, India since 2006. His research interests are Optimisation, Controller design, Active magnetic bearings and bearingless drives.

João Miguel da Costa Sousa is a Full Professor with the Department of Mechanical Engineering (DEM), Instituto Superior Técnico, Universidade de Lisboa, Portugal. He is the Coordinator of the Center of Intelligent Systems, a research unit of IDMEC/IST, a private non-profit association of science, technology and training. He received the Ph.D. degree in electrical engineering from the Delft University of Technology, the Netherlands, in 1998. He has authored and co-authored one book and more than two hundred papers and articles published in journals and conference proceedings. He has supervised more than 40 Ph.D. and M.Sc. students. He participated in more than 20 research projects. Prof. Sousa is an Associate Editor of the IEEE Transactions on Fuzzy Systems, Editor of Mathematics and Computers in Simulation and member of the editorial board from Fuzzy Sets and Systems. He is the Chair of the Fuzzy Systems Technical Committee from the IEEE Computational Intelligence Society.

Ömür Tosun is an associate professor in the Department of International Trade and Logistics in Faculty of Applied Sciences. He has a PhD degree in Production Management from Department of Business Administration in the Faculty of Economic and Administrative Sciences, Akdeniz University, Turkiye. He has a BS in Industrial Engineering and MBA in Production Management. He has an interest on neural networks, optimization, metaheuristic methods and bio-inspired algorithms.

Lefteri H. Tsoukalas received the Ph.D. degree from the University of Illinois–Urbana, Champaign, IL, USA, in 1989. He is a Professor and the Former Head of the School of Nuclear Engineering, Purdue University, West Lafayette, IN, USA, and has held faculty appointments with the University of Tennessee, Knoxville, TN, USA; Aristotle University, Thessaloniki, Greece; Hellenic University, Thessaloniki; and the University of Thessaly, Volos, Greece. He is the Director of the Applied Intelligent Systems Laboratory, Purdue University, which pioneered research in anticipatory algorithms and machine learning applications in nuclear engineering and power grid management. He has three decades of experience in smart instrumentation and control techniques, with over 200 peer-reviewed research publications including the textbook Fuzzy and Neural Approaches in Engineering (Wiley, 1997). Dr. Tsoukalas was a recipient of the Humboldt Prize and Germany's Highest Honor for International Scientists in 2009. He is a Fellow of the American Nuclear Society.

Steffen Udluft received his diploma and PhD in physics from the Ludwig-Maximilians University München, in 1996 and 2000, respectively, and was a postdoctoral researcher at the Max-Planck-Institute for physics from 2000 to 2001. During this time he worked on the neuro-trigger of the H1 experiment for particle physics at DESY, Hamburg. Since 2001 he has been working for Siemens Corporate Technology, and continues to pursue the application of neural networks and other machine learning methods to real word problems. His main research focus is data-efficient reinforcement learning which includes transfer-learning, handling of uncertainty, and generalization capabilities.

B. Venkateswararao was born in Ramabhadrapuram, India in 1978. He received his Bachelor degree in Electrical and Electronics Engineering from College of Engineering, Gandhi Institute of Technology And Management(GITAM) Visakapatnam, Andhra Pradesh, India in 2000, the Master degree in Electrical Power Engineering from the College of Engineering, JNTU, Hyderabad in 2007 and He received his Doctoral degree from Jawaharlal Nehru Technological University, Hyderabad in 2015. He is presently working as Associate Professor in the Department of Electrical and Electronics Engineering, V R Siddhartha Engineering College, Vijayawada. His research interests are Power system stability analysis, FACTS devices, Power system control and power system optimization. He has published several research papers in national and international conferences and journals. He is a member of ISTE and IE.

Susana Vieira is a Professor with the Department of Mechanical Engineering, Instituto Superior Técnico (IST), Universidade de Lisboa, and a senior researcher at the Center of Intelligent Systems, IDMEC. She received the MSc and PhD degrees both in Mechanical Engineering in 2005 and 2010, respectively, from IST, University of Lisbon, Portugal. She was a Teaching Assistant at IST from 2005 to 2006 and in 2009, she was an Invited Teacher at the Erasmus University of Rotterdam, the Netherlands. Her main research area is Soft Computing, more specifically she works in feature selection, fuzzy modeling, fuzzy optimization and metaheuristics. Her research focuses mainly on the development of computational intelligence methods for knowledge data discovery.

Pandu R. Vundavilli received his BTech in Mechanical Engineering from Jawaharlal Nehru Technological University, Kakinada-533003, India and MTech. in Computer Integrated Manufacturing from National Institute of Technology, Warangal-506004, India in 2000 and 2003, respectively. From 2003 to 2005, he worked as a faculty member at the Koneru Lakshmaiah College of Engineering, Vaddeswaram-522502, India. He received his PhD in Mechanical Engineering from Indian Institute of Technology, Kharagpur-721302, India in 2009. He is working at present as Asst. Professor in the School of Mechanical Sciences of IIT Bhubaneswar - 752050, India. His research interests include modeling and simulation of manufacturing systems, robotics and soft computing. He has published around 75 publications in various International and National Journals and Conferences.

Qiang Wang received the BS degree from QuFu Normal University, JiNing, in 2010. He received the MS degree and Ph.D. degree from GuangDong University of Technology (GDUT), GuangZhou, in 2013 and 2017, respectively. He is currently a lecturer at the Yulin normal university, Guangxi, China. His research interests include wireless networks optimization, and signal processing.

Junshan Yang received his B.S. degree from the School of Electronics and Information Engineering of Liaoning University of Technology, PR China, in 2004. He received his M.S. degree from the School of Physics and Telecommunication Engineering of South China Normal University, PR China, in 2008. He received his Ph.D degree with the School of Engineering and Information, Shenzhen University, China. His current research interests include evolutionary computation, bioinformatics, machine learning.

Yijun Yang is currently a research assistant in the School of Computer Science and Engineering, Southern University of Science and Technology. He is a member of SUSTC Learning and Optimization Lab. His current research interests include computational intelligence techniques and their applications.

Jiarui Zhou is a research fellow in HIT Shenzhen Graduate School, China and University of Birmingham, UK.

Zexuan Zhu is a Professor with the College of Computer Science and Software Engineering, Shenzhen University, China. He received his B.Sc degree from the Department of Computer Science and Engineering, Fudan University, China, in 2003 and the Ph.D degree from the School of Computer Engineering, Nanyang Technological University, Singapore, in 2008. His research interests include computational intelligence, machine learning, and bioinformatics. He is an Associate Editor of IEEE Transactions on Evolutionary Computation and IEEE Transactions on Emerging Topics in Computational Intelligence, and serves as the Editorial Board Member of Memetic Computing Journal and Soft Computing Journal. He is also a Vice Chair of the IEEE Emergent Technologies Task Force on Memetic Computing.

Adamu Murtala Zungeru received the PhD, MSc and BEng from Nottingham University, Ahmadu Bello University Zaria Nigeria and Federal University of Technology Minna Nigeria respectively. He was a Research Fellow in the Electrical Engineering and Computer Science Department at Massachusetts Institute of Technology (MIT) USA, where he also obtained a Postgraduate Teaching Certificate. He is currently a senior lecturer at Botswana International University of Science and Technology (BIUST). His research interests are in swarm intelligence, wireless sensor networks, embedded systems, and design of analog and digital electronic circuits. He has published over forty papers in journals and international refereed conferences. He is a member of the IEEE, ACM and AP-S.

Index

G

H

I

L

M

N

O

P

R

S

T

U

V

W

Printed in the United States
By Bookmasters